YEARBOOK OF
EUROPEAN ENVIRONMENTAL LAW

Vol. 1

YEARBOOK OF EUROPEAN ENVIRONMENTAL LAW

Volume 1

H. SOMSEN
Lecturer at the University of Nijmegen
Editor-in-Chief

H. SEVENSTER
Professor at the University of Amsterdam
CURRENT SURVEY EDITOR

J. McCAHERY
Senior Lecturer at Tilburg University
BOOK REVIEW EDITOR

L. KRÄMER
DG Environment Commission of the European Communities
DOCUMENTS EDITOR

T. F. M. ETTY
H. VEDDER
ASSISTANT EDITORS

OXFORD
UNIVERSITY PRESS

*This book has been printed digitally and produced in a standard specification
in order to ensure its continuing availability*

OXFORD
UNIVERSITY PRESS

Great Clarendon Street, Oxford OX2 6DP

Oxford University Press is a department of the University of Oxford.
It furthers the University's objective of excellence in research, scholarship,
and education by publishing world-wide in

Oxford New York

Auckland Bangkok Buenos Aires Cape Town Chennai
Dar es Salaam Delhi Hong Kong Istanbul Karachi Kolkata
Kuala Lumpur Madrid Melbourne Mexico City Mumbai Nairobi
São Paulo Shanghai Taipei Tokyo Toronto

Oxford is a registered trade mark of Oxford University Press
in the UK and in certain other countries

Published in the United States
by Oxford University Press Inc., New York

© Han Somsen 2000

ISBN 0-19-876463-4

Antony Rowe Ltd., Eastbourne

Editorial Committee

Editor's Preface

It may appear self-evident that developments which currently dictate the course of European integration simultaneously determine the face of European Community environmental law. However, the reverse also applies in that an analysis of the evolution of the Union's environmental policy provides a blueprint of the challenges facing the Union more generally. In this crucial respect, European Community environmental law distinguishes itself from other, "vertical" areas of Community concern, which frequently may usefully be studied in relative isolation from any wider context but which, consequently, do not offer such panoramic perspectives of European law.

Quite apart from the paramount significance of a body of law which conditions the present and future behaviour of *all* societal actors (individual, corporate and public), the study of EC environmental law hence acquires significance and purpose also by virtue of the fact that the theories, principles, and practical recommendations to which it gives rise often may be extended to EC law more generally.

From the outset, we have tried to ensure that this *Yearbook* performs both these interrelated tasks. It serves as a reliable and critical source of information concerning European Community environmental law, but also as an antenna registering any tremor occurring in this area but the reverberations of which may be felt beyond its epicentre.

As for the latter, this first volume was conceived at a time when the Treaty of Amsterdam introduced novel concepts, procedures, and instruments which are profoundly to affect the Community's environmental policy, but whose effects at the same time will be felt across most other spheres of Community concern.

A first such concept is formed by the principle of integration which, although already familiar to environmental lawyers, now features in new Article 6 EC and consequently has acquired added legal significance. According to this principle, objectives and principles of the Union's environmental policy must be pursued and implemented in all other Community policies. In this sense, competition policy and the principles governing free movement, for example, simultaneously act as vehicles for the realization of the Union's environmental aspirations. Tensions between these competing objectives are inevitable, however, and have been explored extensively by various authors. Temmink's detailed and illuminating analysis of the accommodation of environmental imperatives in the pursuit of an internal market in goods appears to lend support to the thesis that, indeed, the balance between both goals is gradually evolving in a way consistent with Article 6 EC. However, other core policies may prove more resistant to such an evolution. Verschuuren's article suggests that, although implementation of EC environmental law by self-regulatory means gives rise to identifiable efficiency gains,

competition policy may prove hostile to such innovations. The facility to introduce national, more stringent standards even after harmonization would appear
to fall squarely within the professed policy of integration. Yet, as Sevenster shows,
even though the Treaty of Amsterdam addressed this issue in detail, new Article
95 EC remains ambiguous and less than crystal clear in this respect, reflecting the
continued schizophrenia surrounding the proper equilibrium. Van Calster and
Onida's articles provide alarming evidence that Community efforts to regulate
the generation, disposal, and movements of waste are severely inhibited by the
simple fact that "waste" simultaneously may be a "good" and hence subject to the
provisions governing the free movement of goods.

Quite apart from these self-imposed constraints, regimes governing international trade further limit the Union's freedom of choice in determining the
proper balance between trade and the environment. Krämer's compact and
challenging account of the Community's eco-labelling scheme usefully serves
as an illustration of this concern.

Potentially one of the most innovative concepts catapulted into the arena of
European integration by the Treaty of Amsterdam concerns what may loosely
be termed "flexibility". Many of the articles depart from the premise that future
EC environmental law will increasingly be moulded by concerns which may be
subsumed under this novel concept. Although it is certainly not intended to
dwell on the precise significance and meaning of flexibility, some general
observations may serve to illuminate one of the over-arching themes which
inform a number of contributions to this volume.

In its narrowest sense, flexibility is a concept that refers to the procedures
specified in new Articles 11, 43 and 45 EC. However, just as much as "subsidiarity" has come to represent a normative political concept rather than a
neutral legal notion, the same appears to apply to flexibility which, many
authors feel, is already radically changing the face of EC environmental law. In
the most general of terms, flexibility is a vehicle in response to the reality that
existing and increasing future diversity of local conditions and associated
preferences need to be accommodated in the enlarged Union. Thus conceived, flexibility may be viewed as an operative corollary of the principle of
subsidiarity. Different aspects of this broad and, admittedly, opaque notion of
flexibility are addressed in this volume.

In as far as flexibility operates in the context of the principle of subsidiarity,
it is to manifest itself in the exercise of Community powers and will impact on
the question when Community action is the preferred option. Revesz, relying
on extensive US experience, submits that there should be a presumption in
favour of state action and underlines the conceptual and real shortcomings of
Community intervention. Drawing upon US data he maintains, for example,
that the Union in general should steer clear of regulating processes (as
opposed to products) and that few of the common justifications for harmonization stand up to critical scrutiny.

Once it has been established that the most appropriate level of action is that
of the Community, flexibility is also to influence the choice of regulatory

instruments, processes, and styles. In these cases, flexibility is understood as allowing Member States greater room for manœuvre in tailoring the impact of secondary environmental law to domestic needs and priorities. As part of this discussion, attention is afforded to the proliferation of new instruments in the arena of EC environmental law such as self-regulation (Verschuuren), framework directives, and open-ended standards. As far as open-ended standards are concerned, Scott's article on the Community's Directive on integrated pollution prevention and control (IPPC) offers excellent examples of the associated fundamental problems. Based on an analysis of the operation of the principle of flexibility in the Community's eco-label scheme, Krämer, too, propagates caution in respect of the trend to allow for increasing flexibility in the arena of the Community's environmental policy.

Krämer's stance undoubtedly is inspired by his well-known concern that the Community's environmental laws should be effective in bringing about the results to which it is committed by virtue of the Treaty, prevailing secondary law, and various soft-law instruments. Indeed, the impact of any new principles and procedures on this *acquis* should be a key factor in our assessment of their expediency. However, the constitutional character of the protection of a common heritage dictates that it is as imperative that these new principles operate in a context of transparency and (*ex ante* and *ex post*) accountability as that they are effective in bringing about the desired result.

The evolution of EC environmental law under the influence of the associated concepts of subsidiarity, proportionality, and flexibility may require additional constitutional guarantees to surround Community environmental decision-making. The recently agreed private agreement with the European car industry, a first offspring of the Commission's flirtations with new instruments, gives rise to numerous and obvious questions relating to public participation in environmental decision-making, transparency, and judicial protection. Similarly, when flexibility gives rise to increased levels of discretion vested in public authorities, whilst at the same time the boundaries of these discretionary powers remain vague, the question arises how the exercise of such discretion may be judicially reviewed.

To the extent that this evolution will stimulate the kind of decentralization advocated by Revesz or even localized Community standard-setting which, as Scott suggests, may ensue in the context of the implementation of open-ended standards such as Best Available Technology (BAT), these judicial and administrative guarantees, too, will increasingly have to be situated at national or local level. This in itself constitutes a highly significant development, the precise ramifications of which to a large extent remain speculative at the present time.

Whereas Ward convincingly shows that the Court is gradually tightening its grip on Member States' remedies and procedural rules that are attached to claims based on Community law, thus vesting individuals with rights, my own analysis of the potential of such a system of privatized enforcement is not unambiguously optimistic. Grant and Newell's article on the workings of environmental interest groups in the arena of the Community's environmental policy implies that any disintegration of the Brussels monopoly on Community environmental law-making will also force these groups radically to re-adjust their proven strategies. Given the increasing intricacy of the network of relationships between Community, national, local, public, and private actors which together carry out the Community's environmental policy, this process of re-adjustment represents a challenge of considerable proportion.

Clearly, in view of these various considerations, it becomes crucial to follow developments in national environmental law, as they will increasingly determine both the effectiveness and constitutional legitimacy of the Community's efforts to preserve and protect the environment. It is for this reason that it was decided early on that a section of this *Yearbook* should be devoted to developments at national level. As it will be available on an annual basis, the information may serve to expose recurrent themes concerning the implementation of EC environmental law and any signs of the emergence of a *ius commune* in European environmental law.

I sincerely believe that this *Yearbook* can perform these important objectives to the satisfaction of professionals, academics and students of environmental law. It is a great privilege to have the opportunity to make this contribution, however modest, to the law which is to protect our environment for the benefit of present and future generations.

HAN SOMSEN
Editor-in-Chief

Acknowledgements

That a collection of articles is the fruit of the combined efforts of numerous individuals and organizations comes as no surprise. However, even by accepted standards, this first volume is a remarkable product of pan-European co-operation in one of the most complex fields of European Community law. It truly is impossible to do justice to all those who played a role in realizing this ambitious endeavour. Nevertheless, for this first volume, I permit myself to mention at least those the lives of whom the *Yearbook* has come to dominate to a far greater extent than was ever anticipated.

The idea of producing an annual volume devoted exclusively to European Union environmental law was first floated in 1994 by Ludwig Krämer who, ever since, has lent his considerable intellectual and moral support to the project.

Directorate General XI generously contributed towards the cost of a conference which was held at Warwick University in July 1998 and where some of the papers published in this volume were first discussed. I should like to record my gratitude to Aileen Stockham, conference organizer of the Legal Research Institute, and its director, Professor Michael McConville, for what has been a smoothly organized and very enjoyable conference.

Joseph McCahery and Hanna Sevenster frequently must have questioned the wisdom of their decision to join the editorial team, not to mention their young families to whom I am equally indebted.

I am grateful to the faculty board of the School of Law of Nijmegen University, for its encouragement and financial support. Patricia van Gaalen and Hans Vedder deserve praise for their tireless energy, patience, and good humour under what at best may be described as hectic circumstances.

I am particularly indebted to Thijs Etty, who led by example. He frequently worked late hours and quickly acquired a role far more fundamental than he was led to believe when he first walked into my office to offer his assistance.

Finally, I am only too well aware that the ultimate success of this volume is owed for a great part to the expertise and enthusiasm of its contributors.

HAN SOMSEN
Editor-in-Chief

Contents

REVIEWS OF BOOKS

List of Contributors

Geert van Calster is a Senior Research Fellow at the Institute of Environmental and Energy Law, Collegium Falconis, Catholic University of Leuven and a member of the Brussels Bar. His fellowship at Leuven and his Chevening Scholarship at Oxford University culminated in a PhD thesis entitled *Does the WTO need a Title on the Environment? Lessons learnt from the European Community.* He is practising law at the Brussels offices of Caestecker & Partners/Andersen where he deals mainly with questions of international and EC trade and environmental law. He has published extensively on European and environmental law.

Wyn Grant is Professor at the Department of Politics and International Studies of the University of Warwick. His recent publications include (co-edited with Anthony Perl and Peter Knoepfel *The Politics of Improving Urban Air Quality* (Northampton: Edward Elgar, 1999); *The Common Agricultural Policy* (Basingstoke: Macmillan, 1997); and *Autos, Smog and Pollution Control* (Brookfield: Edward Elgar, 1996). He is a regular contributor to the club magazine of Charlton Athletic Football Club.

Ludwig Krämer is Head of the Waste Management Unit in DG Environment of the European Commission. He has published profusely on wide-ranging issues of European environmental law. His *European Environmental Law* (London: Sweet & Maxwell, 1993), *Focus on European Environmental Law* (2nd edn., London: Sweet & Maxwell, 1997), and *EC Treaty and Environmental Law* (4th edn., London: Sweet & Maxwell, 2000) have become standard texts for academics and practitioners and students.

Peter Newell is a Research Fellow at the Institute of Development Studies based at the University of Sussex, undertaking research, teaching, and consultancy on global environmental issues. He has published widely in the area of environmental politics including a forthcoming book with Cambridge University Press, *Climate for Change: Non State Actors and the Global Politics of the Greenhouse*, and a series of journal articles and book chapters. He is currently researching the governance implications of public–private partnerships in the environmental area.

Marco Onida is an official with the Waste Management Unit of the European Commission. He is involved in the preparation of legislation in the field of waste, particularly packaging waste, hazardous waste, and end-of-life vehicles.

Richard Revesz is a Professor of Law at New York University School of Law, where he directs the Program on Environmental Regulation. He has written extensively about environmental law and policy, particularly concerning federalism and environmental regulation, the design of liability rules for environmental protection, environmental regulation, and public choice, and the theoretical foundations of environmental policy. He is the author or editor of several books, including *Foundations of Environmental Law and Policy* (New York: Oxford University Press, 1997) and *Analyzing Superfund: Economics, Science and the Law*, edited with Richard Stewart (Washington, DC: Resources for the Future, 1995).

Joanne Scott is University lecturer, University of Cambridge and Fellow of Clare College. Her most recent publications include *EC Environmental Law* (London and New York: Longman, 1988), and "Of Kith and Kine: Trade and Environment in the EU and WTO", in J. H. H. Weiler, *The EU, WTO and NAFTA: Towards a Common Law of International Trade* (Oxord: Oxford University Press, 1999).

Hanna Sevenster is Professor of European Environmental Law at the Centre for Environmental Law of the University of Amsterdam and attorney with De Brauw Blackstone Westbroek (The Hague) where she deals in particular with European Community competition and environmental law. She publishes widely in the area of EC law, is a regular contributor to the *Nederlands Tijdschrift voor Europees Recht* (Netherlands Journal of European Law) and editor of the Current Survey of the *Yearbook of European Environmental Law* (Oxford: Oxford University Press).

Han Somsen is Lecturer at Nijmegen University. Since its establishment in 1992 he has been editor and permanent contributor of the *European Environmental Law Review* (Kluwer) and European Adviser of *Water Law* (Wiley). He has published extensively in the area of European environmental law. He edited *Protecting the European Environment* (London: Blackstone Press, 1996) and contributed to numerous journals and books. His monograph, *Effective Enforcement*, is to be published by Oxford University Press shortly. He is editor in chief of the *Yearbook of European Environmental Law* (Oxford: Oxford University Press).

Harrie Temmink is Lecturer in public economic law at the Europa Institute of the University of Utrecht and has published extensively on issues concerning the internal market. He is editor of the *Nederlands Tijdschrift voor Europees Recht* (Netherlands Journal of European Law) and a regular contributor to numerous law reviews.

Jonathan Verschuuren is Professor of European and International Environmental Law at Tilburg University and involved in numerous research projects co-ordinated by the Centre for Legislative Studies of the Schoordijk Institute of Tilburg University. He is a member of the Commission on

Environmental Law of the IUCN and chairperson of the *Tilburg Foreign Law Review*. His numerous publications focus on issues of international, European, and Dutch environmental law.

Angela Ward is Assistant Director of the Centre for European Legal Studies, Cambridge, and is a Fellow of Magdalene College Cambridge. She has published numerous academic articles, and has worked as a practising solicitor in Sydney and Brussels. She is also the director of a substantial aid programme which aims at preparing the Polish judiciary for EU membership.

Environmental Regulation in Federal Systems

RICHARD L. REVESZ*

I. Introduction

In the United States of America (USA), vesting control over environmental regulation at the federal level is most commonly justified both in the legal academic literature and the legislative arena by reference to three distinct arguments. First, advocates of federal control argue that in its absence inter-state competition would result in a "race to the bottom". Secondly, they maintain that federal regulation is necessary to prevent inter-state externalities. Thirdly, proponents of centralization raise the public choice claim that environmental interests will be systematically under-represented at the state level relative to business interests.

This article, which builds upon my prior works in the area,[1] has three major purposes. First, it casts serious doubt on the validity of some of the arguments made in favour of centralizing environmental regulation. Secondly, it shows that, to a large extent, there has been a mis-allocation of responsibility over environmental regulation: the federal government has taken too aggressive a role with respect to matters best handled at the state level, but has been too constrained in its exercise of authority with respect to issues over which it enjoys a distinct comparative advantage. Thirdly, it attempts to extract from the experience in the USA lessons that might be of interest to the European Union (EU) and to the international trading regime.

Section II develops the arguments for a presumption for decentralization, which calls for vesting responsibility over environmental protection at the state rather than federal level, as a result of differences in preferences over environmental protection, as well as differences in the benefits and costs of

* Professor of Law, New York University School of Law. The generous financial support of the Filomen D'Agostino and Max E. Greenberg Research Fund at the New York University School of Law is gratefully acknowledged.

[1] R. L. Revesz, "Rehabilitating Inter-State Competition: Rethinking the 'Race to the Bottom' Rationale for Federal Environmental Regulation" (1992) 67 *New York University Law Review* 1210; R. L. Revesz, "Federalism and Inter-State Environmental Externalities" (1996) 144 *University of Pennsylvania Law Review* 2341; R. L. Revesz, "Federalism and Environmental Regulation: A Normative Critique", in J. Ferejohn and B. Weingast (eds), *The New Federalism: Can the States be Trusted?* (Stanford, Cal.: Hoover Institution Press, 1997); R. L. Revesz, "Federalism and Environmental Regulation: Lessons for the European Union and the International Community" (1997) 83 *Virginia Law Review* 1331; R. L. Revesz, "The Race to the Bottom and Federal Environmental Regulation: A Response to Critics" (1997) 82 *Minnesota Law Review* 535.

such protection. This presumption can be rebutted if decentralization gives rise to some pathology that could be cured through federal regulation.

Sections III to V examine the three most prominent justifications offered in the academic literature and in the legislative histories of the federal environmental statutes in the USA for vesting responsibility over environmental regulation at the federal level. First, the "race to the bottom" rationale posits that states, in an effort to induce geographically mobile firms to locate within their jurisdictions, will offer them sub-optimally lax environmental standards, so as to benefit from additional jobs and tax revenues. Secondly, the problem of inter-state externalities arises because a state that sends pollution to another state obtains the labour and fiscal benefits of the economic activity that generates the pollution, but does not suffer the full costs of the activity. Thus, a sub-optimally large amount of pollution will cross state lines. Thirdly, a public choice claim posits that state political processes will systematically undervalue the benefits of environmental protection or overvalue its costs. I show that these three arguments do not justify the broad role over environmental regulation accorded to the federal government in the USA.

Section VI attempts to define an appropriate federal role. It focuses on the types of federal regulation that may be desirable in light of (1) different types of inter-state externalities (pollution externalities, benefits that accrue outside the jurisdiction in which the need for environmental protection arises, and existence or non-use values placed by out-of-state citizens to certain natural resources); (2) economies of scale; (3) benefits that might flow from uniformity in regulation; and (4) rights-based views concerning the protection of minimum levels of public health. It shows that these arguments justify a far narrower federal role than that embodied in the current environmental statutes.

Section VII shows that much of the criticism of centralized regulation that flows from the preceding analysis of the institutional framework in the USA applies with equal force to the EU. It also underscores the importance for the EU of debates concerning the proper allocation of authority currently waged primarily on this side of the Atlantic.

Section VIII explains why the assessment of centralized intervention is different in the international community from federal systems. It also provides a framework for analysing the desirability of environmentally-based trade restrictions in the international community.

II. A Presumption in Favour of Decentralization

My starting point is a rebuttable presumption in favour of decentralization.[2] This presumption rests on three independent grounds. First, the USA is a large and diverse country. It is therefore likely that different regions have different preferences for environmental protection. Environmental protection entails

---

[2] Section II relies heavily on Revesz, "The Race to the Bottom and Federal Environmental Regulation: A Response to Critics", n. 1 above, 536–8.

an important resource allocation question. We can generally purchase additional environmental protection at some price, paid in the currency of jobs, wages, shareholders' profits, tax revenues, and economic growth. Given the existence of the states as plausible regulatory units, the trade-off reflecting the preferences of citizens of different regions should not be wholly disregarded in the regulatory process, absent strong reasons for doing so.

In the case of some social decisions, such reasons are present. The example of federal civil rights legislation, which trumped deeply held preferences of a large region of the country, is perhaps most prominent. But while I am sympathetic to the argument that the protection of a minimum level of public health ought to be viewed in quasi-constitutional terms and guaranteed throughout the country, as I explain below it would stretch this principle beyond its breaking point to say that it calls for the federalization of every decision having public health consequences.[3]

Secondly, the benefits of environmental protection also vary throughout the country. For example, a stringent ambient standard may benefit many people in densely populated areas but only a few elsewhere. Similarly, a particular level of exposure to a contaminant may be more detrimental if it is combined with exposure to other contaminants with which it has synergistic effects.[4]

Thirdly, the costs of meeting a given standard also differ across geographic regions. For example, a source may have a large detrimental impact on ambient air quality if it is directly upwind of a mountain or other topographical barrier. Similarly, a water polluter will have a far larger impact on water quality standards if it disposes of its effluents in relatively small bodies of water. Climate might also play a role: certain emission or effluent standards may be easier (and cheaper) to meet in warmer weather.[5]

In principle, federal regulation could be attentive to these differences. Such a differentiated approach, however, would require a staggering amount of information. Clearly, the federal government does not have a comparative advantage at gathering such information. Thus, not surprisingly, federal regulation generally imposes uniform requirements throughout the country. Moreover, even when federal regulation imposes disuniform standards, the differences are not explainable by the factors discussed above.[6]

This presumption for decentralization should be overcome, however, if there is a systemic evil in letting states decide the level of environmental

---

[3] See nn. 46–47 below.

[4] See J. E. Krier, "On the Topology of Uniform Environmental Standards in a Federal System— And Why It Matters" (1995) 54 *Modern Law Review* 1226; J. E. Krier, "The Irrational National Ambient Air Quality Standards: Macro- and Micro-Mistakes" (1974) 22 *UCLA Law Review* 323.

[5] See *Chemical Mfrs. Ass'n v. EPA*, 870 F 2d 177 (DC Cir. 1989), cert. denied, 495 US 910 (1990); *Tanners' Council, Inc. v. Train*, 540 F 2d 1188 (4th Cir. 1976); *American Frozen Food Inst. v. Train*, 539 F 2d 107 (DC Cir. 1976); *Hooker Chem. & Plastics Corp. v. Train*, 537 F 2d 639 (2d Cir. 1975).

[6] e.g., the Clean Air Act imposes disuniform ambient standards, determined by whether an area is covered by the Prevention of Significant Deterioration (PSD) or non-attainment programmes. See 42 USC 7473, 7502(c)(2), 7503(a)(1)(A) (1994). These differences turn on what ambient air quality standards regions had at a particular time, rather than differences in preferences, benefits, or costs.

protection that will apply within their jurisdictions. Sections III to V examine, respectively, the strength of the race-to-the-bottom, inter-state externality, and public choice justifications for federal environmental protection.

III. The Race-to-the-bottom Justification

The discussion proceeds in four parts.[7] First, it argues that inter-state competition over environmental standards is, in essence, competition for the sale of goods. Secondly, it shows that the leading economic model of the effects of inter-state competition on the choice of environmental standards shows that interjurisdictional competition leads to the maximization of social welfare, rather than to a race to the bottom. Thirdly, it argues that if game-theoretic inter-action among the states leads to a departure from optimality, the result could be over-regulation or under-regulation; thus, even under this scenario there is no compelling justification for federal minimum standards, which are designed to correct only for under-regulation. Fourthly, it shows that even if states systematically enacted sub-optimally lax environmental standards, federal environmental regulation would not necessarily improve the situation.

A. MARKET ANALOGY

Race-to-the-bottom advocates must clear an initial hurdle. If one believes that competition among sellers of, say, widgets is socially desirable, why is competition among states, as sellers of goods—the right to locate within their jurisdictions—socially undesirable?

[7] Sect. III relies heavily on Revesz, "Rehabilitating Inter-State Competition: Rethinking the 'Race to the Bottom' Rationale for Federal Environmental Regulation", n. 1 above; Revesz, "Federalism and Environmental Regulation: A Normative Critique", n. 1 above, at 99–107. For commentary generally supportive of my approach, see, e.g., D. L. Shapiro, *Federalism: A Dialogue* (Evanston, Ill.: Northwestern University Press, 1995), 42–3, 81–3; J. E. Krier, "Uniform Environmental Standards", n. 4 above, at 1236–7; R. B. Stewart, "Environmental Regulation and International Competitiveness" (1993) 102 *Yale Law Journal* 2039, 2058–9; R. B. Stewart, "International Trade and Environment: Lessons from the Federal Experience" (1992) 49 *Washington & Lee Law Review* 1329, 1371; S. Williams, "Culpability, Restitution, and the Environment: The Vitality of Common Law Rules" (1994) 21 *Ecology Law Quarterly* 559, 560–1.

In the past few months several articles have taken issue with my work on federalism and environmental regulation, particularly with my indictment of the race-to-the-bottom rationale for federal environmental regulation. See K. H. Engel, "State Environmental Standard-setting: Is There a 'Race' and Is It 'to the Bottom' " (1997) 48 *Hastings Law Journal* 271; D. C. Esty, "Revitalizing Environmental Federalism" (1996) 95 *Michigan Law Review* 570; J. D. Sarnoff, "The Continuing Imperative (but Only from a National Perspective) for Federal Environmental Protection" (1997) 7 *Duke Environmental Law & Policy Forum* 225; P. P. Swire, "The Race to Laxity and the Race to Undesirability: Explaining Failures in Competition Among Jurisdictions in Environmental Law" (1996) *Yale Law and Policy Review/Yale Journal on Regulation, Constructing a New Federalism: Jurisdictional Competence and Competition* 67. My response appears in Revesz, "The Race to the Bottom and Federal Environmental Regulation: A Response to Critics", n. 1 above. For more recent criticism, see D. C. Esty and D. Geradin, "Environmental Protectionism and International Competitiveness: A Conceptual Framework" (1998) 32 *Journal of World Trade* 5–46; D. C. Esty and D. Geradin, "Market Access, Competitiveness and Harmonisation: Environmental Protection in Regional Trade Agreements" (1997) 21 *Harvard Environmental Law Review* 265–336.

Indeed, states sell location rights because, even though they might not have the legal authority to prevent firms from locating within their borders, such firms must comply with the fiscal and regulatory regime of the state in which they wish to locate. The resulting costs to the firms can be analogized to the sale price of traditional goods. If federal regulation mandating a supra-competitive price for widgets is socially undesirable, why should it be socially desirable to have federal regulation mandating a supra-competitive price for location rights, in the form of more stringent environmental standards than those that would result from inter-state competition?

It is easy to identify possible distinctions between a state as seller of location rights and sellers of widgets. These differences, however, do not provide support for race-to-the-bottom claims.

First, if individuals are mobile across jurisdictions, the costs that polluters impose on a state's residents will depend on who ends up being a resident of the state; the resulting supply curve is thus far more complex than that of a widget seller. In the context of environmental regulation, however, race-to-the-bottom claims have focused exclusively on the mobility of capital, thereby assuming, at least implicitly, that individuals are immobile. Moreover, it is not clear that individual mobility renders competition among states different from competition among widget sellers. Indeed, even if individuals move in search of the jurisdiction that has the level of environmental protection that they favour,[8] and if there is capital mobility, the choice of environmental standards can nonetheless be efficient.[9]

Secondly, while a seller of widgets is indifferent to the effect of the sale price on the welfare of the goods' purchaser, a state ought to be concerned about the interests of the shareholders of the polluting firm who reside in the jurisdiction, both as individuals adversely affected by pollution and as owners of capital adversely affected by the costs of meeting regulatory requirements. But this difference does not support race-to-the-bottom arguments. Indeed, if some of the regulated firm's shareholders did not reside in the regulating jurisdiction and if capital were immobile, a state could extract monopoly profits by setting suboptimally stringent standards, benefiting its in-state breathers at the expense of out-of-state shareholders. (If capital is mobile, competition eliminates this problem.) Nothing in this account provides support for the opposite proposition: that inter-state competition leads to sub-optimally lax standards.

Thirdly, states are not subject to the discipline of the market. If a producer of widgets consistently sells at a price that does not cover its average costs, it will

---

[8] See C. M. Tiebout, "A Pure Theory of Local Expenditure" (1956) 64 *Journal of Political Economy* 416; T. F. Bewley, "A Critique of the Theory of Local Public Expenditure" (1981) 49 *Econometrica* 713.

[9] W. E. Oates and R. M. Schwab, "Pricing Instruments for Environmental Protection: The Problems of Cross-Media Pollution, Interjurisdictional Competition and Interregional Effects" (Nov. 1987) (unpublished manuscript on file with author), cited in W. E. Oates and R. M. Schwab, "Economic Competition Among Jurisdictions: Efficiency Enhancing or Distortion Inducing?" (1988) 35 *Journal of Public Economics* 333, 337.

eventually have to declare bankruptcy. A state, in contrast, can continue in existence even if it recklessly compromises the health of its residents. This difference merely establishes that a state might undervalue environmental benefits. But such undervaluation can take place even if capital is not mobile: it is a public choice problem rather than a race-to-the-bottom problem.

Fourthly, states do not sell "location rights" at a single-component price; they require that firms comply with a variety of regulatory standards and that they pay taxes. The resulting market is thus more complex than one involving the sale of traditional goods. For example, a jurisdiction that imposes a lax worker safety standard but a stringent pollution standard will be desirable for a labour intensive, non-polluting firm, whereas a jurisdiction with stringent safety and lax pollution standards will be desirable for a capital-intensive polluting firm. It is far from clear, however, why this additional complexity in the market would make inter-state competition destructive. Instead, the example suggests a desirable sorting out of firms according to the preferences of individuals in the various jurisdictions.

In sum, while the analogy between inter-state competition for industrial activity and markets for traditional goods is not perfect, it raises serious questions about race-to-the-bottom claims. At the very least, it should require race-to-the-bottom advocates to bear the burden of identifying relevant differences between the two markets and explaining why they turn otherwise desirable competition into a race-to-the-bottom.

B. ECONOMIC MODELS

Quite to the contrary, and contrary to the prevailing assumption in the legal literature and in the legislative debates, the leading economic model of the effects of inter-state competition on the choice of environmental standards shows that interjurisdictional competition leads to the maximization of social welfare, rather than to a race to the bottom.[10] Oates and Schwab posit jurisdictions that compete for mobile capital through the choice of taxes and environmental standards. A higher capital stock benefits residents in the form of higher wages, but hurts them as a result of the foregone tax revenues and lower environmental quality needed to attract the capital.[11]

In their model, individuals live and work in the same jurisdiction and there are no inter-jurisdictional pollution spillovers. Each jurisdiction produces the same goods, which are sold in a national market. Their production requires

---

[10] Oates and Schwab, "Economic Competition Among Jurisdictions: Efficiency Enhancing or Distortion Inducing?", n. 9 above.

[11] One commentator argues that inter-state competition can lead to detrimental results due to factors such as the excessive discounting of future damages, but provides no argument for why this determination would be performed better at the federal level. See J. H. Cumberland, "Interregional Pollution Spillovers and Consistency of Environmental Policy", in H. Seibert (ed.), *Regional Environmental Policy: The Economic Issues* (New York: New York University Press, 1979), 255. For an argument to the contrary, see W. E. Oates and R. M. Schwab, "The Theory of Regulatory Federalism: The Case of Environmental Management", in W. E. Oates (ed.), *The Economics of Environmental Regulation* (Cheltenham: Edward Elgar, 1996), 319.

capital and labour, and produces waste emissions. The various jurisdictions set a total permissible amount of emissions as well as a tax on each unit of capital. Capital is perfectly mobile across jurisdictions and seeks to maximize its after-tax earnings, but labour is immobile.[12]

Each individual in the community, who is identical in both tastes and productive capacity, puts in a fixed period of work each week, and everyone is employed. Additional capital raises the productivity of workers, and therefore their wages.

Each jurisdiction makes two policy decisions: it sets a tax rate on capital and an environmental standard. Oates and Schwab show that competitive jurisdictions will set a net tax rate on capital of zero (the rate that exactly covers the cost of public services provided to the capital, such as police and fire protection). For positive net tax rates, the revenues are less than the loss in wages that results from the move of capital to other jurisdictions. In contrast, net subsidies would cost the jurisdiction more than the increase in wages that additional capital would generate.

In turn, competitive jurisdictions will set an environmental standard that is defined by equating the willingness to pay for an additional unit of environmental quality with the corresponding change in wages. Pollution beyond this level generates an increment to wage income that is less than the value of the damage to residents from the increased pollution; in contrast, less pollution creates a loss in wage income greater than the corresponding decrease in pollution damages.

Oates and Schwab show that these choices of tax rates and environmental standards are socially optimal. With respect to tax rates, one condition for optimality is that the marginal product of capital—the increase in the output of the goods produced by an additional unit of capital—must be the same across jurisdictions. Otherwise, it would be possible to increase aggregate output, and, consequently, aggregate social welfare, by moving capital from a jurisdiction where the marginal product of capital is low to one where it is high. Because capital is fully mobile, the market will establish a single rate of return on capital. This rate is equal to the marginal product of capital minus the tax on capital. The choice by competitive jurisdictions of a net tax of zero equalizes the marginal product of capital across jurisdictions and is therefore consistent with optimality.

With respect to environmental standards, competitive jurisdictions equate the marginal private cost of improving environmental quality (measured in terms of foregone consumption) with the marginal private benefit. For net tax rates of zero, the marginal private cost is, as noted above, the decrease in wage

---

[12] In a companion, unpublished manuscript, they argue that their conclusion that competition among states produces efficient outcomes holds even if individuals are mobile. See n. 9 above. If individuals are mobile, they will choose where to live, as in the Tiebout model, by reference to their preference for environmental protection. Individuals who are willing to trade off a great deal in wages for better environmental quality will move to jurisdictions that impose stringent controls on industry; individuals who attach less importance to environmental quality will go to dirtier areas.

income produced by the marginal unit of environmental protection. This decrease is also the marginal social cost, since it represents society's foregone consumption. Thus, instead of producing a race-to-the-bottom, competition leads to the optimal levels of environmental protection.[13]

C.   NON-OPTIMALITY AS A RESULT OF GAME-THEORETIC INTERACTIONS

So far, the inquiry has not revealed support for the claim of systematic environmental under-regulation in a regime without federal intervention. It is possible, however, that in particular instances, the game-theoretic inter-actions among the states would lead to under-regulation absent federal intervention. In such cases, federal minimum standards would be desirable. But it is equally plausible that in other instances the reverse would be true: that the game-theoretic interactions between the states would lead to over-regulation absent federal intervention. In such cases, federal regulation would be desirable as well, but in such cases federal maximum standards would be called for. Accordingly, there is no compelling race-to-the-bottom justification for across-the-board federal minimum standards, which are the cornerstone of federal environmental law.

As an example of such game-theoretic interactions, consider, in the Oates and Schwab model, a situation in which states decide to impose a positive net tax rate on capital, perhaps because they cannot finance the provision of public goods through a non-distortionary tax, such as a head tax. In such a situation, environmental standards will be sub-optimally lax because the jurisdiction will continue to relax these standards beyond the optimal level in order to benefit from the additional net tax revenue that results from attracting additional capital.

A corollary, however, is that environmental standards will be sub-optimally stringent if a jurisdiction, perhaps because of the visibility that attaches to attracting a major facility, chooses a tax rate on capital that is less than the cost of the public services that capital requires. Under this scenario, the optimal strategy for the jurisdiction is to strengthen the environmental standards beyond the optimal level so as to reduce the negative fiscal consequences.[14]

Similarly, recent studies relax the assumptions of constant returns to scale and perfect competition, which are a cornerstone of the Oates and Schwab model.[15] Instead, it considers the effects of state regulation on an industry that

---

[13] For empirical evidence suggesting that environmental regulation does not impair competitiveness, see A. B. Jaffe, S. R. Peterson, P. R. Portney, and R. N. Stavins, "Environmental Regulation and the Competitiveness of U.S. Manufacturing: What Does the Evidence Tell Us?" (1995) 23 *Journal of Economic Literature* 132.

[14] There is no consensus in the academic literature on whether, on average, states and localities tax or subsidize capital. See P. Mieszkowski and G. R. Zodrow, "Taxation and the Tiebout Model: The Differential Effects of Head Taxes, Taxes on Land Rents, and Property Taxes" (1989) 27 *Journal of Economic Literature* 1098.

[15] See J. R. Markusen, E. R. Morey, and N. D. Olewiler, "Environmental Policy when Market Structure and Plant Locations are Endogenous" (1993) 24 *Journal of Environmental Economics*

exhibits increasing returns to scale, a condition generally associated with imperfect competition. The conclusions of the model are that, depending on the levels of firm-specific costs, plant-specific costs, and transportation costs, inter-state competition can produce either sub-optimally lax or sub-optimally stringent levels of pollution.

Alternatively, if a firm has market power enabling it to affect prices, it will be able to extract a sub-optimally lax standard. Conversely, if a state has market power, the reverse will be true. In summary, just as there are game-theoretic situations in which inter-state competition produces environmental under-regulation, there are other plausible scenarios under which the result is over-regulation.

D. FUTILITY OF FEDERAL REGULATION

But even if, left to their own devices, states systematically enacted sub-optimally lax environmental standards, federal environmental regulation would not necessarily improve the situation. Race-to-the-bottom arguments appear to assume, at least implicitly, that jurisdictions compete over only one variable—in this case, environmental quality. Consider, instead, the problem in a context in which states compete over two variables—for example, environmental protection and worker safety. Assume that, in the absence of federal regulation, state one chooses a low level of environmental protection and a high level of worker safety. State two does the opposite: it chooses a high level of environmental protection and a low level of worker safety protection. Both states are in a competitive equilibrium, with industry not migrating from one to the other.

Suppose that federal regulation then imposes on both states a high level of environmental protection. The federal scheme does not add to the costs imposed upon industry in state two, but it does in state one. Thus, the federal regulation will upset the competitive equilibrium, and unless state one responds, industry will migrate from state one to state two. The logical response of state two is to adopt less stringent worker safety standards. This response will mitigate the magnitude of the industrial migration that would otherwise have occurred.

Thus, if a race to the bottom exists, federal environmental standards can have adverse effects on other regulatory programmes, in this case, worker safety. On this account, federal environmental regulation is desirable only if its benefits outweigh the costs that it imposes by shifting to other programmes the pernicious effects of inter-state competition.

More generally, the presence of such secondary effects implies that federal regulation would not be able to eliminate the negative effects of inter-state competition, if such negative effects existed. Recall that the central tenet of

and Management 69; J. R. Markusen, E. R. Morey, and N. D. Olewiler, "Competition in Regional Environmental Policies when Plant Locations are Endogenous" (1995) 56 *Journal of Public Economics* 55.

race-to-the-bottom claims is that competition will lead to the reduction of social welfare; the assertion that states enact sub-optimally lax environmental standards is simply a consequence of this more basic problem. In the face of federal environmental regulation, however, states will continue to compete for industry by adjusting the incentive structure of other state programmes.

So, for example, if states cannot compete over environmental regulation, they will compete over worker safety standards. One might respond by saying that worker safety should also be (and is) the subject of federal regulation. But states would then compete over consumer protection laws or tort standards, and so on. And even if all regulatory functions were federalized, the competition would simply shift to the fiscal arena, where the competition would lead to the under-provision of public goods. Thus, the reduction in social welfare implicit in race-to-the-bottom arguments would not be eliminated.

The race-to-the-bottom rationale for federal environmental regulation is, therefore, radically under-inclusive. It seeks to solve a problem that can be addressed only by wholly eliminating state autonomy. In essence, then, race-to-the-bottom arguments are frontal attacks on federalism. Unless one is prepared to federalize all regulatory and fiscal decisions it is far from clear that federal intervention in the environmental arena would mitigate the adverse social welfare consequences of a race to the bottom, if such a race existed.

IV. The Inter-state Externality Justification

The presence of inter-state externalities provides a compelling argument for federal regulation under conditions in which Coasian bargaining is unlikely to occur.[16] A state that sends pollution to another state obtains the labour and fiscal benefits of the economic activity that generates the pollution, but does not suffer the full costs of the activity. Thus, a sub-optimally large amount of pollution will cross state lines.

Several reasons might explain why transaction costs are sufficiently high to prevent the formation of inter-state compacts. First, the baselines are not well defined in the current legal regime. Does an upwind state have the right to send pollution downwind unconstrained? Alternatively, does the downwind state have the right to enjoin all upwind pollution? Secondly, for different pollution problems, the range of affected states will vary, making less likely the emergence of conditions favouring co-operation. For example, in the case of air pollution, the states affected by a source at a particular location will depend to a large extent on the nature of the pollutant and the height of the stack. Thirdly, the causation questions are not likely to be straightforward. Considerable scientific work needs to be undertaken in order to determine what sources of pollution are having an impact on the downwind state, and it

---

[16] In contrast, if the transaction costs were sufficiently low to permit such bargaining, there would be no efficiency-based reason for federal regulation.

makes little sense for these determinations to be replicated with respect to each compact.

The fact that inter-state externalities provide a compelling justification for intervention, however, does not mean that all federal environmental regulation can be justified on these grounds. For environmental problems such as the control of drinking water quality, there are virtually no inter-state pollution externalities; the effects are almost exclusively local. Even with respect to problems for which there are inter-state externalities, such as air pollution, the rationale calls only for a response well targeted to the problem, such as a limit on the amount of pollution that can cross state lines, rather than the control of pollution that has only in-state consequences.

The analysis of the effectiveness of the environmental statutes at remedying inter-state pollution spillovers proceeds by reference to the Clean Air Act—the statute designed to deal with the pollution that gives rise to the most serious problems of inter-state externalities.[17] It examines the statute's ambient and emission standards, which are the core of the regulatory effort, as well as its acid rain provision and inter-state spillover provisions, which are more directly targeted to the problem of inter-state externalities. It shows that federal regulation has been both ineffective and potentially counter-productive.[18]

A. AMBIENT AND EMISSION STANDARDS

The core of the Clean Air Act consists of a series of federally prescribed ambient standards and emission standards. Ambient standards determine the maximum permissible concentration of a particular pollutant in the ambient air, but do not directly constrain the behaviour of individual polluters. Emission standards, in contrast, determine the maximum amount of a pollutant that can be discharged by an individual source.

The federal emission standards are not a good means by which to combat the problem of inter-state externalities. These standards constrain the pollution from each source, but do not regulate the number of sources within any given state or the location of the sources.

Similarly, the various federal ambient air quality standards also are not well targeted to address the problem of inter-state externalities, because they are both over-inclusive and under-inclusive. From the perspective of constraining inter-state externalities at a desirable level, ambient standards are over-inclusive because they require a state to restrict pollution that has only in-state consequences. Concern about inter-state externalities can be addressed by limiting the amount of pollution that can cross inter-state borders. Because some air pollution has only local effects, such externalities can be controlled

---

[17] Sect. IV relies heavily on Revesz, "Federalism and Inter-State Environmental Externalities", n. 1 above; Revesz, "Federalism and Environmental Regulation: A Normative Critique", n. 1 above, 107–20.

[18] Similar criticisms can be raised against the Clean Water Act, which is designed to combat an environmental problem for which the inter-state pollution spillovers are also salient. See Revesz, "Federalism and Inter-State Environmental Externalities", n. 1 above, 2370.

even if the upwind state chooses to have poor environmental quality within its borders.

Conversely, the federal ambient air-quality standards are also under-inclusive from the perspective of controlling inter-state externalities because a state could meet the applicable ambient standards but nonetheless export a great deal of pollution to downwind states because the sources in the state have tall stacks and are located near the inter-state border. In fact, a state might meet its ambient standards precisely because it exports a great deal of its pollution.

The federal ambient and emissions standards could perhaps be justified as a second-best means by which to reduce the problem of uncontrolled inter-state externalities. One might believe that by reducing pollution across the board they reduce inter-state externalities proportionately.

Such a view, however, is incorrect as a matter of both theory and empirical observation. The amount of aggregate emissions is not the only variable that affects the level of inter-state externalities. In particular, two other factors play important roles. The first is the height of the stack from which the pollution is emitted. The higher the stack, the lesser the impact close to the source and the greater the impact far from the source. Thus, absent a federal constraint, states have an incentive to encourage their sources to use tall stacks, as a way to externalize both the health and environmental effects of the pollution and the regulatory costs of complying with the federal ambient standards.

Secondly, the level of inter-state externalities is affected by the location of the sources. In the eastern part of the USA, where the problem of inter-state pollution is most serious, the prevailing winds blow from west to east. Thus, states have an incentive to induce their sources to locate close to their down-wind borders so that the bulk of the effects of the pollution is externalized. They can induce this result, for example, through the use of tax incentives or subsidies, or through permitting and zoning decisions.

The best evidence that states do indeed encourage sources to use tall stacks can be found in the provisions of the SIPs adopted by at least fifteen states in response to the enactment of the Clean Air Act in 1970. These SIPs allowed sources to meet the NAAQS by using taller stacks rather than by reducing emissions.[19] In those SIPs, the permissible level of emissions was an increasing function of the height of the stack.[20] If the stack was sufficiently high, the

---

[19] See Clean Air Act Oversight: Hearings Before the Subcomm. on Environmental Pollution, Sen. Comm. on Public Works (1974) 93d Cong., 2d Sess., 330–1, 337, 357–9 (hereinafter Sen. Comm. on Public Works); R. E. Ayres, "Enforcement of Air Pollution Controls on Stationary Sources Under the Clean Air Amendments of 1970" (1975) 4 *Ecology Law Quarterly*, 441, 452, nn. 28, 30.

[20] e.g., the Georgia regs. that were struck down in *Natural Resources Defense Council* v. *EPA*, 489 F 2d 390, 403–11 (5th Cir. 1974), reviewed on other grounds *sub nom. Train* v. *Natural Resources Defense Council* provided that, for sulphur dioxide, allowable emissions could be proportional to the cube of the stack height, for stacks under 300 feet, and proportional to the square of the stack height for stacks over 300 feet. See Georgia Rules and Regulations for Air Quality Control 270–5–24–.02(2)(g) (1972). A similar formula applied to particulate emissions. See *ibid.*, 270–5–24–.02(2)(m). Thus, a sufficiently high stack would eliminate the need for any emissions reduction.

effects would be felt only in the downwind states and would therefore have no impact on in-state ambient air-quality levels. Through these measures, the states created strong incentives for their firms to externalize the effects of their sources of pollution.

It is true that states had an incentive to externalize pollution even before the enactment of the Clean Air Act in 1970 because, by encouraging tall stacks, states could make other states bear the adverse health effects of pollution. The 1970 provisions, however, created an additional incentive. By encouraging the use of tall stacks, states could also externalize the regulatory impact of the standards, thereby availing themselves, for example, of the opportunity to attract additional sources without violating the NAAQS.

Taller stacks entail higher costs of construction and, possibly, operation. It is therefore conceivable that a state that did not view the externalization of health effects as sufficient by itself to outweigh imposing such costs on in-state firms would reach a different conclusion when tall stacks led to the externalization of both health and regulatory impacts.

More generally, before 1970, the states had not developed extensive regulatory programmes for controlling air pollution. The net benefits of taller stacks, if any, might not have been worth the institutional investment necessary to create a regulatory programme to transmit incentives for such stacks. The Clean Air Act, by requiring states to prepare SIPs, gave them no choice but to create an institutional structure designed to regulate the emissions of industrial sources. With that structure in place, it became comparatively easier to encourage tall stacks.

In addition, the health benefits of reducing the impact of emissions on in-state ambient air-quality levels are external to the firm emitting the pollution. Thus, a firm will take such effects into account only if required to do so by a regulator. In contrast, the regulatory benefits of reducing the impact on in-state ambient air-quality levels can be captured directly by the firms, which, by using taller stacks, need to invest less to reduce their emissions.[21] While before 1970, firms would have expended resources in tall stacks only if required to do so by a state regulatory agency, after 1970 they had an independent incentive for pursuing such a policy.

It is therefore not surprising that the use of tall stacks expanded considerably after 1970. For example, whereas in 1970 only two stacks in the USA were higher than 500 feet, by 1985 more than 180 stacks were higher than 500 feet and twenty-three were higher than 1000 feet.[22] While the ability of states to externalize pollution in this manner is now less of a problem as a result of a system of regulation of stack height that followed the 1977 amendments to the

---

[21] The savings can be substantial. e.g., a study in the early 1970s, when tall stack credits were most prevalent, showed that the cost of complying with regulatory requirements were between $60/kw and $130/kw for a new lime scrubber, as compared with between $4/kw and $10/kw for a tall stack. See Sen. Comm. on Public Works, n. 20 above, 210, 215.

[22] See A. W. Reitze, Jr., "A Century of Air Pollution Control: What's Worked: What's Failed; What Might Work" (1991) 21 *Environmental Law* 1549, 1598; J. R. Vestigo, "Acid Rain and Tall Stack Regulation Under the Clean Air Act" (1985) 15 *Environmental Law* 711, 730.

Clean Air Act, tall stacks remain a means by which excessive pollution can be externalized.

In contrast to the experience with tall-stack provisions, it is difficult to find direct evidence concerning whether states also provided incentives for sources to locate close to their downwind borders, because such incentives are unlikely to be reflected in regulatory documents. There is, however, literature suggesting that such incentives are present in the case of the siting of waste sites.[23] It would thus not be implausible to believe that states acted in the same manner with respect to air pollution facilities.

In summary, far from correcting the problem of inter-state externalities, the Act's ambient and emission standards may well have exacerbated it.

B.   ACID RAIN PROVISIONS

The acid rain provisions of the 1990 amendments are often hailed as a means of reducing inter-state externalities because acid rain is produced by pollution that travels long distances. However, these provisions apply only to the two pollutants that lead to the formation of acid rain: sulphur dioxide and nitrogen oxides. Further, they apply to only one type of facility: electric utilities. Moreover, these provisions are not structured to allocate emissions between upwind and downwind states in a desirable manner.[24]

With respect to nitrogen oxides, the provisions set emission standards for new and existing sources. As discussed above, emissions standards are not a well targeted means for controlling inter-state externalities. With respect to sulphur dioxide, the acid rain provisions establish a system of grandfathered permits, under which existing emitters are assigned, for free, a number of permits equal to their historical emissions, subject to certain constraints. These permits are tradeable in a single national market.

Although these constraints on the grandfathering of permits are likely to reduce the amount of acid rain, particularly after 2000, they make no attempt to allocate emissions between upwind states and downwind states in an optimal way. The acid rain problem manifests itself primarily in the North East, but is caused primarily by emissions from the mid-West. Because the market is national, mid-Western sources can buy, without restriction, permits from the West and the North East. Such trades would have an undesirable impact in the North East. In fact, downwind states are attempting to prevent their sources from selling permits to upwind sources, though such measures may well be struck down on constitutional grounds.

[23] See, e.g., D. E. Ingberman, "Siting Noxious Facilities: Are Markets Efficient" [1995] *Journal of Environmental Economics and Management* S–20, S–23; B. C. Mank, "Environmental Justice and Discriminatory Siting: Risk-Based Representation and Equitable Compensation" (1995) 56 *Ohio State Law Journal* 329, 421; R. B. Wiygul and S. C. Harrington, "Environmental Justice in Rural Communities" (1993–4) 96 *West Virginia Law Review* 405, 437–8; R. Zimmerman, "Issues of Classifications in Environmental Equity: How We Manage Is How We Measure" (1994) 21 *Fordham Urban Law Journal* 633, 650.

[24] See 42 USC 7651–7651o (1994).

C. INTER-STATE SPILLOVER PROVISIONS

Sections 110(a)(2)(D) and 126(b), which date from the 1977 amendments, are the most comprehensive means for controlling inter-state spillovers. These provisions prohibit a state from "contribut[ing] significantly to non-attainment in, or interfer[ing] with maintenance by" any other state with respect to the NAAQS, or "interfer[ing] with measures required by" any other state under the PSD programme.[25]

Unlike the federal ambient and emissions standards, the inter-state spillover provisions are designed to prevent excessive pollution from crossing inter-state borders. Unlike the tall-stack and acid rain provisions, they are designed to deal with the problem comprehensively. Unfortunately, however, both in resolving various threshold issues and in interpreting substantive questions under the inter-state spillover provisions, the administrative practice and case law have rendered these provisions virtually useless as a means of constraining inter-jurisdictional externalities.

The Environmental Protection Agency (EPA), through the resolution of various threshold issues, has blocked the prospects of downwind states complaining about excessive upwind pollution in important ways. First, it has maintained that it cannot predict such impacts more than fifty kilometres (approximately thirty miles) from the source of the pollution, and has summarily rejected the predictions made by downwind states on the basis of longer-range models.[26] Thus, sections 110(a)(2)(D) and 126(b) have been of no use to downwind states challenging pollution from sources not immediately contiguous to their borders.

The second threshold issue relates to the treatment of pollutants that are transformed as they travel through the atmosphere. For example, increased sulphur dioxide emissions upwind have an effect downwind not only on ambient air-quality levels of sulphur dioxide, but also on ambient air quality levels of particulates. The EPA has consistently taken the position, which has been upheld by the courts, that the impact of transformed pollution need not be taken into account in evaluating whether the upwind pollution is excessive.[27] Thus, the phenomenon of acid rain, an important manifestation of the problem of inter-state pollution, has been largely outside the reach of sections 110(a)(2)(D) and 126(b).

Thirdly, the EPA has not set a national ambient air quality standard for sulphates,[28] even though a relative consensus developed within the scientific community in the 1980s concerning the adverse environmental effects of acid

---

[25] See 42 USC 7410(a)(2)(d), 7426(b) (1994).
[26] See, e.g., *New York* v. *EPA*, 716 F 2d 440, 443–4 (7th Cir. 1983); *New York* v. *EPA*, 710 F 2d 1200, 1204 (6th Cir. 1983).
[27] See, e.g., *New York* v. *EPA*, 716 F 2d 440, 443 (7th Cir. 1983); *New York* v. *EPA*, 710 F 2d 1200, 1204 (6th Cir. 1983).
[28] See *Connecticut* v. *EPA*, 696 F 2d 147, 164–5 (2nd Cir. 1982); B. A. Ackerman and W. T. Hassler, *Clean Coal/Dirty Air* (New Haven, Conn.: Yale University Press, 1981), 65–72.

rain.[29] Nor has the EPA promulgated regulations to combat regional haze,[30] despite a statutory obligation under section 169A to do so by 1979. Had the EPA done so, it would have been required by sections 110(a)(2)(D) and 126(b) to take into account the impact of upwind emissions of sulphur dioxide on the downwind ambient air quality levels of sulphates as well as their impact on regional haze.[31]

The EPA's interpretation of the substantive standards of sections 110(a)(2)(D) and 126(b) has further contributed to rendering these provisions ineffective in controlling inter-state externalities. It is useful in this regard to construct a three-category taxonomy defined by reference to whether the downwind state would meet the federal ambient standards if it did not have to face pollution transported from the upwind state and whether the downwind state actually meets the federal ambient standards despite the upwind pollution.

In the first category, the downwind state would meet the federal ambient standards without the upwind pollution, and meets these standards despite the upwind pollution. In the second category, the downwind state would not meet the federal ambient standards even if there were no upwind pollution and, of course, does not meet the standards with the upwind pollution. In the third category, the downwind state would meet the federal ambient standards in the absence of upwind pollution, but does not meet these standards with the upwind pollution; here, the upwind pollution is the but-for cause of the violation of the federal ambient standards. This taxonomy is summarized in Table I.

Table I: Taxonomy of inter-state spillovers

	Violation without upwind pollution	Violation with upwind pollution
Category I	No	No
Category II	Yes	Yes
Category III	No	Yes

As to each of these categories, two questions are relevant. First, should the federal government play a role in controlling the upwind pollution? Secondly, assuming that such a role is appropriate, how should the federal government

---

[29] See J. L. Kulp, "Acid Rain: Causes, Effects, and Control", *Regulation* (Winter 1990), 41–3; V. Lee, "Inter-State Sulfate Pollution: Proposed Amendments to the Clean Air Act" (1981) 5 *Harvard Environmental Law Review* 71–6.

[30] See, e.g., *New York* v. *EPA*, 852 F 2d 574, 578–9 (DC Cir. 1988), cert. denied, 489 US 1065 (1989); *Vermont* v. *Thomas*, 850 F 2d 99, 103 (2nd Cir. 1988).

[31] See, e.g., *New York* v. *EPA*, 852 F 2d 574, 578–9 (DC Cir. 1988), cert. denied, 489 US 1065 (1989); *Vermont* v. *Thomas*, 850 F 2d 99, 104 (2nd Cir. 1988); *New York* v. *EPA*, 716 F 2d 440, 443 (7th Cir. 1983); *New York* v. *EPA*, 710 F 2d 1200, 1204 (6th Cir. 1983).

determine the permissible amount of upwind pollution that can enter the downwind state?

In Category I, absent a violation of the federal ambient standards—either the NAAQS or the PSD increments—the EPA has chosen to place no limits on the upwind pollution. In this situation, the upwind pollution will be unconstrained even if it leads to a violation of a state ambient standard in the downwind state that is stricter than the federal standard. Further, the upwind pollution will be unconstrained even if the downwind state has limited the emissions of its sources in order to preserve a margin for growth that will permit it to attract new industry. Finally, the upwind pollution will be unconstrained even if the downwind state has been unable to set a baseline under the PSD programme, thereby constraining further environmental degradation, because no major source has applied for a permit.[32]

In Category II cases, where the upwind pollution exacerbates a violation of a federal ambient standard in the downwind state, the EPA has never found upwind pollution to meet the "significant contribution" standard and has given little guidance on what factors distinguish a "significant" contribution from an "insignificant" one. In cases involving a single upwind source, the EPA concluded that contributions of 1.5 per cent and of 3 per cent were not excessive.[33] It reached these conclusions with no analysis, apparently basing its determination on the fact that those percentages do not seem particularly large. Nor did the EPA engage in any inquiry as to the cumulative impacts of upwind emissions. In light of the large number of sources that are likely to affect ambient air-quality levels in the downwind state, this approach is quite unprotective of the interests of downwind states.

In Category III, the EPA has indicated that the plain meaning of the statutory phrase "prevent attainment" requires the Agency to deem excessive any upwind pollution that was the but-for cause of a violation of the federal ambient standards in the downwind state. In the only case in which the situation was presented, however, the Agency rejected the downwind claim, stating that it doubted the accuracy of the modelling analysis performed by the downwind state.[34]

In summary, three principal rules emerge from the administrative interpretations of sections 110(a)(2)(D) and 126(b), which have been uniformly upheld by the courts: upwind pollution is never constrained if the downwind state meets the federal ambient standards; upwind pollution that exacerbates a violation of the federal ambient standards in the downwind states is constrained only if the upwind source "significantly contributes" to the violation; and upwind pollution that is the but-for cause of the violation of federal ambient standards in the downwind state is always constrained.

---

[32] See, e.g., *Air Pollution Control District* v. *EPA*, 739 F 2d 1071, 1085–8 (6th Cir. 1984); *Connecticut* v. *EPA*, 656 F 2d 902, 910 (2nd Cir. 1981).

[33] See, e.g,. *Connecticut* v. *EPA*, 696 F 2d 147, 165 (2nd Cir. 1982); *Air Pollution Control District* v. *EPA*, 739 F 2d 1071, 1092–3 (6th Cir. 1984).

[34] See *New York* v. *EPA*, 852 F 2d 574, 580 (DC Cir. 1988), cert. denied, 489 US 1065 (1989).

The combination of these rules leads to illogical and, in practice, unprotective results. Consider first the Category I case of a downwind state that is not violating the NAAQS or the PSD increments. The amount by which the downwind state's ambient air-quality levels are better than the federal ambient standards represents that state's margin for growth. If the downwind state is not able to attract new sources, because, for example, it is experiencing a temporary economic downturn, the rules allow an upwind state to consume the downwind state's margin for growth without constraint. Indeed, the rules even allow an upwind state to consume the downwind state's margin for growth by amending its SIP to permit its existing sources to increase their emissions up to the point at which the federal ambient standards become constraining in the downwind state.[35] Once the air-quality levels in the downwind state reach the level of the federal ambient standards (with the help of the upwind state), the downwind state will be unable to attract any sources without requiring emission reductions from its existing sources. At the extreme, a downwind state with no existing industrial base would be precluded from ever acquiring one.

In contrast, if the downwind state consumes its margin for growth first, either by attracting new sources or by amending its SIP to allow existing sources to pollute more, any increase in the pollution that the upwind state sends downwind would be deemed a violation of sections 110(a)(2)(D) and 126(b). An upwind state without an industrial base at the time that the downwind state reaches the federal ambient standards might be effectively precluded by this rule from attracting any polluting sources in the future if, as a result of the state's geography, any in-state emissions would be likely to migrate downwind.

Accordingly, the margin for growth in the downwind state would be allocated on a "first-come-first-served" basis. Such rules of capture are undesirable; they create incentives for both upwind and downwind states to use the downwind state's margin for growth at a faster rate than is economically desirable, and do not allocate this margin for growth to whichever state values it most highly.

The discussion so far has focussed on a downwind state that intends to use its margin for growth for economic expansion. Instead, states might set state ambient standards that are more stringent than the federal standards because they attach more value to environmental protection. The federal environmental laws emphasize, as explicitly reflected in section 116 of the Clean Air Act, that federal standards are floors and not ceilings, and that, with exceptions not relevant to this discussion, states remain free to enact standards that are more stringent than the federal standards. Indeed, more stringent standards are undesirable only if they are an effort to externalize to other states the costs of pollution control.

---

[35] Of course, this strategy can be followed only if it does not lead to a violation of the federal ambient standards in the upwind state.

Under the current administrative and judicial approach, however, more stringent state ambient standards can be used only to limit the emissions of in-state sources and cannot be invoked, under any circumstances, to constrain upwind emissions. Such a regime creates a disincentive for downwind states to have more stringent state ambient standards: downwind states bear all the costs of such standards (the costs of tougher emissions limitations for in-state sources), but the upwind states can appropriate the benefit by taking the additional opportunities created for the externalization of pollution.

The administrative and judicial approach to Category II situations, in which the upwind pollution aggravates a violation of the federal ambient standards, also is misguided. In Category II cases, the downwind state would be unable to constrain the upwind pollution unless the pollution was deemed a "significant contribution" to the violation. Under the non-attainment provisions of the Clean Air Act, however, the downwind state has an obligation to reduce its emissions until it meets the NAAQS. Thus, absent a "significant contribution" from upwind sources, the full burden of pollution reduction falls initially on the downwind sources, even if upwind reductions would be far less costly.

But once the downwind state made sufficient improvements so that it could meet the NAAQS were it not for the upwind pollution, the situation would change. The upwind pollution would then be the but-for cause of the violation of the NAAQS in the downwind state—a Category III problem. The upwind pollution would be enjoined as "prevent[ing] the attainment" of the NAAQS, even if the cost to the upwind state of doing so were wholly disproportionate to the cost to the downwind state of somewhat more stringent pollution controls. As already indicated, in cases in which all emissions from the upwind state have at least some impact downwind, such a rule would prevent any polluting activity in the upwind state. The downwind state, by reducing its emissions to the point at which it could meet the NAAQS in the absence of the upwind pollution, but no further, could effectively destroy the upwind state's industrial base.

In summary, of the three rules articulated by the EPA and the courts to address the problem of inter-state spillovers, two are overly lenient. In contrast, the third is overly harsh, though, perhaps as a result of its harshness, EPA has failed to apply it to any specific case.

Perhaps the best illustration of the inefficacy of the Clean Air Act's inter-state pollution provision is provided by a dispute in which Kentucky complained about excessive emissions from an electric utility just across the border in Indiana. The Indiana utility was emitting six pounds of sulphur dioxide per million BTU of heat input—a level that reflected no pollution controls at all. In contrast, the electric utility in Kentucky had spent $138 million installing scrubbers in order to meet a standard of 1.2 pounds per million BTU. Moreover, the Indiana utility consumed almost half of the permissible pollution levels in parts of Kentucky. Nonetheless, despite the compelling nature of the facts, the downwind state lost its challenge.[36]

---

[36] See *Air Pollution Control District* v. *EPA*, 739 F 2d 1071, 1092–3 (6th Cir. 1984).

V. The Public Choice Justification

As indicated above, I have not yet tackled in any comprehensive way the public choice analysis of issues concerning federalism and environmental regulation. I have taken a somewhat sceptical view, however, of the assertion, largely undefended in the legal literature, that federal regulation is necessary to correct for the systematic underprotection of environmental quality at the state level.[37]

First, it is not enough to say that state political processes undervalue the benefits of environmental regulation, or overvalue the corresponding costs. Federal regulation is justifiable only if the outcome at the federal level is socially more desirable, either because there is less under-regulation or because any over-regulation leads to smaller social welfare losses.

Secondly, given the standard public choice argument for federal environmental regulation, it is not clear why the problems observed at the state level would not be replicated at the federal level. The logic of collective action would suggest that the large number of citizen-breathers, each with a relatively small stake in the outcome of a particular standard-setting proceeding, will be overwhelmed in the political process by concentrated industrial interests with a large stake in the outcome. But this problem could occur at the federal level as well as at the state level.

In fact, the logic of collective action might suggest the under-representation of environmental groups would be more serious at the federal level. The costs of organizing on a larger scale magnifies the free-rider problems faced by environmental groups. Moreover, because environmental concerns vary throughout the country, there will be a loss in the homogeneity of the environmental interests when they are aggregated at the federal level, thereby further complicating the organizational problems. For example, environmentalists in Massachusetts may care primarily about air quality whereas environmentalists in Colorado may rank the environmental implications of water allocation as most important. Other things being equal, state-based environmental groups seeking, respectively, better air quality in Massachusetts and a more environmentally sensitive allocation of water in Colorado are therefore likely to be more effective than a national environmental group seeking, at the federal level, better environmental quality with respect to both of these attributes.

In contrast, the situation is likely to be different for industry groups. For many environmental problems, an important portion of the regulated community consists of firms with nation-wide operations. For such firms, operating at the federal level poses no additional free-rider problems or loss of homogeneity.

It is possible, however, that the additional organizational problems faced by environmental groups at the federal level are outweighed by benefits arising

---

[37] Sect. V relies heavily on Revesz, "The Race to the Bottom and Federal Environmental Regulation: A Response to Critics", n. 1 above, 542–3, 558–61.

from the fact that the clash of interest groups takes place before a single legislature, a single administrative agency, and, in part, as a result of the exclusive venue of the DC Circuit over important environmental statutes, in a single court.[38] One can imagine models under which public choice problems are, indeed, ameliorated at the federal level—a task that none of my critics has taken on. The problem, though, is that such models are unlikely to provide a good account of reality.

For example, if one assumed that beyond a certain threshold, additional resources do not increase a group's probability of being successful in the political process, and if this threshold at the federal level is sufficiently lower than the sum of the corresponding thresholds at the state level, it may be that environmental groups would not be at a disadvantage at the federal level even if they were at a disadvantage in the states. In this case, the economies of scale of operating at the federal level more than outweigh the increased free-rider problems.

The assumptions behind such a model, however, are not particularly plausible. The threshold concept might properly describe certain costs associated with effective participation in the regulatory process. For example, with respect to the regulation of a particular carcinogen, each group might need to hire a scientist to review the regulator's risk assessment. It may well be the case that a certain minimum will secure the services of a competent scientist and that devoting additional resources to the problem would be of little, if any, use. Thus, for costs of this type, the marginal benefit of additional expenditures is zero, or close to zero, regardless of the other party's expenditures.

The structure of other costs, however, is likely to be quite different. For example, with respect to access to the legislative process, the standard public choice account is that the highest bidder prevails.[39] Thus, the benefit that a party receives from its expenditures is a function of the expenditures of the other party. Unless the costs of this type are quite small, the economies of scale of operating at the federal level are unlikely to outweigh the additional free-rider problems. Finally, if the relevant public-choice interactions are characterized as involving the diffuse interests of breathers or other environmental beneficiaries on one side and the concentrated interests of industrial firms on the other side, the debate over which forum is relatively better for the environmentalist interests is not of great practical importance. What is important, instead, is that both fora are bad for these interests as a result of the diffuse nature of their interests. As a result, given this characterization of this problem, it is difficult to explain, in public choice terms, why there would be any environmental regulation at all.[40]

---

[38] See R. L. Revesz, "Environmental Regulation, Ideology, and the D.C. Circuit" (1997) 83 *Virginia Law Review* 1717.

[39] See S. Peltzman, "Toward a More General Theory of Regulation" (1976) 19 *Journal of Law and Economics* 211; G. J. Stigler, "The Theory of Économic Regulation" (1971) 2 *Bell Journal of Economics* 3.

[40] Swire acknowledges this difficulty with his argument: "[i]n light of the straightforward public choice analysis presented here, the puzzle remains how environmental protection ever succeeds in the political process".

For this reason, the most plausible public-choice explanations for environmental regulation posit that regulated firms obtain benefits from such regulation in the form of rents and barriers to entry, or that certain regions in our country can obtain from the regulatory process advantages relative to other regions. An extensive public-choice literature suggests that the impetus for environmental regulation sometimes comes, implicitly or explicitly, from the regulated firms themselves, which can obtain rents and barriers to entry that give them an advantage over their competitors.[41] At other times, the advocates are particular regions of the country, which hope to obtain a comparative advantage with respect to other regions.[42]

When the relevant interactions are seen in this manner, the case for federal regulation on public-choice grounds is considerably weakened.[43] A more definitive conclusion, however, must await further sustained analysis.

VI.   Toward Desirable Federal Intervention

The preceding discussion shows why the three principal justifications for federal intervention are unlikely to justify an absolute displacement of state authority.[44] Nonetheless, there is an important role for federal intervention to correct various pathologies that otherwise would result.

(1) *Inter-state externalities:* the preceding discussion has focussed on pollution externalities, principally air pollution that crosses state lines, and shown why the existence of such externalities provides a compelling reason for federal regulation. Other externalities that merit federal regulation arise with respect to different environmental problems. For example, to the extent that certain endangered species are located in a particular state, the costs of protection are largely concentrated in that state. The benefits of preservation, however, accrue nationally, or, for that matter, globally. Similarly, out-of-state citizens place value on the existence of certain natural resources—even resources that they never plan to use. Such existence, or non-use, values provide a powerful justification for federal control over exceptional natural resources such as national parks.

---

[41] See N. O. Keohane, R. L. Revesz, and R. N. Stavins, "The Choice of Regulatory Instruments in Environmental Policy" (1998) 22 *Harvard Environmental Law Review* 313, 348–51.

[42] See B. P. Pashigian, "Environmental Regulation: Whose Self-Interests are Being Protected?" (1985) 23 *Economic Inquiry* 551.

[43] See R. van den Bergh, "The Subsidiarity Principle in European Community Law: Some Insights From Law and Economics" (1994) 1 *Maastricht Journal of European and Comparative Law* 337, 346–8; R. van den Bergh, "Subsidiarity as an Economic Demarcation Principle and the Emergence of European Private Law" (1998) 5 *Maastricht Journal of European and Comparative Law* 129, 148–51.

[44] Sect. VI relies heavily on Revesz, "Federalism and Environmental Regulation: A Normative Critique", n. 1 above, 121–5; Revesz, "The Race to the Bottom and General Environmental Regulation: A Response to Critics", n. 1 above, 543–5.

(2) *Economies of scale:* advocates of federal regulation often maintain, though without much empirical support, that centralization has strong economies of scale advantages. The economies of scale argument is most plausible in the early stages of the regulatory process, particularly with respect to the determination of the adverse effects of particular pollutants through risk assessment. Indeed, there is little reason for this determination to be replicated by each state. In this area, however, the federal government appears to have substantially under-invested. The force of the rationale, however, is far less compelling at the standard-setting phase. At this stage, not only are the savings from eliminating duplication of efforts likely to be much lower, but centralization will have serious social costs as a result of the difficulty of setting standards that are responsive to the preferences and physical conditions of different regions.[45]

(3) *Uniformity:* as previously discussed, federal environmental standards are generally minimum standards. The states remain free to impose more stringent standards if they wish. Some standards that apply to pesticides and mobile sources such as automobiles,[46] however, are both floors and ceilings: they pre-empt both more stringent and less stringent state standards. Uniformity of this sort can be desirable for products with important economies of scale in production. In such cases, disparate regulation would break up the national market for the product and be costly in terms of foregone economies of scale. The benefits of uniformity, however, are less compelling in the case of process standards, which govern the environmental consequences of the manner in which goods are produced rather than the consequences of the products themselves. Indeed, unlike the case of dissimilar product standards, there can be a well-functioning common market regardless of the process standards governing the manufacture of the products traded in the market.

(4) *Protection of minimum levels of public health:* there is a powerful notion, informed in part by constitutional considerations, that a federal polity should ensure all its citizens a minimum level of environmental protection. At some level, this justification is compelling: a minimum level of health ought to count as a basic human right, in the same manner as minimum levels of education, housing, or access to employment. There are two major problems, however, with justifying federal environmental regulation in this manner. First, federal environmental regulation seeks to limit the risk of exposure to particular pollutants or from particular sources, rather than limiting aggregate levels of environmental risk. As a result, such regulation is both over-inclusive (it regulates more than that which has a claim to quasi-constitutional legitimacy) and under-inclusive (it makes no effort to determine aggregate exposure levels;

---

[45] See nn. 2–6 above.
[46] See 7 USC 136v(b) (1994) (pesticides); 42 USC 7416 (1994) (mobile sources).

therefore some individuals may in fact be below the minimum). Secondly, because environmental risks are only one component of health risks, it is difficult to understand why the federal government should have such a pre-eminent role in environmental regulation when it does relatively little with respect to the provision of general health care. In fact, investments in preventive measures such as immunizations or pre-natal care would have a far larger impact on health than investments in environmental regulation. Thus, the justification for federal regulation based on the need to guarantee a minimum level of health calls for a radically different form of regulation from that currently in effect: one that focuses on aggregate environmental health risks and the inter-actions between environmental health risks and other health risks.[47]

VII. Lessons for the European Union

The legal issues concerning centralized environmental regulation are framed somewhat differently in the EU from that in the USA.[48] Two differences are particularly salient: the justifications for centralized intervention and the legal status of the debates over the proper allocation of authority. This section focuses solely on these two legal differences and does not attempt to address political, institutional, or historical differences.

The presence of inter-jurisdictional externalities has played a role in justifying centralized intervention in the EU, as it has in the USA.[49] By relying predominantly on ambient standards and emission standards as the primary tools of environmental policy, the EU's efforts to control inter-state externalities are subject to the same criticisms as the federal environmental statutes in the USA.

The other prominent justification offered in the European context for centralized regulation is that harmonization of environmental laws promotes the

---

[47] Some federal role with respect to environmental regulation might also be justified by the federal government's responsibility to implement obligations flowing from international treaties.

[48] Sect. VII relies heavily on Revesz, "Federalism and Environmental Regulation: Lessons for the European Union and the International Community", n. 1 above, 1338–41.

[49] See, e.g., R. van den Bergh, M. Faure, and J. Lefevere, "The Subsidiarity Principle in European Environmental Law: An Economic Analysis", in E. Eide and R. van den Bergh (eds.), *Law and Economics of the Environment* (Oslo: Juridisk, 1996), 121; R. B. Stewart, "Environmental Law in the United States and the European Community: Spillovers, Cooperation, Rivalry, Institutions" [1992] *University of Chicago Law Forum* 41, 45; M. L. Schemmel and B. de Regt, "The European Court of Justice and the Environmental Protection Policy of the European Community" (1994) 17 *Boston College International and Comparative Law Review* 53, 80; M. M. T. A. Brus *et al.*, "Balancing National and European Competence in Environmental Law" (1994) 9 *Connecticut Journal of International Law* 633; K. Lenaerts, "The Principle of Subsidiarity and the Environment in the European Union: Keeping the Balance of Federalism" (1994) 17 *Fordham International Law Journal* 846, 880–1.

establishment of a common market;[50] this justification has not been nearly as prominent in federalism debates in the USA.

The harmonization rationale has some force in the case of product standards. Indeed, a product cannot trade freely throughout a common market if states within the market can exclude it on environmental or health and safety grounds. Harmonization arguments, however, have also been invoked to justify the vesting of centralized responsibility over process standards, such as environmental ambient and emissions standards. There are several serious problems with extending the argument in this manner.[51]

First, as long as product standards are harmonized, there can be a well-functioning common market regardless of the stringency of the process standards governing the products' manufacture. Thus, more accurately, the argument must call for the harmonization of the products' production costs, so as to deny a comparative advantage to states with lax environmental standards.

The second problem, however, is that the costs of complying with environmental regulation, or, for that matter, the costs of complying with any regulation, are only one component of the total costs of production. Other components include a state's investments in infrastructure, health care, and education, as well as its wages, labour productivity, and access to raw materials. These factors, which can have a significant effect on production costs, are unlikely to be (or are incapable of being) the subject of the EU's harmonization efforts. Thus, rather than eliminating cost differences, the harmonization of environmental standards has the effect of conferring a competitive advantage on states with lower non-harmonizable components of costs.

Thirdly, the harmonization argument cannot be used, as it has in the EU, to justify both uniform ambient standards and uniform emissions standards. A centralized regulatory regime consisting only of uniform ambient standards, which permits the states to allocate the pollution control burden among existing and new sources in any way they see fit, would confer a competitive advantage on the states with the smaller industrial base. Indeed, states with lower

---

[50] See, e.g., A. Haagsma, "The European Community's Environmental Policy: A Case Study in Federalism" (1989) 12 *Fordham International Law Journal* 311, 355; O. Lomas, "Environmental Protection, Economic Conflict and the European Community" (1988) 33 *McGill Law Journal* 506, 511; G. Close, "Harmonisation of Laws: Use or Abuse of the Powers Under the EEC Treaty?" (1978) 3 *European Law Review* 461, 470.

[51] Despite its weak intellectual pedigree, it is not surprising that the harmonization argument has been influential. The European Union (EU) (then known as the European Economic Community (EEC)) was established by the Treaty of Rome in 1957 (Treaty Establishing the European Economic Community, 25 Mar. 1957, 298 UNTS 11) (hereinafter EC Treaty). This treaty did not contain any specific rules dealing with environmental protection. Environmental regulation between 1957 and 1986 was based principally on Art. 94 EEC, which authorizes the issue of directives, "for the approximation of such provisions laid down by law, regulation or administrative action in Member States as directly affect the establishment or functioning of the common market" *ibid.*, 54. Thus, centralized involvement had to be justified by reference to the benefits of harmonization. The Treaty of Rome was amended by the Single European Act (SEA) in 1986, [1987] OJ L169/1, and by the Treaty on European Union (the Maastricht Treaty) in 1992 (Treaty Establishing the European Community (TEU), 7 Feb. 1992 [1992] OJ C224/1, [1992] CMLR 573 (hereinafter EC Treaty). Now, Arts. 95 and 174–6 EC provide the EU with explicit authority to promulgate environmental standards.

pollution output could offer their sources less stringent emissions standards without violating the ambient standards. The addition of centralized emissions standards moderates this comparative advantage but does not wholly eliminate it. Highly industrialized states, where the centralized ambient standards constrain further growth, would be unable to attract new sources without imposing additional costs on existing sources.

In light of these weaknesses, it is not surprising that recent European scholarship has sought to re-characterize the quest for harmonization in race-to-the-bottom terms. Commentators have argued, as have race-to-the-bottom advocates in the USA, that the goal of centralized intervention is to protect states from the pressure to impose sub-optimally lax environmental standards as a means of attracting jobs and tax revenues.[52] But, obviously, the weaknesses of the race-to-the-bottom rationale for centralized environmental regulation are not confined to this side of the Atlantic.[53]

In addition, the legal status of the debates concerning the strength of the rationales for centralized environmental regulation is also different in the EU and the USA. In the USA, the choice between federal and state regulation (except when state regulation is coupled with trade restrictions) is, for the most part, a matter of policy. The constitutional constraints are extremely weak, even after the Supreme Court's decisions in *New York* v. *United States*,[54] *United States* v. *Lopez*,[55] and *Printz* v. *United States*.[56]

In the EU, in contrast, the subsidiarity principle adopted in the Maastricht Treaty in 1992 permits action at the federal level "only if and insofar as the objectives of the proposed action cannot be sufficiently achieved by the Member States and can therefore, by reason of the scale or effects of the proposed action, be better achieved by the Community".[57] Thus, in the EU, the subsidiarity principle constitutionalizes the inquiry concerning the level of government at which responsibility for environmental regulation should be allocated. Although commentators are divided about the likely role of the European Court of Justice in enforcing the subsidiarity principle, some believe

---

[52] See L. Krämer, *E.C. Treaty and Environmental Law* (2nd edn., London: Sweet & Maxwell, 1995), 62; Lenaerts, n. 51 above, 881; van den Bergh, Faure, and Lefevere, n. 50 above; see also Stewart, n. 50 above, 45.

[53] See Sect. II above.

[54] 505 US 144 (1992) (holding that Congress may not require states to enact or administer a federal programme).

[55] 115 S Ct. 1624 (1995) (holding, for the first time in over 50 years, that Congress exceeded its authority under the Commerce Clause).

[56] 117 S Ct. 2365 (1997) (holding that Congress may not compel state officers to execute federal laws).

[57] See EC Treaty, n. 52 above, Art. 5. A similar principle had applied exclusively to environmental regulation, between 1986 and 1992, under Art. 174(4) EC of the Single European Act in 1986. See *ibid.*, Art. 174(4) EC as in effect in 1986.

For discussion of the application of the subsidiarity principle to environmental law, see L. J. Brinkhorst, "Subsidiarity and EC Environmental Policy" (1993) 8 *European Environmental Law Review* 20; Lenaerts, n. 50 above; Van den Bergh, Faure, and Lefevere, n. 50 above; W. P. J. Wils, "Subsidiarity and EC Environmental Policy: Taking People's Concerns Seriously" (1994) 6 *Journal of Environmental Law* 85.

that the principle is fully justiciable.[58] The unsettled state of the doctrine lends particular significance to the strength of the various rationales for federal intervention. As a result, the debates concerning the proper allocation of authority over environmental regulation currently being waged primarily on this side of the Atlantic may well acquire an even greater salience in the EU.

VIII.   Lessons for the International Community

Section A explains the analytical differences between the paradigmatic federal and international cases for centralized regulation. Section B explains why, even for the same type of case, the assessment of the desirability of centralized intervention is different in the two situations.[59]

A.   ANALYTICAL DIFFERENCES BETWEEN THE PARADIGMATIC FEDERAL AND INTERNATIONAL CASES

Some commentators maintain that the cases for centralized intervention in federal systems and in the international community are analytically analogous. For example, in a recent article, Daniel Farber argues that "free trade and environmental regimes have much in common".[60] He adds:

Notably, the rationale for both the trade and environmental regimes is the fear that a "prisoner's dilemma" may lead to a race to the bottom, whether of trade restrictions or environmental laxity. It turns out that both kinds of races can occur only under particular—and rather similar—circumstances. Thus, the appropriate conditions for multilateral trade regimes are similar to those for multilateral environmental regimes.[61]

Before exploring why these two types of measures are analytically distinct, it is useful to define with some precision what Farber must mean by "free trade" and "environmental" regimes. The structures of these two regimes can best be understood by reference to the two-by-two matrix shown in Table II.

The rows in the table indicate that a jurisdiction's standard can be either a product standard, which regulates the environmental consequences of the product itself, or a process standard, which regulates the environmental consequences of the industrial process through which the product is produced. The table's columns indicate whether, in addition to being enforced against

---

[58] Commentators are divided about the role of the European Court of Justice (ECJ) in subsidiarity inquiries. See, e.g., Lenaerts, n. 50 above, 894 (Court could merely require reasons for federal action); A. G. Toth, "A Legal Analysis of Subsidiarity", in D. O'Keefe (ed.), *Legal Issues of the Maastricht Treaty* (London: Chancery Law Publishers, 1994), 37, 48 (subsidiarity principle raises political questions); J. Steiner, "Subsidiarity Under the Maastricht Treaty", in *Legal Issues of the Maastricht Treaty*, above, 49, 58 (subsidiarity principle is fully justiciable).

[59] Sect. VIII relies heavily on Revesz, "Federalism and Environmental Regulation: Lessons for the European Union and the International Community", n. 1 above, 1332–5, 1341–5.

[60] D. A. Farber, "Environmental Federalism in a Global Economy" (1997) 83 *Virginia Law Review* 1283–4.

[61] *Ibid.*, 1284–5.

domestic producers, the standards are also enforced by means of trade restrictions.[62] In the case of product standards, a trade restriction would bar the entry into the jurisdiction of products that violate the jurisdiction's product standard. In the case of process standards, a trade restriction would bar the entry into the jurisdiction of products manufactured through an industrial process that violates the jurisdiction's process standards.

The paradigmatic case of a "free trade" regime is the regulation, by a federal or international authority, of overly stringent product standards that are coupled with trade restrictions. Such measures are sometimes motivated by a desire to reduce the negative effects of a product that are external to its purchaser. For example, a product's price might not fully reflect the cost of disposing of its packaging. Similarly, the consumption of the product (as is the case, for example, with tobacco products) might have negative effects on the health of third parties, or on the public health system. Alternatively, the restriction might be adopted at the behest of in-state producers of the product, who might be able to meet the more stringent product standard more cheaply than their out-of-state counterparts. The reason for federal regulation or international regulation is the concern that the jurisdiction externalizes, to individuals and firms outside the jurisdiction, too many of the costs of meeting its product standard.[63]

In contrast, the paradigmatic case of an "environmental" regime is the regulation, by a federal or international authority, of overly lax process standards not enforced by means of trade restrictions. The concern here is that the jurisdiction imposes unacceptable environmental consequences upon its residents.[64]

As Table II shows, these two types of measures are not exclusive; the table reveals the existence of two other categories. Product standards need not be coupled with trade restrictions. Such measures are not commonplace, however, because domestic producers would be put at a disadvantage compared to their out-of-state counterparts, and the benefits of the standard would be defeated if the consumption of imports became prevalent.

Similarly, process standards can be coupled with trade restrictions. Such measures are not part of the legal regimes of the USA and the EU, but they are becoming a prominent feature of international trade disputes.[65]

---

[62] A jurisdiction might attempt to enforce its standards only by means of trade restrictions, exempting domestic producers. Such discriminatory measures would fall foul of any plausible system of trade regulation. Thus, Table I does not contemplate this possibility. A complete description of the problem, however, would require a two-by-two-by-two matrix.

[63] See Stewart, "International Trade and Environment: Lessons from the Federal Experience", n. 7 above, 1334–5.

[64] Farber's terminology is somewhat confusing. Both regimes have environmental consequences. In one case, the purpose of the higher level intervention is to pre-empt overly lax environmental regulation whereas in the other it is to pre-empt overly stringent environmental regulation. Similarly, both regimes have trade consequences. Constraints on coupling overly stringent product standards with trade restrictions expands the market for products manufactured by states with less stringent standards. Constraints on overly lax process standards expand the market for products manufactured in states with more stringent process standards by reducing a differential in production costs.

[65] See nn. 70–72 below (discussing the *Tuna-Dolphin* case).

Table II: A Taxonomy of Regulatory Standards

		Enforcement through trade restrictions	
		Yes	No
Type of Standard	Product	"Free trade" regime	
	Process		"Environmental" regime

"Free trade" and "environmental" regimes are different in three important respects: (1) the winners and losers, both in-state and out-of-state, from the regulatory regime; (2) the instances in which there is a divergence between the in-state calculus and the global social calculus concerning the desirability of the regulatory measures; and (3) the impact of public choice considerations. These differences severely undercut the force of the analogy between the two types of regimes.

First, the two types of measures produce different winners and losers. Within the regulating jurisdiction, a product standard coupled with trade restrictions imposes costs on consumers, who must pay higher prices for the product. In turn, it confers benefits on the victims of the externality, who suffer fewer adverse consequences. It also confers benefits on producers of the product within the jurisdiction if they have a comparative advantage in meeting the jurisdiction's product standard, or to in-state producers of substitute products. In deciding whether to impose the regulatory measure, a welfare-maximizing jurisdiction would weigh these benefits to environmental victims and producers against the costs to consumers.

The jurisdiction would not concern itself, however, with the effects of the measure outside its borders, which are likely to be negative. Out-of-state producers will have a smaller market in which to sell their products, leading to a loss of jobs, profits, and tax revenues in that jurisdiction. In addition, out-of-state consumers will face higher prices if there are economies of scale in production.

In contrast, the winners and losers, both in-state and out-of-state, are different in the case of process standards not coupled with trade restrictions. As with product standards, in-state victims of environmental externalities are beneficiaries of the regulatory measure. In-state producers, however, must bear higher operating costs. Thus, here, there is a divergence between the interests of in-state producers and environmental beneficiaries, which were aligned for product standards coupled with trade restrictions. Moreover, as a result of the higher operating costs, industrial plants may move to a state with less stringent process standards, leading to fewer jobs, lower wages, and lower tax revenues in the state adopting the process standard. In assessing the desirability of a particular process standard that is not coupled with trade restrictions, a state must strike a different balance, weighing the standard's health benefits against its labour and fiscal costs.

Secondly, in the case of product standards coupled with trade restrictions, there is the possibility of divergence between the in-state calculus of the importing jurisdiction and the global social calculus: the regulatory measure that maximizes the jurisdiction's welfare might not maximize the overall welfare. Indeed, the jurisdiction imposing the restriction will not concern itself with the negative impact of the restriction on out-of-state producers and consumers. Thus, left to its own devices, a welfare maximizing jurisdiction might impose restrictions that reduce the global social welfare.

In contrast, in the case of process standards not coupled with trade restrictions, there is no divergence between the in-state calculus and the global social calculus (difference in net benefits; the choice that maximizes the jurisdiction's welfare would also maximize the overall welfare; get rid of costs). Even though a decision to weaken or strengthen a process standard may have consequences outside the jurisdiction, in the form of industrial inflow or outflow, respectively, these consequences do not give rise to the type of externality that reduces the global social welfare. The process standard can be thought of as a component of the price charged by the jurisdiction for the right to locate within its borders. The external effect is thus the result of the normal competitive mechanism for the reallocation of resources in response to changes in prices. Thus, the weakening or strengthening of a state environmental standard gives rise to a pecuniary externality, with no adverse social welfare consequences, rather than a true or technological externality.[66]

Thirdly, public choice considerations suggest that the two types of measures would be the product of political pressures from distinct groups. Disproportionate political influence on the part of environmental beneficiaries would lead to overly stringent product and process standards. In contrast, disproportionate political influence on the part of manufacturers might lead to overly stringent product standards but overly lax process standards.

Undoubtedly, under certain conditions jurisdictions will reach the socially optimal result, absent higher-level intervention, with respect to both product and process standards. There are also some similarities in the instances in which higher-level intervention is appropriate. Nonetheless, the paradigmatic models of the two situations are analytically distinct. Inattention to those differences is likely to impede the development of desirable public policy concerning when a jurisdiction's decision-making processes ought to be displaced.

---

[66] Nonetheless, if the jurisdiction cannot pursue a welfare maximizing strategy, as a result perhaps of the presence of distortionary taxes, its choice of process standard might have distortionary effects elsewhere. For a discussion of the difference between technological externalities and pecuniary externalities, see W. J. Baumol and W. E. Oates, *The Theory of Environmental Policy* (2nd edn., Cambridge: Cambridge University Press, 1988), 29–31.

B.   DESIRABILITY OF FEDERAL INTERVENTION IN FEDERAL SYSTEMS AND THE INTERNATIONAL COMMUNITY

The issues concerning the desirability of centralized intervention are different, in two important respects, in the international community from federal systems. First, in the international community, there is only weak capacity for centralized environmental standard-setting and virtually no capacity for centralized environmental enforcement. Secondly, the differences in wealth and economic development are far more salient in the international community than in federal systems.

As a result of the lack of a viable system of environmental standard-setting and enforcement, there are stronger arguments in the international community than in federal systems for allowing countries to impose environmentally-based trade restrictions. Even where centralized regulation might be preferable, for example as a result of inter-jurisdictional externalities, state regulation coupled with trade restrictions might be the best available outcome if centralized regulation is not feasible, or if it is not feasible in an enforceable manner.

The different treatment of process standards in federal systems and in the international community is therefore not surprising. In both the USA and the EU, state-imposed trade restrictions have been coupled with product standards but not with process standards.[67] Instead, environmental regulation with respect to processes has been the domain of the federal government. There is little justification for allowing a state to impose a process standard designed to change the environmental behaviour of another state when a centralized authority can do so directly.

In contrast, process standards have been coupled with trade restrictions in the international community—the USA's restrictions on the import of certain tuna products at issue in the *Tuna Dolphin* case is probably the best known example.[68] Even though the Secretariat of the General Agreement on Tariffs and Trade (GATT), the WTO's predecessor, took a sceptical view with respect to the permissibility of such measures,[69] the issue continues to draw the body's attention[70] and may well be decided differently in future negotiating rounds.

The second important difference between the systems of the USA and the EU on the one hand and the international community on the other arises as a result of the more extreme differences in wealth and levels of economic development in the international community. This factor, coupled with the lack of

---

[67] See Stewart, "International Trade and Environment: Lessons from the Federal Experience", n. 7 above, 1342.

[68] See *United States: Restrictions on Imports of Tuna* (1993) GATT BISD (39th Supp.), 155.

[69] See GATT Secretariat, Trade and Environment, GATT/1529, 10 (3 Feb. 1992), in *World Trade Materials*, Jan. 1992, 37, 50 ("In principle, it is not possible under GATT's rules to make access to one's own market dependent on the domestic environmental policies or practices of the exporting country").

[70] See WTO Secretariat, Report of the WTO Committee on Trade and Environment, PRESS/TE 014, 2–10, 39–42 (14 Nov. 1996).

a viable, widespread system for economic redistribution in the international community, implies that the distributional consequences of each policy ought to play a far more salient role in evaluating their relative desirability.

For example, in a federal system of relatively homogenous states, it might be desirable to adopt policies that lead to the maximization of social welfare without undue concern about how the costs and benefits of such policies are distributed across different geographic subdivisions. Indeed, federal governments regulate in many areas, and the distributional consequences may well even out across programmes. Thus, it may not be sensible to compromise the social welfare properties of each programme in order to achieve a better programme-specific distribution. Moreover, even if such evening out of the aggregate distributional consequences does not occur, it is likely to be more desirable to redistribute through a system of taxes and subsidies than by compromising the efficiency of the various regulatory programmes. The situation is different in the international community with its larger differences in wealth and economic development, and lesser opportunities for redistribution.

A full analysis of when process standards coupled with trade restrictions ought to be permissible in the international community obviously cannot be undertaken here. The following taxonomy, however, seeks to provide a useful way to begin to analyse the relevant issues.

The first element of this taxonomy is defined by reference to the geographic scope of the physical effects of the pollution that gives rise to the trade restriction. Six situations are relevant:

(a) purely domestic effects in the exporting country;
(b) physical spillovers into the importing country;
(c) physical spillovers into third countries;
(d) impairment of existence values in the importing country;
(e) impairment of existence values in third countries; and
(f) effects on the global commons.

In the first situation, if the effects of the pollution are confined to the exporting country, trade restrictions are hardest to justify. Producers in the importing country may be upset that one factor of production is cheap in the exporting country, but restrictions imposed for this reason are unlikely to be welfare enhancing. Moreover, given that the costs of production have many non-harmonizable components, such as wages, labour productivity, infrastructure, and educational systems, it is not clear why a single factor should be singled out for special treatment.[71]

A sufficiently egregious disregard for human health can be thought of as akin to the violation of a basic human right, and therefore sanctionable.[72] (The use of child labour might be seen as an example of such a violation.) Many environmental disparities between exporting and importing countries, however, do not give rise to problems of this magnitude.

---

[71] But see nn. 77–79 below (discussing legislative proposal and views of Vice President Gore).
[72] See nn. 47–48 above.

In the second situation—the case of physical spillovers—trade restrictions might be the only way for the importing country to protect itself. In the USA, the permissibility of such restrictions is sometimes determined by comparing the welfare gains in the importing state with the corresponding welfare losses in the exporting state.[73] In the international community, however, the distributional concerns discussed above complicate the inquiry.

In the third situation—where the physical spillovers affect third countries—the importing country's trade restriction might nonetheless increase the global social welfare. Because the importing country is not affected by the pollution, however, one might be concerned that the asserted environmental reason for the restriction is a mere subterfuge, masking a protectionist motivation.

With respect to the fourth and fifth situations, there is no analytical reason for treating existence values, also known sometimes as non-use values, differently from physical spillovers. Citizens of the importing country might suffer a real loss in utility from learning about the destruction of a valuable natural resource abroad, even if they never planned to visit it. The claims of citizens of wealthy countries for trade measures to protect their existence values might not seem particularly sympathetic if the costs fall on citizens of far poorer countries, whose very livelihood might be at stake. Moreover, the controversy surrounding the use of the contingent valuation methodology, which is used to value existence values, makes problematic any attempt to weigh the interests of the various jurisdictions.[74] As a result, trade measures motivated by the impairment of existence values are likely to be viewed as less legitimate than trade measures motivated by physical spillovers.

Finally, with respect to the global commons, in some cases trade measures will be expressly permitted by international treaties.[75] Such treaties, however, often take a long time to negotiate (and an even longer time to result in the imposition of specific obligations). In the interim, unilateral trade measures may well be the best available way to protect the global commons.

The second element of the classification system is defined by reference to how the environmental standards in the exporting and importing countries compare to those that would maximize social welfare in the respective jurisdictions. The relevant categories are set forth in Table III.

To illustrate this table by means of an example, consider the following situation, which is consistent with the box labelled "g". A's actual standard is ten parts per million (ppm) of a pollutant, whereas its optimal standard is twelve ppm; thus, A's actual standard is more stringent than its optimal standard. In turn, B's actual standard is eight ppm (more stringent than A's actual standard) but its optimal standard is six ppm (thus, B's standard is less stringent than its optimal standard).

[73] See Revesz, "Federalism and Inter-State Externalities", n. 1 above, 2405–8.
[74] For an overview of the issues, see P. R. Portney, "The Contingent Valuation Debate: Why Economists Should Care" (1994) 8 *Journal of Economic Perspectives* 3.
[75] For a summary, see R. L. Revesz, *Foundations of Environmental Law and Policy* (New York: Oxford University Press, 1997), 305.

Table III: Comparison of the stringency of environmental standards in countries A (exporting) and B (importing)

		B		
		Laxer than optimal	*Optimal*	*More stringent than optimal*
A				
	Laxer than optimal	a	b	c
	Optimal	d	e	f
	More stringent than Optimal	g	h	i

In the event that *B*'s environmental standards are more stringent than *A*'s, should *B*'s use of trade measures be appropriate merely because its standards are more stringent than *A*'s? Such an approach was embodied in the proposed International Pollution Deterrence Act,[76] which would have authorized the imposition of countervailing duties equal to the amount that the foreign firm would have to expend in order to comply with the US standards.[77] Similarly, Vice-President Gore wrote, while he was still a senator: "[j]ust as government subsidies of a particular industry are sometimes considered unfair under the trade laws, weak and ineffectual enforcement of pollution control measures should also be included in the definition of unfair trading practices".[78] The problem with this approach is that it would authorize the erection of trade barriers even when the disparity in the environmental standards is justified by differences in the preferences for environmental protection, differences in the costs of pollution control, and differences in the extent to which pollution produces adverse health and environmental effects in the two countries.

Alternatively, should trade measures be appropriate only in situations a, b, and c, in which *A*'s standards are laxer than optimal? Such an approach would recognize the reasons why it is desirable for different countries to have different levels of environmental protection.

Or should *B* be barred from using trade measures in situations a, d, and g because its own standards are laxer than optimal, even though *A*'s are laxer still? Such an approach would create incentives for *B* to adopt socially desirable standards.

In situations c, f, and i, where *B*'s standards are more stringent than optimal, should *B* be permitted to use trade measures only if its optimal standards are more stringent than *A*'s standards? An affirmative answer might be predicated on the undesirability of allowing *B* to penalize other countries as a result of its

[76] S. 984, 102d Cong. (1991).
[77] *Ibid.*, 3–4.
[78] A. Gore, *Earth in the Balance* (Boston, Mass.: Houghton Mifflin Com., 1992), 343.

own public choice problems that lead it to adopt suboptimally stringent standards.

IX. Conclusion

In summary, in a well designed system, the allocation of authority between the federal government and the states would look very different from the way it does now. The federal government currently performs many functions that would better be discharged at the state level, and fails to perform some functions that can only be effectively carried out at the federal level. Perhaps this gap results in part from confusion over the strength of the race-to-the-bottom, inter-state externality, and public choice justifications for federal environmental regulation, which this article hopes to help dispel. The analysis of these issues in the domestic context also has important implications for the EU and the international community.

Flexibility in the Implementation of EC Environmental Law

JOANNE SCOTT*

I. Introduction

This article addresses the theme of Member State flexibility in the implementation of Community environmental law. It does so against the backdrop of the proportionality principle. This theme is explored, and the issues arising exemplified, by reference to a single example: Council Directive 96/61/EC concerning Integrated Pollution Prevention and Control (IPPC).[1] Originally proposed in 1993 in accordance with the priorities identified in the fifth Environmental Action Programme, this Directive represents a self-conscious expression of the application of the proportionality principle. To this end it is presented as leaving "as much freedom as possible" to Member States in implementation.[2] This "freedom" is conceived in both substantive and institutional terms. Member States enjoy considerable autonomy not only in determining the scope and distribution of the pollution abatement burden, but also in constructing institutional arrangements for achieving implementation. Implementation of the IPPC Directive is to be achieved, at the latest, by 30 October 1999.[3]

The concept of proportionality is multi-faceted. Closely related to the more recently conceived principle of subsidiarity, it too is concerned to ensure that "decisions are taken as closely as possible to the citizens of the Union".[4] At its simplest proportionality requires that "the Community shall not go beyond what is necessary to achieve the objectives of the Treaty".[5] It is concerned with the "intensity" of Community action. It is conceived as militating in favour of (framework) directives rather than detailed measures, and requires that these leave as much scope for national decision as possible, where appropriate providing Member States with alternative ways to achieve the objectives pursued. It provides, in addition, that care be taken to respect well-established national arrangements and the organization and working of Member States' legal

* Lecturer, University of Cambridge, Fellow of Clare College, and Jean Monnet Fellow (1998–9) European University Institute, Florence. Many thanks to Han Somsen and Gràinne de Bùrca for their generous help.

[1] [1996] OJ L257/26.
[2] COM(93)423 final, 11. See also COM(95)88 final and COM(96)306 final.
[3] N. 1 above, Arts. 21(1) and 22.
[4] Second recital, "Protocol on the Application of the Principles of Subsidiarity and Proportionality" annexed to the Treaty of Amsterdam.
[5] Art. 5 EC (formerly Art. 3b EC).

systems. In all respects the constraints which it imposes upon the Community institutions are defined functionally, having regard to considerations of effectiveness in the achievement of the objectives pursued and proper enforcement of the measure.[6]

This article will examine the IPPC Directive through the lens of proportionality. It turns first (section II) to issues of substantive flexibility, and considers how much room for manœuvre Member States enjoy in defining the nature and scope of the obligations laid down in the Directive. Section III goes on to examine the issue of procedural flexibility in implementation and the constraints, if any, which Member States face in terms of the organization and design of implementation processes. This latter section highlights a degree of tension between subsidiarity and proportionality as currently defined, and argues in favour of a higher degree of procedural prescription in implementation in the interests of legitimacy and the realization of meaningful subsidiarity.

II.   Substantive Flexibility in Implementation

In thinking about substantive flexibility in the implementation of Community environmental law three factors emerge as of critical importance in influencing the scope of Member State autonomy: (a) choice of legal basis; (b) choice of policy instrument at Community level; and (c) the nature and scope of any exceptions laid down. Each of these will be discussed in the context of the IPPC Directive.

A.   CHOICE OF LEGAL BASIS

It is readily apparent, on the basis of the text of the EC Treaty itself, that the legal basis upon which any Community act is predicated will have important implications in terms of Member State flexibility in implementation. Particularly significant in the environmental sphere is the distinction, in terms of the scope of Community legislative competence, between Articles 95 (formerly Article 100a) EC and 175 (formerly Article 130s) EC. Under the former the Community may enact either minimum or exhaustive harmonization measures, whereas under the latter (the legal basis of the IPPC Directive) Member States are always, in principle, entitled to maintain or introduce more restrictive protective measures.[7] In the face of such minimum harmonization, Member States are obliged merely to respect the "floor" of obligations laid down in the Community measure. In the regulatory space above that floor Member States enjoy substantive autonomy subject, in the context of Article 175 EC to two legal constraints.

---

[6] N. 4 above, paras. 6 and 7.

[7] Art. 176 (formerly Art. 130t) EC. It is important to note that even in the case of measures adopted under Art. 95 EC which take the form of exhaustive harmonization measures, the safeguards provided for under paras. 4–6 apply. These are discussed in detail in the article by H. G. Sevenster at p. 291.

First, stricter measures enacted within a Member State must be notified to the Commission.[8] Any failure to do so will represent a breach of Community law, rendering the Member State concerned liable to proceedings pursuant to Article 226 (formerly Article 169) EC. Less certain is the legal status of such measures pending notification and the question whether Member States are authorized to apply stricter measures prior to their notification. This question has assumed enormous significance in the wake of the European Court's famous *CIA Securities* judgment.[9] Here a failure to notify the Commission of proposals to adopt new technical specifications at national level, as required under the 1983 Notification Directive,[10] was said to render the technical regulations concerned inapplicable, and unenforceable against individuals, even in proceedings between private parties. The Directive was considered such as to confer rights upon individuals, upon which they could rely before national courts, such courts being obliged to decline to apply the non-notified measures. Nonetheless, in this case, while the notification procedure laid down did not require a Commission decision approving the national measure, it did empower the Commission, except in urgent cases, to delay adoption of these measures.[11] The Commission does not enjoy such authority under Article 176 EC, and the situation here appears more akin to that in the earlier *Enichem Base* case.[12] Here, by way of contrast, a failure to notify under the 1975 Directive on Waste was not deemed to be such as to affect the lawfulness of the rules in question or to give rise to individual rights.[13] That the Waste Directive neither required Commission approval of the notified measures, nor laid down any procedure for Commission monitoring of such measures, was a factor cited by the Court in justifying this conclusion. Thus, though the matter cannot be considered to be conclusively settled, it does appear that a failure to notify under Article 176 EC will not deprive existing or new national norms of legal effect. Nonetheless it is important to emphasize that many such measures may also have to be notified under the 1983 Notification Directive. This extends to draft "technical specifications", these being defined as specifications contained in a document laying down the characteristics required of a product. The concept of product regulation is broadly defined here to include, *inter alia*, quality and performance standards as well as labelling and packaging requirements.[14]

[8] Cf Art. 95 EC where the Member State is not only obliged to notify the Commission but to secure Commission confirmation of the measure in question. A Member State is not authorized to apply such national provisions until it has obtained such a decision. See Case C–41/93, *French Republic v. Commission* [1994] ECR 1–1829, para. 30.

[9] Case C–194/94, *CIA Securities International SA v. Signalson SA and Securitel SPRL* [1996] ECR I–2201.

[10] Council Dir. 83/189/EEC laying down a procedure for the provision of information in the field of technical standards and regulations [1983] OJ L109/8.

[11] *Ibid.*, Art. 9(1) and (2).

[12] Case 380/87, *Enichem Base and Others v. Commune di Cinisello Balsamo* [1989] ECR 2491.

[13] *Ibid.*, para. 23.

[14] For a recent decision of the European Court on the scope of this concept, see Case C–13/96, *Bic Benelux SA v. Belgium* [1997] ECR I–1753, where an obligation to affix specific distinctive signs to products subject to an environmental tax was deemed to constitute a technical specification.

The second constraint arising in this context is more significant and more complex. More stringent national measures must be compatible with the EC Treaty.[15] Thus, as Weatherill expresses it, while the Community legislative act in question represents the "floor" of Member State obligations, the "ceiling" is constituted by the Treaty itself. Member State substantive autonomy is confined to the regulatory space in between. Thus, for example, national measures must be compatible with Community policies in areas such as the Single Market, competition law, and taxation. This has implications not only for the level of protection which may be pursued, where the national measure concerned falls within the scope of Community law, but also for the range of environmental policy instruments available to Member States, and the circumstances in which these may be deployed. Many of the issues arising are discussed in some detail in other contributions to this volume.[16] These articles exemplify the range, breadth, and intensity of the Treaty constraints applying.

One set of constraints is, however, not discussed but merits brief consideration in view of the nature and significance of the limits to Member State substantive autonomy which they may imply. These arise by virtue of the Community's participation in international law regimes, and notably in the World Trade Organization (WTO) established in 1994. This was concluded by the Community, as regards matters within its competence,[17] by Decision 94/800/EC, the preamble to which provides:

Whereas where Community rules have been adopted in order to achieve the aims of the Treaty, Member States may not, outside the framework of the common institutions, enter into commitments liable to affect those rules or alter their scope.[18]

Annexed to the WTO Agreement are a number of multilateral agreements on trade in goods. Included among these is the GATT 1994, the Technical Barriers to Trade Agreement (TBT), and the Agreement on the Application of Sanitary and Phytosanitary Measures (SPS). Binding on the Member States, these agreements severely restrict their ability to apply national standards *vis-à-vis* third-country imported goods.[19] Both the SPS and the TBT Agreements take the world trading system beyond a discrimination-based approach to the assessment of the legitimacy of applying national standards to imported goods. This is readily illustrated by reference to the recent "hormones" decision of the WTO Appellate Body.[20] Here non-discriminatory Community

[15] This constraint will also apply under Art. 95 EC where the Community act in question contains a "minimum harmonization clause" permitting Member States to enact stricter measures. In practice, under Art. 95 EC, this will frequently be accompanied by a free circulation clause permitting the free movement of goods complying with the minimum standards laid down. Thus, Member States are free to apply stricter standards only to domestic goods or production.

[16] See especially the article by J. Verschuuren at p. 103, on the use of environmental agreements and the constraints implied by EC competition law. See also the article by H. Temmink at p. 61, on the free movement of goods and the principles governing Community internal market law and their implications for national environmental law and policy.

[17] *Opinion 1/94* [1994] ECR I–5267.　　　　　　　　　　　[18] [1996] OJ L336/1.

[19] See, in particular, Art. 2.2 TBT and 3.1 SPS.

[20] "EC Measures against Meat and Meat Products (Hormones)", published on the internet at: http://www.wto.org.

standards were found to be contrary to the SPS Agreement on the basis that they were not based upon a risk assessment as laid down in Article 5(1) of the Agreement. The Community measures as developed and applied failed to satisfy the standards of scientific rationality required where SPS measures are applied in such a way as to restrict international trade.

Thus, it is one thing for Community Member States to enact stricter protective measures pursuant to a minimum harmonization directive. It is quite another for the resulting stricter standards to be applied to imported goods. Where these goods originate in the Community, or are in free circulation therein, the discipline of Articles 28–30 (formerly Articles 30–36) EC will apply, along with the concomitant principles of necessity, proportionality, and least restrictive means. In the case of third-country goods, Member States must respect international agreements to which the Community is party including, crucially, the WTO Agreement on Trade in Goods and its constituent parts. Thus, at both Community and international level, rules have emerged which seek to reconcile the regulatory diversity accompanying a minimum harmonization approach, with the free movement of goods. Consequently Member State autonomy in implementation, implied by the enactment of minimum standards at Community level, is circumscribed where stricter national standards purport to apply to imported goods.

B.   CHOICE OF POLICY INSTRUMENT FOR ENVIRONMENTAL PROTECTION

Much Community environmental law consists of measures which lay down legally binding standards to be met by the Member States. Environmental standards take a variety of forms but are generally subsumed within the label "command and control". Such standards may regulate ambient environmental quality (ambient standards), product quality (product standards), or production processes (process standards). Whereas ambient standards lay down concentration ceilings for a given pollutant in a given environmental medium (for example, air), product and process standards may be either "performance" or "specification" based.[21] Performance standards are characterized by Ogus as "output" standards, requiring "certain conditions of quality to be met at the point of supply, but leav[ing] the supplier free to choose how to meet those conditions".[22] Specification standards, by contrast, take the form of "input" standards and may, for example, regulate product composition or alternatively stipulate technical requirements to be satisfied by industrial plants.

Within the sphere of command and control regulation, the policy instrument selected at Community level has a substantial bearing upon the scope of Member State substantive flexibility in implementation. It will be immediately

[21] A. Ogus, *Regulation: Legal Form and Economic Efficiency* (Oxford: Oxford University Press, 1994), 150–1.
[22] *Ibid.*, 151.

apparent that it is ambient standards which are the least prescriptive in substantive terms and the most respectful of Member State autonomy in decision-making. Recourse to such standards confers considerable discretion on the Member States in terms of how to distribute the pollution abatement burden implied. Overall environmental quality must comply with the limit values laid down but the nature of the specific steps required to achieve this result is left in the hands of the Member States. Thus, for example, in order to achieve the required improvement in air quality, steps may be taken to reduce emissions from industrial plants and/or to regulate private use of motor vehicles. Equally the required reduction may be achieved through recourse to instruments of command and control at national level, or through the introduction of economic incentives (positive or negative) which encourage rather than demand a change in behaviour on the part of economic actors or consumers. In this sense Member States retain considerable discretion in terms of the choice of policy instrument for the implementation of ambient standards in Member States though, as will be seen, discretion which may be curtailed from time to time by virtue of the case law of the European Court.

It is not surprising in the light of the above to discover that support for ambient standards in Community law has been growing. Thus, the Molitor Report endorsed the Community's "new approach" to environmental regulation "which stresses the setting of general environmental targets whilst leaving the Member States and, in particular, industry the flexibility to choose the means of implementation".[23] Similarly, the Union of Industrial Employers' Confederations of Europe (UNICE) Regulatory Report identified as a priority for reforming environmental regulation the need to promote intervention which is "goal-based, with specific goals and objectives being consistent across both the EU and other OECD countries".[24] Proponents of an ambient-based approach to environmental regulation at EU level look to economic theory in support of their position, arguing that such standards offer substantial benefits in terms of cost-effectiveness. In view of the flexibility which such standards accord in terms of the distribution of the pollution abatement burden, Member States can ensure that the lowest cost route to compliance is achieved. It may be argued further that geography as well as economics favours recourse to ambient standards. By focusing upon the overall quality of the receiving environment even uniform ambient standards are sensitive to geographic variation in terms of assimilative capacity and disparities in terms of the environmental problems to be addressed.

Turning for a moment to the IPPC Directive, it is apparent that ambient standards play an important role in the integrated pollution regime which it constructs. They represent a baseline below which Member States are not entitled to sink.[25] Nonetheless, as will be observed shortly, such standards repre-

[23] COM(95)288 final/2, 54.

[24] "Releasing Europe's Potential Through Targeted Regulatory Reform" (Brussels: UNICE, 1995). UNICE is the Union of Industrial and Employers' Conferations of Europe.

[25] N. 1 above, Art. 10 of the Directive. It is notable that in the Commission's original Proposal compliance with ambient standards would, in certain circumstances, release installations from

sent just one of a wide variety of command and control instruments endorsed by this measure. The Directive and the preparatory documents leading to it are unusually explicit in their endorsement of the value of flexibility in implementation, and tolerant of variation in Member State response. But even so, this Directive does not represent the final triumph of an ambient-based approach in Community law. Before turning to consider this Directive in more detail, from the point of view of the policy instruments which it deploys, it is necessary to consider why it might be that the Community is less than unequivocal in its preference for ambient standards.

Environmental regulation through recourse to ambient standards is difficult to reconcile with the origins of Community environmental law. In view of the absence of specific Community competence in this sphere until the entry into force of the Single European Act in 1987, environmental intervention came to be justified partly in terms of its contribution to levelling the competitive playing field between Member States, and hence its contribution to the common market project. But ambient standards, unlike product or process standards, are differentiated in their impact according to geographic and environmental considerations. Thus, the United Kingdom (UK) with its fast flowing rivers, strong winds, and well-mixed tidal waters, enjoys a high environmental assimilative capacity. Consequently uniform ambient standards may imply a reduced economic burden for the UK, relative to some of its EU partner states. Add to this the fact that compliance with ambient standards may be promoted not through a reduction in overall output of polluting emissions, but through the export of pollution, and the limits of ambient standards, both in terms of inter-state equity and harmonization of conditions of competition, are all too apparent.

Policy considerations aside, there may also be legal reasons why ambient standards have not won a more convincing victory in the EU. These are discussed by Jans in his text-book on Community environmental law where he examines aspects of the European Court's case law concerning the implementation of environmental law directives which might be seen as undermining the flexibility generally associated with recourse to ambient standards.[26] He cites a series of cases in which the Court examined, and denied, the adequacy of national measures implementing Community directives laying down ambient quality standards. It did so, first of all, on the basis that implementation must be achieved by mandatory rules (and not administrative circulars) binding on third parties as well as the administration in order to ensure that "individuals are in a position to know with certainty the full extent of their rights in order to rely on them where appropriate, before the

the obligation to comply with emission standards established at national level according to the application of BAT. Finally, however, Community ambient standards represent the bottom line, but where BAT-based emission standards imply a higher level of protection these must be complied with also.

[26] J. H. Jans, *European Environmental Law* (The Hague–Boston, Mass.–London: Kluwer Law International, 1995), 130–1.

national courts . . . [and] that those whose activities are likely to give rise to nuisances are adequately informed of the extent of their obligations".[27] Jans notes that this approach seems to imply that such directives establishing ambient limit values are intended to impose obligations directly on individuals, and that the European Court may mean to insist that national legislation implementing such standards must "translate environmental quality standards into, for example, emission limit values" which are binding *vis-à-vis* specific sources of the polluting emissions. This, he points out, "would be a very free interpretation of the obligation to transpose environmental quality standards".[28]

Secondly, the Court found that "the general nature of the Directive [establishing ambient quality standards] cannot be satisfied by a transposition confined to certain sources of the exceeding of the limit values which it lays down";[29] in this case plants requiring authorization by the administration. Here the implication seems to be that not only do Community-level ambient standards require translation at national level into more specific standards binding individual polluters, but also that such standards must be binding with respect of all sources of the pollutant in question rather than merely one category thereof.

This discussion highlights not only confusion about the nature of ambient standards in Community law, but also the significance of legal context in thinking about flexibility in implementation. While it might be possible, as many have done, to draw up a generalized taxonomy of standards and to identify the unique and important characteristics of each, ultimately flexibility in implementation depends also upon how the various instruments for environmental protection are constructed, especially by the relevant courts. The very fact that the European Court demands that directives be implemented by measures which are legally binding, and hence that conformity be achieved in law as well as in fact, operates immediately to circumscribe Member State flexibility. Thus, for example, at least in so far as implementation is designed to achieve the minimum standards laid down by a directive, recourse to economic instruments, rather than command-and-control techniques, may well be legally precluded in so far as these cannot guarantee, in law, particular patterns of behaviour on the part of economic actors or consumers. According to the Amsterdam guidelines, the limits to the application of the proportionality principle are reached where this threatens to impede the effective enforcement of Community law. The European Court, as self-styled guardian of the Community legal order, steps in to police this contested border, and in so

---

[27] Case C–59/89, *Commission* v. *Germany* [1991] ECR I–2607 para. 23.

[28] N. 26 above, 130. Jans also gives two alternative explanations. The first is that the Court may have intended that such standards be "transposed into national law in such a way that they create a general obligation under which it becomes illegal to cause pollution in excess of the European quality standard". This, Jans suggests, is hardly practical. The second is that "the Court does not appreciate the difference between emission standards and quality standards and has attempted to equate them as far as implementation is concerned".

[29] N. 27 above, para. 22.

doing may, from time to time, alter the nature of the political bargain as to the nature and extent of Member State autonomy in implementation.

Returning now to the IPPC Directive, it is necessary to examine more closely the range of instruments for environmental protection deployed therein, and to consider the flexibility which these accord to the Member States. The Directive is predicated upon the requirement that the operation of new installations of the kind listed in Annex I is contingent upon the granting of a permit. Applications for permits are to include, as a minimum, the information laid down in Article 6 of the Directive, and permits granted must lay down conditions which guarantee compliance with the requirements of the Directive. Included among these requirements are the broadly defined "general principles" laid down in Article 3. However, at the heart of the IPPC regulatory framework lies Article 9. Article 9(3) requires that permits include emission limit values for pollutants which are likely to be emitted from the installation concerned in "significant quantities", in particular, those listed in Annex III. Thus, the Directive imposes an obligation upon Member States to introduce performance standards for installations operating within their territory.[30] This reflects the basic ethos of the Directive, namely the belief that:

the setting of emission limit values can generally best be done at local level, taking into account appropriate environmental conditions. The same standards are not always appropriate at each and every location in the Community.[31]

While emission limit values are to be set within the Member States, a number of constraints apply. First, and crucially, these measures "shall be based on the best available techniques, without prescribing the use of any technique or specific technology, but taking into account the technical characteristics of the installation concerned, its geographical location and the local environmental conditions".[32] This concept of "best available techniques" or BAT represents the cornerstone of the Directive albeit, as noted above, that it applies against a backdrop of continued reliance upon Community-level ambient standards. BAT, like its better known cousin BATNEEC (best available technology not entailing excessive costs), is a kind of specification standard but one which has been adapted to reflect economic exigencies as well as technical progress. As such, these have come to be known as "benefits-based" specification standards, and are beloved of those espousing the value of efficiency in environmental regulation. In the case of BAT, economic considerations creep into the equation as a result of the definition of "available" laid down in Article 2(11) of the IPPC Directive. This is defined as those techniques:

developed on a scale which allows implementation in the relevant industrial sector, under economically and technically viable conditions, taking into consideration the costs and advantages, whether or not the techniques are used or produced inside the Member State in question, as long as they are reasonably accessible to the operator.

---

[30] This provides further that such emission standards may be supplemented or replaced by equivalent parameters or technical measures, injecting further flexibility into the Directive.
[31] N. 2 above, 12.   [32] N. 1 above, Art. 9(4) of the Directive.

More generally, in determining BAT special consideration is to be given to the factors listed in Annex IV. These are to be taken into account generally, or in specific cases, "bearing in mind the likely costs and benefits of a measure and the principles of precaution and prevention". It is immediately apparent that BAT accords considerable flexibility to the Member States. Two restraining factors should however be emphasized. First, as seen, Article 2(11) defines BAT according to industrial sector rather than individual plant, at least when it comes to the question of economic or technical viability, and to the assessment of relative costs and advantages. It would not, it would appear, be open to a Member State to require lower emission limits in respect of an individual plant within a given industrial sector on the basis of the unusually poor economic profile or tight operating margins of that specific plant. This requirement that BAT be conceptualized at the level of industrial sector, rather than individual plant, would appear to imply further that (subject to considerations of reasonable accessibility) costs and advantages be assessed for the sector as a whole and not according to the circumstances or location of a single plant. This reading is confirmed by the explanatory memorandum accompanying the original Commission proposal for this Directive. Here it is noted that:

BAT should be considered at the level of the industrial sector and should weigh the environmental benefit of setting standards based on BAT with the cost (or the benefit) to industry of implementing BAT. Whatever the technique, *if it is affordable for an average operator in the industrial sector concerned*, then the emission limit values achievable by that technique should be required for all operating at a similar scale in that sector, and derogations should not be given for individual operators, unless the conditions set out in . . . the Directive apply.[33]

Nonetheless there is ambiguity about the level at which BAT is to be assessed. We know that it is to be determined on a sectoral basis in terms of the "average operator", but the result attained will depend upon the geographic level at which this is conceived. It may well be that, in the course of implementing the Directive, Member States will designate competent authorities operating at regional or local level. In some Member States regional governments will enjoy (constitutionally guaranteed) responsibility for implementation and so the relevant competent authority will inevitably operate at a sub-national level. While the Directive makes it clear that it is for the competent authorities to establish emission limit values, and that in so doing they may take various factors into account (including geographical location and local environmental conditions), the Directive provides simply that these limit values are to be based on BAT. It does not prescribe the level at which BAT is to be conceived or make it clear how much autonomy Member States enjoy in this respect. Thus, when the Commission observes that the setting of emission limits can best be done at a local level, it is not clear whether "local" in the context of BAT implies national rather than Community, or whether various conceptions of BAT may be applied within a single Member State, and conse-

---

[33] N. 2 above, 5 (emphasis added).

quently even within a given industrial sector. Article 11 provides that the competent authority is to follow, or to be informed of, developments in BAT. It may be argued that this implies a passive rather than an active role for such authorities, made responsible for the application of BAT, rather than for defining its substance.

This discussion about the level at which BAT is to be conceived has important implications from the perspective of the geographic dimension of economic and social cohesion.[34] The IPPC Directive, with its emphasis upon BAT, appears to endorse the emergence of different standards in different Member States, with consideration of costs and advantages capable of reflecting, nationally, economic context and relative levels of economic development. However, it is less certain that BAT, in the context of IPPC, is sensitive to regional and local economic context.[35] This is no doubt an argument which will, in due course, be played out before a court, be it national or European. That the Community, in preparing its policy on the environment, is obliged to take account of the economic and social development of the Community as a whole and the balanced development of its regions will be but one factor to consider in defining a conception of BAT which seeks to reconcile flexibility with effectiveness and considerations of inter-regional, as well as international, equity.

The second, less direct, constraint inhibiting Member States in their construction of BAT is to be found in Article 18 of the Directive. This provides that the Council may, in the circumstances set out, establish Community-level emission standards where a need for Community action has been identified,[36] and also that existing Community emission standards shall continue to be applied as minimum standards in respect of Annex I installations. Thus, not only does the flexibility inherent in BAT operate against a backdrop of ambient standards introduced at Community level, but also within the framework of the "regulatory overhang" implied by new and existing Community performance standards. In this respect the Commission's explanatory memorandum observes that:

Where broadly comparable [emissions] limits are set across the Community and where the effect on competitiveness is minimal . . . there may not always be a need for harmonization at Community level. Where, however, standards are very different, so affecting competitiveness, future proposals under the framework of this [IPPC] Directive are much more likely in order to ensure the effective functioning of the internal market.[37]

---

[34] Arts. 158–162 EC and the Commission's *First Cohesion Report*, COM(96)542, where it seeks to define the concept of economic and social cohesion, identifying a social dimension and a geographic dimension. The geographic dimension is, in turn, understood as encompassing a national (cohesion between Member States) and a regional (cohesion between regions) dimension.

[35] Other than to the extent that the scale of activities may differ in the more or less developed regions of the Community thus, if the Commission's conception in the explanatory memorandum represents a correct interpretation of Art. 2(11), permitting differentiation of emission standards from locality to locality within a single Member State.

[36] In so doing it is to act in accordance with the procedures laid down in the Treaty.

[37] N. 2 above, 12.

Thus, there is, written into the legislation an inducement for Member States to conceive and apply the concept of BAT in good faith. Whether viewed as threat or safeguard, Article 18(1) represents a stark reminder to the Member States that the issue of the choice of policy instrument(s) for environmental protection has not been settled once and for all. Flexibility, according to the Commission's perspective, must be earned.

C.   EXCEPTIONS IN COMMUNITY ENVIRONMENTAL LAW

It is indicative of the breadth of Member State discretion in the implementation of the IPPC Directive that this measure does not itself contain any exceptions to the obligations laid down. Where obligations are defined sufficiently loosely the need for exceptions may be obviated, with Member State concerns being accommodated within the rules themselves. Nonetheless, as noted above, in certain respects the IPPC Directive is parasitic upon earlier Community legislation notably, though not only, those listed in Annex II. The authorization systems laid down in these measures are to apply, without prejudice to the exceptions provided for in the Large Combustion Plant Directive,[38] in respect of Annex I activities, until such a time as the relevant measures have been adopted pursuant to Article 5 of the Directive. Reference to the Large Combustion Plant Directive serves as a reminder of the salience of negotiated exceptions in Community environmental law. The Directive is riddled with exceptions, particularly in the case of emission limits for new plants.[39] Thus, for example, Article 5(2) and (6) introduces a degree of flexibility for Member States burning indigenous sold fuels or lignite, permitting cost considerations to enter into the equation. More strikingly is the country-specific exception articulated in Article 5(3). This provides that Spain may, until the end of 1999, authorize new solid-fuel power plants (so long as they are commissioned before the end of 2005) which do not meet the emission standards laid down in Annexes III–VII, subject to the requirement that these installations respect a sulphur dioxide limit value which is some 60 per cent higher than the generally applicable limit and, in the case of plants burning indigenous solid fuels, that they achieve a desulphurization rate of at least 60 per cent (as opposed to the 90 per cent reduction generally required for plants of this size). No minimum requirements are to apply to these plants in the case of emissions of nitrogen oxides and dust.[40] Such plants might be anticipated to have a life expectancy of around forty years. Thus, this derogation, though temporary, is of enormous significance, environmentally and economically.

[38] Council Dir. 88/609/EEC [1998] OJ L336/1.

[39] In respect of existing plants see Art. 3(5) of the Directive where the Commission, subject to Council control, is empowered to modify Member State emission ceilings and targets laid down in Annexes I and II.

[40] Art. 5(3) of the Directive provides that total authorized capacity of such plants must not exceed 2,000 MW in the case of plants burning indigenous solid fuel, 7,500 (or 50% of total new capacity authorized by the end of 1999, where this is lower) in the case of plants burning imported solid fuel.

Like the IPPC Directive, the Large Combustion Plant Directive was adopted on the basis of Article 175 (formerly Article 130s) EC. While, since the entry into force of the Maastricht Treaty, decision-making in this sphere is largely premised upon qualified majority voting in Council, in the case, *inter alia*, of measures significantly affecting a Member State's choice between different energy sources and the structure of its energy supply, unanimity is still required. In the shadow of the veto, Community intervention is characterized by an unusually high degree of flexibility deriving either (or both) from the open-ended nature of the rules themselves, or from the breadth of the negotiated exceptions to those rules.

D.   SUBSTANTIVE FLEXIBILITY: CONCLUSION

This section has sought to exemplify, by reference to the IPPC Directive, the nature and scope of Member State discretion in the implementation of EC environmental law. Whereas the language of implementation might appear to imply the mechanical pursuit of pre-ordained ends, the IPPC case-study demonstrates the importance of implementation in substantive terms, and of the choices which Member States exercise within the framework of implementation. Adopting the language of Selznick, implementation constitutes "governance" rather than "management" in the sense that it implies more than merely justifying decisions according to the contribution they make to settled ends, but also a crucial role for Member States in defining the ends to be pursued.[41] Certainly, in implementing directives, Member States "govern" within parameters established by Community law but, as observed, changing patterns of regulation at EU level are such to permit wide variation in Member State response. What is clear is that when the Community speaks it does not silence the Member States. When the Community governs it does not govern alone. Substantive flexibility in implementation is real and governance consequently multi-levelled. It is against this backdrop that this article now turns to consider a related issue, namely the question of *how* Member States govern in an implementation context and, in particular, the degree of flexibility which they enjoy in constituting the processes and procedures associated with the implementation task.

III.   Flexibility in Implementation: Procedural Perspectives

By and large the Community, and particularly the European Court, has adopted a position of watchful agnosticism when it comes to national procedures for the implementation of Community law. Subject to limits which are functionally determined according to considerations of effectiveness in the application and enforcement of Community law, Member States have been

---

[41] This is a distinction adopted by P. Selznick, *The Moral Commonwealth: Social Theory and the Search for Community* (Berkeley, Cal.: University of California Press, 1992), 290.

permitted considerable autonomy in determining, internally, the distribution of implementing authority and the rules according to which that authority is to be exercised.[42] Thus, for example, in the absence of specific provisions stating the contrary, it is for the Member States, in the light of their own constitutional and administrative practices, to determine the role to be played by sub-national authorities in the implementation of Community law. Nonetheless, the European Court insists, there are only as many "Member States" as there are state members and consequently legal responsibility for implementation under Article 226 EC rests with central government regardless of prevailing territorial relations within that state, and regardless of the legal or practical capacity of central government to control the activities of sub-national political actors.[43] Equally that, for example, the UK chooses to implement (most) directives by way of delegated legislation (in the form of regulations) pursuant to the European Communities Act 1972[44] is a matter of considerable indifference to the Community. That this implies attenuated parliamentary involvement in the legislative process is neither here nor there from the perspective of the European Court. For this Court, process is relevant only to the extent that it impinges upon outcome and, in particular, to the extent that it is such as to preclude the emergence of implementing norms which comply with its favoured principles of "full effectiveness, legal certainty and effective judicial protection".[45] Implementing measures must be legally binding, sufficiently clear and precise, and, where appropriate, susceptible to enforcement on the part of individuals before their national courts.[46] Beyond this, the identity of the implementing authority, and the credibility of its claim to authority, is a matter for the Member States.

This position of watchful agnosticism, underwritten by considerations of effectiveness, is borne out by the principle of proportionality as enunciated in the Amsterdam guidelines. These provide, "[r]egarding the nature and the extent of Community action", that "[w]hile respecting Community law, care should be taken to respect well established national arrangements and the organization and working of Member States' legal systems".[47] This perspective is further reflected in the Declaration adopted by the Amsterdam Conference to the Protocol on the application of the principles of subsidiarity and proportionality.[48] This reiterates that "the administrative implementation of Community law shall in principle be the responsibility of the Member States in accordance with their constitutional arrangements".

Thus we see, as the very organization of the Treaty suggests, that proportionality is tied to a specific conception of subsidiarity; that which has been

---

[42] For a good discussion of the limits to this autonomy, highlighting the many uncertainties which remain, see Jans, n. 26 above, and S. Prechal, *Directives in European Community Law* (Oxford: Oxford University Press, 1995), especially part 5.

[43] Cases 227–230/85, *Commission* v. *Belgium* [1988] ECR 1.

[44] S. 2(2). See also Sched. 2 which lays down limitations in this respect.

[45] Prechal, n. 42 above, 95.   [46] *Ibid.*, 90.

[47] N. 4 above, para. 7.   [48] [1997] OJ C340/140.

called "procedural subsidiarity".[49] This, like proportionality, is concerned with what the Community should or should not do, rather than how Member States should or should not do it. It, like proportionality, is concerned to delimit the proper scope of Community intervention according to considerations of effectiveness in the achievement of the objectives pursued. Each assists in establishing the proper parameters of EC level governance, but not in shaping patterns of governance within the Member States themselves.

There are, however, important signs that the Community's absolute commitment to watchful agnosticism may be waning. There are indications that as the principle of proportionality bites, enhancing Member States' substantive flexibility in implementation, the Community is beginning to take a greater interest in the procedures and processes associated with implementation. As the Community backs off in substantive terms, it is seeking to exercise greater control over the manner in which implementation decisions are adopted within Member States. Substantive flexibility may be accompanied by stricter procedural prescription. This is most clearly, but not only, apparent in an area outside environmental policy but of profound importance for it; Community structural funding, which represents an important component of the Community's strategy for economic and social cohesion.[50] Here implementation occurs within the framework of "partnership", implying a form of governance which is both multi-level and multi-actor. While decisions about the scale of funding available, and its distribution between Member States, continue to be adopted at Community level, within an inter-governmental framework, decisions relating to the allocation of funding for specific programmes and projects, and relating to the management of funding received, are adopted by "the partnership". While this implies a role for Community-level institutions—specifically the Commission—this role is not an exclusive one. The Commission is to act in close consultation with the Member State concerned and the competent authorities and bodies including, within the framework of each state's national rules and current practices, the economic and social partners designated by the Member State at national, regional, local, or other level.[51] In its current proposals for the reform of the structural funds, the Commission is committed to strengthening and consolidating the partnership principle, with a view to promoting a broader and deeper conception of it. Breadth, in this context, relates to access to the partnership and the range of actors participating within it. The Commission emphasizes that "[t]he participation of regional and local authorities, environmental authorities, and economic and social partners, including non-governmental organizations, must be guaranteed by Member States".[52] Depth, on the other hand, refers to the

---

[49] See A. Scott, J. Peterson, and D. Millar, "Subsidiarity: A 'Europe of the Regions' v. the British Constitution" (1994) 32 *Journal of Common Market Studies* 46.

[50] On the link between structural funding and environmental policy see J. Scott, *EC Environmental Law* (London and New York: Longman, 1998), 128–47.

[51] Council Reg. (EEC) No. 2081/93 [1993] OJ L193/5, Art. 4(1).

[52] See the memorandum accompanying the Commission's Proposal for a Regulation reforming the structural funds, published on the internet at: http://europa.eu.int/comm/dg16/index-eu.htm.

need to involve the various partners throughout the various stages of the development planning process. Still, however, the definition of partnership proposed in the reform regulation is imbued with considerable flexibility. Article 8(1) provides:

Community action shall contribute to corresponding national operations. They shall be drawn up in close consultations, hereinafter referred to as the "partnership", between the Commission and the Member States, together with:

— the regional and local authorities and other competent authorities;
— the economic and social partners;
— the other competent bodies.

Each Member State shall within its own institutional, legal, and financial system, choose and designate the most representative partners at national, regional, local, or other level referred to in the first indent through as wide an association as possible including, where appropriate, the bodies active in the field of environment and in the promotion of equal opportunities between men and women.

This flexibility notwithstanding, the conceptual and practical significance of this concept should not be ignored. In an area such as this where the Community has shed ever greater responsibility for decision-making, assuming today an essentially strategic role, its willingness to devolve authority to the Member States has been contingent in at least two respects. First, implementation decisions are adopted within the Member States, but in the sight of the Commission. The Commission has a seat at the negotiating table, thus reflecting the Community interest in implementation.

Secondly, while the partnership is to adopt its own rules of procedure, its composition is at least loosely determined by Community law. The Community seeks not merely to secure its own position within the partnership but also, *inter alia*, the participation of sub-national government and the social and economic partners. These are issues to which we will return, notably from the perspective of the legitimacy of governance in the EU. Before doing so, however, it is necessary to re-enter the environmental sphere proper, and to look again to the case of the IPPC Directive. In so doing it will be possible to ascertain the extent to which (if any) Member State procedural flexibility in implementation has been curtailed.

Member States are to adopt the implementing measures necessary to comply with the IPPC Directive no later than three years after its entry into force. Such national measures are to contain a reference to the Directive or to be accompanied by such a reference on the occasion of their official publication. The Member State concerned is obliged to inform the Commission of the measures adopted, and to communicate to it the text of the main provisions.[53] While responsibility for achieving conformity with the Directive, in law and in fact, rests at the door of the Member States, it is the "competent authority"—

---

[53] N. 1 above, Art. 21 of the Directive.

the authority, authorities, or bodies responsible under the legal provisions of the Member States—designated by Member States which shall be "responsible . . . for carrying out the obligations arising from this Directive".[54] As seen above in the previous section, the tasks incumbent upon the "competent authority" are many and varied. This concept of a competent authority made responsible pursuant to a Community directive is one which is encountered throughout Community environmental law. The concept is rarely defined in legislation and, where it is, it is rarely defined with any greater precision than in the IPPC Directive.[55] That is to say, quite simply, that Member States enjoy considerable autonomy in establishing or identifying the appropriate body or bodies. Attempts to persuade the Court to restrict this autonomy in the name of effectiveness have conspicuously failed. Thus, in *Traen*, the European Court held that the 1975 Directive on Waste:[56]

does not lay down any restrictive criteria concerning the "competent . . . authorities to be responsible, in a given zone, for the planning, organization, authorization and supervision of waste-disposal operations", which are to be established or designated by the Member State. The Member States are therefore unrestricted in their choice of such authorities.[57]

Consequently, it was held to be open to the Member State concerned (in the guise of the Flemish Region) to designate the director of a water-purifying company, set up by the public authorities, as the competent authority within the meaning of that Directive.

In a subsequent case, also concerning the 1975 Directive on Waste, Advocate General Jacobs observed that "excessive division of responsibility for carrying out the duties listed in Article 5 of the directive may jeopardize the achievement of the directive's aims and is not therefore permissible".[58] There is, however, nothing in the case law of the Court which obliges Member States to designate an authority at any particular level of government, be it central, regional, or local. Nor indeed is there any authority to suggest that the body designated need form part of the government at all. This is, *par excellence*, the land of watchful agnosticism. Yet the issue of the identity of the implementing authority is the beginning, not the end, of the story of procedural flexibility.

---

[54] *Ibid.*, Art. 2(8) of the Directive.
[55] See, however, e.g., Art. 18 EMAS, where the Member State is charged with ensuring that the composition of the competent bodies is such as to guarantee their independence and neutrality.
[56] Council Dir. 75/442/EEC [1975] OJ L194/39.
[57] Cases 372–374/85, *Ministere Public v. Oscar Traen and Others* [1987] ECR 2141, para. 17.
[58] Case C–359/88, *Criminal Proceedings against E. Zanetti and others* [1990] ECR 1–1461, para. 30 and, for the ECJ judgment [1990] ECR I–1509, paras. 18–20. This raises interesting issues in relation to the discussion above (part one) about the level at which the substance of BAT is to be defined. In the event that it is accepted (and this is, in my view, unlikely) that it is for the relevant competent authority, at whatever level, to define (rather than merely apply) BAT standards, then there may conceivably come a point at which "excessive division of responsibility" would impair realization of the objectives underlying the directive. If BAT may imply very different things in different localities, and if there is no limit to the "localness" of the level at which this is defined, then considerations of economic viability begin to veer towards a plant specific rather than an average operator approach.

Crucial too is the manner in which the competent authority is to exercise its powers, and it is here that Community-level procedural constraints begin to bite. Two provisions in the Directive merit particular consideration in this respect.

First, Article 15 is concerned with access to information and public participation in the permit procedure. Article 15(1) provides that, without prejudice to the Directive on Access to Environmental Information (and subject to the restrictions laid down in Articles 3(2) and (3) thereof),[59] applications for permits are to be made available to the public for an appropriate period of time, in order that the public be given an opportunity to comment upon these before the competent authority reaches its decision. An application for a permit must include the details laid down in Article 6, as well as a non-technical summary thereof. The permit decision having been adopted, it too must be made available to the public along with subsequent updates and a copy of the permit granted.

Secondly, where a Member State is aware that the operation of an installation is likely to have significant negative effects on the environment of another Member State, or where a Member State likely to be significantly affected so requests, the Article 6 information submitted pursuant to the permit application must be made available to the other Member State at the same time as it makes it available to its own nationals. Such information is to serve as a basis for consultations between these states. In such cases the applications are also to be made available for an appropriate period of time to the public of the Member State likely to be affected so that it will have the right to comment on them before the competent authority reaches its decision.[60]

In neither of these respects is the IPPC Directive unique. A significant number of Community environmental acts provide for such public and transboundary consultations.[61] In some cases these may even go further than the IPPC Directive in procedural terms. Thus, for example, the amended EIA Directive requires not only that the public be informed of any decision to grant or refuse development consent, making available to the public the content of the decision and any conditions attached thereto, but also that the public be informed of the "main reasons and considerations on which the decision is based".[62] Moreover, since its inception, the EIA Directive has laid down the cir-

---

[59] Council Dir. 90/313/EEC [1990] OJ L158/56. It is important to note, in view of the discretion which Member States enjoy in designating the competent authority or authorities, that while Art. 3(1) of this Directive lays down the obligations binding "public authorities", Art. 6 of this Directive provides that "Member States shall take the necessary steps to ensure that information relating to the environment held by bodies with public responsibilities for the environment and under the control of public authorities is made available on the same terms and conditions as those set out in Arts 3, 4 and 5".

[60] On transboundary effects, see Art. 17 IPPC, n. 1 above.

[61] See, e.g., Council Dir. 85/337/EEC [1985] OJ L175/40 as amended by Council Dir. 97/11/EEC [1997] OJ L73/5 (Environmental Impact Assessment); Council Dir. 82/501/EEC [1982] OJ L230/1 (as amended) on Major Accident Hazards—the so-called "Seveso Directive"; and Council Reg. (EEC) No. 1836/93 on Eco-Management and Audit [1993] OJ L168/1.

[62] Council Dir. 97/11/EC, n. 61 above, Art. 9(1).

cumstances in which Member States "*shall* enter into consultations" regarding transboundary effects, albeit that the detailed arrangements for implementing this obligation are to be determined by the Member States themselves.[63] The IPPC Directive, by contrast and tendentiously, provides merely that the transboundary exchange of information "shall serve as the basis for any consultations necessary in the framework of the bilateral relations between the two Member States on a reciprocal and equivalent basis". Both the EIA and the IPPC Directive provide for transboundary co-operation where the project in question is *likely* to have significant (negative in the case of the IPPC Directive) effects on the environment of another Member State, while in the setting of the Seveso Directive the threshold for the transboundary provision of information is set at a lower level. In the event of the possibility of a major accident of the kind envisaged by the Directive, with transboundary effects, the *potentially* affected Member State is entitled to receive sufficient information to ensure application of the relevant provisions of the Directive.[64]

The point here, however, is not to engage in an in-depth comparison of the various procedural constraints laid down in the directives under discussion. It is rather simply to note first that these exist, and secondly that they exist in a form which is consistently open-ended, leaving substantial, though variable, autonomy to the Member States in establishing detailed arrangements. Yet, for all that, the argument here is that such procedural constraints relating to implementation process are of immense importance. At a practical level this is readily apparent and may be illustrated by reference to the IPPC Directive. Though the nature and scope of the public participation required is barely defined in this Directive, it does unequivocally require public consultation in some form. For a number of Member States, in the context of the authorization of industrial plants, this will imply more public consultation than has hitherto been required. Thus, for example, at present no such consultation is required in either Denmark or Ireland, and whereas in Sweden there is, in practice, normally a public hearing, public opinion does not formally have to be taken into account. It is, however, upon the conceptual significance of such developments that the remainder of this section will concentrate. Whatever their shortcomings in terms of current scope and definition, such developments raise important issues in thinking about law, legitimacy and governance in the European Union.

---

[63] N. 61 above, Art. 7 of the Environmental Impact Directive, as amended.

[64] N. 61 above (Seveso Directive), Art. 13. See also Council Dir. 90/220/EEC [1990] OJ L117/15, Art. 13, which provides for information exchange between Member States in the context of authorizing the placing on the market of genetically modified organisms. Where the competent authority in any one Member State raises an objection, and where the competent authorities concerned cannot reach agreement within the time limit laid down, authority to take the decision passes from the relevant authority in the Member State concerned to the Commission or the Council, acting in accordance with a regulatory committee procedure. Thus, the Directive invites consensual, negotiated resolution of the issue as between Member States, but against a backdrop of the possibility of Community intervention where the required transboundary co-operation fails to produce agreement between states.

First, it can be argued that the introduction, at Community level, of certain
kinds of procedural constraints on the manner in which Member States implement Community law will facilitate the subsidiarity principle, in that they
diminish the need for substantive Community regulation of the issue at hand,
or at least the intensity of that regulation. Over recent years, above all in the
environmental sphere, the concept of subsidiarity has been approached
through the lens of transboundary (negative) externalities or spillovers. That
activities in one Member State are capable of spilling over to another Member
State is frequently cited as a justification for Community-level intervention. In
the presence of such spillover effects the *de facto* capacity of Member States to
protect the environment is undermined. As the concept of spillovers has
expanded to encompass not only physical but economic externalities,[65]
Community environmental law has been rationalized not only in terms of
managing physical inter-dependence between states but also in terms of preventing competition between the rules of the Member States and, ultimately,
a destructive and short-sighted regulatory "race to the bottom".[66] Though less
fashionable than it once was, and no doubt exaggerated in its scope and intensity, the competitive deregulation thesis is hard to dismiss out of hand. Market
integration, accompanied by political fragmentation, does undeniably generate "a gap between the formal domain of political authority and the actual
economic system of production, distribution and exchange" and does consequently serve "to limit or undermine the actual power or scope of national
political authorities".[67] On the other hand, uncritical acceptance of the thesis
will take the steam out of subsidiarity, generating momentum in favour of a
harmonized Community- (or even higher) level regulatory response. Thus, in
confronting the level of governance issues, we appear to face an unsavoury
choice between, on the one hand, ostensible national autonomy undermined
by the realities of international interdependence and, on the other, effective
but remote regulation at the level of the European Union.

This dilemma has its origins in the construction of a stark choice between a
totally co-ordinated supranational regulatory response and a totally fragmented response at the level of the individual Member State. Member States
either act together, within the framework of the European Union, or they act
alone. The IPPC Directive serves to illustrate that this choice is excessively
stark. It offers a glimpse of an "in-between" according to which Member States
exercise substantive choices at national (or sub-national) level but in so doing

---

[65] See also W. P. J. Wils, "Subsidiarity and EC Environmental Policy: Taking People's Concerns
Seriously" (1994) 6 *Journal of Environmental Law* 85. Wils argues that three categories of spillovers
may be such as to justify Community-level intervention: physical, economic, and psychic. This
last category refers to situations in which the environmental sensibilities of citizens in one
Member State are offended by activities in another, resulting in a decline in their psychological
well-being. For a discussion of this, see Scott, n. 50 above, 10–18.

[66] See the article by R. L. Revesz, at p. 1 in this volume, for a critical commentary on this subject.
For an interesting and thoughtful account of the same issues in the social policy sphere, see C.
Barnard, "EC 'Social' Policy", in P. Craig, and G. de Búrca (eds.), *The Evolution of EU Law* (Oxford:
Oxford University Press, 1999), 479–516.

[67] D. Held, *Political Theory and the Modern State* (Cambridge: Polity, 1989), 229.

are required to consider not only national interests, but also with "out-of-state interests".[68] The latter find a secure voice in "domestic" decision-making, by virtue of procedural constraints imposed by Community law. In the case of the IPPC Directive such "out-of-state interests" are permitted access to decision-making in another Member State where the operation of an installation in the one state is likely to have significant negative effects in the other. This wording is, in principle, sufficiently open-ended to extend not merely to situations involving physical spillovers, but also to those where environmental quality in one state is threatened indirectly, due to the economic consequences of regulatory decisions adopted, or about to be adopted, in another (not necessarily neighbouring) state. Hence, such provisions providing for transboundary co-operation, though generally conceived against a backdrop of physical interdependence between states, may be construed more broadly to reflect the environmental consequences of economic spillover effects.

Following this argument through, albeit still at a very general level, it is apparent that were Community law to structure domestic decision-making in such a way that it be genuinely responsive to out-of-state interests, the mere fact of inter-dependence between states, be it physical or economic, would not suffice in and of itself to justify Community level intervention. While the presence of externalities—frequently distant not only in time but in space— may undermine the capacity of one state to control its "own" environment, regulation of Member State implementation procedures may serve to increase the transparency of transboundary externalities, and to guarantee a place for transnational considerations, albeit in a national setting. Such procedural requirements serve to situate decision-making within the Member States in a European context, enhancing the audibility of voices from outside the relevant Member State and increasing awareness of, and sensitivity to, the transboundary consequences of domestic decisions. Thus, by denying Member States unqualified procedural autonomy, it may be possible to expand the range of substantive choices over which they may exercise control; thus contributing to the realization of subsidiarity, the aim of which is to ensure that decisions be taken as closely as possible to the people. By constraining the manner in which Member States reach decisions it may be possible to close, partially at least, the "gap" between the political "national", and the environmental and economic "transnational", without necessitating a transfer of power to a higher level of political authority.

Moving on, in so far as the IPPC Directive seeks to shape procedural arrangements for implementation, it not only facilitates realization of subsidiarity, but also the capacity of this doctrine to contribute to the

---

[68] M. Poiares Maduro, *We, the Court: The European Court of Justice and the European Economic Constitution* (Oxford: Hart Publishing, 1998), 172. Here, the author is proposing an interesting thesis in relation to the application of Art. 28 EC, based in part upon procedural considerations in terms of *how* Member States arrive at their regulatory choices and the range of non-national interests which find voice within this process.

Community's much vaunted "quest for legitimacy".[69] Subsidiarity demands legislative self-restraint on the part of the Community. It does so on the basis that, other things being equal, considerations of legitimacy in governance favour political and legal authority being left in the hands of the Member States. The concept of subsidiarity, as it has developed in Community law, essentially assumes, at the level of the Member States, the "connection between authority and consent".[70] What we find, however, in the IPPC Directive are seeds of an approach which insists upon compliance with certain minimum standards of propriety in governance. These take us beyond the quest for "blanket legitimacy" associated with the overall organization of the state, into the realm of "legitimacy in depth" where the processes by which individual decisions are adopted are constrained on the basis of normative considerations. At least two values may be identified as underpinning the procedural requirements structuring implementation in the case of the IPPC Directive, even if these values are not explicitly acknowledged and are only gently endorsed. The first process value implicit in the Directive is that of participation, and the second is deliberation.

Participation speaks to the issue of access (in terms of breadth and depth) to the political process. The IPPC Directive, though largely neutral on the issue of the identity of the actors responsible for achieving implementation, and in terms of the power relations between them, does regulate access in one respect. As noted above, it insists, unequivocally, upon public consultation prior to the adoption of any decision to grant or deny permit applications. Public participation through consultation, is further to be facilitated by guaranteeing access to information, including non-technical information.

The concept of deliberation is less easy to define, more difficult to assess empirically, and certainly more normatively contested.[71] It is an idea which has received considerable attention in, and beyond, Community law circles over recent years. In the EU setting it is in the context of the implementation of Community legislation that the value of deliberation has been highlighted, and ambitious descriptive and normative claims made on its behalf. These discussions have, however, been largely confined to implementation at the

---

[69] On the link between subsidiarity and the quest for legitimacy, see G. de Bùrca, "The Quest for Legitimacy in the European Union" (1996) 59 *Modern Law Review* 349–76.

[70] N. 41 above, 268.

[71] P. Fitzpatrick, "Consolations of the Law: Community and Deliberative Politics", paper presented at workshop on "Law and Deliberative Politics", Bielefeld, 26–27 Feb. 1999 (manuscript supplied by author). Fitzpatrick identifies Habermas as the "main patron saint" of deliberative approaches, while recognizing that "some place is given to Rawls and his paradoxical ability to be situationally deracinated". In thinking about deliberation, Fitzpatrick draws upon J. Elster (ed.), *Deliberative Democracy* (Cambridge: Cambridge University Press, 1998). See also, for a discussion of deliberation within the civic republican tradition, the special issue of the *Yale Law Journal* on republicanism and law, (1998) 97 *Yale Law Journal* 8; a special issue on this subject. See also E. O. Eriksen, *Deliberative Democracy and the Politics of Pluralist Society* (ARENA Working Paper No 6/94), concerning, in particular, the work of Juergen Habermas and Joshua Cohen.

hands of EU "comitology" committees.[72] In this context deliberation has been conceived as follows:

Participants engage in collective reasoning on the merits of public policy; the substance of the discussion involves attempting to achieve some larger public good, independent from (but not necessarily inconsistent with) what is desirable for the participants themselves. Participants make use of information in order to persuade others; at least legislators themselves maintain open-mindedness and willingness to be convinced by others' analyses of the merits; and the legislators themselves are committed to making their final decisions on policy proposals in accordance with their judgment on the merits.[73]

Hence, deliberation speaks to the formation of political preferences, as well as to the shaping of political outcomes. The preferences of those participating in decision-making are viewed not merely as exogenous to the political process, to be received and aggregated by passive agencies of authority, but as born of the experience of dialogue and exchange. In addition deliberation is understood as privileging critical reason, over power, and aspiring in the direction of decision-making by consensus rather than by bare majority.

Rightly or wrongly deliberation has been endorsed by many as central to conceptions of good governance. Hence the willingness of Community law to promote deliberative politics at the level of Member State implementation serves to bolster the legitimacy of governance at this level, and consequently to enhance the normative value of subsidiarity. Of course, there are the sceptics albeit that, as Peter Fitzpatrick notes, even their observations often serve, by focussing upon the "pathologies of deliberation", to affirm "a healthy norm".[74] While this is not the place to debate the merits of a deliberative polity, it is important to acknowledge the centrality of deliberation in academic discourse on the theme of legitimacy. Alongside values such as participation, community, and civility, deliberation has emerged, glorious in its indeterminacy, as a means of thinking normatively about law, legitimacy, and governance, both in and beyond the majoritarian state.

It is notable in this respect that an argument can be made, albeit tentatively, that the IPPC Directive promotes deliberative practices, especially in so far as it establishes a framework (discussed earlier) for transboundary co-operation

[72] See C. Joerges, and J. Neyer, "From Intergovernmental Bargaining to Deliberative Political Processes: The Constitutionalization of Comitology" (1997) 3 *European Law Journal* 273, and C. Joerges and E. Vos (eds.), *Social Regulation through European Committees: Empirical Research, Institutional Politics, Theoretical Concepts and Legal Developments* (Oxford: Hart Publishing, (1999)). See also, in the context of Member State implementation of Community structural funds, J. Scott, "Law, Legitimacy and Governance: Prospects for 'Partnership'" (1998) 36 *Journal of Common Market Studies* 175. It is notable, in terms of comitology as an aspect of the implementation debate, that though Art. 19 provides for the establishment of a committee to assist the Commission, its powers are limited to those laid down in Art. 15(3); namely the drawing up of the format and particulars needed for the transmission of information relating to principal emissions and sources responsible, to be published every three years, on the basis of data supplied by the Member States. On the recent Proposal for a Council Decision amending procedures for the exercise of implementing powers conferred by the Commission, COM(1998)380 final.

[73] Cited in C. Joerges, "Good Governance Through Comitology", in Joerges and Vos, n. 72 above.

[74] N. 71 above.

and consultations between Member States. Moreover, the various mechanisms laid down for the exchange of information[75] may similarly be conceived
as sowing the seeds of deliberation, by encouraging the re-visiting of decisions
already adopted (preferences already formed); for example, those relating to
the definition of BAT, and the requirement that permit conditions be periodically reconsidered and updated.[76] Yet it would be misleading to push these
arguments too far, and it is unnecessary to do so for the purposes of this article. The argument here is less about what has been realized so far in terms of
reinforcing legitimacy through giving expression to values such as participation and deliberation than about what could, potentially, be achieved, and
where this might lead us in our appreciation of the proportionality principle,
and its implications for Community law.

IV. Procedural Perspectives: Conclusion

This third section has addressed the theme of procedural flexibility in implementation in the context of the application of the proportionality principle. It is
based on a recognition that proportionality, as currently defined, favours
Member State procedural autonomy in implementation, and that the European
Court has done little to impede this. Nonetheless it has argued, at a descriptive
level, that even now Member State procedural autonomy in implementation is
not absolute. This is exemplified by reference to the IPPC Directive in that this
lays down procedures for public consultation and for transboundary co-operation between states. This section has also argued, at a normative level, in favour
of Community constraints on the nature of the processes and procedures associated with the implementation task. It has done so on the basis that Member
States, in exercising ever broader substantive policy choices, should be required
to confront the European dimension of the issue at hand, and to be responsive
to the transboundary consequences of domestic decisions. Moreover, if the
Community is exercising legislative restraint in the name of legitimacy, thus
enhancing (or at least not curtailing) the substantive autonomy of the Member
States, it is not unreasonable for the Community to demand compliance with
minimum standards of good governance at the level of the Member States. Two
specific values were highlighted in this respect: participation and deliberation.
Others may be preferred. Nonetheless it is important to note that the two values
cited find expression in a wide variety of institutional settings, and may be nour-
ished by any one of a large number of mechanisms. They do not militate in
favour of a particular institutional response, or imply the emergence of a
Community "blueprint" for defining implementation arrangements. Such values constrain, but do not exclude, procedural flexibility in implementation. If in
the past, the challenge for Community law has been to balance demands for
autonomy and effectiveness in implementation, the challenge today is to
embrace also considerations of legitimacy.

---

[75] N. 1 above, Arts. 11 and 16.   [76] N. 1 above, Art. 13 of the Directive.

From Danish Bottles to Danish Bees: The Dynamics of Free Movement of Goods and Environmental Protection— a Case Law Analysis

HARRIE TEMMINK*

I. Introduction

Over the past decade or so, interest in the potential conflict between the free movement of goods, regulated by Articles 28–30 (formerly Articles 30–36) EC and national environmental law has increased considerably. This is reflected both in the case law of the European Court of Justice (ECJ) and in legal literature.[1] While earlier examples exist in which the ECJ explores the relationship between the free movement of goods and environmental policy,[2] it is the *Danish Bottles* case which has served as a landmark decision.[3] In this judgment, the ECJ made an assessment of a Danish regulation on returnable bottles, under the regime of Articles 28–30 EC, finding that the Danish legislator was entitled to introduce a system of deposit-and-return for drink containers that aims to protect the environment, provided it pursues a "reasonable" degree of protection. As regards the requirement that importers and manufacturers could only use bottles that were authorized, the Danish system was viewed as too excessive and therefore as contravening Article 28 (formerly Article 30) EC. Simply put, the ruling implies that environmental imperatives must be taken into consideration but not necessarily at the "highest level".

It is easy to see that the free movement of goods represents an essential cornerstone of the internal market. Article 14 (formerly Article 7a) EC defines the internal market as an "area without internal frontiers", which at the same time represents a core goal of the EC Treaty. The concept of the internal market is

---

* Lecturer in public economic law, Europa Instituut, University of Utrecht.

[1] See L. Krämer, "Environmental Protection and Article 30 EEC Treaty" (1993) 30 *Common Market Law Review* 111; D. Emiray, "The Movement of Goods in a Green Market" [1994] *Legal Issues of European Integration* 73; J. H. Jans, *European Environmental Law* (The Hague–Boston, Mass.–London: Kluwer Law International, 1995), 197–235; L. Krämer, *E.C. Treaty and Environmental Law* (3rd edn., London: Sweet & Maxwell, 1998), 139–59. See in general P. Oliver, *Free Movement of Goods in the European Community* (3rd edn., London: Sweet & Maxwell, 1996); J. Scott, *EC Environmental Law* (London: Longman, 1998).

[2] Case 172/82, *Inter-Huiles* [1983] ECR 555; Case 240/83, *Procureur de la République* v. *Association de Défense des Brûleurs d'Huiles Usagées* [1985] ECR 531.

[3] Case 302/86, *Commission* v. *Denmark ("Danish Bottles")* [1988] ECR 4607.

not limited to the cross-border flow of goods between Member States, how-ever. Rather, as is commonly understood, the proper functioning of the internal market requires also the maintenance of equal conditions of competition for undertakings operating within the internal market.[4] The elimination of obstacles to the free movement of goods is hence crucial for the smooth functioning of the internal market, in turn a *conditio sine qua non* for the ongoing process of European economic integration.[5]

At the same time, environmental policy is also recognized as an important objective in the EC Treaty, particularly following amendments by the Treaty of Amsterdam.[6]

It is all too common for fundamental goals to conflict and, likewise, there exists a potential for environmental policies of Member States to undermine the concept of the internal market. Conflict may occur, for example, where environmental standards are imposed on products, amounting to product bans although, as *Danish Bottles* shows, this conflict also emerges in contexts where more intricate environmental regulations are at issue.[7]

In essence, the Treaty provisions concerning free movement of goods are straightforward. The non-tariff Treaty provisions consist of Articles 28–30 EC, covering quantitative restrictions and measures having equivalent effect on imports and exports between Member States.[8] Articles 28 and 29 EC state that Member States may not restrict imports and exports of goods. Article 30 EC contains a catalogue of possible justifications which, crucially for our purposes, includes the protection of the health of humans, animals, or plants. The ECJ has further increased the possibilities of justifying trade restrictions on

---

[4] The ECJ endorses this view. See Case C–300/89, *Commission* v. *Council ("Titanium Dioxide")* [1991] ECR I–2867 (on the legal basis of European environmental legislation). See also Case C–233/94, *Germany* v. *European Parliament and Council* [1997] ECR I–2405. On the notion "common market" see Case 15/81, *Gaston Schul* [1982] ECR 1409 (para. 33). On the notion "common market" as opposed to "internal market", see P. J. G. Kapteyn and P. VerLoren van Themaat, *Introduction to the Law of the European Communities* (3rd edn., ed. and rev. by L. Gormley, The Hague–London–Boston, Mass.: Kluwer Law International, 1998), 122–4.

[5] See in more detail A. Schrauwen, "Marché Intérieur—Recherches sur une notion", dissertation, University of Amsterdam (1997). See also K. Mortelmans, "The Common Market, the Internal Market and the Single Market, What's in a Market?" (1998) 35 *Common Market Law Review* 101.

[6] Art. 2 EC provides, among others, that the Community shall have as its task the promotion of sustainable development of economic activities and a high level of protection and improvement of the environment. See G. Van Calster and K. Deketelaere, "Amsterdam, the Intergovernmental Conference and Greening the EU Treaty" [1998] *European Environmental Law Review* 12.

[7] A great deal of European environmental legislation would never have been adopted had it not been for the threat posed by national environmental legislation to the establishment and proper functioning of the internal market, which is also evidenced by the preambles of environmental directives and regulations based on Arts. 94 and 95 (formerly Arts. 100 and 100a) EC. See on the fundamental relationship between trade barriers, distortions of competition, and the need for harmonization the authoritative study by E. Rehbinder and R. Stewart, *Environmental Protection Policy* (Berlin–New York: Walter de Gruyter, 1985), Vol. 2 of the *Integration Through Law* series.

[8] The term "goods" for the purpose of the Treaty was examined in *Wallonian Waste* (Case C–2/90, *Commission* v. *Belgium ("Wallonian Waste")* [1992] ECR I–4431). The ECJ had to decide whether recyclable, non-recyclable, and non-reusable waste constituted "goods" in the sense of the Treaty. It established that "objects which are shipped across a frontier for the purposes of commercial transactions are subject to Art. 28 EC, whatever the nature of those transactions" (para. 26). This wide definition covers waste that has a "negative" economic value.

imports and, in this case law, also recognized environmental protection as a "mandatory requirement" that may have precedence over the free movement of goods.

As a general rule, exceptions to fundamental principles must be interpreted restrictively and the ECJ obviously imposes strict conditions in order for such national environmental measures to be justified.[9] Neither is the prerogative of Member States to invoke a justification eternal. This power is lost once an environmental directive has reconciled the "mandatory requirement", or one of the general interests enumerated in Article 30 EC, with the internal market objective.

Since the ECJ plays such a decisive role in locating the balance between free movement of goods and environmental objectives, in this chapter the recent legal developments in the case law of the ECJ will be more fully explored. Although the case law in the field of Articles 28–30 EC is sometimes understood by commentators as being an established body of jurisprudence (which may be true for certain traditional policy fields, such as foodstuffs), in the field of the environment, law is in its development stage and issues yet have to be fully crystallized. Many fundamental questions hence remain unresolved regarding the scope of the prohibitions of Articles 28 and 29 EC and the conditions under which environmental measures may be justified (sections III–VI). Before turning to these issues, I shall first discuss the situations in which Articles 28–30 EC apply (section II).

Importantly, the balance between the free movement of goods and environmental imperatives also plays a role in the determination of the scope of application of the new flexibility clause laid down in Article 11 EC. We shall consider the relevance of this clause for environmental issues in the light of the provisions on the free movement of goods (section VII).

As part of the customs union, the EC Treaty also covers tariff aspects of the free movement of goods. Article 25 (formerly Articles 12–17) EC prohibits customs duties and charges having equivalent effect on the trade of goods between Member States. Article 90 (formerly Article 95) EC prohibits internal taxation which discriminates against imports from other Member States, or any form of protection for similar or competing domestic products. When the use of fiscal instruments in environmental policy is considered, it follows that these Treaty provisions have to be taken into account. By way of illustration, Article 90 EC does not preclude differentiated rates of internal taxes on electricity according to the manner in which it is produced, in so far as that system is inspired by environmental considerations. However, Article 90 EC is breached where taxes on imported and similar domestic products are calculated on the basis of discriminatory criteria resulting in higher taxes being levied on imported products.[10] Although hence of considerable interest for

---

[9] See Case 113/80, *Commission* v. *Ireland ("Irish Souvenirs")* [1981] ECR 1625.

[10] See the important example of Case C–213/96, *Proceedings against Outokumpu Oy* [1998] ECR I–1777. See G. Van Calster, "Ook voor milieufiscaliteit geldt een strikte non-discriminatieregel" [1998] *Nederlands Tijdschrift voor Europees Recht* 205. The ECJ rejected the argument that fiscal

national and Community environmental policy, these tariff provisions will not be afforded further separate attention.[11]

II. Applicability of the Regime of Articles 28–30 EC

A. APPLICATION TO NATIONAL ENVIRONMENTAL MEASURES

It is useful briefly to recall the circumstances under which the provisions on the free movement of goods generally apply. Initially, it must be established whether an environmental issue is regulated by a directive or a regulation. The application of Articles 28–30 EC is unambiguous in the situation in which the Community legislator has not, or not yet, adopted harmonization measures in the form of directives or regulations. In such cases, in adopting or applying national regulations, Member States are free to establish environmental standards in as far as these respect the margins posed by Articles 28–30 EC. This regime applies irrespective of the question whether such provisions emanate from central, regional, or local government.[12]

It is also possible that a national measure only partially falls within the scope of a directive or regulation. This implies that for the remainder (the part which has not yet been subject to harmonization) the measure needs to be considered in the context of Articles 28–30 EC. This process requires a complex and in-depth assessment of the subject matter, the wording, and the objectives of both the European and the national provisions in question,[13] and in particular of the material scope of the Community provision.

The *Wallonian Waste* case offers a useful illustration of the mechanics of this process. The ECJ assessed an absolute ban on the import of waste into Wallonia in the context of Directive 84/631/EEC, in so far as the ban applied to hazardous waste and hence fell within the scope of that Directive.[14] To the

discriminations could be justified by environmental considerations in similar fashion to the "mandatory requirement" case law established in the context of Art. 26 EC. See on this point the Opinion of Jacobs AG.

[11] See the Communication of the Commission on environmental taxes and charges within the common market [1997] OJ C224/6. See also W. De Wit, *Nationale milieubelastingen en het EG-Verdrag* (Deventer: Kluwer 1997).

[12] Good examples in the case law are Case 380/87, *Balsamo ("Enichem Base")* [1989] ECR 2491, and Case C-2/90, *Wallonian Waste* (n. 8 above). An interesting complication for the application of Arts. 28–30 EC occurs when one region decides to establish an environmental measure that creates a barrier to intra-Community trade and other regions do not take protective measures. In *Wallonian Waste*, the ECJ did not examine the effect of the Wallonian import ban on waste on trade between the Flemish and the Wallonian regions, despite the fact that the Commission had also challenged this flow of goods. Probably, the ECJ considered that this was an internal situation not covered by Art. 28 EC. On the role of (national) decentralized administrations in the application of Community law, see J. W. van de Gronden, *De implementatie van het EG-milieurecht door Nederlandse decentrale overheden* (Deventer: Kluwer, 1998) See the book review section below.

[13] See Cases 141–143/81, *Holdijk* [1982] ECR 1299. In this ruling, the ECJ held that, in the absence of specific provisions on the protection of animals in a common market organization and in other Community legislation, a Member State can in principle take measures to protect animals that are covered by the common market organization at issue (paras. 12–13).

[14] [1986] OJ L181/13 (as amended).

extent that the ban applied to non-hazardous waste, where no Community legislation applied, the contested rules were assessed under Articles 28–30 EC.[15]

A similar, more recent example, is provided by *Harpegnies*,[16] which concerned the authorization of plant protection products already marketed in another Member State. Although the referring Belgian court did not properly categorize the products at issue, the ECJ distinguished pesticides as plant protection products for agricultural use, which are covered by Community legislation,[17] and other plant protection products used for non-agricultural purposes where no secondary legislation was yet in force.[18] The question whether a second authorization was lawful under EC law was answered within the framework of the Directive for the former category, but in the context of Article 28 EC in respect of the latter group of pesticides.[19]

In both examples, the material scope, the products dealt with in the directives at issue, determined the tri-lateral relationship between national law, primary, and secondary Community law.

Interestingly, in *Compassion* the starting point was the general interest covered by the relevant provisions of secondary Community law. The ECJ concluded that a national restriction on the export of veal calves could not be justified by the protection of the health of animals as mentioned in Article 30 EC, because this interest had already been covered by Council Directive 91/629/EEC Laying Down Minimum Standards for the Protection of Calves.[20] The ECJ proceeded, nevertheless, to examine whether a Member State could rely on the protection of public policy or public morality, as safeguarded by Article 30 EC, in order to restrict the export of calves to another Member State. Since matters relating to the protection of public policy or public morality were not covered by the Directive, they belonged to a non-harmonized area.[21]

---

[15] Case C–2/90, *Wallonian Waste* (n. 8 above). Dir. 75/442/EEC on Waste ([1975] OJ L194/39) did not apply because the dir. does not refer specifically to trade in waste between Member States. The case arose before the adoption of Council Reg. (EEC) 259/93 on the supervision and control of shipments of waste within, into and out of the European Community [1993] OJ L30/1.

[16] Case C–400/96, *Criminal proceeding against Jean Harpegnies*, judgment of 17 Sept. 1998, not yet reported.

[17] Council Dir. 91/414/EEC of 15 July 1991 concerning the placing of plant protection products on the market [1991] OJ L230/1.

[18] Dir. 98/8/EC of the European Parliament and of the Council of 16 February 1998 concerning the placing of biocidal products on the market [1998] OJ L123/1, had not yet been adopted when the facts in the main proceedings took place.

[19] Case C–400/96, *Criminal proceedings against Jean Harpegnies*, n. 16 above, paras. 13–22. Similarly, Case 125/88, *Criminal proceedings against Nijman* [1989] ECR 3533 (para. 14). For more examples, see Jans, n. 1 above, 94–8.

[20] [1991] OJ L340/28.

[21] Case C–1/96, *The Queen* v. *Minister for Agriculture, Fisheries and Food, ex parte Compassion in World Farming Ltd* [1998] ECR I–1251 (paras. 65–68). The argument was not accepted by the ECJ (see sect. VI.A). The subject could have been covered by Reg. (EEC) 805/68, which regulates the market in beef and veal (n. 13 above). The ECJ examined the Regulation and held that a ban on the export of calves would interfere with the proper functioning of the common organization of the market, but it did not draw the conclusion that an export ban thus must be incompatible with the Regulation (see, to that effect, Case 218/85, *Cerafel* v. *Le Campion* [1986] ECR 3513). Instead, the

In summary, harmonization essentially seeking to reconcile conflicting interests at European level, the balance between free movement and environmental goals should be examined with reference to the harmonization measure and national environmental measures can thus only exist within the boundaries posed by the relevant directive or regulation.[22] Yet, the harmonization process should not be equated with uniformity of national laws. Rather, directives are flexible instruments of environmental policy, leaving policy margins to national authorities.[23] Since harmonization of national environmental regulations has expanded considerably in the last two decades, it comes as little surprise that numerous environmental cases were recently dealt with by the ECJ where national environmental law was measured against both primary and secondary EC law. Given the complexity of the issues involved, a closer examination of the ECJ's case law bearing upon the continued importance of Articles 28–30 EC after harmonization appears merited. In this regard, four basic conceptions serving to determine the reserved powers of Member States following harmonization may be inferred from the ECJ's case law.

First, even if Community legislation has formally been adopted, the regime of Articles 28–30 EC fully applies and Member States hence still enjoy competence to adopt provisions justified by Article 30 EC when the implementation period has not yet expired[24] or when the harmonization measure requires that more detailed rules must be adopted in order for the Community measure to be applicable.[25]

ECJ referred to *Holdijk* (n. 13 above) and the specific circumstances under which this ruling was delivered. Without further motivation, it then proceeded to examine the Dir. See on this point paras. 41–46, and Sevenster, "Dierenbeschermingswet Sneuvelt op Richtlijn" (1998) 4 *Nederlands Tijdschrift voor Europees Recht* 105.

[22] See for examples in the environmental field Case C–169/89, *Criminal proceedings against Gourmetterie Van den Burg* [1990] ECR I–2143 (restriction on the importation and marketing of the "dead red grouse"); Case C–5/94, *The Queen* v. *Ministry of Agriculture, Fisheries and Food, ex parte Hedley Lomas (Ireland) Ltd* [1996] ECR I–2553 (restriction on export of sheep); Case C–37/92, *Vanacker* [1993] ECR I–4947 (Dir. on waste) and Case C–422/92, *Commission* v. *Germany* [1995] ECR I–1097 (directives on waste).

[23] Art. 249 EC states that a directive shall be binding, as to the result to be achieved, upon each Member State to which it is addressed, but shall leave to the national authorities the choice of form and methods.

[24] Case 35/76, *Simmenthal* [1976] ECR 1871; Case 251/78, *Denkavit Futtermittel* [1979] ECR 3369. See also AG Léger in his Opinion in Case C–350/97, *Wilfried Monsees* v. *Unabhängiger Verwaltungssenat Kärnten et al.*, delivered on 17 Dec. 1998. Central to this case was the question whether geographical and temporal restrictions on the transport of animals are allowed under Arts. 28–30 EC. Council Dir. 95/29/EC of 29 June 1995 on the modification of Dir. 91/628/EEC on the protection of animals on their transport [1995] OJ L148/52, was not taken into consideration, because the implementation period had not yet expired at the time the facts took place. Nevertheless, Léger AG invoked the Directive when he examined the proportionality of the measure in question under Art. 28 EC and considered less trade-restrictive measures to achieve the goal (para. 40). During the implementation period, Member States must refrain from any measure that may seriously threaten the fulfilment of the Directive's aims: see Case C–129/96, *Inter-Environnement Wallonie* [1997] ECR I–7411. This makes the introduction of new trade restrictions that are covered by a directive but are not in conformity with it questionable, even when they may be justified under Art. 28 EC or the "mandatory requirement" case law.

[25] In Case C–67/97, *Criminal proceedings against Ditlev Bluhme (Danish Bees)*, judgment of 3 Dec. 1998, not yet reported, concerning a Danish trade restriction on particular bees, Council Dir.

Secondly, the question whether the subject matter has been dealt with exhaustively must be answered. This issue, associated with what is sometimes referred to as the principle of estoppel or the principle of pre-emption, directly bears upon the division of competences between the Community and Member States.[26] The ECJ has consistently held that Member State recourse to Article 30 EC or the doctrine of mandatory requirements ceases to be possible as soon as the Community legislator has provided for exhaustive harmonization of the measures necessary to achieve the specific interest which the Member State invokes.[27]

This aspect of the relationship between Articles 28–30 EC and secondary legislation may be usefully illustrated on the basis of *Compassion*.[28] One of the questions addressed in that case was whether a Member State may rely on Article 30 EC in order to justify restrictions on the export of live veal calves, given that Directive 91/629/EEC provides for harmonization. The Advocate General and the ECJ delivered fundamentally different opinions. According to the Advocate General, the Directive did not have the effect of completely removing the competence which Article 30 EC allows Member States to adopt necessary provisions on grounds of the protection of the life and health of animals, because it gives Member States a broad discretion to grant derogations for very long periods.[29] The ECJ did not agree. It followed from the wording of the Directive, its context, and the objectives which it pursues, that it lays down minimum common standards for the protection of calves that are confined for the purposes of rearing and fattening. Therefore, the ECJ held that "in adopting the directive the Community legislature laid down *exhaustive* common minimum standards".[30] In other words, the United Kingdom (UK) could not rely on Article 30 EC for reasons relating to the protection of the health of animals, because this general good had already been fully covered by the Directive. Derogations are

---

91/174/EEC of 25 Mar. 1991 laying down zoötechnical and pedigree requirements for the marketing of pure-bred animals and amending Dirs. 77/504/EEC and 90/425/EEC [1991] OJ L85/37, did not apply. Art. 6 of the Directive provides that detailed rules for application of the Directive are to be adopted in accordance with the so-called "committee" procedure, but no such rules have been adopted in relation to bees. The legislation at issue was therefore examined under Arts. 28–30 EC, paras. 10–13.

[26] See H. G. Sevenster, *Milieubeleid en Gemeenschapsrecht—Het interne juridische kader en de praktijk* (Deventer: Kluwer, 1992), 18–20.

[27] See, in particular, Case C–169/89, *Gourmetterie Van den Burg*, n. 22 above (concerning the exhaustive character of Dir. 79/409/EEC on wild birds, see para. 8); Case C–5/94, *Hedley Lomas*, n. 22 above (on the exhaustive character of Dir. 74/577/EEC on stunning of animals before slaughter, para. 18) and Case C–323/93, *Centre d'Insémination de la Crespelle* v. *Coopérative de la Mayenne* [1994] ECR I–5077 (on the exhaustive character of Dirs. 87/328/EEC, 88/407/EEC, and 91/174/EEC on the health conditions in intra-Community trade in bovine semen, see paras. 31–35).

[28] Case C–1/96, *Compassion*, n. 21 above, para. 47.

[29] AG Léger, Opinion in *Compassion* (paras. 61–70). See Art. 3(4) of the Directive.

[30] Case C–1/96, *Compassion*, n. 21 above, para. 56, emphasis added. See also para. 63 of this ruling.

justified within the framework of the Directive, which does not foresee in a ban on the export of live veal calves.[31]

The third variable impacting on Member States' reserved powers after harmonization involves an analysis of *harmonization technique*. In determining the harmonization technique employed, it is crucial to distinguish the question what subject is addressed in a directive, and whether the directive exhaustively regulates the powers of the Member States, from the issue regarding the reserved powers of Member States. "Exhaustive harmonization" rules out the possibility for Member States to apply more protective standards than fixed in the Community Directive in case of total harmonization but, as *Compassion* shows, not in case of minimum harmonization. Harmonization is said to be total when a directive provides for a complete system of regulation in a particular field.[32] Total harmonization is especially important in the context of product standards. The free movement of goods is difficult to reconcile with residual national powers to deviate from the provisions of a directive. Minimum harmonization, by contrast, is a technique which allows Member States to adopt (environmental) standards more stringent than prescribed by the Community act.[33] In *Compassion*, by virtue of Article 11(2) of Directive 91/629/EEC, Member States were entitled to adopt stricter measures for the protection of calves than those laid down in the Directive. According to this provision, however, such measures are permitted only if they relate to cattle farms falling within the jurisdiction of the Member State in question, and if they are in compliance with the general rules of the Treaty, such as those pertaining to the free movement of goods. A ban on exports imposed on account of conditions prevailing in other Member States complying with the minimum standards of the Directive hence falls outside the derogation of Article 11(2).[34]

---

[31] It must be observed that the terminology of the ECJ on the exhaustiveness of directives is not very consistent. In *De Agostini*, for instance, the ECJ refers to "partial harmonization" in respect of the provisions co-ordinated by the TV Directive (Joined Cases C–34–36/95, see n. 75 below, para. 32). In *Norbrook*, the ECJ uses the word "exhaustively" in order to define the extent to which the conditions for granting marketing authorizations for certain medical products have been harmonized (Case C–127/95 [1998] ECR I–1531, para. 32). In *Nilsson* the ECJ points out that zoötechnical and pedigree conditions relating to intra-Community trade in bovine semen have been fully harmonized under Dirs. 87/328/EEC and 91/174/EEC. It followed that a Member State may not obstruct the use in its territory of the semen of pure-bred bulls where they have been accepted for artificial insemination in another Member State on the basis of tests carried out in accordance with a Community decision (Case C–162/97, *Criminal proceedings against Gunnar Nilsson et al.*, judgment of 19 Nov. 1998, not yet reported, para. 41). It is to be hoped that the ECJ will pay more attention to the use of a consistent terminology.

[32] See, e.g., Case 148/78, *Ratti* [1979] ECR 1629 (on the marketing of solvents and Dir. 73/173/EEC).

[33] See on both types of harmonization Jans, n. 1 above, 89–118. See for harmonization techniques in general, P. J. Slot, "Harmonization" (1996) 21 *European Law Review* 378.

[34] Case C–1/96, *Compassion*, n. 21 (paras. 57–60). In *Hönig*, the ECJ established that Dir. 88/166/EEC of 25 Mar. 1986 laying down minimum standards for the protection of laying hens kept in battery cages [1988] OJ L74/83, permits Member States to lay down stricter national rules regarding the cage area for hens. Arts. 28–30 EC did not apply as the German legislation was confined to German territory and no intra-Community trade was involved (Case C–128/94, *Hönig* v. *Stadt Stockack* [1995] ECR I–3389).

Similarly, in *Aher-Waggon*, the ECJ was asked whether the German refusal to grant registration for a propeller-driven aircraft previously registered in Denmark, on the ground that it exceeded maximum noise levels permitted in Germany, was compatible with Directive 80/51/EEC on the Limitation of Noise Emissions from Subsonic Aircraft[35] and the principles of the free movement of goods under Article 28 EC. The Directive merely lays down minimum requirements; according to Article 3(1), each Member State shall ensure that all aeroplanes that fall within the categories of this provision are certified in accordance with requirements "which are at least equal" to the standards specified in Annex 16/5 to the Convention on International Civil Aviation. The Directive thus allows Member States to impose stricter noise limits, but only in so far as these are compatible with Article 28 EC.[36]

In *Compassion* and *Aher-Waggon*, the minimum harmonization character was inferred from the content and the wording of the directives at issue. However, it is equally possible that the reserved powers of Member States follow from the legal basis of a Community measure. Article 95(4) EC (which serves as a basis for internal market measures) and Article 176 EC (the legal basis for autonomous environmental measures) permit Member States, under certain conditions, to apply more stringent national environmental provisions after adoption of a European harmonization measure. Article 176 EC adds that such measures must be compatible with the EC Treaty, which assumes that they must be in conformity with Article 28–30 EC. Pursuant to Article 95(4) EC, on the other hand, the more stringent national provisions must be based on grounds of major needs referred to in Article 30 EC or relating to protection of the environment. The Commission has to verify whether the more stringent national measures are not a means of arbitrary discrimination or a disguised restriction on trade between Member States.[37] The language of Article 95(4) EC hence seems to indicate that the test of Articles 28–30 EC plays a role here as well. Article 95(4) EC has been applied by Member States in order to justify more stringent environmental measures only sporadically and, thus far, guidance of the ECJ clarifying this element of Article 95 (4) EC is lacking.[38]

The scope of both provisions continues to be subject to lively debate. It has been argued that Articles 95(4) and 176 EC imply that all Community measures based on Articles 95 and 175 EC pursue minimum harmonization.

---

[35] [1980] OJ L18/26, as amended by Council Dir. 83/206/EEC of 21 Apr. 1983 [1983] OJ L117/15.

[36] Case C–389/96, *Aher-Waggon GmbH* v. *Federal Republic of Germany*, judgment of 14 July 1998, not yet reported (paras. 15–16). Unlike AG Cosmas, the ECJ did not pay attention to the possibility that the registration of a second-hand civil propeller-driven aircraft might not even fall within the ambit of the Directive, because Art. 3(1) only obliges Member States to respect the noise standards when the aeroplanes in question are newly registered in its territory.

[37] This terminology seems to be derived from the second sentence of Art. 28 EC.

[38] After Amsterdam, according to the revised Art. 95a(6) EC the Commission must not only verify whether the more stringent national rules amount to arbitrary discrimination or a disguised restriction on trade, but also whether they constitute "an obstacle to the functioning of the internal market". See on this ambiguous wording and, in general, the scope of Art. 95a(4) EC the article by Sevenster at p. 291 of this volume.

Another, less compelling, view is that reliance on these provisions is no longer possible if the Community measure in question is a manifestation of total harmonization.[39] This interesting and important issue could have been settled in *Dusseldorp*, where the question arose whether a regulation based on Article 175 EC leaves room for more stringent national measures. The ECJ was not obliged to answer this question, however, as the national measure proved incompatible with Article 29 EC.[40] Other case law suggests that the ECJ is not eager to accept that after harmonization Member States may apply more stringent environmental measures to imported products meeting the minimum standards fixed by a directive.[41]

The fourth and final consideration concerns the situation in which directives and regulations are implemented and/or applied in the national legal order, usually by means of legislative measures. A directive, and hence also national implementing legislation, may involve the issuing of individual authorizations by (decentralized) administrative bodies. Crucially, such authorizations must not only respect the provisions of the Community directive and the national implementing legislation, but also the Treaty provisions relating to goods. The significance of this obligation has become particularly clear in the case law of the ECJ on the interpretation of waste directives.[42]

---

[39] On Art. 95 EC, see the discussion by Jans, n. 1 above, 104–5. The most persuasive argument in favour of the first view is that the Treaty provisions always take preference over secondary legislation.

[40] Case C–203/96, *Chemische Afvalstoffen Dusseldorp BV et al.* v. *Minister van Volkshuisvesting, Ruimtelijke Ordening en Milieubeheer*, judgment of 25 June 1998, not yet reported (paras. 35–50). Jacobs AG in his Opinion of 23 Oct. 1997 similarly argued that the question did not need to be resolved in that case (paras. 70–74).

[41] See for instance Case C–11/92, *R.* v. *Secretary of State for Health, ex parte Gallaher Ltd et al.* [1993] ECR I–3545. Such a requirement goes beyond the obligations imposed by the Directive and thus will contravene Art. 28 or 29 EC (see Case C–369/89, *Piageme* v. *Peeters* [1991] ECR I–2971, on language requirements on foodstuffs and "total harmonization" Dir. 79/112/EEC). From the point of view of environmental protection, it is hence important that minimum harmonization rules actually do take as a reference a high level of environmental protection, rather than the "lowest common denominator". Art. 95(3) EC instructs the Commission to take as a base a "high level" of environmental protection, health and safety protection, and consumer protection while proposing internal market harmonization. Following Amsterdam, the Parliament and the Council must now also "seek to achieve this objective". Moreover, the Commission shall take into account in particular any new development based on scientific facts.

[42] The case law is, unfortunately, not very consistent. In Case C–37/92, *Vanacker* (n. 22 above) the ECJ does not explicitly assess the relevant French implementation provision under Arts. 28–30 EC. It states that "since the question of the collection of waste oil has been regulated in a harmonized manner at Community level by the Directive, any national measure relating thereto must be assessed in the light of the provisions of the Directive and not of Arts. 30 to 36 EC" (para. 9). This is surprising, since in previous case law concerning the same Directive, the ECJ interpreted both the Directive(75/439/EEC [1975] OJ L194/31) and Art. 29 EC (see Case 172/82, *Inter-Huiles* (n. 2 above)); Case 295/82, *Rhône Alpes Huiles* [1984] ECR 572; Case 173/83, *Commission* v. *France* [1985] ECR 491). However, the ECJ referred to those judgments and concluded that it had decided in these cases "that the national legislation which established a system of approval by zones, was incompatible with the Directive in question and with the rules concerning the free movement of goods because it precluded the exportation of waste oil" (para. 11). The conclusion in *Vanacker* is that the national provision in question, which was similar to the ones at issue in the previous cases, is incompatible only with the Directive.

B. RELEVANCE FOR ENVIRONMENTAL MEASURES OF COMMUNITY
ORIGIN

It thus appears that the Treaty provisions concerning the free movement of goods remain relevant even if it is clear that the subject matter falls within the scope of secondary Community legislation.[43] Although directives or regulations sometimes explicitly refer to the Treaty provisions on the free movement of goods,[44] such clauses are superfluous; secondary legislation should always be in conformity with provisions of the EC Treaty, as these are a *lex superior*.[45] That the prohibition of quantitative restrictions and measures having equivalent effect also applies to environmental measures adopted by the Community institutions is an issue which has been prominent in the case law on the Community's regime relating to waste. Rulings such as *Wallonian Waste* and *Dusseldorp* raised the question whether certain provisions of the EU legislation on waste are perhaps incompatible with the Treaty provisions on the free movement of goods.[46] From these judgments it may be deduced, however, that the ECJ leaves more margin for the provisions of the Community legislator than for measures adopted by national authorities.[47]

---

[43] See in particular Case 15/83, *Denkavit Nederland* v. *Hoofdproduktschap voor Akkerbouwprodukten* [1984] ECR 2171 (para. 15), and Case C–51/93, *Meyhui* v. *Schott Zwiesel Glaswerke* [1994] ECR I–3879 (para. 11). See also Case 172/82, *Inter-Huiles* (n. 2 above).

[44] e.g. Reg. (EEC) 805/68 of the Council of 27 June 1968 on the common market organization of the market in beef and veal ([1968] I OJ Spec. Ed. 187) prohibits in the second indent of Art. 22(1) any quantitative restriction or measure having equivalent effect in the internal trade of the Community. See for this provision *Compassion* (n. 21 above).

[45] One might conceive this relationship in terms of Arts. 28–30 EC being a *lex generalis* and the harmonization measure a *lex specialis*, which derogates from the primary provisions. However, it is submitted that the interpretation of the *lex specialis* should be carried out in the light of the *lex generalis*. Specific problems may occur when a policy area is covered by secondary legislation which represents a restatement of current case law on the free movement of goods. This might hinder the judicial development of the Treaty provisions. An example is the exhaustion of trade mark rights embodied in Art. 7 of Dir. 89/104/EEC of 21 Dec. 1988 to approximate the laws of the member states relating to trade marks [1984] OJ L40/1. See on this issue E. Gippini-Fournier's comments on Case C–352/95, *Phyteron International SA* v. *Jean Bourdon SA* [1997] ECR I–1729 in (1998) 35 *Common Market Law Review* 962. A similar problem could occur in the field of waste.

[46] See, for instance, P. Von Wilmowsky, "Waste Disposal in the Internal Market: the State of Play after the Court's Ruling on the Walloon Import Ban" (1993) 30 *Common Market Law Review* 564.

[47] See Oliver, n. 1 above, 49. See also U. Scheffer, *Die Marktfreiheiten des EG-Vertrages als Ermessensgrenze des Gemeinschaftsgesetzgebers* (Frankfurt am Main: Peter Lang, 1997). It should be remembered that the ECJ so far has never declared a provision in a harmonization measure incompatible with Art. 28 or 29 EC. In the recent *Safety Hi-Tech* case the ECJ upheld the prohibition on the use and marketing of HCFCs which was designed to protect the ozone layer in Reg. (EC) 3093/94 of 15 Dec. 1994 on substances that deplete the ozone layer [1994] OJ L333/1. According to the ECJ, the prohibition established by the measure was proportionate in the light of Art. 28 EC (Case C–284/95, *Safety Hi-Tech Srl* v. *S. & T. Srl*, judgment of 14 July 1998, not yet reported). Tariff provisions of Arts. 23, 25 EC, and the former Art. 13 EC were held to be incompatible with secondary EC legislation. See, e.g., Case C–363/93, *Lancry* v. *Direction Générale des Douanes* [1994] ECR I–3957, on the invalidity of a Council decision which authorized France to maintain levies on imports into the overseas departments.

III.   The Scope of Article 28 EC and Environmental Measures

Article 28 EC forbids Member States to introduce or maintain quantitative restrictions on imports from other Member States and all measures having an equivalent effect. The ECJ has consistently held, since its well-known *Dassonville* case,[48] that:

All trading rules enacted by Member States which are capable of hindering, directly or indirectly, actually or potentially, intra-Community trade are to be considered as measures having an effect equivalent to quantitative restrictions.

In subsequent cases, the ECJ has dropped the requirement that the obstacle is caused by a *trading* rule,[49] thereby potentially placing all types of national measures, including environmental measures, under the umbrella of the prohibition of Article 28 EC.

The *Dassonville* formula was reinforced in the no less famous *Cassis de Dijon* case.[50] The ECJ adopted the principle of mutual recognition of national regulations, a principle departing from the presumption that imported goods are lawfully manufactured and marketed in another Member State. In the absence of European harmonization, legal obstacles that obstruct the importation of such goods and which are the consequence of distortions between national legislation constitute measures of equivalent effect prohibited by Article 28 EC. Examples are rules relating to designation, form, size, weight, composition, presentation, labelling, and packaging of products. This is so even if those rules apply without distinction to imported and domestic products. Thus, whereas in *Dassonville* the focus was still on the product standards of the Member State of importation, in *Cassis de Dijon,* the emphasis shifted to the principle that goods need in the first place to be produced and brought on the market in conformity with the standards of the Member State of origin.

Striking examples in the case law of the ECJ regarding national environmental measures caught by the prohibition of Article 28 EC include provisions on the regulation for returnable bottles,[51] an import ban on waste,[52] and an import ban on live freshwater crayfish.[53] Recently, the ECJ defined, as a trade restriction within the meaning of Article 28 EC, the requirement that the registration of an aircraft is made conditional upon noise emission limits[54] and a legal provision "prohibiting biocidal products which have not been previously

---

[48] Case 8/74, *Procureur du Roi* v. *Dassonville* [1974] ECR 837, para. 5.

[49] See most recently the *Spanish Strawberries* ruling (n. 84 below).

[50] Case 120/78, *Rewe Zentrale* v. *Bundesmonopolverwaltung für Branntwein* ("*Cassis de Dijon*") [1979] ECR 649.

[51] Case C–302/86, *Danish Bottles* (n. 3 above).

[52] Case C–2/90, *Wallonian Waste* (n. 8 above).

[53] Case C–131/93, *Commission* v. *Germany* ("*German crayfish*") [1994] ECR I–3303.

[54] Case C–389/96, *Aher-Waggon* (n. 36 above).

authorized from being marketed, acquired, offered, put on display or sale, kept, prepared, transported, sold, disposed of for valuable consideration or free of charge, imported or used".[55]

The scope of Article 28 EC was also at issue in the case law following *Keck* and in *Spanish Strawberries*, the implication of which for national environmental measures will be discussed next.

B.   LIMITING THE SCOPE OF ARTICLE 28 EC: *KECK* AND ENVIRONMENTAL MEASURES

The *Dassonville* definition of the notion of measures having equivalent effect to a quantitative restriction has a very wide scope. Indeed, there is hardly any measure of trade policy that has not, at least potentially, had an influence on intra-Community trade. In fact, Article 28 EC is inapplicable only when the effect on imports is too uncertain or overly hypothetical.[56]

The broad concept of a measure having equivalent effect has given rise, in the 1980s, to ECJ judgments which lacked clarity as to the determination of its boundaries. The cases concerned national legislation which did not directly affect imports, but could have the effect to restrict the volume of trade because it affected marketing opportunities for imported products. Examples are rules on advertising and competition, rules that reserve the sale of products to certain categories of merchants and even rules that restrict the opening hours of shops or prohibit trading on Sundays. All the national rules at issue in these cases applied without distinction to domestic and imported goods. The ECJ employed concepts that deviated from the classic *Dassonville* formula.[57] The ambiguity in the ECJ case law in turn led to conflicting decisions of national courts in the UK[58] and reform proposals designed to alter the scope of Article 28 EC.[59]

---

[55] Case C–400/96, *Criminal proceedings against Jean Harpegnies*, n. 16 above (para. 30). See also Case C–293/94, *Brandsma* [1996] ECR I–3159.

[56] See, e.g., Case C–93/92, *CMC Motorradcenter v. Baskiciogullari* [1993] ECR I–5009 (on pre-contractual information obligations).

[57] The saga on the regulation of trading hours has become the most notorious example. In *Torfaen* the ECJ ruled that the regulation of the opening hours of shops could have a trade-restricting effect but left it to the national courts to decide whether the measures were proportionate (Case 145/88, *Torfaen Borough Council* [1989] ECR 3851). On the other hand, in *Conforama* and *Marchandise* the ECJ took the position that measures prohibiting employment in shops on Sundays were justified and in accordance with the proportionality criterion (Case C–312/89, *Union départementale des syndicats CGT de l'Aisne v. SIDEF Conforama et al.* [1991] ECR I–997; Case C–322/89, *Marchandise et al.* [1991] ECR I–1047). This was subsequently confirmed in Stoke-on-Trent concerning opening hours of shops (Case C–169/91, *Council of the City of Stoke-on-Trent v. B & Q* [1992] ECR I–6635). In *Quietlynn*, it was held that national legislation prohibiting the sale of sex articles from unlicensed sex establishments did not have a connection with intra-Community trade (Case C–23/89, *Quietlynn Ltd v. Southend-on-Sea BC* [1990] ECR I–3059).

[58] See A. Arnull, "What Shall We Do on Sunday?" (1991) 16 *European Law Review* 112.

[59] See especially E. White, "In Search of the Limits of Article 30 of the EEC Treaty" (1989) 26 *Common Market Law Review* 235.

Spurred on by these events, in 1993, the ECJ delivered its "dramatic judg-ment"[60] in *Keck*.[61] The ECJ departed from previous case law as it had become necessary to "re-examine and clarify" its case law regarding Article 28 EC. The ECJ decided that the application to products from other Member States of national provisions restricting or prohibiting certain selling arrangements is not such as to hinder trade within the meaning of the *Dassonville* formula. Such rules henceforth would fall outside the scope of Article 28 EC, provided that they apply to all affected traders within the national territory and they affect in the same manner, in law and in fact, the marketing of domestic prod-ucts and of those from other Member States. The rationale behind *Keck* is that, where those conditions are fulfilled, the application of such rules to the sale of products from another Member State meeting the requirements laid down by that state is not by nature such as to prevent their access to the market or to impede access any more than it impedes access of domestic products.

Keck caused considerable turmoil. Much criticism was based on the pre-sumption that the *Keck* ruling would undermine the internal market objec-tive.[62] However, the point of departure after *Keck* must be that the ECJ has not sacrificed the *Dassonville* formula and that distinctly applicable measures remain fully within the scope of Article 28 EC. Furthermore, within the cate-gory of indistinctly applicable measures, those which are product-related continue to be caught by Article 28 EC. Physical or direct environmental instruments like product bans (e.g. a ban on phosphates in detergents), prod-uct standards (e.g. maximum noise allowances), licensing systems etc. are hence still to be considered as quantitative restrictions or measures having an equivalent effect.[63] The same holds true for bans on the distribution of prod-ucts in a certain part of national territory.[64] The post-*Keck* examples include rules on packaging and designation,[65] rules regulating the name under which a product may be marketed,[66] and rules pertaining to the characteristics of a product.[67]

But a second group of measures should be assessed under the new prin-ciples. Despite the failure to provide a clear definition, the ECJ qualified as

---

[60] Oliver, n. 1 above, 100.

[61] Cases C–267/91 and C–268/91, *Criminal proceedings against Bernard Keck and Daniel Mithouard* [1993] ECR I–6097.

[62] See especially A. Mattera, "De l'arrêt 'Keck': L'obscure clarté d'une jurisprudence riche en principes noveteurs et en contradictions" [1994] *Revue du Marché Unique Européen* 117. See, how-ever, R. Joliet, "The Free Circulation of Goods: the Keck and Mithouard Decision and the New Directions in the Case Law" (1995) 1 *Columbia Journal of European Law* 436 (also published in (1994) 113 *Journal des Tribunaux* 145).

[63] A. Epiney, "Die Maßstabsfunktion des Art. 30 EGV für nationale umweltpolitische Maßnahmen. Zu den Rückwirkungen der neueren Rechtsprechung des EuGH zu Art. 30 EGV im Bereich des Umweltrechts" [1995] *Zeitschrift für Umweltrecht* 24. See for a recent example the judgment in the *Aher-Waggon* case, n. 36 above (registration of aircraft exceeding a maximum noise level).

[64] As has been observed by the AG in para. 20 of his Opinion in *Danish Bees* (Case C–67/97, n. 25 above). See also Cases C–277/91, C–318/91, and C–319/91, *Ligur Carni et al.* [1993] ECR I–6621.

[65] Case C–470/93, *Mars* [1995] ECR I–1923.

[66] Case C–315/92, *Estée Lauder ("Clinique")* [1994] ECR I–317.

[67] Case C–17/93, *Van der Veld* [1994] ECR I–3537.

provisions restricting or prohibiting certain selling arrangement rules on resale at a loss,[68] advertising rules,[69] the exclusive right for retailers to sell certain products,[70] and trading hours legislation.[71] Thus, it seems that measures determining how and under what conditions products are sold constitute "certain selling arrangements" which are no longer caught by the prohibition of Article 28 EC. The crucial point is that the selling arrangement rules fall outside the scope of Article 28 EC only if they do not have a discriminatory effect. Meanwhile, whereas the interpretation of the notion of "different treatment in law" is relatively unambiguous,[72] the proper meaning of the phrase "different treatment in fact" is less clear.[73]

Five years after *Keck*, the new doctrine has become established case law.[74] What is the implication of this doctrine for environmental measures? In *TV-Shop* the question arose whether the prohibition on using the words "environmentally friendly" or similar imprecise phrases implying that a detergent is beneficial for the environment in a television broadcast could be considered a hindrance in the sense articulated in Article 28 EC.[75] The ECJ applied the *Keck* formula and ruled that a ban on misleading advertising is a national measure restricting or prohibiting certain selling arrangements which, as such, is not covered by Article 28 EC. Yet, this case is easily distinguished for being an advertising or unfair competition case, rather than a genuine environmental case.

Certainly, *Danish Bees* is an environmental case. The Danish government argued that the prohibition on keeping certain bees on the island of Læsø should be regarded as relating to a selling arrangement within the meaning of the *Keck* judgment. The ECJ, however, found that the legislation in question concerned the intrinsic characteristics of the bees and therefore was not to be regarded as a selling arrangement.[76] In other words, the legislation was product-related and did not concern the conditions of sale.

Despite the lack of any clear European (and national) examples of its application, it is submitted that the *Keck* case law cannot be omitted in a discussion

---

[68] Cases C–267, 268/91, *Keck* (n. 61 above).

[69] Case C–292/92, *Hünermund* [1993] ECR I–6787; Case C–142/93, *Leclerc-Siplec* [1995] ECR I–179; Cases C–34–36/95, *De Agostini & TV-Shop* (n. 75 below).

[70] Case C–391/92, *Commission* v. *Greece ("Greek Baby Food")* [1995] ECR I–1621 (exclusive right for pharmacists to distribute processed milk for infants); Case C–387/93, *Banchero* [1995] ECR I–4663 (national monopoly on tobacco sales); Case C–162/97, *Criminal proceedings against Gunnar Nilsson et al.*, n. 31 above (requirement of authorization for insemination activities).

[71] *Inter alia*, Cases C–401, 402/92, *'t Heukske* [1994] ECR I–2199 and Cases C–69, 258/93, *Punto Casa* [1994] ECR I–2355.

[72] Case C–320/93, *Lucien Ortscheit GmbH* v. *Eurim-Pharm Arzneimittel GmbH* [1994] ECR I–5243.

[73] See Case C–391/92, *Commission* v. *Greece ("Greek Baby Food")*, n. 70 above, and Cases C–34–36/95, *Konsumentenombudsman (KO)/De Agostini (Svenska) Förlag AB and TV-Shop i Sverige AB* [1997] ECR I–3843.

[74] R. Barents, "Old and New Trends in the Court's Case Law on Foodstuffs" (1998) 8 *European Food Law Review* 127.

[75] Cases C–34–36/95, *De Agostini & TV Shop*, n. 73 above

[76] Case C–67/97, *Ditlev Bluhme*, n. 24 above (para. 21).

on the relationship between Articles 28–30 EC and environmental issues.[77] The consequences of *Keck* may hence be usefully illustrated on the basis of a hypothetical case study. Assume that at national level policy-makers decide that the adverse effect of firework displays on the environment should be combated. In principle, there are several possible instruments which can be considered, but which may fall within the scope of Article 28 EC, if applied to imported fireworks.[78] The *Dassonville* formula certainly applies when the marketing of fireworks is made conditional upon compliance with certain environmental standards related to the chemicals used, as these would amount to ordinary "product-related" standards. The *Keck* formula will apply, however, when the display of fireworks is prohibited only during certain periods. Such a situation is thus no longer caught by the prohibition of Article 28 EC as it regulates "certain selling arrangements". The same probably holds true if the sale of fireworks is made conditional upon the possession of a licence by the retailer. The ruling in *Greek Baby Food* indeed indicates that national provisions channelling the distribution of products in principle fall outside the ambit of Article 28 EC. Prior to 1993, however, such instruments would have been considered to be measures having equivalent effect.[79] Uncertainty about the applicability of Article 28 EC remains when national measures do not impose requirements on retailers or limit the permitted times of display, but instead target consumers, for instance by prohibiting firework displays without a prior licence. After *Keck* it remained unclear how price measures that are imposed in order to discourage consumers are to be assessed.[80]

Not unlike the European Commission in its fifth Environmental Action Programme, national policy-makers may also increasingly prefer the instruments of social regulation as a means of improving public awareness about the environmental burden posed by fireworks. Yet, in this context, the freedom of commercial communication is clearly at stake. Where retailers and other traders are encouraged to provide environmental information to the public on a purely voluntary basis, *Dassonville* or *Keck* would seem to be inapplicable because the effect on intra-Community trade would remain too uncertain or even hypothetical. If, on the other hand, the environmental information is compulsory, the legality of the scheme will come to depend on the question

---

[77] Krämer, for instance, does not even mention the *Keck* judgment in the context of the free movement of goods. See L. Krämer, *EC Treaty and Environmental Law* (London: Sweet & Maxwell, 1998), 139.

[78] There is no EC harmonization of fireworks, although both legal and illegal trade in fireworks between the Member States is considerable due to different safety standards (e.g. between Belgium and the Netherlands). Dir. 93/15/EC of the Council of 5 Apr. 1993 on the marketing and control of explosives for civil use [1993] OJ L121/20, excludes fireworks from the scope of application. See on product policy and the environment H. Temmink, "National Product Oriented Environmental Policy and EC Law—The Dutch Example" (1993) 2 *European Environmental Law Review* 213.

[79] See Case C–369/88, *Delattre* [1991] ECR I–1487; Case C–60/89, *Monteil and Samanni* [1991] ECR I–1547; Case C–271/91, *Société Laboratoire* [1993] ECR I–2899.

[80] See Cases C–267, 268/92, *Keck* (n. 61 above); Case C–63/94, *Groupement national des négociants en pommes de terre de Belgique* v. *ITM Belgium SA et al.* ("*Belgapom*") [1995] ECR I–2467, and, recently, Case C–120/95, *N. Decker* v. *Caisse de maladie des employés privés* [1998] ECR I–1831.

whether the information has to be displayed on the packaging itself (labelling) or, alternatively, the trader is free to provide the information either on the packaging, in a leaflet, or at the point of sale. If environmental information needs to be attached in the form of a label, it thereby directly impacts on the physical features of a product and, consequently, the rule creates a trade restriction in the sense of Article 28 EC. *Keck* does not alter the ECJ's case law relating to labelling. Where such a physical link is not compulsory, the information requirement probably no longer falls within the scope of Article 28 EC. This may be deduced from the case law concerning advertising following *Keck*, in which advertising has been considered a "selling arrangement". Whereas according to previous case law such a ban would certainly be assessed under Article 28 EC, it follows from the same case law that a ban on advertising for fireworks no longer falls within the ambit of Article 28 EC.[81]

In the light of this analysis, national regulation on environmental information on products must be examined differently after *Keck*. This conclusion follows from the rationale of *Keck*, which is to limit the applicability of Article 28 EC to those measures that create obstacles to the free movement of goods and hinder the access to transfrontier markets. However, the rigid formal distinction between product-related rules and rules on certain selling arrangements can give rise to rather arbitrary results, as was illustrated by the difference between compulsory information on the product itself and rules relating to "the periphery" of the sale of fireworks. It has therefore been suggested that the ECJ should alter its present case law and bring rules on commercial information (product information, advertising) within the scope of Article 28 EC.[82] Thus far, the ECJ has not embraced this stance.

C.   EXTENDING THE SCOPE OF ARTICLE 28 EC: *SPANISH STRAWBERRIES*

As has been shown, Article 28 EC applies to state measures or conduct that obstruct the free movement of goods. The ECJ has extended the notion of the "state" so as to include private associations with powers based on public law.[83] *Spanish Strawberries* shows that not only by positive actions, but also by failing to take adequate measures, a Member State may contravene Articles 28 and 10 EC.[84] This extension of the scope of Article 28 EC may have important implications in the sphere of the environment.

In *Spanish Strawberries*, the Commission brought an action against France because it had failed to take all necessary and proportionate measures to prevent the obstruction by actions of private individuals of the free movement of fruit and vegetables. These actions, initiated by angry French farmers,

---

[81] Cf the case law mentioned in n. 68 above with the pre-*Keck* ruling in Case C–362/88, *GB-Inno v. Confédération du Commerce Luxembourgeois* [1990] ECR I–667.

[82] See Opinion of Jacobs AG in *Leclerc-Siplec* (n. 69 above). See also T. Todino and T. Lüder, "La jurisprudence 'Keck' en matière de publicité: vers un marché unique inachevé?" (1995) *Revue du Marché Unique Européen* 171.

[83] See for instance Cases 266/87 and 267/87, *Royal Pharmaceutical Society* [1989] ECR 1295.

[84] Case C–265/95, *Commission v. French Republic ("Spanish Strawberries")* [1997] ECR I–6959.

including an organization known as "*Co-ordination Rurale*", consisted, *inter alia*, of the interception of lorries transporting agricultural products in France, the destruction of their loads, violence against lorry drivers, threats against French supermarkets selling agricultural products originating in other Member States, and the damaging of those goods on display in shops in France. The campaigns were directed particularly at strawberries originating from Spain and tomatoes from Belgium. They had a systematic character and lasted for more than a decade.

The ECJ, in a judgment of 9 December 1997, ruled for the first time that Article 28 EC not only requires that Member States abstain from adopting measures or conduct liable to constitute an obstacle to trade but also, when read in conjunction with the principle of Community loyalty laid down in Article 10 EC, that they take all necessary and appropriate measures to ensure that that fundamental freedom is respected in their territory. The fact that a Member State abstains from taking action or, as the case may be, fails to adopt adequate measures to prevent obstacles to the free movement of goods created by its nationals aimed at products originating from other Member States is just as likely to obstruct intra-Community trade as any positive act.[85] In the light of a number of specific factors, and given the frequency and seriousness of the incidents cited by the Commission, the ECJ concluded that the measures adopted by the French Government were manifestly inadequate to ensure freedom of intra-Community trade in agricultural products.

The ruling is remarkable,[86] for although the obstruction to the free movement of goods was caused by private parties, the Commission did not invoke the cartel provision of Article 81 EC against the farmers, something which, admittedly, would have posed practical difficulties. The articulation of an action against the individual farmers on the basis of Article 28 EC would have been equally problematic, however, since the horizontal effect of this provision is unclear[87] and, in any event, would have necessitated a complex and costly operation. Due to these circumstances, the Commission instead decided to bring an action against the Member State, France. Since it was not France itself that imposed the obstruction, the infringement of the French authorities could not be based solely on Article 28 EC. However, Article 10 EC states that Member States shall facilitate the achievement of the Community's tasks and that they shall abstain from any measure which may jeopardize the attainment of the objectives of the Treaty. This obligation plays a fundamental

---

[85] A logical consequence is that the ECJ refers to the *Dassonville* formula without mentioning the word "measures" (para. 29).

[86] See for comments K. Mortelmans, "Artikel 5 juncto Artikel 3 EG: een nieuwe route voor vrij verkeer van goederen" (1998) 47 *Ars Aequi*, 200; B. J. Drijber, "Hof houdt lidstaat aansprakelijk voor niet-optreden tegen sancties van particulieren" (1998) 4 *Nederlands Tijdschrift voor Europees Recht* 101; C. Denys, case note in (1998) 7 *European Environmental Law Review* 179.

[87] Case 58/80, *Dansk Supermarked* [1981] ECR 181 (para. 17). See also Case C–16/94, *Dubois* [1995] ECR I–2421 (para. 20). See in general M. Quinn and N. MacGowan, "Could Article 30 Impose Obligations on Individuals?" (1987) 12 *European Law Review* 163.

role in filling loopholes by imposing responsibilities on Member States *vis-à-vis* the actions of individuals within their jurisdiction.[88]

Social eruptions like the French riots may be relevant in an environmental context, too. A related example is provided by the consumer boycott of French products as a result of the French nuclear tests on Mururoa, which was supported by campaigns by numerous European environmental and consumer groups.[89] However, it is not likely that, on the basis of *Spanish Strawberries*, the Commission would have a high probability of success in bringing an action. The criteria of the ECJ are strict and minor incidents appear insufficient to condemn a Member State on this basis. The ECJ requires that the incidents be frequent and serious and that the measures taken by Member States be manifestly inadequate. Although how exactly these criteria are to be further developed remains to be seen, the message of the ECJ is clear. Member States are under a specific obligation to prevent private parties from infringing the free movement of goods. There is no reason why the same principle should not apply equally where private parties are obstructing other freedoms with environmental implications.[90]

The impact of *Spanish Strawberries* may well extend beyond the application of Article 28 EC. Thus, a more interesting question is whether the ruling also affects the existing obligation of Member States to take all appropriate measures to ensure that private parties act in compliance with secondary environmental law. It is well known that the ECJ has consistently refused to afford directives horizontal direct effect,[91] and that Member States often fail adequately to implement and enforce the environmental directives.[92] It has been

---

[88] In the field of competition policy, the ECJ has considered that Arts. 81 and 82 EC, read in conjunction with Art. 3(g) EC, imply that the Community shall ensure a system whereby competition in the internal market is not distorted, and Art. 10(2) EC requires Member States not to introduce or maintain in force measures that could deprive those provisions of their effectiveness. This would be the case, in particular, if a Member State were to require or favour the adoption of agreements and behaviour contrary to the competition provisions or to reinforce their effects. See Case 311/85, *Vlaamse Reisbureaus* [1987] ECR 3801 (para. 10), and, recently, Case C–35/96 *Commission* v. *Italy*, judgment of 18 June 1998, not yet reported. This case law is particularly important in situations where Member States use environmental agreements to pursue environmental policy.

[89] Not without success. Due to these actions, the import of French wines into the Netherlands after nuclear tests dropped considerably, as happened with Dutch tourists going to France for their holidays. See *De Volkskrant*, 9 Jan. 1999.

[90] If private actions contribute to the creation of trade barriers, the question arises whether private organizations like environmental groups may also invoke justifications like the protection of the environment before a national court against other private organizations (e.g. polluting industry). See on this role for private environmental groups, the Communication of the Commission on the enforcement of environmental law, COM(96)500 final. The ECJ gave an affirmative answer in *Bosman*, in the context of Art. 39 EC (free movement of workers). It held that "[t]here is nothing to preclude individuals from relying on justifications on grounds of public policy, public security or public health. Neither the scope nor the content of those grounds or justifications is in any way affected by the public or private nature of the rules in question" (Case C–415/93, *Bosman* [1995] ECR I–4921, para. 86).

[91] e.g. in Case C–91/92, *Faccini Dori* [1994] ECR I–3325. The case law has been widely criticized; see P. Craig, "Directives: Direct Effect, Indirect Effect and the Construction of National Legislation" (1997) 22 *European Law Review* 519.

[92] See fifteenth Report on the Application of EC law—1997, C250/1, especially at 49–71.

submitted that *Spanish Strawberries* may pave the way for a supplementary instrument for the enforcement of EC environmental legislation.[93]

Consider the case where industrial establishment acts in breach of an environmental directive.[94] *Spanish Strawberries* opens the opportunity for private organizations to proceed to a national court and invoke the particular provision in the directive, read in conjunction with Article 10 EC, in order to oblige the Member State to take immediate and adequate measures in order to prevent the infringement, e.g. in the form of an injunction. This is especially interesting in the context of the wide-spread use of national policies based on tolerance and persuasion where the authorities, as a matter of policy, do not take coercive action in response to all individual breaches of environmental law because of a number of additional and extraneous policy considerations.[95] This alternative, national avenue for the enforcement of environmental directives has several attractions, in so far as it is likely to lead to effective and efficient enforcement that minimizes the level of polluting activities. Whether the ECJ will be prepared to extend the principles underlying *Spanish Strawberries* to these situations remains to be seen. Further exploration of the parameters may be required to determine, in particular, when a Member State has been "manifestly inadequate" to ensure the implementation and enforcement of a directive.[96]

IV. Recent Developments Regarding Article 29 EC and National Environmental Measures

Article 29 (formerly Article 34) EC prohibits restrictions on exports and, even though the wording in the Article is identical to that of Article 28 EC, the ECJ has given a different, more restrictive, meaning to Article 29 EC. According to *Groenveld* and *Oebel*, a national measure having equivalent effect to quantitative restrictions, in the context of exports, is prohibited if two cumulative conditions are satisfied. First, the national measure must have as its specific object or effect the restriction of patterns of export. Secondly, the measure must dis-

---

[93] C. Denys case note in (1998) 35 *European Environmental Law Review* 181.

[94] As an example the proposed Directive on the burning of waste ([1998] OJ C372/11) can be indicated.

[95] Institutionalized in Dutch environmental law as "*gedoogbeleid*", but equally prevalent in other jurisdictions. See K. Hawkins, *Environment and Enforcement* (Oxford: Oxford University Press, 1984).

[96] Prior to *Spanish Strawberries*, the Commission launched a proposal for a regulation on the functioning of the internal market in relation to the free movement of goods among the Member States. The Regulation was adopted on 7 Dec. 1998 (Reg. (EC) No. 2679/98 [1998] OJ L337/8). It provides the Commission with a mechanism for obliging a Member State to take all necessary and proportionate measures to remove within a certain period of time obstacles to the free movement of goods in the sense of Arts. 28–30 EC, caused by its action or failure to act. The Regulation was finally adopted in a much weaker version than the original Commission draft. Nevertheless, it may be worthwhile for the Commission to investigate the possibilities of taking a similar initiative to deal with serious breaches of environmental EC legislation where Member State actions are "manifestly inadequate".

criminate in such a way as to provide a special advantage for national production or for the domestic market of the state in question.[97]

The ECJ has frequently dealt with the assessment of environmental measures in the context of Article 29 EC. Examples include export bans on waste,[98] the obligation for producers to deliver poultry offal to a local authority,[99] and restrictions on the export of sheep.[100] While export restrictions inspired by environmental grounds are becoming increasingly common, the scope of the prohibition on export restrictions remains ambiguous, which at the same time may explain why national courts often ignore the application of Article 29 EC.[101]

Crucial for the application of Article 29 EC is the discriminatory element of the measure. The *Groenveld/Oebel* definition hence differs from the *Dassonville* formula with regard to the effect of the measure at issue. Thus, rules which apply, in the terminology of the ECJ, "without distinction" may fall within the scope of Article 28 EC, but according to current case law will not fall within the prohibition of Article 29 EC.

When the *Dusseldorp* judgment is referred to in this context, there are no problems which emerge. The ECJ referred to its "settled case law" and to the *Groenveld/Oebel* doctrine, and concludes that "it is plain" that the object and effect of the Dutch provisions that prohibit export of oil filters unless the processing of oil filters abroad is superior to that performed in the Netherlands, is to restrict export and to provide a particular advantage for national production.[102]

Much less clear, however, is the situation in *Compassion*, a judgment delivered about six months earlier. In that case, British animal welfare bodies with a particular interest in the prevention of cruelty to farm animals asked the Minister of Agriculture, Fisheries, and Food to prohibit or restrict the export of calves for rearing in veal crates. The Minister replied, *inter alia*, that the UK did not have the power to restrict the export of veal calves. The ECJ established, without further reasoning, that a ban or restriction on the export of live calves from one Member State to other Member States constitutes a quantitative restriction on exports contrary to Article 29 EC.[103] One wonders why the issue of the scope of Article 29 EC was not raised during the proceedings. There is no doubt that a ban or restriction on the export of calves to other Member States complies with the first condition of the *Groenveld/Oebel* formula, but it certainly does not follow that the measure results in a difference in treatment leading to a particular advantage for domestic production since, in the UK, the

---

[97] Case 15/79, *Groenveld v. Produktschap voor Vee en Vlees* [1979] ECR 3409; Case 155/80, *Oebel* [1981] ECR 3147.

[98] Case 172/82, *Inter-Huiles* (n. 2 above).

[99] Case 118/86, *Nertsvoederfabriek Nederland* [1987] ECR 3883.

[100] Case C–5/94, *Hedley Lomas* (n. 22 above).

[101] M. Jarvis, *The Application of EC Law by National Courts. The Free Movement of Goods* (Oxford: Clarendon Press, 1998), 135 and 145–9.

[102] Case C–203/96, *Dusseldorp*, n. 40 above (paras. 40–42).

[103] Case C–1/96, *Compassion*, n. 21 above (para. 39).

veal crate system was already prohibited.[104] There exist numerous other examples, where the relationship between an export ban and a favouring of domestic production was not satisfactorily resolved.[105]

The ECJ's approach towards the ambit of Article 29 EC has already met considerable criticism,[106] and it has been urged to find a coherent interpretation without placing all export restrictions within the scope of Article 29 EC.[107] It has been submitted, for example, that export restrictions for agricultural products that are covered by a common market organization should be assessed under the *Dassonville* definition from Article 28 EC and not under the *Groenveld/Oebel* formula.[108] It has been suggested that the *Groenveld/Oebel* test should be slightly reworded so as to cover any measure which has the object or effect of extending less favourable treatment to exports other than goods intended for the domestic market, even if this discrimination is not apparent on its face.[109] However, as *Compassion* shows, the ECJ has so far not been prepared to alter its definition. The result is that difficulties remain when a Member State seeks to justify export restrictions for the purpose of environmental protection within the meaning of the "mandatory requirement" or "rule of reason" case law (see section VI B).

V.   *Pistre*: Internal Situations Covered by Articles 28 and 29 EC?

Articles 28 and 29 EC prohibit trade restrictions between Member States. According to settled case law, those provisions do not apply to situations

---

[104] See also Sevenster in her commentary in (1998) 4 *Nederlands Tijdschrift voor Europees Recht* 105.

[105] In Case C–47/90, *Delhaize Frères* v. *Promalvin* [1992] ECR I–3669, the ECJ held that the obligation to bottle wine in the region of production contravened Art. 29 EC. It has been suggested that such an obligation does not favour national production or the domestic market. Nevertheless, it may also be argued that the obligation does have a positive impact on regional bottling activities. A better example is Case 273/82, *Jongeneel Kaas* v. *Netherlands* [1984] ECR 43. National legislation imposing quality requirements on exports was held to fall within Art. 29 EC, although the measures did not seem to favour domestic production. On the relation between the interpretation of Arts. 28 and 29 EC, Jans has observed the following curious consequence of the *Pistre* rule (see n. 118 below). The ECJ accepted that Art. 28 EC could be invoked when the facts of a case are confined to a single Member State. The French legislation in question required an authorization in order to market certain agricultural products bearing a label with references to the word "mountain". In as far as the French law also applies to exports, such an authorization will not be considered as a quantitative export restriction in the sense of Art. 29 EC since there is no discrimination favouring domestic production. Yet, if the same trader, instead of exporting the foodstuffs, places them on the domestic market, he may invoke Art. 28 EC. The relation between Art. 29 and Art. 28 EC then becomes arbitrary. See J. H. Jans, case note in (1998) 46 *Sociaal-Economische Wetgeving* 113.

[106] W. H. Roth, "Wettbewerb der Mitgliedstaaten oder Wettbewerb der Hersteller? Plädoyer für eine Neubestimmung des Art. 34 EGV" [1995] *Zeitschrift für das gesammte Handelsrecht* 78.

[107] Oliver, n. 1 above, 120. See also Barents, case note in [1993] *Sociaal-Economische Wetgeving* 671.

[108] See on the difference between the application of Art. 29 EC with and without the presence of a common market organization, Van Calster, case note in (1997) 2 *Columbia Journal of European Law* 135. See also Case 190/73, *Criminal proceedings against J.W.J. van Haaster* [1974] ECR 1123.

[109] See Oliver, n. 1 above, 121.

which are purely internal in the sense that they concern only domestic products marketed on national territory.[110] Consequently, it is not possible to invoke Article 28 or 29 EC in order to challenge discrimination by Member States against their own domestic production.[111] Such "reverse discrimination" is not prohibited by Community law, at least, not as long as there are no exhaustive harmonization rules.[112]

For national environmental legislation to fall within Article 28 or 29 EC, a transfrontier element such as the importation and exportation of goods should hence be established. Intra-Member State restrictions on the movement of waste, which concern trade between regions in one and the same Member State, must also be judged in this context.

However, recent case law suggests that the ECJ is employing a more subtle approach as regards the principle of "purely internal situations". Influenced by the notion of Community citizenship,[113] it is in the area of the free movement of persons that this new case law is developing in particular. Yet, in the field of the free movement of goods, the case law concerning tariff barriers is undergoing a remarkable evolution too. In *Kos*,[114] the ECJ was asked whether an *ad valorem* charge on imports and exports from the Dodecanese islands constitutes a prohibited charge having an equivalent effect to customs duties within the meaning of Articles 23 and 25 (formerly Articles 9, and 12–17) EC. The communal tax also applied to goods leaving the Dodecanese islands for another part of Greece. As regards the compatibility of these charges, the ECJ concluded that a charge levied at a regional frontier by reason of the dispatch of goods from one region to another within the same state constitutes an obstacle to the free movement of goods which is at least as serious as a charge levied at the national frontier by reason of the export of goods from all the territory of a Member State. The logic underlying *Kos* is the concept of a customs union, which prohibits the partitioning of national markets through tariff barriers. The judgment undoubtedly has implications for the compatibility of regional charges on harmful products with these tariff provisions.[115] Perhaps an even more interesting question is whether identical reasoning of the ECJ should not also apply in the context of Articles 28 and 29 EC. After all, these provisions pursue the same fundamental objective of the free movement of goods in the context of the internal market.

---

[110] Joined Cases 314–316/81 and 83/82, *Waterkeyn* [1982] ECR 4337; Case 286/81, *Oosthoek's Uitgeversmaatschappij* [1982] ECR 4575; Case 355/85, *Cognet* [1986] ECR 3231.

[111] See, e.g., Case 98/86, *Ministère public* v. *Mathot* [1987] ECR 809 (para. 9).

[112] The existence of harmonization measures may play a role while assessing purely internal situations. See Cases C–225–227/95, *Kapasakalis*, judgment of 2 July 1998, not yet reported (purely internal situation in which Dir. 89/48/EEC on a general system for the recognition of higher-education diplomas awarded on completion of professional education and training of at least three years' duration [1989] OJ L019/16, does not apply).

[113] See in particular Case C–85/96, *Martínez Sala* [1998] ECR I–2691.

[114] Casse C–485, 486/93, *Simitzi* v. *Kos* [1995] ECR I–2655 (para. 21). See also Case C–163/90, *Legros et al.* [1992] ECR I–4624 (para. 16); and Case C–363/93, *Lancry* (n. 48 above).

[115] See for the compatibility of environmental taxes the *Outokumpu Oy* case (n. 10 above).

Support for this viewpoint may be found in *Leclerc-Siplec*.[116] A French court made a preliminary reference on the compatibility of an advertising rule with Article 28 EC, even though the facts did not evidence a transfrontier element. More particularly, the French broadcasting networks TF 1 and M6 refused to broadcast an advertisement for fuel sold at supermarkets of the French retailer Leclerc, on the ground that French legislation prohibits the broadcasting of televised advertisements for the distribution sector. The ECJ nevertheless proceeded to apply the *Keck* formula, possibly because it was for the national court to decide on the facts, which could reveal that the fuel was imported. Indeed, the judgment explicitly refers to the importation of goods from other Member States.[117]

A new dimension to this discussion has been introduced following the *Pistre* case.[118] In that case, French managers were prosecuted for marketing various pork products which were labelled to include the word *montagne* (mountain) or *Monts de Lacaune* (the mountains of Lacaune) without prior authorization, as required by French legislation. The companies manufactured the products in France, and they were exclusively marketed on French territory. The French Cour de Cassation nevertheless enquired, *inter alia*, whether such an authorization could constitute a measure having equivalent effect contrary to Articles 28 and 30 EC. The French government, the Commission, and the Advocate General pointed out that the facts in the main proceedings were confined to French territory since the prosecutions in question had been brought against French nationals and concerned French products marketed on French territory. Articles 28 and 30 EC should therefore not apply.

However, the ECJ decided otherwise. It confirmed that a national measure does not fall within the ambit of Article 28 EC when the application of such measure does not have an actual link to the importation of goods. Nevertheless, the important observation was added that Article 28 EC cannot be considered inapplicable merely because all the facts of the specific case before the national court are confined to a single Member State.[119] Even in such a situation, the application of the national measure may have effects on the free movement of goods between Member States, in particular when the measure in question facilitates the marketing of goods of domestic origin to the detriment of imported goods. In such circumstances, the application of the measure, even if restricted to domestic producers, in itself creates and maintains a difference of treatment between those two categories of goods, hindering, at least *potentially*, intra-Community trade.[120]

---

[116] Case C–142/93, *Leclerc-Siplec* [1995] ECR I–179.

[117] See paras. 21–23 of Case C–142/93 (n. 68 above). In *Keck* there was no indication that in the factual situation the French ban on resale at a loss applied to imported products. See also Case C–292/92, *Hünermund* (n. 68 above) and Cosmas AG in his Opinion (paras. 12–16) in Case C–63/94, *Belgapom* (n. 80 above).

[118] Cases C–321–324/94, *Criminal proceedings against Jacques Pistre et al.* [1997] ECR I–2343.

[119] See on this element also the *Oosthoek* ruling (n. 110 above).

[120] Paras 44–45, emphasis added.

Pistre was confirmed in *Foie Gras*, where the ECJ established that Article 28 EC cannot be considered "inapplicable simply because at the present time there are no actual cases with a connection to another Member State".[121] The cases appear to suggest that an environmental measure may fall within the scope of Article 28 EC, and also Article 29 EC, even in the absence of concrete evidence of trade between Member States. An abstract assessment of the nature of a measure may suffice to place the measure under the regime concerning the free movement of goods. In *Pistre*, French legislation did not expressly exclude imported products from the system, so that imports could be caught by the prohibition too.[122] Hence, there is no reason why this reasoning should not apply in respect of regional trade rules, in particular concerning movements of waste between national regions.

That this is more than a mere theoretical prospect is usefully illustrated by recent Dutch cases concerning movements of waste within the Netherlands in the context of Article 29 EC, which at the same time serve to underline the confusion still surrounding the issue. In *Heijmans*[123] the Provincial Executive of the Province of North Brabant rejected an application for an exemption under the *Verordening bedrijfsafvalstoffen Noord-Brabant 1992* (North Brabant Industrial Waste Regulation 1992) for the transport of sludge residues from the province of Noord-Brabant to the province of Noord-Holland. From the facts, no intra-Community trade dimension emerged and, consequently, both the Rechtbank (district court) in 1994 and the president of the Afdeling Bestuursrechtspraak Raad van State (Administrative Disputes Division of the Council of State) in 1995 ruled that the question of the compatibility of the decision with Articles 28 and 29 EC did not arise. This line of thought was confirmed in the *BFI* case[124] in 1996: a refusal of the transport of waste from one Dutch province (Noord-Holland) to another (Zuid-Holland) was held to lack any element of intra-Community trade.

Strikingly, following appeal against the judgment of the district court of 's-Hertogenbosch in *Heijmans*,[125] the same division of the Council of State came to the opposite conclusion on 25 July 1996. It held that the decision not

---

[121] Case C–184/96, *Commission* v. *France ("Foie Gras")*, judgment of 22 Oct. 1998, not yet reported (para. 17). Both the *Pistre* and *Foie Gras* rulings were delivered by a chamber of the ECJ.
[122] Para. 46 of the *Pistre* ruling.
[123] Rechtbank, 's-Hertogenbosch, 29 Nov. 1994, AWB 94/3338 BELEI and AWB 94/4545. See J. H. Jans, "Dutch Idiosyncrasies and the Direct Effect of EC Law" (1996) 23 *Legal Issues of European Integration* 93 (especially 94–6). President of the Afdeling Bestuursrechtspraak Raad van State, *Heijmans Milieutechniek BV* v. *Gedeputeerde Staten van Noord-Brabant*, 6 Apr. 1995, K01.95.005 [1996] AB Rechtspraak Bestuursrecht 28 (annotation by Backes). The president only implicitly referred to the Treaty provisions on the free movement of goods.
[124] President of the Afdeling Bestuursrechtspraak Raad van State, *BFI Afvalverwerkingstechnieken* v. *Gedeputeerde Staten van Noord-Holland*, 14 Oct. 1996, F03.96.0793; Kort Geding 1997, No. 24; (1997) 24 Milieu & Recht 46 (annotation by Jans).
[125] Afdeling bestuursrechtspraak Raad van State, *Heijmans Milieutechniek BV* v. *Gedeputeerde Staten van Noord-Brabant*, 26 July 1996, H01.95.0016, Backes, 1996) AB Rechtspraak Bestuursrecht 425; Jans (1996) 23 *Milieu & Recht* 134. The Council of State came to the conclusion that the decision could not be justified under Art. 30 EC, because environmental protection is not mentioned as a general good in that provision.

only restricted exports of waste to other provinces within the Netherlands, but also impeded exports to other Member States. Moreover, it was held that national and transfrontier trade in waste were treated differently in a way which favoured domestic (local) waste industry. Hence, the decision was incompatible with Article 29 EC and could therefore not be upheld. A similar conclusion was reached in *Wubben*[126] in 1995, which arose after an appeal against a refusal to issue a licence for the collection of chemical waste. Under the *Wet Chemische Afvalstoffen* (Law on Chemical Waste), the collection of chemical waste without a licence was prohibited. Wubben held a licence in two provinces but wanted to extend its activities to the province of Noord-Holland. His application was refused on the ground that he did not operate a compulsory disposal installation on the territory of that province. Whereas Wubben was a Dutch company with disposal installations in the Netherlands only, The Council of State, on the basis of *Inter-Huiles*, did not hesitate to annul the refusal as being contrary to Article 29 EC.

These examples illustrate the difficulty national courts face in the application of the internal situation principle enunciated by the ECJ. It remains to be seen what the implications of *Pistre* will be. It is submitted that the Council of State rulings of 25 July 1996 and the *Wubben* judgment were right; the abstract way of reasoning and the holistic approach towards the national or regional regulation, appears to be the proper approach.

The first similar case arising before the Council of State after *Pistre* was the *Icova* case[127] of 24 December 1998. Once again, the Council of State was asked to rule on a refusal to authorize the exportation of waste from Noord-Holland to the province of Zuid-Holland on the basis of the Noord-Holland *Provinciale Milieuverordening Noord-Holland* (Provincial Environmental Regulation). The case is interesting, also because several provisions of the EC Treaty were invoked in order to challenge the refusal. Referring to *Kos*, the applicant argued that the ECJ considers the partitioning of national markets in regions as contrary to the principle of the free movement of goods. *A fortiori*, the case law on the tariff provisions in the Treaty should also apply in the context of Articles 28–30 EC. The Council of State rejected the argument. Analysing *Lancry* and *Kos*,[128] the Council observed that in those cases the transfrontier element was established by the fact that the charges in question were levied both on products imported from other Member States and domestic products. According to the Council, it is questionable whether the charges in *Kos* would also have been considered as prohibited charges having equivalent effect if they had been levied on intra-regional trade only. Since the provision in the

---

[126] Afdeling Bestuursrechtspraak Raad van State, *Wubben Oliebewerking BV* v. *Minister van VROM*, 3 Aug. 1995, G05.93.2561 (1996) AB Rechtspraak Bestuursrecht 27; Jans, (1996) 23 *Milieu & Recht* 21. See on this Dutch case law, M. Jarvis, *The Application of EC Law by National Courts. The Free Movement of Goods* (Oxford: Oxford University Press, 1998), 168–73. Jarvis also mentions similar difficulties encountered by French courts.

[127] Afdeling Bestuursrechtspraak Raad van State, *Icova BV* v. *Gedeputeerde Staten van Noord-Holland*, 24 Dec. 1998, E03.96.1394, not yet reported.

[128] See n. 114 above.

Provincial Environmental Regulation explicitly excluded from its application the export of waste outside national territory, the refusal only affected trade within the Netherlands and therefore could not be considered as an export restriction in the sense of Article 29 EC.

It is not clear why *Pistre*, after all a case on non-tariff barriers, has been apparently overlooked. Although the export of waste was expressly excluded in the Provincial Environmental Regulation, the judgment could have reinforced the argument that the ECJ also places potential influences on intra-Community trade within the scope of Article 29 EC. *Pistre* indeed still departs from the idea of a transfrontier movement of goods, but the case may be seen as a move towards a less stringent interpretation by the ECJ of the notion of "frontier" in the sense of the Treaty.[129]

It is also regrettable that the Council (acting as a court of final appeal) did not refer the case to the ECJ pursuant to Article 234 (formerly Article 177) EC in order to clarify the compatibility of inter-regional barriers with Articles 28 and/or 29 EC. A test case, for instance on the scope of the abstract assessment, might begin to clarify the jurisprudence discussed.

VI. Exceptions

A. THE SCOPE OF ARTICLE 30 EC IN THE ENVIRONMENTAL CASE LAW OF THE COURT OF JUSTICE

Article 30 EC contains a list of possible public interest concerns that may justify to restrict the free movement of goods. It provides that Articles 28–29 EC shall not preclude prohibitions or restrictions that are justified on grounds of, *inter alia*, the protection of health or life of humans, animals, or plants. It has been noted before that the ECJ advocates a strict interpretation of the exceptions enumerated in Article 30 EC. As a result, environmental measures are only justified by Article 30 EC if they have a direct influence on the protection of humans, animals, or plants. In *Dusseldorp*,[130] the ECJ considered that an export restriction for oil filters cannot be justified under this provision, if the processing of oil filters in other Member States and their shipment over a greater distance for export do not pose a threat to the health and life of humans. In *Aher-Waggon*,[131] concerning noise standards as a condition for

---

[129] Furthermore, *Pistre* may have an impact on the possibility of challenging reverse discrimination. The Court seems to have softened the refusal to prohibit reverse discrimination. It is useful to point out that the question in *Pistre* appears to have been prompted by the need for the national court to assess the applicants' argument on reverse discrimination. Their argument was that if the national law is unenforceable *vis-à-vis* imports by virtue of being in breach of Art. 30 EC, it should also be rendered unenforceable *vis-à-vis* domestic products since domestic products would otherwise be in a less favourable situation than imports. See the Opinion of Jacobs AG, para. 34. See for a more detailed treatment of *Pistre*, H. Weyer, "Freier Warenverkehr, rein innerstaatliche Sachverhalte und umgekehrte Diskriminierung" (1998) 33 *Europarecht* 435.
[130] Case C–203/96, *Dusseldorp*, n. 40 above (para. 46).
[131] Case C–389/96, *Aher-Waggon*, n. 36 above (para. 19).

aircraft registration, the ECJ recognized that noise emissions can form a threat to the public and noted that stricter noise standards than those fixed by a minimum directive may be justified by considerations of public health and environmental protection, in that Germany, a very densely populated state, attached special importance to ensuring that its population is protected from excessive noise emissions. *Aher-Waggon* is remarkable, since it could be argued that, as far as public health is concerned, excessive noise emissions are already combated by the Directive.

In *Compassion*,[132] the ECJ examined whether a Member State may rely on Article 30 EC for reasons related to the protection of public policy or public morality in order to restrict the export of veal calves to other Member States. In that case, an environmental group had invoked these grounds on the basis that those exports may provoke a reaction in national public opinion against the maintenance of a method of rearing animals which is considered cruel. The ECJ stated that, in reality, public policy and public morality had not been invoked as separate justifications but as a guise for justifications relating to the protection of animal health, already covered by the harmonizing directive. This is a reasonable interpretation since it avoids the perverse logic of not allowing an environmental measure to be justified on environmental grounds but accepting it on grounds of public policy or public morality.[133]

Once it is established that a national measure may be justified in the light of the derogations mentioned in Article 30 EC, it is settled case law that, subject to the limits imposed by the Treaty, Member States are free to decide upon the level of protection of human health and life they wish to pursue.[134] In reality, however, the ECJ often decides for itself whether in a specific situation a national rule contravenes the aims of Article 30 EC, with or without reference to the necessity and proportionality tests.

In *Harpegnies*,[135] the ECJ ruled that, since biocidal products are used to combat organisms harmful to human or animal health and liable to damage natural or cultivated products, they inevitably contain dangerous substances. This consideration sufficed to justify a prohibition to market these products without prior authorization under Article 30 EC.

The *Danish Bees* case[136] concerned restrictions on the keeping of bees other than brown bees (*Apis mellifera mellifera*) on the small and remote Danish island of Læsø. In this case, national measures to preserve an indigenous animal population with distinct characteristics were considered to contribute to the maintenance of bio-diversity by ensuring the survival of the population concerned, which could be justified by Article 30 EC.

---

[132] Case C–1/96, *Compassion*, n. 21 above (paras. 65–68).

[133] As has been observed by Sevenster, "Dierenbeschermingswet Sneuvelt op Richtlijn" (1998) 4 *Nederlands Tijdschrift voor Europees Recht* 105. See also K. Mortelmans, "Vrij verkeer in de EG en de gezondheid van dieren: laat je niet kisten" (1998) 47 *Ars Aequi* 709.

[134] Case C–1/90 and C–176/90, *Aragonesa de Publicidad Exterior* v. *Departamento de Sanidad* [1991] ECR I–4151.

[135] Case C–400/96, *Harpegnies*, n. 16 above (paras. 31–33, with reference to the *Brandsma* case, n. 54 above). The proportionality principle, however, was not satisfied.

[136] Case 67/97, *Danish Bees*, n. 25 above (paras. 33–34).

It can be deduced from this judgment that the population in question does not need to be in immediate danger of extinction for the derogation to be justified. It is immaterial, according to the ECJ, whether the object of protection is a separate subspecies, a distinct strain within any given species or merely a local population. The main test under Article 30 EC is that the populations involved have characteristics distinguishing them from others. Therefore, they may be protected either in view of a risk of extinction that is more or less imminent or, in the absence of such a risk, even on account of scientific or other interest in preserving the pure population at the location concerned. One might expect, on the basis of these considerations, that the ECJ would have proceeded with an examination of the relationship between the measure and the bee population involved. As regards the existence of a threat to the subspecies *Apis mellifera mellifera* on the island of Læsø, the Commission argued that this was an evidential matter that should be determined by the national court. The Advocate General also considered that the effectiveness and the appropriateness of the measures adopted by Denmark should be determined by the national court.[137] The ECJ avoided this question and ruled that the Danish preservation measures were justified without taking into consideration these factual issues. This case law reinforces the impression that Member States enjoy a wider margin to establish a high level of protection under the Treaty provisions than under the "mandatory requirements" case law. This issue will be discussed in more detail in the following sections.

B.   THE SCOPE OF ENVIRONMENTAL PROTECTION AS A MANDATORY REQUIREMENT

The broad interpretation of a trade restriction within the meaning of Article 28 EC and the restrictive interpretation of Article 30 EC created a tension in the case law. By virtue of the so-called "rule of reason" or "mandatory requirement" case law,[138] the ECJ has addressed this tension by adding to the grounds mentioned in Article 30 EC rules that are justified in order to satisfy mandatory requirements (such as the protection of the consumer and the protection of fair trading practices). For the first time, the ECJ recognized in the *Danish Bottles* case the protection of the environment as a mandatory requirement that can justify restrictions on the free movement of goods. The case law has further developed in the *Wallonian Waste*[139] ruling and in subsequent judgments.

---

[137] Hence, in order to establish whether the sub-species still survived in a relatively pure state or whether the population of Læsø had already been substantially corrupted by in-breeding with other bees: see the Opinion of Fennelly AG, delivered on 16 June 1998 (para. 34).

[138] Case 120/78, *Cassis de Dijon*, n. 50 above.

[139] Case C–2/90, *Wallonian Waste* (n. 8 above). See also Case C–389/96, *Aher-Waggon* (n. 36 above), where the ECJ did not refer to previous case law on the "rule of reason", although it accepted the German considerations of public health and environmental protection as justifying a trade barrier (para. 19). See, for other recent examples of case law where the ECJ deals with the "rule of reason", Cases C–321–324/94, *Pistre* (n. 118 above); Case C–203/96, *Dusseldorp* (n. 40 above); Case C–67/97, *Danish Bees* (n. 25 above); Case C–284/95, *Safety Hi-Tech* (n. 47 above).

i. The Condition that Environmental Measures should Apply "Without Distinction"

The difference between the Treaty exceptions and the doctrine of mandatory requirements resides in the circumstance that the latter is conditional upon the absence of any discrimination. Article 30 EC, on the other hand, provides that the national restrictive or prohibitive measures are not permitted if they are used as a means of arbitrary discrimination or a disguised restriction on trade between Member States.[140] The ECJ applies a much more stringent condition if a Member State attempts to justify a restrictive measure on the basis of "mandatory requirements". In such a case, the national measure must apply without distinction to imported and domestic products. The scope of this condition is far from clear and the case law of the ECJ leaves room for different interpretations. Besides, the impression emerges that if the ECJ can circumvent the application of the "without distinction" condition in more difficult situations, it will do so. The most notorious example is provided by the *Wallonian Waste* ruling. To the surprise of many, the ECJ upheld a total ban on all waste imports into Wallonia despite the fact that the measure clearly favoured Wallonian waste to the detriment of imported waste. The ECJ ruled that, given the particular nature of waste and in the light of the principle that environmental damage should as a matter of priority be remedied at source, as enshrined in Article 174(2) EC and the Basle Convention, waste had to be disposed of as near as possible to the place where it is produced, in order to limit as far as possible the transport of waste. The ECJ reasoned that it is for each region, municipality, or other local authority to take appropriate steps to ensure that its own waste is collected, treated, and disposed of. Thus, the disputed measures could not be regarded as discriminatory.[141]

The ECJ was presented with an excellent opportunity to clarify its case law on the "indistinct applicability" criterion in *Danish Bees*, where it could have

---

[140] The second sentence of Art. 30 EC "is designed to prevent restrictions on trade based on the grounds mentioned in the first sentence of Art. 30 EC from being diverted from their proper purpose" (Case 34/79, *Henn and Darby* [1979] ECR 3795). The ECJ explicitly stated that this provision is an expression of the principle of proportionality. The power of the Member States to prohibit imports from other Member States must be restricted to what is necessary to achieve the objectives of protection being legitimately pursued under Art. 30 EC. See Case C–400/96, *Harpegnies*, n. 16 above (para. 34), and also sect. VI.C. The same logic applies to export restrictions.

[141] Case C–2/90, *Wallonian Waste*, n. 8 above (para. 36). See the critical comments by Hancher and Sevenster, case note in (1993) 30 *Common Market Law Review* 351. Case law outside the environmental area confirms the rather arbitrary way in which the ECJ sometimes interprets the condition that measures should apply "without distinction". Especially in the field of measures on taxes, the case law is lacking in clarity. Cf, for instance, Case C–204/90, *Bachmann* [1992] ECR I–249, and Case C–484/93, *Svensson* [1995] ECR I–3955. See also Tesauro AG in his Joined Opinion in Case C–120/95, *Decker* (n. 80 above) and Case C–155/96, *R. Kohll* v. *Union des caisses de maladie* [1998] ECR I–1931 (paras. 45–50). He invited the ECJ to make a clear statement on the "without distinction" condition in the cases in question, which concerned national regulations that made reimbursement of medical costs incurred in other Member States subject to prior authorization from the insurer, and denied such reimbursement where authorization had not been obtained. The ECJ solved the cases by focusing on the economic nature of the measures in question and hence did not have to deal with the delicate question whether the national provision applied "without distinction".

applied the *Wallonian Waste* doctrine to an environmental case. A Danish provision prohibited the keeping of nectar-gathering bees other than brown bees on the island of Læsø. It was also forbidden to introduce onto the island any living domestic bees. The question thus emerges whether this was a measure that applied without distinction.

The ECJ declared that the Danish provision was justified on the basis of Article 30 EC. Hence, an examination of the discriminatory character of the Danish legislation was not necessary. However, the Opinion of Advocate General Fennelly is interesting. It drew attention, in referring to *Wallonian Waste*, to the special factors which may apply in respect of national environmental rules. The measure at issue in *Danish Bees* was designed to protect a particular population of the subspecies *Apis mellifera mellifera* in its native geographical area, where it has allegedly developed a number of distinctive morphological characteristics. It attempted to do so by way of preventive action against cross-breeding with the golden bee and even with brown bees from non-local populations. Doubts remained whether the Læsø brown bee population was sufficiently distinctive to merit protection against in-breeding with other populations. Nevertheless, the Advocate General took the view that the measure could be treated, at least for the purpose of an analysis of its effect on trade in *golden* bees, as an indistinctly applicable measure. The acceptance of the existence of material differences implied that the exclusion of the latter was not discriminatory in character.[142]

Whether the measure is "without distinction" in relation to non-indigenous *brown* bees does not become clear from the Opinion. Unlike *Wallonian Waste*, where support was drawn from the principles of "self-sufficiency and proximity", recognized in European and international environmental law, and despite the fact that the precautionary principle and the principle that preventive action should be taken (both set out in Article 174(2) EC) could have served a similar purpose, the Advocate General failed to provide for such an "additional" principle. The only reference he made was to the method laid down in the Rio Convention on Conservation of Bio-diversity through the Establishment of Areas in which a Population Enjoys Special Protection.[143]

Another recent case where the ECJ failed to address the question of the nature of a national measure is *Aher-Waggon*. As has been seen, this case concerned national legislation which made the first registration in national territory of aircraft previously registered in another Member State conditional upon compliance with stricter noise standards than those laid down in a Community directive. However, aircraft which obtained registration in national territory before the directive was implemented were exempt from this rule. The ECJ justified the trade barrier thus created by considerations of public health (Article 30 EC) and environmental protection, without examining the character of the provision. However, the non-discriminatory nature of the measure is not unambiguous as it would appear that aircraft suffer a difference

---

[142] Opinion of Fennely AG, delivered on 16 June 1998 (paras. 22–25).
[143] See also the ECJ in the *Danish Bees* ruling, n. 25 above (para. 36).

in treatment according to the country of registration. It was exactly because of this inequality that Aher-Waggon appealed against the refusal and that the Bundesverwaltungsgericht referred a question to the ECJ under Article 234 EC. The ECJ did not appear to consider this an important issue, perhaps because under Article 30 EC discriminatory measures can be justified. If this is true, however, it remains unclear why the ECJ involved the doctrine of mandatory requirements in its reasoning in the first place.[144]

ii. *Protection of the Environment as a Ground for Justifying Export Restrictions?*

We have seen that environmental protection is a mandatory requirement within the meaning of the rule of reason, provided that the measure is applicable without distinction. This implies that the protection of the environment can never be invoked in order to justify measures covered by the prohibition of Article 29 EC since, according to the *Groenveld/Oebel* formula, such measures can *ipso facto* only fall within the scope of that provision if such measures are discriminatory. Indeed, until now the ECJ has never ruled that an export restriction is justified because the measure in question protects the environment or any other general good recognized as a "mandatory requirement".

However, the ECJ's formalistic approach is problematic. According to Article 30 EC, export restrictions are only justified in the face of a serious threat to the health of humans, animals, and plants. This means, for instance, that measures restricting the export of waste with a negative environmental impact but that do not endanger public health cannot be justified under Article 30 EC.[145] A solution for this dilemma may be found in either of two ways: the ECJ alters the definition of "measure having equivalent effect" in the context of Article 29 EC (see section IV), or it relaxes the rule that "mandatory requirements" cannot be invoked in respect of measures that are "distinctly applicable".

The *Dusseldorp* ruling sheds new light on the issue. The Dutch government submitted that export restrictions on oil filters could be justified, *inter alia*, by an imperative requirement relating to the protection of the environment. The measure in question was also designed to enable AVR Chemie AV, responsible for waste management, to operate in a profitable manner with sufficient raw material. Although the ECJ rejects the measure in view of its economic nature, it is remarkable that it observes that this is so "even if the national measure in question could be justified by reasons relating to the protection of the environment".[146] It may be inferred that the ECJ does not rule out the justification of export restrictions on the basis of environmental protection. Indeed, it is hard to believe that the phrase is a "slip of the tongue", without independent significance, since the Advocate General had drawn explicit attention to the

---

[144] Case C–389/96, *Aher-Waggon*, n. 36 above (para. 19).
[145] See for a critical approach Oliver, n. 1 above, 122.
[146] Case C–203/96, *Dusseldorp*, n. 40 above (para. 44), emphasis added.

question.[147] On the other hand, the statement is not very forceful. It may be that the ECJ perhaps did not find that *Dusseldorp* was the right opportunity to introduce a new line of authority and now awaits a proper test case to develop further its case law.[148]

C.   THE PRINCIPLES OF NECESSITY AND PROPORTIONALITY

Generally, the ECJ only accepts the application of Article 30 EC or the "mandatory requirement" justification if the national measure is proper to protect the interest at stake (*necessity*) and if no national measure is possible which has a less restrictive effect on intra-Community trade (*proportionality*).[149] In preliminary rulings where the necessary factual information is not at its disposal, the ECJ usually leaves it to national courts to decide the matter. However, if the information is sufficient, rather than leaving the final decision to the national court, the ECJ will settle the issue itself.[150] Remarkably, in environmental cases this is often what the ECJ has preferred to do.[151] This is an important point, since the level of environmental protection permitted will usually hinge on the proportionality test, as is illustrated by *Danish Bottles*. In more recent cases, the necessity condition proved a stumbling block. In this respect, consider *Dusseldorp*, where the Netherlands invoked Article 30 EC concerning the protection of the health and life of humans. The ECJ ruled that the processing and shipment of oil posed no threat to health.[152]

The *Harpegnies* ruling confirms that the principle of mutual recognition is also used in this context. Mutual recognition in this case did not apply to standards, but to procedures. A Member State is free to require a biocidal product, which has already received approval in another Member State, to undergo a fresh procedure of examination and approval. However, the principles of proportionality and necessity require that they must take account of technical or chemical analyses or laboratory tests which have already been carried out in

---

[147] Opinion of Jacobs AG in *Dusseldorp* (paras. 89–91). He did not take a stance on the discriminatory character of the rule, but dismissed the argument put forward by the Netherlands because, in his opinion, it had not been shown that the transport of waste in question in itself posed an environmental threat.

[148] This opportunity may be provided by Case C–209/98, *FFAD-Entreprenøforening* (pending) [1998] OJ C234/22, concerning Danish legislation begging comparisons with the Dutch legislation in the *Dusseldorp* case.

[149] See, in general, N. Emiliou, *The Principle of Proportionality in European Law* (London: Kluwer, 1996), 227–65. The causal connection and the requirement of proportionality are not always given the same meaning by the ECJ. See Jans, n. 1 above, 215–22. The necessity criterion is usually so clear that the ECJ often does not refer to it. Even the proportionality test is not always explicitly applied. See *Wallonian Waste* (n. 8 above), where the ECJ does not explicitly apply the proportionality test to the Belgian law in question.

[150] See Case C–210/96, *Gut Springenheide GmbH, Rudolf Tusky v. Oberkreisdirektor des Kreises Steinfurt–Amt für Lebensmittelüberwachung*, judgment of 16 July 1998, not yet reported, paras. 30–31. The case concerned misleading information on packs of eggs. Obviously, in direct actions (Art. 226 EC) the ECJ must always settle the issue itself.

[151] See Case C–118/86, *Nertsvoederfabriek Nederland* (n. 99 above); Case C–302/86, *Danish Bottles* (n. 3 above); Case 125/88, *Nijman* (n. 16 above).

[152] Case C–203/96, *Dusseldorp*, n. 40 above (para. 46).

another Member State.[153] In *Danish Bees*, the ECJ summarized both tests as the question whether the national legislation was necessary and proportionate in relation to its aim of protection, or whether it would have been possible to achieve the same result by less stringent measures. On the basis of the Rio Convention and secondary Community law on bio-diversity, the ECJ concluded that the measure in question was appropriate in relation to the aim pursued.[154] The fact that the ECJ's solution was perhaps not that obvious can be concluded from the Opinion of the Advocate General, who recommended leaving it to the national court to assess the proportionality of the national measure.[155]

D.   MEASURES OF A NON-ECONOMIC NATURE

The ECJ has consistently held that purely economic justifications cannot mandate barriers to the fundamental principle of the free movement of goods. This may be different when the economic implications are an integral and necessary part of the justified environmental measures.[156] This established case law is particularly important for trade measures concerning waste. Member States often restrict the export of waste in order to guarantee the supply for national waste disposal installations, thus ensuring that they can operate in a profitable manner. Environmental and economic motives go hand in hand and the question is where to draw the line if barriers to the free flow of goods result.

In *Dusseldorp*, the Netherlands argued that an export ban on oil filters was necessary in order to ensure sufficient raw materials and business to enable AVR Chemie, responsible for waste management, to operate in a profitable manner and to ensure a sufficient supply of oil filters for use as fuel. The ECJ rejected this argument, finding it sufficient to point out that settled case law supported the view that purely economic aims cannot justify barriers to the fundamental principle of the free movement of goods.[157] The judgment presupposes that the ECJ does not accept the primary justification of the

---

[153] Case C–400/96, *Harpegnies*, n. 16 above (para. 35). This was established case law: see Case 272/80, *Frans-Nederlandse Maatschappij voor Biologische Producten* [1981] ECR 3277, and Case C–293/94 *Brandsma* (n. 55 above).

[154] Case C–67/97, *Danish Bees*, n. 25 above (paras. 35–37), with reference to Case 124/81, *Commission* v. *United Kingdom* [1983] ECR 203.

[155] Opinion of Fennelly AG, paras. 34–35. Similarly Léger AG's Opinion in Case C–350/97, *Monsees*, n. 24 above (paras. 34–44). See also Cases C–438/97, *Warnecke et al.* [1998] OJ C72/7, and C–20/98, *K.H. Meinert* [1998] OJ C94/11 (pending).

[156] The classic example is Case 72/83, *Campus Oil Limited* v. *Minister for Industry and Energy* [1984] ECR 2727. See also Case 118/86, *Nertsvoederfabriek Nederland*, n. 99 above (para. 15). The conflict between environmental and economic considerations can also be found in secondary legislation. Where the regime of Arts. 28–30 EC departs from the rule that trade barriers must be eliminated and the exception that environmental considerations may prevail, in the Birds Directive (Dir. 79/409/EEC [1979] OJ L103/1) the opposite occurs. As a rule, a Member State should take all appropriate measures like the indication of special protective zones. An exception may be based on economic interests (see Arts. 2 and 4). See on this conflict of interests Case C–57/89, *Leybucht* [1991] ECR I–883; Case C–355/90, *Santoña* [1993] ECR I–4221 and Case C–44/95, *Lappel Bank* [1996] ECR I–3805. See also Art. 6(4) of the Habitat Directive, 92/43/EC ([1992] OJ L206/7).

[157] Case C–203/96, *Dusseldorp*, n. 40 above (para. 44).

Netherlands, i.e. that the export ban was necessary in order to ensure the protection of the environment. Yet this conclusion is debatable, for at least two reasons. First, it could be submitted that, from a holistic environmental perspective, the export restrictions are not of an economic nature but necessary to ensure a sufficient supply and avoid environmentally unsound recovery or disposal of the wastes concerned.[158] Moreover, in the light of considerations on the application of the competition provisions of Articles 82 and 86 (formerly Articles 86 and 90) EC, the reasoning may be inadequate. A Member State acts in breach of the prohibitions laid down in Article 86 EC on public undertakings and Article 82 EC on abuse of a dominant position if it adopts any measure which enables an undertaking on which it has conferred exclusive rights to abuse its dominant position. The ECJ stated that the export prohibition had the effect of favouring AVR Chemie by enabling it to process waste intended for processing by a third undertaking and which therefore resulted in the restriction of outlets in a manner contrary to Article 86(1) EC in conjunction with Article 82 EC. However, such a restriction may be justified by a general economic interest within the meaning of Article 86(2) EC. Indeed, the Netherlands invoked this provision and reiterated that the rules in question were intended to reduce the costs of the undertaking responsible for the incineration of dangerous waste and thus to enable it to be economically viable. The argument appears similar to that rejected in the context of Articles 29–30 EC. However, the ECJ did not reject it *prima facie*, but invited the Dutch government to prove before the national court that the objective (the task of general economic interest) could not be achieved equally well by other means. If the government succeeds in proving the necessity of the measures in question, then the curious result will be that, on the one hand, the economic nature of a measure cannot justify barriers to the free movement of goods, but, on the other hand, would not rule out justifications pursuant to the Treaty provisions concerning competition. It is difficult to see how such a result is compatible with case law suggesting that the Treaty provisions on free movement and competition should be consistent. Indeed, in *Corsica Ferries*, the ECJ held that, if the conditions for application of Article 86(2) EC are satisfied, a trade restriction in the context of the free movement (in this case of services, Articles 49–55 (formerly Articles 59–66)) EC is ruled out.[159]

E.   EXTRA-TERRITORIAL EFFECT OF ENVIRONMENTAL MEASURES: AN ISSUE UNRESOLVED

The ECJ has yet to provide a clear answer to the delicate question whether Member States may justify trade restrictions by relying on Article 30 EC or the "mandatory requirement" case law of the ECJ in order to protect the

---

[158] See G. Van Calster, "Court Criticizes Restrictions on Free Movement of Waste" (1999) 24 *European Law Review* 170–84.

[159] See Case C–266/96, *Corsica Ferries France SA v. Gruppo Antichl Ormeggiatori del Porto di Genova Coop.arl et al.*, judgment of 18 June 1998, not yet reported (para. 59).

environment in another Member State.[160] Although this issue of extra-territoriality could have been settled in recent environmental cases, the ECJ failed to address it.

In both *Hedley Lomas* and *Compassion*, the measure restricting export had its cause within the Community, but outside the territory of the Member State which had adopted it (or had been asked to adopt it). In *Hedley Lomas*, the British export ban would have an effect on the treatment of animals to be slaughtered in Spain. The ECJ ruled that Directive 74/577/EEC on Stunning of Animals before Slaughter[161] excluded recourse to Article 30 EC, and therefore the question concerning extra-territoriality did not arise.[162] In *Compassion*, the ECJ could simply refer to Article 11(2) of Directive 91/629/EEC on the Protection of Calves[163] which permits Member States to maintain or apply stricter provisions *within their territories*. In conjunction with the exhaustive character of the Directive, this excluded the extra-territorial nature of the export measure proposed.[164] In *Dusseldorp*, the ECJ reasoned that the argument put forward by the Dutch government, to the effect that the export restriction on oil filters was necessary in order to protect public health, would only be relevant "if the processing of oil filters in other Member States and their shipment over a greater distance as a result of their being exported posed a threat to the health and life of humans".[165] It may be inferred that, had the processing and shipment resulted in a proven threat to health, the ECJ would have authorized the country of export to protect public health in other Member States.[166]

It is widely assumed that the ECJ is unwilling to accept the extra-territorial effect of protective measures. Indeed, Advocate General Jacobs is strongly opposed to extra-territoriality and has argued in his Opinions in *Hedley Lomas* and *Compassion* for a strict limitation of the scope of Article 30 EC.[167] Some commentators have criticized the attitude of the ECJ[168] and others have proposed alternatives.[169] It is surprising that the ECJ has yet to provide a satisfactory answer to this problem. Hitherto, the ECJ has been able to circumvent the matter by choosing alternative solutions and perhaps it awaits a more ideal test case to elaborate a statement of principle.

[160] Cases 172/82, *Inter-Huiles* (n. 2 above); Case 118/86, *Nertsvoerders Nederland* (n. 99 above); Case 169/89, *Gourmetterie Van den Burg* (n. 24 above); Case C–3/91, *Exportur SA* v. *LOR SA et Confiserie du Tech* [1992] ECR I–5529. See on the relevant case law Jans, n. 1 above, 231–5.

[161] [1974] OJ L316/10.   [162] Case C–5/94, *Hedley Lomas* (n. 22 above).

[163] [1996] OJ C085/19.   [164] Case C–1/96, *Compassion* (n. 22 above).

[165] Case C–203/96, *Dusseldorp*, n. 40 above (para. 46), emphasis added.

[166] J. H. Jans, case note in (1998) 25 *Milieu & Recht* 293.

[167] Opinion in *Hedley Lomas* (paras. 33–39); Opinion in *Compassion* (paras. 86–93).

[168] L. Krämer, *E.C. Treaty and Environmental Law* (London: Sweet & Maxwell, 1998), 155 (who favours the view that Member States may take measures to protect the environment outside their own jurisdiction, as long as the measure is neither discriminating nor disproportionate); Jans, n. 1 above, 231–5 that transfrontier application of Art. 30 EC is in principle possible, but Member States are primarily responsible for their own territory.

[169] Sevenster defends the view that, even if there exists a Community measure that covers the subject matter, a Member State may adopt measures to safeguard general interests in other Member States, as long as the measures are necessary and proportionate. See H. G. Sevenster, *Eco-imperialisme binnen de Europese Unie: een juridisch probleem?* (Deventer: Kluwer, 1998).

VII. Flexibility in Environmental Regulation and Free Movement of Goods

The Treaty of Amsterdam foresees in a new concept designed to allow for flexible integration.[170] This section will analyse the relationship between the regime concerning the free movement of goods and this new concept allowing for flexible environmental integration. The impact may be measured in two ways. First, the restrictions that Articles 28–30 EC impose on the realization of flexible integration can be examined. Secondly, it may be argued that after flexible harmonization the Treaty provisions on the free trade in goods continue to be relevant.

Let us begin by exploring the concept of flexible integration. A provision in the Treaty on European Union[171] and a specific flexibility clause in Article 11 EC introduce a concept allowing Member States which intend to establish closer co-operation between themselves to make use of the institutions, procedures, and mechanisms laid down by the EC Treaty.[172] The concept does not foresee in a new legal basis *stricto sensu* and it does not extend the competences of the Community institutions. However, it may be considered an important instrument for those Member States which, within the framework of the EC/EU Treaties, wish to go further in the area of environmental protection than is possible in the face of the reservations of a minority of Member States. Indeed, the concept of closer co-operation has been negotiated as an alternative to manifestations of flexible integration as constituted by the Schengen model (outside the EU framework), "opting-out" methods like the Social Protocol (inside the EU framework), and also in order to alienate fears that the impending enlargement with Member States unable to maintain high levels of protection, in the short term, would stagnate further integration in the Union. Outsiders are not totally excluded, however, since the flexibility system allows them to become party to such co-operation at any stage, provided they comply with the basic decision and with the decisions taken within that framework. They are also empowered to take part in the deliberations on the matters concerned, although they cannot take part in the adoption of decisions.[173]

At first sight, the conditions for flexibility established by the new Treaty provisions appear to make flexible environmental integration a troublesome

---

[170] See, e.g., C. D. Ehlermann, "Différenciation, flexibilité, coopération renforcée: les nouvelles dispositions du traité d'Amsterdam" [1997] *Revue du Marché Unique Européen* 53; J. A. Usher, "Flexibility—The Amsterdam Provisions", conference paper (University of Groningen, 1997); E. Steyger, "Flexibility and the 'acquis communautaire'", conference paper (University of Amsterdam, 1998); H. Kortenberg, "Closer Cooperation in the Treaty of Amsterdam" (1998) 35 *Common Market Law Review* 833–54; H. Gaja, "How Flexible is Flexibility under the Amsterdam Treaty?" (1998) 35 *Common Market Law Review* 871.

[171] A new title VII (Arts. 43–45 EC) will be inserted which applies to the whole consolidated TEU and the EC Treaty.

[172] Another specific provision relates to co-operation in the third pillar: Art. 40 (formerly Art. K 12) EC.

[173] Arts. 43(1)g EC and 44 TEU.

prospect, in particular when it concerns co-ordination of national environmental measures falling within the ambit of Articles 28 and 29 EC.

Thus, the flexibility provisions contain both substantive and procedural conditions for closer co-operation, most of which appear self-evident. As a procedural condition, the co-operation must at least concern a majority of Member States, after a proposal from the Commission. The Council must authorize closer co-operation in accordance with the procedures laid down in the specific provisions. A member of the Council may "for important and stated reason of national policy" oppose the granting of an authorization.[174] As a result, the Commission or any Member State can veto closer co-operation, which already undermines the force of the concept of flexibility.

Further qualifications emerge when the substantive conditions enumerated in Article 43 EU and Article 11 EC are analysed. As Ehlermann has observed, what is particularly striking is that the (cumulative) enumeration of the conditions has been formulated in a negative way. Rather than specifying the policy areas where closer co-operation is permitted, it is stated where it is not possible and what principles need to be respected.[175]

First, there are conditions regarding the competence to co-operate on certain subjects. The co-operation proposed must be aimed at furthering the objectives of the Union and at protecting and serving its interests, and may not concern areas which fall within the exclusive competence of the Community.[176] Environmental protection is one of the objectives of the EU Treaty where, it is commonly agreed, the Community does not possess exclusive competence. These conditions hence do not stand in the way of closer co-operation in the field of autonomous environmental measures.

A debate already taking place in the context of the principle of subsidiarity, which does not apply when a policy area falls within the exclusive jurisdiction of the Community (Article 5 (formerly Article 3b) EC), is whether the Community has exclusive competence in the area of the free movement of goods. Opinions still differ on the notion of "exclusive jurisdiction", but there are persuasive arguments for considering internal market matters as falling within the exclusive powers of the Community.[177] If this position is correct, the scope for closer co-operation on environmental measures that are related to trade in goods may prove fairly limited.

Furthermore, closer co-operation must remain within the limits of the powers conferred upon the Community by the Treaty and is only permitted where the objectives of the Treaties cannot be attained by applying the relevant procedures laid down therein.[178] This means not only that the limits for closer

---

[174] Art. 11(2) EC.

[175] C. D. Ehlermann, "Les nouvelles disposition du traité d'Amsterdam" [1997] *Revue du Marché Unique Européen* 53, at 70.

[176] Art. 43(1) TEU and Art. 11(1) EC.

[177] C. Caliess, "Der Schlüsselbegriff der 'ausschließlichen Zuständigkeit' im Subsidiaritätsprinzip des Art. 3 b II EGV" (1995) 5 *Europäische Zeitschrift für Wirtschaftsrecht* 693; A.G. Toth, "The Principle of Subsidiarity in the Maastricht Treaty" (1992) 29 *Common Market Law Review* 1079.

[178] Art. 11(1)d EC and Art. 43 (1)c TEU.

environmental co-operation correspond with the competences of, in particular, Articles 94, 95, and 175 EC, but that every alternative to adopt measures within the regular framework of these provisions must have been exhausted. To be sure, it will not be easy to determine at what point all other means have failed. Will this occur only after complete deadlock in the conciliation committee, or is an earlier moment possible? And what will happen if the Commission, despite the request of certain Member States, refuses to launch a proposal for an environmental measure on the basis of Article 95 EC?[179]

An important bottleneck for closer co-operation could be the condition that the proposed co-operation may not affect the *acquis communautaire* and the measures adopted under the other provisions of the Treaty. Co-operation may not "constitute a discrimination or a restriction of trade between Member States" nor "distort the conditions of competition between the Member States".[180] The flexibility provisions also lay down that the proposed co-operation may not "affect Community policies, actions or programmes nor the competences, rights, obligations" and "the competences, rights, obligations and interests of those Member States which do not participate therein".[181] These requirements seem reasonable, as it must be ensured that closer co-operation does not lead to a regression in the integration process.[182] Current EC law is equally based on this principle. For instance, as was observed in section II, more stringent national measures then prescribed by Community legislation must always be in conformity with the primary EC provisions of Articles 28–30 EC. However, it is difficult to imagine a subject that falls within the sphere of Community law that does not have any effect on the *acquis communautaire*. Taken literally, every act of closer co-operation on a subject that belongs to Community competences will, one way or another, affect Community policies, actions, or programmes, and will also influence the position of non-participants. This by definition is the case when prior agreement on the basis of the regular procedures is not reached, since in such cases the interests of the non-participants are at stake, which presumably is exactly the reason agreement could not be reached. On the other hand, it is hard to believe that *any* effect rules out closer co-operation since, in the alternative, the flexibility provisions become entirely superfluous. Clearly, a balance must be found.

Environmental measures that fall within the jurisdiction of the Treaty, but are not yet subject to Community policy, will usually have an effect on the free movement of goods and, consequently, may restrict trade and distort competition. Does this imply that such measures may not be adopted under the flexibility mechanism? The fundamental question becomes whether any

---

[179] Consequently, a request for a proposal may be made under the flexibility mechanism, but then the Commission can (again) refuse if it motivates its decision, see Art. 11(2) EC.

[180] Art. 11(1)EC. The formulation of the first requirement is clearly based on the conditions of Arts. 30 and 95(6) EC.

[181] Art. 11(1)b EC and Art. 43(1)e TEU.

[182] H. Kortenberg, "Closer Cooperation in the Treaty of Amsterdam" (1998) 35 *Common Market Law Review* 846.

difference between national regulatory frameworks must be considered as distorting competition. If this is the case, there can be no flexibility which leads to differences in legislation between Member States.[183] This would practically exclude all product related environmental measures.

Perhaps the answer should depend on the nature of the measure under consideration. When closer co-operation is shaped in the form of a non-binding instrument of Community law, such as a recommendation, competition distortions will be much less profound than if binding instruments are proposed. Hence, voluntary action will be more likely to be in conformity with the conditions set forth by the flexibility provisions.

Furthermore if a binding instrument (such as a directive) is considered, the situation may depend upon the assessment of the measure under the regime of Articles 28–30 EC. Before harmonization at European level, Member States enjoy the power to invoke the exceptions embedded in Article 30 EC and the "rule of reason" in order to justify barriers to trade. If co-operating Member States wish to adopt an environmental measure under Article 11 EC that is clearly covered and justified by the general good of protecting the environment or the life and health of animals and plants, it can be argued that such a measure is a lawful measure under EC law.[184] Consequently, although flexible harmonization may influence trade between Member States and lead to a distortion of competition, the situation is less problematic than before harmonization, from a Community law point of view. It may be argued that this makes such a measure compatible with the conditions of Articles 43 and 11 EC, even though the result of closer co-operation will be that some Member States will preside over legislation that differs from that of other Member States. In such cases, the co-operating Member States make use of competences which they retained, which is in line with established doctrine regarding the harmonization process.[185] Community legislation on the basis of Articles 94 and 95 EC in areas such as the environment claims authority because it is justified or eliminates distortion of competition. Indeed, many existing environmental directives already contain specific and different rules for one or more Member States or regions of a particular Member State.[186]

Even after a Community act has been adopted on a regular basis (where all Member States participate) there may be room for flexible co-operation in order to achieve further integration. This is particularly so when the regular harmonization process is not exhaustive or when the harmonization tech-

---

[183] See J. A. Usher, "Flexibility—The Amsterdam provision", conference paper (University of Groningen, 1997), 23.

[184] Of course, it must be clear that such a "flexible" directive does not, for instance, lead to discrimination against products of non-participant states if such a possibility does not exist under Art. 30 EC or the "rule of reason".

[185] Cf E. Steyger, "Flexibility and the acquis communautaire", conference paper (University of Amsterdam, 1998), 4.

[186] For instance, taking safeguard measures in order to tackle specific problems in the region. See, e.g., Art. 20 of Dir. 80/778/EEC on the quality of water for human consumption [1980] OJ L229/1.

nique leaves Member States the competence to enact more protective rules than foreseen in a directive. Under current EC law, as long as Articles 28–30 EC are respected, nothing stands in the way of closer co-operation between Member States with a view to "filling" the policy margin left by a (minimum) harmonization directive. This may be so pursuant to Article 95(4) EC or a specific harmonization clause in a directive. After all, the harmonization technique has been carefully considered by the Member States in the decision-making process, which expresses itself in a clause authorizing them to establish more stringent environmental standards. For the sake of European integration, this possibility is better realized within a Community framework (the flexibility mechanism) than outside it.

The role of Articles 28–30 EC *after* flexible harmonization emerges in the context of the question whether the co-operating Member States continue to be able to rely on Article 30 EC or the "rule of reason" in order to justify trade barriers.[187] In my opinion, the answer should be in the affirmative if the conditions that are established under Article 30 EC, the "rule of reason", the conditions laid down in the flexible directive and the conditions of the flexibility provisions of the Treaty, are respected.

Although it goes beyond the purpose of this contribution to elaborate upon these points, perhaps the following conclusions may be drawn. At first sight, the many conditions laid down in the flexibility provisions of the Amsterdam Treaty appear to restrict severely the policy areas which are amenable to closer co-operation. This is due to certain procedural elements, in particular the exclusion of areas where the Community has exclusive competence and the condition that the flexible action cannot affect the interests of outsiders or the *acquis communautaire*. It is submitted, however, that it certainly cannot be ruled out that in practice, after the coming into force of Amsterdam, these conditions will not completely stifle closer co-operation in the environmental field, even where it concerns product standards or occurs subsequent to Community harmonization. It is also submitted that the regime on the free movement of goods remains of interest after flexible harmonization has been agreed upon. Whether all this will encourage or discourage the use of the new flexibility mechanism in environmental policy remains to be seen. To be sure, political will may be just as important as legal constructions.

VIII. Conclusion

The ECJ case law addressing the relationship between the internal market and environmental imperatives is expanding rapidly, especially in the context of the regime concerning the free flow of goods. The overall tendency in the ECJ's case law indicates a readiness to give a considerable degree of support to

---

[187] See also E. Steyger, "Flexibility and the acquis communautaire", conference paper (University of Amsterdam, 1998), 5.

environmental arguments.[188] It is, however, difficult to assess the degree of "greenness" of the judgments delivered in search for the balance between the free movement of goods, an objective that finds its basis primarily at European level, and environmental protection, a goal to be achieved by the European and national administrations simultaneously. It is also important to note that often the most crucial case law did not directly concern environmental law, as is well illustrated by judgments such as *Spanish Strawberries*, *Keck*, and *Pistre*. The obvious implication of these judgments is that the broader the ECJ interprets the prohibitions on restrictions on imports and exports of goods, the less scope remains for national environmental policy.

Likewise, it is interesting to see that the cases concerning environmental measures have an impact on the general scope of Articles 28–30 EC. Judgments like *Danish Bottles*, *Wallonian Waste*, and, more recently, *Hedley Lomas*, *Compassion*, and *Dusseldorp* are either classic case law or, at least, constitute important rulings for the interpretation of the regime on the free movement of goods. A good example is the significance of *Wallonian Waste* for the development of the condition that measures, in order to be justified, should apply "without distinction".[189]

Case law concerning "open standards" like Articles 28, 29, and 30 EC has been developed mainly on a case-by-case basis. For this reason, many unresolved questions continue to surround the issue of the compatibility of environmental provisions with the fundamental freedom of trade in goods, something which continues to surprise. Some of these relate to formal, technical questions, such as the scope of Article 29 EC and the possible application of the rule of reason in the context of export restrictions (*Dusseldorp*), or the requirement that trade restrictions established in order to protect the environment may only be invoked if the measure in question applies "without distinction" (*Danish Bees*, *Aher-Waggon*). Yet, other unresolved problems are much more fundamentally related to the concept of the internal market, such as the debate on the extra-territoriality of exceptions (*Compassion*, *Dusseldorp*) and the application of Articles 28–30 EC to internal situations (*Pistre*). The main challenge for the ECJ in future years must therefore be to develop a more coherent and transparent case law on the free movement of goods and the environment.

---

[188] P. Sands, "The European Court of Justice: An Environmental Tribunal?", in H. Somsen (ed.), *Protecting the European Environment: Enforcing EC Environmental Law* (London: Blackstone Press, 1996), 23–35.

[189] Indeed, this case seems also to have an impact on the interpretation of the provisions on the free movements of services. See Case C–275/92, *H.M. Customs and Excise* v. *Schindler* [1994] ECR 1039.

EC Environmental Law and Self-Regulation in the Member States: in Search of a Legislative Framework

JONATHAN VERSCHUUREN*

I. Introduction

In the European Union, there exists a movement among Member States gradually to abandon rigid environmental standards of a command-and-control type, which traditionally have regulated private industry, in favour of creating room for industry to select the most cost-effective measures to protect the environment. The regulatory objectives are usually set forth in legislation or in individual permits. Yet, the realization of these aims is often determined by a negotiating process within a branch of industry or with individual companies in conformity with environmental agreements or individual eco-management plans. The movement away from command-and-control-type environmental regulation to self-regulation hence involves Member States setting goals which are then flexibly satisfied at the level of industry by private actors.

The instrument of self-regulation, and in particular environmental agreements, is widely used throughout the Community, as is evidenced by the 1996 Communication from the Commission on Environmental Agreements.[1] In view of proven advantages of self-regulation, the Commission is now promoting the use of environmental agreements at national level.[2] For various reasons, however, in many Member States objections have been voiced against the use of self-regulation in general and environmental agreements in particular. In a comparative study, Golub concludes that the transparency and legal status of many agreements are ambiguous.[3] As will be shown below, such

---

* Professor of European and International Environmental Law at the Centre for Legislative Studies, Tilburg University (Netherlands).

[1] Communication from the Commission to the Council and the European Parliament on environmental agreements, 27 Nov. 1996, COM(96)561 final (hereinafter "the Communication"). The Commission concludes that the use of agreements with industry in the area of environment policy has become more common in practically all Member States since the beginning of the 1990s. Cf. S. Krieger, "Die Empfehlung der Kommission über Umweltvereinbarungen" (1997) 21 *Europäische Zeitschrift für Wirtschaftsrecht* 648 and J. C. Bongaerts, "The Commission's Communication on Environmental Agreements" (1997) 6(3) *European Environmental Law Review* 84–86.

[2] Commission Recommendation (EC) 96/733 of 9 Dec. 1996 concerning environmental agreements implementing Community directives [1996] OJ L333/59.

[3] J. Golub, "New Instruments for Environmental Policy in the EU, Introduction and Overview" in J. Golub (ed.), *New Instruments for Environmental Policy in the EU* (London–New York: Routledge, 1998), 14–15.

controversies are often associated with the proper relationship between self-regulation and existing national or Community legislation.

The central question addressed in this article is the relationship between the Commission's Recommendation on the use of environmental agreements and national use of self-regulation against the background of existing national and EC command-and-control legislation. Is the existing regulatory system compatible with instruments of self-regulation and, if the answer is in the negative, how should the new legislative framework be given shape?

In analysing this question, section II will commence with a brief review of the relevant Commission documents relating to environmental agreements and other Community initiatives relating to self-regulation. This will be followed by a short exposition on the advantages and disadvantages of self-regulation in environmental law in general and European environmental policy and law in particular (section III). If the use of self-regulation is to be encouraged, a legislative framework must be designed so as to limit the drawbacks of self-regulation whilst fully exploiting its advantages. An attempt will be undertaken, in section IV, to analyse the proper role of state legislation to realize this objective by way of one specific example, Directive 94/62/EC on Packaging and Packaging Waste.[4] This Directive was implemented in the Netherlands by means of an environmental agreement. It will be argued that significant lessons can be learned from Dutch experience with the use of flexible instruments for future EC environmental law (section V).

II. Self-regulation in European Community Environmental Policy and Law

A. ENVIRONMENTAL AGREEMENTS: EC POLICY DOCUMENTS

Although the European debate on self-regulation reached its apotheosis in 1996, with the publication of the Communication and Recommendation on Environmental Agreements, the use of self-regulatory instruments was first advocated in the fifth environmental action programme.[5] In reality, however, the Community proved reluctant, affording industry scope in effect to develop its rules, and the emphasis on regulation of the command-and-control type remained largely unchallenged. The hesitance unreservedly to embrace self-regulation is illustrated by the Council Resolution on the environment and sustainable development, of 1993.[6]

---

[4] [1994] OJ L365/10.

[5] Towards Sustainability, A European Community Programme of Policy and Action in Relation to the Environment and Sustainable Development, COM(92)23 final—Vol. II, 29.

[6] See Resolution of the Council and the Representatives of the Governments of the Member States, meeting within the Council of 1 Feb. 1993 on a Community programme of policy and action in relation to the environment and sustainable development—A European Community programme of policy and action in relation to the environment and sustainable development [1993] OJ C138/1 para. 19: "Whereas previous environmental measures tended to be prescriptive in character with an emphasis on the 'thou shalt not' approach, the new strategy leans more towards a

It was in 1996 that self-regulation was unambiguously promoted by the Commission when it proclaimed, in the Communication from the Commission to the Council and the European Parliament on environmental agreements, that at a national level, Member States should have the opportunity to conclude environmental agreements, provided that these do not interfere with internal market requirements and competition rules.[7] At European level, the Commission pledges that the transparency and credibility of environmental agreements will be ensured.[8]

The Communication was followed by the Recommendation concerning environmental agreements implementing Community directives in December. Interestingly, the Recommendation includes conditions against which a draft agreement can be tested. Thus, for example, the Recommendation advocates that agreements should take the form of an enforceable contract, specify quantified objectives, and be accessible for the public. Elsewhere in this chapter, it will be argued that such guidelines should become an integral part of the legislative framework (section IV).

The Recommendation was welcomed by the Council which, in a Resolution of 7 October 1997, recognized that environmental agreements must set specified objectives, be transparent, reliable, and enforceable.[9] Particularly noteworthy is the fact that the Council encourages the Commission to indicate in its proposals for directives which provisions could be implemented by environmental agreements. If this is to give rise to systematic references to self-regulation in environmental directives, as a necessary consequence one might expect national environmental law to undergo a fundamental change in the next century.[10] This begs the question how the regulatory framework in future EC environmental directives should be formulated, to which we shall turn in section IV.

B. SELF-REGULATION IN EC ENVIRONMENTAL LAW

Thus far, Community environmental law only very rarely has explicitly required or allowed the use of self-regulation or of other alternative means of implementation. A contemporaneous example is the Council proposal for a Directive on Limitation of Emissions of Volatile Organic Compounds due to the Use of Organic Solvents in Certain Industrial Activities:[11]

'let's work together' approach. This reflects the growing realization in industry and in the business world that not only is industry a significant part of the (environmental) problem, it must also be part of the solution. The new approach implies, in particular, a reinforcement of the dialogue with industry and the encouragement, in appropriate circumstances, of voluntary agreements and other forms of self-regulation. Nevertheless, Community action is and will continue to be an important element in the avoidance of distortions in conditions of competition and preservation of the integrity of the Internal Market".

[7] COM(96)561 final, para. 48 at 25.   [8] See n. 8 below.
[9] Council Resolution (EC) 97/C 321/02 of 7 Oct. 1997 on environmental agreements [1997] OJ C321/6.
[10] Evidence that this practice is emerging is further provided by the recently proposed ELV Directive. (see in detail Onida at p. 253).
[11] COM(96)538 final [1997] OJ C99/32, as revised by COM(98)190, [1998] OJ C126/8.

whereas alternative approaches to reduction may allow the objectives of this Directive to be achieved more effectively than by implementing uniform emission limit values; whereas, therefore, Member States may be exempted from compliance with the emission limits, if they implement a national plan, which will, within the time frame from implementation of this Directive, lead to an at least equal reduction in emission of organic compounds from these processes and industrial installations.

Besides directives which authorize Member States to employ environmental agreements for the purpose of their implementation, some regulations promote self-regulation in the sense that they contain procedural provisions designed to harmonize self-regulation in the Union. The Regulations on a Community Eco-label Award Scheme[12] and a Community Eco-Management and Audit Scheme (EMAS)[13] constitute such examples, both schemes having originated from business itself. The Regulations establish a procedural framework intended to stimulate these and to promote self-regulation, albeit on a strictly voluntary basis. It has even been observed that companies which have their site registered under EMAS usually already "decided to face up to the environmental challenge".[14]

C.   ENVIRONMENTAL AGREEMENTS AT COMMUNITY LEVEL

Whilst self-regulation is thus promoted as a suitable tool for the implementation of environmental directives, the Commission also advocates concluding environmental agreements at Community level.[15] In the Communication, the Council correctly observed that there are only three binding policy instruments (regulations, directives, and decisions).[16] Agreements, in contrast, are non-binding, for example in the form of letters of intent or policy declarations, and will normally meet little objection, as long as these agreements do not fundamentally interfere with national environmental law.[17] In this context, it should be recalled that Article 5 (formerly Article 3b) EC states that the Community only acts within the limits of the power conferred upon it by the Treaty (attribution of powers) and that its actions may not go beyond what is necessary to achieve the objectives of Treaty (proportionality). Together with the principle of subsidiarity, these provisions guarantee that the Member States have the freedom to develop their own policy and legislation in areas not covered by the exclusive competence of the Community.[18]

---

[12] Reg (EEC) 880/92 of 23 Mar. 1992, [1992] OJ L99/1.

[13] Reg (EEC) 1836/93 of 29 June 1993 [1993] OJ L168/1.

[14] K. Taschner, "Environmental Management Systems: The European Regulation" in J. Golub (ed.), *New Instruments for Environmental Policy in the EU* (London: Routledge, 1998) 217.

[15] See n. 8 above.   [16] COM(96)561 final, para. 41 at 23.

[17] On the significance of soft law in the European Community see generally J. Karl, "Zur Rechtswirkung von Protokollerklärungen in der Europäischen Gemeinschaft" (1991) 46 *Juristenzeitung* 593. See also F. Snyder, *Soft Law and Institutional Practice in the European Community* (EUI Working Paper Law No. 93/5); see further Case C–322/88, *Grimaldi Fonds Maladies Professionelles* [1989] ECR 4407, where the Court seized jurisdiction to interpret a soft-law instrument.

[18] Environmental policy is not covered by the exclusive competence of the Community.

The environmental agreement concluded by the Commission and the European automobile industry in July 1998 is the first example of an environmental agreement at Community level.[19] The European Automobile Manufacturers Association (ACEA) has committed itself to an objective of 140g/km emission for CO_2, in return for which the Commission will refrain from proposing binding legislative measures. To attain the policy goals previously formulated[20] as well as new emission objectives under the Kyoto Protocol, the Commission concluded the non-binding agreement. The agreement was supported by the Council,[21] but militated against the European Parliament's explicit demand to impose binding measures on the automobile industry.[22]

Whereas the Commission can conclude non-binding agreements only in so far as these do not encroach upon Member States' reserved powers, it might still be warranted to persuade industry or other private parties voluntarily to act in conformity with the principle of sustainability. Although self-regulation has numerous advantages and hence certainly must be developed further, we should remain realistic in our expectations. It will be shown that the use of self-regulation at European level may prove even more complex and hazardous than at national level.

III. Advantages and Disadvantages of Self-regulation: General Observations

A. ADVANTAGES OF SELF-REGULATION

The disadvantages of command-and-control-type regulation have been thoroughly explored in the context of the debate on European harmonization and the regulation of economic activities.[23] Especially from a perspective of economic efficiency, these appear compelling and relate to the fact that uniform reduction targets and technologies are imposed, ignoring the variable pollution abatement costs facing individual firms, depending on such factors as age and location of a plant.[24] Also, command-and-control regulation stifles innovation as firms are forced to switch over to expensive equipment, regardless of the existence of other, sometimes more effective, solutions at lower cost.[25] Thus, it has been observed, command-and-control regulation "has evolved into a morass of complex, contradictory, and essentially unenforceable requirements that overwhelm regulators and regulated alike".[26]

---

[19] COM(98)495, reproduced at p. 573.   [20] COM(95)689 and COM(96)248.
[21] Council conclusions on the Commission Communication, published on the Internet at: http://europa.eu.int/comm/dg11/co2/co2_coun.htm.
[22] Recently again formulated in the Parliament's Resolution on climate change in the run-up to Buenos Aires, published on the Internet at: http://europa.eu.int/comm/dg11/co2/ co2_reso.htm.
[23] See G. Majone, *Regulating Europe* (London: Routledge, 1997); N. Cunningham and P. Grabosky, *Smart Regulation* (Oxford: Clarendon Press, 1998).
[24] Golub (n. 3 above), 3.   [25] *Ibid.*, 4.
[26] R. I. Steinzor, "Reinventing Environmental Regulation: The Dangerous Journey from Command to Self-control" (1998) 22 *Harvard Environmental Law Review* 117. For an elaborate

Consensus regarding the drawbacks of command-and-control regulation is paralleled by the long list of advantages of self-regulation which have been spelled out in numerous publications on the subject.[27] In its Communication, the Commission identifies three core benefits of self-regulation; the encouragement of a pro-active approach from industry, cost-effectiveness, and speedier realization of objectives.[28] It appears useful briefly to explore the most important advantages of self-regulation,[29] most of which are also spelled out in the Commission's Communication on the environmental agreement with the European automobile industry.

First, by virtue of its nature, self-regulation allows optimal use to be made of the knowledge and expertise present within a society (industry, agriculture, etc.). Business enjoys a significant advantage *vis-à-vis* the state in terms of technical and organizational knowledge of their own processes and the best ways to limit their negative environmental impact.[30] To take the CO_2 emissions by cars as an example, the automobile industry is best placed to determine what is technically feasible with regard to fuel efficiency. They are encouraged pro-actively to employ the most efficacious way to reduce CO_2 emissions by cars.[31]

Secondly, self-regulation is characterized by a minimum of procedural constraints and hence can easily be adapted compared to parliamentary procedures usually required for amendments of command-and-control-type legislation. Flexibility is also ensured because of the relatively small circle of actors involved in the process, further facilitating any necessary changes to the regime. On this issue of flexibility, the Commission notes:[32]

Where companies participate in environmental agreements, licensing authorities may be able to issue less detailed and target based licenses, leaving the company the scope to find the most efficient way of achieving the targets. Moreover, the company may not need to apply for a license for every change in the process. Flexibility also encourages creative solutions and technological innovation.

A third argument in favour of self-regulation is that it leads to higher compliance rates. Thus, because there exists a direct relation between those who

analysis of command-and-control regulation, cf K. Webb, *Pollution Control in Canada: The Regulatory Approach in the 1980s, Administrative Law Series* (Ottawa: Law Reform Commission of Canada, 1988).

[27] Extensive references to the literature in this field are reproduced in European Environmental Agency, *Environmental Agreements, Environmental Issue* (Copenhagen: European Environmental Agency, Series No. 3 Vol 1, 1997) 88–91.

[28] COM(96)561 final, paras. 7–9 at 7–8.

[29] See Th. G. Drupsteen, P. C. Gilhuis, C. J. Kleijs-Wijnnobel, S. D. M. de Leeuw, and J. M. Verschuuren, *De toekomst van de Wet milieubeheer* (Deventer: W.E.J. Tjeenk Willink, 1998) 247.

[30] As is shown by the case studies described in K. A. Strasser, "Preventing Pollution" (1996) VIII *Fordham Environmental Law Journal* 1, 16–22. In particular his example of Zytec Corporation and its problems with cleaning newly manufactured circuit boards is illuminating: instead of conceptualizing a certain environmental problem as a cleaning problem, in the way the existing legislation would have led it to, it devised a more innovative and fundamental solution (20–2).

[31] The encouragement of a proactive approach from industry is the first advantage in the Commission's Communication on environmental agreements, COM(96)561 final, para. 7 at 7.

[32] COM(96)561 final, no. 8 (7).

conceive the rules and those bound by them, preparedness to comply may be expected to be higher than is the case with command-and-control-type legislation.[33]

Associated with these advantages is a fourth advantage, namely that costs for industry are lower because it is left free to opt for the measures it judges to be the most appropriate to reach given goals. Compliance costs are reduced as a result too.[34]

In addition, the active and direct participation of the actors involved may be regarded as a more direct form of democracy helping to bridge the gap between government and its citizens.[35] Instead of the traditionally confrontational relationship between the Commission and industry, the European automobile industry has now become directly involved in the rule-making process.[36]

Finally, the visibly more active role of business, industry, or branches of industry in preserving the environment helps to improve their image and may stimulate consumers to purchase products of companies with such a positive image, or even persuade banks and insurance firms to do business with those companies.[37] Self-regulation hence may stimulate firms pro-actively to develop environmental programmes.[38]

B.   LIMITATIONS OF SELF-REGULATION

Obviously, self-regulation as an instrument of environmental policy has a number of inherent limitations, or "risks", which have to be borne in mind before a process of self-regulation is embarked upon.[39] The Commission identifies out three crucial conditions for self-regulation:

— all parties must be determined and committed to pursue well-defined environmental objectives,
— agreements must be enforceable,
— free rider behaviour must be discouraged.

To be sure, there are more extensive limitations to the self-regulatory approach which shall now be briefly explored.[40]

Environmental management is characterized by strong conflicts of interests. Businesses aim at maximizing profits, which requires a minimum of state

---

[33] J. C. Ruhnka and H. Boerstler, "Governmental Incentives for Corporate Self-Regulation" [1998] *Journal of Business Ethics* 309–26.

[34] One of the three advantages mentioned in the Commission's Communication, COM(96)561 final, para. 8 at 7.

[35] Golub (n. 3 above), 6.   [36] *Ibid.*, 6.   [37] *Ibid.*, 5.

[38] More extensively on this topic: S. Sharma and H. Vredenburg, "Proactive Corporate Environmental Strategy and the Development of Competitively Valuable Organizational Capabilities" [1998] *Strategic Management Journal* 729–53.

[39] COM(96)561 final, para. 10 at 8.

[40] This list is also based on earlier research on the topic by the author for the Dutch Ministry of Housing, Spatial Planning and the Environment, and has been published in *Drupsteen et al.* (n. 28 above), 249.

intervention in their activities. Local residents and environmental action groups, however, aspire to live in a clean and healthy environment. Government, on the other hand, is pursuing even more general interests. Self-regulation harbours the risk that industry and business may come to dominate the regulatory process and such other, more general, interests become marginalized in the process.

Although participation of industry in the regulatory process may be an efficacious way to reduce industrial pollution,[41] individuals and NGOs are no match for industry in the elaboration of self-regulatory rules, if they are involved at all.[42] Public support for self-regulation will be undermined by unilateral proclamations by branches of industry, without the participation of other parties in the formation of these rules. For these and other reasons of a political, strategic, and technical nature, environmental interest groups are therefore likely to prefer command-and-control instruments.[43]

Since so many actors (profit and non-profit) can create, implement, and enforce rules, by nature self-regulation is more fragmented and diffused than state legislation. This has several possible implications: the quality and legal force of rules may differ, they may be inaccessible or lack transparency and mutual coherency.

All this, in turn, creates a real risk of new legislative measures interfering with self-regulation. State regulation hangs over the sphere of self-regulation like the sword of Damocles. Private entities entering into an environmental agreement with the Commission or at national level with the Department of the Environment can never be confident that a binding policy instrument on the same subject will not be adopted after all, for instance if parliament strongly insists upon such binding rules. This prospect appears realistic in the case of CO_2 emissions by private cars. The European Parliament insists on the use of enforceable instruments and calls upon all parties involved in the decision-making process to expedite the adoption of a directive introducing a tax on energy and CO_2 emissions, and a directive restructuring the Community framework for the taxation of energy products.[44] In the environmental agreement with the European automobile industry, the right of the Community or its Member States to exercise its prerogatives in the field of fiscal policy has been upheld.[45] Such "legislative threats" may frustrate the successful development of an effective regime of self-regulation.[46]

---

[41] D. S. Grant II, "Allowing Citizen Participation in Environmental Regulation: An Empirical Analysis of the Effects of Right-to-Sue and Right-to-Know Provisions on Industry's Toxic Emissions" (1997) 78 *Social Science Quarterly* 871.

[42] They lack sufficient countervailing powers: M. Aalders and T. Wilthagen, "Moving Beyond Command-and-Control: Reflexivity in the regulation of Occupational Safety and Health and the Environment" (1997) 19 *Law & Policy* 432.

[43] N. O. Keohane, R. L. Revesz, and R. N. Stavins, "The Choice of Regulatory Instruments in Environmental Policy" (1998) 22 *Harvard Environmental Law Review* 364.

[44] Parliament's Resolution on climate change in the run-up to Buenos Aires (n. 21 above).

[45] COM(98)495.   [46] Steinzor (n. 25 above), 200–1.

Free-rider problems also may seriously undermine the effectiveness of self-regulation, as is acknowledged by the Commission.[47] Not all individual companies in a given branch may be bound by the self-regulatory rules, simply because they are not members of any of the contracting parties. Even if a company is a member of a contracting party, the question remains whether the individual company will actually adopt the obligations agreed by the contracting parties. In both cases it may be tempting to avoid the obligations, in order to obtain a competitive advantage over participants in the scheme.[48] Free-rider problems will occur especially where a branch is not well organized.

The reverse situation may also occur: a strong group of companies or a single company with a dominant position may impose its rules on other subordinate companies, giving rise to distortions of competition or even to cartels.

A further question that may be asked is whether contracting parties should be expected to possess the kind of panoramic vision which solutions to environmental problems require. It appears reasonable to suggest that in reality often the scale of the environmental problems at issue far exceeds their resources.

Also, whereas self-regulation may increase the likelihood of compliance, on the other hand, by its nature, contracting parties cannot easily be forced to live up to the agreements, although the law of contract may sometimes be used to enforce an agreement. Within a branch organization it is even more difficult to enforce rules on individual members, and third parties (free riders) cannot be forced to comply with self-regulation at all. The controversy between the Commission and the European Parliament on the agreement with the automobile industry has focused on this issue. Parliament strongly criticizes the fact that no provision has been made for the eventuality that manufacturers who are members of ACEA may fail to comply with their commitments under the agreement.[49]

At a more general level, the private character of self-regulation may undermine the potential for judicial review. Whereas the exercise of public (environmental) powers usually is amenable to judicial review, self-regulatory agreements can rarely be invoked in court, at least not in the administrative courts most accessible to individual citizens and environmental action groups and best equipped to test actions and decisions against environmental legislation. With regard to EC law in particular, this poses real problems. National environmental legislation is often influenced by EC environmental law or even specifically designed to implement it. As is well known, national implementing rules taking the form of self-regulation, do not normally satisfy the parameters articulated in the case law of the European Court of Justice.

[47] COM(96)561 final, para. 12 at 9.
[48] In the Netherlands this has proved to be a real problem: see J. W. Biekart, "Negotiated Agreements in EU Environmental Policy" in J. Golub (ed.), *New Instruments for Environmental Policy in the EU* (London–New York: Routledge, 1998) 186.
[49] Parliament's Resolution on climate change in the run-up to Buenos Aires (n. 21 above).

Environmental directives have to be transposed into binding provisions of national law, fully satisfying the requirements of clarity and legal certainty and affording recourse of interested parties to the courts. The result intended by the directive has to be ensured not only in fact, but also in law, i.e. by legally binding rules within a statutory framework.[50] The Commission has summarized these rules as follows:

> where Directives intend to create rights and obligations for individuals, for instance by setting limit values of general application aimed to protect human health, the transposing acts need binding force and appropriate publicity. Only in this case can the persons concerned be able to ascertain the full extent of their rights, relying on them, where appropriate, before the national courts. Moreover, the fact that a practice is consistent with the protection afforded under a Directive does not justify the failure to implement that Directive in the national legal order. Member States therefore are required to take binding action and may not rely on the recognition of unilateral commitments on the part of industry.[51]

In addition, as has already been briefly alluded to, self-regulation could lead to the formation of cartels, which in turn may be incompatible with Articles 81 and 82 (formerly Articles 85 and 86) EC.

It has been seen that the Community must respect Member States' reserved powers. As a result, in this area of reserved powers the Community at best may act by means of "soft law" that does not interfere with national policy. In such cases too, however, in view of Article 5 (formerly Art. 3b) EC, the Community should take care to respect Member States' prerogatives and hence it is advisable to include a provision in any agreement to the effect that any sanctions imposed must be in accordance with national law.

In conclusion, the potential risks associated with self-regulation are both numerous and compelling. However, the legislature and executive, both at national and EU level, can and should play a constructive role in minimizing these risks. Self-regulation by no means implies that public authorities can afford a "hands-off" approach. Rather, in order to overcome the many risks associated with self-regulation and for self-regulation really to become an effective tool to protect the environment, pro-active government is required.[52] A framework is needed within which self-regulation can operate, either in the form of a generic law or by the executive on an *ad hoc* basis, for instance in a permit. Such a system amounts to what I shall term "conditional self-regulation".

---

[50] Cf Jans and the case law mentioned there: J. H. Jans, *European Environmental Law*, European Monographs (Groningen: Wolters-Noordhoff, 1995), 125 and recently Case C–340/96, *Commission* v. *the UK and Northern Ireland*, 24.4.99 (not yet reported).

[51] COM(96)561 final, para. 31 at 20, referring to the ECJ in Case C–29/84, *Commission* v. *Germany* [1985] ECR I–1661 and Case C–339/87, *Commission* v. *The Netherlands* [1990] ECR I–851.

[52] Biekart (n. 48 above), 187.

IV. Conditional Self-regulation

A. A LEGISLATIVE FRAMEWORK FOR SELF-REGULATION

A legislative framework for self-regulation exists only in part at European level. In specific areas of environmental self-regulation, such as environmental management within business and eco-labelling, rules have been laid down in regulations on allowing voluntary participation by companies in the industrial sector in a Community eco-management and audit scheme (EMAS)[53] and a Community eco-label award scheme respectively.[54] Otherwise, however, an elaborate framework, designed specifically to regulate the process of self-regulation, does not exist.

An appropriate starting point in our search for such a framework is constituted by the Commission's Communication and related publications, from which a number of parameters may be distilled, designed to promote self-regulation whilst minimizing risks associated with its use:

— EC law must leave room for self-regulation;
— general substantive standards should be fixed in a legislative framework;
— the legislation must promote commitments to be clear and binding (which hence must be monitored and enforced) and discourage "free rider" behaviour, and;
— the legislation should ensure transparency and a role for third parties.

In the remainder of this section, these parameters will be discussed one by one. Obviously, for self-regulation to take place, both at a national and at European level, it is essential that secondary EC law should leave sufficient scope for self-regulation.[55] Directives that are very detailed and strict and require Member States to use direct regulation for their implementation may effectively rule out self-regulation or even the use of contracts (UK water supply case). According to the European Court of Justice, directives must be implemented by means of binding legal instruments, unless a directive determines otherwise.[56] In the Communication, the Commission pledged to leave more room for implementation by means of environmental agreements:[57]

Whenever regulatory action becomes necessary for the Commission, the Commission will carefully consider whether certain provisions of these legislative measures will allow for implementation by binding environmental agreements and will include, if appropriate, such provisions in its proposals.

An illustrative example of this approach is the proposal for a Council Directive on Emissions of Volatile Organic Compounds Due to the Use of

---

[53] Reg. (EEC) No. 1836/93 of 29 June 1993 [1993] OJ L168/1.
[54] Reg. (EEC) No. 880/92 of 23 Mar. 1992 [1992] OJ L99/1.   [55] COM(96)561 final, para. 33 at 21.
[56] See, for instance, Case 97/81, *Commission* v. *The Netherlands* [1982] ECR I–1819 and Case C–361/88, *Commission* v. *Germany* [1991] ECR 2567 Case C–340/96, *Commission* v. *the UK and Northern Ireland*, note 50, above.
[57] COM(96)561 final, para. 48 at 25.

Organic solvents in certain industrial activities, mentioned earlier.[58] Instead of obliging Member States to use a permit system, the proposal in more general terms refers to an "authorization", which is a procedure by which the competent authority reaches a decision, which may be in the form of a permit, but also an environmental agreement. The proposal gives the following definition:

Authorization ... means a procedure by which the competent authority grants authorization to operate all or part of an installation, by means of a written decision or decisions.

Obviously, at all times provisions of EC law must be complied with. As has been seen, in this regard the strict formulation of Article 81 (formerly Article 85) EC could prove problematical.[59] This invites the consideration whether the inclusion of an exception relating to the protection of the environment, additional to those currently enumerated in paragraph three of this provision, may be justified. We shall briefly return to this question below.

In order to ensure that generally accepted minimum standards of environmental protection are safeguarded in processes of self-regulation, the legislator should legally oblige the actors involved in self-regulation to attain these standards. Such an obligation should in part be based on, or influenced by, goals fixed by national or European public authorities. Important principles laid down in international treaties and declarations (such as the 1992 Rio Declaration), the EC Treaty, and national legislation should also be taken account of for this purpose. Generally accepted principles such as the precautionary principle must form the basis of any rule, also when this rule is made by business itself. In this way, environmental interests are sufficiently taken into account. The legislator may even codify these principles with a view to ensuring their legal relevance for all environmental decisions.[60]

Self-regulation must lead to the realization of certain environmental goals and, therefore, a legislative framework must ensure that the commitments are clear and binding (monitored and enforced) and discourage "free-rider" behaviour.[61] In order to ensure that the self-regulated enter into binding commitments,[62] it is necessary for legislation to perform the function of the metaphorical big stick.[63] The "threat" of statutory standards if the self-regulatory process fails to produce the desired results must be sufficiently deterrent for all businesses involved. The threat of statutory standards will stimulate the conclusion of substantive commitments and reduce the danger of a large number of free riders. Where statutory standards already exist, business may be urged to commit itself to pro-active measures and realistic

---

[58] COM(96)538 final [1997] OJ C99/32, as revised by COM(98)190 [1998] OJ C126/8.

[59] COM(96)561 final, para. 28 at 17–18.

[60] R. A. J. Van Gestel and J. M. Verschuuren, "Artikel 21 Grondwet en de noodzaak van zelfregulering in het milieurecht: naar een andere betekenis van sociale grondrechten?" in H. R. B. M. Kummeling, and S. C. Van Bijsterveld (eds.), *Grondrechten en zelfregulering* (Deventer: W. E. J. Tjeenk Willink, 1997) 149–50.

[61] COM(96)561 final, para. 20 at 13; Golub (n. 3 above), 14; Biekart (n. 48 above), 186.

[62] COM(96)561 final, para. 19 at 12.   [63] Golub (n. 3 above), 14.

deadlines. Businesses tempted by free-rider behaviour will realize that exclusion from the process of self-regulation will mean that they will have to adhere to the possibly more rigid statutory rules.

Another way of discouraging free-rider behaviour is by affording parties the right to request statutory authority to be conferred upon the agreement. For example, in the Netherlands such a possibility exists in the Environmental Management Act.[64]

Monitoring and enforcing environmental agreements in principle should be arranged in the agreement itself and should be the responsibility of the parties involved. The agreement can be monitored by the parties themselves, as long as there exist sufficient guarantees that this is done reliably and accurately.[65] Agreements should be concluded in contractual form, so that the law of contract can be used for their enforcement.[66] Parties can also resort to some alternative form of dispute resolution, provided that the competent complaints authority can actually impose its decisions upon the contracting parties. The role of state authorities should be confined to policing the monitoring and enforcing activities of the parties. This has been referred to as "systems enforcement": public inspectors monitor the operation of self-control systems.[67] These monitoring mechanisms, and indeed the entire monitoring system, should be promoted and supported by statutory law.

The legislative framework should also be designed with a view to providing procedural guarantees aimed at minimizing risks relating to openness and accountability.[68] Since environmental protection is of common concern, it is unacceptable when environmental policy is made behind closed doors. It is reasonable to presume that access to information provides a strong impetus for companies not to stay behind, or to perform even better than others for reasons of market opportunities or public relations.[69]

Also, in order to secure the widest public support, where this is feasible, important stakeholders in the field of environmental protection should be allowed to participate in the conclusion of agreements, or at least have the opportunity to comment on draft versions.[70] This is important not only for directly affected stakeholders, such as neighbours of an individual plant subject to a self-regulatory regime aimed at reducing toxic emissions, but also when the state is contemplating such measures for an entire industrial branch. In the latter case, it is conceivable that an important national environmental

---

[64] See Art. 15.36 of the Act. So far, this provision only refers to so-called "waste disposal fees" (these are levies imposed on products by the producers themselves, enabling them to take back and recycle their products when disposed of by consumers), but such a provision could be given a much broader scope.

[65] COM(96)561 final, para. 22 at 13.   [66] *Ibid.*, para. 26 at 16.

[67] Aalders and Wilthagen (n. 42 above), 431.

[68] More generally, see J. Black, "Constitutionalising Self-Regulation" (1996) 59 *Modern Law Review* 24–55; COM(96)561 final, para. 23 at 14.

[69] Biekart (n. 48 above), 186.

[70] COM(96)561 final, para. 18 at 11–12. See more extensively, C. L. Hartman and E. R. Stafford, "Green Alliances: Building New Business with Environmental Groups" (1997) 30 *Long Range Planning* 184–96.

interest group becomes a party to the agreement, or at least is informed about the negotiations or invited as an observer.

As for the crucial issue of access to justice, here there is a role for government as well. Command-and-control regulation normally can be reviewed in (administrative) courts. In the case of self-regulation, this is usually not the case, since there simply will be no state measure to be reviewed. Evidently, it is important that self-regulatory rules or decisions are reviewable and hence, for example, can be tested against national or European legislation, and there are ways to achieve this. Parties involved could for instance be obliged to create some kind of alternative dispute resolution, such as a complaints authority or an arbitration committee. In this way, self-regulatory rules can be tested without administrative courts having to intervene.[71] In extreme cases, whenever a self-regulatory agreement is considered to amount to a wrongful act, the matter can be taken to civil courts, although it is doubtful whether for third parties such as environmental interest groups this can realistically be regarded as a satisfactory avenue.[72]

B.   CASE STUDY: IMPLEMENTATION OF DIRECTIVE 94/62/EC IN THE NETHERLANDS

As has been seen, numerous conditions need to be satisfied for self-regulation to be effective. This may now usefully be illustrated by the way in which environmental agreements implemented Directive 94/62/EC on Packaging and Packaging Waste[73] in the Netherlands, a Member State where a great deal of experience exists with environmental agreements.

Although Article 3(12) of this Directive provides a definition of a voluntary agreement,[74] it does not unambiguously allow for implementation by self-regulation. Article 22 simply states that Member States shall bring into force the laws, regulations, and administrative provisions necessary to comply with the Directive. In order to resort to self-regulation for its implementation and guarantee that the objectives of the Directive are fulfilled, if necessary by compelling the relevant companies to reach the objectives, the Netherlands has opted to implement the Directive by environmental agreement in conjunction with legislation. In this way, obstacles posed by enforcement and monitoring, free riding and the circumstance that implementation by environmental agreement might not satisfy minimum standards articulated by the European Court have been negotiated.

---

[71] Obviously, such a body should be set up in such a way as to satisfy the criteria elaborated by the ECJ, as regards the notion of "any court or tribunal" in the context of Art. 234 (formerly Art. 177) EC.

[72] In the Netherlands, administrative courts are easier to access than civil courts. They are also more competent fully to review administrative decisions.

[73] [1994] OJ L365/10.

[74] "The formal agreement concluded between the competent public authorities of the Member State and the economic sectors concerned, which has to be open to all partners who wish to meet the conditions of the agreement with a view to working towards the objectives of this Directive."

The process of implementation of this Directive in the Netherlands may be summarized as follows. First, an environmental agreement was concluded by the Ministry of the Environment and large employers' associations and branch organizations on 15 December 1997.[75] This was the follow-up to an earlier agreement, concluded in 1991. Although this latter agreement was signed by a fairly large group of 150 companies from the packaging industry, there remained a group of free riders. As a result, several targets for specific waste streams were never met.[76] In addition, monitoring industry's performance was chaotic and data proved difficult for third parties to obtain.[77]

In the second agreement, a wide range of measures was covered, including recycling and recovery of packaging materials, the prevention of litter, obligations for contracting parties to inform their members on prevention of waste and to inform the public on progress with the reduction of waste. It also provides for the setting up of a Packaging Commission to monitor implementation of the agreement. Parties are obliged to evaluate compliance with the agreement which, if problems emerge, for instance when one of the parties does not comply with the agreement, leads to deliberations on the agreement by the parties involved. Whenever there are differences which cannot be resolved by the Packaging Commission, parties have to apply to an arbitration committee. Since the agreement is a contract, parties can also seise a court in case of non-compliance by one of the other parties.

In the same period, however, based on the Environmental Management Act, the legislator enacted the Order on Packaging and Packaging Waste of 30 June 1997 (hereafter "the Order").[78] This Order constituted precise transposition of the Directive and obliged manufacturers and importers of products, *inter alia*, to recover and recycle certain percentages by weight for each packaging material, percentages that are identical to those mentioned in the Directive. Crucially, however, the Order also states, in Article 2, that manufacturers and importers are exempted from the obligations arising from the Order if they have joined an agreement with the Ministry for the Environment. Compared to the Order, the advantages for contracting manufacturers are twofold.

First, they are no longer individually bound by the obligations of the Order, but have to fulfil the Directive's objectives as a group. Thus, the combined manufacturers of plastic packaging have to reach a target, rather than manufacturers individually. As a result, manufacturers of different types of packaging may compensate for each other's strengths and weaknesses. An example may illustrate this. Presume that one manufacturer may achieve good results recycling glass, but has difficulties meeting the target for plastic. Further, presume that another party to the agreement does better in recycling plastic. Together they may comply with the goals set in the Directive. Although this isolated example may appear futile, with about 80 per cent of the manufacturers and importers

---

[75] "Packaging Covenant II" [1997] *Nederlandse Staats Courant*, No. 247 at 38.
[76] Biekart (n. 48 above), 181.   [77] See n. 74 above.
[78] [1997] *Nederlandse Staats Courant*, No. 125 at 14.

expected to sign the agreement, the potential advantage for individual manufacturers is clearly significant.

Secondly, the goals have to be realized by 30 June 2001 instead of 1 August 1998, and hence manufacturers have more time to adapt their products to the new packaging rules. Importantly, the date of 30 June 2001 is derived from the Directive and in this sense the Order is much stricter than the Directive.[79]

Bearing in mind the risks involved in self-regulation summarily discussed above, this dual approach (simultaneous implementation by national legislation and by environmental agreement) has a number of compelling advantages:

1. compliance with Directive 94/62/EC is secured as its obligations are fulfilled, either by the Order or by the agreement;
2. whereas the initial agreement of 1991 produced serious free-rider problems, resulting in a failure to achieve targets for specific waste streams,[80] the new agreement fills this gap. Those not signing the agreement are obliged to comply with the Order, which contains rules stricter than those laid down in the agreement and hence serves as the metaphorical stick.
3. the goals are formulated clearly in both the agreement and the Order and the results are initially monitored and enforced by the contracting parties themselves. Public authorities will monitor the entire system and may intervene whenever objectives are not fulfilled or a party does not comply with the agreement. When certain manufacturers or importers (or groups of manufacturers) do not comply with the agreement, the latter may exclude these manufacturers or importers, in which case they must comply with the Order.[81] These obligations may be enforced by administrative and criminal enforcement instruments. Also, all parties (including the ministry), can seise a court for breach of contract.
4. the agreement encourages efficient use of resources as it introduces flexibility for manufacturers and importers;
5. compliance costs for manufacturers and importers are reduced, and;
6. the agreement enjoys widespread support from manufacturers and importers, which in turn may be expected to result in positive repercussions in the sphere of compliance.

---

[79] The Directive itself also opens up the possibility of stricter national rules in Art. 6(6): "Member States which have, or will, set programmes going beyond the targets of para 1 (a) and (b) and which provide to this effect appropriate capacities for recycling and recovery, are permitted to pursue those targets in the interest of a high level of environmental protection, on condition that these measures avoid distortions of the internal market and do not hinder compliance by other Member States with the Directive. The Member States shall inform the Commission thereof. The Commission shall confirm these measures, after having verified, in cooperation with the Member States, that they are consistent with the considerations above and do not constitute an arbitrary means of discrimination or a disguised restriction on trade between Member States."

[80] Biekart (n. 48 above), 181.   [81] See Art. 2(3) of the Order.

Two final issues need briefly to be considered. First is the problem that there is only a limited role for environmental protection organizations or other third parties in the formation and subsequent enforcement of the agreement. Although environmental organizations were represented during the negotiations leading to the agreement, there are few procedural safeguards in the Order or the agreement. According to the agreement, the contracting parties are obliged to compile a public annual report on the progress as regards implementation of the agreement. Yet, it has transpired that not all the results are fully accessible to the general public and it may be concluded that, as with the agreement of 1991, these problems have yet to be fully resolved.[82]

A possibly more complex problem relates to any distortions of competition that may arise from this approach. Thus, the advantages afforded to contracting parties could be deemed to be contrary to Article 81(1)[83] EC and Article 82 (formerly Article 85(1) and Article 86) EC.[84] In the light of the Commission's Communication,[85] this possibility should be given serious consideration. Although a detailed analysis of the relationship between these provisions and the use of environmental agreements falls outside the scope of this article, the Commission's Notice in the *DSD* case[86] suggests that it applies the competition rules in environmental matters without any special consideration for the subject matter at issue.

As is well known, exemptions to the prohibition of Article 81(1) (formerly Article 85(1)) EC may be granted by the Commission under paragraph 3, if an agreement contributes to improving the production or distribution of goods or to promoting technical or economic progress, while allowing consumers a fair share of the resulting benefit, and which does not impose restrictions

---

[82] Biekart (n. 48 above), 181.

[83] Art. 81(1) (formerly Art. 85) EC reads as follows: "The following shall be prohibited as incompatible with the common market: all agreements between undertakings, decisions by associations of undertakings and concerted practices which may affect trade between Member States and which have as their object or effect the prevention, restriction or distortion of competition within the common market, and in particular those which: (a) directly or indirectly fix purchase or selling prices or any other trading conditions; (b) limit or control production, markets, technical development, or investment; (c) share markets or sources of supply; (d) apply dissimilar conditions to equivalent transactions with other trading parties, thereby placing them at a competitive disadvantage; (e) make the conclusion of contracts subject to acceptance by the other parties of supplementary obligations which, by their nature or according to commercial usage, have no connection with the subject of such contracts."

[84] H. G. Sevenster, "Milieu en mededinging" [1997] *Nederlands Tijdschrift voor Europees Recht* 183. For an extensive review on the question whether or not environmental agreements can be allowed in the light of Art. 81 (formerly Art. 85) EC, cf H. G. Sevenster, "De geoorloofdheid van milieubeleidsafspraken in Europees perpectief", in M. V. C. Aalders and R. J. J. Van Acht (eds.), *Afspraken in het milieurecht* (Zwolle: W. E. J. Tjeenk Willink, 1992), 73–93. See also F. O. W. Vogelaar, "Towards an Improved Integration of EC Environmental Policy and EC Competition Policy: An Interim Report" in Barry and Hawk (eds.), *International Antitrust Law & Policy* (The Hague: Kluwer, 1995) 529–63; A. V. Steinbeck, "Umweltvereinbarungen und Europäisches Wettbewerbsrecht" (1998) 6 *Wirtschaft und Wettbewerb* 554–66; D. Ehle, *Die Einbeziehung des Umweltschutzes in das Europäische Kartellrecht* (FIW-Schriftenreihe Heft 168, Cologne: Carl Heymanns Verlag, 1996).

[85] COM(96)561 final, para. 28 at 18.

[86] Notice pursuant to Art. 19(3) of Council Reg. (EC) No. 17/62 implementing articles 85 and 86 of the Treaty, [1962] OJ Sp. Ed. 204/62, p. 87, Case IV/2 34.439—DSD [1997] OJ C100/4.

which are not indispensable to the attainment of these objectives and if they do not afford such undertakings the possibility of eliminating competition in respect of a substantial part of the products in question. The question whether or not the agreements concluded under the new Dutch Packaging Order are permitted in the light of these EC competition rules, will remain unclear until the Commission has passed judgment on these agreements. If the provisions of Article 81 (formerly Article 85) EC prove substantially to obstruct the application of an effective instrument securing a high level of environmental protection in the Union, ultimately a discussion about any necessary amendments of Article 81 EC may prove unavoidable.

V. Conclusion

In its 1996 Communication on Environmental Agreements, the Commission acknowledged that self-regulation in environmental policy and law has many advantages and therefore must be promoted. However, as has been shown, there are numerous drawbacks which need to be addressed for the potential of self-regulation to be fully realized. In this chapter, an attempt has been undertaken to contribute to such a discussion, partly by drawing upon Dutch experience, where environmental agreements were pioneered and which partly served as a model for the Communication. The ensuing analysis has revealed that, whereas the advantages of self-regulation at times are compelling, potential and real drawbacks remain to be resolved. In this regard, the Dutch model offers promising and constructive insights, and gives rise to a number of general propositions.

First and most importantly, potential risks of self-regulation can be reduced or even eliminated where it is supported by a strong legislative framework. Evidently, secondary EC law should leave room for self-regulation by explicitly allowing Member States to implement the provisions of a directive by environmental agreement or some other self-regulatory instrument. This means that directives should not impose certain instruments at the exclusion of others, and should not be unnecessarily detailed. Directives should hence specify the goals that should be attained by a given date, but the exact forms and methods should be left to Member States, which may enter into negotiations between the parties involved with the purpose of concluding an environmental agreement.

Secondly, in order to ensure that generally accepted standards of environmental protection are not obscured in the process of self-regulation, the legislation must articulate substantive standards. Such legislation must require commitments to be clear and binding which must also be monitored and enforced.

Thirdly, the legislation must discourage free-rider behaviour, for instance by stipulating that certain statutory rules come to apply if a firm does not take part in the self-regulatory process, or does not comply with the agreements.

A fourth and final role of the statutory framework is to ensure transparency and to involve third parties (especially environmental protection associations) in the process, including forms of review by judicial or arbitral bodies. The latter includes possibilities to have an agreement tested by some judicial or arbitration body.

Whereas, as has been shown, not all problems have yet been solved, it is submitted that the case of the implementation of Directive 94/62/EC on Packaging and Packaging Waste in The Netherlands by the Order as well as by the agreement shows that it is possible to create such a constellation.

European Community Eco-Labelling in Transition

LUDWIG KRÄMER*

I. Introduction

European Community environmental policy and law have developed progressively over the last twenty-five years, initially in the absence of an express legal foundation in the EC Treaty. This legal basis was inserted eventually by the Single European Act in 1987 and implied that national environmental policy and law were not to be replaced by Community action, but merely complemented by it. Since, however, from the very start, the establishment of a common market—in present terminology "internal market"—constituted one of the Community's principal objectives, it soon had to face the question how to integrate environmental requirements with the principles governing the free circulation of goods.[1]

This article addresses the EC's approach to eco-labelling which, over the last two decades, has evolved considerably. There have been a number of environmental labels that have appeared at Community level. It should be noted that their common feature is that they inform consumers and users of the environmental characteristics of products, thereby allowing an informed and considered purchase of those products.

The following examples of EC environmental labels may be mentioned by way of illustration:

— the label "dangerous to the environment" for chemical substances;[2]
— the label "collect separately" for certain batteries;[3]
— the label "organic" for biologically produced agricultural products;[4]
— the progressively introduced energy label informing on energy and water consumption and noise levels of electrical household appliances;[5]
— the label informing consumers about food products containing genetically modified organisms.[6]

---

* Head of Unit, DG IX (now DG Environment), E3, "Waste" of the European Commission. The opinions expressed are personal to the author.

[1] For a full account of this issue, see H. Temmink at p. 61 of this volume.
[2] Dir. 79/831/EEC [1979] OJ L259/10, amending Dir. 67/548/EEC [1967] OJ L196/1.
[3] Dir. 91/157/EC [1991] OJ L78/38, as amended by Dir. 93/86/EC [1993] OJ L264/51.
[4] Reg. (EC) No. 2092/91 [1991] OJ L198/1.   [5] Dir. 92/75/EC [1992] OJ L297/16.
[6] Reg. (EC) No. 258/97 [1997] OJ C43/1.

124   *Ludwig Krämer*

Current subjects of discussion in the Council and the European Parliament are labels for recyclable packaging[7] and the fuel consumption of cars.[8] Schemes to introduce a uniform symbol for environmentally friendly products were first developed at Member State level, in particular in Germany and Sweden. A 1987 request by the European Parliament to create a Community label for clean products in the context of Community waste management policy remained without follow-up.[9] Fearing that the scheme in operation in Germany might pose a threat to the completion of the internal market by 1992, France and the United Kingdom in 1987 called for the introduction of a Community-wide eco-labelling scheme. In response, the Council invited the Commission to submit a proposal for an eco-label scheme,[10] which was eventually adopted unanimously in the Council relatively quickly.[11]

In the second part of this article, the scope of the EC eco-label will be examined. This is followed in Part III by a discussion of some problems of international trade and eco-labelling. Following that, aspects of consumer information (Part IV) and flexibility (Part V) will be considered. Finally, some conclusions about the future of Community eco-labelling are drawn.

II.   The Scope of Regulation (EC) 880/92

The objectives of the EC eco-label award scheme are formulated as follows:

— to promote the design, production, marketing and use of products which have a reduced environmental impact during their entire life cycle;

[7] Commission Proposal [1996] OJ C382/10.   [8] Commission Proposal [1998] OJ C305/2.
[9] Resolution of 19 June 1987 [1987] OJ C190/154.
[10] Resolution of 7 May 1990 [1990] OJ C122/2. Commission Proposal [1991] OJ C75/23, amended by [1992] OJ C12/16.
[11] Reg. (EC) No. 880/92 on a Community eco-label award scheme [1992] OJ L99/1; see W. Bank, *The European Eco-label and International Trade. The Compatibility of the Eco-label with the GATT* (Brussels: European Environmental Bureau, 1995); K. Dawkins, "Ecolabelling: Consumer Right-to-know or Restrictive Business Practice?" in R. Wolfrum (ed.), *Enforcing Environmental Standards: Economic Mechanisms as Viable Means?* (Berlin: Springer, 1996), 501; E. Eiderström, "Ecolabels in EU Environmental Policy" in J. Golub (ed.), *New Instruments for Environmental Policy in the EU* (London–New York: Routledge, 1998), 190; B. Jadot and N. de Sadeleer (eds.), *Le label écologique et le droit* (Brussels: Story Scientia, 1992); B. Jadot, "Les systèmes communautaires d'attribution de label écologique et de management environnemental et d'audit. Une voie d'avenir ou un trompe-l'oeil?" in P. Renaudière and P. van Pelt (eds.), *Développements récents du droit communautaire de l'environnement* (Diegem: Kluwer Editorial, 1995), 111; K. Krisor, "Présentation du règlement concernant un système communautaire d'attribution de label écologique" in B. Jadot and N. de Sadeleer (eds.), *Le label écologique et le droit* (Brussels: Story Scientia, 1992), 27; F. Maniet, "Le label écologique et la protection des consommateurs" in Jadot and de Sadeleer (eds.), above, 89; G. Roller, "Le label écologique allemand: 'l'ange bleu' " in Jadot and de Sadeleer, above, 1; G. Roller, "Der 'Blaue Engel' und die 'Europäische Blume' " (1992) 2 *Europäische Zeitschrift für Wirtschaftsrecht* 499; J. Salzman, *L'étiquetage écologique des produits dans les pays de l'OCDE* (Paris: OECD, 1991); D. Vandermeersch, "Les labels écologiques et les règles de concurrence et de la libre circulation des marchandises au sein de la CEE", in Jadot and de Sadeleer, above 113; T. von Dannwitz, "Umweltzeichen der EG und Umweltzeichen in Deutschland", in H. W. Rengeling (ed.), *Handbuch zum europäischen und deutschen Umweltrecht* (Cologne: Heymann, 1998), 1314; H. Ward, "Trade and Environment Issues in Voluntary Eco-labelling and Life Cycle Analysis" (1997) 7 *Review of European Community & International Environmental Law* 139.

— to provide consumers with better information on the environmental impact of products.[12]

The scheme is voluntary and awarded to applicants on request. The eco-label bears a logo represented by a flower consisting of a corolla of petals in the form of twelve EC stars, encircling an "E" for Europe. The Regulation does not apply to food, drinks, or pharmaceuticals. Although relating exclusively to products, Regulation (EC) No. 880/92 was nonetheless based on Article 175 (formerly Article 130s) EC. It endeavoured to establish uniform criteria for the award of an eco-label, "to apply throughout the Community" and expressly stipulated that "uniform application of criteria and compliance with procedures should be ensured throughout the Community".[13] Simultaneously, however, it stated that "existing or future independent award schemes can continue to exist".[14] This juxtaposition of Community and national eco-labelling schemes obviously is at the expense of efforts to eliminate—real or perceived—barriers to the free circulation of goods stemming from national eco-labelling schemes.

Ecological criteria are to be fixed for product groups. Each product group has to include "all competing products which serve similar purposes and which have equivalence of use".[15] The Regulation itself does not fix any priorities for product groups. Instead, such initiatives emanate from the Commission, either at its own initiative or following a request from a Member State. A Member State may also develop ecological criteria for a specific product group and submit them to the Commission for further consideration. Although such a national initiative is, evidently, not legally binding, it may have a considerable impact on the final form of the Community criteria.

The criteria have to be based on a "cradle-to-grave" approach as defined in Article 1, as well as on a number of general principles for ecological criteria laid down in the Regulation. The specific criteria for a product group are normally fixed for a period of three years and must be precise, clear, and objective so as to ensure their uniform application and a high level of environmental protection.

Before formally submitting a proposal, the Commission consults the principal interest groups of industry and commerce (including trade unions) and consumer and environmental organisations within a consultation forum.[16] The Commission's Proposal is then submitted to a committee, which is composed of the representatives of Member States and chaired by the Commission. In terms of its structure, composition, and procedure, this committee mirrors the committees for the adaptation of Community directives to technical and scientific progress, which are based on Article 202 (formerly

---

[12] Reg. (EC) No. 880/92 [1992] OJ L99/1, Art. 11.

[13] Reg. (EC) No. 880/92 (n. 11 above), recitals 6 and 9.

[14] Reg. (EC) No. 880/92 (n. 11 above) recital 7; this recital, though, continues: "the aim of this Regulation is to create the conditions for ultimately establishing an effective single environmental label in the Community".

[15] *Ibid.*, Art. 5.　　　　　　　　　　　　[16] *Ibid.*, Art. 6.

Article 145) EC, and where Member States' votes are weighed according to Article 205 (formerly Article 148) EC. As a result, no specific requirement exists as to the qualification of the committee's members. When the committee approves a proposal by a qualified majority, the Commission adopts the proposal by decision. If such a majority is not reached, the proposal is submitted to the Council, which decides within three months by qualified majority. Where such a decision has not been taken within that time-span, the decision is taken by the Commission.[17]

The application for the award of an eco-label for a specific product is made by the manufacturer or the Community importer and addressed to the competent body of the Member State where the product is manufactured, first marketed, or imported. This competent body must be independent and neutral and assesses whether the product conforms to the general eco-label principles laid down in the Regulation and to the specific criteria fixed for the specific product group.[18] The decision to award or refuse a label is communicated to the Commission and the other Member States. In case of diverging opinions of different competent bodies, the Commission shall revert to the committee procedure described above.[19] The actual use of the label is the subject of a contract between the competent body and the applicant.[20]

Guidelines have been adopted relating to costs and fees for the application and the award of the label,[21] the use of the eco-label in advertising, and the confidentiality of certain information.

Article 18 of the Regulation stipulates that the Commission should, within five years, review the eco-label scheme in the light of the experience gained and propose appropriate amendments. The Commission made such a proposal at the end of 1996,[22] which at the same time gave insights in the operation of the scheme. At the time of writing, this proposal was still under consideration by the Council and the European Parliament. Its adoption, which is not anticipated before 2000, will probably be under the new Article 175(1) EC to which the co-decision procedure, and hence qualified majority voting, applies.

III. Regulation (EC) No. 880/92 and International Trade

A. BARRIERS TO TRADE

Soon after its adoption, Regulation (EC) No. 880/92 was challenged on the basis of possible conflicts with the provisions of international trade law, although no formal complaints have hitherto been registered. Since participation of producers in the system is voluntary, at first glance such incompatibil-

---

[17] Reg. (EC) No. 880/92 (n. 11 above) recital 7, Art. 7.
[18] *Ibid.*, Art. 9.   [19] *Ibid.*, Art. 10.
[20] See the form of a model contract [1993] OJ L243/13.
[21] See Guidelines for the Fixing of Fees [1993] OJ L129/23.
[22] COM(96)603 of 11 Dec. 1996 [1997] OJ C114/9.

ities may appear unlikely. However, a number of issues need to be addressed before a final judgement can be made.

The first such issue is posed by Article 5 of the Regulation, which provides that "the specific ecological criteria for each product group shall be established using a 'cradle-to-grave' approach". Whereas Regulation (EC) No. 880/92 refers only to products, Article 5 also requires an assessment of the ecological circumstances under which the materials for the product were obtained. Examples are paper kitchen towels, toilet paper, or copying paper, products for which the EC has fixed ecological criteria.[23] During the elaboration of these criteria, the question was discussed whether the paper should contain a certain percentage of recycled paper and whether the fibres of virgin paper had to originate from sustainable forestry. In particular the Brazilian and the American paper pulp industries intensely lobbied the Community against the inclusion of any such criteria, arguing that such a clause would harm sustainable forestry in the Third World and favour European producers.[24] Although the Community rejected these arguments, it is striking that in its recent decisions on paper it no longer expressly requires or favours the use of recycled paper.[25]

It is conceivable that European paper producers use more recycled paper fibres than American producers. Nevertheless, it is difficult to see how such a clause could be discriminating in the sense of the rules of the World Trade Organisation (WTO); the clause applies to all paper, irrespective of its origin,[26] and WTO rules allow states or state organisations to fix their own level of environmental protection as long as this does not amount to discrimination. Any state may therefore provide for measures which afford preference to recycled paper fibres over virgin paper fibres without fear of being accused of discrimination. Indeed, it is a generally recognized objective of EC waste policy to promote the recycling of waste over the use of virgin raw materials. Furthermore, as the EC system is voluntary, and hence paper which contains virgin paper only fibres may be freely imported into the Community, there cannot seriously be any question of direct or indirect discrimination. Also, it should be noted that the notion of "sustainable forestry" is devoid of legal substance, since as yet there are no objective, universally recognized criteria to define the

---

[23] Decision 94/924/EC [1994] OJ L364/24; Decision 94/925/EC [1994] OJ L364/32; Decision 96/467/EC [1996] OJ L192/26; Decision 98/94/EC [1998] OJ L19/77.

[24] Written Questions E–300/93 by Amadeo [1995] OJ C145/40; E–909/95 by Siso Cruellas [1995] OJ C209/31.

[25] See Decisions 96/467/EC and 98/94/EC (n. 23 above).

[26] See, however, Dawkins, n. 11 above, 510: "preferences for recycled paper products over virgin pulp would discriminate against sustainable plantation forestry; it is at least debatable that farmed pulpwood from Brazil could be as ecologically sound as the energy-intensive remanufacture of post-consumer paper and the related disposal of the de-inked wastes in Denmark"; see also 516: "eco-labelling is, by definition, discriminatory".

In my own opinion, there is no discrimination in the legal sense of the term, since access to the Community market is not forbidden or restricted for Brazilian paper; the voluntary eco-label scheme is an added environmental value.

notion.[27] Moreover, Decisions 96/467/EC and 98/94/EC merely require a commitment to respect certain international guidelines on sustainable forestry, but remain vague in terms of their detailed implementation. Claims invoking international trade rules thus seem to have been of a political rather than of a legal nature. This is reflected by the fact that there is hardly any legal literature calling into question the compatibility of Community policy on paper with WTO rules.[28]

At international level, labelling issues arose in the first tuna–dolphin decision involving GATT provisions. In the underlying dispute, the USA had prohibited the import of tuna fish caught with nets which also killed dolphins swimming with the tuna fish. Furthermore, the USA had also allowed tuna fish products sold in the USA to be labelled "dolphin-free", a practice which Mexico challenged on the basis of GATT rules. As regards the label—the other issues need not be discussed here—the GATT dispute resolution panel found, in its decision of 6 September 1991, that the labelling provisions did not contradict GATT rules for the following reasons:

— the label was not mandatory but voluntary. Thus, tuna fish could be sold with or without the label;
— if the label gave any advantage to domestic products, this did not result from governmental intervention, but from the free choice of consumers;
— access to the label was available to Mexican and other countries' manufacturers in the same way as to USA producers.

Although the panel's findings—as well as those of the second tuna panel, which were, as regards labelling, practically identical to those of the first panel—were never officially approved by the GATT authorities, it is submitted that the panel's rulings apply to the Community eco-label scheme, as indeed to most other existing eco-label schemes. Thus, the Community scheme complies with all three conditions which the panel laid down for the legality of a labelling scheme under GATT rules. For the remainder, the tuna–dolphin scenario is not comparable to the Community eco-labelling scheme,[29] as the USA prohibited the import of tuna fish which was caught with particular nets, whereas the Community eco-label scheme has no such direct impact on imports or the free circulation of goods generally.

Although it is neither viable nor desirable to discuss the question whether the Agreement on Technical Barriers to Trade (TBT) could apply to eco-labelling schemes, it is submitted that similar conclusions apply.

---

[27] It should be noted that the Netherlands, some years ago, failed in their attempt to limit the import of tropical wood to such wood which came from sustainable forestry, because no solution was found for determining "sustainable forestry".

[28] Dawkins, n. 11 above, at 569, reports an eco-label standard in the Netherlands, which required a 100% recycled fibre content.

[29] Dawkins, n. 11 above, 518, is of a different opinion.

Another issue which should be addressed relates to Article 6 of the Regulation, pursuant to which the Commission must consult the principal interest groups. Obviously, the representatives of industry and trade at Community level are predominantly Community producers and traders. Hence consultation could indirectly lead to bias in favour of practices which correspond to European production methods. Due to pressure from third countries, the proposal for a revision of Regulation (EC) No. 880/92 therefore provides that producers from third countries may directly ask for the award of an eco-label and that "interested parties inside or outside the Community shall be treated on an equal footing".[30]

Related to the issue of consultation is the more substantive one that eco-label schemes tend to be tailored to domestic products, production standards, and environmental standards.[31] This at the same time explains why Member States favour maintaining national eco-labelling in tandem with the Community scheme. For example, where a state does not produce nuclear energy but obtains a large share of its energy from solar energy, for its eco-scheme it will be inclined to rate the use of solar energy more favourably than nuclear energy. Since there are no internationally recognized methods of undertaking an objective "cradle-to-grave" assessment of products,[32] the criteria to some extent will remain a function of national preferences.

It is for this reason that eco-labelling schemes are likely to continue to occupy an important place in international trade discussions. Third-country producers will fear additional barriers caused by the costs of participation in such schemes, inadequate access to information, exclusion from the selection process for products, and the general lack of transparency.[33]

IV. Consumer Information

A. SIX YEARS OF EXPERIENCE

The EC eco-label scheme has had a difficult take-off. During the first years of its existence, controversies within the Commission on the appropriateness of ecological criteria fixed by public authorities at Community level led to an almost complete paralysis in the development of these criteria. Eventually, the intervention of Member States in the Council resolved the situation by the end of 1994. Nevertheless, the development of ecological criteria progressed only

---

[30] Since the Commission's proposal for a review of the eco-label award scheme (n. 22 above), intended to privatize the labelling award scheme, it did not provide any longer for a consultation procedure of private interests.

[31] See Dawkins, n. 11 above, 503.

[32] The Commission in COM(96)603 (n. 22 above), para. 25, lists 10 ISO standards which are in preparation, concerning environmental labelling and life cycle assessment.

[33] See also Banki, n. 11 above.

slowly, mainly because trade and industry could not muster much enthusiasm for an eco-label favouring the top 10 or 20 per cent of a given product group. Consequently, by the end of 1998, only about 230 products had obtained an eco-label. It can safely be said that consumer awareness of the eco-label thus has been disappointing. The Commission is not a marketing body or economic operator and in the past therefore has done little to promote the use of eco-labels. The proposal for a review of the eco-label scheme suggested privatizing the eco-label scheme and, consequently, requested Member States to promote awareness campaigns for consumers, "specifically aimed at promoting the use of the Community eco-label". Although the Commission itself has not yet undertaken much to promote such campaigns, the need for such marketing measures thus at least seems to be recognized.

B.   COMMUNITY AND NATIONAL ECO-LABELLING SCHEMES

The proliferation of the label is one of the principal disappointments of the Community eco-label scheme, which also competes with national eco-label schemes. Regulation (EC) No. 880/92 proclaimed, however, that "while existing or future independent award schemes can continue to exist, the aim of this Regulation is to create the conditions for ultimately establishing an effective single environmental label in the Community".[34] However, since 1992, the number of national eco-label schemes has increased rather than fallen[35] and the resistance of Member States to abandoning their national schemes continues to be considerable. Some national schemes—the German "Blue Angel", the Scandinavian "Nordic Swan", the Dutch scheme—being much more widely used and better known by consumers than the Community scheme, there may be little incentive to substitute those successful schemes for a less successful one. Also, as has been seen, the national eco-label may be hoped to favour national production, which may be a realistic prospect particularly in the area of food, although Regulation (EC) No. 880/92 does not apply to food and drink.[36]

From a consumer's perspective, however, the proliferation of different eco-label schemes can only be confusing. When a single product bears two, three, or even four different quality labels, the ecological message for the consumer is, to say the least, ambivalent. In addition, nothing prevents a producer of a product not bearing an eco-label from advertising the ecological properties of the product. It is clear that consumers often trust national eco-label schemes more than schemes emanating from international bodies. This is not surprising since, as yet, there exists no true "Community" public opinion, and infor-

---

[34] Regulation (EC) No. 880/92 (n. 14 above), recital 7.

[35] COM(96)603 (n. 22 above), paras. 10 and 19 mentions eco-label schemes in 7 Member States; with the exception of the Scandinavian (1989) and the German (1977) system all these systems were set up after 1991 (France 1992; Netherlands 1992; Austria 1991; Spain 1993).

[36] Reg. (EC) No. 880/92 (n. 12 above), Art. 2. See also Reg. (EC) No. 2092/91 [1991] OJ L198/1, which allows products that come from organic agriculture to bear the label "organic".

mation conveyed by national governments or bodies is therefore also more readily accepted.

The Commission's review proposal did not suggest replacing national eco-label schemes by a single Community scheme, but merely that the former should only apply, after a period of five years, "to product groups for which no specific Community eco-label criteria are established". Thus, wherever ecological criteria are developed at Community level, national criteria will progressively disappear.

The European Parliament agreed to the Commission's proposal. However, it added the requirement that the Community criteria had to be at least as stringent as the most onerous national criteria.[37] This proviso is inspired by past experience at Community level, where ecological standards are the fruit of political compromise of committee members which vote on these standards as governmental representatives.[38] Community decision-making thus does not always guarantee that optimal solutions are found.

C.   PRIVITAZING THE ECO-LABELLING SCHEME

Since the Commission itself does not necessarily possess the required technical and scientific know-how as regards different product groups, the elaboration of studies is of only limited value. It is thus that the ecological criteria for a product group are not, in all cases, optimal from an environmental perspective. The Commission, in its proposal for a review of the scheme, therefore proposed the adoption of the decisions on the ecological criteria, no longer by the Commission itself, but by a European eco-label organization (EEO) which was to be created for this purpose. The EEO was to be composed of the national competent bodies which at present are in charge of awarding the eco-label to a specific product. The EEO would receive mandates from the Commission to elaborate ecological criteria for product groups. The consultation of interested parties, however, was to be undertaken by the Commission, which would publish the criteria once it was satisfied that the terms of the relevant mandate had been complied with. This would have allowed the Commission to approve or reject the results of the EEO's work and thus exert political influence on the elaboration of ecological criteria, even though, overall, the influence of Member States on the eco-label scheme would have been strengthened.

Neither the European Parliament nor the Council found the idea of setting up an EEO attractive. Parliament was of the opinion that the EEO would be too expensive and that the Commission should retain its role as technical co-ordinator and political mediator. It also doubted that Member States' competent bodies would be capable of running the eco-label scheme at Community level autonomously. Parliament thus instead suggested the setting up of a

---

[37] European Parliament, n. 11 above.

[38] This point is stressed by T. von Dannwitz, "Umweltzeichen in der EG und Umweltzeichen in Deutschland" in H. W. Rengeling (ed.), *Handbuch zum europäischen und deutschen Umweltrecht* (Cologne: Heymann, 1998), ch. 40, para. 18.

technical committee by and within the Commission, which should fix the ecological criteria. Members of the committee were to be the national competent bodies and representatives of interested parties. Although, at the time of writing, the Council had not yet decided on the structure of the decision-making body, several Member States expressed the opinion that the Commission could not and should not give up its responsibility for Community decisions on ecological criteria.

D.   GRADED LABELS

The different ecological criteria for products refer to a number of factors[39] with which a product has to comply in order to obtain the label. In its proposal for a reviewed scheme, the Commission suggested a graded label: where a product fulfilled only some of the ecological criteria—but passed a general "minimum test"—it would receive one eco-flower. Where it complied with more criteria, up to three flowers could be awarded. The Commission was of the opinion that this graded label would increase flexibility and provide for better consumer information.[40]

The European Parliament rejected the idea of several flowers, but instead proposed the use of written information on the positive environmental effects of the product.[41] Consumer organizations, too, have expressed doubts about the efficiency of a graded label.[42] Whether the Council and the European Parliament will actually introduce a graded label, is as yet uncertain. The introduction of supplementary written information as well as a logo will require an adaptation of the label to each national language and thus certainly undermine some of the advantages of a Community-wide eco-label.

V.   Flexibility in Regulation (EC) No. 880/92

A.   THE MONITORING BODY

When questions of flexibility, subsidiarity, and proportionality are at issue, the first enquiry should certainly be whether an eco-label scheme which is set up and run by Community public authorities is desirable at all. Thus, one could argue, in particular, that the decision on such a scheme be left to market forces. Examples are differentiated taxation—as is the case, for example, with leaded petrol—rules on the composition and make-up of products, labelling requirements, information and education measures, etc. Compared to some of these measures, which are clearly more interventionist, an eco-label involv-

---

[39] See, for instance, Decision 98/488/EC [1998] OJ L219/42 on soil improvers, which fixed criteria for heavy metal concentrations, nutrient loadings, general labelling, product performance, salmonella content, and nuisances.

[40] Commission COM(96)603 (n. 22 above), para. 28.

[41] Opinion of the European Parliament [1998] OJ C167/118.

[42] See Opinion by the Economic and Social Committee (ESC) [1997] OJ C296/77, para. 3.1.

ing a supplementary public quality award to environmentally less harmful products and which limits this award to the top 15 per cent, 20 per cent or 25 per cent of products of a given product group, appears an appropriate instrument to promote the objectives of environmental policy. Since the Community revolves around the maintenance of an internal market where goods circulate freely, it seems mistaken to rely on considerations of subsidiarity to hold that eco-labelling schemes should be set up only at national level. On the contrary, different ecological criteria for identical product groups or a refusal to grant an eco-label to a product which has already received an eco-label in another Member State inevitably leads to confusion and is counter-productive from an environmental as well as from an internal market perspective.

The Commission's proposal for Member States' competent eco-labelling bodies to monitor and run the Community eco-labelling scheme is not justifiable either, at least not by virtue of the principle of subsidiarity. Indeed, hitherto, no precedent exists for formal Member State structures organizing environmental matters at Community level. The only body which could be considered in this respect is IMPEL, an inter-governmental co-operation network which deals with environmental implementation questions. However, this network is informal, has no decision-making function, and has not been set up by any legal Community decision. Moreover, in view of Article 175 EC, the implementation of Community environmental law belongs to Member States' competence. It would hence constitute a completely new development, if Community environmental structures were taken care of by Member States at Community level at the expense of Community institutions or bodies.

B. LEGAL BASIS

Considerations of flexibility certainly prevailed when Article 175 EC rather than Article 95 EC was chosen as a legal basis for Regulation (EC) No. 880/92. The Regulation concerns products, and one of its objectives is to create, in the long term, a Community-wide uniform eco-label scheme. The "centre of gravity" theory, which governs the question of the correct legal basis for secondary EC environmental law,[43] does not appear to support this outcome, since Regulation (EC) No. 880/92 is predominantly a product-related measure. Neither is it readily conceivable for Member States to fix more stringent ecological criteria pursuant to Article 176 EC for a product group, once there is a Community decision on ecological criteria for this product group. The question whether national eco-schemes should be allowed to co-exist is not a problem related to the legal basis, as legislation based on Article 95 (formerly Article 100a) EC may also provide for minimum harmonization. The Commission's proposal not to allow other national eco-labelling criteria for those product groups for which Community ecological criteria have been

---

[43] See in more detail L. Krämer, *EC Treaty and Environmental Law* (3rd edn., London: Sweet & Maxwell, 1986), at 86 ff.

fixed also points at the direction of progressively introducing a Community wide eco-labelling scheme.[44]

In conclusion, the choice of Article 175 EC as the legal basis demonstrates the importance attached to maintaining a maximum amount of national flexibility in controlling the impact of Regulation (EC) No. 880/92.

C. OTHER EXAMPLES OF FLEXIBILITY

The minimum provisions laid down in the Regulation have not been complemented by other Community provisions. For instance, there are no indications to suggest that public authorities involved in public procurement should have a bias in favour of products with an eco-label. Neither have the Community institutions taken any steps to favour, in their own purchasing decisions, eco-labelled products or to promote the use of eco-labelled products in other ways.

Another attempt to introduce even more "flexibility" into the system was the proposal to introduce a graded label, which in part has already been discussed above. No final decision has yet been taken by the Community institutions, but it appears that the idea already has been abandoned by the Commission. A graded label, where up to three flowers are given on the basis of the different environmental criteria (noise, energy consumption, water use, etcetera) certainly allows more information to be conveyed than at present is the case. The question remains whether more information helps or rather confuses consumers and whether it allows producers to comply more easily with the scheme's requirements. Producers might prefer a graded system, if it allows them to obtain the eco-label more easily, in other words where the standards are relaxed. However, for the purpose of lowering of standards, a graded label is not indispensable. At present a graded eco-labelling scheme does not exist anywhere in the world.

The Commission's proposal also contains other provisions designed to introduce greater flexibility into the eco-labelling scheme, such as the possibility of reviewing the ecological criteria after three years (which allows the validity period to be prolonged according to the circumstances), allowing access to the scheme also for retailers of products which are marketed under their own trade name, the introduction of an indicative assessment matrix for the ecological criteria,[45] and reduction of the fees for the attribution of the label. These aspects will not be discussed here, since their final incorporation into the Community eco-labelling scheme as yet is uncertain.

---

[44] [1992] OJ L99/1 (n. 11 above), Art. 11.

[45] COM(96)603 (n. 22 above) Annex I: "a product shall be assessed before the production, at the production, at distribution, at use and at reuse, recycling or disposal; the assessment shall concern air quality, water quality, soil protection, reduction of waste, energy saving , management of natural resources, prevention of warming up of the atmosphere, protection of the ozone layer, environmental safety, noise and protection of the ecosystems".

VI. Conclusion

From this summary analysis of the Community eco-labelling scheme, it appears that its legal framework is largely appropriate for the objectives it is designed to serve and, in any event, is on the point of being amended so as to fulfil these functions. Trade-related problems are minor and also the information which is conveyed to consumers and users is, by and large, adequate.

Two interrelated issues should be considered. On the one hand, the Community eco-label is a label which *not only* aims at achieving a high level of environmental protection. Indeed, Article 5 of Regulation (EC) No. 880/92 points out that the determination of ecological criteria shall be based on the use of clean technology "as far as possible" and that these shall reflect "where appropriate" the desirability of maximizing product life. This wording illustrates that the commitment to pursuing a high level of environmental protection is not absolute. This is reflected by the Commission's publications, on the basis of which it appears doubtful that between 10 and 15 per cent of a given product group could actually obtain the eco-label.

The Community eco-labelling scheme obviously also suffers from the fact that it is hardly known. The award of approximately 250 eco-labels in six years clearly is unsatisfactory, a state of affairs which will have to change in the future. The Commission has in the past done too little to promote the eco-label. The reluctance from industry and trade associations to support a system which benefits only a small part of their members has not been compensated for by individual companies participating in the eco-scheme. Any such doubts about the quality of the EC eco-label may undermine its chances of succeeding. In addition, in a number of Member States, where consumers and users might be ready to buy and use products that are equipped with an eco-label, the Community scheme has to compete with national systems which are not integrated into the national administration and are hence perhaps perceived as more neutral and objective.

This last aspect invites the question whether a Community body which monitors the eco-system and which is perceived as less political than the European Commission could serve to reinvigorate the scheme. Current efforts by the Commission to have the scheme monitored by the national competent bodies which are neutral and independent point in this direction. An alternative option would be to attribute this task to the European Environmental Agency in Copenhagen, set up in 1990.[46] Regulation (EC) No. 1210/90 expressly provides, in Article 20, that in the future the question will be considered whether the Agency should take over such tasks. In its proposal for the review of the eco-labelling scheme, however, the Commission rejected this idea.[47] It argued that the Agency possessed neither the necessary structures nor the expertise, and that its internal decision-making procedures were not adequate for the eco-labelling scheme. These arguments in themselves are not

---

[46] Reg. (EC) No. 1210/90 [1990] OJ L120/1.   [47] COM(96)603 (n. 22 above), para. 34.

compelling since a simple amendment of the Regulation could provide for the necessary structure and also ensure co-operation between national competent bodies and Community authorities. In the long term, such a solution could prove more promising than the scheme proposed by the Commission.

Yet, this summary examination should not obscure the fact that, in the final analysis, the problematic reception of the Community eco-labelling scheme may merely reflect the reality that as yet, and despite emerging notions of European citizenship, concepts of "Community" public opinion or "European" consumers, on which ultimately the success of a European eco-label scheme rest, remain unrealized.

Judicial Review of Environmental Misconduct in the European Community: Problems, Prospects, and Strategies

I. Introduction

Courts have always been central to the success of the "new legal order" created by the treaties founding the European Community. In particular, the constitutional method of construction employed by the European Court of Justice[1] secured the establishment of a "federal" legal system,[2] and one which was characterized by the enjoyment by private parties of expansive bundles of rights when enforcing Community law in national courts. This has been crucial in securing the effective application of Community law at Member State level, by facilitating the recruitment of domestic courts as principal organs in safeguarding the faithful implementation of EC rules and policy.

This article will canvass some of the contemporary initiatives of the European Court which are aimed at ensuring the full enforcement of EC rules in Member State legal systems, and assess their utility for private parties seeking full application of EC environmental directives in national law. [3] In particular, the European Court of Justice is instituting ever tighter control over Member State remedies and procedural rules that are attached to claims based on Community law, which includes the development of Member State liability in damages for breach of measures vesting individuals with rights. It will be illustrated here that these developments afford Member State judges an

* Assistant Director, Centre for European Legal Studies, Cambridge. Fellow of Magdalene College, Cambridge.

[1] For a classic criticism of this case law, see E. Stein, "Lawyers, Judges, and the Making of a Transnational Constitution" (1981) 75 *American Journal of International Law* 1.

[2] For a further classic study of the constitutional foundations of the EC see J. H. H. Weiler, "The Community System: The Dual Character of Supranationalism" (1981) 1 *Yearbook of European Law* 267.

[3] I will not be examining the impact of well known notions such as the doctrine of direct effect or sympathetic interpretation, as their role in the enforcement of EC environmental measures has been ably documented elsewhere. See in particular L. Krämer, "Direct Effect of EC Environmental Law", in H. Somsen (ed.), *Protecting the European Environment: Enforcing Environmental Law* (London: Blackstone, 1996), 99.

enhanced opportunity to set aside barriers to the effective enforcement of environmental directives when they are breached by government authorities. Further, one recent Court of Justice decision suggests that rules pertaining to Member State remedies and procedural rules may also apply in cases in which one private party seeks to enforce a directive against another, the so-called "horizontal" scenario for application of directives in national law. If this were so, this case law might be prayed in aid by applicants seeking an effective remedy when a directive laying down environmental standards is breached by a private sector actor.

It will be further argued that, somewhat paradoxically, these developments carry the potential to highlight shortcomings in the Community legal system when it comes to the opportunity for private parties to bind Community institutions to their constitutional duty to integrate environmental protection requirements when formulating other Community policies. This is a relatively new development, given that the obligation of Article 174 (formerly Article 130(r)) EC, was first inserted into the EC Treaty in the 1986 Single European Act, and it was only then that failure to take account of environmental implications became a self-evident ground of review of Community legislation.[4]

The difference between standards of protection afforded to private parties, when challenging Community, as opposed to Member State, misconduct, was illustrated for the first time in *Greenpeace*,[5] in which the Court of Justice denied standing under Article 230(4) (formerly Article 173(4)) EC to three environmental interest groups and several private citizens who wished to challenge a Commission decision to fund the construction of two power plants in the Canary Islands.[6] The developer of the power stations had failed to institute an environmental impact study in alleged breach of Directive 85/337/EEC on the Assessment of the Effects of Certain Public and Private Projects on the Environment,[7] with potential culpability on the part of the Commission arising

---

[4] See the Opinion of Cosmas AG in Case P–321/95, *Stichting Greenpeace Council* v. *Commission* [1998] ECR I–1651 (hereafter referred to as *Greenpeace*), para. 62, where he asserts that Art. 230(2) (ex Art. 174(2)) EC imposes "on the Community institutions a specific and clear obligation which could be deemed to produce direct effect in the Community legal order", and that provisions on the EC Treaty concerning the environment are not "mere proclamations of principle".

[5] Case P-321/95, *Stichting Greenpeace Council* v. *Commission* [1998] ECR I–1651.

[6] The alleged decision to disburse a tranch of 12 million Euros to fund the project was made pursuant to a Decision (which in turn had been made pursuant to Council Reg. (EEC) No. 1787/84 on the European Regional Development Fund [1984] OJ L169/1, as amended by Council Reg. (EEC) No. 3641/85 [1985] OJ L350/40) granting Spain financial assistance from the European Regional Development Fund (ERDF), up to a maximum of 108,578,419 Euros, to build the power stations. The payments were to be made in four tranches. The applicants challenged the second of these payments. Note that the *Greenpeace* case was the second attempt by an environmental group to challenge Commission funding for projects which had been approved which breached environmental standards. The first, however, failed due to the absence of a clear decision on the part of the Commission declining to review assistance already provided to the relevant project. Issues pertaining to standing, and the applicants' right to an effective remedy, were not addressed in the case. See Case T–461/93, *An Taisce—The National Trust for Ireland and WWF UK* v. *Commission* [1994] ECR II–733, which was unsuccessfully appealed to the ECJ as Case C–325/94 P, *An Taisce—The National Trust for Ireland and WWF UK* v. *Commission* [1996] ECR I–3727.

[7] [1985] OJ L175/40 (hereafter referred to as the Environmental Assessment Directive).

from both Article 174 (formerly Article 130r(2)) EC, and its further elaboration in Article 7 of Council Regulation (EEC) No. 2052/88 on the tasks of the structural funds and their effectiveness and on co-ordination of their activities.[8] However, despite the global trends towards expanding opportunities for public interest environmental groups (including developments of this kind in the national courts of Member States), the European Court of Justice adhered to its traditional, somewhat restrictive, interpretation of Article 230(4) EC[9] and denied the applicants' standing to sue. It would therefore seem, at this early stage, that the movement towards close scrutiny of rules which impede access to justice in Member State courts, in cases concerning the failure of Member State government authorities to comply with EC law, has not yet influenced Court of Justice policy in the context of effective judicial review under Article 230(4) EC.

Finally, a brief discussion will ensue of a further development in the case law which tends to immunize Community institutions from public accountability for decisions affecting the natural environment. This concerns *WWF UK*[10] in which the Court of First Instance vested private citizens with only a restricted right of access to information concerning possible infringement of Community law by Member States.[11] This means that there will continue to be restricted public accountability for Commission decisions to refrain from bringing Article 226 (formerly Article 169) EC proceedings against Member States for alleged breach of EC environmental law.

II. Enforcement of EC law Through National Courts: Current Developments and their Relevance to Environmental Litigation

As is well known, all organs of Member State government, including judicial bodies, are bound under Article 10 (formerly Article 5) EC to secure that obligations arising under the EC Treaty are implemented in good faith.[12] It is beyond doubt that this general duty applies in full to enforcement of Community environmental measures. The ethos that underpins this principle rests, at least in part, on the need for uniform enforcement of Community law throughout the Member States. An example of its operation in the context of

---

[8] [1988] OJ L185/9.

[9] Under Art. 230(4) (ex Art. 177(4)) EC decisions which are not addressed to private parties, including all measures of a general nature, can only be challenged if they are "of direct and individual concern" to the applicant. This provision has been interpreted in a notoriously conservative fashion, with seminal cases including Case 25/62, *Plaumann* v. *Commission* [1963] ECR 95; Joined Cases 789 and 790/79, *Calpak* v. *Commission* [1980] ECR 1949. For two prominent commentaries criticizing the case law see C. Harlow, "Towards a Theory of Access for the European Court of Justice" [1992] *Yearbook of European Law* 213 and Arnull, "Private Applications and the Action for Annulment under Article 173 of the EC Treaty" (1995) 32 *Common Market Law Review* 1.

[10] Case T-105/95 *WWF UK (World Wild Life Fund for Nature)* v. *Commission* [1997] ECR II–313. For a case commentary see P. Kunzlik (1997) 9 *Journal of European Law* 321.

[11] Decision 94/90/EC on public access to Commission documents [1994] OJ L46/58.

[12] This provision was held to apply to courts in Case C–106/89, *Marleasing* [1990] ECR 4156.

EC environmental law emerged relatively recently, in a well-known Court of Justice decision concerning Directive 79/409/EEC on the Conservation of Wild Birds (the Birds Directive).[13] In this case, the Court of Justice firmly subjugated economic interests to the imperative of conservation of bird life,[14] with Advocate General Fennelly advising the Court of Justice that Member States should be prevented from interpreting the Directive in a way that would generate an economic advantage (when compared with environmentally diligent Member States) through failure to comply with ecological obligations.[15]

One of the areas in which the Court of Justice has crafted particularly imperative rules concerns Member State remedies and procedural rules. In short, there has been a general, if not entirely consistent, shift in Court of Justice case law towards disapplication of national remedies and procedural rules which render Community law impossible in practice or excessively difficult to enforce (the principle of effectiveness), or which afford a less favourable remedy than that which would apply to analogous claims of a purely domestic nature (the principle of non-discrimination).[16] Further, it will be shown, these principles, taken together, have rather assumed the appearance of a rule of thumb, as it is becoming difficult to predict which types of domestic sanctions and procedural rules will breach its parameters. It is my submission, therefore, that the prevailing uncertainty in the law carries the potential to empower national judges, particularly in the context of EC environmental law. Given the propensity, for example, of obstructive rules on standing, restrictive time limits, and awkward rules on the computation of damage (to name but a few problems) to thwart judicial enforcement of EC environmental directives, Court of Justice rulings which have led to disapplication of obstructive

---

[13] [1979] OJ L103/1.

[14] Case C–44/95 *Regina* v. *Sec. of State for the Environment, ex parte Royal Society for the Protection of Birds* [1996] ECR I–3805. See also commentary by J. D. C. Hart (1997) 9 *Journal of European Environmental Law* 168, and footnote by Gerd Winter, 179–80.

[15] Case C–44/95, n. 14 above, 3839–41. See further Hart, n. 14 above, 174.

[16] See, e.g., Case 45/76, *Comet BV* [1976] ECR 2043; Case 33/76, *Rewe* [1976] ECR 1989. Note that Member States are entitled to attach criminal penalties to enforcement of a directive, provided that the principles of effectiveness and non-discrimination are respected, and that it is proportionate and dissuasive. For an example of the operation of this principle in the context of the disposal of waste, see Joined Cases C–58/95, C–75/95, C–112/95, C–119/95, C–123/95, C–135/95, C–140/95, C–141/95, C–154/95, and C–157/95, *Criminal proceedings against Sandro Gallotti and Others* [1996] ECR I–4345. Numerous academic commentaries have been written on ECJ regulation of Member State remedies and procedural rules. See, e.g., J. Lombay and A. Biondi, *Remedies for Breach of EC Law* (Chichester: Wiley, 1997); M. Andenas and F. Jacobs, *European Community Law in English Courts* (Oxford: Oxford University Press, 1998); Prechal, "Community Law in National Courts" (1998) 35 *Common Market Law Review* 681; W. van Gerven, "Bridging the Gap Between Community and National Laws: Towards a Principle of Homogeneity in the Field of Legal Remedies" (1995) 32 *Common Market Law Review* 679; A. Ward, "Effective Sanctions in EC Law: A Moving Boundary in the Division of Competence" (1995) 2 *European Law Journal* 205; B. Fitzpatrick and E. Szyszczak, "Remedies and Effective Judicial Protection in Community Law" (1994) 57 *Modern Law Review* 434; D. Curtin and Mortelmans, "Application and Enforcement of Community Law by the Member States: Actors in Search of a Third Generation Script" in D. Curtin and T. Heukels (eds.), *Institutional Dynamics of European Integration* (Dordrecht: Martinus Nijhoff Publishers, 1994); E. Szyszczak, "European Community Law: New Remedies, New Directions?" (1992) 55 *Modern Law Review* 215.

national rules concerning sanctions and procedures could be a particularly powerful tool in the hands of the private petitioner. Liberal interpretation by national judges of Court of Justice case law in this field could overcome some of the most tenacious barriers to the award of a judicial remedy to correct environmental wrongs.

In addition, as mentioned above, suggestions are emerging in the case law of attenuation of the prohibition on horizontal enforcement of directives, which might prove particularly useful in claims in which victims of breach of EC environmental law seek a direct remedy against the perpetrator of environmental misconduct, as opposed to a government agency which has breached a regulatory duty. This development has arisen in a Court of Justice ruling concerning the availability of "effective remedies" for breach of Directive 76/207/EEC on the Implementation of the Principle of Equal Treatment for Men and Women as Regards Access to Employment, Vocational Training, and Promotion, and Working Conditions (Equal Treatment Directive)[17] by a private-sector actor.[18] Its possible ramifications in environmental litigation will be discussed in detail below.

A.   COURT OF JUSTICE REVIEW OF OBSTRUCTIVE MEMBER STATE REMEDIES AND PROCEDURAL RULES

Since the mid-1980s, the Court of Justice has been increasingly inclined to order the disapplication of Member State remedies and procedural rules for breach of its guidelines in this field. In particular, frequent recourse has been made to the principle of effectiveness, and indeed the vast majority of cases in which national law was found wanting have concerned breach of this rule.[19] As a result, the Court of Justice has, in effect, set aside a large number of rules emanating from the domestic plane that might have otherwise frustrated effective enforcement of individual rights.

Some examples will illuminate this point. In the *San Giorgio*[20] decision, the Court of Justice ruled that an onerous rule of evidence enshrined in Italian law rendered recovery of an unlawfully levied charge excessively difficult, and therefore incompatible with the EC Treaty. In the landmark *Johnston*[21] decision, it was held that the right to a judicial remedy to enforce rights based on EC law was a fundamental principle of the Community legal system, and that a United Kingdom (UK) law that hampered judicial review of the Equal Treatment Directive breached this principle. In *Cotter and McDermott*,[22] an Irish prohibition on unjust enrichment which would have allowed the state to escape payment of benefits in breach of the Directive concerning equal

---

[17] [1976] OJ L39/40.   [18] Case C–180/95, *Draehmpaehl* v. *Urania* [1997] ECR I–2195.

[19] Note however, that the *Draehmpaehl* case, *ibid.*, is also of importance in that the principle of non-discrimination is discussed (and applied) by the ECJ.

[20] Case 199/82, *Amministrazione delle Finanze dello Stato* v. *San Giorgio* [1983] ECR 3595.

[21] Case 222/84, *Johnston* v. *Chief Constable of the Royal Ulster Constabulary* [1986] ECR 1651.

[22] Case C–377/89, *Cotter and McDermott* v. *Minister for Social Welfare and Attorney-General* [1991] ECR I–1155.

treatment in matters of social security, failed when tested against the principle of effectiveness. While the well-known *Emmott*[23] case prevented the same government from escaping its responsibilities with respect to the same Directive by reference to national time limit for bringing proceedings. It was held in *Emmott* that, until a directive had been properly transposed, applicants would be uncertain about the scope of their rights. Therefore, the Irish limitation period for bringing proceedings could not begin to run until the Equal Treatment Directive had been implemented in Irish law.

French law was found wanting in the *Deville* decision,[24] when the Court of Justice held that a national legislature may not, following a judgment from the Court of Justice confirming that domestic legislation was incompatible with the EC Treaty, adopt a procedural rule which specifically reduced the possibility for recovery of illegally levied charges. Later, it was held in the *Peterbroeck*[25] case that a Belgian time-limit on the raising of new arguments on appeal could not be applied to new arguments based on Community law that had not been heard at first instance. While the *Van Schijndel*[26] case suggested that any domestic rule in the Netherlands that obliged courts or tribunal to raise points of law of their motion must also apply when binding rules of Community law were relevant to a case. Finally in *Fantask*[27] a Danish rule pertaining to "excusable error", which would have allowed the taxation authorities to evade the duty to refund a charge levied in breach of an EC directive, was held to render Community law impossible in practice to enforce.

Some of the principles cited above have been subject to adjustment in subsequent Court of Justice case law. In particular, it now seems clear that, contrary to the findings in the *Emmott*[28] case, reasonable time-limits for bringing proceedings will not normally precipitate breach of the principle of effectiveness,[29] nor is it certain that Member State rules prohibiting unjust enrichment will always fall foul of the principle.[30] However, the trend toward closer Court of Justice review of Member State remedies and procedural rules remains

---

[23] Case C–208/90, *Emmott* v. *Minister for Social Welfare* [1991] ECR I–4269.

[24] Case 240/87, *Deville* v. *Administration des Impôts* [1988] ECR 3513. For a more recent and detailed discussion of the *Deville* principle see, e.g., Case C–343/96, *Nitexport Srl* v. *Amministrazione delle Finanze dello Stato*, judgment of 9 Feb. 1999, not yet reported.

[25] Case C–312/93 [1995] ECR I–4599.

[26] Joined Cases C–430/93 and C–431/93 [1995] ECR I–4705.

[27] Case C–188/95 [1997] ECR I–6783.   [28] See n. 23 above.

[29] On the basis of the *Fantask* case (n. 27 above) it would seem that the *Emmott* prohibition on the application of national time limits in cases involving unimplemented directives will only operate when a Member State government has discouraged the applicant from bringing proceedings in good time. This is supported by, e.g., Joined Cases C–279/96, C–280/96, and C–281/96, *Ansaldo Energia and others*, Case C–231/96, *Edis* v. *Ministero delle Finanze*, Case C–260/96, *Ministero delle Finanze* v. *Spac SpA* (not yet reported judgments of the ECJ of 15 Sept. 1998).

[30] National rules prohibiting unjust enrichment of traders seeking repayment of unlawfully levied charges were upheld in Case C–212/94, *FMC* [1996] ECR I–389. For a more detailed deliberation on this point see Cases C–192–218/95, *Comateb* [1997] ECR I–1655. See generally P. Dougan, "Cutting your Losses in the Enforcement Deficit: A Community Right to the Recovery of Unlawfully Levied Charges" in A. Dashwood and A. Ward (eds.), *The Cambridge Yearbook of European Legal Studies* 1 (1998), 233.

potent, and carries significant consequences in the field of Community environmental directives.

Their effect, in plain terms, is as follows. It is beyond doubt that the above principles apply to environmental directives that satisfy the preconditions for direct effect. So, for example, if enforcement of a directive of this kind[31] were being frustrated by an unreasonably short limitation period, restrictive rules on standing,[32] or an evidential rule which favoured an authority which was opposed to judicial application of an environmental directive, the principle of effectiveness could be invoked, and result in the disapplication of the relevant obstructive rule.

One Court of Justice case concerning environmental law has already raised this issue, and the ruling of the Court pointed to the award of a remedy when it may not otherwise have been available under national law. In *Kraaijeveld*[33] the applicants sought the annulment of a decision of the South Holland Provincial Executive, in which approval had been given to a modification to zoning plans concerning dyke reinforcement. The problem in terms of procedural law lay in the fact that the applicants had failed to invoke Directive 85/337/EEC on the Assessment of the Effect of Certain Public and Private Projects on the Environment,[34] a measure which tended to suggest that the project in issue could not proceed in the absence of an environmental impact study. Instead, the national judge raised concerns over the relevance of the Directive to the case. There was some doubt, therefore, whether the national court seised of the dispute was empowered to raise points of Community law of its own motion.

After interpreting the scope of the Directive, and concluding that projects of the kind described by the national court fell within its terms, it was decided that the Dutch government had failed properly to implement the Environmental Assessment Directive.[35] The Court of Justice intimated that the relevant provisions of the Directive vested individuals with rights[36] before

---

[31] The difficulty of proving direct effect with respect to environmental directives is discussed by Krämer, n. 3 above. He argues, e.g., at 123–4 that, despite contrary indications in the ruling of the ECJ in Case C–236/92, *Difesa della Cava* [1994] ECR I–485, Art. 4 of Dir. 75/442/EEC on waste ([1975] OJ L194/39) will ordinarily have direct effect.

[32] For detailed discussion see Geddes, "Locus Standi and EEC Environmental Measures" (1992) 4 *Journal of European Law* 29. For a discussion of recent developments in the French courts, in which restrictive national laws were disapplied to secure proper enforcement of the Birds Directive n. 13 above; see P. Cassia and E. Saulnier, "La loi du 3 juillet 1998 sur la chasse et le droit communautaire: 'error communis facit jus'?", *Europe* No. 7, 1999; E. Saulnier, "La loi du 3 juillet 1998 sur la chasse et le droit communautaire: 'error communis facit jus'?", *Revue de Droit Rural* No. 275, Aug.–Sept. 1999, forthcoming.

[33] Case C–72/95, *Aannemersbedrijf P.K. Kraaijeveld BV and others* v. *Gedeputeerde Staten van Zuid-Holland* [1996] ECR I–5403.

[34] [1985] OJ L175/40.   [35] See in particular paras. 21–53.

[36] See n. 4 above, para. 56. Elmer AG, in terms which were more imperative than those employed by the ECJ, concluded that Art. 2(1) of the Directive had direct effect. See in particular paras. 64–74 of the Opinion. The direct effect of Arts. 2, 3, and 8 of the Environmental Assessment Directive was upheld by the ECJ in Case C–431/92, *Commission* v. *Germany* [1995] ECR I–2189. See the Opinion of Cosmas AG in *Greenpeace*, n. 4 above, para. 58 of his Opinion. Note that the direct effect of relevant provisions of the Environmental Assessment Directive was not contested by the Commission in *Greenpeace*. See para. 35 of the Opinion of Cosmas AG.

turning to the relevance of the applicant's failure to raise the Directive in proceedings before the national court. The Court of Justice, after reminding the national court of its Article 10 (formerly Article 5) EC duty "to ensure the legal protection which persons derive from the direct effect of provisions of Community law"[37] cited, *inter alia*, the *Van Schijndel*[38] ruling in support of the following proposition:

where, pursuant to national law, a court must or may raise of its own motion pleas in law based on a binding national rule which were not put forward by the parties, it must, for matters within its jurisdiction, examine of its own motion whether the legislative or administrative authorities of the Member State remained within the limits of their discretion under Articles 2(1) and 4(2) of the Directive, and take account thereof when examining the action for annulment.[39]

The *Kraaijeveld*[40] case neatly illustrates the utility of recourse to Court of Justice rulings concerning Member State remedies and procedural rule in order to secure effective enforcement of EC environmental measures. It suggests that national judges are bound to take account of environmental directives that vest individuals with rights, even if they have not been alluded to by the parties. This principle will apply, at the very least, when national law contains a facility for judges to raise points of law of their own motion.

In addition, Court of Justice rulings concerning Member State remedies and procedural rules have generated, in the hands of private parties, an entitlement to the award of two specific remedies before national courts. It is now beyond doubt that natural and legal persons that do have the right to enforce unimplemented environmental directives on the domestic plain will also be entitled to an interim order to protect their claim, even if this would not ordinarily be available under the domestic law of the Member State in which the case is brought.[41] Secondly, all EC rules that vest individuals with rights are susceptible to challenge under the rules formulated by the Court of Justice concerning Member state liability in damages for breach of EC law.[42]

---

[37] Opinion of Cosmas AG, para. 58.　　[38] N. 26 above.　　[39] *Ibid.*, para. 60.
[40] N. 33 above.
[41] Case C–213/89, *The Queen* v. *Secretary of State for Transport, ex parte Factortame Limited and others* [1990] ECR I–2433.
[42] Joined Cases C–6/90 and C–9/90, *Francovich and Bonifaci and others* v. *Italian Republic* [1991] ECR I–5357; Joined Cases C–46/93 and C–48/93, *Brasserie du Pêcheur SA* v. *Germany* and *The Queen* v. *Sec. of State for Transport, ex parte Factortame and others* [1996] ECR I–1029 (hereafter referred to as *Brasserie du Pêcheur*); Case C–392/93, *The Queen* v. *HM Treasury, ex parte British Telecommunications plc* [1996] ECR I–1631; Joined Cases C–178/94, C–179/94, C–188/94, C–189/94, and C–190/ 94, *Dillenkofer* v. *Federal Republic of Germany* [1996] ECR I–4845 (hereafter referred to as *Dillenkofer*); Case C–5/94, *The Queen* v. *Ministry of Agriculture, Fisheries and Food, ex parte Hedley Lomas Ireland* [1996] ECR I–2553 (hereafter referred to as *Hedley Lomas*). For commentaries on this case law see, e.g., W. van Gerven, "Bridging the Unbridgeable: Community and National Torts Law after Francovich and Brasserie" (1996) 45 *International and Comparative Law Quarterly* 507; Convery, "State Liability in the United Kingdom after Brasserie du Pêcheur" (1997) 34 *Common Market Law Review* 603; case commentary on state liability cases by P. Oliver (1997) 34 *Common Market Law Review* 635.

The ramifications of the state liability rules in the field of environmental law have been well documented elsewhere.[43] However, it is submitted that several points merit emphasis, especially in the context of the capacity of the rule to enhance the discretion of national judges to secure rigorous enforcement of EC environmental measures. Under the principles enunciated by the Court of Justice, state liability for damages will be activated under the following circumstances:

— when there has been a breach of EC law vesting individuals with rights;
— the breach of the law is sufficiently serious; and,
— there is a causal link between the breach of the law and the damage sustained.[44]

Domestic rules relating to state liability, including procedural rules, will continue to operate under this rubric, provided that they do not render Court of Justice rules on this topic impossible or excessively difficult to enforce, and provided that they are not less favourable than the rules that would apply in analogous domestic claims for damages.[45] However, the Court of Justice has squarely rejected the idea that domestic concepts of fault which go beyond the parameters of those implied by the state liability case law can have any role to play in the award of damages for breach of individual rights.[46] That being so, private parties seeking compensation for loss arising from failure of Member States to implement individual rights enshrined in environmental directives will no longer be required to overcome difficulties inherent in domestic rules requiring proof of fault on the part of the wrongdoer.[47]

A further notable feature of the three-part test is that compensation is payable not only for EC measures that satisfy the conditions for direct effect, but also for measures which vest individuals with rights, even though the Court of Justice has provided no clear indication of how this distinction might be drawn.[48] Therefore, national judges will be entitled to consider the award of compensation for all EC environmental directives of this kind. Therefore, it seems likely, on the basis of the *Kraaijeveld*[49] ruling, that breach of Articles 2(1) and 4(2) of the Environmental Assessment Directive will be susceptible to review for damages, as will any other environmental directive which vests individuals with rights, even if it is not directly effective.[50] Equally, the Court of

---

[43] H. Somsen, "Francovich and its Application to EC Environmental Law", in H. Somsen (ed.), n. 3 above.

[44] *Brasserie du Pêcheur*, n. 42 above, para. 368.

[45] *Ibid.*, para. 67. See also *Hedley Lomas*, n. 42 above, para. 31.

[46] *Brasserie du Pêcheur*, n. 42 above, para. 79.

[47] Note also that domestic rules on damages that supply more generous levels of protection will not be displaced by Community law principles on state liability. See *Brasserie du Pêcheur*, n. 42 above.

[48] The distinction was introduced into the case law in *Francovich*, n. 42 above. See generally Oliver, n. 41 above.

[49] N. 33 above.

[50] For a review of EC directives that may attract state liability in damages see H. Somsen, n. 3 above, 144–9.

Justice has held that Directive 80/68/EEC on the Protection of Groundwater Against Pollution Caused by Certain Dangerous Substances[51] is directly effective,[52] which suggests that breach of its terms could activate an action for damages in national courts.

In addition, the Court of Justice has confirmed that a total failure to implement a directive amounts *per se* to a serious breach of a Member State's obligations under the EC Treaty.[53] Equally, therefore, complete failure to implement an environmental directive that vests individuals with rights will be sufficient to ground a claim in state liability. With respect to adequate implementation of directives, the Court of Justice has provided a series of factors which national judges are entitled to take into account when deciding whether a sufficiently serious breach has arisen.[54] One of these factors warrants special emphasis, as it will be of critical importance to actions for damages concerning breach of EC environmental law.

It has been held that national judges should take account, *inter alia*, of the attitude of the Commission in deciding whether or not misconduct on the part of Member States is sufficiently grave to warrant a claim for damages.[55] Thus far actions brought by the Commission against Member States under Article 226 EC for breach of their duty to implement environmental directives have been the most important mechanism for securing compliance. Now, however, that they have assumed new significance. A judgment from the Court of Justice confirming breach of Article 10 EC and Article 249 EC implementation duties will provide powerful evidence before national courts that misconduct on the part of Member States is "sufficiently" serious to support a claim in damages under the state liability principles.[56]

In addition, Commission Decision 94/90/EC introducing a Code of Conduct on Public Access to Commission and Council Documents[57] carried great potential to assist such claims, as the Code of Conduct vests citizens with an entitlement to information concerning a wide range of Commission activities. If private parties were able to obtain information under the Code of Conduct which indicated that the Commission had been of the view that breach of an implementation duty was serious, but that it had refrained from bringing Article 226 EC proceedings for reasons unrelated to the gravity of the breach, the opinion of the Commission could be tabled as evidence in an action for damages instituted by private parties before Member State courts.[58] However, as will be illustrated in section III below, the ruling of the Court of First Instance in *WWF UK*[59] has confirmed that the Code of Conduct has been

---

[51] [1980] OJ L20/43.

[52] Case C–131/88, *Commission* v. *Germany* [1991] ECR I–825. See also the discussion by Cosmas AG in *Greenpeace*, n. 4 above, para. 54 of the Opinion.

[53] See in particular *Dillenkofer*, n. 42 above.

[54] *Brasserie du Pêcheur*, n. 41 above, para. 56.   [55] *Ibid.*

[56] Case C–237/90, *Commission* v. *Germany* [1992] ECR I–5973; Lenz AG in Case C–337/89, *Commission* v. *United Kingdom* [1992] ECR I–6103 suggested that the ruling to the effect that the UK had failed to fulfil the obligations arising out of the Drinking Water Directive could provide a basis for damages.

[57] N. 11 above.   [58] N. 10 above.   [59] N. 10 above.

restricted, in some respects, to a requirement to give adequate reasons. This has limited its utility for private parties seeking information on why the Commission has refrained from bringing proceedings under Article 226 EC. This development, therefore, may have adverse consequences in terms of collation of evidence to prove that a Member State breach of Community law is "sufficiently serious" in actions for damage brought by private parties through Member State courts.

Finally, the most awkward stumbling block to obtaining a remedy in damages for breach of EC environmental law rests with the issue of causation of damage. The Court of Justice had held that this third element of the state liability rules is a matter for the exclusive decision of domestic judicial authorities, and one which should be determined entirely by reference to national law.[60] It is submitted that Community-wide rules on state liability are unlikely to be of any utility in enforcing directives that are designed to preserve endangered species or to protect ecosystems. For example, a private citizen seeking damages for failure of a Member State properly to implement the Birds Directive[61] would have difficulty in proving that they suffered any quantifiable loss, that was directly caused by the Member State's breach of its Community obligations. Similarly, even if an applicant were able to prove a sufficiently serious breach of the Environmental Impact Assessment Directive, flexibility at the national level on the concept of "damage" would be required before an applicant would be in a position to make use of Community state liability rules.

This may not, however, be an insurmountable difficulty. For example, Advocate General Elmer argued in the *Kraaijeveld*[62] case that Article 6(2) of the Environmental Impact Assessment Directive vests individuals with a directly enforceable right to express their opinion on projects which are likely to have adverse effects on the environment. It is quite conceivable that denial of this right could occasion loss to an applicant, especially if they have a strong "individual relationship" with the territory affected.[63] Persons who had enjoyed, over a long period of time, "a quality of life" which might be severely affected by the grant of planning permission[64] may be able to quantify this loss, and convince a national judge that it is recoverable under the state liability principles. Equally, loss of revenue from tourism activities, a lowering in the value of real estate, or an adverse effect on local industries

---

[60] *Brasserie du Pêcheur*, n. 42 above, para. 65. See also *Hedley Lomas*, n. 42 above, para. 30. But see, more recently, Case C–319/96, *Brinkmann Tabak fabriken GmbH* v. *Skatteministeriet*, judgment of 24 Sept. 1998, not yet reported, in which the ECJ took jurisdiction over the causation issue.

[61] N. 13 above. Note that the ECJ has held that Art. 9 of the Birds Directive has direct effect. See Case C–118/94, *Associazione Italiana per il WWF* v. *Regione Veneto* [1996] ECR I–1233, and the opinion of Cosmas AG in *Greenpeace*, n. 4 above, para. 55.

[62] N. 4 above, para. 70 of his Opinion. See also the Opinion of Cosmas AG in *Greenpeace*, n. 4 above, paras. 58 and 59.

[63] Cosmas AG in *Greenpeace*, n. 4 above, para. 107, argued in favour of assessing an applicant's "individual relationship" with the contested act in deciding whether standing to review environmental measures should be granted under Art. 230(4) EC.

[64] *Ibid.*, para. 108.

might be viewed by national courts as "damage" that falls within the rubric of state liability principles.[65]

In addition, there may be substantial scope for instituting state liability claims in the event of serious breach of directives laying down quality standards for air and water.[66] If, for example, a citizen were to sustain some form of physical harm as a result of a Member State's failure properly to implement Directive 80/68/EEC on the Protection of Groundwater Against Pollution Caused by Certain Dangerous Substances[67] (a measure which, as noted above, has been held to be directly effective), they should have less difficulty in proving that the damage sustained was caused by the failure of the Member State to observe its duties under the EC Treaty.

B.   CONTEMPORARY MODIFICATION OF THE PROHIBITION ON HORIZONTAL DIRECT EFFECT OF DIRECTIVES

Additional support for private parties seeking the enforcement of EC environmental directives in national courts can be found in a recent case concerning horizontal direct effect of directives. As is well known, in the early 1990s, the European Court of Justice unequivocally scuppered speculation that its case law had evolved to a point which vested national judges with authority to enforce unimplemented EC directives in actions of a purely private nature. It had been argued that, due to the development of the doctrine of sympathetic interpretation, the obligations on Member State judges to interpret national law in conformity with EC directives (in so far as it was possible to do so)[68] meant that horizontal direct effect of directives was being introduced "by the back door".[69] However, in 1994, the Court of Justice ruled in the seminal

---

[65] Note that these were the interests invoked by the individual applicants in *Greenpeace*, but which failed to vest them with individual concern under Art. 230(4) EC. See in particular the Opinion of Cosmas AG, paras. 110–113.

[66] There are numerous directives in these fields. See, e.g., Council Dir. 80/778/EEC relating to the quality of water intended for human consumption [1980] OJ L229/1; Dir. 79/869/EEC concerning methods of measurements and frequencies of sampling and analysis of surface water intended for the abstraction of drinking water [1979] OJ L271/44; Dir. 76/464/EEC on pollution caused by certain dangerous substances discharged into the aquatic environment [1976] OJ L129/3.

[67] [1979] OJ L20/43.

[68] See, in particular, Case 14/83, *von Colson* [1984] ECR 1891; Case 79/83, *Dorit Harz* [1984[ECR 1921; Case C–106/89, *Marleasing* [1990] ECR 4135. For a discussion of the operation of the doctrine of sympathetic interpretation in the context of an environmental directive, see Case C–202/94, *Criminal Proceedings Against Godefridus van der Feesten* [1996] ECR I–355; Case C–44/95, *Regina* v. *Secretary of State for the Environment, ex parte Royal Society for the Protection of Birds*, n. 14 above; Case C–168/95, *Arcaro* [1996] ECR I–4705 (which confirms that the doctrine of sympathetic interpretation cannot be used in order to aggravate criminal liability); Case C–379/92, *Peralta* [1994] ECR 3453; Joined Cases C–304/94, C–330/94, C–342/94, and C–224/95, *Tombesi and Others* [1997] ECR I–3561.

[69] See, e.g., Meade, "The Obligation to Apply European Law: Is Duke Dead?" (1991) 16 *European Law Review* 490; Emmert and Periera de Azevedo, "L'effet horizontal des directives et la jurisprudence de la CJCE: un bâteau ivre?" (1993) 29 *RTDE* 503. For the most detailed study of the effect of dirs. in national law see S. Prechal, *Directives in European Community Law—A Study of Directives and Their Enforcement in National Courts* (Oxford: Oxford University Press, 1995).

Faccini Dori[70] case that the rule on sympathetic interpretation was not absolute. It was held that if the doctrine could not afford an adequate remedy in actions in which one private party sought to enforce a directive against another, the party suffering loss due to inadequate implementation should sue the defaulting Member State for damages under the state liability principle.

The prohibition on horizontal direct effect of directives has ramifications in the environmental sector in the field of civil liability. If a private party were to breach, for example, a directive concerning water or air quality, and the relevant directive had not been properly transposed into national law, individuals suffering loss as a result should sue the relevant Member State for damages, rather than seek redress in a civil suit against the entity which has acted in breach of rules laid down in directives.

These principles, however, may have been modified in a 1997 case concerning equal treatment between men and women. The plaintiff in *Draehmpaehl* v. *Urania*[71] sought reparation for damage allegedly suffered as a result of discrimination on grounds of sex, in breach of Articles 2 and 3 of the Equal Treatment Directive.[72] The dispute concerned discrimination in the context of appointment to a vacant post. Mr Draehmpaehl had made an unsuccessful application for a position that was advertised by the defendant in terms which indicated that only women need apply for the vacant post.

Mr Draehmpaehl was of the view that, due to the refusal of Urania to engage him, he had suffered discrimination on grounds of sex, in access to employment. He therefore brought proceedings before the *Arbeitsgericht Hamburg*, where it was indeed held that the substance of his claim had been made out. The Arbeitsgericht had no difficulty in reaching the conclusion that the advertisement posted by the defendant was not gender-neutral, as it was clearly addressed to women. However, the case became more complicated when it came to the quantum of damages payable to Mr Draehmpaehl. While German law correctly reflected Articles 2 and 3 of the Equal Treatment Directive by preventing employers from discriminating against workers on grounds of sex,[73] the remedy proffered by German law may have been wanting. Mr Draehmpaehl was entitled to recover only three months' wages by way of compensation, which he argued to be inadequate in order to secure his rights under the Equal Treatment Directive.

The Court of Justice had some sympathy with this view, and, consistently with past cast law, held that a national ceiling on the payment of damages would be incompatible with Community law, provided that Mr Draehmpaehl would have been appointed to the position, but for the discriminatory advertisement.[74] More interesting for present purposes, however, was the failure of the Court of Justice to address the issue of horizontal direct effect of directives. It might be assumed that this was crucial to the case, given that Mr

---

[70] Case C–91/92 [1994] ECR I–3325.   [71] N. 18 above.   [72] [1976] OJ L39/40.
[73] Para 611a(1) of the *Bürgerliches Gesetzbuch* (hereafter referred to as the German Civil Code).
[74] N. 18 above, paras. 32–34.

Draehmpaehl was seeking enforcement of the Equal Treatment Directive against a private-sector actor. However, rather than refer to this case law, the Court of Justice recalled that Member States are obliged to supply an effective remedy to enforce EC directives,[75] and that Member States are bound to guarantee that real and effective judicial protection is afforded by domestic sanctions that are utilized to secure enforcement of directives.[76]

Therefore, *Draehmpaehl* v. *Urania* provided significant, albeit subtle, developments in the law on enforcement of directives in domestic legal systems. It suggested that, in some circumstances, private parties will be entitled to invoke the Community right to an effective remedy to enforce rights enshrined in a directive when their claim is brought, not against an emanation of the state, but against a private legal entity.[77]

The ruling of the Court of Justice in the *Draehmpaehl* case might prove a useful weapon in the hands of individuals seeking an adequate remedy for breach of EC environmental law. The case may mean that if a private undertaking has failed to meet standards laid down in an environmental directive individuals and other legal entities suffering loss as a result thereof should be entitled to call on the *Draehmpaehl* ruling in support of an action against the perpetrator. A strict interpretation of the case would suggest that, even in actions involving private parties *inter se*, national judges will be required to disapply any national rules which prevent the award of a remedy which secures real deterrent effect against breach of directly effective directives.[78]

III. Challenging Acts of Community Institutions in the Context of EC Environmental Law

A.   PRIVATE PARTIES AND INDIVIDUAL PETITION TO THE COURT OF FIRST INSTANCE

In contrast to promising developments that have occurred with respect to judicial review before national courts, private parties continue to confront difficulties when seeking an effective remedy, when they challenge unlawful

---

[75] N. 18 above, paras. 24–26.   [76] *Ibid.*, para. 24.

[77] For a detailed commentary on the case see A. Ward, "New Frontiers in Private Enforcement of EC Directives" (1998) 23 *European Law Review* 65.

[78] Cf *Arcaro*, n. 68 above, in which the ECJ expressly held, in the context of a case concerning criminal enforcement of an environmental directive, that "a directive may not by itself create obligations for an individual and that a provision of a directive may not therefore be relied upon as such against such a person": at 4729 of the ruling. Note that, more recently, the ECJ ruled in Case C–185/97, *Coote* v. *Granada Hospitality Ltd.*, judgment of 22 Sept. 1998, not yet reported, that it was answering questions on judicial protection in the context of a horizontal action between private parties "for the purposes of *interpreting* national provisions transposing the directive" (emphasis added, at para. 19). It is submitted, however, that the *Coote* case does not preclude the possibility that the right to an effective remedy is a general principle of law that operates independently of the doctrine of direct effect. See P. Dougan, "The Equal Treatment Directive, Remedies and Direct Effect", *European Law Review* (forthcoming); A. Ward, *Judicial Review and the Rights of Private Parties EC Law* (Oxford: OxfordUniversity Press, 2000).

conduct of Community institutions, whether such misconduct concerns failure to protect the natural environment or some other type of wrong. In particular, restrictive rules on standing which operate under Article 230(4) EC,[79] subsisting problems with the action for validity instituted before national courts, and the tight parameters of Article 288(2) (formerly Article 215(2)) EC non-contractual liability of Community institutions[80] have tended to frustrate private parties seeking to call EC institutions to account for allegedly unlawful conduct.

This case law is beginning to have ramifications in the field of environmental law, most notably due to the Article 174 EC obligation on EC institutions to integrate environmental protection requirements in other fields of Community policy. This duty has been reflected in secondary Community legislation, such as Article 7 of Regulation (EEC) No. 2052/88 concerning Community structural funds.[81] It provides that the institutions are bound, in dispersing these funds, to comply with "the provisions of the Treaties, with the instruments adopted pursuant thereto and with Community policies, including those concerning environmental protection".[82] This means that a Community institution that acts in violation of this duty may be sued under European administrative law.[83] However, while Community institutions and Member States enjoy an automatic entitlement to bring claims of this kind before the Court of Justice,[84] the same is not true for private parties. The difficulties facing private parties seeking judicial review before the Court of Justice and the Court of First Instance came to the fore last year in the *Stichting Greenpeace* case.[85]

Three environmental interest groups, and private citizens describing themselves variously as local residents, farmers, fishermen, and owners of tourism operations in the Canary Islands, sought the annulment, under Article 230 EC, of a Decision of the EC Commission releasing certain structural funds to support the construction of two power stations in the Canary Islands. They argued that the Commission had breached Regulation (EEC) No. 2052/88, in that the funds were released in the absence of institution of environmental impact studies, which in turn precipitated infringement of the Environmental Impact Assessment Directive. However, before these issues could be examined, the applicants were obliged to satisfy highly restrictive rules on *locus standi* that are imposed on private parties under the fourth paragraph of Article 230 EC.

---

[79] For a detailed discussion see Arnull, n. 9 above, and Harlow, n. 9 above.

[80] For cases laying down foundation principles on Art. 288(2) EC liability, see Case 5/71, *Zuckerfabrik Schöppenstedt* v. *Council* [1971] ECR 975; Joined Cases 83, 94/76, 4, 15, 40/77, *HNL* v. *Council and Commission* [1978] ECR 1209; Case 238/78, *Ireks-Arkady* v. *Council and Commission* [1979] ECR 2955. For a most detailed account of Art. 288(2) EC case law see T. Heukels and A. McDonnell (eds.), *The Action for Damages in Community Law* (The Hague–Boston, Mass.–London: Kluwer Law International, 1997).

[81] [1988] OJ L185/9.   [82] *Ibid.*

[83] For the most detailed study of this topic see J. Schwarze, *European Administrative Law* (London: Sweet & Maxwell, 1992).

[84] Art. 230(1) EC.   [85] N. 4 above.

The Court of Justice has, for many years, made a highly restrictive interpretation of the words "individual concern" which appear in Article 230(4) EC. With respect to all EC measures, save for decisions which are specifically addressed to the applicant, private parties are obliged to prove that they belong to a "closed category".[86] If, on the other hand, the impugned measure affects the applicant in only "a general and abstract fashion and, in fact, like any other person in the same situation"[87] they will be denied standing to sue. Moreover, the Court of Justice has also held that:

The possibility of determining more or less precisely the number or even the identity of the persons to whom a measure applies by no means implies that it must be regarded as being of individual concern to them, as long as it is established that such application takes effect by virtue of an objective legal or factual situation defined by the measure in question.[88]

The test for individual concern has been satisfied in only a small number of cases,[89] despite repeated calls for liberalization of standing rules under Article 230(4) EC.[90]

Unfortunately the applicants failed to satisfy the test for standing under Article 230(4) EC, nor was the Court of Justice sympathetic to submissions that the provision's rules should be changed to allow for public-interest environmental litigation. First, in the context of the standing of the individual citizens who sought to challenge the Commission's decision, counsel for the applicants had called on the Court to refrain from applying restrictive case law on standing that had been formulated in the context of "economic issues and economic rights",[91] and that account needed to be taken of "the nature and specific character of the environmental interest underpinning the action".[92] To this the Court of Justice replied that a Community decision concerning the financing of power stations only indirectly affected rights arising under the Environmental Impact Assessment Directive,[93] which implied that, if any "special" rule were to be formulated to reflect the peculiarities of this sector, it would not apply to the case at hand. This might be taken as a finding that the applicants had failed to prove that the decision to finance the power stations was not of "direct" concern to the applicants, which is a further requirement of Article 230(4) EC.[94]

Secondly, cogent submissions were made to the effect that the restrictive approach to standing exercised by the Court of First Instance and the Court of

---

[86] e.g. Joined Cases 789 and 790/79, *Calpak* v. *Commission* [1980] ECR 1949. See also n. 9 above.

[87] *Greenpeace*, n. 4 above, para. 28.

[88] See, e.g., Case C–209/94 P, *Buralex* [1996] ECR I–615, para. 24; and Case C–264/91, *Abertal and Others* v. *Council* [1993] ECR I–3265, para. 16.

[89] e.g. Case 11/82, *Piraiki-Patraiki and others* v. *Commission* [1985] ECR 207; Case C–152/88, *Sofrimport* v. *Commission* [1990] ECR I–2477; Case C –309/89, *Codorniu SA* v. *Council* [1994] ECR I–1853.

[90] See, e.g., Arnull, n. 9 above, and Harlow, n. 9 above.

[91] N. 4 above, para. 17.

[92] *Ibid.*

[93] *Ibid.*, para. 31.

[94] On direct concern see, e.g., Case 69/79, *Alcan* v. *Commission* [1970] ECR 385; *Piraiki-Patraiki*, n. 89 above. Cf the Opinion of Cosmas AG in *Greenpeace*, n. 4 above, para. 64, where he indicates the requirements of direct concern were satisfied.

Justice conflicted with (i) trends in the case law of the Member States (and decisions of one foreign jurisdiction), which were increasingly sympathetic to public interest environmental litigation;[95] (ii) declarations on environmental matters made by Community institutions and Member State governments on environmental matters;[96] (iii) affirmations in Court of Justice case law itself, in which it had been held that environmental protection is "one of the Community's essential objectives",[97] and that Community environmental legislation can create rights and obligations for individuals;[98] and (iv) developments in international law favouring preservation of the natural environment.[99] These submissions, however, were not alluded to by the Court of Justice in its ruling.

Thirdly, the applicants proposed an alternative interpretation of the fourth paragraph of Article 230 EC. For actions in which breach of environmental obligations is in issue, it was suggested that the applicant should be required to demonstrate that:

— he has personally suffered (or is likely personally to suffer) some actual or threatened detriment as a result of the allegedly illegal conduct of the Community institution concerned, such as a violation of his environmental rights or interference with his environmental interests;
— the detriment can be traced to the act challenged; and
— the detriment is capable of being redressed by a favourable judgment.[100]

The Court of Justice, however, continued to apply a restrictive approach to the issue of individual concern. It was held that "where, as in the present case, the specific situation of the applicant was not taken into consideration in the adoption of the act, which concerns him in a general and abstract fashion, and, in fact, like any other person in the same situation, the applicant is not individually concerned by the act".[101]

---

[95] *Greenpeace*, n. 4 above, para. 20. The foreign jurisdiction referred to was the USA, with reference being made to *Sierra Club* v. *Morton*, 405 US 727, 31 L Ed.2d 636 643 (1972). The applicants argued that if their claim had been brought in any one of the Member States it would have been declared admissible. They relied on the Final Report on Access to Justice (1992) prepared by the ÖKO-Institute for the Commission in support for this contention. On the liberal interpretation of the Canadian equivalent to "direct and individual concern" by its Federal Court see McLeod-Kilmurray, "*Stichting Greenpeace* and Environmental Interest before the Community Judicature: Some Lessons from the Federal Court of Canada" in A. Dashwood and A. Ward (eds.), *Cambridge Yearbook of European Legal Studies* 1 (1998) 269.

[96] *Greenpeace*, n. 4 above, para. 21.

[97] *Ibid.* See also Case 240/83, *Procureur de la République* v. *Association de Défense des Brûleurs d'Huiles Usagées* [1985] ECR 531, para. 13, and Case 302/86, *Commission* v. *Denmark* [1988] ECR 4607, para. 8.

[98] *Ibid.*, see, e.g., Case C–131/88, *Commission of the European Communities* v. *Federal Republic of Germany* [1991] ECR I–0025.

[99] *Ibid.*, para. 22. The applicants referred, *inter alia*, to the Fifth Environmental Action Programme ([1993] OJ C138/1), principle 10 of the Rio Declaration, ratified by the Community at the UN Conference of 1992 on Environment and Development, to Agenda 21, adopted at the same conference, the Council of Europe Convention on Civil Liability for Damage resulting from Activities Dangerous to the Environment.

[100] No. 4 above para. 23.   [101] *Ibid.*, para. 28.

But perhaps the most troubling aspect of the Court's decision was the manner in which it dealt with arguments pertaining to the rights of the applicant to an effective judicial remedy. It had been contended that the approach that had been adopted by the Court of First Instance had created a legal vacuum since environmental interests were by their very nature common and shared. Given that those interests are liable to be held by a potentially large number of individuals, there could never be a "closed class" of applicants who would satisfy the traditional test for individual concern.[102] Moreover, the applicants argued that the possibility of bringing proceedings in Spanish courts for inadequate enforcement of the Environmental Impact Assessment Directive did not cure access-to-justice difficulties, as such proceedings bore no relation to the unlawful conduct of Community institutions in disbursing structural funds in violation of an obligation to protect the environment.[103]

The Court of Justice, however, concluded that, even if the applicants were denied standing under Article 230(4) EC, they would not be denied effective judicial protection.[104] It noted that the applicants had brought proceedings before Spanish courts that were aimed at correcting the failure of Spanish government authorities to enforce the Environmental Impact Assessment Directive, and that therefore both these domestic actions and the claim for Article 230 EC review were based on the same rights. That being the case, it was concluded that "those rights are fully protected by national courts which may, if need be, refer a question to this Court for a preliminary ruling under Article 234 (formerly Article 177) EC".[105]

It is respectfully submitted that this finding is grounded on false premises. While it is true that the substantive rights asserted by the applicant before both courts were similar, the solution proffered by the Court of Justice left them with a remedy against only one perpetrator of unlawful conduct, namely Spanish government authorities. Community institutions, on the other hand, have been granted scope to breach statutory duties to comply with environmental standards, safe in the knowledge that it will be nearly impossible for private parties to contest their conduct directly before the Court of First Instance. Further, the abovementioned refusal of the Court of Justice to take account of developments unfolding at the national level, in which Member State courts are increasingly inclined to grant standing to private citizens to enforce environmental protection measures, creates a dangerous double standard, and at the very least an impression that the notion of "effective judicial protection" is taken more seriously by Member State courts than in Community courts. The anomaly is further compounded by the fact that, as was illustrated in section II, the applicants have a veritable battery of arguments at their disposal in actions brought before national courts to correct Member State breach of environmental measures, which would include

---

[102] N. 4 above, para. 18.   [103] *Ibid.*, para. 19.   [104] *Ibid.*, para. 32.
[105] *Ibid.*, para. 33. Cf the Opinion of Cosmas AG who argued in paras. 71–75 that the availability of a remedy under national law in no way acted as a bar to *locus standi* under Art. 230(4) EC.

litigation brought before Spanish courts for government breach of the Environmental Impact Assessment Directive.

Finally, the Court of Justice rejected submissions that would have vested the three environmental interest groups with standing.[106] It was held, in keeping with past case law, that the members of these associations were not individually concerned by the measure.[107]

While Advocate General Cosmas in *Greenpeace* also advised against granting standing to sue under Article 230(4) EC in the circumstances before him, he advanced views that were more sympathetic to public-interest environmental litigation than the ruling adopted by the Court of Justice. Even though the Advocate General asserted that Community law did not recognize an *actio popularis* in environmental matters,[108] and that the applicants were not entitled to challenge the premise that the fourth paragraph of Article 230 EC, as interpreted by the Court of Justice, should not apply to claims concerning preservation of the environment,[109] he nonetheless observed that the Court of Justice had seen fit in the past "to ease the procedural obstacles, when the specific nature of a case so requires, for the sake of affording more comprehensive judicial protection".[110] The Advocate General shared the view that the three environmental interest groups should not be vested with special standing rights under Article 230(4) EC,[111] but formulated a test which would allow certain private citizens standing to sue under Article 230(4) EC when challenging measures passed by EU institutions that are detrimental to the natural environment. He argued that it is possible for a Community act affecting the environment to impact on both an open and closed class of individuals, with the latter being comprised of persons who are geographically proximate to the intervention in the environment,[112] or who are gravely affected by it in a manner which distinguishes them from others.[113] For the Advocate General, the critical factor in defining this closed class was the applicants' "individual relationship to the contested act".[114] He concluded, however, that the individual applicants in the case at hand had failed to satisfy this test, as they had only vaguely relied on the fact that they lived "very close" to the construction sight

---

[106] For a summary of these submissions see the Opinion of Cosmas AG, paras. 116–117. Note that it was held in Case C–142/95 P, *Associazione Agricoltori della Provincia di Rovigo and Others* v. *Commission* [1996] ECR I–6669 that local residents did not enjoy a right to participate in proceedings concerning a Commission decision approving funding for the protection of residents and the natural environment of a specific region in Italy. On this basis they were denied standing to sue to review the decision.

[107] N. 4 above, para. 29. Past cases in which this principle has been upheld include Joined Cases 67/85, 68/85, and 70/85, *Van der Koy and others* v. *Commission* [1988] ECR 219; Case C–313/90, *CIRFS and others* v. *Commission* [1993] ECR I–1125.

[108] *Greenpeace*, n. 4 above, para. 53 of the Opinion.

[109] No. 4 above, para. 76 of the Opinion.

[110] *Ibid.*, para. 68. The AG cited Case 294/83, *Les Verts* [1986] ECR 1339 in support of this proposition.

[111] *Ibid.*, paras. 114–118.   [112] *Ibid.*, para. 104.

[113] *Ibid.*, para. 106. The AG cited Case C–358/89, *Extramet Industrie* v. *Council* [1991] ECR I–2501, and *Codorniu*, n. 88 above, in support of this proposition.

[114] *Ibid.*, para. 107.

of the power plants, and had failed to show why effects on arable production, fishing, and tourism would be so severe as to vest them with a right to standing. Equally general and abstract, said the Advocate General, were the applicants' claims that harm to health would result from the project.[115]

It would seem, therefore, that amendment to Article 230 EC will be necessary if private parties are to be entitled to bind Community institutions, through judicial channels, to their duty to take account of environmental ramifications when elaborating Community policies. This contrasts markedly with the policy pursued by the Court of Justice in the context of its case law concerning Member State remedies and procedural rules, with respect to which the Court of Justice was equally bereft of a mandate in the foundation treaties to elaborate detailed principles. The plain meaning of these texts has thus failed to deter the Court of Justice from making deep incursions into national law in the field of Member State remedies and procedural rules, and these principles have obliged national courts to exercise a great deal of ingenuity, and even create new remedies that would not otherwise exist under national law. Given that the Court of Justice has asserted that effective judicial protection is a "fundamental right" in the Community legal order,[116] and the high standards required of Member States in the context of compliance with environmental measures, it may be viewed as somewhat surprising that the Court withdrew from taking a more innovative approach in the *Greenpeace* case.

Further, it is respectfully submitted that the action for validity under Article 234 (ex Article 177) EC is an imperfect remedy, and one that fails to ensure that Community institutions will be held responsible at the judicial level if they fail to comply with Article 174 EC and secondary legislation which reflects its terms. First, applicants are only entitled to question the validity of a Community rule if there is a national measure in place which implements it.[117] Such a measure may not exist in all cases, and indeed in *Greenpeace* it was by no means clear that Spanish authorities had promulgated a measure which the applicants could have challenged at the domestic level in order to contest the validity of the Commission decision releasing structural funds.[118] Secondly, even if such a measure did exist, national judges do not have the authority to declare a Community measure invalid, and must instead refer a question to the Court of Justice under Article 234 EC if they have serious doubts about the validity of the measure.[119] At the very most, national judges are entitled to issue an interim order (but this is discretionary)[120] which means that applicants can wait for up to two years for an order of the Court of Justice declaring a measure invalid. Thirdly, Advocate General Cosmas in the *Greenpeace* case argued that the protection afforded by national courts in validity proceedings is not as far-reaching and comprehensive as that avail-

---

[115] N. 4 above, para. 112. [116] *Johnston*, n. 21 above.

[117] For a detailed discussion see the Opinion of Tesauro AG in Case C–63//89, *Les Assurances du Crédit* v. *Council and Commission* [1991] ECR 1–799.

[118] See the Opinion of Cosmas AG, n. 4 above, para. 74.

[119] Case 314/85, *Foto-Frost* [1987] ECR 4199.

[120] e.g. Joined Cases C–143/88 and C–92/89, *Zuckerfabrik* [1991] ECR I–415.

able under Article 234 proceedings. This was so because the former "could not extend to cover the issue of legality of the financing *per se* or *a fortiori*, lead to the setting aside of the Commission decision to continue financing".[121] Nor is an action for damages under Article 288(2) (formerly Article 215(2)) EC a practical solution. The Court of Justice has intimated in the past that it will be reluctant to entertain actions claiming damages against Community institutions, which are in principal designed to contest the legality of Community measures. Such actions are more properly brought through national courts under the validity mechanism, or under Article 230(4) EC when standing so allows.[122]

B.   PRIVATE PARTIES AND ACCESS TO INFORMATION ON COMMISSION DECISIONS CONCERNING INFRINGEMENT PROCEEDINGS

Finally, Court of Justice case law has fallen short of providing an absolute guarantee that Commission investigations into possible Member State breach of EC environmental measures are conducted under conditions of transparency. In the one decision in which the Court has been called on to interpret Commission Decision 94/90/EC on Public Access to Commission Documents in the context of a complaint concerning EC environmental law, the Decision was read conservatively, and in a manner which guaranteed that negotiations that precede the adoption of Article 226 EC proceedings are undertaken under conditions of secrecy.

In *WWF UK*,[123] the applicants sought the release of documents held by the Commission concerning an investigation into an alleged breach of EC environmental law by the Irish government, who had sought Commission support via EC structural funds to build a visitors' centre in a national park. A Commission Decision giving the green light to the project had been unsuccessfully challenged by the applicants (*inter alia*), due to an unsurprising failure to satisfy the rules on standing under Article 230(4) EC.[124] They therefore sought further information under Decision 94/90/EC concerning the Commission's approval of the relevant project. This in turn was refused, so the applicant sought a second action for annulment, this time on the basis of the decision refusing access to documents.

While the Court of Justice confirmed that Decision 94/90/EC conferred on third parties' legal rights which the Commission was bound to respect,[125] it drew a distinction between documents which protect the public interest (including Commission investigations) and those which protect the interests of the Commission in ensuring confidentiality of its internal deliberations.[126] It was only with regard to the latter type of document that the Commission was

---

[121] N. 4 above, para. 74 of the Opinion.   [122] See *Les Assurances du Crédit*, n. 117 above.

[123] N. 10 above. For a detailed commentary on the case see Kunzlik, n. 10 above, 333 ff.

[124] Case T–461/93, *An Taisce and WWF UK* v. *Commission* [1994] ECR II–733; Case C–325/94 P, *An Taisce and WWF (UK)* v. *Commission* [1996] ECR I–3727.

[125] N. 10 above, para. 55.

[126] These are the two exceptions laid down in the Decision to an entitlement to access to documents of EC institutions.

held by the Court to be required to strike a balance between the interests of the citizen in obtaining access to those documents, and its own interests in protecting the confidentiality of deliberations. With regard to the "public interest" concerning documents relating to investigation into a possible breach of Community law, the Court held that the Commission was only required to indicate the reasons for which the documents detailed in the request for information were related to possible infringement proceedings.[127] If the Commission has satisfied this duty, and has supplied adequate reasons,[128] it seems likely that applicants will be refused any further information.

The secrecy with which the Commission conducts investigations has been subject to wide criticism, not least of which has emanated from the House of Lords Select Committee on the European Communities, which has lamented the difficulty in following the progress of complaints made to the Commission, let alone the problem of accessing enough information to engender confidence in how they are being handled.[129] One commentator has echoed this criticism in more strident terms. It has been suggested that the conferral of EU citizenship by the Maastricht Treaty might have carried a concomitant expectation that such citizens might have a right to participate in, and expect greater transparency from, the work of EC institutions. This was said to be particularly important in the context of environmental issues, in which Commission investigations can play a pivotal role in the ignition of public debate.[130] The rules formulated by the Court of Justice in *WWF UK*, however, provide only flimsy support for these ambitions. Further, as has already been noted, information supplying an indication of the Commission's view on the seriousness of a Member State breach of EC environmental measures would be most useful to private parties wishing to bring a claim for damages in national courts with respect to such a breach.

IV. Conclusion

Therefore, as can be seen from the above discussion, there is a great deal of scope for national judges to harness principles that have been formulated by the Court of Justice in order to maximize enforcement of EC environmental measures at the national level. Both rigorous rules pertaining to the adequacy of Member State remedies and procedural rules, and new developments concerning sanctions that might attach to horizontal enforcement of directives,

---

[127] N. 10 above, para. 64.

[128] Note, however, that it was held in *WWF UK* that the Commission had, on the facts of that case, breached its duty to provide adequate reasons under Art. 253 EC. The principles and approach of *WWF UK* have subsequently been affirmed. See, e.g., Case T–124/96, *Interporc Im- und Export GmbH* v. *Commission*, CFI judgment of 6 Feb. 1998; Case T–14/98, *Heidi Hautala* v. *Council*, CFI judgment of 19 July 1999.

[129] Ninth Report on "Implementation and Enforcement of Environmental Legislation" Session 1992–3, HL Paper 53–1. Cited by Kunzlik, n. 10 above, 338.

[130] Kunzlik, n. 10 above, 336.

will assist the Member State judge who is minded to subject obstructive domestic principles to close review for breach of higher norms of Community law. In particular, the formulation of specific remedies, and most notably the sanction of compensation for damage that has evolved through state liability principles, might be a particularly useful tool in the hands of those seeking justice in the field of environmental protection.

The same cannot be said, however, with respect to the range of principles which private parties are entitled to invoke in order to call Community institutions to account for environmental misconduct. This sector has inherited the traditional limitations to Article 230(4) EC review that have long applied in other sectors of Community activity. As a consequence it seems unlikely that Community courts will ever be in a position to give judgment on the substance of a case in which breach of environmental law is alleged under Article 230 EC, due to the difficulties which applicants will experience in obtaining standing to sue. This situation is far less than ideal, and calls into question the coherence of a Community legal order which purports to vest individuals with effective judicial remedies to protect their rights.

The Legal Framework for the Regulation of Waste in the European Community

GEERT VAN CALSTER*

I. Introduction

This article examines European Community (EC) legislation on waste and waste management. Over the years, the Community's approach to waste has changed dramatically, but has not always been consistent. This article shows how the regime has evolved, examines the directives regulating waste and how future EC waste policy may evolve. The second section involves a detailed analysis of the Framework Directive. In section III the framework for the regulation of hazardous waste is reviewed and possible amendments are assessed. In the following section, section IV, the extensive framework concerning the shipment of waste between Member States and the import of waste into the EC is reviewed. Section V offers an analysis of the Packaging and Packaging Waste Directive. In sections VI–IX, the rules relating to landfill, incineration, waste oils and other specific regimes are analysed. Other specific regimes are not dealt with as they are addressed sufficiently elsewhere in this volume. The article concludes in Section X.

II. The EC Framework Directive on Waste

This section provides an analysis of Directive 75/442/EEC[1] which is commonly referred to as the "Framework Directive" of EC waste policy. Yet, it only genuinely deserves this title following the 1991 amendments,[2] since Article 2 of the original text excluded "waste covered by specific Community rules" from its scope of application. The text now states that "specific rules for particular instances or supplementing those of the Directive on the management of particular categories of waste may be laid down by means of individual Directives" (Article 2(2)). Thus, the Framework Directive, as amended, has

---

* Senior Research Fellow, Institute of Environmental and Energy Law, Collegium Falconis, K.U.Leuven; Member of the Brussels Bar, Caestecker & Partners. The author would like to thank Michael Rose, partner at S. J. Berwin, for his comments on an earlier version of this article, as well as Derrick Wyatt Q.C. (St. Edmund Hall, Oxford University) for sharing his thoughts on the definition of waste in particular. The contents of this article remain the sole responsibility of the author.

[1] Council Dir. 75/442/EEC of 15 July 1975 on waste (the Framework Directive) [1975] OJ L194/39.

[2] Council Dir. 91/156/EEC of 18 Mar. 1991 amending Dir. 75/442/EEC [1991] OJ L78/32.

become the *lex generalis* of EC waste legislation. Its principles apply to all categories of waste unless otherwise provided in specific legislation. However, far from merely specifying general principles, the Directive contains specific and far-reaching obligations for Member States. Moreover, the general waste-management principles of the Framework Directive are crucial for the interpretation of other EC legislation in this area.

The aim of the Directive is to protect the environment, improve the quality of life, and avoid disturbances of the internal market. The 1991 amendments were introduced for the following reasons:

— *Lack of Community definition of waste.* The Directive defined waste as "any substance or object which the holder disposes of or is required to dispose of pursuant to the provisions of national law in force". Reference to national law clearly frustrated Community harmonization efforts. Directive 91/156/EEC amending Directive 75/442/EEC on waste[3] now stresses the need for a common terminology (third recital).
— *Lack of a clear choice in favour of re-use.* Article 3 of the Framework Directive called upon Member States to encourage prevention and recycling. In line with the 1989 Commission Communication on a Community strategy for waste management,[4] Directive 91/156/EEC now aims to establish a clear hierarchy in waste policy (fourth recital).
— *Community self-sufficiency in waste disposal.* The Council wanted to pursue a more co-ordinated approach by ensuring that the Community as a whole becomes self-sufficient in waste disposal. To this end, individual self-sufficiency of all Member States is regarded instrumental (seventh recital).
— *Lack of strict control measures.* Article 8 foresaw a permit system for installations or undertakings treating, storing, or tipping waste on behalf of third parties. Undertakings treating their own waste and those collecting or transporting waste on behalf of third parties were only to be "supervised". The amendments introduce strict controls on all undertakings involved in waste management (tenth recital).

A.   SCOPE OF APPLICATION: DEFINITION OF WASTE—"RECOVERY" AND "DISPOSAL"

i.   *The Theory: Article 1, Annex I and the European Waste Catalogue*

Article 1(a) of the Framework Directive defines waste as "any substance or object in the categories set out in Annex I which the holder discards or intends or is required to discard". The provision goes on to state that "the Commission,

---

[3] [1991] OJ L78/32.
[4] Communication from the Commission to the Council and the European Parliament of 18 Sept. 1989 on a Community strategy for waste management, COM(89)934; see also Council Resolution of 7 May 1990 on waste policy [1990] OJ C122/2, which endorses the Commission Communication.

acting in accordance with the procedure laid down in Article 18, will draw up, not later than 1 April 1993, a list of wastes belonging to the categories listed in Annex I. This list will be periodically reviewed and, if necessary, revised by the same procedure". The "holder" is defined as anyone who has physical control over the waste, including the generator, exporter, waste broker, recycler, etcetera. Article 2(a)–(b) exclude certain substances from the scope of application.[5]

Category Q16 ("any materials, substances or products which are not contained in the above categories") reflects the inclusive nature of the Annex. If a substance *expressis verbis* has been included in the list, the Community legislator considers it to be "waste" provided, of course, that the other conditions of Article 1 are met: the holder discards or intends or is required to discard the substance concerned. If a substance does not figure in the list, it falls under Q16 and it will be considered waste should it meet the aforementioned conditions.

The aim of introducing a Community-wide definition of waste has been frustrated in practice. First, category Q13 ("any materials, substances or products whose use has been banned by law") enables Member States to maintain some sort of a national definition of waste. Although Q13 does not specify which legislator is entitled to introduce such ban, it may be assumed that both the Community's and Member States' competence in this matter have been recognized.[6] Q13 should not lead to grave concern, however. Often, Member States are eager to regulate the use or storage of a product which they consider to be a waste, but a straightforward ban might not be the remedy sought.

Secondly, the definition of waste under the Framework Directive is far from clear and the predicted disputes over its exact meaning have not failed to materialize. One reason for the difficulty is the intrinsic interchangeable character of "waste". What is a waste for one producer is a valuable resource for another: waste of the industrialized world might be prime material for developing countries, and one and the same production process might now use resources which it previously discarded.

The Commission has been instructed by Article 1(a) to draw up what is referred to as the "European Waste Catalogue" (EWC) and has done so by Decision 94/3/EC.[7] As with the waste Annex of the Framework Directive, the EWC should be regarded as a confirmative list, albeit in more detail. Products figuring on the list should be regarded as waste, provided they meet the other

---

[5] (a) Gaseous effluents emitted into the atmosphere; (b) where they are already covered by other legislation: (i) radioactive waste; (ii) waste resulting from prospecting, extraction, treatment and storage of mineral resources and the working of quarries; (iii) animal carcasses and the following agricultural waste: faecal matter and other natural, non-dangerous substances used in farming; (iv) waste waters, with the exception of waste in liquid form; (v) decommissioned explosives.

[6] N. De Sadeleer, *Le droit communautaire et les déchets* (Brussels: Bruylant, 1995), 239; and C. de Villeneuve, "Les notions de 'déchets' et de 'déchets dangereux'; les définitions proposées par la Commission des C.E." (1990) 13 *Aménagement-Environnement*, 14–18.

[7] Commission Decision 94/3/EC of 20 Dec. 1993 establishing a list of wastes pursuant to Art. 1(a) of the Framework Directive on Waste [1994] OJ L5/115.

requirements of Article 1.[8] To be sure, the list is not exhaustive. The EWC is a non-exhaustive list of wastes that is to be a reference nomenclature, providing a common terminology throughout the Community designed to improve the efficiency of waste management activities.[9]

ii. Negative Indication: Products with an Economic Value are not Excluded

Evidently, the question what is "waste" and which substances are merely "products" is of paramount importance. Taking the legal base and the purpose of the directives into account, the ECJ has hinted that the legislator envisaged a broad application of the Directive.[10] From the outset, Community waste directives were not just meant to create a level playing-field for producers of waste and for economic operators. It follows from Article 174 (formerly Article 130r) EC that they are also designed to protect the environment.

These considerations have led the European Court of Justice (ECJ) to rule that a substance of which its holder disposes may constitute waste even when it is capable of economic reutilization.[11] National legislation that defines waste in such a way as to exclude substances and objects that can be reutilized is incompatible with the Framework Directive.[12]

iii. Positive Indication: The Objective Qualities of the Good v. the Intention of the Holder?

Ideally, the question whether a substance is a threat to public health or a danger for the environment should be a matter of objective analysis.[13] In practice, however, this may be impossible: asbestos, for example, which once appeared completely harmless, now has proved to be extremely dangerous. In any event, that a definition of waste should be "objective", i.e. independent of the intention of the holder, is hard to sustain in view of the subjective definition of waste (Article 1(a)), which includes the terms "intends to discard".

With respect to the issue of the "intention" of the holder, the rationale behind the introduction of the term "to discard" is crucial. Commentators have turned to linguistic analyses to explain the term, even comparing the various linguistic versions of the Directive. The original Directive used the term "to dispose of", which was abandoned in subsequent amendments. Indeed, "to dispose of" has a negative connotation, referring to materials that one

---

[8] See also the headnote of the Annex to Decision 94/3/EC (4): "the inclusion of a material in the EWC does not mean that the material is a waste in all circumstances. The entry is only relevant when the definition of waste has been satisfied".

[9] *Ibid.* (3) and (6).

[10] See Joined Cases 372–374/85, *Openbaar Ministerie* v. *Oscar van Traen and others* [1987] ECR 2141, at para. 7.

[11] Joined Cases C–206/88 and C–207/88, *Criminal proceedings against Vessoso and Zanetti* [1990] ECR 1461, at para. 8.

[12] Case C–422/92, *Commission* v. *Germany* [1995] ECR I–1097, at para. 22, and Case C–359/88, *Criminal proceedings against E. Zanetti et al.* [1990] ECR 1509, at para. 13. See also Joined Cases C–304/94, C–330/94, C–342/94, and C–224/95, *Criminal Proceedings against Euro Tombesi et al.* [1997] ECR I–3561, at paras. 47–52.

[13] See the Opinion of Jacobs AG in *Vessoso and Zanetti*, n. 11 above, at para. 22.

wants to get rid of, which could give rise to the impression that the Community aimed only at regulating waste for disposal. As noted, the ECJ has unequivocally stated that this is not the case. In fact, the Directive draws no distinction according to the intentions of the holder disposing of the waste.[14] It could be argued that the aim of the Framework Directive might be jeopardized if the application of the Directive were dependent on the question whether the holder intended to exclude all economic reutilization by others of the substances or objects of which he disposes.[15]

In response to the Directive's broad scope, certain Member States, notably Germany,[16] wished to exclude all waste with an economic value. The Council decided against this course of action. The use of the term "to discard" was designed to ensure that there would be no doubt about the implication of waste that has economic value. To be sure, extensive linguistic analysis of this term has been rather unproductive.[17] It is submitted that a proper understanding of the concept does not wholly rest on the idea that the holder intends to exclude any possibility of recovery. Nor does it presuppose that an object is released to a third party or that the holder of the waste abandons the title to it.[18] Instead, a more inclusive and robust approach to the concept is required.

iv. A Way Out of the Impasse: The Euro Tombesi Bypass

This section examines a proposal of Advocate General Jacobs that may offer a way around the impasse posed by the definition of waste. In his Opinion in *Euro Tombesi*, Advocate General Jacobs provides an alternative route that builds upon the seemingly more specific terms "recovery" and "disposal". Because Advocate General Jacobs' approach circumvents pussy-footing around the concept "to discard", I have referred to it as the *Euro Tombesi* bypass.[19]

The Advocate General's starting point is that the ECJ's broad interpretation has not been altered by the 1991 amendments to the Framework Directive,[20] and that little is to be gained from considering the common meaning of the term "discard",[21] since the Framework Directive clearly extends both to substances and objects that are disposed of and to those that are recovered.

---

[14] *Vessoso and Zanetti*, n. 11 above, at para. 11.

[15] *Ibid.*, at para. 12.   [16] De Sadeleer, n. 6 above, 263.

[17] Evidently, linguistic analysis is imperative in the interpretation of all (on the face unclear) Community legislation; see this author's analysis, "The EU's Tower of Babel—The Interpretation of Multi-lingual Texts by the ECJ" in A. Barav and D. Wyatt (eds.), *Yearbook of European Law—1997* (Oxford: Clarendon Press, 1998).

[18] J. Fluck, "The term 'Waste' in EU Law" (1994) 3 *European Environmental Law Review* 81.

[19] Opinion of Jacobs AG of 24 Oct. 1996 in Joined Cases C–304/94, C–330/94, C342/94, and C–224/95, *Criminal proceedings against Euro Tombesi and others* [1997] ECR I–3561. See G. van Calster, "The EC Definition of Waste: The *Euro Tombesi* Bypass and Basel Relief Routes" [1997] *European Business Law Review* 137. See also J.R. Salter, "The meaning of 'Waste' in European Community Law" (1997) 6 *European Environmental Law Review* 14.

[20] Jacobs AG in *Euro Tombesi*, n. 20 above, at para. 40. This had already been underlined by the ECJ in *Commission* v. *Germany*, n. 12 above.

[21] Jacobs AG in *Euro Tombesi*, n. 20 above, at para. 50.

The scope of the term "waste" thus depends on what is meant by "disposal operation" and by "recovery operation".[22]

There is of course an element of circularity in this approach, as Advocate General Jacobs himself admits.[23] In essence, he creates the circle by defining waste through the definition of disposal and recovery,[24] which in turn are activities relating to waste. Interestingly this method is also found back in the OECD definition of waste,[25] which does not employ the notion of discarding, but hinges on the intended destination of a material.

The Directive defines "recovery" as "any of the operations provided for in Annex II, B", and "disposal" as "any of the operations provided for in Annex II, A" (Article 1(f) and (e)).[26] The Annexes have last been amended in 1996.[27] As is noted in their headnotes:

This Annex is intended to list disposal/recovery operations such as they occur in practice. In accordance with Article 4 waste must be disposed of/recovered without endangering human health and without the use of processes or methods likely to harm the environment.

The lists are not exhaustive but reflect the methods "such as they occur" in practice.

In its judgment in *Euro Tombesi*,[28] the ECJ happily took up Advocate General Jacobs' suggestion that the instant case did not in fact require elaborate deliberating. It sufficed that in the case at issue the national legislation was quite clearly in violation of Community law.[29] Nevertheless, the ECJ implicitly adopted the approach of Advocate General Jacobs by suggesting that the way forward was to turn to the concepts of "recovery" and "disposal" instead of hovering around the exact meaning of "to discard".[30]

---

[22] Jacobs AG in *Euro Tombesi*, n. 20 above, at para 50. See also P. Morrens and P. de Bruycker, "Het Europese afvalstoffenbegip" (1997) 6 *Tijdschrift voor Milieurecht* 418; they pointed to the appeal of an inverse approach (defining waste through recovery and disposal, rather than through "to discard").

[23] *Ibid.*, 55.

[24] Jacobs AG has developed this reasoning only with respect to recovery, which was at stake in the national legislation involved. There is, however, no reason for not following such reasoning for waste in general, through the combined definitions of disposal and recovery.

[25] OECD Council Decision C(88)90.

[26] These definitions differ substantially from the original Directive which defined "disposal" as "the collection, sorting, transport and treatment of waste as well as its storage and tipping above or under ground, and the transformation operations necessary for its re-use, recovery or recycling". This definition was simultaneously very broad (including recovery) and narrow. For instance, activities such as seabed disposal were not covered. See de Villeneuve, n. 6 above, 16.

[27] Commission Decision 96/350/EC of 24 May 1996 adapting Annexes IIA and IIB to Council Dir. 75/442/EEC on waste [1996] OJ L135/32, an almost exact copy of the Decision of the OECD Council of 27 May 1988 on transfrontier movements of hazardous wastes, C(88)90, amended on 28 and 29 July 1994 by Decision C(94)152.

[28] N. 19 above.

[29] See R. Macrory, "European Court Decision on Meaning of 'Waste' " [1997] *ENDS-Report*, 43–4.

[30] See also in particular the express confirmation by the ECJ in para. 27 of *Inter-Environnement*, that "to discard" encompasses both disposal and recovery operations (Case C–129/96, *Inter-Environnement Wallonie ASBL* v. *Région Wallonne* [1997] ECR I–7411).

Despite the Advocate General's suggestion in *Euro Tombesi* (i.e. to define waste through the concepts of recovery and disposal) specific legal practice concerns as well as interpretative problems for national courts remain. First, it will be crucial to distinguish between the two types of operation. For instance, and as we shall see in more detail below, the prior authorization (permit) procedure of the Framework Directive is substantially different for the two categories of waste management.[31] In its 1996 Community Waste Strategy,[32] the Commission suggests that the principles of self-sufficiency and proximity apply only to waste for disposal and not to waste for recovery. This view has been confirmed by the ECJ in *Dusseldorp*.[33]

Secondly, it remains important to distinguish "recovery", a waste management operation, from residues and by-products of production processes, as well as "secondary raw materials" which economic operators wish to keep outside the waste management regime. The latter, although referred to in Article 3.1(b)(i) of the Framework Directive (as amended), are not as such defined in the Directive.[34] When these products are "(re-)used" by the same manufacturer, or by other manufacturers within one and the same economic grouping, are they to be regarded as waste? Commissioner Bjerregaard (environment) defined "secondary raw materials" as "those materials which come out of a recycling, re-use, reclamation or other recovery process, while until then the materials have to be regarded as waste. Thus, materials that still must undergo a recovery operation could in principle not come under the notion of secondary raw materials."[35]

"Take-back" schemes are equally problematic.[36]

The Commission may introduce specific rules for secondary raw materials on the basis of Article 2(2) of the Framework Directive.[37] So far, it has shown no intention to that effect. In view of the confusion, the European Parliament (EP) proposed to introduce a specific regime for secondary raw materials. It proposed to insert a clause which would oblige the Community to adopt specific measures, notably for the metal industry.[38]

In brief, secondary raw materials form a particular challenge for the definition of waste; and no specific legislative intervention is to be expected soon. As

---

[31] See de Sadeleer, n. 6 above, 277 ff.

[32] Communication from the Commission of 30 July 1996 on the review of the Community strategy for waste management—draft Council resolution on waste policy. The Council has endorsed the Commission's text with some nuances: [1997] OJ C76/1. See the author's note "Communication on Community Waste Strategy Lacks Specificity" (1996) 8(18) *Eurowatch* 3–4.

[33] N. 162 below.

[34] An *ad hoc* group of the Technical Adaptation Committee for waste legislation is currently assessing the need for the EC to introduce specific legislation. International developments, in particular within the OECD, are closely followed.

[35] Question of B. Cassidy MEP [1997] OJ C138/44.

[36] See A. M. Welker and D. Geradin, "Waste from Electrical and Electronic Equipment: Producer Responsibility: A Review of Initiatives in the EC" (1996) 5 *European Environmental Law Review* 341.

[37] See EP Opinion concerning the Commission proposal for a Directive amending Directive 75/442/EEC [1989] OJ C158/232, at 233.

[38] Trade in scrap metal is considerable, especially between industrialized countries and the developing world.

a result, legal practice and the courts are left with dealing with the interpretive issues involved. That a residue is used by one and the same manufacturer should have no influence on the characterization of a substance as "waste". It thus seems justified to take the view, similar to Advocate General Jacobs, that where a residue cannot be used in a normal industrial process without undergoing a recovery operation such as those listed in Annex IIB, it must be regarded as waste, until such time as it is recovered. The consignment of a residue to a process designed to transform it or certain components into a usable raw material constitutes a recovery process.[39]

Taking the ordinary meaning of the term "recovery" as a starting-point, Advocate General Jacobs suggested in *Euro Tombesi* that what is entailed is a process by which goods are restored to their previous state or transformed into a usable state or by which certain usable components are extracted or produced. Goods that are transferred to another person and put to continual use in their existing form are not "recovered" and are therefore not wastes.[40] In *Inter-Environnement*, he built upon these conclusions,[41] suggesting that a by-product or a residual product does not constitute waste if it was destined for direct use in a further process in its existing form, in other words if it was not destined for disposal or consignment to a recovery operation prior to its continued use.

In support of this argument, Advocate General Jacobs refers to work in the OECD,[42] implying that there is general consensus among OECD countries that it is relevant to consider whether the use of a residual product or by-product as a substitute for another material or ingredient is as environmentally sound as that of the material or ingredient which it is replacing. This meant that where, owing to the fact that it is a residue, by-product, secondary raw material, or other material resulting from an industrial process, a material—or the process which it undergoes—does not meet normal health or environmental requirements or standards, it must be considered waste. In so far as a material is wholly interchangeable with another product and requires no additional regulation or supervision beyond that applicable to the product it is replacing, it is, in the Advocate-General's view, unnecessary for it to be classified as waste.

Interestingly, Advocate General Jacobs suggests in *Euro Tombesi* that, in light of the degree of specificity of the Directive itself,[43] it must be left to the Member States in some respect to develop more detailed criteria for applying

---

[39] Jacobs AG in *Euro Tombesi*, n. 19 above, at para. 53. [40] *Ibid.*, at para. 52.

[41] Which he rephrased as "where a residue cannot be used in a normal industrial process without undergoing a recovery operation such as those listed in Annex IIB, it must be regarded as waste, until such time as it is recovered": Case C–129/96, *Inter-Environnement Wallonie ASBL* v. *Région Wallonne* [1997] ECR I–7411.

[42] Discussion paper on guidance for distinguishing waste from non-waste, issued by the OECD Waste Management Policy Group, ENV/EPOC/WMP(96)1; see also OECD final guidance document for distinguishing waste from non-waste, ENV/EPOC/WMP(98)1/REV1.

[43] The author takes it that this is the meaning of "as the Directive stands at present", in Jacobs AG's conclusions in *Euro Tombesi*, n. 19 above, 56.

the term "recovery operation" to the various situations which may occur in practice.[44]

The reasoning of Advocate General Jacobs in *Inter-Environnement* at the same time raised the question of the precise nature of the *Euro Tombesi* bypass. Does recourse to the notions "recovery" and "disposal" do away with the notion "to discard" as a cumulative condition for a substance to be regarded as waste? In the light of the bypass' circularity one could argue that it does. Advocate General Jacobs' reference to the OECD document seems to hint at such a conclusion as well. Of course, the objectivity of this approach is appealing.[45] Preliminary questions referred to the ECJ by a Dutch administrative court might offer the occasion for the ECJ to shed its light on this question. The court has asked the ECJ whether the mere fact that a substance is being subjected to one of the processes included in Annex IIB amounts to this substance having been discarded.[46]

In *Inter-Environnement*, the ECJ merely gave the national court the guidance which was strictly necessary: that substances forming part of an industrial process may constitute waste within the meaning of the Framework Directive. It added as an important *obiter*, however, that its conclusion does not undermine the distinction which must be drawn between waste recovery and normal industrial treatment of products which are not waste.[47] This may suggest that the ECJ is prepared to follow Advocate General Jacobs' reasoning and the view that there is a class of goods for which no recovery operation is necessary for them to be included in the normal industrial cycle, without risk to the environment. In other words, the concept of "recovery" would be given a restrictive interpretation.[48] The Commission has announced that it would rather postpone reviewing the EC's definition of waste, in particular with respect to "secondary raw materials", until talks at the international level had been finalized.[49] Advocate General Jacobs would seem to be the token forward, now that the ECJ appears to shun the ball.[50] Since the OECD has published its long awaited guidance document, it is time for the Commission and Member States' experts to take up the challenge.

---

[44] *Ibid.* See, e.g., the judgment of the High Court of Justice (Chancery Division) of 9 Nov. 1998 in *Shipment Regulation Mayer Parry Recycling Ltd* v. *The Environment Agency*.

[45] See A. van Rossem, "Nieuwe ontwikkelingen in het Europese afvalstoffenrecht?" (1998) 4 *Nederlands Tijdschrift voor Europees Recht* 20.

[46] See van Rossem and Jans, n. 30 above; and B. Veldhoven, "The Concept of Waste: Wood Chips used as Substitute Fuel" (1998) 7 *European Environmental Law Review* 149.

[47] N. 30 above, 58 ff. It is uncertain whether the obiter implies that the ECJ might share Jacobs AG's view (see n. 44 above) that the detailed contents of what "recovery" entails should be left to the Member States (this is suggested by van Rossem and Jans, n. 30 above), or a mere reminder that this fell outside the reply to be given to the national court.

[48] Van Rossem, n. 45 above.   [49] Question of Cassidy MEP [1997] OJ C138/44.

[50] Despite Jacobs AG's express invitation to do so; see his Opinion in *Inter-Environnement* (n. 41 above, at para. 69), where he pleads for legal certainty. See also H. Somsen, case note in (1998) 7 *European Environmental Law Review* 87; and B. Deltour, case note in (1998) 21 *Aménagement/Environnement* 131.

B.   MEMBER STATES' OBLIGATIONS UNDER THE DIRECTIVE

i.   Waste Hierarchy and General Obligations

Article 3 reflects the hierarchy within the Community waste strategy.[51]
Member States should, respectively, take measures to encourage:

(1) the prevention or reduction of waste production and its harmfulness
     (mainly through R&D);[52]
(2) the recovery of waste by means of recycling, re-use or reclamation of any
     other process with a view to extracting secondary raw materials; and
(3) the use of waste as a source of energy.[53]

The EP wanted to tie Member States to quantitative limits of reduction but was
not supported by the Commission.[54]

Article 4 enumerates the environmental values that Member States are to
protect. They are required to take the necessary measures to ensure that waste
is recovered or disposed of without risk to water, air, soil, and plants, and
animals; without causing a nuisance through noise or odours; and without
adversely affecting the countryside or places of special interest. Member
States also have to take all necessary measures to prohibit the abandonment,
dumping, or uncontrolled disposal of waste. Article 4 imposes a legal duty to
design and enforce concrete measures so that waste is recovered or disposed
of without risk to the human health and the environment.[55] It does not, however, require the adoption of *specific* measures or a particular method of waste
disposal, and is hence not sufficiently precise to be capable of conferring
rights which an individual may rely on against a Member State.[56]

---

[51] The 1989 Strategy, n. 4 above, and the 1996 version, COM(96)399 [1997] OJ C76/1.

[52] Art. 3 does not prevent Member States' authorities from completely banning the marketing
of certain products, for instance plastic bags: see Case C–380/87, *Enichem Base and others* v.
Commune di Cinisello Balsamo [1989] ECR 2491. The applicants' arguments in this case related
also to Treaty Articles with respect to the free movement of goods (Art. 28 (formerly Art. 30) EC ff.).
Unfortunately, the ECJ did not go into this argument, since the Italian court which had asked the
preliminary question had not raised this issue.

[53] Disposal of waste through incineration, especially if it does not coincide with energy recovery, is not the Commission's preferred option. The Commission still expresses substantial doubt
about this technique in its 1996 Communication. See M. Rose, "Review of the Community Waste
Strategy" (1996) 27 *The Warmer Bulletin* 9.

[54] Amended Commission proposal [1989] OJ C 326/6. Quantified targets are included in EC legislation on packaging waste.

[55] Case C–45/91, *Commission* v. *Greece* [1992] ECR I–2509.

[56] Case C–236/92, *Comitato di Coordinamento per la Difesa Della Cava and others* v. *Regione
Lombardia and Others* [1994] ECR I–483, note by M. Reddish, (1994) 3 *European Environmental
Law Review* 307–10. Individuals can thus not rely on this provision to challenge a permit granted.
To be fair, this judgment interpreted Art. 4 of the unamended Directive. There is no reason, how-
ever, to assume that the ECJ's appraisal with respect to the general obligations of the Directive
would have changed following the 1991 amendments.

ii.   Community Self-sufficiency and the Proximity Principle

Article 5 contains the principle of self-sufficiency,[57] according to which Member States have to take appropriate measures, in co-operation with other Member States where this is necessary or advisable, to establish an integrated and adequate network of disposal installations, taking account of the "best available technology not involving excessive costs". The network must enable the Community as a whole to become self-sufficient in waste disposal and the Member States to move towards that aim individually, taking into account geographical circumstances or the need for specialized installations for certain types of waste. The network must also enable waste to be disposed of in the nearest appropriate installations, by means of the most appropriate methods and technologies in order to ensure a high level of protection. The latter means that the so-called "proximity principle" is laid down in the EC Framework Directive, albeit in a specific form. Waste need not *per se* be disposed of in the nearest installation. This installation needs to employ the most appropriate methods and technologies in ensuring a high level of protection of the environment and health.

iii.   Waste-management Plans

Article 7 obliges Member States to draw up waste-management plans which must at the very least cover the type, quantity, and origin of waste to be recovered or disposed of; general technical requirements; any special arrangements for particular wastes; and suitable disposal sites or installations. In addition, they *could* deal with the persons empowered to carry out the management of waste; the estimated costs of recovery and disposal operations; and appropriate measures to encourage rationalization of the collection, sorting, and treatment of waste.

Article 7(3) provides that Member States are entitled to prevent movements of waste which are not in accordance with their waste-management plans. The policy should be appreciated in the light of the internal market. Member States are required by Article 5 to take the principle of self-sufficiency into account in their waste-management policies. Imports and/or exports of waste might endanger the self-sufficiency of a Member State, and it would appear that Article 7(3) provides that imports or exports may be lawfully prohibited in the name of self-sufficiency. Yet, as is exemplified by *Dusseldorp*, this conclusion might be premature since it does not take account of the relationship between the Framework Directive and other Community principles, such as the free movement of goods.

The process by which Member States notify the Commission of their national waste-management plans has not functioned successfully, despite the Commission's insistence.[58]

[57] See J. Jans, "Self-Sufficiency in European Waste Law?" (1994) 3 *European Environmental Law Review* 223.
[58] IP/97/890.

iv.   Procedural and Administrative Requirements for Waste Management

Generally, any holder of waste is required to have it handled by a waste collector, or by an undertaking which carries out the operations listed in Annex II A
or B. The holder may also recover it or dispose of it himself, in accordance with
the provisions of the Directive (Articles 8–11). Articles 9–12 contain a system of
prior authorization; undertakings involved in the disposal and/or recovery of
waste, have to obtain a permit in accordance with Article 6.

The prior authorization (permit) procedure is substantially different for the
two categories of waste management.[59] The permit requirement for *waste disposal* discussed earlier (Article 9) refers to Articles 4, 5, and 7. The permit
requirement for *recovery* (Article 10) refers to Article 4 only. This could lead to
a conclusion that the room for manœuvre for Member States under Article 9 is
wider than under Article 10. It has been suggested[60] that the absence in Article
10 of any reference to Article 7 excludes Member States' competence to refuse
a permit on any of the grounds mentioned in that Article. In other words,
whilst a permit for a disposal installation may be refused on organizational
grounds (e.g. the network of disposal installations provides sufficient capacity
to deal with that Member States' waste), this would not apply to recovery operations. However, such an interpretation is problematic. To be sure, Article 9
refers to Article 7, whereas Article 10 does not. However, Article 7 refers to
waste-management plans in general, so that it becomes somewhat perverse to
construe a *lex specialis vis-à-vis* Article 7. It appears more plausible that both
are on the same footing in terms of legislative hierarchy.

Another difference between the permit system for recovery and disposal
operations is the absence, in Article 10, of any indication of what the permit
should cover. Article 9 (disposal), on the other hand, lists a number of issues
which need to be covered by the permit. As stated in Article 9, the permit may
be issued for a limited period only.

Undertakings that have received a permit need to be inspected (Article 13)
and have to keep appropriate records (Article 14). The duty to keep a record
may be extended to producers of waste (Article 14). Article 11 creates a possibility of exempting from the permit requirement establishments or undertakings carrying out their own waste disposal at the place of production, and
establishments or undertakings that carry out waste recovery. This may occur
only if the authorities have adopted general rules for each type of activity. More
specifically, this means that rules be drafted specifying the types and quantities of waste, the conditions under which the activity in question may be
exempt from the permit requirements,[61] and the methods of disposal or recovery that must be complied with. It is important to note that the undertakings
exempted are subject to registration (Article 11(2)).

---

[59] See de Sadeleer, n. 6 above, 277 ff.   [60] See *ibid.*
[61] These rules have to be notified to the Commission: Art. 11(3).

v. Polluter Pays Principle

Pursuant to Article 15, in accordance with the polluter pays principle, the cost of disposing of waste must be borne by the holder, and/or by the previous holders or the producer of the product. The Directive does not indicate how this provision should be applied. Article 15 constitutes the first instance of the polluter pays principle being introduced into Community law.[62]

III.   Toxic and Dangerous Waste—"Hazardous Waste"

A.   GENERAL FRAMEWORK AND THE DEFINITION OF "HAZARDOUS WASTE"

i. Build-up to the Current Situation

Directive 78/319/EEC on Toxic and Dangerous Waste[63] defines "toxic and dangerous waste" as "any waste containing or contaminated by the substances listed in Annex to this Directive of such a nature, in such quantities or in such concentrations as to constitute a risk to health or the environment". "Waste" was defined in the same manner as in the original Framework Directive. The Annex was entitled "List of toxic or dangerous substances and materials" and stated in a headnote: "the following list consists of certain dangerous substances and materials selected as requiring priority consideration".

Neither the Directive nor the Annex specified the "quantities" or the "concentrations" in which the substances were deemed to constitute a risk. The effect was to deregulate the definition: it was up to national authorities to lay down provisions with respect to these concentration limits. Unsurprisingly, a number of Member States failed to do so.[64]

That the definition of hazardous waste called for harmonization became especially apparent in the context of the transboundary movements of waste.[65] After the EP had called upon the Commission to act,[66] the Commission tabled a proposal on 16 August 1988.[67] The EP proposed a number of amendments,[68] most of which were rejected by the Commission.[69] The Council subsequently amended the proposal on a number of crucial issues,

---

[62] See K. Vandekerckhove, "The Polluter Pays Principle in the European Community", in A. Barav and D. Wyatt, *Yearbook of European Law—1993* (Oxford: Clarendon Press, 1994), 203–62.

[63] [1978] OJ L84/43.   [64] See de Villeneuve, n. 6 above, 14–18.

[65] The prior notification system under Dir. 84/631/EEC on the supervision and control within the European Community of the transfrontier shipment of hazardous waste [1984] OJ L326, depended on the term. See R. Hunter, "The Problematic EU Hazardous Waste List" (1995) 4 *European Environmental Law Review* 83.

[66] Resolution of the European Parliament on the treatment of waste in the EC [1984] OJ C127/67.

[67] COM(88)391 [1988] OJ C295/8.

[68] Opinion of the EP of 25 May 1989 [189] OJ C158/238. The Parliament, *inter alia*, proposed to opt for a regulation rather than for a directive.

[69] COM(89)560 [1990] OJ C42/19.

including the definition of hazardous waste, and the text was adopted on 12 December 1991 as the Hazardous Waste Directive.[70]

Based on Article 175 EC,[71] it is a directive as meant in Article 2(2) of the Framework Directive, a *lex specialis* for hazardous waste, although the Directive does not as yet apply to domestic waste, the limitations of the scope of application of the Framework Directive do *not* apply to the Hazardous Waste Directive.[72] Consequently, even if Community or national legislation is introduced for any of the specific categories of waste enumerated in Article 2(1)b of the Framework Directive (thereby removing this waste from the scope of application of the Framework Directive), the provisions of the Hazardous Waste Directive will apply to such categories provided, of course, that they meet the definition of "hazardous waste". Importantly, the Commission is planning to extend the scope of the Hazardous Waste Directive to household waste. A majority of Member States already operate a system of separate collection and/or delivery of at least some hazardous domestic waste. The Commission proposes to require Member States to collect hazardous domestic and similar waste in separate fractions by professional waste collectors, or delivered in separate fractions to specialist collection facilities. To assist households and other producers to identify the waste concerned, manufacturers would be obliged to mark their products with a relevant symbol.[73]

As is also evidenced by the ninth recital to the Directive, the text aims to introduce a precise and uniform definition. In this regard, "hazardous waste" means:

wastes featuring on a list to be drawn up in accordance with the procedure laid down in Article 18 of the Framework Directive on the basis of Annexes I and II to this Directive, not later than six months before the date of implementation of this Directive. These wastes must have one or more of the properties listed in Annex III. The list shall take into account the origin and composition of the waste and, where necessary, limit values of concentration. This list shall be periodically reviewed and if necessary amended by the same procedure, and,
any other waste which is considered by a Member State to display any of the properties listed in Annex III. Such cases shall be notified to the Commission and reviewed in accordance with the procedure laid down in Article 18 of the Framework Directive with a view to adaptation of the list. (Article 1(4))[74]

Importantly, the definition of waste based on a list of features was introduced by the Council. Annex IA is quite straightforward: wastes displaying any of the properties listed in Annex III and which consist of any of the materials listed in

---

[70] [1991] OJ L377/20. Dir. 91/689/EEC repeals Dir. 78/319/EEC, n. 63 above.

[71] Formerly Art. 130s EC.

[72] de Sadeleer, n. 6 above, 308.

[73] "Brussels plans separate collections for hazardous municipal waste" [1997] *ENDS-Report* 41–2.

[74] Using three Annexes is inspired by OECD work on the matter. See Decision of the OECD Council of 27 May 1988 on transfrontier movements of hazardous wastes, C(88)90, amended on 28 and 29 July 1994 by Decision C(94)152. See also N. de Sadeleer and J. Sambon, "The Concept of Hazardous Waste in European Community Law" (1997) 6 *European Environmental Law Review* 9.

Annex IA are hazardous. Annex IB combines three Annexes, namely IB, II, and III. Thus, the wastes which are listed in Annex IB (which contain any of the constituents of Annex II and have any of the properties described in Annex III) are deemed to be hazardous. Waste number 40 of Annex IB, which refers to "any other wastes which contain any of the constituents listed in Annex II and any of the properties listed in Annex III", renders Annex IB into an open Annex. Nevertheless, the Annexes only deal with the hazardous character of "wastes". Whether the substances enumerated are in effect "wastes", is to be determined in the light of the Framework Directive (Article 1(3) of the Hazardous Waste Directive).

The prior establishment of an inclusive and binding list of hazardous wastes was required and the Commission was instructed to draw up a list of hazardous wastes on the basis of the Annexes. Work on this list had to be finalized no later than six months before the entry into force of the Directive. Yet this proved a difficult and controversial task, in part since the Commission never favoured the idea of introducing a binding list of hazardous wastes. Although Commission officials did undertake various attempts to draw up such a list, these efforts were all fruitless. Eventually, the Commission issued a proposal to revise the definition of the term "hazardous wastes", and to delay the repeal of Directive 78/319/EEC, in order to prevent a legal vacuum.[75] It explained the failure by stating that such a list is unfeasible since, according to the Commission, a waste featuring on the list is automatically hazardous in all circumstances, which does not necessarily correspond to reality. It therefore proposed to modify the definition by direct reference to the hazardous properties.[76]

The EP[77] and the Council opposed this view. The new definition of waste would in effect reinstate the provisions of the previous Directive, leaving too much power to Member States. The Commission reluctantly issued a new proposal, reinstating the definition of waste as it had been adopted in the Hazardous Waste Directive and proposing to delay repealing Directive 78/319/EEC.[78] The latter was done by Directive 94/31/EC,[79] delaying the withdrawal until 27 June 1995. The Commission subsequently proposed a list

[75] Commission Proposal of 21 Sept. 1993 for a Council Directive amending Dir. 91/689/EEC on hazardous waste [1993] OJ C271/16.

[76] The definition put forward by the Commission read: "any substance or object belonging to the categories or generic types of waste set out in Annex I, taking into account the constituents referred to in Annex II, and which display one or more of the properties listed in Annex III". Under this proposal, the Commission was still to draw up a list of hazardous wastes, however not prior to the entry into force of the Directive. The Community list proposed by it was to take into account the origin and the composition of the waste and, where necessary, limit values of concentration. Once the list had been established, any decision by a Member State to consider categories of waste as hazardous waste would have had to be notified to the Commission *and* reviewed in accordance with the Committee procedure laid down in the Framework Directive.

[77] EP Opinion of 6 Dec. 1993 on the Commission proposal for a Directive amending Dir. 91/689/EEC on hazardous waste [1993] OJ C329/377.

[78] Amended Commission proposal of 28 Dec. 1993 for a Directive amending Dir. 91/689/EEC on hazardous waste, COM(93)696 [1994] OJ C51/4.

[79] [1994] OJ L168/28.

of hazardous wastes to the Committee referred to in Article 18 of the Framework Directive, which is a so-called "3A Committee".[80] This Committee did not agree with the Commission proposal, after which the Council had to decide the issue.[81]

The list of hazardous wastes the Council adopted differs considerably from the Commission proposal. The Commission seemed very reluctant to list concrete, identifiable types of waste. It referred to the requirement of the Directive that the wastes contain one or more of the properties listed in Annex III. In order to guarantee this, the Commission said, it would have been necessary to combine the generic types listed in Annex IB with the appropriate concentration limit values for each constituent in Annex II, which had yet to be determined.

ii. Annexes I and II in Conjunction with Annex III—EC List of Hazardous Waste

The Council adopted yet another approach in Decision 94/904/EC,[82] where the core element is the burden of proof. The lists of hazardous wastes included in the Annex are considered to display one or more of the properties of Annex III of the Hazardous Waste Directive (Article 1 of the Decision).[83] It is up to the holder of the waste, or to any other interested party, to prove that such is not the case.[84] However, the Decision is not very clear about the procedure for providing this proof nor about the requirements which are to be fulfilled. More clarity must be provided by the Hazardous Waste Directive and by Decision 94/904/EC. First, the fourth recital to the Council Decision states that Member States may make provisions, in exceptional cases, to determine on the basis of documentary evidence provided in an appropriate way by the holder, that a specific waste on the list does not display any of the properties listed in Annex III.

Secondly, Article 1 of the Decision lays down concentration limits for items H3 to H8 of Annex III. It therefore seems that anyone wishing to prove the non-hazardous character of the relevant wastes, may do so by establishing that the limits of Article 1 are not exceeded. Finally, Annex III refers to criteria laid

---

[80] "Comitology" is EC jargon for part of the legislative procedure, involving varying degrees of Member States' input.

[81] Commission proposal of 21 Sept. 1994 for a Council Decision establishing a list of hazardous waste pursuant to Art. 1(4) of Council Dir. 91/689/EEC on hazardous waste, COM(94)156. Some suggest (e.g. R. Hunter, n. 65 above, 86) that the Commission deliberately handed an incomplete version to the Committee to provoke its opposition. The Commission was hoping that either the Council subsequently would not find the qualified majority needed to change the Commission's proposal, or the Council would be forced to bear responsibility for the final list.

[82] Council Decision 94/904/EC of 22 Dec. 1994 establishing a list of hazardous waste pursuant to Art. 1(4) of Council Dir. 91/689/EEC on hazardous waste [1994] OJ L356/14.

[83] Should the "concentrations" approach have been followed, as was suggested by the Commission, Member States' authorities would have had to prove that the threshold concentrations were exceeded. See J. Sambon and N. de Sadeleer, "Le concept de déchets dangereux en droit communautaire", (1995) 18 *Aménagement-Environnement* 146.

[84] In other words, contrary to the European Waste Catalogue (n. 8 above), the hazardous waste list has direct legal effect. See Hunter, n. 65 above, 84.

down in other Community legislation, and to relevant testing methods. These criteria will naturally play a role in the burden of proof.

Hence, the Council has circumvented the issue of clarity by reversing the burden of proof.[85] Also, it has been rightly suggested that the list of hazardous wastes should be read in conjunction with the list of wastes which has been established under the Framework Directive.[86] Decision 94/904/EC follows the classification of Decision 94/3/EC[87] and includes only a limited number of the headings and subheadings entitled "hazardous wastes". This allows for clarification of the list by way of *a contrario* reasoning.[88] Clearly, prior to judging the hazardous character, the definition of waste as such needs to be satisfied. The introductory note to Decision 94/904/EC underlines this, where it states "inclusion in the list does not mean that the material or object is a waste in all circumstances. The entry is only relevant when the definition of waste according to Article 1(a) of the Framework Directive has been satisfied, unless Article 2(1)b of the Directive applies" (introductory note, at 2).

The EC hazardous wastes list is likely to be amended in the light of the Basel Convention on Transboundary Movement of Wastes. This Convention foresees a ban on the export of hazardous wastes for recovery to non-OECD states. Progress on the definition of hazardous wastes in the framework of the Convention will probably necessitate a broadening of the EC list.[89]

Unsurprisingly, the process of working out a definition of "hazardous wastes" by the parties to the Basel Convention has turned out to be quite a challenge. The debate on this issue has taken place within the Technical Working Group, and the results were discussed at the meeting of the parties at the end of February 1998. In an Annex to the Convention, the hazardous waste list (List A) bans the export of wastes containing arsenic, lead, mercury, asbestos, and dozens of other chemicals and substances. The non-hazardous waste list (List B) exempts from the ban those wastes that can be safely recycled or re-used, including scrap iron, steel, or copper, certain electronic assemblies, non-hazardous chemical catalysts, paper, and textile wastes. The ban and the Annexes need further ratification by a minimum number of parties, in order for them to enter into force.[90] For the EC, however, the Annexes have already entered into force.

iii. *Any Other Waste which is Considered by a Member State to Display Any of the Properties Listed in Annex III and Article 176 EC*

Apart from dangerous wastes listed in Annexes I and II *in conjunction with* Annex III, Article 1(4) defines hazardous wastes as "any other waste which is

---

[85] Criticized by Hunter, n. 65 above, 87 ff.   [86] De Sadeleer, n. 6 above, 302.

[87] N. 7 above.

[88] *Contra* Hunter, n. 65 above, 86, who dismisses the list as "vague and over-broad".

[89] See "Progress on Hazardous Waste List Points to Broadening of EC Rules" [1997] *ENDS-Report* 40.

[90] See Report of the fourth Meeting of the Conference of the Parties to the Basel Convention, Malaysia, 23–27 Feb. 1998—Implementation of Decisions II/12 and III/1 (exports of hazardous wastes)—Lists of hazardous wastes, UNEP/CHW 4/35.

considered by a Member State to display any of the properties listed in Annex III". Member States are required to notify such cases to the Commission, which will review them in accordance with the procedure laid down in Article 18 of the Framework Directive.[91] The wording seems to suggest that the so-called "review" of Member States' additions merely represents a stock-taking exercise. In theory this threatens the harmony of the EC definition, although in practice one might wonder why Member States would be tempted to add substances to the list of hazardous wastes. Indeed, the Community list itself is quite broad, and the burden of proof protects the authorities from having to document substantially each single case before being able to classify the waste as "dangerous".

The legal basis of the Directive, Article 175 EC, may cause further complications. Article 176 EC states that "the protective measures adopted pursuant to Article 175 EC shall not prevent any Member State from maintaining or introducing more stringent protective measures". Although such measures must be compatible with the Treaty, Article 176 EC does allow for a flood of national regulations which could endanger the Directives' harmonizing efforts.[92] In practice, this threat does not seem to have materialized, however.

B. MEMBER STATES' OBLIGATIONS

An obligation which has been assigned considerable weight is the requirement that Member States prohibit the mixing of different categories of hazardous waste or the mixing of hazardous waste with non-hazardous waste by the establishments and undertakings concerned (Article 2(2)). Mixing may be allowed, however, provided all necessary measures are taken to ensure the safety of all environmental resources listed in Article 4 of the Framework Directive. Any such operation must be covered by a specific authorization in the permit of the operator involved (Article 2(3) of the Hazardous Waste Directive in conjunction with Articles 9–11 of the Framework Directive). Particular attention must be paid to improving safety during disposal or recovery. Should waste already be mixed with other waste, substances, or materials, where technically and economically feasible (Article 2(4)), separation must be effected.

The Framework Directive (Article 11(1)(a)) authorizes Member States to exempt from the permit requirement establishments or undertakings which carry out their own waste disposal at the place of production and recovery activities. This possible derogation may *not* be granted for hazardous wastes (Article 3(1)). The possible exemption for undertakings carrying out waste recovery (Article 11(1)(b)), however, has been sustained for hazardous wastes subject to a number of requirements.

---

[91] See "DETR Consults on Changes to EC Hazardous Waste List" [1997] *ENDS-Report.*

[92] On the issue of stricter national environmental measures, see T. L. Joseph, "Preaching Heresy: Permitting Member States To Enforce Stricter Environmental Laws Than the European Community" (1995) 20 *The Yale Journal of International Law* 227, and further references therein.

The inspection obligation of Article 13 of the Framework Directive (with respect to disposal, recovery, and transport undertakings) has been extended to producers of hazardous waste (Article 4(1)). Inspections concerning collection and transporting operations have to pay specific attention to the origin and the destination of the waste (Article 5(2)). Undertakings which dispose of hazardous waste and/or recover it, as well as producers of hazardous waste and all establishments and undertakings transporting, must keep a record of the data listed in Article 14 of the Framework Directive (Article 4(2)). Member States are required to send the Commission all relevant information of the establishments concerned in the format that was determined by Commission Decision 96/302/EC of 17 April 1996.[93]

Hazardous waste that is collected, transported, and/or temporarily stored is subject to the relevant international and Community labelling requirements (Article 5(1)). In the general national waste-management plans (imposed by the Framework Directive) or separately therefrom, the authorities need to draw up plans for the management of hazardous waste. The Commission has to compare these plans and has to make its analysis available to the Member States which request it (Article 6). It also has to include a chapter on the implementation of the Hazardous Waste Directive in its report to the institutions (Article 8(1) and (2)). It should be noted that temporary derogations from the Directive may be enacted by the Member States should this prove necessary in the event of emergency or grave danger. Member States have to keep the Commission informed of any such measures (Article 7).

C.   PROPOSED AMENDMENTS

This section reviews some of the amendments that, if implemented, will extend the scope of application of the Hazardous Waste Directive. The amendment is intended to include "hazardous municipal waste" in the provisions of the Directive. Clearly, such waste will have to be collected separately. The aim is twofold. First, the Commission and interested parties have pointed to the health and environmental risks of disposing of hazardous municipal wastes without proper safeguards. This is especially true for hazardous liquids and for products containing heavy metals. Secondly, including such waste in the Directive, coupled with the duty to collect such wastes separately, is to render the process of treating and recovering not just these wastes but also the non-hazardous fraction of household wastes more economically viable.[94]

In a draft proposal, the term "hazardous municipal wastes" has been defined as not only waste produced by households, but also by "commercial, industrial, institutional and other hazardous waste which, because of its nature or composition, is similar to hazardous waste from households".[95]

---

[93] [1996] OJ L116/26.

[94] "Brussels Plans Separate Collections for Hazardous Municipal Waste" [1997] *ENDS-Report* 41–2.

[95] *Ibid.*

Member States will be obliged to ensure that such waste is collected in separate loads by professional waste collectors or delivered in separate loads to specialist collection facilities. The undertakings involved will have to register with the authorities. Producers and holders of hazardous municipal waste will have to be informed of the need to collect the waste separately.

Products that become or could become hazardous municipal waste will have to be labelled as such. The products subject to this requirement will be indicated through amending the EC hazardous waste list.[96]

It will take some time for this amendment to be put in place. A formal proposal by the Commission has yet to be tabled. Member States are divided on the issue. Quite a number already have systems in place which provide for the separate collection of (part of) the municipal waste stream. Others fear the extra costs.[97]

Industry and consumer organizations alike point to the difficulties surrounding the provision on labelling, and drafting of the list of products that will be made subject to the labelling requirement undoubtedly will prove to be controversial.[98] Moreover, the label would have to be streamlined with other labelling requirements, e.g., under Regulation (EC) No. 880/92 on a Community eco-label award scheme (the Eco-Label Regulation),[99] or with respect to the Packaging and Packaging Waste Directive.

IV. Shipments of Waste

A.   GENERAL FRAMEWORK AND SOURCES OF INSPIRATION

This section examines the legal framework that regulates the shipment of waste. It should be noted that Regulation (EC) No. 259/93 on the Supervision and Control of Shipments of Waste Within, Into, and Out of the European Community (Waste Shipment Regulation)[100] replaces Dir. 84/631/EEC,[101]

---

[96] Note 82 above.

[97] See "Cost Question Looms for Municipal Hazardous Waste Proposals" [1997] *ENDS-Report* 39–40.

[98] Europe's trading partners would like to have a say in the drafting of the list. The USA in particular is worried that yet another labelling requirement might amount to a barrier to trade.

[99] Reg. (EC) No. 880/92 of 23 Mar. 1992 [1992] OJ L99/1.

[100] Council Reg. (EC) No. 259/93 of 1 Feb. 1993 [1993] OJ L30/1. See also S. Crousse, F. Haumont, L. Horn, P. Lewisch, L. van Portvliet, and J. Timsit, "The EC Waste Shipment Regulation in Practice: Cross-border Waste Shipment as Exemplified by Selected Member States of the European Union" (1997) 6 *European Environmental Law Review* 143; X. Debroux, "La réglementation des mouvements transfrontaliers de déchets" (1997) 7 *Revue du Marché Unique Européen* 69–105; N. de Sadeleer, "La circulation des déchets et le Marché unique Européen", (1994) 4 *Revue du Marché Unique Européen* 108; J-P. Hannequart, "Droit Européen et droit belge relatif aux transferts transfrontaliers de déchets" (1990) 13 *Aménagement/Environnement* 68 ff.; J. Sommer, "Les déchets, de l'autosufficance et de la libre circulation des marchandises" (1994) 4 *Revue du Marché Commun et de l'Union Européenne* 247; A. Veldkamp, "Communautaire ontwikkelingen inzake in-, uit- en doorvoer van afvalstoffen", (1994) 3 *Tijdschrift voor Milieurecht* 80.

[101] Dir. 84/631/EEC of 6 Dec. 1984 on the supervision and control within the EC of the transfrontier shipment of hazardous waste. See Hannequart, *ibid.*, 68 ff.; and J. Sommer, "Les déchets, de l'autosuffance et de la libre circulation des marchandises" (1994) 4 *Revue du Marché Commun et de l'Union Européenne* 247.

which only applied to transfrontier shipments of *hazardous* waste. It ran into difficulties, particularly on the lack of a uniform definition of "hazardous waste".[102] The Waste Shipment Regulation was also intended to integrate a number of international developments, in particular the provisions of the Lomé Convention[103] and the Basel Convention.[104] Work in the Council was undoubtedly also influenced by the Seveso affair,[105] as well as by ECJ case law.[106] A source of inspiration may also have been OECD activities themselves.[107] Generally, the institutions reasoned that for part of the waste streams at least, standard economic activity (i.e. waste trade) leads to greater environmental protection.[108] The institutions opted for a regulation rather than for a directive to guarantee simultaneous and harmonious application in all Member States.[109]

The OECD view[110] is that the recovery of valuable raw materials from wastes is an integral part of the international economic system, and that well-established international markets and techniques exist for collecting and processing such wastes. Transfrontier shipments are a necessary tool to make use of adequate recovery facilities in other countries. To this end, the OECD decision has installed a three-tiered control system which has directly influenced the EC Regulation:

— wastes destined for recovery operations included in the *green list* of wastes are merely subject to all existing controls normally applied in commercial transactions;[111]

---

[102] Dir. 78/319/EEC (n. 63 above) in effect left it to the individual Member States to define the concept of "hazardous waste". Thus, whether a waste fell within the control procedure of Dir. 84/631/EEC could well differ according to whether one adopted the view of the Member States of import/export alternatively. See A. Bloch, "Afval definiëren bij invoer, doorvoer en uitvoer" (1992) 1 *Tijdschrift voor Milieurecht* 13.

[103] In particular Art. 39 of the ACP–EEC Convention of 15 Dec. 1989 [1991] OJ L229/3.

[104] Convention of 22 Mar. 1989 on the Control of Transboundary Movements of Hazardous Wastes and their Disposal (1989) 28 *International Legal Materials* 649.

[105] In 1982, 41 barrels of dioxine-contaminated waste "disappeared" from a factory in Seveso, Italy. They were to be found in France eight months later, in a ramshackle building. This and other scandals led the Community to adopt a Community Waste Strategy, n. 4 above.

[106] Especially Case C–2/90, *Wallonian Waste* [1992] ECR I–4431. The ECJ upheld the complete import ban of non-hazardous wastes into the Walloon Region of Belgium and took some controversial decisions with respect to, in particular, the discriminatory nature of the ban.

[107] See the Decision-Recommendations of the OECD Council on Transfrontier Movements of Hazardous Waste, 1 Feb. 1984, C(83)180; Decision-Recommendation of the OECD Council on Exports of Hazardous Wastes, C(86)64; Decision of the OECD Council on Transfrontier Movements of Hazardous Wastes, C(88)90, amended by Decision C(94)152; Decision-Recommendation of the OECD Council on the Reduction of Transfrontier Movements of Wastes, C(90)178; Decision of the OECD Council concerning the Control of Transfrontier Movements of Wastes Destined for Recovery Operations, C(92)39, amended by Decision C(93)74, amended by Decision C(94)153 and C(94)154 and by Decision C(95)155.

[108] Waste is recyclable not just as a raw material, but also as a source of energy.

[109] See Commission proposal of 26 Oct. 1990 for a Council Regulation on the supervision and control of shipments of waste within, into, and out of the European Community, COM(90)415, [1990] OJ C289/9. Despite the direct effect of the Regulation, difficulties remain in practice: see Crousse, Haumont, Horn, Lewisch, van Portvliet, and Timsit, n. 100 above.

[110] C(92)39, n. 107 above.

[111] The Decision foresees that exception has to be made for those wastes on the green list which are contaminated by other materials to an extent which increases the risks associated with the

— wastes included in the *amber list* may be shipped, subject to the consent of the competent authorities of the countries involved. Consent may be tacit;
— finally, transfrontier shipments of wastes included in the *red list* may only go ahead after prior written authorization by the authorities concerned.

An important development has occurred in the framework of the Basel Convention.[112] The third Convention of the parties (September 1995) adopted a formal amendment of the Treaty.[113] Article 4A now prohibits the export of hazardous wastes from OECD to non-OECD states, for disposal immediately and for recovery as at 31 December 1997. The fourth conference of the parties to the Convention (March 1998) has adopted the (non-exhaustive) lists which make the amendment operational.[114] However, due to a lack of ratifications of the amendment, it has not yet entered into force. In the EC, however, the amendment has taken effect and the list of hazardous wastes now adopted will soon be formally integrated into the EC shipments of waste regime.

The EC Regulation is based on Article 175 EC.[115] The guiding principles are:

— the principle of self-sufficiency "taking into account geographical circumstances or the need for specialized installations for certain types of

wastes sufficiently to render them appropriate for inclusion in the amber or red list, when taking into account the criteria listed in Annex II to the Decision.

[112] See "Waste Exporters Lose Battle of Geneva—but the Fight over Scrap Metal Goes On" [1994] *ENDS-Report* 15; and *Agence Europe*, 10 Mar., 27 Apr. and 28 Apr. 1995.

[113] In accordance with Art. 17 of the Treaty, the amendment binds only those countries which have ratified it. Moreover, some countries have expressed a formal reservation as regards the amendment.

[114] Even after the adoption of the lists, Annexes I and III to the Convention remain the essential factors characterizing wastes as hazardous. Annex I includes, on the one hand, 18 categories of "waste streams" (typically referring to specific activities), and 26 specific constituents that are deemed to make wastes hazardous; Annex III contains a list of hazardous characteristics. Wastes which are included in Annex I are considered hazardous, *unless* they do not possess any of the characteristics enumerated in Annex III; moreover, wastes are also "hazardous" if they are considered such by national legislation. Decision IV/9 of the Conference of the Parties introduces two new Annexes. Annex VIII contains the wastes that are characterized as hazardous; Annex IX contains the wastes that are characterized as not hazardous. Explanatory notes to the lists explicitly provide that the Annexes are not exhaustive. They are intended as an expeditious means of determining whether, in principle, a waste is hazardous for the purposes of the Convention. The Technical Working Group that developed the Annexes is instructed to review the lists to keep them up to date with current developments, which are to be signalled by the parties themselves. See Report of the Fourth Meeting of the Conference of the Parties to the Basel Convention, Malaysia, 23–27 Feb. 1998, UNEP/CHW.4/35.

[115] The ECJ rejected an appeal by the EP that the text had to be based on Art. 95 EC: Case C–187/93, *European Parliament* v. *Council* [1994] ECR I–2857. The Commission had based its proposal on Arts. 95 (harmonization in the field of the internal market) and 133 EC (external trade policy). The Council decided to base the Regulation solely on Art. 175 EC. The ECJ sustained the use of the latter, citing its case law that in choosing between Arts. 95 and 175 EC, the preponderant aim and content of the legislation concerned are decisive. The ECJ did not assess whether Art. 133 EC should have been included. Although the Regulation has a clear environmental goal, it does have an enormous impact on the international movement of wastes. See J. Bouckaert, "De juridische basis van Verordening 259/93" (1995) 4 *Tijdschrift voor Milieurecht* 19; and Sommer, n. 101 above.

waste". Thus, the self-sufficiency principle need not lead to an absolute application of the proximity principle;

— different procedures apply depending on the type of waste[116] and its destination, including whether it is destined for disposal or recovery;

— Member States are allowed to object to movements of waste in order to protect the environment, including having an option to take measures prohibiting generally or partially, or objecting systematically to shipments of waste for disposal; and,

— exports of waste for disposal to third countries are prohibited, taking into account the Basel Convention and OECD Decisions. Shipments of waste for recovery listed on the "green list", however, are generally excluded from the control procedures.

B.   SCOPE OF APPLICATION

The Regulation applies to shipments of waste within, into, and out of the Community. The concept of waste is based on the notion set forth within the Framework Directive. Together with specific exclusions,[117] the Regulation also includes a cryptic provision with respect to the "green list of wastes", included in Annex II. These wastes allow for relatively easy techniques of treatment. Shipments of waste destined for recovery and listed in the green list are excluded from the Regulation, except for the following:

- Article 11(b)–(e) remain applicable (see Article 1(3)(a)), as do Article 17(1)–(3) (see Article 1(3)(a)) as well as Articles 25 and 26 (see Article 1(3)(e)). Article 11 deals with the information to be provided to the authorities.[118] Article 17 contains provisions with regard to export to non-OECD states. Articles 25 and 26 contain take-back provisions in the event of illegal traffic. Member States may apply these provisions in the event of illegal trafficking of green list wastes, or should the Framework Directive be contravened;

- Commission and Member States' representatives may decide that a procedure be set in place for part of the green list wastes. This may be

[116] The Regulation includes a green, amber, and red list of waste; the lists are adapted by Commission Decision, in co-operation with Member States' experts.

[117] The Regulation does not apply to (see Art. 1(2)): the offloading to shore of waste generated by the normal operation of ships and offshore platforms, including waste water and residues, provided that such waste is the subject of a specific binding international instrument; shipments of civil aviation waste; shipments of radioactive waste as defined in Art. 2 of Dir. 92/3/Euratom of 3 Feb. 1992 on the supervision and control of shipments of radioactive waste between Member States and into and out of the Community; shipments of waste mentioned in Art. 2(1)(b) of the Framework Directive, where they are already covered by other relevant legislation; shipments of waste into the Community in accordance with the requirements of the Protocol on environmental protection to the Antarctic Treaty.

[118] Art. 11(1): in order to assist the tracking of shipments of waste for recovery listed in Annex II, they shall be accompanied by the following information, signed by the holder: (a) the name and address of the holder; (b) the usual commercial description of the waste; (c) the quantity of the waste; (d) the name and address of the consignee; (e) the operations involving recovery, as listed in Annex II.B to the Framework Directive; (f) the anticipated date of shipment.

justified, *inter alia*, if the wastes concerned exhibit any of the hazardous characteristics listed in Annex III of the Hazardous Waste Directive (Article 1(3)(c)). Such wastes are treated as if they had been listed in Annex III or IV of the Waste Shipment Regulation and are listed in an Annex II(a); and,

- in exceptional cases, the shipment of wastes listed in Annex II may, for environmental or public health reasons, be controlled by Member States as if they are listed in Annex III or IV. The Commission has to be notified and other Member States informed. The Commission may subsequently confirm such action by adding such wastes to Annex II.A (see Article 1(3)(d)).[119]

Otherwise, green list wastes are subject to all provisions of the Framework Directive, but not to the Waste Shipment Regulation.[120] The exclusion of these wastes is to prevent a flood of notifications which might hinder the authorities in checking shipments involving real risks, and to provide for a source of profit for the recycling industry.

The Commission Decision, which adapted the list in 1994,[121] included a headnote stating that, "regardless of whether or not wastes are included on this list, they may not be moved as green wastes if they are contaminated by other materials to an extent which (a) increases the risks associated with the waste sufficiently to render it appropriate for inclusion in the Amber or Red lists, or (b) prevents the recovery of the waste in an environmentally sound manner".[122] It remains unclear how this will be applied in practice. Given the vagueness of the criteria, private parties arguably are not bound by the headnote, except in the most extreme cases.[123] In a 1998 Decision the Commission once more adapted the green list.[124]

C. SHIPMENTS OF WASTE BETWEEN MEMBER STATES

i. *Waste Intended for Disposal*

The procedure set up by the Waste Shipment Regulation for the shipment of wastes between Member States, intended for disposal, centres around prior notification (Articles 3 ff.).

a. Information to be Provided by the Notifier The notifier[125] who intends to ship waste for disposal from one Member State to another and/or pass it in

---

[119] By proposing this inclusion to the Committee set up by Art. 18 of the Framework Directive.

[120] The Waste Shipment Regulation refers expressly to Arts. 10 and 11 of the Framework Directive (duly authorised facilities) and to Arts. 8, 12, 13, and 14.

[121] Commission Decision 94/721.EC, adapting pursuant to Article 42(3), Annexes II, III and IV to Council Regulation (EEC) No. 259/93 on the supervision and control of shipments of waste within, into and out of the EC [1994] OJ L288/36.

[122] This note is based on the OECD Decision, n. 107 above.

[123] See Hunter, n. 65 above, 84.

[124] Commission Decision 98/368/EC, adapting pursuant to Article 42(3), Annexes II and III to Council Regulation (EEC) No. 259/93 on the supervision and control of shipments of waste within, into and out of the European Community [1998] OJ L165/20.

[125] Art. 2(g): "notifier means any natural person or corporate body to whom or to which the duty to notify is assigned, that is to say the person referred to hereinafter who proposes to ship waste or have waste shipped: (i) the person whose activities produced the waste (original producer); or (ii) where this is not possible, a collector licensed to this effect by a Member State or a registered or licensed dealer or broker who arranges for the disposal or the recovery of waste; or (iii) where these

transit through other Member States must notify the authority of destination[126] and send a copy of the notification to the authorities of dispatch[127] and of transit,[128] and to the consignee.[129] A consignment note has to be used which is issued by the authority of dispatch.[130] The notifier has to have a contract with the consignee which has to include the obligation of the notifier to take the waste back, if the shipment has not been completed as planned, or if it has been effected in violation of the Regulation (Articles 25–26); and the obligation of the consignee, to provide as soon as possible and no later than 180 days following the receipt of the waste, a certificate to the notifier that the waste has been disposed of in an environmentally sound manner.[131]

b. Further Procedures—Objections   The authority of destination has thirty days following dispatch of the acknowledgement[132] to take its decision authorizing the shipment, with or without conditions, or refusing it (Article 4). Authorization can only be given in the absence of objections on its part or on the part of the other authorities. The decision has to be sent to the notifier with copies to the other authorities (Article 4(2)(a)). Authorities of dispatch and transit may raise written objections within twenty days following the acknowledgement, and/or may lay down written conditions in respect of the transport of waste within their jurisdiction. These conditions are entered into the consignment note and may not be more stringent than those laid down in respect of similar shipments occurring wholly within their jurisdiction (i.e. principle of non-discrimination) and they have to take due account of existing

persons are unknown or are not licensed, the person having possession or legal control of the waste (holder); or (iv) in the case of import into or transit through the Community of waste, the person designated by the laws of the State of dispatch or, when this designation has not taken place, the person having possession or legal control of the waste (holder)." In other words, except in unavoidable cases, it will be for the initial producer to make the notification. However, so as not to impose an excessive burden on small and medium-sized enterprises, provision is made for the possibility of an approved collector giving notification for them.

A competent authority of the state of dispatch may fulfil this notification requirement itself, should national legislation and procedure so provide. However, Art. 3(8) excludes this possibility in the event that this authority itself has objections against the waste. Should this be the case, it has immediately to inform the notifier of any such objections.

[126] Art. 2(m): "state of destination means any state to which a shipment of waste is planned or made for disposal or recovery, or for loading on board before disposal sea without prejudice to existing conventions on disposal sea".

[127] Art. 2(l): "state of dispatch means any state from which a shipment of waste is planned or made".

[128] Art. 2(n): "state of transit means any state, other than the State of dispatch or destination, through which a shipment of waste is planned or made".

[129] Art. 2(h): "consignee means the person or undertaking to whom or to which the waste is shipped for recovery or disposal".

[130] See Commission Decision 94/774/EC concerning the standard consignment note referred to in Council Reg. (EC) No. 259/93 on the supervision and control of shipments of waste within, into, and out of the European Community [1994] OJ L310/70.

[131] In the event of waste to be shipped between two establishments under the control of the same legal entity, the contract may be replaced by a mere declaration by the entity in question undertaking to dispose of the waste.

[132] Within three working days upon notification, the competent authority of destination has to send an acknowledgement to the notifier.

agreements, in particular relevant international conventions.[133] Should the authorities be satisfied that their objections have been properly addressed and that the transport conditions will be met, the notifier has to be informed immediately. After any essential change in the conditions of the shipment, a new notification must be made (Article 4(4)).

The *Member States* may raise only the following objections (Article 4(2)(c)): They may, "in accordance with the Treaty" prohibit generally or partially or object systematically to shipments in order to implement the principles of proximity, priority for recovery, and self-sufficiency in accordance with the Framework Directive (Article 4(3)(a)(i)). "In accordance with the Treaty" refers to the principles of non-discrimination and proportionality. Member States have to apply such measures without discriminating between their nationals and those of other Member States, or between nationals of different Member States. Moreover, the measure must be proportionate to the legitimate aim sought.[134] This possibility, however, does not apply in the case of hazardous waste (as defined in the Hazardous Waste Directive)[135] produced in a Member State of dispatch in such a small quantity overall per year that the provision of new specialized disposal installations within that state would be uneconomic (Article 4(3)(a)(ii)). In the event of objections, the Member State of destination has to liaise with the Member State of dispatch to try to resolve the issue. If there is no satisfactory solution, either state may refer the matter to the Commission, which will determine the issue.

Authorities of dispatch and destination may raise objections if the shipments are not in accordance with the Framework Directive, especially Articles 5 and 7 (the principle of self-sufficiency), or where the installation has to dispose of waste from a nearer source and the competent authority has given priority to this waste, or in order to ensure that shipments are in accordance with waste management plans (Article 7 of the Framework Directive). The authorities have to take into account geographical circumstances or the need for specialized installations for certain types of waste (Article 4(3)(b)).

Finally (Article 4(3)(c)), *all authorities* may object to the shipment if the notifier or the consignee was previously guilty of illegal trafficking;[136] or if the shipment conflicts with national law and/or international obligations of the Member State(s) concerned.

Once the notifier has received authorization from the authority of destination, the shipment can go ahead (Article 5(1)). All undertakings involved complete the consignment note. Within three working days following receipt of the waste, the consignee is required to send copies of the completed consignment

---

[133] Art. 32 states that the international transport conventions listed in Annex I to which the Member States are parties shall be complied with in so far as they cover the waste to which the Regulation refers. It would seem justified to refer to this list also for the application of Art. 4(2)(d).

[134] This exception has to be interpreted in the light of ECJ case law on Arts. 28–30 (ex Arts. 30–36) EC.

[135] N. 70 above.

[136] In this case, the competent authority of dispatch may refuse all shipments involving the person in question in accordance with national legislation.

note to the notifier and to the authorities. As soon as possible, and not later than 180 days following the receipt of the waste, the consignee must dispatch a certificate of disposal to the notifier and to the authorities.

c. Waste for Recovery   In essence, consent for the shipment of wastes for recovery from the amber list may be tacit, whilst for the red list, consent must be explicit, in writing, prior to the shipment:

- *Amber list*
  The same procedure applies as for waste destined for disposal, *mutatis mutandis* (Article 6). For instance, the consignment note must include relevant data with respect to the planned recovery operation.

  The authorities have thirty days following dispatch of the acknowledgement *to object* to the shipment (Article 7), for instance should they suspect that waste which is in effect destined for disposal would be shipped as waste destined for recovery. Written consent may be provided in a period shorter than thirty days. Within twenty days following the dispatch of the acknowledgement, conditions in respect of the transport of waste can be laid down. Generally, long-term authorizations are possible for a specific recovery facility (Article 9), allowing subsequent shipment to be merely notified. Such decisions may be limited to a specific period of time and they may be revoked at any time, and Member States of transit and dispatch may object.

  The *authorities of destination and dispatch* may only object to the shipment for any of the following reasons:

  - the Framework Directive, in particular Article 7; or,
  - if it is not in accordance with national laws and regulations relating to environmental protection, public order, public safety, or health protection; or
  - if the notifier or the consignee has previously been guilty of illegal trafficking; or
  - if the shipment conflicts with obligations resulting from international conventions concluded by the Member State(s) concerned; or
  - if the ratio of the recoverable and non-recoverable waste, the estimated value of the materials to be finally recovered or the cost of the recovery and the cost of the disposal of the non-recoverable fraction do not justify the recovery under economic and environmental considerations. Experience with the predecessor of the current Regulation showed that parties will try to brand their waste as "recoverable", even if it is largely unsuited for any kind of recovery.[137]

  The *authorities of transit* may only raise reasoned objections to the planned shipment based on the second, third, and fourth of the aforementioned reasons.

[137] Veldkamp, n. 100 above, 82.

The shipment may go ahead after the thirty-day period has expired only if no objection has been lodged. Tacit consent, however, expires within one year from that date. Where the authorities decide to provide written consent, the shipment may be effected immediately after all necessary consents have been received. The procedure then proceeds as has been set out above.

- *Red list and non-assigned waste*
Shipments of waste for recovery listed in Annex IV and of waste for recovery which have not yet been assigned to Annex II, Annex III, or Annex IV must follow the same procedures, except that the consent of the competent authorities concerned must be provided in writing prior to commencement of shipment (Article 10). Also, there are no general authorizations as in Article 9 possible for these types of waste.

d. Shipment of Waste for Disposal and Recovery between Member States with Transit via Third States   Article 12 outlines a procedure of information to be submitted to the authorities of third states. Obviously, no such shipment can go ahead without the express authorization of the authorities concerned. The authority of destination has to wait for consent, "where appropriate", before giving its authorization.

D.   SHIPMENTS OF WASTE WITHIN MEMBER STATES

The Council opted against including intra-Member State traffic of waste, mainly for reasons related to the principle of subsidiarity.[138] Member States have to establish an "appropriate system" for the supervision and control of shipments of waste within their jurisdictions (Article 13), taking account of the need for coherence with the Community system established by the Regulation. This may be realized, for instance, by simply copying it.

E.   EXPORTS OF WASTE OUTSIDE THE COMMUNITY

i. Waste for Disposal

Article 14 prohibits all exports of waste for disposal,[139] except those to EFTA states which are also parties to the Basel Convention.[140] Exports of waste for disposal to an EFTA country is also banned if the EFTA country of destination prohibits imports of such wastes or where it has not given its written consent to the specific import of this waste, or if the authority of dispatch in the Community has reason to believe that the waste will not be managed in accordance with environmentally sound methods in the EFTA country of destination concerned.

---

[138] The Commission originally proposed to impose a notification duty for all shipments, even for cases involving a single Member State. See COM(92)121, [1992] OJ C115/4.

[139] The original proposal did not distinguish between disposal and recovery, a distinction which was introduced at the instigation of the EP.

[140] Iceland, Liechtenstein, Norway, and Switzerland.

The procedure is similar to shipments of waste within the EC, with some modifications (Article 15), including longer time-limits. Objections have to be based on Article 4(3).

ii. Waste for Recovery

a. Annex V List of Wastes   According to Article 16, all exports of waste for recovery listed in Annex V[141] are prohibited except those to:

— countries to which the OECD decision applies; and to
— other countries which are Parties to the Basel Convention; and/or
— with which the Community, or the Community and its Member States, have concluded bilateral or multilateral or regional agreements or arrangements in the sense of Article 11 of the Basel Convention; or
— with which individual Member States have concluded bilateral agreements prior to the date of application of the Regulation.[142] The latter have to be compatible with Community legislation and in accordance with Article 11 of the Basel Convention. They have to be notified to the Commission and they expire when agreements are concluded with the Community as a whole.[143] For both exceptions, any such exports are however prohibited from 1 January 1998 onwards.

The absolute prohibition of exports of wastes listed in Annex V to non-OECD countries represents the implementation, in the EC, of Decision III/1 of the Convention of the Parties to the Basel Convention.[144] Annex V shall be decisive for the scope of the export prohibition. The Commission is to review and amend Annex V,[145] taking into consideration the wastes figuring on the Community hazardous wastes list[146] and the work of the Working Groups of the Basel Convention.[147] For the moment, Annex V consists of all wastes figuring in the amber and red lists of wastes.[148] In any event, regardless of Annex V developments, exports will remain prohibited if the country concerned prohibits all imports of such wastes or where it has not given its consent to their specific import; and if the authority of dispatch has reason to believe that the waste will not be managed in accordance with environmentally sound methods.

---

[141] Inserted by Art. 1 of Council Reg. (EC) No. 120/97 amending Reg. (EC) No. 259/93 on the supervision and control of shipments of waste within, into, and out of the European Community [1997] OJ L22/14.

[142] The Community has exclusive competence as regards shipments involving third countries.

[143] Art. 16(2)(d): "agreements which individual Member States have concluded must guarantee an environmentally sound management" (Art. 11 of the Basel Convention). This procedure now seems less relevant, given the forthcoming absolute ban.

[144] Prepared by Decision II/12. The EC has formally approved the amendments to the Basel Convention: Council Decision of 22 Sept. 1997 on the approval, on behalf of the Community, of the amendment to the Convention on the control of transboundary movements of hazardous wastes and their disposal (Basle Convention), as laid down in Decision III/1 of the Conference of the Parties [1997] OJ L272/45.

[145] Following the procedure of Art. 18 of the Framework Directive.   [146] N. 82 above.

[147] See nn. 90 and 114 above.   [148] Art. 2 of Reg. (EC) No. 120/97, n. 141 above.

As noted, the Fourth Conference of the Parties to the Basel Convention has adopted the (non-exhaustive) lists of hazardous wastes, which makes the export ban to non-OECD countries operational. The Commission has adopted a proposal for the Council formally to adopt Annexes VIII and IX to the Basel Convention.[149] In accordance with its competence to adapt Annex V to the Waste Shipments Regulation, the Commission has not waited for the actual implementation of the new Annexes to the Basel Convention in the EC. Commission Regulation (EC) No. 2408/98[150] has adapted Annex V to the Regulation, which now comprises three classification systems:

— Annexes VIII and IX to the Basel Convention; Annex IX (listing those wastes which are considered as non-hazardous for the purposes of the Basel Convention, and thus not covered by the export ban under the Basel Convention) is however included for clarification purposes only;
— the EU list of hazardous wastes;[151] and
— the amber and red lists of wastes annexed to the Waste Shipments Regulation.

The latter two classes are an application of the Basel Convention's authorization for parties to take measures that go further than the Convention's provisions. However, Annex V provides that in the event of conflict or discrepancy between the classification under the Basel Convention and the classification under EU legislation, the former prevails. This provision is designed not to prevent Annex IX from taking effect. It is motivated by the view that the lists of the Basel Convention reflect the most recent work on the issue. The Regulation expressly considers that in the future further-reaching measures may indeed be taken.

b. Annex II List of Wastes: Green List The Regulation includes a contested procedure with respect to the export of "green list" wastes (Annex II) to non-EFTA countries. Article 17 foresees that the Commission notifies the green list of wastes to every country to which the OECD Decision does not apply. The Commission then requests written confirmation that such waste is not subject to control in the country of destination and that the latter will accept categories of such waste to be shipped without the application of the procedures for Annex III or IV wastes. Alternatively, the country concerned may indicate whether such waste should be subject to any of the procedures included in the Regulation. In absence of this confirmation, the Commission is instructed to make "appropriate proposals". The Commission determines, in consultation

---

[149] Commission proposal of 6 Nov. 1998 for a Council decision on the approval, on behalf of the Community, of the amendment of Annex I and the adoption of new Annexes VIII and IX to the Convention on the Control of Transboundary Movements of Hazardous Wastes and their Disposal (Basel Convention), as laid down in Decision IV/9 of the Conference of the Parties, COM(1998)634. See also n. 114 above.

[150] Commission Reg. (EC) No. 2408/98 amending Annex V to Council Reg. (EC) No. 259/93 on the supervision and control of shipments of waste within, into, and out of the European Community [1998] OJ L298/19.

[151] Laid down in Decision 94/904/EC, n. 82 above.

with the country of destination, which of the controls shall apply. That is, the Commission looks either to the procedures set forth in Annex III or IV or to the procedures laid down in Article 15 (exports of waste for disposal).[152]

For those countries that have either not responded, or that have indicated that they do not wish to receive some or all types of green-list wastes, the Commission proposed to apply the red-list procedure (prior authorization of the authorities of destination required). It justified this proposal by observing that a unilateral decision by the EC completely to prohibit such shipments would be too inflexible and would have unduly adverse effects on trade. In the Commission's view, some of the countries concerned might not have been fully aware of the significance of their decision for those parts of their industrial sector which can use green-list wastes for transformation and further processing. Moreover, the Commission argued against absolute import prohibitions of "waste". It insisted that some of the substances included in the green list might not be considered "waste" under the legislation of the country concerned. A blank refusal of substances on the list thus might have undesirable consequences.

For all these reasons, the Commission opted for the red-list procedure, which would have allowed non-OECD countries flexibility in dealing with import requests, whilst at the same time establishing strict monitoring. The proposal received fierce criticism. The Commission proposal suggested that in applying the red-list procedure, shipments could in effect have gone ahead with the authorization of the non-OECD country concerned. This could have violated the Basel Convention depending on the definition, by the parties to the Convention, of "hazardous wastes".

Answering allegations that the EC was trying to circumvent the Convention, the Commission replied that it does not consider the green list of wastes to contain hazardous substances.[153] This highlights the very essence of the dispute. More generally, whereas the OECD and the EC stress the *risk* of a certain substance, normally associated with its handling, the Basel Convention focuses on the *hazard* of a substance, through its inherent characteristics. Interestingly, the ACP–EU Joint Assembly[154] opposed any weakening of the Basel Convention particularly through allowing selected non-OECD countries to continue importing hazardous wastes from OECD countries.[155] Following severe criticism, the Commission amended its proposal. For those countries that indicate they do not wish to receive some or all types of green-list waste, the Commission decided to "respect the wishes of these countries" and not to allow the exports concerned. For countries that have not responded, the

---

[152] See Commission Decision 94/575/EC determining the control procedures under Reg. (EC) No. 259/93 as regards certain shipments of waste to certain non-OECD countries [1994] OJ L220/15.

[153] "Commission Finally Proposes Ban on Hazardous Waste Exports" [1995] *ENDS-Report* 42.

[154] Set up in the framework of the Lomé Convention, which deals with the relationship between a number of African–Caribbean–Pacific states and the EU.

[155] Resolution of the ACP–EU Joint Assembly of 20 Mar. 1997 on hazardous waste [1997] OJ C308/61, at para. 5.

proposal maintains the red-list route.[156] The Council has adopted its Common Position that follows the Commission proposal.[157]

In any event, where waste of the green list is exported it must be destined for recovery operations within a facility which, under applicable domestic law, is operating or is authorized to operate in the importing country. In the absence of a control procedure, the control of this requirement is in effect left to the importing country concerned.

c. Annex III (Amber List), IV (Red List), and Non-assigned Wastes   Where waste listed in Annex III (amber list) is exported from the Community for recovery to countries and through countries to which the OECD Decision applies, Articles 6–8 and 9(1), (3)–(5), i.e. the procedure applicable to export of wastes for recovery within Member States, apply *mutatis mutandis*. Where the waste for recovery is listed in Annex IV (red list), or has not yet been assigned to Annex II, III, or IV, and is exported for recovery to or through countries to which the OECD Decision applies, Article 10 applies by analogy, i.e. the procedure for export for recovery between Member States, but without the possibility of tacit consent. Where waste for recovery listed in Annexes III and IV and waste for recovery which has not yet been assigned to Annex II, III, or IV is exported to and through countries to which the OECD Decision does not apply, the same procedure applies as for the export out of the EC of wastes destined for disposal (Article 15, except for paragraph (3)). Reasoned objections may be raised in accordance with Article 7(4) only (shipments of waste for recovery between Member States), save as otherwise provided for in bilateral or multilateral agreements.[158]

iii. Export of Waste to ACP States

Article 18 prohibits all exports of waste to ACP states. This does not prevent a Member State to which an ACP state has chosen to export waste for processing from returning the processed waste to the state of origin. In such a case, a specimen of the consignment note, together with the stamp of authorization, must accompany each shipment. This export ban conforms with Article 39 of the Lomé IV Convention, which prohibits exports of all wastes listed in Annexes I and II of the Basel Convention.

It is important to note that the green list of wastes is generally *not* covered by the Regulation's requirements. The Commission proposal dealing with the exports of wastes on the green list[159] expressly provides that those wastes on

---

[156] Amended Commission proposal of 26 Jan. 1998 for a Council Regulation establishing common rules and procedures to apply to shipments to certain non-OECD countries of certain types of waste, COM(97)685.

[157] Common Position 48/98 of 4 June 1998 with a view to adopting a Council Regulation establishing common rules and procedures to apply to shipments to certain non-OECD countries of certain types of waste [1998] OJ C333/1.

[158] Note the difference with exports of wastes destined for disposal, where exceptions have to be based on Art. 4(3). This provides more room for exceptions.

[159] N. 156 above.

the green list which are considered as hazardous under the Basel Convention are effectively banned from export to ACP states.

i.   Imports of Waste for Disposal

Imports into the Community of waste for disposal are prohibited. Exception is made for imports:

— from EFTA countries which are parties to the Basel Convention;
— from other countries which are:

- either Parties to the Convention; or
- with which the Community, or the Community and its Member States, have concluded bilateral or multilateral agreements or arrangements compatible with Community legislation and in accordance with Article 11 of the Basel Convention. The agreements have to guarantee that the disposal operations are carried out in an authorized centre and comply with the requirements for environmentally sound management; or
- with which individual Member States have concluded bilateral agreements or arrangements prior to the date of application of the Regulation, compatible with Community legislation and in accordance with Article 11 of the Basel Convention, containing the same guarantees as referred to earlier and guaranteeing that the waste originated in the country of dispatch and that disposal will be carried out exclusively in the Member State which has concluded the agreement or arrangement. These agreements expire when agreements or arrangements are concluded by the Community or by the Community and the Member States (Article 19); or
- in accordance with Article 19(2). Member States are authorized to conclude bilateral agreements after the date of application of the Regulation, should such waste not be managed in an environmentally sound manner in the country of dispatch. The same guarantees as referred to in the previous paragraph need to be provided. The Commission has to be notified of any such agreements, prior to their conclusion.[160]

All non-EFTA countries, from which imports are allowed, must present a request beforehand to the Member State of destination on the basis that they do not have and cannot reasonably acquire the technical capacity and the necessary facilities in order to dispose of the waste in an environmentally sound manner. The authority of destination has to prohibit the import if it has reason to believe that the waste will not be managed in an environmentally sound

---

[160] The Commission has strongly criticized this loophole. See de Sadeleer, n. 6 above, 497.

manner on its territory (Article 19(3) and (4)). Article 20 involves a procedure which is similar to the procedure of Article 4 (shipments of waste destined for disposal, between Member States), although it has extended time limits. The shipment may be effected only after the notifier has received authorization from the competent authority of destination.

ii. Imports of Waste for Recovery

Imports of waste for recovery into the Community are prohibited except those from countries to which the OECD decision applies, or from other countries under the conditions referred to earlier with respect to waste destined for disposal (Article 21). In the latter case, relevant control procedures apply by analogy (Article 22).

G.   OTHER PROVISIONS

Title VI of the Regulation deals with the transit of waste from outside and through the Community for disposal or recovery outside the Community. The remainder of the Regulation contains a number of provisions, for instance with respect to the take-back guarantee in the event of incomplete shipment and treatment (Article 25), illegal trafficking (Article 26), spot checks of shipments (Article 30), co-operation with the Basel Convention (Articles 40–41), and reporting requirements. Importantly, Article 27 requires that all shipments of waste covered by the scope of the Regulation are provided with a financial guarantee or equivalent insurance covering costs for shipment, including take-back cases. Such guarantees are returned after proof has been furnished that the operation has been completed successfully.

H.   SOME TOPICAL ISSUES AND THE VIEW OF THE ECJ

Importantly, recent case law of the ECJ has limited the application of the principles of self-sufficiency and proximity to waste destined for disposal. In *Dusseldorp*, the ECJ rebuked the Dutch government for over-enthusiastically restricting waste exports. The ECJ determined that the principles of self-sufficiency and proximity, laid down in the Framework Directive and in the Waste Shipments Regulation, did not apply to shipments of waste for recovery. Dutch reliance on Article 176 EC failed since the ECJ did not accept imperative reasons for derogating from Article 29 (formerly Article 34) EC. Finally, the existence of a waste agency with exclusive rights to handle certain waste management operations was held to be incompatible with Article 86(1) (formerly Article 90(1)) EC. The judgment in *Dusseldorp* constitutes a highlight in the assessment of the dichotomy between the protection of the environment and the internal market. The decision contains certain illuminating statements with respect to the application of the *Cassis de Dijon* rule in the context of Article 29 EC. The facts underline that in the waste management sector, increasing use is being made of restrictions on exports and of exclusive rights.[161]

The classification of mixed types of wastes also remains problematic. A recent judgment by the ECJ does not seem to have resolved the issue. In *Beside*, the ECJ held that a "small" quantity of materials not included in the green list does not alter the classification of the complete batch as belonging to the green list. It did not indicate how the qualification "small" should be interpreted, but left this for national courts to settle. The case highlights again that the realization of harmonized definitions in the waste sector is all but running smoothly.[162]

V. Packaging and Packaging Waste

A.   ORIGINS OF THE DIRECTIVE

Requirements with respect to packaging have a direct influence on the internal market and the question whether Member States should be allowed to enforce stricter measures than their neighbours is particularly complex. Prior to 1994, the Council dealt with the subject of packaging in Directive 85/339/EEC on Containers of Liquids for Human Consumption.[163] This Directive was not working satisfactorily, since differences in its implementation prevented the smooth functioning of the internal market. The German packaging ordinances are a case in point. The state-supported collection and recovery system led to an influx of packaging waste in the German market. Similarly, economic operators were less interested in collecting the waste on their own territory, since they found supplies outside Germany.[164]

Typically, Community action in this sector involves a balancing act between environmental protection and free movement of goods. Although the latter is undoubtedly a pillar of Community policy, a high level of environmental protection has gradually been introduced as a principle of similar importance.

---

[161] See the author's note "ECJ Rebukes Restrictions to Free Movement of Waste" (1999) 25 *European Law Review* 178–84 re Dusseldorf, case C–203/96. See also A. van Rossem and H. G. Sevenster, "Hof beantwoordt vragen Afdeling over afvalregime" (1998) 4 *Nederlands Tijdschrift voor Europees Recht* 196. Similar issues are raised in a case against Germany (limitations to the shipments of waste destined for cement-kiln incineration): see "Commission Decides Further Step in Legal Action against Germany on Waste Shipments" IP/98/876.

[162] Case C–192/96, *Beside BV and IM Besselsen* v. *Minister van Volkshuisvesting, Ruimtelijke Ordening en Milieubeheer*; see van Rossem and Sevenster, n. 161 above, at 196–8. See also the judgment of the High Court, Queen's Bench Division, of 22 May 1997 in *R* v. *Environment Agency, ex parte Dockgrange Limited and Another*, which concerned the mixture of various wastes occurring on the green list; the High Court decided that the Regulation, on a proper interpretation, does not imply that a mixture of wastes, all of which are individually assigned to the green list of wastes, is not, by reason of the fact of the mixture alone, to be treated as unassigned waste, subject to red-list procedures.

[163] [1985] OJ L176/18.

[164] The Commission's opinion with respect to the German scheme was published in the Official Journal: Commission Notice IV/34493 [1997] OJ C100/4.

Thus, solving the conflict by a mere hierarchy of norms has become impossible.[165] An early good illustration of this dichotomy is provided by *Danish Bottles*.[166]

The Commission submitted its proposal on 15 July 1992.[167] The text was amended[168] to take account of the views expressed by the Economic and Social Committee (ESC).[169] The EP[170] and the Council adopted its Common Position on 4 March 1994.[171] Parliament subsequently rejected the Common Position,[172] which forced the issue into so-called conciliation talks, where Council and Parliament are to try to reach a compromise. In the case of the Packaging Directive, a deal was struck. In this regard Germany, the Netherlands, and Denmark were outvoted, and Directive 94/62/EC was approved in December 1994.[173] The Directive aims to harmonize national measures concerning the management of packaging and packaging waste in order to provide a high level of environmental protection, and to ensure the functioning of the internal market (Article 1(1)).

B. SCOPE OF APPLICATION AND OBJECTIVES—HIERARCHY OF PRINCIPLES

The Directive covers all packaging placed on the market in the Community and all packaging waste (Article 2).[174] "Packaging" means all products made of any materials of any nature to be used for the containment, protection, handling, delivery, and presentation of goods from raw materials to processed goods from the producer to the user or the consumer (Article 3(1)). "Packaging waste" refers to any packaging or packaging material covered by the definition of waste in the Framework Directive,[175] excluding production residues (Article 3(2)).

Member States considered whether, in line with the Community waste-management strategy,[176] it was appropriate to express a preference for dealing

---

[165] This conclusion has been reinforced by the Treaty of Amsterdam, which has included "sustainable development" as an objective of both the EU and the EC, and which has strengthened the principle of a high level of environmental protection. More details are given in G. van Calster and K. Deketelaere, "Amsterdam, the IGC and Greening the EU Treaty" (1998) 7 *European Environmental Law Review* 12.

[166] Case C–302/86, *Commission* v. *Denmark* [1988] ECR 4607. See further the article by H. Temmink at p. 61 above.

[167] Commission proposal for a Council directive on packaging and packaging waste COM(92)278 [1992] OJ C263/1.

[168] Amended Commission proposal for a directive on packaging and packaging waste COM(93)416 [1993] OJ C285/1.

[169] [1993] OJ C129/1.   [170] [1993] OJ C194/154.

[171] Common Position 13/94 adopted by the Council on 4 Mar. 1994 with a view to adopting an EP and Council Directive on packaging and packaging waste [1994] OJ C137/65.

[172] [1994] OJ C205/163.

[173] Dir. 94/62/EC on packaging and packaging waste [1994] OJ L365/10. See J. Golub, "State Power and Institutional Influence in European Integration: Lessons from the Packaging Waste Directive", *EUI Working Paper*, No. 96/3 (Florence: European University Institute, 1996), 34.

[174] Packaging which is produced in the EC, but exported, is not covered by the Directive.

[175] N. 1 above.   [176] N. 4 above.

with packaging waste. The importance of such a hierarchy extends beyond the policy level. A number of Member States had already put in place national packaging waste programmes, including the use of voluntary agreements with industry.[177] These initiatives contained national recycling and/or production targets, going far beyond what was technically and politically feasible, especially for southern Member States. If prevention were placed at the top of the hierarchy, the legitimacy of national prevention targets under Community law would be boosted. In contrast, the absence of any hierarchy indicates that all alternatives are to be considered equal. High re-use targets, for instance, are then to be dismissed, especially should they hinder free movement of packaging.[178]

The original proposal did not contain a preference.[179] Since there was no generalized agreement on "Life Cycle Analysis" methodology and interpretation, the Commission felt that prevailing uncertainty prevented authorities from preferring any single option. Therefore, prevention of packaging waste by reducing the amount of packaging was put forward as the only tool of which the environmental soundness was certain.[180] The EP did express a clear preference for re-use and recycling[181] but the Commission rejected this in its amended proposal, citing the pre-existing hierarchy in the Framework Directive, as well as the need for flexibility. The Council inserted the idea of a hierarchy into its Common Position, but it did not fully agree with the EP. The priority for prevention was clearly expressed. Rather than citing re-use and recycling as preferable to recovery, the Council considered re-use, recycling, and recovery equivalent.

The final text reads: "this Directive lays down measures aimed, as a first priority, at preventing the production of packaging waste and, as additional fundamental principles, at re-using packaging, at recycling and other forms of recovering packaging waste and, hence, at reducing the final disposal of such waste" (Article 1(2)).

---

[177] For an overview, see the Commission Proposal, n. 167 above, and de Sadeleer, n. 6 above, 371–81. See further the article by J. Verschuuren at p. 103 above.

[178] T. Demey, J-P. Hannequart, and K. Lambert, *Packaging Europe* (Brussels: Brussels Instituut voor Milieubeheer, 1996), 99.

[179] Recital 5 of the Commission Proposal (n. 167 above): "as long as life-cycle assessments justify no clear hierarchy, reusable packaging and recoverable packaging waste and, in particular, recyclable packaging waste are to be considered as equally valid methods for reducing the environmental impact of packaging".

[180] Europe's packaging industry maintains that this is still the case. See *Use of Lifecycle Assessment (LCA) as a Policy Tool in the Field of Packaging Waste Management*, Discussion Paper (Brussels: European Organisation for Packaging and the Environment, 1996), 5.

[181] Recital 5 to the EP's opinion (n. 170 above): "until scientific and technological progress is made with regard to recovery processes, reuse and recycling should be considered preferable in terms of environmental impact; . . . life-cycle assessments should be completed as soon as possible to justify a clear hierarchy between reusable, recyclable and recoverable packaging".

C. PREVENTION, RE-USE, RECYCLING, AND RECOVERY

i. Prevention

It is observed that prevention of the production of packaging, and prevention of packaging waste is the first priority.

The former is dealt with rather concisely. Article 4(1) requires Member States to take preventive measures apart from those introduced by the Directive (which are related to the prevention of packaging waste). Prevention of packaging as such is dealt with more extensively at policy level,[182] as well as in the Framework Directive.

The prevention of packaging waste is defined in terms of the "essential requirements" of Article 9. This Article obliges Member States to ensure that three years from the date of entry into force of the Directive, packaging may be placed on the market only if it complies with all essential requirements defined by the Directive, including Annex II. Specific Community standards are to be developed which already meet these requirements (Article 10) and pre-existing Community standards which do so are published in the Official Journal, together with equivalent national standards. Annex II contains the "essential requirements on the composition and the re-usable and recoverable, including recyclable, nature of packaging". Unfortunately, the Annex consists of vague, general criteria, which require harmonization in order to be effectively applied.[183] Nonetheless, it imposes far-reaching conditions, including the requirement that packaging be designed, produced, and commercialized in such a way as to permit its re-use or recovery, including recycling, and to minimize its impact on the environment when it is disposed of. From 30 June 1996, Member States have had to presume compliance with all requirements of the Annex of packaging which complies with the aforementioned standards. From 31 December 1997, packaging has been able to be placed on the market only if it complies with the essential requirements. The question remains how these requirements are to be controlled and enforced in the period prior to the establishment of a set of standards.[184] CEN, the European standardization body, has been given the mandate to develop such standards.[185] Its work is being delayed by the need to create standards which both meet the requirements of the Directive and provide industry with workable solutions.[186]

---

[182] For instance, in the Communication from the Commission on the review of the Community Strategy for Waste Management—Draft Council Resolution on Waste Policy, COM(96)399, where the responsibility of the producers of waste is singled out as a main element of the new Community strategy. The Council adopted a resolution which integrates the Commission Communication: Council Resolution on a Community Strategy for Waste Management [1997] OJ C76/1. See also the EP with respect to this Communication [1996] OJ C362/241.

[183] Demey, Hannequart, and Lambert, n. 178 above, 61 ff.   [184] *Ibid.*, 63 ff.

[185] Commission mandate to CEN of 8 Mar. 1996 for standardization and a study related to packaging and packaging waste.

[186] *CEN Annual Report, 1997–8* (Brussels: CEN, 1998), 13.

ii.   Re-use, Recycling, and "Other Forms of Recovering Waste"

Re-use, recycling, and "other forms of recovering waste" constitute the additional fundamental principles of packaging waste policy. Attempts to define the precise meaning of this concept are probably self-defeating. It would seem that a negative description is the most adequate: none of the alternatives mentioned enjoys priority.

Article 5 merely states, with respect to re-use,[187] that Member States may encourage systems of packaging, which can be re-used in an environmentally sound manner, in conformity with the Treaty. The length of this Article is deceptive, as it is a principle of utmost importance. Article 5 acknowledges that the principle of re-use, albeit not a binding Community principle of packaging waste policy, may be introduced by Member States as a priority in their national policies. Member States' competence, however, is limited to packaging for which re-use is feasible in an environmentally sound manner. Moreover, national measures may not infringe the Treaty. Contrary to Article 15 (economic instruments), Article 5 does not expressly recall the environmental objectives of the Treaty, but merely refers to "the Treaty" in general. This underlines that full weight should be given to principles such as the free movement of goods and free competition. The assessment of proportionality in particular will be predominant.[188]

Article 7 obliges Member States to establish systems to provide for the return and/or collection of used packaging and/or packaging waste from the consumer, other final users, or from the waste stream in order to channel it to the most appropriate waste management alternatives, as well as for the re-use or recovery including recycling of the packaging and/or packaging waste collected. This is a general obligation with direct influence on the promotion of re-use. That the "systems" could take the form of voluntary agreements is indicated by the subsequent condition of Article 7: the systems must be open to all economic operators of the sectors concerned and to the participation of the competent public authorities. They have to apply to imported products under non-discriminatory conditions, including the detailed arrangements and any tariffs imposed for access to the systems, and they generally have to be designed so as to avoid barriers to trade or distortions of competition.[189]

---

[187] Art. 3(5): "Re-use" is "any operation by which packaging, which has been conceived and designed to accomplish within its life cycle a minimum number of trips or rotations, is refilled or used for the same purpose for which it was conceived, with or without the support of auxiliary products present on the market enabling the packaging to be refilled; such re-used packaging will become packaging waste when no longer subject to re-use".

[188] See G. de Búrca, "The Principle of Proportionality and its Application in EC Law", in A. Barav and D. Wyatt (eds.), *Yearbook of European Law—1993* (Oxford: Clarendon Press, 1994), 105, a good reminder of the pitfalls which any proportionality test entails. See also B. Jadot, "Mesures nationales de police de l'environnement, libre circulation des marchandises proportionnalité" [1990] *Cahiers de Droit Européen* 427.

[189] See F. O. W. Vogelaar, "Verpakkingen en verpakkingsafval. De Richtlijn 94/62/EG en haar tenuitvoerlegging in Nederland", in K. Deketelaere and L. F. Wiggers-Rust (eds.), *Actualiteiten Europees Milieurecht* (Bruges: Die Keure, 1997), 95, who assesses Dutch implementation of the Directive by way of an environmental agreement with industry.

Industrial and commercial property rights need to be protected. By specifically mentioning re-use as a specific "fundamental principle", and by allowing Member States to develop re-use systems (Article 5), the Directive *de facto* identifies re-use as a priority. Still, this suggestion might be at odds with the fact that re-use has been laid down as an "additional fundamental principle", along with recovery and recycling.

Article 6 imposes concrete recovery[190] and recycling[191] targets:

— no later than five years from the implementation date, between 50 per cent as a minimum and 65 per cent as a maximum by weight of the packaging waste has to be recovered;
— within this general target, and within the same time limit, between 25 per cent as a minimum and 45 per cent as a maximum by weight of the totality of packaging materials contained in packaging waste has to be recycled with a minimum of 15 per cent by weight for each packaging material.[192]

No later than ten years from the same date, a percentage of packaging waste has to be recovered and recycled, which is to be determined by the Council (by qualified majority) with a view to increasing substantially the targets mentioned. Moreover, the first target has to be reviewed every five years, by the Council acting by a qualified majority. This is also the case after the first five-year period (i.e. before the end of the ten-year period of substantial review), which ends on 30 June 2001 (Article 6 in conjunction with Article 22).

The following exceptions have been allowed:

— *Greece, Ireland, and Portugal* may decide to attain, no later than five years from the date of implementation, lower targets but shall attain at least 25 per cent for recovery (Article 6(5)). They may also postpone the attainment of those targets to a later deadline which cannot exceed 31 December 2005.[193] These exceptions do not extend to the revised targets (after the ten- to five-year period);
— Member States which have or will set programmes going beyond the targets and which provide appropriate capacities for recycling and recovery are permitted to pursue those targets (Article 6(6)). They must avoid distortions of the internal market and they must not hinder compliance by other Member States with the Directive. The Commission has to confirm these measures after having verified that they meet the conditions and do not constitute an arbitrary means of discrimination or a disguised

[190] Art. 3(6): "recovery" is any of the applicable operations provided for in Annex II. B to the Framework Directive, n. 2 above.

[191] Art. 3(7): "recycling" is "the reprocessing in a production process of the waste materials for the original purpose or for other purposes including organic recycling but excluding energy recovery".

[192] The minimum level for each material prevents Member States from reaching the target by just tackling "easy" packaging waste, such as paper and glass.

[193] Included because of their specific situation, respectively the large number of small islands, the presence of rural and mountain areas, and the current low level of packaging consumption.

restriction on trade. This provision has already triggered controversy. Its relation with Article 95 (formerly Article 100a) EC is the most contested.

1. First, Article 6(6) cannot constitute a "safeguard clause" in the sense of Article 95(10) (previously Art. 100A(5)) EC. The latter refers only to provisionary measures whereas the provision in the Packaging Directive clearly envisages long-term programmes.
2. The former Article 100a EC allowed Member States to maintain stricter national standards but held that they could not introduce new ones. The Directive applies to pre-existing and future programmes. In this sense, the Directive goes further than the former Article 100a(4) EC.[194]
3. On the other hand, it introduces stricter conditions namely with respect to the facilities for recycling and recovery. It does not indicate how this should be interpreted, and it would seem logical to interpret this provision in the light of the other conditions, in particular relating to the internal market. This would suggest that the capacities of other Member States must be taken into account, provided there is some sort of a formal agreement between the countries concerned, relating to import/export of the waste. One of the very concerns which led to the Directive was that an influx of packaging waste on the territory of a Member State might prevent this State from recovering its own waste in an environmentally sound manner. This must be borne in mind when assessing the programmes concerned.

In practice, the conditions imposed by the Directive would seem to limit national ambitions.

— Since the Directive is based on Article 95 EC,[195] Member States may maintain stricter national standards which were introduced prior to the Directive. The application thereof must not be a means of arbitrary discrimination, or a disguised restriction on trade.[196] Could the Commission (in the review procedure) or the ECJ (should it come to a challenge of a national programme) review the very level of environmental protection sought? One interpretation suggests that Member States are entitled to set 100 per cent recycling targets, e.g., for certain types of products. Community review would then focus on the necessity of the measure for the level pursued, and assessing whether there are no less trade-restrictive means that would achieve the same level of protection.[197]

---

[194] Art. 95(4) EC has been amended following the Amsterdam Treaty, and now expressly allows the introduction of new measures: see van Calster and Deketelaere, n. 165 above.

[195] A legal base which was not this time contested by the Council.

[196] From the extensive literature on this matter, see for instance Joseph, n. 92 above; R. D. Sloan, "Exemptions from Harmonisation Measures under Art. 100a(4) EC: The Second Authorisation of the German Ban on PCP" (1995) 4 *European Environmental Law Review* 45; B. M. Veltkamp, "Lidstaat wikt, Commissie beschikt: toepassing Artikel 100A, lid 4, EG" (1996) 2 *Nederlands Tijdschrift voor Europees Recht* 113.

[197] *Contra*: De Búrca, n. 188 above. Her analysis indicates that the ECJ does review Member States' discretion, whereby the level of discretion appears to vary according to the interest pursued (note that this author's analysis concerns the application of generally Art. 28 EC, i.e. not in the context of environment directives in particular).

Fluctuation in the targets and the exceptions have been criticized,[198] because, in effect, no penetrating rate of harmonization is ensured. It is therefore uncertain whether the Directive corresponds to the kind of harmonization needed for the realization of the internal market (Article 95 EC).

Apart from concrete targets, Member States have to, where appropriate, encourage the use of materials obtained from recycled packaging waste for the manufacturing of packaging and other products (Article 6(2)).

D.   OTHER PROVISIONS

An important element with a view to the free movement of goods is the marking and identification system. The 1996 Commission proposal for a Directive on Marking of Packaging and on the Establishment of a Conformity Procedure for Packaging[199] introduces a Community-wide marking system for packaging, and aims to harmonize the assessment of national packaging measures. The latter part describes the procedure whereby the manufacturer or his authorized representative ensures and declares that his packaging satisfies the essential requirements.

The Commission had in fact attached a marking proposal to its original text. It provided for different symbols for re-usable packing, recoverable packing, and packaging made partly or entirely of recycled materials. The Council was of the opinion that it came too early. The issue is linked to the aforementioned problem of the hierarchy of policy principles. Differing labelling for, say, re-use and recycling inevitably leads the consumer to think that one of the options is more environmentally friendly than the other. It was decided that this issue needed further study, and the Commission was instructed to come up with a new proposal, to be adopted not later than two years after the entry into force of the Directive. In its 1996 proposal the Commission proposed a specific symbol for re-usable and for recyclable packaging only. The use of the symbols would be compulsory for all manufacturers wishing to use a symbol to indicate the recyclable content of their product. The text does not foresee that packaging bearing the mark should contain a minimum percentage of recycled material. All national symbols would disappear. The text is likely to provoke intense debate.

Apart from the marking system by way of symbols, Article 8(2) states that packaging should indicate the nature of the packaging materials used. The Commission has established the numbering and abbreviations on which the identification system is based.[200] This system is voluntary in a first stage, subject to revision to establish whether to introduce it on a binding basis.

---

[198] See for instance Demey, Hannequart, and Lambert, n. 178 above, 45.

[199] COM(96)191 [1996] OJ C382/10.

[200] Commission Decision of 28 Jan. 1997 establishing the identification system for packaging materials pursuant to EP and Council Dir. 94/62/EC on packaging and packaging waste [1997] OJ L50/28.

The use of economic instruments was a widely debated issue in the conciliation talks. Article 15 instructs the Council to adopt economic instruments to promote the implementation of the objectives set by the Directive. In the absence of such measures, Member States are allowed, in accordance with, *inter alia*, the polluter pays principle and the obligations arising out of the Treaty, to adopt measures to implement those objectives. This provision puts more emphasis on the environmental goals of the Treaty than the proposal of the EP, which wanted to include the classic "internal market provision", that these instruments must not lead to distortion of competition, obstruction of the free movement of goods, or discrimination against imported goods. Belgium, which was drafting its legislation concerning ecological taxes on, *inter alia*, various forms of packaging, objected, stating that inclusion of this provision would have made national eco-taxes and other economic instruments questionable in the light of the Treaty Articles with respect to the internal market. The more general reference in the final text to "Treaty obligations", as well as the express citation of the Community's environmental policy, should offer enhanced protection of these economic instruments in the balancing-act with the internal market.[201]

Article 11 imposes concentration levels of heavy metals in packaging. Member States are required to establish databases, facilitating the Commission's monitoring of the packaging (waste) market and of Member States' compliance with the Directive.[202] Although Member States were obliged to implement the Directive before 30 June 1996 (Article 22), many failed to do so, especially with respect to the recovery targets. They have to inform the Commission of the national measures implementing the Directive.[203]

The recently appointed head of the Commission's environment services has begun studying the role of industry in the revision of the Directive. The Commission is due to publish its proposal for a revised target by mid-2000. It would like to take industry's role in drafting the text further than the traditional consultation rounds.

E.   TENSIONS WITH THE INTERNAL MARKET

The Packaging and Packaging Waste Directive is at the forefront of current discussions with respect to hindrance of the free movement of goods in the name of environmental protection. Both the Directive itself and national measures implementing it have to be assessed in the light of the Treaty provisions which form part of the "Trade and the Environment" debate: Articles 28 (ex Article

[201] See Demey, Hannequart, and Lambert, n. 178 above, 117 ff.; and de Sadeleer, n. 6 above, 400.

[202] See Commission Decision 97/138/EC of 3 Feb. 1997 establishing the formats relating to the database system pursuant to EP and Council Dir. 94/62/EC on packaging and packaging waste [1997] OJ L52/22.

[203] See Commission Decision 94/741/EC of 24 Oct. 1994 concerning questionnaires for Member States' reports on the implementation of certain directives in the waste sector [1994] OJ L296/42 and Council Dir. 91/692/EEC standardizing and rationalizing reports on the implementation of certain directives relating to the environment [1991] OJ L377/48.

30),[204] 81–82 (ex Articles 85–86),[205] 87 (ex Article 92)[206] and 90 (ex Article 95) EC.[207] It has been argued that the Directive itself may be at odds with the principles of free movement of goods, laid down in Article 28 ff. EC, as well as with the requirements of Article 95(4). This could be the case, for instance, where the text prevents exports of packaging waste in the event of high national standards. Most problematic, however, are those national measures which aim to promote re-use of packaging. The Danish,[208] German,[209] and Luxembourg[210] systems are currently under Commission scrutiny.[211]

[204] See, *inter alia*, D. Chalmers, "Environmental Protection and the Single Market: An Unsustainable Development. Does the EC Treaty Need a Title on the Environment?" (1995) 21 *Legal Issues of European Integration* 65; D. Geradin, "Balancing Free Trade and Environmental Protection—the Interplay between the ECJ and the Community Legislation" in J. Cameron, P. Demaret, and D. Geradin (eds.), *Trade and the Environment: The Search for Balance* (London: Cameron May, 1994), 204; L. Krämer, "Environmental Protection and Art. 30 EEC Treaty", (1993) 30 *Common Market Law Review* 111; C. London and M. Llamas, *EC Law on Protection of the Environment and the Free Movement of Goods* (London: Butterworths, 1995); A. Long, "The Single Market and the Environment: The European Union's Dilemma: The Example of the Packaging Directive" (1997) 6 *European Environmental Law Review* 214; D. A. Reid, "Trade and the Environment: Finding a Balance—The European Union Approach" (1996) 5 *European Environmental Law Review* 144; *Idem*, "The Packaging and Packaging Waste Directive" (1995) 4 *European Environmental Law Review* 239; A. Schmidt, "Trade in Waste Under Community Law" in Cameron, Demaret, and Geradin (eds.), above, 184; H. Temmink, "From Danish Bottles to Danish Bees: The Dynamics of Free Movement of Goods and Environmental Protection—a Case Law Analysis", at p. 61 this volume; A. Veldkamp, "Community Waste Policy and the Internal Market: Conflicting Interests?" in M. Faure, J. Vervaele, and A. Weale (eds.), *Environmental Standards in the European Union in an Interdisciplinary Framework* (Antwerp: Maklu, 1994), 219; A. Weale, "Environmental Protection, The Four Freedoms and Competition among Rules", in Faure, Vervaele, and Weale (eds.), above, 73.

[205] See, *inter alia*, P. Bennett, *Anti trust? European Competition Law and Mutual Environmental Insurance*, Working Papers (Oxford: University of Oxford—School of Geography, 1998); L. Gyselen, "The Emerging Interface between Competition Policy and Environmental Policy in the EC" in Cameron, Demaret, and Geradin (eds.), n. 204 above, 242; R. Jacobs, "EEC Competition Law and the Protection of the Environment" (1993) 20 *Legal Issues of European Integration* 37; T. Portwood, *Competition Law and the Environment* (London: Cameron May, 1994); M. Rose, "The Environment and Competition: The European Perspective", paper for the 1996 Madrid Conference of the Union Internationale des Avocats, Environmental Law Commission; F. O. W. Vogelaar, "Towards an Improved Integration of EC Environmental Policy and EC Competition Policy: An Interim Report" in B. Hawk (ed.), *Towards an Improved Integration of EC Environmental Policy and EC Competition Policy: An Interim Report* (New York: Fordham Corporate Law Institute, 1995) 529.

[206] See, *inter alia*, J. Jans, "State Aid and Arts. 92 and 93 of the EC Treaty: Does the Polluter Really Pay?" (1995) 4 *European Environmental Law Review* 108; G. van Calster, "State Aid for Environmental Protection: Has the EC Shut the Door?" (1997) 1 *Environmental Taxation & Accounting* 38–51.

[207] See, *inter alia*, A. Criscuolo, "Environmental Policy and Fiscal Policy in the Community: The Challenge of National Eco-taxes—the Belgian Case" (1998) 2 *Environmental Taxation & Accounting* 3, 52–70 (Part 1), No.4 (1998), 10–30 (Part 2); W. de Wit, *Nationale milieubelastingen en het EG-Verdrag* (Deventer: Kluwer, 1997), 442. See also the author's note, "Ook voor milieufiscaliteit geldt een strikte non-discriminatieregel" Case C–213/96, *Outokumpu Oy*, *Nederlands Tijdschrift voor Europees Recht* 205–9.

[208] Until recently, the case was notorious for the Commission's hesitation in bringing it to court.

[209] P. Queitsch, "Rechtliche Problemfelder der Verpackungsverordnung" (1995) 15 *Umwelt- und Planungsrecht* 246. The contentious element of the German packaging laws, are the so-called "re-use quotas", which in practice oblige beverage manufacturers to use a certain number of refillable containers. As with the Danish laws, the Commission has not been eager to tackle this politically sensitive case head on.

VI.   Landfill of Waste

A.   A WINDING ROAD TO THE CURRENT PROPOSAL

Landfill of waste is a disputed method for disposing of waste. The Commission submitted a proposal for a directive on landfill on 22 July 1991. In 1995, a Common Position was reached by the Council. The EP did not find the level of environmental protection in the Common Position sufficient and therefore, on 22 May 1996, rejected it. It objected to the high number of derogations on the grounds that they severely limited the effect of the Directive. The Parliament particularly objected to the exclusion of more than 50 per cent of EC territory by the derogation for areas with a population density of fewer than thirty-five persons per square kilometre. The Commission subsequently withdrew its proposal. In June 1996 the Council invited the Commission to present a new proposal on the landfill of waste as soon as possible.[212]

B.   THE 1997 PROPOSAL OF THE COMMISSION

The current regime was initiated by a Commission Proposal of 5 March 1997.[213] The text is to a large extent based on the principles and provisions of the 1991 proposal, designed in particular to woo the EP. The new elements are: the reduction of the landfilling of biodegradable waste; the requirement that waste be pre-treated before it is landfilled, a ban on the disposal of used tyres, the requirement that the costs of landfilling be increased, a prohibition on co-disposal of (non-)hazardous waste, an improvement of the general requirements for all classes of landfills and stricter conditions for existing landfills, and more restricted exemptions for remote areas.

The proposal applies to waste in the sense of the Framework Directive, as amended,[214] with a few very specific exceptions (Article 3). All landfills are covered by the Directive, i.e. any "waste disposal site for the deposit of waste on to or into land, including internal waste disposal sites (i.e. landfill where a producer of waste is carrying out its own waste disposal at the place of production)". Excluded are "facilities where waste is unloaded in order to permit its preparation for further transport for recovery, treatment or disposal elsewhere, and temporary (i.e. less than one year) deposit of waste prior to recovery, treatment or disposal" (Article 2(f)). Article 4 classifies all landfills into one

---

[210] Luxembourg is planning to introduce environmental levies which seem to favour re-use and domestic producers; similar problems exist in Germany. See J. Bongaerts, "Taxation of One-way Fast Food Packaging Waste: How to Wrap Up Environmental Policy Objectives in Fiscal Instruments?" (1997) 1(4) *Environmental Taxation & Accounting* 34–43.

[211] More details are given in G. van Calster, "De Europese verpakkingsrichtlijn: Oorsprong, inhoud en verhouding met het EG-Verdrag", in Deketelaere and Wiggers-Rust, n. 189 above, 1.

[212] IP/97/181.

[213] Commission Proposal of 5 Mar. 1997 for a Council Directive on the landfill of waste, COM(97)105. See the results in n. 220 below.

[214] Nn. 1 and 2 above.

of three classes: landfills for hazardous,[215] non-hazardous,[216] and inert[217] waste.

Article 5 establishes uniform waste acceptance criteria, based on the afore-mentioned classification. First, it sets targets for the reduction of biodegradable municipal waste going to landfill, finally leading to a reduction in 2010 of such waste going to landfills to 25 per cent of the total amount (by weight) of the 1993 level.[218] Furthermore, certain wastes are not acceptable for landfill. These are liquid waste (unless it is inert and a permit is granted); explosive, corrosive, oxidizing, highly flammable, or flammable waste in the sense of the Hazardous Waste Directive,[219] infectious hospital or clinical waste; whole used tyres, as at two years from the date of entry into force of the Directive, and shredded tyres five years from that date (excluding in both instances bicycle tyres and tyres with an outside diameter above 1,400 mm),[220] and, finally, all other waste which does not fulfil the acceptance criteria determined in accordance with Annex II.[221] Article 5 prohibits the dilution or mixture of waste solely in order to meet the waste acceptance criteria; treatment is allowed should this be necessary to consolidate the waste or to stabilize it.

Article 6 provides for more restrictions. Only waste that has been subject to treatment may be landfilled, only hazardous waste that fulfils the criteria set out in Annex II may be assigned to a hazardous waste landfill, landfill for non-hazardous waste may only be used for municipal waste and for non-hazardous wastes of any other origin and, finally, inert waste landfill sites may only be used for inert wastes. Article 7 introduces a specific permit procedure for landfill sites. Applications must contain, *inter alia*, a hydrogeological and geological description, a plan for closure and aftercare, and details concerning the financial security by the applicant. The permit conditions must include, *inter alia*, a description of the class of landfill; a list of defined types and quantities of waste; details of requirements for the preparation and the operation of the site and of monitoring and control procedures (Article 9).

In line with the "polluter pays principle", the Commission would like to require Member States to increase the costs of landfilling. The proposed

---

[215] Art. 2(c): see Decision 94/904/EC, n. 82 above.

[216] Art. 2(d): i.e. all waste which is not hazardous.

[217] Art. 2(e): i.e. waste that does not undergo any significant physical, chemical, or biological transformations. Inert waste must not dissolve, burn, or otherwise physically or chemically react, biodegrade, or adversely affect other matter with which it comes into contact in a way likely to give rise to environmental pollution or to harm human health. The total leachability and pollutant content of the waste and the ecotoxity of the leachate must be insignificant.

[218] Art. 2(b): i.e. waste from households, as well as commercial, industrial, institutional, and other waste which, because of its nature or composition, is similar to waste from households.

[219] N. 70 above.

[220] This prohibition is a result of the "priority waste stream group" of used tyres, which reached its conclusions in 1993. Priority waste streams were those groups of waste (including, for instance, demolition waste and electronic waste) to which the Commission had granted priority treatment. This approach has been abandoned in the latest Community waste strategy.

[221] Annex II contains the general principles for acceptance of waste, the various classes of landfills, and the guidelines outlining preliminary waste acceptance procedures to be followed until a uniform waste classification and acceptance procedure has been adopted.

Article 10 obliges them to fix the rates for waste disposal in such a way as to include all costs involved in the setting up and operation of the landfill, including the aftercare and site closure costs. This provision aims to introduce "life-cycle-analysis" in the price structure of landfills. Article 11 deals with waste-acceptance procedures (see Annex II), and Article 12 concerns the control and monitoring procedures in the operational phase. Article 13 includes details with respect to the closure procedure. It provides for instance that, after closure, the operator remains responsible for the maintenance of the site, for the monitoring and analysing of landfill gas emissions, and for the control of leachate from the site into the groundwater, as long as the competent authority considers that the landfill is likely to cause a hazard for the environment. Annex III contains details of the monitoring procedure.

The Commission proposes to require Member States to implement the Directive before 30 June 2000 (Article 18). Existing landfills will have to present the authorities with a conditioning plan for the site that will guide the authorities' decision whether the operations may continue (Article 14). Contrary to the Common Position of the Council which was reached under the previous proposal, the current proposal does not contain a Community exemption for remote areas, but leaves room for a Member State exemption instead. Article 3(3) enables Member States to declare, at their own initiative, (parts of) some Articles inapplicable to:

— landfill sites for non-hazardous wastes or inert waste with a total capacity of 10,000 tons, serving islands, where this is the only landfill on the island and where this is exclusively destined for the disposal of waste generated on that island; or to

— landfill sites for non-hazardous wastes or inert waste in isolated settlements with difficult access, if the landfill site is destined for the disposal of waste generated only by that isolated settlement. Such settlement should have no more than 500 inhabitants per municipality and no more than five inhabitants per square kilometre, and with no access road that can be used by heavy goods vehicles of 3.5 tons above, and where the distance to the nearest urban agglomeration with at least 250 inhabitants per square kilometre is not less than 50 kilometres.

The Proposal has to pass quite a number of hurdles before it was entered into the statute books. Those Member States which rely heavily on landfill, including notably the UK, were vigorously opposing it.

In February 1998, the Parliament adopted a number of amendments, which closely followed the report of the EP's environment committee[222] on the matter. The latter had proposed that the EP amend the text considerably. Importantly, the EP would like the Community to recognize expressly landfill as the last resort in the Community's waste hierarchy. This issue is sensitive, since a 1996 study commissioned by the Community seemed to conclude that

---

[222] Report on the Proposal for a directive on the landfill of waste, A4–0026/98, 30 Jan. 1998 (*Rapporteur* Caroline Jackson MEP).

incineration was even more environmentally unsound than landfill.[223] This suggestion was badly received in those Member States that have invested heavily in incineration installations. Should the Community, at the instigation of the EP, now recognize landfill as the worst option, other states would be equally opposed (including the UK). Therefore, this suggestion was not likely to be accepted by the Council although it was included in an amended proposal by the Commission.[224]

The EP also suggested that, failing harmonization of existing and future landfill taxes in the Member States, the Community should step in and introduce a Community-wide tax on waste intended for landfill tips. Such a move would do away with the distortions that sometimes occur due to the existence of a variety of landfill taxes throughout the Member States. The Commission did not include this part of the Parliament's Opinion in its amended proposal. In what appears to be an understatement, it said that it "is not expected to put forward a proposal on economic instruments",[225] and it does not want to be tied to such a far-reaching commitment in sector-specific legislation such as the landfill proposal.

Equally, the Committee had suggested that there be no time limit on the liability of landfill site operators for damage caused by their activities. The amended Commission proposal includes a minimum period of thirty years after closure, during which the operator of the site is responsible for monitoring landfill gas and leachate from the site. The new text now also suggests that Member States should not introduce a shorter time-limit for liability for damage caused by the site than normally foreseen under the national liability regime. However, no directions and/or obligations are included that would amount to harmonizing Member States' liabilities regimes. This is of course not surprising since the environmental liability regime is an altogether separate and even more complicated issue.

Once the EP had issued its Opinion on the matter,[226] the Council reached an agreement on the Commission's proposal.[227] In fact, the Council had already reached agreement, prior to the EP's Opinion on the text.[228] The text is weaker than the Commission's original proposals. Nevertheless, it contains a number of principles which in particular the UK and some other Member States originally objected to. The provisions of the Common Position are based on the principle of classification of landfills according to the types of waste they accept: non-hazardous, hazardous, or inert waste. The classification is cou-

---

[223] European Commission, DG XI, Cost-benefit analysis of the different municipal solid waste management systems: objectives and instruments for the year 2000 (Coopers & Lybrand, Centre for Social and Economic Research on the Global Environment (Brussels: CSERGE, 1997)).

[224] Amended Commission proposal for a directive on the landfill of waste, COM(98)189, [1998] OJ C126/11.

[225] *Ibid.*, at para. 3.

[226] European Parliament Minutes of 19 Feb. 1998—Proposed amendments to the Commission proposal for a Council dir. on the landfill of waste (A4–0026/98).

[227] 2101st Council meeting—Labour and social affairs, 3 June 1998, PRES/98/179 (formal adoption of the Common Position).

[228] 2062nd session of the Council—16 Dec. 1997, PRES/97/399.

pled with a differentiation in the procedures for issuing acceptance permits, and for control and monitoring of the site during the operational and the closure phases. Hazardous waste which has been rendered non-hazardous would also be subject to specific requirements.

Certain types of wastes would as such be excluded from acceptance in landfills (liquid waste; explosive, combustible or flammable wastes; hospital wastes and other infectious clinical wastes; and any other type of waste which does not fulfil the acceptance criteria defined in the Directive). Importantly, the proposal introduces a quantified reduction strategy for the landfill of biodegradable municipal waste. A reduction would have to be realized of this type of waste accepted for landfill to 75 per cent (2006), 50 per cent (2009), and 35 per cent (2016) of the tonnage produced in 1995. The Directive will enter into force in 1999, and the figures would be reviewed in 2014, when an additional four years may be granted to those Member States which rely heavily on landfill sites (including the UK).

All waste would have to undergo treatment before going to landfill, except where this "would not further the objectives of the Directive" (i.e. a concession to the UK, which makes the pre-treatment requirement rather hollow) or, in the case of inert waste, would not be technically feasible. Member States are urged to levy a waste disposal and landfill dumping charge. The charge should at least cover the costs involved in the setting up and operation of the site. Exemptions may be granted to landfill sites for non-hazardous or inert waste, serving small islands which have only a single landfill site with a total capacity of less than 15,000 tonnes, or serving isolated settlements (no more than 500 inhabitants and with difficult access). In all likelihood, the EP will reject the Council's text in second reading. It remains to be seen what the reaction of the Commission will then be.[229]

---

[229] The 1991 Commission attempt to introduce a directive on the landfill of waste ended with the retraction of the proposal by the Commission itself, after the Parliament and Council disagreed with respect to the main elements of the text. The current Directive was adopted in Apr. 1999 ([1999] OJ L182/1). It establishes varying dates for three classes of landfills: those for hazardous, non-hazardous, and inert wastes. These duties include in particular the types of waste that may be accepted in the site. All landfill sites are moreover subject to general criteria, laid down in the Annex. Member States have to provide the Commission with a strategy that ensures that, by 17 July 2006, biodegradable municipal waste going to landfill is reduced to 75% of the total amount (by weight) of such waste produced in 1995; by 17 July 2009, this figure must be brought down to 50%; and by 17 July 2016, it must be 35%. The figures may be amended by the Council along the way.

Member States that put more than 80% of their municipal waste to landfill in 1995 may postpone the aforementioned dates for up to 4 years, provided, however, that the figure of 35% is reached no later than 2019.

A number of materials must not go to landfill: they include liquid waste; explosive, corrosive, oxidizing, and flammable waste; hospital and clinical wastes; and tyres (subject to a number of conditions). All waste that does go into landfill must be treated to ensure that the waste acceptance criteria and procedures (specified in the Annex) are met. The price charged by the operator must ensure that all his obligations under the Directive will be met, including his estimated cost of the closure and the after-care of the site for at least 30 years. The operator is responsible for the after-care of the site, and the authorities are obliged to keep a financial security for as long as they deem necessary to ensure due after-care. The Directive does not in itself detail any specific liability regime. National law and/or relevant Community regulations apply.

Member States may at their own option declare the main elements of the Directive inapplicable

VII.   Incineration of Waste

A.   INCINERATION AND THE WASTE HIERARCHY

Generally, EC institutions are suspicious of incineration as a valuable waste-management tool. In 1990 the Council was still carefully optimistic. In its Resolution on waste policy[230] it stated that "provided it is subject to adequate standards, incineration can be a useful means of reducing the volume of waste and recovering energy". The Commission was far less enthusiastic in its 1996 Communication on the review of the Community waste strategy,[231] especially in a draft version of this document dated 11 January 1996.[232] In the latter, the Commission did not hide its position where it stated that "preference should be given to the recycling of material over energy recovery operations". A variety of reasons led it to this conclusion. First, purely as a matter of policy, leaving the option open of incinerating waste might, in the eyes of the Commission, have a discouraging effect on the prevention of waste. Secondly, the Commission, in a controversial move, claimed that from a technical point of view incineration is less energy efficient and/or more polluting than re-use or recycling. Further, by separating the waste at source, which is required if one is to give preponderant weight to prevention and recycling, end-users and consumers are actively involved in waste management. Leaving wastes to be incinerated would make them less aware of the need to decrease the generation of waste. Finally, the Commission expressed the opinion that it is not desirable to establish energy strategies which rely heavily on waste supplies.

In the final text of the Commission Communication, preference for recycling was scaled down under considerable pressure from industry and from Member States. Incineration with energy recovery could be preferable in certain cases, should the circumstances so require. The Commission no longer claimed that scientific data prove the technical environmental disadvantages of incineration. This uncertainty has been underlined by the Council Resolution which endorses, with nuances, the Commission Communication.[233] The Council states that "as regards recovery operations, . . . the choice of option in any particular case must have regard to environmental and economic effects", but it considers that "at present, and until scientific and technological progress is made and life-cycle analyses are further developed,

---

to landfill sites for non-hazardous or inert wastes with a total capacity of not more than 15,000 tonnes, or with an annual intake not exceeding 1,000 tonnes serving islands, where this it the only landfill on the island, and where it is exclusively destined for the disposal of waste generated on the island. Once, however, the total capacity of that landfill has been reached, any new landfill site established on the island has to comply with all the requirements of the Directive Member States also have this option for landfill sites for non-hazardous or inert waste in isolated settlements, if the site is destined for the disposal of wastes generated only by that isolated settlement.

Existing landfills must meet the requirements of the Directive, at the latest on 17 July 2009.

[230] N. 4 above.   [231] *Ibid.*   [232] See Rose, n. 53 above.
[233] N. 182 above.

re-use and material recovery should be considered preferable and insofar as they are the best environmental options". While the preference for material recovery seems to have been watered down, it has nonetheless been sustained. Moreover, the Council has expressed its explicit concern about large-scale movements within the Community of waste for incineration with or without energy recovery.[234]

There is no EC regime that deals with the incineration of waste in general. Instead, there are two specific directives with respect to the incineration of waste from municipal waste plants and one dealing with the incineration of hazardous waste. Apart from these regimes, waste incineration is subject to the Framework Directive, including its general requirement that waste be disposed of without endangering human health and without using processes or methods which could harm the environment.[235]

Incineration on land and at sea is classified as a disposal operation under Annex II A of the Framework Directive (D10 and D11 respectively). It should be noted that the use of waste principally as a fuel or other means of generating energy is viewed as a recovery operation under Annex II B to the Directive (R9). Thus the former are subject to the permit requirements of Article 9 of the Framework Directive, whilst the latter falls under Article 10. Moreover, both plans for the disposal of toxic and dangerous waste by incineration, and for the treatment by incineration of other solid and liquid waste, are subject to the permit requirement of Article 3 of Directive 84/360/EEC on the Combating of Air Pollution from Industrial Plants.[236] This includes careful design of these installations. Finally, the Directive on Integrated Pollution Prevention and Control (IPPC) provides a further legal basis for the regulation of emission limits.[237]

Ever since 1990, the Council urged the Commission to come forward with a proposal dealing with the incineration of industrial waste.[238] The Commission has now issued a proposal for a directive on the incineration of non-hazardous waste to replace the two directives on the incineration of municipal waste and to include non-hazardous industrial waste.[239] The Council repeated its wish for new legislation on waste incineration in its 1997 Resolution.[240]

A new blow to the use of incineration may have been administered by a 1997 study which was commissioned by the Commission. The main objective of the

[234] Likewise: the EP in its Resolution of 14 Nov. 1996, n. 182 above.
[235] Art. 4 of the Framework Directive, as amended, n. 2 above.
[236] Dir. 84/360/EEC of 28 June 1984 [1984] OJ L188/20. On the link between air pollution control and waste management with respect to incineration, see de Sadeleer, n. 6 above, 411 ff.
[237] Council Dir. 96/61/EC of 24 Sept. 1996 concerning integrated pollution prevention and control [1996] OJ L257/26. Annex II to this Directive, in conjunction with Arts. 18 and 20(b), allows for the introduction of Community-wide emission limit values for, *inter alia*, air pollution from new and existing municipal waste incineration plants; the incineration of hazardous waste; pollution caused by waste from the titanium oxide industry; the disposal of waste oils; and the treatment of hazardous waste. So far, the Commission has not proposed any (additional) emission requirements for any of the enumerated sectors, and it does not seem willing to do so in a nearby future.
[238] Council Resolution of 7 May 1990, n. 4 above.
[239] Report from the Commission of 8 Nov. 1995 on waste management policy, COM(95)522.
[240] N. 51 above.

study was to assess the environmental and economic costs and benefits of different methods of recycling, re-using, incineration (with and without energy recovery), and landfilling municipal solid waste (MSW). Several important conclusions were explicated. With respect to economic costs, the study suggests that the unit costs of collecting MSW are significantly higher in rural areas than urban areas; that the costs of semi-automatic sorting/processing are two and a half times those of manual processing; that incineration with heat and power recovery consistently results in the lowest costs; and that the economic costs of landfill are, as expected, higher in urban areas.

With respect to environmental costs and benefits, the analysis concludes that recycling offers the most significant net environmental benefits in all Member States, although the benefits vary considerably due to differences in transport costs, energy savings, and the mix of recycled products. The net environmental benefits of recycling also vary considerably between materials. The largest benefits are associated with the recycling of metals and glass whilst the recycling of plastic film gives rise to net environmental costs. That municipal composting of organic waste results in net environmental costs most of which are associated with transport. This suggests that home composting would be more attractive from an environmental perspective. Also incineration with energy recovery leads to significant net environmental benefits if it replaces a marginal power source (assumed to be the relatively highly polluting coal-fired power stations), but produces significant net costs if it replaces the EU average power source. Landfill has small net environmental costs both with and without energy recovery.[241] The study also seems to suggest that waste incineration, even with energy recovery, should come at the very bottom of the waste hierarchy, even after mere landfill.

Opposition to this conclusion has been voiced by the industry concerned and by some Member States, which have invested heavily in research and infrastructure for waste incineration plants. These include the Flemish region of Belgium and certain *Länder* in Germany.

B.   PREVENTION OF AIR POLLUTION FROM MUNICIPAL WASTE PLANTS

Both Directive 89/369/EEC on the Prevention of Air Pollution from New Municipal Waste Incineration Plants[242] and Directive 89/429/EEC on existing Plants[243] concern "municipal waste", i.e. "domestic refuse, as well as commercial or trade refuse and other waste which, because of its nature or composition, is similar to domestic refuse" (Article 1(3)). Another important component is the definition of "municipal waste-incineration plant" as "any technical equipment used for the treatment of municipal waste by incineration, with or without recovery of the combustion heat generated, but excluding plants used specifically for the incineration of sewage sludge, chemical,

---

[241] Note 223 above.   [242] [1989] OJ L163/32.   [243] [1989] OJ L203/50.

toxic and dangerous waste, medical waste from hospitals or other types of special waste, on land or at sea, even if these plants may burn municipal waste as well" (Article 1(4)). Installations which burn principally combustibles other than waste, and only in an accessory manner municipal waste, are caught.[244] "New" installations are those for which the authorization to operate was granted after 1 December 1990. "Existing" installations are those for which the first authorization to operate was granted before that date.

The two pillars of the regime are permit requirements including emission limits and a number of operational obligations. The emission limits which are laid down in Directive 89/369/EEC will have to be met in stages by existing installations (Article 3 ff. of Directive 89/429/EEC), leading to identical limits for new and for existing installations by 1 December 2000 (Article 2(ii) of Directive 89/429/EEC). However, plants with a nominal capacity equal to or more than six tonnes of waste per hour, i.e. quantitatively the most important ones, had to meet the limits by 1 December 1996. The emission limits concern total dust, certain heavy metals, and three chemical substances (i.e. hydrochloric acid (HCl), hydrofluoric acid (HF), and sulphur dioxide (SO_2)). Member States may lay down emission limit values for other pollutants other than those mentioned in the Directive, according to the local circumstances and taking into account the best available technologies not entailing excessive costs (Article 3(4) of Directive 89/369/EEC).[245] The operational requirements include the minimum temperature to be reached in the combustion process, as well as a minimum injection of oxygen and concentration levels for carbon monoxide and organic compounds (Article 4). A sudden drop in the process' temperature has to be covered by auxiliary burners (Article 7), and severe sanctions are provided for in the event of a breach of the permit requirements, including the withdrawal of the permit (Article 8).

Finally, since the Directives are based on Article 175 EC, Member States may maintain or introduce more stringent measures in accordance with Article 176 EC. As noted, the Commission has recently presented a new initiative, which should result in a general directive on the incineration of waste. Almost all waste which is not caught by the Hazardous Waste Incineration Directive is to fall under the new initiative, and two existing directives on municipal waste are to be abolished. Stricter emission limits will apply (dioxin and furan emissions are targeted in particular). Both new and existing plants will have to conform to these new limits. As in the Hazardous Waste Incineration Directive, the proposed Directive introduces specific provisions for co-incineration.[246]

C.   INCINERATION OF HAZARDOUS WASTE

Technically speaking, incineration of hazardous waste poses more risks than the incineration of non-hazardous waste. However, especially in conjunction

---

[244] Contrary to what the Commission originally suggested: [1988] OJ C75/4.

[245] BATNEEC: See n. 267 below.

[246] Commission Proposal of 7 Oct. 1998 for a Council Directive on the Incineration of waste [1998] OJ C372/11.

with the Community monitoring system of shipments of waste, hazardous waste which is to be incinerated is easier to keep track of. In combination with the regime for hazardous waste,[247] the formalities surrounding shipments of waste provide economic operators with a more or less accurate picture of the waste they are dealing with. Like the directives on the incineration of municipal waste, Directive 94/67/EC on the Incineration of Hazardous Waste[248] focuses on emission limits and on operational requirements. The purpose of incineration plants is to reduce the pollution-related risks of hazardous waste through a process of oxidation, to reduce the quantity and volume of the waste, and to produce residues that can be re-used or disposed of safely.

The scope of application of Directive 94/67/EC has caused controversy. "Hazardous waste" is defined as in the Hazardous Waste Directive.[249] Certain substances are excluded, either because they are covered by other Community legislation[250] or for specific reasons.[251] "Incineration plants" means any technical equipment used for the incineration by oxidation of hazardous wastes with or without recovery of the combustion heat generated, including plants burning such wastes as a regular or additional fuel or any industrial process (Article 2(2)). However, Article 3(3) excludes "co-incineration" plants from a substantial number of the Directive's provisions.[252] These are plants which are not intended primarily to incinerate hazardous wastes and which are being fed with hazardous wastes. Their use is widespread in the cement industry. If the heat resulting from the incineration of hazardous waste is no higher than 40 per cent of the total heat released in the plant at each moment of the operation, the exemptions apply (Article 3(3)). Throughout the following paragraphs, the most important provisions for co-incineration plants will be mentioned alongside the general regime. Member States may make all requirements of the Directive applicable to co-incineration as well.

The guiding principle for the incineration of hazardous wastes is that a level of incineration as complete as possible should be achieved (Article 6). The permit which is required by the Framework Directive may only be granted if all conditions of Directive 94/67/EC are satisfied. Permits which are granted must list the types and quantities of hazardous wastes which may be (co-)incinerated, as well as the total capacity of the plant (Article 3(1)–(2)). The operator must perform extensive checks prior to the treatment of the waste, so as to ensure that he is aware of all properties of the waste and to ensure its safe handling (Article 5). Article 6 contains the minimum operational levels of temperature and oxygen injection. All incineration plants have to be equipped with burners which switch on automatically when the temperature of the combus-

---

[247] N. 70 above.

[248] [1994] OJ L365/34. See A. Layard, "The 1994 Directive on the Incineration of Hazardous Waste, 'Substitute Fuels' and Trans-Scientific Choices" (1997) 6 *European Environmental Law Review* 16.

[249] N. 70 above.   [250] For further details, see Art. 2(1) of the Directive.

[251] For instance, hazardous waste resulting from the exploration for and the exploitation of oil and gas resources from off-shore installations and incinerated on board.

[252] The most contentious aspect of the Directive's regime; see Layard, n. 248 above.

tion gases falls below the relevant minimum temperature. Both the minimum levels and the requirement of automatic burners are covered by the exemption for co-incinerators, however, which is unfortunate.[253] The limit values for carbon monoxide concentrations, which are laid down in Article 6(5), do extend to co-incinerators.

Article 7 lays down emission limit values for dust, organic carbon, hydrogen chloride, hydrogen fluoride, and sulphur dioxide, as well as for heavy metal emissions and their compounds (Article 7(1)). Article 7(2) concerns the emissions of dioxins and furans. The entry into force of the requirements with respect to these substances was dependent on the establishment of a harmonized measurement method. The method for measuring dioxins has now been agreed upon.[254] The Commission is of the view that the emission limits for dioxins are now enforceable, whereas some Member States argue that the delay has made the limits illegal.[255]

For co-incineration, the limit values are set against only that part of the volume of exhaust gas resulting from the incineration of hazardous waste, following the criteria laid down in Annex II. Failing this, co-incineration plants would have all too easily been able to meet the requirements. The necessity of a permit for waste water discharge from the incinerator plant, as well as the other requirements of Article 8 with respect to such discharges, does not apply to co-incineration. Article 9 applies to standard incinerators and co-incinerators alike, and requires environmentally sound dealing with the residues from the incineration operation, in line with Directives 75/442/EEC and 91/689/EEC. The transport and storage of dry residues have to take place in closed containers; transport routes have to be analysed with a view to the safe transport of the different substances; and any heat which is generated by the incineration process should be used as far as possible. Articles 10–11 contain specifications on the measurement and monitoring, but they do not apply to co-incinerators. Co-incinerators are not exempt from the possible sanctions under Article 12.

New incinerators (permit granted on or after 31 December 1996) have to meet the operational standards and emission limits from the beginning of 1997; existing plants have to do so by 1 June 2000 (Article 13 in conjunction with Article 18).[256] The Commission tabled a proposal at the end of 1997, which seeks to limit the emissions into water of heavy metals (cadmium and mercury in particular) and dioxins.[257] The proposal complements the provisions of Directive 94/67/EC, which until then were limited to limit values for air emissions.

[253] Layard, n. 248 above, 18.

[254] Commission Decision 97/283/EC of 21 Apr. 1997 on harmonised measurement methods to determine the mass concentration of dioxins and furans in atmospheric emissions in accordance with Art. 7(2) of Dir. 94/67/EC on the incineration of hazardous waste [1997] OJ L113/11.

[255] See "Agreement on Dioxin Tests for Incinerators" [1997] *ENDS-Report* 37.

[256] See "DOE's Proposals for Implementing Incineration Directive" [1997] *ENDS-Report* 37.

[257] Commission proposal of 21 Nov. 1997 for a Council directive amending Dir. 94/67/EC on incineration of hazardous waste, COM(97)604 [1998] OJ C1316. See "Commission proposes amendment to the Directive on hazardous waste incineration", IP/97/1048.

D. MOVEMENTS OF WASTE DESTINED FOR INCINERATION AND THE INTERNAL MARKET

The investments that some Member States have made in incineration plants are provoking an interesting debate with respect to the free movement of waste and the internal market. A number of Member States have invested heavily in new incineration plants. Some of them, notably Denmark, have complained that the influx of wastes from other Member States is taking up the full capacity of their installations. Denmark claims that this has forced it to increase the amount of its waste that is landfilled. In the face of over-capacity of their incinerators other Member States, such as Germany and the Flemish Region of Belgium, are seeking to limit the export of wastes destined for incineration from their territory.

Interestingly, both the Commission[258] and Advocate-General Jacobs[259] have expressed the opinion that the principles of self-sufficiency and proximity do not apply to shipments of wastes destined for recovery, but merely to those destined for disposal. This interpretation has now been confirmed by the ECJ.[260] Should the incineration of waste with energy recovery be regarded as a disposal operation and not, as the current EC position seems to be, a recovery operation, the aforementioned Member States could use this as an argument in order to restrain the free movement of wastes.

Disputes which are similar to those in the context of the Packaging and Packaging Waste Directive are likely to emerge should the Member States concerned effectively hinder such transport.

VIII. Waste Oils

Community directives on waste oils[261] were the first pieces of EC waste legislation. Most waste oil contains heavy metals such as zinc, lead, and chromium. Upon combustion, some of these contaminants are emitted into the ambient environment. Apart from the environmental hazards involved, the mere disposal of them is a waste of resources since many waste oils are re-usable and/or recyclable. A specific feature of this type of waste is also that it is widely distributed among citizens. For instance, many individuals replace the oil of their vehicles themselves, causing specific problems in collection and storing. Directive 75/439/EEC was based on internal market considerations,[262] and on

---

[258] N. 51 above.

[259] Opinion of Jacobs AG of 23 Oct. 1997 in Case C–203/96, *Chemische Afvalstoffen Dusseldorp and Others* v. *VROM* (1998) ECR I–4075.

[260] N. 161 above.

[261] Council Dir. 75/439/EEC of 16 June 1975 on the disposal of waste oils [1975] OJ L194/23; amended by Dir. 87/101/EEC of 22 Dec. 1986 [1987] OJ L42/43.

[262] In the absence of specific environmental provisions in the Treaty, the Dir. was based on Arts. 94 and 308 EC. This is the case with all environmental measures of the first generation. See, e.g., X. Debroux, "Le choix de la base juridique dans l'action environnementale de l'Union Européenne" (1995) 31 *Cahiers de droit Européen* 383.

the protection of the environment and the health of citizens.[263] Finally, recycling of the oils would be conducive to a fuel supply policy. Directive 75/439/EEC lacked specificity, especially in the control system, and it was generally considered too lax. Directive 87/101/EEC was to remedy these shortcomings.

"Waste oils" are defined as "any mineral-based lubrication or industrial oils which have become unfit for the use for which they were originally intended, and in particular used combustion engine oils and gearbox oils, and also mineral lubricating oils, oils for turbines and hydraulic oils" (Article 1). Contrary to the original text, synthetic oils (which do not consist of hydrocarbons) are excluded from the scope of the Directive, as are waste oils containing more than 50 ppm of PCB/PCT. They are regulated by the Community legislation on PCB/PCTs. Oils are to be considered waste once and so long as they become unfit for the use for which they were originally intended.

Member States have to ensure that waste oils are collected and disposed of without causing any avoidable damage to man and environment (Article 2).[264] The text seems to accept that a 100 per cent environmentally safe management of waste oils is impossible. This is also reflected in the BATNEEC obligation with respect to permits. The hierarchy of methods of managing waste oils is again a particularly sore point. Commission services favoured regeneration, i.e. "any process whereby base oils can be produced by refining waste oils, in particular by removing the contaminants, oxidation products and additives contained in such oils" (Article 1). Article 3 of the original Directive did not express a preference, stating that recycling should be favoured, either by regeneration or by combustion (other than for destruction). The Commission proposal[265] suggested inserting the obligation to ensure to a maximum extent the management of waste oils by way of regeneration. Many Member States objected on the ground that combustion (with energy recovery) was widespread in the EC. The final text is subtly in favour of regeneration, whilst leaving Member States the option of treating waste oils by combustion. Technical, economic, and organizational constraints may lead them to favour combustion, which will occur in environmentally acceptable conditions (Article 3).

Clearly, Member States are required to prohibit all discharge of waste oils into inland surface water, ground water, territorial sea water, and drainage systems; all deposits and/or discharges of waste oils harmful to the soil and all uncontrolled discharges of residues resulting from the processing of waste oils; as well as all processing of waste oils causing air pollution which exceeds the level prescribed by existing provisions (Article 4).

The Directive provides for a unique state-monitored back-up system for the collection and management of waste oils. From the outset, the Council

[263] In the first Community Action Programme on the environment, the introduction of a directive on waste oils had been identified as a priority.

[264] This requires Member States to set up a set of legal obligations and control measures: Case C–366/89, *Commission v. Italy* [1993] ECR I–4201, at para. 17.

[265] Commission Proposal of 24 Jan. 1985, COM(84)757 [1985] OJ C58/3.

predicted that the normal functioning of the market might not always guarantee complete and safe collection and management. Depending on market circumstances (supply, demand, and consequently price), economic operators might not be interested in the setting up and/or maintenance of a complete collection system. Therefore, Article 5 enables Member States in the event of market failure to ensure that one or more undertakings carry out the collection and/or disposal of waste oils offered to them by holders, where appropriate in the area assigned to them by the competent authorities. If a person holding waste is unable to manage waste oils in an environmentally sound manner, he must place the waste at the disposal of an undertaking referred to in Article 5.

Indemnities may be granted to the undertakings concerned for the service rendered, provided they do not exceed annual uncovered costs, taking into account a reasonable profit. Indemnities may not cause any significant distortion of competition or give rise to artificial patterns of trade (Article 13). They may be financed, *inter alia*, by a charge imposed on waste oils or products which, after use, are transformed into waste oils, taking into account the polluter pays principle (Article 14).

These back-up provisions expressed doubts about the satisfactory functioning of a market-based economic system when it comes to environmental resources. From a legal point of view, the system constitutes a challenge to the EC's state aid rules, as well as to the gradual dismantling of state monopolies and the granting of exclusive rights to enterprises. The ECJ has had to clarify these provisions in the light of the free movement of goods, and in view of the relationship between the Treaty and harmonized legislation.

The control system for enterprises engaged in the management of waste oils depends on their activities. Undertakings that are involved in the collection of waste oils only have to be made subject to registration only (Article 5(4)). Member States must supervise these undertakings properly, but they are free to decide whether a permit system needs to be set in place.[266] They have to ensure that during storage and collection, holders and collectors do not mix waste oils with PCBs and PCTs or with toxic or dangerous waste (Article 10(1)). Any undertaking which disposes of waste oils must obtain a permit (Article 6) and must be inspected periodically (Article 13). A permit for such an undertaking may only be granted if all appropriate environmental and health protection measures have been taken, including "use of the best technology available, where the cost is not excessive", commonly referred to as "BATNEEC".[267] The regeneration of waste oils containing PCBs or PCTs is forbidden, unless the process makes it possible either to destroy or to reduce them

---

[266] Art. 1(5) of the Commission Proposal included a permit duty for all undertakings involved in the processing of waste oils, including those collecting the waste.

[267] Best Available Technology Not Entailing Excessive Costs. See C. Billiet, " 'BAT' et 'BATNEEC': quelques faits et réflexions" (1995) 18 *Aménagemment/Environnement* 71. Reference to BATNEEC in this context is to be seen as a guideline for the authorities, not as a right for undertakings. Member States are not *obliged* to give a permit to an undertaking involved in the disposal of waste oil, should all economically viable measures have been taken. See J. Jans, "Toetsing van de afvalolie-richtlijn" (1993) 2 *Tijdschrift voor Milieurecht* 251.

so that the regenerated oils do not contain them beyond a maximum limit, to be imposed by national authorities but in any event not exceeding 50 ppm (Article 10(3)).[268]

Special provisions are included for those installations where waste oils are used as fuel. The Commission wanted to prohibit the combustion of waste oil in installations with a thermal input of less than one megawatt (MW). This proposal was inspired by the problems which emerged with the implementation of the 1975 Directive. In most Member States many small installations were operating. In fact, a substantial number of producers of waste oil (factories and so on) also combust this waste and use it as a fuel for part of their operations. The Commission was particularly concerned that, for most of these small installations, the introduction of new technologies would not be economically viable. However, because of the very existence of many small installations in most Member States, and in the aftermath of the oil crisis, ministers were not inclined to agree with the proposed ban.

The Directive now distinguishes between plants with a thermal input of more or less than three MW. Combustion of oils in plants with a thermal input of three or more MW has to meet the emission limit values set in the Annex (Article 8(1)(a)).[269] For plants with a thermal input of less than three MW, it is left to the Member States to take appropriate measures. At the very least, they have to ensure that, as for installations with an input of more than three MW, the residues of the operation are disposed of in accordance with the relevant legislation on toxic and dangerous waste, and that the oil used as fuel does not contain any toxic or dangerous substances, and does not contain PCB/PCT in concentrations beyond 50 ppm (Article 8(2)).

The Directive foresees a reporting duty for undertakings (Article 11). Any establishment producing, collecting, and/or disposing of more than a fixed amount of waste oil needs to fulfil the requirements. The threshold is set by the Member States but may not exceed 500 litres. The undertakings concerned must keep relevant records and submit these to the authorities. Article 16 enables Member States to introduce stricter national measures with respect to any of the requirements. This may include a ban on the combustion of waste oils.[270]

---

[268] In a statement annexed to the Directive, the Council underlined that this is a maximum limit and that Member States should make every effort to stay well below this limit.

[269] Notwithstanding the provisions of Dir. 84/360/EEC on the combating of air pollution from industrial plants [1984] OJ L188/20. The Annex contains 10 pollutants. Member States may any time set more stringent limit values than those included in the Annex. They may also set limit values for substances other than those foreseen in the Annex.

[270] This express authorization was inserted in 1986, after it had been recognized by the ECJ: Case 240/83, *Procureur de la République* v. *Association de défense des brûleurs d'huiles usagées (ADBHU)* [1985] ECR 531.

IX.   Other Specific Regimes

The following headings deal with some[271] specific (existing or proposed) EC waste regimes. Given their highly specific character, we hereinafter recall their guiding principles only.

A.   PCBS / PCTS

PCBs (polychlorinated biphenyls) and PCTs (polychlorinated terphenyls), (hereinafter conjunctly referred to as "PCBs")[272] have been widely used in appliances[273] and buildings because of their insulating and flame-retardant properties. Once their hazardous character became known,[274] Community action was taken. Directive 76/403/EEC[275] on the Disposal of Polychlorinated Biphenyls and Polychlorinated Terphenyls concerned only the *disposal* of PCBs. Restrictions on the use of PCBs were included in the legislation on the marketing and use of dangerous substances.[276] Directive 85/467/EEC amending for the sixth time (PCBs/PCTs) Directive 76/769/EEC on the approximation of the laws, regulations, and administrative provisions of the Member States relating to restrictions on the marketing and use of certain dangerous substances and preparations[277] prohibits all new uses of PCBs and the second-hand sale of equipment containing them, with a few exceptions. In 1988, the Commission sent a proposal to the Council which was to deal with the handling and disposal of PCBs which were in circulation before the 1985 ban.[278] After lengthy negotiations and procedural complications, an amended text was finally adopted by the Council in 1996.[279] The purpose of the Directive is radical: it is intended to approximate the laws of the Member States on the controlled disposal of PCBs, the decontamination or disposal of equipment containing PCBs, and/or the disposal of used PCBs in order to eliminate them completely (Article 1). PCBs include mixtures containing PCBs in a total of

---

[271] No separate attention will be afforded to the proposed Directive on end of life vehicles (ELVs), as the proposal is discussed extensively by M. Onida, "Challenges and Opportunities in EC Waste Management: Perspectives on the Problem of End of Life Vehicles", at p. 253 of this volume. See for instance also the Commission Proposal of 17 July 1998 for a Council Directive on port reception facilities for ship-generated waste and cargo residues, COM(98)452, inspired by the regime of the International Convention for the Prevention of Pollution from Ships 1973 and the 1978 Protocol thereto ("Marpol 73/78").

[272] Community Directives include both PCBs and PCTs under the term "PCBs".

[273] Electrical and hydraulic equipment, especially transformers and condensers.

[274] PCBs are persistent organic pollutants. They accumulate in the food chain (via the tissue of plants and animals) and they are barely biodegradable. Upon combustion, they release highly toxic dioxins and they are probably carcinogenic. See de Sadeleer, n. 6 above, 333.

[275] [1976] OJ L108/41.   [276] Dir. 76/769/EEC [1976] OJ L262/201.

[277] [1985] OJ L269/56.

[278] See S. P. Johnson and G. Corcelle, *The Environmental Policy of the European Communities* (London: Kluwer, 1995), 212.

[279] Council Dir. 96/59/EC of 16 Sept. 1996 on the disposal of polychlorinated biphenyls and polychlorinated terphenyls (PCB/PCT) [1996] OJ L243/31.

more than 0.005 per cent by weight. Waste oils containing less than 50 ppm of PCBs fall within the scope of the Waste Oil Directive.

Member States must ensure that used PCBs are disposed of and equipment containing PCBs is decontaminated or disposed of as soon as possible. For equipment that contains more than five litres of PCBs, decontamination and/or disposal must be effected at the latest by the end of 2010 (Article 3 in conjunction with Article 4). This obligation, as phrased in the Directive, extends to the smallest amounts of PCBs which would still be apparent in the equipment concerned. This will lead to huge financial implications for the Member States and for the operators involved. As yet, it is uncertain how far exactly Member States should go in pursuing this "total cleansing" goal. By 16 September 1999, Member States had to provide the Commission with detailed inventories of equipment which contains more than five litres of PCBs (Article 4), along with national plans for the decontamination and/or disposal of inventoried equipment and the PCBs contained therein (Article 11).

Until they are decontaminated, taken out of service, and/or disposed of, the maintenance of transformers containing PCBs may continue only if the objective is to ensure that the PCBs they contain comply with technical standards or specifications regarding dielectric quality and provided that the transformers are in good working order and do not leak. No PCBs may be separated from such transformers, for the re-use of the PCBs, and the transformers may not be topped up with PCBs (Article 5). Subject to these conditions, transformers containing between 0.05 per cent and 0.005 per cent by weight of PCBs may be used beyond the 2010 deadline, to be disposed of at the end of their useful lives (Article 9).

All undertakings engaged in the decontamination and/or the disposal of PCBs are subject to a permit requirement under Article 9 of the Framework Directive.[280] Incineration of PCBs is subject to the Hazardous Waste Incineration Directive. Other methods of disposal may be accepted provided they achieve equivalent environmental safety standards—compared with incineration—and fulfil the technical requirements referred to as best available techniques (Article 8). In line with the proximity principle, shipments of (equipment containing) PCBs may go ahead between Member States, in the light of the small number of adequate installations in the EC and taking into account the most environmentally sound option.

B.   BATTERIES AND ACCUMULATORS CONTAINING CERTAIN DANGEROUS SUBSTANCES

Directive 91/157/EEC[281] is based on Article 95 EC and targets the differences in the national regulations concerned. The distortion of the internal market was especially obvious in the light of the introduction by various Member

---

[280] N. 2 above.
[281] Dir. 91/157/EEC of 18 Mar. 1991 on batteries and accumulators containing certain dangerous substances [1991] OJ L78/38.

States of a requirement for manufacturers to ensure a collection system for used batteries.

The Directive targets batteries which contain specified levels of cadmium, lead, and mercury. Member States had to prohibit, after 1 January 1993, the marketing of alkaline manganese batteries for prolonged use in extreme conditions (e.g. temperatures below 0° C or above 50° C, exposed to shocks) containing more than 0.05 per cent of mercury by weight, and of all other alkaline manganese batteries containing more than 0.025 per cent of mercury by weight. Alkaline manganese button cells and batteries composed of button cells are exempted from this prohibition (Article 3).

Article 6 obliges Member States to set up programmes in order to achieve the following objectives: reduction of the heavy-metal content of batteries and accumulators; promotion of marketing of batteries and accumulators containing smaller quantities of dangerous substances and/or less polluting substances; gradual reduction, in household waste, of spent batteries and accumulators covered by Annex I;[282] promotion of research aimed at reducing the dangerous-substance content and favouring the use of less polluting substitute substances in batteries and accumulators, and research into methods of recycling; and separate disposal of spent batteries and accumulators covered by Annex I. The first such programmes were to cover the 1993–7 period and have come up for review.

The requirement of separate collection has been detailed in Article 4. Steps need to be taken to ensure that spent batteries and accumulators are collected separately with a view to their recovery or disposal, and that they are marked in the appropriate manner, together with the appliances into which they are incorporated. The marking must include indications concerning the separate collection; where appropriate, recycling; and the heavy-metal content.[283] Member States may introduce measures such as economic instruments in order to encourage recycling. These measures must be introduced after consultation with the parties concerned, be based on valid ecological and economic criteria, and avoid distortions of competition (Article 7). Batteries and accumulators may not be incorporated into appliances unless they can be readily removed, when spent, by the consumer (Article 5). This does not apply to the categories of appliance included in Annex II.

The Batteries Directive will be reviewed significantly. The Commission is not satisfied with the result of the 1991 Directive, which in effect has led to a variety of measures in the Member States, creating a lot of confusion. The Commission has drafted a proposal to replace the Directive with a new text along the follow-

---

[282] Annex I contains the batteries and accumulators covered by the Directive: 1. Batteries and accumulators put on the market as from 18 Sept. 1992 and containing: more than 25 mg mercury per cell, except alkaline manganese batteries; more than 0.025% cadmium by weight; more than 0.4% lead by weight. 2. Alkaline manganese batteries containing more than 0.025% mercury by weight placed on the market as from 18 Sept. 1992.

[283] Detailed arrangements for the marking have been included in Commission Dir. 93/86/EC adapting to technical progress Council Dir. 91/157/EEC on batteries and accumulators containing certain dangerous substances [1993] OJ L264/51.

ing lines.[284] All batteries will be covered, new marketing restrictions will be introduced, cadmium batteries will be progressively removed from the market, all batteries will have to be collected separately from household waste, collection and recycling targets will be set in place, and electrical appliances will need to be redesigned to ensure that all batteries may be removed.

C.   WASTE FROM ELECTRICAL AND ELECTRONIC EQUIPMENT

The management of waste from electrical and electronic equipment is high on the Commission's priority list. It is expected to issue a proposal on the subject in the near future (probably by spring 2000). Brussels has witnessed a considerable interest in what a proposal might entail. Reportedly, the focus of the expected proposal is very much on prioritizing re-use. Commission drafts have suggested an 80 to 90 per cent take-back rate for large household goods, office equipment, and dispensing machines, such as freezers, fridges, washing machines, computers, etc. 40 to 60 per cent is proposed for smaller household goods (including televisions and lamps). Crucially, between 70 and 90 per cent of large household goods, IT equipment, and some other goods would have to be recycled into new equipment. A recycling figure of between 40 and 60 per cent is proposed for smaller household goods such as televisions. The use of lead would be banned. As the proposals are still very much in a drafting stage, it is difficult to predict any real details. It is certain, however, that any text will have to face fierce opposition on both sides of the Atlantic.[285]

D.   WASTE FROM THE TITANIUM DIOXIDE INDUSTRY

Titanium dioxide is a white pigment, used in the fabrication of paints and plastics. The receiving environment of waste from the titanium dioxide industry is mainly the aquatic environment. The management of the relevant waste is intertwined with the legislation concerning water pollution, and will not be discussed here.[286] EC legislation on this substance has also been relevant for the more general issue of the choice of legal basis, following a challenge in the ECJ of the legal basis of Directive 89/428/EEC.[287]

---

[284] "Commission Aims to Step Up Battery Recycling" [1997] *ENDS-Report* 42–3; "Tough Recycling Targets in EC Proposal on Batteries" [1997] *ENDS-Report* 41.

[285] American manufacturers in particular claim that the Community initiative would amount to a barrier to trade, and have threatened WTO action.

[286] Dir. 78/176/EEC of 20 Feb. 1978 on waste from the titanium dioxide industry [1978] OJ L54/19; Dir. 82/883/EEC of 3 Dec. 1982 on procedures for the surveillance and monitoring of environments concerned by waste from the titanium dioxide industry [1982] OJ L378/1; Dir. 83/29/EEC of 24 Jan. 1983 amending Dir. 78/176/EEC on waste from the titanium dioxide industry [1983] OJ L32/28; Dir. 89/428/EEC of 21 June 1989 on procedures for harmonising the programmes for the reduction and eventual elimination of pollution caused by waste from the titanium dioxide industry [1989] OJ L201/56; Dir. 92/112/EC of 15 Dec. 1992 on procedures for harmonising the programmes for the reduction and eventual elimination of pollution caused by waste from the titanium dioxide industry [1992] OJ L409/11.

[287] Case C–300/89, *Commission* v. *Council* [1991] ECR I–2867. See R. Barents, "The Internal Market Unlimited: Some Observations on the Legal Basis of Community Legislation" (1993) 31

X. Conclusion

The foregoing discussion of the legal framework of waste in the EC suggests that, in an important sense, the work of the Commission and the ECJ has reached a mature stage. Indeed, the regulatory materials we have just canvassed illustrate that the early weaknesses in the regime, associated with the definitions of waste, recovery, and hazardous waste have now been extensively reconsidered and modified, leading to a more effective system of control. Moreover, this article has considered some of the new initiatives of the Commission in order to illustrate the new approaches and legal instruments the Commission is developing in its attempt to regulate waste across the EU.

Common Market Law Review 85; J. Robinson, "The Legal Basis of Environmental Law: Commission v Council, Case 300/89" (1992) 4 *Journal of Environmental Law* 109; H. Somsen, case note in (1992) 30 *Common Market Law Review* 140.

Environmental NGOs and EU Environmental Law

PETER NEWELL AND WYN GRANT*

I. Flexible Deregulation

The 1990s in Europe have been hailed as the era of the regulatory state. Ever since what was identified as the fiscal crisis of the state, governments have sought to reconcile the dilemma of meeting electoral demands for action to tackle public-policy problems without increasing the burden on taxpayers. Regulation offers a way out of that dilemma because the transaction costs can be relatively low and the costs of regulation are borne by the regulated. However, this sets up a new set of pressures, as the regulated complain that they are disadvantaged by more procedurally onerous or substantively rigorous regimes than exist elsewhere. Regulation then becomes perceived as a competitiveness issue. Anthony Giddens, in discussing the concept of the new mixed economy in an analysis of Labour's Third Way has defined it in terms of a balance between regulation and deregulation.[1]

With any type of bureaucratic apparatus, there is a danger of the means becoming the ends. Traditional forms of command-and-control regulation may generate very high transaction costs without leading to any impact on environmental outcomes. For example, a programme to increase the average number of vehicle riders in Los Angeles eventually had to be abandoned because it involved a substantial staff being employed to track what was happening at over 5,000 work sites. As one respondent commented, "[t]hat's an awful lot of file space, an awful lot of people opening envelopes".[2] Economists have argued that rather than employ large numbers of people to attempt to devise, enforce, and monitor complex regulations, it is more efficient to use the price mechanism to influence behaviour.

There was a substantial American debate on deregulation in the 1980s, which was influential both through the transmission of ideas and through the increased pressures for competitiveness generated through an increasingly integrated international economy. In March 1995, President Clinton and

* Peter Newell is a Research Fellow at the Institute of Development Studies based at the University of Sussex. Wyn Grant is Professor at the Department of Politics and International Studies at the University of Warwick.

[1] A. Giddens, "After the Left's Paralysis" (1998) 1 *New Statesman*, 18, at 19.

[2] W. Grant, "Improving Air Quality: Lessons from California" in D. Banister (ed.), *Transport Policy and the Environment* (London: Routledge, 1998), 204, at 211.

Vice-President Gore unveiled the "reinventing environmental regulation" initiative designed to encourage collaboration between industry and regulators and greater use of market mechanisms. Vice President Gore saw the key problem as reconciling the end of the era of big government with the need to continue protecting the environment. President Clinton subsequently emphasized the need for the responsible reinvention of regulations, replacing an inflexible approach by one that identified priorities.[3]

Collier identifies a number of forces which sharpened deregulatory pressures at the EU level.[4] The single market programme embodied a deregulation philosophy designed to strengthen the competitiveness of European industry. The subsidiarity doctrine became increasingly influential and offered at least the possibility of loosening regulatory intervention at Member State level. Another important factor was the position of European industry, which saw over-regulation as leading to higher costs, greater uncertainty, and the imposition of disproportionate administrative burdens.[5]

The Fifth Environmental Action Programme, in 1992, called for a strengthening of the dialogue with industry and the encouragement of voluntary agreements and other forms of self-regulation. It was argued that the general public and the social partners should become more actively involved in the development and practical implementation of environmental policy.[6] This theme was taken up by the influential European Round Table of industrialists (ERT) in 1993, which called for significant changes in the European regulatory framework. In 1994, Bernard Delogu, a senior DG XI official, stated that future legislation would be strongly influenced by the concept of market forces and less dependent on command-and-control legislation. He cited the EU's voluntary schemes for eco-labelling and environmental management and auditing as examples of this new trend.

As German concerns about eroding competitiveness grew, an Anglo-German coalition, combining business leaders and politicians, pressed the case for an examination of whether regulation was burdening companies. At the 1994 European summit it was agreed to establish a group of experts to examine the impact of EU and national legislation on employment and competitiveness. The subsequent Molitor Report chose to look at environmental regulation as only one of four sectors examined. The report advocates a new approach to environmental regulation "which stresses the setting of general environmental targets whilst leaving the Member States and, in particular, industry the flexibility to choose the means of implementation".[7] In particular, the group argued that "any new proposal should be accompanied by a careful

---

[3] W. Grant, "Large Firms, SMEs, Environmental Deregulation and Competitiveness" in U. Collier (ed.), *Deregulation in the European Union: Environmental Perspectives* (London: Routledge, 1998), 147, at 159–60.

[4] U. Collier, "The Environmental Dimensions of Deregulation: an Introduction", in Collier (ed.), n. 3 above, 3.

[5] G. Porta, "Environmental Policy Instruments in a Deregulatory Climate: The Business Perspective", in Collier (ed.), (n. 3 above), 165, at 167.

[6] *Ibid.*, 170.   [7] Quoted in Collier (n. 3 above), 15.

analysis of whether or not market-based methods could be employed to achieve the same goals; where a market-based approach is feasible, any departures from it should be justified".[8]

This was followed by a Regulatory Report, issued by the European business organization, the Union of Industrial Employers Confederation in Europe (UNICE). Although in some cases companies sought deregulation, they in particular wanted targeted changes to improve the quality and harmonization of regulations. There was no one solution, but regulation should be goal-based with specific goals and objectives being consistent with those of the United States of America and Japan. Particular emphasis was placed on industry statements on the use of negotiated agreements to restore and protect the environment.

Considerable interest was displayed in Dutch experience where a deregulation action programme had been adopted in 1983, not so much to change goals, but to develop alternatives to more traditional instruments. Regulatory space has been restructured around "a point of equilibrium between concern for environmental quality on the part of economic actors and improved economic competitiveness of firms as a result of increased responsiveness to market forces".[9] Of course, the equilibrium point in the Netherlands could be rather different from that in other Member States. Flexibility could be a cover for the re-emergence of greater policy divergence rather than the development of a common approach within the EU to shared environmental problems. Liefferink and Mol argue that "as the old curative and reactive policies increasingly turn into preventive ones, polluters are more and more directly involved in the formulation and implementation of policy measures".[10] If polluters have indeed internalized new norms, this could well be a process that will lead to more effective outcomes in terms of the quality of water and air and the reduction of waste.

However, if this process is to be a rounded one, rather than simply offering industry institutional opportunities to shape the implementation of environmental policies to suit its agenda, NGOs need to be involved in the process as well. Large firms with their regulatory affairs divisions and their well-resourced interest associations are better placed to engage in this process than most NGOs. The asymmetry of power between business organizations and NGOs may imply that a "facilitating" state is in fact facilitating the goals of business to the exclusion of wider social goals. Given the transformation of states, through the process of globalization, into "competition states which privilege business objectives, what impact can NGOs hope to make?"[11] For, while it is clear that the role of industry representatives in the policy process will increase, in terms of their proactive contribution to "regulation" through voluntary codes and self-regulation, it is less clear what the shifting dynamics

---

[8] *Ibid.*   [9] *Ibid.*, 11.

[10] D. Liefferink and A. P. J. Mol, "Voluntary Agreements as a Form of Deregulation? The Dutch Experience" in Collier (n. 3 above), 181, at 184.

[11] P. Cerny, *The Changing Architecture of Politics* (London: Sage, 1991).

of environmental policy in Europe mean for environmental non-governmental organizations (ENGOs).

The shift to a deregulatory agenda creates a number of challenges for NGOs (non-governmental organizations). In ecological terms, there is the environmental impact of measures such as energy market liberalization, introduced under the rubric of deregulation, as part of the internal market programme. The effect, if it is to follow the trend of other nationally-based forms of energy market liberalization (such as in the United Kingdom (UK)), will be to lower the price of fuels, increase consumption, and therefore make more difficult the implementation of the sort of energy saving and energy efficiency measures that NGOs are calling for.

The shift to voluntary codes implied by this agenda also means that governmental mechanisms of oversight on compliance that have traditionally formed the first point of contact for NGOs in lobbying for more effective policy are reduced. The withdrawal of institutional oversight of companies may be replaced increasingly by the direct monitoring of corporate activity by ENGOs which may report directly to the Commission, operating as informal information clearing houses on the implementation efforts of the companies across Europe. This sort of task will more likely be performed by nationally based NGOs in the first instance, rather than EU-level umbrella groups of the sort explored in this article, whose activities are geared much more exclusively to Brussels-level lobbying. Instances of implementation failure by companies identified by national members may nevertheless be communicated to the Commission via umbrella groups.

The shift towards self-regulation and voluntary codes may therefore thrust NGOs, however inadequately resourced or trained to perform the task, into a watchdog capacity, not necessarily on behalf of, but in conjunction with, the Commission. Whether their activities will come to be regarded as a nuisance or a useful supplement to the Commission's own efforts to oversee the implementation of (self-)regulation and co-ordination of practice remains to be seen. Some ENGOs such as Greenpeace also clearly have a longer history of performing this sort of "watchdog" exposé function than others, though the increasing professionalization of the organization means that they are becoming wary of coming into conflict with businesses, for fear of being dragged before the courts as a result of direct action. The *enfants terribles* of the environmental movement now have assets which can be frozen. The point is that as the flexible deregulation agenda proceeds, it can be expected that NGOs, depending very much on their preferred strategy and ideology, will seek increasingly to engage directly with companies themselves, rather than lobby the institutions of the Community or even national governments to "regulate" them. They will nevertheless continue to report their findings, perhaps in the form of exposés, to those institutions as part of a multi-pronged strategy and will therefore play an important part in making the compliance process more transparent. This is exactly the sort of function that NGOs have carved out for themselves in international conventions on environmental questions where their input is drawn upon by an international board of evaluators of countries' implementation measures. Such a role is officially recognized under international law as legitimate and important to the overall success of the agreement.[12] Hence past experience suggests that where countries use voluntary programmes with industry to help achieve emissions targets, NGOs help to inform international secretariats about the pace and depth of implementation.

The challenge posed by "flexible regulation" comes on top of a range of difficulties which ENGOs already face in seeking to influence the environmental policy of the European Community. Hence, while flexible deregulation creates some new challenges, for the most part it seems the overall effect may be to exacerbate some of the difficulties groups already face.

II. NGOs and EU Environmental Policy

A.   THE NATURE OF THE BEAST: THE CHALLENGE OF EU LOBBYING

Despite a rapidly expanding literature on the role of NGOs in world politics, relatively little has been written on the engagement of international NGOs in the European environmental policy-making process.[13]

It is particularly notable that the paucity of literature in this area is not reflective of the growth in the number of NGOs based in Brussels. In other words, academic interest has not kept pace with the expansion in environmental group activity at EU level. There has been an enormous growth of permanent environmental group representation in Europe. Often groups pool their resources as the case of the self-proclaimed G7 (the seven largest environmental umbrella groups operating in Brussels) and the European Environment Bureau (EEB) bears out. The largest international NGOs such as Greenpeace, Friends of the Earth, and World Wide Fund for Nature (WWF), all have branches in Brussels to co-ordinate their campaigns. They are also often part of single issue coalitions which attempt to represent a range of NGOs in a particular issue area. Climate Network Europe (CNE), the subject of the case study below, is an example of such a coalition.

Whilst there are a number of studies of the activities of national NGOs, this is an inadequate basis for comprehending the unique role of interest groups in the EU because, as Grande notes, "the European system of interest mediation

---

[12] P. Newell, "The International Politics of Global Warming: A Non-Governmental Account", PhD Thesis, University of Keele (1997).

[13] T. Princen and M. Finger, *Environmental NGOs in World Politics* (London: Routledge, 1994); P. Wapner, "Politics Beyond the State: Environmental Activism and World Civic Politics" (1995) 47 *World Politics* 311–40. Exceptions are S. Mazey and J. Richardson, "Environmental Groups and the EC: Challenges and Opportunities" (1992) 1 *Environmental Politics* 109–28, and D. Rucht, "'Think Globally, Act Locally?' Needs, Forms and Problems of Cross-national Cooperation among NGOs" in D. Liefferlink *et al.* (eds.), *European Integration and Environmental Policy* (London: Belhaven Press, 1993), 75–95.

has its own specific features".[14] The European model of a multinational, neo-federal, and open decision-making process presents NGOs with a number of distinct challenges.[15] This system creates agenda-setting possibilities, but also structural weaknesses. Mazey and Richardson argue that the strengths include an ability to build Europe-wide coalitions of interests. Many Europe-wide organizations have meetings every four to six weeks in order to exchange information and ideas.[16] Added to this is a sense in which the NGOs organized at Brussels level (albeit at different speeds and with different emphasis) are pushing in the same direction from a common platform. In contrast it can be argued that many industries are in competition with one another even where gathered loosely under the umbrella of a federation. In other words there are perhaps fewer intra-interest rivalries among NGOs. A further factor which may enhance the influence of ENGOs is their perceived ability (perceived by the Commission at least) to contribute to the process of European integration, albeit not to the same degree as industry federations. NGOs are perceived to help the Commission to do its job. The small size of the Commission causes it to be very dependent upon outside sources for information and expertise. The size of the Commission also limits its oversight in matters of implementation: a role which NGOs are in a position to supplement. Having the resources to both devise and implement practical solutions is "particularly important in certain areas of the EC where local administrations may not be the best agents for service delivery".[17] In general, NGOs benefit from the fact that there is a tradition of close relations between DG XI and NGOs founded on mutual support. Mazey and Richardson note that "without NGO support, DG XI might have died in its early years".[18] DG XI is therefore keen to cultivate networks of support to bolster its position within the Commission power structure.

Too heavy a dependence upon DG XI is simultaneously, however, a structural weakness of environmental organizations in Brussels. Their other key point of access, the European Parliament, despite the ongoing attempts to strengthen its hand in the policy process, remains poorly equipped to deliver significant policy reform in the environmental area. Another aspect of the close relationship between NGOs and DG XI is the direct and indirect (via contracts) financial support that NGOs receive from the Commission. The EEB, founded because DG XI needed an NGO movement as a counter-weight to industry lobbies, is funded by the Commission to hold seminars and round-tables. This may compromise their position as critics of the way the EU makes environmental law. Some NGOs are said to have been tamed by this process.[19] The provision of Commission funding for the EEB is thought to shape its less confrontational lobbying approach,[20] and subsidies to the groups undermine

---

[14] E. Grande, "The State and Interest Groups in a Framework of Multi-level Decision-making: The Case of the European Union" (1996) 3 *Journal of European Public Policy* 318–38, 321.
[15] Mazey and Richardson (n. 13 above).   [16] *Ibid.*   [17] *Ibid.*, 123.
[18] *Ibid.*, 121.   [19] *Ibid.*, 122.
[20] J. McCormick, *The Global Environmental Movement* (London: Belhaven Press, 1989).

the critical potential of the bureau *vis-à-vis* the Commission.[21] Its status under Belgian law means it must avoid overt political stances and must reach a compromise between the differing tactics of its member organizations and the different national political styles of lobbying.

The nature of the relationship has attracted fire from other quarters too. Industry, in particular, has been critical of what it considers to be "agency capture" by NGOs of DG XI. In addition to what was said above about the weakness of the Commission being a strength for the NGOs in terms of establishing a dependency upon their expertise and input, the organizational weakness of DG XI also means that the NGOs' influence does not stretch as far as that of their industry counterparts, who enjoy strong relations with the more powerful DG III. Because of this, industry groups are in a stronger overall position within the policy-making process. It is also possible to question the extent to which "agency capture" really occurs at EU level.[22] As Mazey and Richardson argue, "in practice, it is virtually impossible for any single interest . . . to secure exclusive access to the relevant officials, let alone to secure exclusive influence".[23]

A further structural weakness of NGOs is the lack of resources which would enable them to participate in the policy process from initiation to implementation. Keeping track of policy initiatives is a major undertaking for groups, made easier by the pooling of resources within Europe-wide networks. Following the development of policy is made more difficult, however, by the fact that policy with a significant bearing on the environment emerges simultaneously from a number of Directorates General, creating a monitoring problem of huge proportions for often poorly financed NGOs. Only the better resourced NGOs, such as WWF, are able to orchestrate their activities so that they are in a position to lobby a number of DGs simultaneously, and oversee the development of policy across a range of areas of relevance to "the environment". The WWF, for example, has lobbied the EU on its development cooperation policy both with third parties (such as African–Caribbean–Pacific countries (ACP) and Asian and Latin American countries (ALA)) and within the Community, channelled through the regional and cohesion funds and the PHARE programme for Central and Eastern Europe. It has also lobbied for reform of programmes addressed by powerful DGs which have an enormous environmental impact, such as the Common Agricultural Policy (CAP).[24] The process of following the life-course of a policy from initial development to implementation and maintaining good contacts with influential actors is complicated by the high turnover of Commission staff.[25]

---

[21] In 1992 DG XI spent roughly 6.5 million ECU on NGOs. Approximately 10% of this funding is set aside for the running costs of these groups (core-funding). As a result up to half the group's annual budget comes from the EC (see Rucht, n. 13 above).

[22] Grande (n. 14 above), 322.

[23] S. Mazey and J. Richardson (eds.), *Lobbying in the EC* (Oxford: Oxford University Press, 1993), 10.

[24] See Mazey and Richardson (n. 13 above).   [25] *Ibid.*

The influence of NGOs upon the direction and content of EU environmental law is also relative. The increasingly effective representation at Brussels level of interests counter to their own aims severely curtails the impact of the lobbying efforts of "green" groups. The fear that the presence of powerful industry groups will undermine the power of NGOs is fanned by the simultaneous pressures upon DG XI to talk to industrial interests and upon the environmental unit of DG III to play a greater part in the development of Community environmental policy.[26] In addition, the resources that industry groups provide the Commission with are to some extent more important for its purposes. As Rucht notes, "if NGOs refused to co-operate with the Commission, this would not really pose a threat to the credibility of the rules and regulations it must prepare; but this would not be the case where the Commission depends upon the input of expertise from industry lobbyists".[27] The wider point is that industry lobbies are often better resourced with personnel to provide the Commission with up-to-the-minute responses to its requests for information. The industry federation has a staff of 140 compared with the European Environment Bureau whose full-time staff numbers three.[28]

Added to this are a number of problems which all ENGOs face, but which appear to be exacerbated in the European context. Environmental campaigns are notoriously subject to the ups and downs of what has been referred to as the "issue attention cycle" and environmental issues are easily displaced on the public agenda by other issues considered to be more important.[29] The fact that the European Presidency system allows for frequent rotation of priorities in the environmental area makes it especially difficult for NGOs to pursue a sustained campaign over time.[30] The degree of influence they are able to have will vary according to the priorities of the Presidency. CNE may be considered to have more influence during the Dutch presidency than under the Irish because the Dutch Presidency made climate change a priority area for action. The fact that the Dutch, Luxembourg, and British Presidencies have all

---

[26] D. Wilkinson, "Towards Sustainability in the European Union? Steps within the European Commission Towards Integrating the Environment into Other Policy Sectors" (1997) 6 *Environmental Politics* 153–74.

[27] Rucht (n. 13 above), 89. [28] *Ibid.*, 83.

[29] A. Downs, "Up and Down with Ecology: The Issue Attention Cycle" (1972) 28 *Public Interest* 38–50.

[30] That said, much of the business is inherited from the previous Presidency, so there is some continuity despite scope to influence the direction and pace of Council business. Six-month Presidencies mean that countries may start an initiative or complete one, but rarely see them through all their stages. Hence for environmental NGOs, at each stage of the policy they may be dealing with a different set of personnel with whom good relations have to be cultivated on an ongoing basis. To get round some of these problems, the UK secured an agreement with its three successors as President of the Environment Council to conduct an audit against common criteria and targets of progress each country makes during its sixth months, intended to overcome the problem of countries holding the Presidency launching only short-term initiatives. The "troika" system that is supposed to operate is also designed to promote co-operation between the preceding, incumbent, and succeeding Presidencies. However the resistance of smaller Member States wary of domination of their Presidency by larger partners has lessened the intended impact of the system.

emphasized climate change in their programmes has made rotation less disruptive. Influence then depends on the strength of groups in the Presidency Member State and the nature of their relations with the most powerful government organs within that country. It will be up to these groups to press upon the incoming Presidency the importance of including environmental concerns in their programme of activity. This is made easier by the fact that "the government concerned knows that within six months it is difficult to achieve much and will be open to suggestions".[31]

Access and influence also of course rest upon wider trends in global politics, so that, for example, the Commission is more likely to encourage the participation of NGOs when it is under pressure to formulate a policy position in the run up to a round of international negotiations, or when its policies have been questioned by third parties. The credibility gap that the USA and others have been keen to highlight in the climate policy of the European Union has led to greater input from NGOs in helping to formulate policy proposals that will ensure the EU sticks to its 15 per cent CO_2 reduction target. International pressure upon the EU to sustain the momentum of the negotiations as the industrialized party with the most advanced target creates a catalyst for policy innovation which will benefit the profile and influence of NGOs, particularly those in a position to offer technical expertise on how to achieve emissions cuts.

Many of the problems which plague effective EU environmental policy also make co-operation between NGOs at the European level difficult. It is not just differences in priority between northern and southern Member States, but also East–West differences as the accession of new members proceeds. The weakness of the environmental movement in CEE (Central and Eastern Europe)[32] will leave an important vacuum where checks and balances are urgently required on the nature of post-transition development and the EU's role in accelerating that development. Suspicions have been raised that aid to CEE is guided by the interests of consultants and manufacturers of "clean technology" in western Europe.[33] In the climate change case there is already pressure upon countries of CEE to sign up to joint implementation and "hot air" trading schemes which seek to capitalize upon the comparatively low costs of investing in emission reductions in those countries. There clearly remains an important need for NGOs in these areas to act as an environmental watchdog over the enlargement process.

---

[31] *The European Citizen* No. 8 (1991), 12.

[32] P. Hardi, "East Central European Policy-making: The Case of the Environment" in O. Höll (ed.), *Environmental Cooperation in Europe* (Boulder, Colo.: Westview Press, 1994); S. Baker, "The Scope for East-West Cooperation" in A. Blowers and P. Glasbergen (eds.), *Environmental Policy in an International Context: Prospects* (London: Open University Press, 1996).

[33] B. Connolly and M. List, "Nuclear Safety in Eastern Europe and the Former Soviet Union" in R. Keohane and M. Levy (eds.), *Institutions for Environmental Aid* (Cambridge, Mass.: MIT Press, 1996).

B. EUROPEAN INSTITUTIONS AND ENVIRONMENTAL NGOS

By being part of the legal policy-making process, NGOs also perform a political function. They help the institutions of the Community to uphold the myth of the involvement and representation of "civil society" in the policy-making process. By consulting with NGOs, the Commission is able to claim that "society" has a voice in Community policy debates, that "public" stakeholders have been consulted and lent their approval, that the policy-making process itself is somehow open, transparent, democratic even. NGOs help to sustain this idea by coalescing with this process, which the Community uses to defend itself against the charge of a "democratic deficit" existing in Community politics. It is also true that when groups decide to press their demands within the EU rather than at the state level, there is an institutional implication in that it enhances the legitimacy of the European policy as an arena for authoritative decision-making.[34]

Lobbying the institutions of the Community serves a number of functions for NGOs nevertheless. It becomes especially important when national governments are adopting more recalcitrant positions and therefore recourse to the institutions of the EC is often strategic. It serves certain short-term goals that cannot be met by national-level lobbying. Mazey and Richardson[35] note "[i]n the environmental sector, groups at the national level are often in conflict with their own national administrations and hence see the EC as an alternative arena in which to exercise influence". Grant notes, for example, "the case against Britain's 'dirty' drinking water was fuelled by information from environmental interest groups".[36] Sometimes NGOs can play the Commission off against their national government and *vice versa* in order to extract the greatest gain in terms of environmental policy reform. This process can jeopardize close relationships with national government departments nurtured over many years, but it can also bring about effective results. In a legal sense, the resort to the use of the European Court of Justice (ECJ) by groups such as Friends of the Earth in the face of a "laggard" and Europhobic Thatcherite government in the UK is one manifestation of this trend.[37] In this case relations with the government were not strong and so the risk posed by bringing Brussels on side was one worth taking.

Despite this, Lauber argues "the European Community as a political structure offers substantially fewer opportunities for the environmental movement than the more advanced of its Member States".[38] Environmental organizations

[34] G. Marks and D. McAdam, "Social Movements and the Changing Structure of Political Opportunity in the European Union" in G. Marks, F. Scharpf, P. Schmitter, and W. Streeck (eds.), *Governance in the European Union* (London: Sage, 1996).

[35] Mazey and Richardson (n. 13 above) 116–17.

[36] W. Grant, "Pressure Groups and the European Community: An Overview" in Mazey and Richardson (n. 23 above), 27–48 at 28.

[37] A number of British groups such as FoE (Friends of the Earth) also complained to the Commission about the British government's handling of various road schemes such as the M11 link.

[38] V. Lauber, "The Political Infrastructure of Environmental Politics in Western and Eastern Europe" in Höll (n. 32 above), 257.

have no right to information, no right to be consulted in advance of a measure taken by Community organs, and no right of standing before the European Court of Justice (they can only file complaints according to Articles 173/175 of the EC Treaty). NGOs are of course consulted, but only on an informal basis and when the Commission seeks information or support for specific projects. Often consultation is sought on proposals which are effectively a *fait accompli* and where a seal of approval rather than meaningful input and direction is sought.

NGOs are denied the same privileges as business, labour, and consumer groups, reflecting both the goals of the Community and the groups designated as important at the time of the drafting of the Treaty in the late 1950s.[39] This includes business and consumer groups and interested parties central to the process of European integration. Changes such as the Directive on the Freedom of Access to Information on the Environment which came into effect on 1 January 1993 and the establishment of the European Environment Agency, said to "create an important point of access for the environmental lobbies to Community institutions",[40] may make it easier to participate meaningfully in EC policy-making on the environment in the future.

Nevertheless, the fact remains that "[i]n contrast to groups in various other policy areas, NGOs have no formal rights regarding the policy process in the EC".[41] The process is *ad hoc* and arbitrary so that who gets what information and who is invited to which committee meeting are often political decisions made by Commission officials. Contact between NGOs and the Commission is often on the basis of informal contacts. Rucht describes a reactive process whereby NGOs respond to Commission proposals having little choice but to adopt the agenda and gain access to information as quickly as possible.[42] This is not to suggest that NGOs do not have an impact upon the Commission's agenda. National NGOs in "lead" states from the green "troika" are in a position to set the Commission's agenda. Often this will be reflected by the promotion of broad principles like the "precautionary principle" within EU policy debates, which has been used in German law since the late 1980s. The evolution of the Large Combustion Plant Directive and the Packaging Directive within the EU also displayed regulatory replication from German policy which NGOs lobbied for. We see through this process the diffusion from the national to the Community level of the indirect influence of strong environmental lobbies from powerful Member States.[43] Nevertheless, the Commission itself is relatively insulated from public opinion (access to which is a key point of leverage for NGOs), such that the need for the sort of public approval of Community action which NGOs are able to mobilize is less pressing.

It is very difficult for groups to find out early enough in the policy process which proposals are being prepared by which section of a

---

[39] *Ibid.* (n. 38 above). [40] *Ibid.* (n. 38 above), 258.
[41] Rucht (n. 13 above), 88. [42] *Ibid.*
[43] A. Sbragia, "Environmental Policy: The 'Push-Pull' of Policy-making" in H. Wallace and W. Wallace (eds.), *Policy-making in the European Union* (3rd edn., Oxford: Oxford University Press, 1996).

Commission department. Relying on formal consultations is rarely enough and most lobbying is done on an informal basis at "social" gatherings and conferences. To be effective groups have to lobby simultaneously at the national and European levels.[44] This is where groups like CNE come in. They can orchestrate a Europe-wide campaign of activities with their member groups lobbying in the national capitals of laggard states which may be obstructing the passage of an item of legislation. To be effective, it is also necessary to put pressure on all institutions on a simultaneous basis which is difficult for poorly resourced organizations. Despite claims by the Commission that a proposal has left its hands, it continues to perform an ongoing role in the policy process (in relation to amendments put forward by the Parliament etc.) and needs to be continually lobbied. Keeping up with the frequent changes of personnel within the Commission is also difficult, a tracking process made all the more difficult by the volume of short-term part-time staff where the rate of turnover is very high.

The European Parliament is thought to be more sensitive to the interests of NGOs and therefore provides a key point of contact in the policy process. The representation of Greens in the EP and policy entrepreneurs such as Von Blottnitz willing to sponsor environmental reforms provide a potential veto point for measures aimed at the further deregulation of environmental policy. But the overall impact of such stalling has to be viewed in the context of the relative impotence of the EP despite the formal strengthening of its powers, and the powerful backing that the deregulatory agenda enjoys. Perhaps the best way for NGOs to influence the Parliament is to draft a text in the form of a resolution, amendment, or question. This involves lobbying the *rapporteurs* of the committees asked for an opinion by the Commission. Failing this, NGOs then try to find an MEP willing to put down an amendment on their behalf. It is difficult to mobilize sufficient support for a proposal however, given that, to stand a good chance of being accepted, amendments need the support of both the Socialist and European People's Party groups (the two largest groupings).[45] The parliamentary intergroups provide one focal point for bringing MEPs together from different countries and parties.

The hardest task for NGOs, however, is influencing the Council of Ministers. Voting patterns often follow the "push/pull" formulae[46] where northern Member States vote in favour of environmental legislation and poorer southern members vote against it. The best opportunity for NGOs at this stage is to co-ordinate lobbying with national members. It is often too late, however, to modify proposals before the Council, and the politics essentially centre on inter-state bargaining. Lobbying the Council directly is difficult because Council working papers are officially confidential even though leaked extensively. Lobby groups often get most of their information from Member States that are willing to engage with interest-group concerns. Council reports containing redrafts of Commission proposals giving the position of national

---

[44] *The European Citizen* (n. 31 above).   [45] *Ibid.*   [46] Sbragia (n. 43 above).

delegations and mentioning their reservations on particular clauses are an essential lobbying tool in the hands of NGOs. These help to identify who the stalling partners are despite public proclamations by those governments suggesting they are pushing for stronger environmental action. One other channel of influence is for NGOs to organize a press conference in the run up to a session of the Council as a way of expressing views about a draft directive and attempting to keep public attention focused on its progress in the hope that this will encourage the adoption of more far-reaching action.

III. Forms of Influence

A. THE EUROPEAN DIMENSION

In general, it is possible to divide up the roles of NGOs at this level into agenda-setting/pressure mobilization, expertise, monitoring/enforcement. We address the respective influence activities in the following sections.

i. *Agenda-setting/Pressure Mobilization*

Besides general awareness-raising and pressure mobilization among the public at the national level, agenda-setting also refers to the ability of NGOs to project ideas into the institutional arena and create policy problems, some of which are filtered through deliberate non-decision-making processes.[47] Others, perhaps because they resonate with existing interests and agendas, manage to secure a place on the policy agenda. The promotion of COGEN (combined heat and power generated electricity) in recent Commission documents, for example, is the result of NGOs (alongside the COGEN industry itself) projecting the use of COGEN as a "win-win" solution to climate change and the Community's energy needs without imposing new costs on industry. In most cases it is argued that NGOs enjoy greatest influence within national policy arenas, where policy responses develop first.[48] It is at this stage of the policy process when the problem is defined, expertise sought, and the need for international action discussed, that policy positions are developed. NGOs are therefore able to shape expectations about the nature of the policy that should be developed.

In a reactive policy situation, NGOs are in many ways able to set the pace of political change and assert their preferred interpretations of what the issue means and what degree of action may be appropriate, whilst governments are deciphering their own preferences or interests in the debate. It is arguably harder to do in an EC context where the range of policy-relevant "usable" interpretations is much narrower and the goals of policy more clearly defined.

---

[47] P. Bachrach and M. Baratz, "Two Faces of Power" (1962) 56 *American Political Science Review* 947.
[48] A. Rahman and A. Roncerel, "A View from the Ground Up" in I. Mintzer and J. Leonard (eds.), *Negotiating Climate Change* (Cambridge: Cambridge University Press, 1994), 239.

ii. Expertise

Those NGOs likely to have the greatest role in shaping EU environmental law are those that are considered to have significant reserves of human and financial resources, advance intelligence of policy proposals, good contacts, and an ability to provide policy-makers with sound information and advice. The extent to which institutions call upon NGOs for their input is a function of the degree to which they have access to other sources of research and information and, in broader terms, whether NGOs have assets which they think they can make use of. Mazey and Richardson note "reputations for expertise, reliability and trust are key resources in lobbying in Brussels as elsewhere".[49] Eurogroups that are at once "representative" and expert are those that are likely to be called upon most by the Commission. Grant notes that environmental "think-tanks" and policy research institutes (such as the Institute for Environmental Policy) make an important contribution to the policy agenda at EC level in this respect.[50]

Richardson finds similarly in relation to EU water policy that NGOs' strength is that "they can out-match the big chemical companies in some respects simply because the groups access a different range of scientific expertise than even a large chemical company can command".[51] On the basis of this "many of the other key players admit that they themselves are usually reacting to the agenda set by environmentalists".[52] Environmentalists can create a megaphone effect for scientific findings in the policy process.[53] This is certainly the case for CNE which, within its ranks, can call upon expertise in the scientific, economic, and technological aspects of the issue, which will all be useful to the Commission at different stages of the policy-making process. This explains why CNE was invited to be part of the Commission expert group on a monitoring mechanism for reducing Community CO_2 emissions. This is not of course, a one-way process and it is probable that the European Environment Agency will be a valuable official source of information on how well companies are implementing their self-declared commitments, as well as providing NGOs with the technical resources to support their case for stronger environmental measures.

It is notable however that the nature of policy advice demanded by the Commission changes over time, so that, while input from scientific experts is required at the start of the policy process as a way of validating the existence of a potential problem worthy of attention and requiring of a policy response, latter stages of policy formation are more likely to be informed and influenced by the opinions and input of economists.[54] It is less likely that many NGOs

[49] Mazey and Richardson (n. 13 above), 110.   [50] Grant (n. 36 above).
[51] J. Richardson, "EU Water Policy: Uncertain Agendas, Shifting Networks and Complex Coalitions" (1994) 3 *Environmental Politics* 161.
[52] *Ibid.*, 161.   [53] *Ibid.*, 139–68.
[54] A. Liberatore, "Facing Global Warming: The Interactions between Science and Policy-making in the European Community" in M. Redclift and T. Benton (eds.), *Social Theory and the Global Environment* (London and New York: Routledge, 1994), 190.

have the sort of expertise that the Commission demands at this stage and therefore their input is likely to be reduced. The levels at which emission reductions will be set, the time-frames that will be employed and the extent to which technologies are in place that can realistically bring about the desired reductions are questions which industry groups, with more "hands-on" experience, are more likely to be able to answer than "green" groups. The overriding concern of the Commission as the policy develops, as the carbon tax debate bears out, will be the impact the proposal may have upon the competitiveness of European industry rather than how far the policy reflects the severity of the issue implied by the science or the extent to which it adequately responds to the degree of public concern surrounding the issue (issues which NGOs often highlight).

iii. Monitoring/Enforcement

"Whistle-blowing" activity by NGOs helps to notify the Commission of instances of non-compliance at the national level. Grant notes, for example, "the case against Britain's 'dirty' drinking water was fuelled by information from environmental interest groups".[55] Because these groups perform this function for the Commission, the Commission in turn is keen to maintain an unofficial monitoring function for them in helping to bridge the "implementation gap" between European-level legislation and national and local implementation.

As part of this process, groups have taken the opportunity to expose Member States' inability to fulfil their commitments. Greenpeace International's report, "The EC's Next Global Warming Factories", published in April 1994, showed how EU proposals to build new power plants may overwhelm the Union's goal of returning CO_2 to 1990 levels by the year 2000.[56] CNE was also approached by the CSD (Commission on Sustainable Development), the international body responsible for overseeing the implementation of the Rio agreements, to produce a report assessing the effectiveness of climate policy in western Europe in order to evaluate the Community's success in meeting the goals of the Convention.[57]

B. THE CLIMATE DIMENSION

Particular issue areas not only give rise to different coalitions of interest or policy communities, they also have a significant effect on the patterns of influence that emerge in that policy area. The issue of global climate change, for example, presents CNE (the subject of the case study below) with a particularly difficult set of obstacles and challenges. Besides the very many scientific uncertainties that attend global warming, which make it harder to develop a

---

[55] Grant (n. 36 above), 28.   [56] "Power Plants Pilloried", *Acid News* (1994), 2.
[57] P. Newell, "Climate Politics in Western Europe: Regional and Global Dimensions" Earth Council Report, available on the Internet at: <http://www.ecouncil.ac.cr/rio/focus/report/english/climate.htm>.

consensus upon appropriate policy action,[58] there are also the economic costs that are perceived to be involved, and the scale of economic restructuring (in terms of energy production and consumption) that may be implied by efforts to decrease the output of greenhouse gas emissions. The interests that will be affected by such change are also among the most powerful in the global economy.[59] This brings environmental organizations campaigning on climate change up against some of the most powerful lobbies in Europe, such as Eurelectric, Europia, and UNICE (Union of Industrial Employers Confederations in Europe).[60] There is also a long time-lag between the time when action is taken to reduce the onset of global warming, and the observable effects of such action. This factor disinclines governments to take potentially very costly action, the benefits of which will not be seen for many decades, and for which they will not receive direct credit.

The relative absence of convenient "techno-fixes" with which to combat the problem closes further potential channels of influence, in terms of group advocacy of simple solutions to the problem.[61] It is easy to contrast this scenario with the case of ozone depletion, where the issue was replacement and substitution. With regard to climate change, the issue is arguably "dissipating" business and not "different" business.[62] It needs to be acknowledged therefore that global warming brings its own set of unique and particularly perplexing challenges to NGOs.

C. THE PROBLEM OF ASSESSING INFLUENCE

It is often hard to assess the impact of a particular campaign or of a particular environmental NGO upon EU environmental law because each of the actors involved in policy-making wants to claim success and influence for himself. Pressure groups may be inclined to exaggerate the degree of influence they have been able to exert, and Member States and/or institutions of the Community are as likely either to claim NGO successes for themselves or to recast events in a light which reflects well on their role.

A group's influence is often manifested by the acceptance of its ideas which capture the political imagination where there exists a "window of opportunity" for a new interpretation. If a concept or policy which NGOs are advocating resonates with an existing policy discourse, or institutional need, then it has a greater chance of being adopted. The notion of "contraction and convergence"

---

[58] E. Skolnikoff, "The Policy Gridlock on Global Warming" (1990) 79 *Foreign Policy* 77–93.

[59] P. Newell and M. Paterson, "A Climate for Business: Global Warming, the State and Capital" (1998) 5 *Review of International Political Economy* 629–704.

[60] L. Collie, "Business Lobbying in the European Community: The Union of Industrial and Employers' Confederations of Europe, in Mazey and Richardson n. 23 above, 213.

[61] That is not to say that groups have not attempted to emphasize the use of clean and energy efficient technologies. Greenpeace, e.g., has been exposing those retail stores not accepting its climate-friendly "Greenfreeze" refrigeration system (Greenpeace Business, *Potential Impacts of Climate Change on Health in the UK* (London: Greenpeace, 1994)).

[62] I. Rowlands, *The Politics of Global Atmospheric Change* (Manchester: University Press, 1995), 137.

promoted by the Global Commons Institute (GCI, see below) and adopted by MEPs suggests that this is the case, and the concept of "ecological moderniza-tion"[63] which promotes the idea that growth and environmental protection are compatible through the pursuit of "win-win" policy options has been used widely in policy debates in the Commission.

The fact that many of the most influential groups are also those closest to governments, those whose policy prescriptions are more easily accommo-dated within existing frameworks further complicates an assessment of influ-ence. In these instances it is hard to detect the distinctive impact of groups. It is more difficult to assess which policies can be explained in terms of NGO influence, and which in their initiation or subsequent development drew nothing from NGO pressure, but were incremental changes that a Member State or the Commission would have made anyway.

In considering the strengths and weaknesses of NGO lobbying in Brussels, it is very difficult to generalize, and one has to be careful to discriminate between "insiders" and "outsiders". Some NGOs are consulted or granted a greater degree of access to the Commission than others. There are few settled and institutionalized patterns of consultation and the Commission is still in the process of developing its consultation and co-ordination procedures, dri-ven by the need to "rationalize" the consultation process. In general, however, it seems that the following factors, taken together, help to account for the degree of influence that NGOs have at the European level.

One key determinant of the degree of influence that an NGO will be able to exert over policy can be expected to be the closeness of its relationship to prin-cipal decision-making bodies and actors. CAN-UK members, for example, have frequent meetings with UK representatives from Brussels and with the Secretary of State for the Environment, before meetings of the EU Council of Ministers.[64]

Some governments have also been more positive in encouraging NGO par-ticipation in policy formulation than others. The relationship between groups and the administration that they are seeking to influence is also of course in a state of flux, with different governments being more or less sensitive to the demands made of them by environmentalists. The presence of political parties such as *Die Grünen* in Germany also enable far more co-operative relations to develop between the government and NGOs, assisted by a generally more receptive government attitude to environmentalist concerns. NGO influence is contingent not only upon groups' relationships with particular governments or parties, but also particular government departments and how influential those departments then are in the overall policy process.[65] Hence, whilst NGOs may be able to nurture positive relations with environment depart-ments, the overall influence of this department compared with trade and

---

[63] A. Weale, *The New Politics of Pollution* (Manchester: University Press, 1992).
[64] F. Weir (Former Climate Campaigner, Friends of the Earth UK), quoted in Newell (n. 12 above).
[65] Newell (n. 12 above).

industry ministries for example, may be limited. This trend reflects the inter-departmental power relations at Brussels level, discussed above. It is also notable that different presidencies encourage the participation of NGOs to different degrees. Following the Rio summit and the emphasis in Agenda 21 on the need to involve all stakeholders in the formulation of policy, the German presidency was keen to ensure greater participation by "green" groups.[66]

Access is also a function of a group's lobbying style. The Brussels lobbying style serves to exclude NGOs that pursue a more confrontational campaigning style. Interactions are preferred with groups which are "responsible", implying those willing to co-operate with the Commission without resorting to publicity to benefit their cause. There is still a perception among some Commission officials that environmentalists are obstructionist, anti-growth, and overly reliant upon the media to attack decision-makers and companies.[67] To the extent that the Commission is able to set the terms of engagement with NGOs, some NGOs may be faced with a strategic dilemma whereby, in order to gain "insider" status with the Commission, they have to drop their more confrontational approach to campaigning, whereas by doing this they may alienate their traditional membership base which is supportive of those tactics. This sort of dilemma is more likely to face groups like Greenpeace than more "conservative" groups like WWF. Rucht claims that working within the EC bureaucracy is less suited to the campaign practices of Greenpeace, which prefers to pursue more confrontational public-oriented campaigns through, amongst other things, media coups.[68] Media-oriented public campaigns against the EU "seed list" which Greenpeace was active in orchestrating, brought unwanted publicity to a controversial issue area, and are unlikely to endear the group to policy-makers who prefer more conciliatory participation. As other writers in other issue areas have noted however,[69] the simultaneous presence of insider and outsider NGOs creates a "good cop/bad cop" presence, where policy-makers make more concessions to the good cops in order to reward positive engagement and deter "deviant" NGO behaviour. The irony of course is that the good cops would not make so much ground if it were not for the more threatening tactics of the "bad cops". The fringe activity of groups like Greenpeace may therefore benefit those NGOs working within the EU system to affect change.

Because of this approach, Rucht notes that the Greenpeace office established in Brussels in 1988 is less effective at influencing EU decision-making processes than other groups operating at this level.[70] The basis of his argument is that the organization tends to stand apart from other alliances, and is therefore less co-ordinated with other NGOs in Brussels and "less adapted to the

---

[66] R. Würzel, "The Role of the EU Presidency in the Environmental Field: Does It Make a Difference which Member State runs the Presidency?" (1996) 3 *Journal of European Public Policy* 282–3.

[67] Mazey and Richardson (n. 13 above), 126.   [68] Cited in Rucht (n. 13 above).

[69] J. Audley, *Green Politics and Global Trade: NAFTA and the Future of Environmental Politics* (Washington DC: Georgetown University Press, 1997).

[70] Cited in Rucht (n. 13 above).

task of lobbying and negotiating with EC bureaucrats".[71] By contrast, groups such as WWF are said to have a closer relationship with DG XI than many other environmental lobbies.[72] Hence, while WWF has set a limit of between 10 and 15 per cent on funding from public agencies, Greenpeace has abstained from asking the EC for money on the basis that this would compromise the group's autonomy of operation.[73] As was mentioned above, the human and financial resources a group can bring to bear in seeking to influence the development of a policy will also affect the impact it is able to make because access to these resources allows campaigners to "follow" an issue from initiation through to implementation, fund quality research, and maintain a higher profile. Better-resourced NGOs are in a position to lobby and monitor the activity of all parts of the Brussels system on an ongoing basis and deal more effectively with the volume of activity generated by the institutions of the Community.

And yet the issue of climate change in Brussels provides a powerful counter-point to the convenience of the "insider/outsider" formulations of influence where groups with more resources and which are more conservative are closer to the centres of decision-making, and therefore more influential. The case of the GCI (Global Commons Institute) illustrates the influence that a small and low-resourced group can have upon policy, suggesting that access and reserves of resources do not of themselves confer influence. The group was successfully able to promote the idea of "contraction and convergence" (between high and low greenhouse gas emitters respectively) which MEP Tom Spencer from the GLOBE group (Global Legislators for the Global Environment) adopted and promoted in the international climate-change negotiations. This case suggests it is often relations between individual legislators and policy entrepreneurs that shape the success of a policy proposal or campaign. Hence it not so much the relationship between GLOBE and GCI as the personal relationship between Aubrey Meyer and Tom Spencer MEP that is the important dynamic. It also suggests the importance of ideas able to capture the imagination of policy-makers which better resourced groups do not have a monopoly over.

It is not useful therefore to assess the influence and impact of NGOs against the yardsticks we employ to gauge corporate influence where financial resources are paramount. NGOs play on policy-makers' perceptions that they represent some notion of the public interest or at least that their motives transcend the narrow profit-making goals of their corporate counterparts. It is their perceived legitimacy and the symbolic potency of their ideas and the popularity of their values that encourage policy-makers to take them seriously. The forms of leverage they exercise are altogether different, therefore, from those which business groups are able to mobilize.

To test some of these ideas in practice the case of CNE is used to explore the role of NGOs in affecting the development of EU climate policy. The case is not representative of environmental pressure group activity in the EU generally,

---

[71] *Ibid.*, 85–6.   [72] Sbragia (n. 43 above), 245.
[73] Mazey and Richardson (n. 13 above), 122.

but it does serve to highlight a number of issues raised by the above discussion, particularly in relation to Europe-wide coalitions of interest.

IV. Case Study: Climate Network Europe

CNE was created in 1989 at the height of international concern about the possible threat posed by the increasing concentrations of greenhouse gases in the atmosphere. The European office of the CAN network was established to produce recommendations for the European Parliament on climate related matters. CNE has seventy-three non-governmental member organizations, but also "builds partnerships with winner industries trade associations, local authorities and other sectors of society on initiatives such as eco-tax reform, renewable energies and energy efficiency".[74] CNE acts as an information service on climate policy developments and produces a quarterly mailing for its member organizations containing information about EU policy and the UN climate negotiations. CNE is also home to possibly the largest climate-related library in Europe with over 2,000 publications related to every aspect of climate change. CNE seeks to raise public awareness about climate change, which it does through media work with member organizations and the organization of seminars in EU countries to support national NGOs in their work on climate change issues.[75] CNE has been centrally involved in the EU climate policy debate from its earliest stages in the late 1980s through to the current day, where it is now regarded as the definitive NGO voice on climate-related matters at Brussels level. CNE monitors and encourages the implementation of polices and measures that combat climate change as well as working with national NGOs to do the same at Member State level.[76] The lobbying work at Brussels level is focused on policies relating to energy efficiency and standards, integrated resource planning, CO_2/energy taxes, renewable energies, and transport policy. CNE was also part of the "G7" large NGO networks based in Brussels that had an input into the inter-governmental conference (IGC) revising the Maastricht Treaty. The group had an input into the report "Greening the Treaty 2" which was published and presented at the hearing of the European Parliament on the IGC.[77]

CNE is part of a global Climate Action Network (CAN) which has other regional branches in Africa, Latin America, Asia, and North America. Hence, the position of CNE is bolstered by its position within a global network. By being part of a global lobby they are able to push on all fronts, which is important when the evolution of EU policy is conditional upon how policy develops in the USA or Japan. By being part of a global coalition that achieved some success in bringing about the Convention and affecting its contents,[78] they have

---

[74] Climate Network Europe, "Climate Network Europe" (1998), available on the Internet at: <http://www.climatenetwork.org/CNE.html>.
    [75] *Ibid.*   [76] *Ibid.*   [77] *Ibid.*   [78] Newell (n. 12 above).

shaped the EU requirements, given that a key part of environmental law on climate change derives from the international level.

The pooling of (often scarce) resources, sharing media and political contacts, expertise, staff, information, and money help to diffuse the burden of campaigning at the European level for groups that would either prefer to focus their campaigning energies in other areas or to have only an indirect European presence. It also enables groups to draw on campaigning strengths in different aspects of the issue. Within CNE for example, Greenpeace is considered to be an authority on the scientific and human aspects of climate change,[79] WWF in relation to the impacts of climate change upon biodiversity[80] and EURACE (European Association for the Conservation of Energy) and Energy 21 on energy efficiency issues, while Friends of the Earth (FoE) focus on nuclear issues, so that a range of dimensions of the climate change problem are covered.

The burden of performing CNE's European-wide mandate is aided by such an implicit division of labour. The breadth of concerns captured by such a coalition can be regarded as a positive asset. Presenting a united front on climate change issues from a diversity of NGOs across Europe carries symbolic value. And yet, the very many differences of expertise and lobbying emphasis and tactics found within a broad coalition like CNE can also be considered a weakness. Such diversity makes efficient policy-making within the organization difficult and conflicts of emphasis may ensue. Bringing all members on board all the time is a difficult exercise, in financial and human resource terms.

CNE works closely with other relevant organizations on the Brussels scene such as Transport and Environment Europe (T&E). Rucht also notes that the directors of the four "big" offices in Brussels (EEB, CEAT, WWF, Greenpeace) meet roughly every six weeks to exchange information and co-ordinate activities. Indeed the overall structural disadvantage of NGOs in the Brussels system makes co-ordination imperative, encouraging groups to act in concert rather than against each other.[81]

CNE has sought to consolidate its position in the EU climate-change debate through the pursuit of alliances with corporate lobbies. These partnerships open up new avenues of influence and help to tilt the balance towards those in favour of environmental action. CNE has been able to foster an alliance with a number of influential clean energy companies and trade associations such as EUROACE (European Association for the Conservation of Energy), the European Wind Energy Association, and COGEN (Cogeneration) in calling for more action on climate change.

Attempting to draw in Member States from southern parts of the Community, as a way of undermining the generally recalcitrant position of

---

[79] Greenpeace (n. 61 above).

[80] World Wide Fund for Nature, "Intensifying Efforts on the Berlin Mandate" (position statement 1996); A. Markham, *Some Like it Hot: Biodiversity and the Survival of Species* (Geneva: WWFI, 1994).

[81] Rucht (n. 13 above).

southern Mediterranean states on this issue, has been a further strategy pursued by the group. CNE provides valuable support for south Mediterranean and North African groups where there is lack of awareness about climate-change issues, a lack of input at European level, and where resource constraints are even sharper.[82] CNE is able to represent these voices and perspectives at the European level, so that other dimensions of the climate-change issue than would be pressed upon Member States by northern NGOs get an airing such as the repercussions for water supply and desertification for example.

The fact that CNE operates without a popular mandate (even if its member organizations rely on public support) means it is inevitably an élite lobbying outfit. This undoubtedly affects the sort of campaigns CNE undertakes. Whilst they may be targeted at popular audiences and they are intended to stimulate popular engagement with the climate-change issue, the group does not have to be sensitive to supporter concerns and therefore its work can be more focused on the demands of policy-makers. It is perhaps useful to think of the organization as the top tier of a wedding cake with the mass membership organizations at the base providing the indirect popular mandate and much of the stability, but CNE, for most policy-makers in Brussels, is the first point of contact on climate related matters. This is not to suggest, of course, that groups belonging to the coalition do not also lobby the EU in their own right, alongside their involvement in CNE co-ordinated campaigns.

CNE has used its permanent presence in Brussels to nurture a range of contacts with the EU which it draws upon in advancing action on climate change. Often the organization is invited to attend meetings by Community representatives as it is widely regarded as *the* European NGO voice on climate change. This means it is expected to participate in conferences on a wide range of matters from clean coal and solar power to building standards and cars. Given this, it is especially important to reach out and form alliances with groups like Transport and Environment Europe on the Auto Oil programme to cover important areas where their expertise may be low. CNE has good access to MEPs, such as McNally and Von Blottnitz, who will sponsor policy reforms on their behalf. Although predominantly from weaker parts of the bureaucracy, such contacts are a key part of their influence. In this regard, Matláry describes "an identifiable and small network of people in the EP and the Energy Directorate that interact between themselves and with key interest groups".[83] The relationship runs (at least) two ways of course, so that MEPs also strengthen their hand through association with the NGOs and use them to bolster coalitions of support for controversial proposals. Once again the organization of the system requires NGOs to organize in a particular way. Indeed the formation of coalitions such as CNE is prompted by external pressure from the Commission upon interest groups to "scale up" as part of the rationalization of

[82] P. Newell, "Climate Change in the Mediterranean: The NGO Dimension" in *Sustainable Mediterranean* (Brussels: EC Press, 1996), 12–13.

[83] J. M. Matláry, *Energy Policy in the European Union* (Basingstoke: Macmillan 1997).

NGO consultation at Brussels level.[84] By rationalizing interest-group activity the Community affects the extent form and direction of pressure-group activity.[85]

Nevertheless, and despite the proliferation of Brussels-based umbrella groups, because the central decision-making institution, the Council of Ministers, is a forum characterized by inter-state bargaining, pressure-group activity is "still heavily weighted in favour of working with national governments".[86] Individual groups use the representation and access to information that membership of CNE provides as just one avenue for the furtherance of their interests. In most cases however, the transnational route does not replace the national route, and "the relationship between the two routes is still rather complementary".[87] In other words, NGOs will continue to represent themselves on some occasions or even simultaneously be represented by umbrella organizations alongside other NGOs. Interest groups will not take the political risk of relying on one channel of access alone.[88] Hence, as Grande argues, the plurality of institutions and actors offers a multitude of access points to the decision-making process that requires groups to employ a range of strategies in order to pursue their interests successfully. Grande quotes Butt "the master-lobbyist, like the chess-master, must be able to play several games at once at different tables, as far a field as Strasbourg, Luxembourg, Brussels as well as in his national capital".[89] Only the larger, better resourced groups however will be able to "cover" all centres and levels of authority. Hence for a small outfit like CNE attempting to influence a diffuse decision-making complex like the EU is an especially difficult task.

In this regard "the exact combination of channels that is used, and the relative emphasis that is placed upon them, will depend on the particular issue being addressed".[90] This makes it particularly difficult to generalize across different "sectors" of interest-group activity and emphasize both the value of case study approaches[91] and approaches sensitive to the way in which policy problems define the shape and nature of the politics (and therefore actors) that engage with the policy problem.[92] The nature of the "policy community" or more informal and unstable "network" depends upon the issue in question and the actors it brings together in strategic alliance. For CNE relations with DG XI, the renewable, cogeneration, and efficiency industry lobbies and with particular MEPs suggest it is part of a pro-climate action policy community. Rather than being a strategic alignment of interests to serve a particular policy goal, it is a more long-term reconciliation of settled interests in a relatively institutionalized set of supportive relations. Nevertheless a limitation upon

---

[84] Mazey and Richardson (n. 13 above).   [85] Grant (n. 36 above).   [86] *Ibid.,* 28.

[87] J. Greenwood, J. Grote, and K. Ronit (eds.), *Organised Interests and the EC* (London: Sage, 1992).

[88] Grant (n. 36 above).   [89] Grande (n. 14 above) quotes Butt (1983:23).

[90] Grant (n. 36 above), 29.

[91] J. Greenwood and K. Ronit, "Interest Groups in the European Community: Newly Emerging Dynamics and Forms" (1994) 17 *West European Politics* 31–52.

[92] Newell (n. 12 above).

the scope of CNE's influence in this regard is that the community is made up of northern European governments, NGOs, and industries. That this is the case would not be surprising to Sbragia who finds that "policy networks rarely cross the 'leader-laggard' divide".[93]

The reliance of the Community upon implementation at national level affords opportunities for domestic influence through familiar channels where actors are known and operate according to recognized "rules of the game". At the same time a combination of factors such as the need to keep open a plurality of channels, the Commission's preference for Euro-actors, the increased use of qualified-majority voting which means it is no longer sufficient to rely on nurturing a national veto and the increasing points of access to the Commission, all mean that transnational strategies remain important for NGOs seeking to affect EU environmental law. Umbrella groups will need to try to overcome some inherent difficulties. Often umbrella groups remain quite poor because most resources are kept at the national level for groups' key activities.[94] Resource constraints are exacerbated by the fact that groups relaying information and co-ordinating activities over a large geographical area incur higher communication and travel costs. In this respect Grant[95] argues that in general such groups are inadequately resourced in relation to the range and complexity of tasks they attempt to undertake; they largely react to an agenda set by the Commission, and they often have difficulty in reconciling divergent national interests of the member organizations. This often means that Euro-groups are unable to agree on anything more than "lowest common denominator" positions. As will be shown below, the first two generalizations in particular apply to CNE. With the last point, whilst there are divergences in approach to the climate change issue among CNE's membership, there seems to be sufficient common agreement on the proper focus of the organization's activities to prevent inter-group conflict and rivalry of the sort found among profit-seeking competitive business entities. CNE is not constrained on a day-to-day basis by needing to ensure that it is not going beyond the mandate set for the organization by its membership. This means it can go beyond lowest common denominator positions because the operating structure of the organization means that input from member organizations is infrequent and often *ad hoc*, despite "board" meetings several times a year where activities and campaigns are reported and future directions charted. The advisory committee, composed of representatives of western European NGOs, provides input on CNE's goals and priorities. For the most part however, the daily work of the group proceeds in a relatively autonomous fashion without continual oversight from members.

Essentially though, given the importance of the Council of Ministers in the climate-change debate because of the requirement for unanimous voting on tax questions and issues of energy use and supply, the politics of global warming as they operate at the European level are to a large degree settled by rela-

[93] Sbragia (n. 43 above), 254.   [94] Rucht (n. 13 above).   [95] Grant (n. 36 above).

tions between national governments. On a national level the cases of Italy, Germany, and the UK[96] serve to illustrate that state-industry politics are the deciding force in the success of climate institutions even where they operate within an EU policy framework. The national politics which shape EU climate policy are not set in stone of course, and different administrations, particularly in the "push" states,[97] can have a transformative effect on the direction and content of EU climate law. Sbragia[98] argues "the importance attached to environmental protection in Brussels is determined in significant measure by the domestic politics of the 'green' Member States". The idea of "ecological modernization"[99] and the precautionary principle (*Vorsorge-Prinzip*) which had taken root in German domestic policy discourse achieved salience in EU debates on environmental policy articulated by DG XI.[100] The desire of "troika" states to have domestic standards of environmental protection adopted by all other Member States is partly, of course, a function of wanting to protect domestic industries from the competitive advantage enjoyed by those Member States not undertaking similar levels of pollution control. It is about dispersing the costs of environmental regulation and cannot solely therefore be attributed to the influence of national NGOs.[101]

New governments nevertheless provide fresh opportunities to press for a change of emphases at the European level in relation to climate policy, as the case of the "New Labour" administration in the UK highlights. An incoming Presidency can also be lobbied with a view to transforming the EU's policy agenda. The Danish environment minister, for example, under pressure from the Danish World Wildlife Fund, used the Presidency to support the integration of environmental and regional policy.[102] For umbrella groups like CNE operating at the European level, influence then rests on the ability of well-organized national groups to press their influence upon governments with significant leverage in EU environmental policy.

Given the failure of most initiatives designed to combat climate change,[103] it would be tempting to suggest that the influence of CNE has been negligible because of the difficulty in establishing direct impacts upon environmental law. Their influence operates in more subtle ways however. It is about education, nurturing contacts, and lobbying with industry groups that may have more influence than themselves, but whose position is supported by CNE. The sorts of influence CNE can lay claim to operate over the longer term (they are a relatively new organization) are less visible (often the lobbying takes place behind closed doors) and are channelled in disparate ways, so that assessing

---

[96] A. Marchetti, "Climate Change Politics in Italy" in T. O'Riordan and J. Jaeger (eds.), *The Politics of Climate Change* (London: Routledge, 1996), 298; C. Beuermann and J. Jaeger, "Climate Change Politics in Germany: How Long will any Double Dividend Last?", in *ibid.*, 186; T. O'Riordan and E. Rowbotham, "Struggling for Credibility: The United Kingdom's Response", in *ibid.*, 228.
[97] Sbragia (n. 43 above).   [98] *Ibid.*, 237.   [99] Weale (n. 63 above).
[100] Sbragia (n. 43 above).
[101] J. Golub, *Global Competition and EU Environmental Policy* (London: Routledge, 1997); D. Vogel, "Trading Up and Governing Across: Transnational Governance and Environmental Protection" (1997) 4 *Journal of European Public Policy* 556–71.
[102] Sbragia (n. 43 above).   [103] Collier (n. 4 above); Newell (n. 57 above).

the overall effect of these various activities is a difficult task. Their influence is also relative, given that they are a small outfit under-staffed and under-resourced, constantly competing for new resources to sustain their existence and taking on an issue unprecedented in scale and complexity and up against many of the most powerful European industrial lobbies.

When thinking about the political influence of a group like CNE, it is important to remember that CNE is run by political entrepreneurs who spend much of their time fighting for the survival of their organization putting together grants, justifying the value-added part is provided to members to fund bodies such as the Stockholm Environment Institute (SEI).[104] Smaller groups constantly face difficulties financing the running costs of their offices which makes longer-term planning very difficult. To assume that a group like CNE has the luxury to be able to sit back on a regular basis and reflect on how best to exert their influence or how the changing architecture of EU politics may impact upon the way it, as an organization, operates is to misunderstand the day-to-day operation of a small single-issue Brussels-based umbrella organization.

V. Conclusion

There would appear to be little doubt that NGOs constitute an important force for political change, by helping to overcome social inertia and bureaucratic resistance to policy reform. They initiate institutional change and can articulate the norms which they feel should underpin environmental policy. Through exercise of their bargaining assets, NGOs can secure a place in policy deliberations, though of themselves these assets do not guarantee for NGOs a degree of direct influence over policy.

In general it is during the earlier stages of policy-formation and agenda-setting and at the end of the policy cycle when proposals come to be implemented that NGOs seem to have most impact upon the course and shape of EU environmental law. Grant argues,[105] "[t]he most successful route for NGOs to exert influence may be at either end of the policy process: influencing the construction of the policy agenda and highlighting implementation deficiencies". Confirming this, Grande argues[106] "there are phases in which the negotiation process is not accessible to interest groups". In the preliminary (agenda-setting) stage, the decision-making process is (relatively) open to interest-group advice and demands and the Commission seeks to reach out to all affected parties. It does this as a way of gathering information about the preferences of major actors and draw upon insights into the technical aspects of the issue. Involvement of groups at this stage also assists the Commission in organizing and mobilizing support for proposals in negotiations with the

---

[104] Whilst CNE is managed by the Stockholm Environment Institute, it also receives financial support from the Danish government and the EU.

[105] Grant (n. 36 above), 44.   [106] Grande (n. 14 above), 330.

Council and Member States. The degree of success for the NGO depends, then, upon the "policy receptivity of the Union, particularly the Commission, to issues salient to the group".[107] When decisions move to the Council however, decision-making becomes less accessible and transparent and negotiations are in the hands of ministers. Here, unless government representatives have been "captured" by a group in advance of the meeting, the horse-trading that follows will proceed largely unaffected by their influence.[108] It should also be recalled that Council meetings are only "the most spectacular instances of closure in the European policy-making process. There are several less spectacular occasions when Commission officials and national representatives retire for deliberations or the preparation of a proposal".[109] Once initial agreement has been reached, there is scope again for consultations with interest groups, only in so far as their demands do not upset what may be a fragile consensus. Nevertheless such consultations help to fine tune the agreements, anticipate criticism and reactions and therefore to ensure their acceptability.[110]

Hence, in spite of the fact that the Commission has stood up to powerful Member States on environmental issues and provided the environmental lobby (or certain parts of it) with financial support,[111] that the ECJ has come to be regarded as pro-environment in its interpretation of the law, and that the EP has displayed a strong environmental consciousness, it can only be concluded that NGOs have not enjoyed a substantial degree of success in advancing their goals at the European level. It is clearly not enough to note then, as Marks and McAdam do, that "environmentalists have confronted a Union that, with the exception of the Council, has shown itself to be both attitudinally sympathetic and structurally open to the interests of the movement".[112] For these authors, the structure of political opportunity was offered by the EU is one that NGOs should easily be able to adapt to. They note "there exists a real affinity between the tactics practiced historically by the movement and the institutional openings afforded environmentalists by the emerging EU structure. Most NGOs in Europe . . . have been dominated by a combination of legal, electoral and lobbying strategies; the precise mix encouraged by the relative openness of the European Court, Parliament and the emerging policy community in Brussels".[113] And yet there is clearly a difference between being permitted formal access to the Union in various formal and legalistic guises and being afforded the real decision-making authority to make a significant political impact that both changes the EU's agenda and contributes to the alleviation of environmental degradation. It also needs to be recalled that the Brussels policy style does not suit a number of NGOs and is appealing only to those with the resources to exploit most fruitfully the opportunities it affords.

---

[107] Marks and McAdam (n. 34 above), 115.   [108] Grande (n. 14 above), 331.
[109] *Ibid.*   [110] *Ibid.*
[111] In 1990 50 million ECU was made available to NGOs for projects and research aimed at protecting the environment (Marks and McAdam (n. 34 above), 115).
[112] Marks and McAdam (n. 34 above), 114.   [113] *Ibid.*, 115.

One (ongoing) source of leverage for NGOs is that the Community does seem to be keen to retain legitimacy as a leader in environmental issues as a way of raising its popularity with the European public and also as a way of projecting leadership in international affairs. Continuing concern about the environment expressed in polls of public opinion (such as Eurobarometer surveys), together with the fact that these problems simply will not go away (and, if anything, will continue to get worse) mean that exogenous factors will also continue to ensure that the environment remains on the Community's policy agenda. The final factor which will ensure an ongoing role or NGOs in the Community is the comparative weakness of DG XI in the overall structure of environmental policy-making within the Union, which means that it is constantly looking out for new allies to bolster its position and create constituencies of support for its policy agenda. This suggests it will continue to reach out to NGOs, exploiting their expertise and access to popular constituencies.

There is no winning formula for success at Brussels level *per se*. As Rucht notes, "[c]oherent, well-staffed and truly international organizations such as the WWF and Greenpeace have been quite successful according to their own criteria. But in relative terms, more informal, under-staffed and loosely co-ordinated transnational groups such as Climate Action Network, have also been successful".[114] This, we would argue, is because they are perceived by their members to perform a useful service above and beyond what the groups could perform on their own, and because the institutions of the Community regard their input as constructive and useful. It was clear from the early part of the article however, that flexible deregulation will add to the many challenges which NGOs already face in trying to make a difference to the content and orientation of EU environmental law.

---

[114] Rucht (n. 13 above), 91.

Challenges and Opportunities in EC Waste Management: Perspectives on the Problem of End of Life Vehicles

MARCO ONIDA*

I. Introduction

This article examines a number of questions related to a recent European Community (EC) proposal in the field of waste management. In order to provide a focus, it will concentrate on a number of issues when attempting to seek a justification for Community action. This focus means that the survey will be selective. It will look to the choice of the most appropriate instrument, how the consultation process works, the choice of the correct legal basis, and the contents of the instrument. I would like to think that, by focusing on these issues, practical policy guidance might be provided, especially with regard to the legal and administrative problems of waste-management policy. At the same time, this survey is intended to serve the purpose of introducing to a broader audience the policy issues of Community waste management in the internal market, and how new ideas and instruments may be needed in order to produce effective long-term results. Waste-management in the context of rigorous economic and legal analysis is a challenging subject. An overriding (but not only) concern is how waste-management policy affects economic interests. The analysis of these issues allows, for our purposes, a unique opportunity to describe how the legislative process works at the European Commission level and to assess its subsequent evolution at the implementation stage. This article has four sections. Section II starts with an analysis of the proposed Directive on End of Life Vehicles (ELV). Section III then proceeds to discuss the problems faced by Member States and the potential economic impact of the proposed legislation, including the legal basis of the legislation and its implementation. Finally, Section IV deals with a number of specific legal issues raised by the Proposal, in particular the dichotomy between "products" and "waste", and the provisions concerning the collection and recovery of Euros. Section VI serves to draw some general conclusions.

* Waste Management Unit, DG XI, European Commission. The views expressed in this article are those of the author and do not necessarily reflect those of the Commission.

II.   The ELV Proposal and its Making

A.   THE WORK INSIDE THE COMMISSION

The proposal for a Community Directive on ELV is the result of many years of work and negotiation both within the Commission and between the Commission and other actors and institutions (e.g. governmental and non-governmental organizations (NGOs)). Since its inception in the mid-1970s, European waste legislation has developed in two different but complementary directions. On the one hand, the Community has established general rules for the management of all waste (general objectives and principles of waste management, planning, licensing, and control requirements).[1] On the other hand, policymakers have set out rules for specific types of waste (e.g. waste oils,[2] batteries and accumulators,[3] packaging[4]) and for waste treatment operations (e.g. incineration,[5] landfilling[6]). The choice of the specific types of waste to be regulated depends on both environmental and internal market considerations.

Although there are now a substantial number of EC directives, as well as a regulation on waste, it is submitted that EC waste legislation requires further development. This can be accomplished by adapting existing texts to scientific and technical progress and by promulgating new pieces of legislation. In this context, a number of "waste streams" have been identified as being of primary importance, and these waste streams therefore form part of the present work of the Commission or other EC institutions.[7]

It was following the adoption by the Commission of a Communication on a Community strategy for waste management[8] in 1989, and the Council Resolution of 1990[9] (inviting the Commission to establish action programmes for particular types of waste), that ELVs were identified as one of the new waste streams to be regulated. Preparatory work within the Commission began shortly thereafter, mainly in the form of research and open discussions with all the actors concerned. The drafting process commenced within the Commission during 1995. A preliminary draft was produced in October 1995

---

[1] Council Dir. 75/442/EEC on waste [1991] OJ L78/39, as last amended by Commission Decision 96/350/EEC [1996] OJ L135/32; Council Dir. 91/689/EEC on hazardous waste [1991] OJ L377/20, as last amended by Council Dir. 94/31/EC [1994] L 168/28; Council Reg. (EC) No. 259/93, on the supervision and control of shipments of waste within, into, and out of the European Community, as amended [1993] OJ L30/1; [1994] OJ L228/36; [1996] OJ L304/15; [1997] OJ L22/14.

[2] Council Dir. 75/439/EEC [1975] OJ L194/23, amended by Council Dir. 87/101/EEC [1987] OJ L42/43.

[3] Council Dir. 91/157/EEC [1991] OJ L78/38, amended by Commission Dir. 93/86/EEC [1993] OJ L264/51.

[4] European Parliament and Council Dir. 94/62/EC [1994] OJ L365/10.

[5] Council Dir. 89/369/EEC [1989] OJ L163/32; Council Dir. 89/429/EEC [1989] OJ L203/50; Council Dir. 94/67/EC [1994] OJ L365/34.

[6] Council Dir. 1999/31 [1999] OJ L182/1.

[7] ELVs, waste from electrical and electronic equipment, used tyres, organic waste, construction and demolition waste are some examples.

[8] SEC(89)934 of 18 Sept. 1989.   [9] [1990] OJ C122/2.

and was subsequently discussed with experts from Member States, industries, and NGOs. A second draft was produced in February 1996, which, following one and a half years of discussions, resulted in the final Proposal being adopted by the Commission on 9 July 1997.[10]

It is thought that the main reason for such a lengthy process was largely due to the number of vested interests, which made it difficult to reach a compromise. Yet, the conflict between environmental and economic interests was, to a certain extent, reflected in the discussions within the various Commission services (in particular the Directorates General for the Environment, Industry, and Economic Affairs). Certain elements of the Commission Proposal have been inspired by the recommendation given by a Project Group. The aim of the Project Group was to facilitate discussion of all the possibilities, and to produce an agreed proposal for the Commission. At the outset, it was made clear that this process could not interfere with the exclusive initiative power of the Commission, as set out in the EC Treaty. On 23 February 1994, the Project Group (whose members were neither appointed nor fully representative of the interests in question) presented a strategy document to the Commission, and invited the Commission to use it as a basis for a proposal for a directive.

In spite of the shared objective, the Project Group focused mainly on the theoretical aspect of the issues, avoiding most details. In this regard, the strategy proposed to the Commission contains only a general set of objectives. Unfortunately, the question of how to implement these proposals was not made very explicit. This result was probably inevitable, given that a consensus on the general issues is easier to forge than an overlapping consensus on concrete questions, such as the allocation of financial responsibilities. The exclusion of certain interests from the Project Group aggravated the policy-making process. Dissenting from the Project Group were many associations (particularly from the dismantling and recycling sector) which voiced their concerns at the time that the Commission began drawing up the proposal for a directive. It must be pointed out that industrial interests were, at least from a quantitative standpoint, better represented in the Project Group than the environmental and consumer interests.

Notwithstanding the lengthy discussions within the Commission, an agreement between the Directorates-General for the Environment and for Industry was achieved in June 1997. Subsequently, a joint proposal was presented to the Commission by the two commissioners representing the respective services (i.e. Bjerregaard and Bangemann). This meant that only one "Special Cabinet Chiefs' " meeting, which prepares the adoption of decisions by the *Collège* and where representatives from the twenty Cabinets sit, was required. The Proposal was then adopted unanimously during the weekly Commission meeting of 9 July 1997. Despite the fact that only a single Special Cabinet Chiefs' meeting was necessary to achieve a consensus, this meeting once again revealed the depth of the interest-group competition at stake. In this

---

[10] COM(97)358 [1997] OJ C337/3.

respect, the contrasting views at the Special Cabinet Chiefs' meeting echoed the views of the Member States showing that the border between the actions of the Commission and the political activity of the Council was not, in this case, very well marked.

B.   A BRIEF SUMMARY OF THE PROPOSAL

This section provides a brief summary of the main provisions of the ELV Proposal. A more detailed analysis can be found in the sections below, referring to the specific legal issues.

Initially it should be stressed that the Proposal applies to all passenger vehicles containing up to nine seats (M1) and to commercial vehicles not exceeding 3.5 tonnes (N1). With the exception of the provisions on prevention (Article 4) and on quantified targets (Article 7), the Proposal applies to two- and three-wheeled motor vehicles, and to motor caravans (Article 3).

In line with the waste hierarchy established at Community level,[11] the Proposal's first objective is the prevention of the quantity and hazardous nature of waste from vehicles. The Commission seeks to achieve this objective by requiring producers of materials and vehicles to incorporate the concepts of design-for-dismantling and design-for-recycling into their products (Articles 7(4) and 4(1)(b) and (c)). Moreover, this goal is further supported by the requirement that forbids certain substances contained in vehicles from entering the shredding process. It is also apparent that the requirement of not allowing these substances to be landfilled or incinerated will further secure the pursuit of the Commission's policy objective. The Proposal provides that such substances must therefore be entirely recyclable or phased out in new vehicles (Article 4(2)), and finally makes producers responsible for the financial consequences of putting vehicles which are not recyclable and recoverable up to a pre-set level (Article 5(4)) on the market.

The Proposal requires Member States to ensure the collection (Article 5) and environmentally sound treatment of all ELVs (Article 6). It states that Member States shall ensure that economic operators (i.e. all economic actors in the automotive chain, from producers of materials to recyclers) develop the appropriate collection infrastructures (Article 5(1)). Furthermore, Member States are required to establish a system based on certificates of destruction and permits (Article 5(3)). This strategy requires that a vehicle owner, in order to be relieved of taxes and national duties, must receive a certificate of destruction, showing that the vehicle has been delivered to an authorized centre for dismantling, before the vehicle can be removed from the public register. Only those centres which comply with the environmental requirements can be permitted to operate and issue the certificates of destruction.

The collection and treatment requirements are complemented by the obligation on economic operators to achieve short- and long-term quantified tar-

---

[11] Communication of the Commission on the review of the Community strategy for waste management, COM(96)399.

gets for re-use, recycling, and recovery of ELVs (Article 7(2)).[12] A number of accompanying provisions complete the Proposal, such as a code of standards for recyclable components (Article 8(1)), another on dismantling manuals (Article 8(3)), and one on information requirements (Article 9).

III.   The Problems Raised

A.   EC ACTION OR NATIONAL INITIATIVES

In order to discuss whether or not action at EC level is required, it is necessary first to examine the problems that arise in this context. It is submitted that the problems are of a twofold nature: environmental externalities (between eight and nine million vehicles are discarded every year in the EU) and economic problems. On a pragmatic level, these problems require a strategy for dealing with: (1) the vehicles which are abandoned in the environment (up to 7 per cent of the total number of ELVs); (2) the pollution caused by dismantling and recycling operations (particularly due to the presence of hazardous substances in vehicles); (3) the hazardous waste created by the shredding process (representing up to 10 per cent of the total quantity of hazardous waste generated yearly in the EU);[13] and (4) the export of ELVs to countries which have lower standards than those existing within the EU.[14]

It is argued that the economic problems may be especially severe. More specifically, they concern the declining profitability of the recycling business due to the decrease in steel prices and the increase in disposal costs for non-recovered materials. Furthermore, Member States that impose stricter environmental standards involuntarily affect the viability of the recycling business in their territory. Moreover, ELVs tend to be transported to Member States where treatment is cheaper (because environmental standards are lower). In this context, operators located in more environmentally ambitious countries may lose out to their competitors in other countries who rely on "externalities" at the expense of the environment.

i.   *The Situation in Member States*

The environmental and economic problems highlighted above are common to all Member States, although there are differences pertaining to local, economic, and geographic conditions. Due to the presence of these differences,

---

[12] "Recycling" indicates the recycling of the material contained in ELVs; "recovery" is a wider term, which includes both recycling and incineration with energy recovery.

[13] Shredder residues are considered hazardous waste, both by the Basel Convention and by Reg. (EC) No. 259/93 (amber List, code AC 190). An application by some Member States to classify this waste as hazardous in Council Decision 94/904/EC (the European Hazardous Waste List [1994] OJ L356/14) is presently being dealt with by the Commission.

[14] No precise figures are available, but it has been estimated that, to give an example, between 50% and 70% of German ELVs were exported in 1995, mainly to Eastern Europe. Anon., "Ab nach Polen" (1996) 5 *DM Das Private Wirtschafts Magazine* 12; *Current Basic Data Reflecting the Overall Ecological and Economic Context of the ELV Issue*, Final report (Paris: Institute for European Environmental Policy, 1996), 134.

some Member States have already enacted, or are on the verge of enacting, leg-islation in the ELV sector.

The legislator in Sweden enacted an ordinance on Producer Responsibility for Vehicles,[15] which came into force on 1 January 1998, making vehicle pro-ducers and importers responsible for the take-back at no cost to consumers and for the environmentally-sound recovery of ELVs registered after 31 December 1997. Previously, the Swedish legislator had enacted a Scrapping Act which has been in place since 1975. This Act obliges producers to pay a sum of approximately 81 Euros (151 ECU until 1997) and entitles final owners of ELVs to a scrapping premium of 58 Euros (between 58 and 175 ECU until 1997, according to the state of the ELV).

A scrap levy was recently introduced in the Netherlands.[16] This levy of approximately 125 ECU (75 Euros since 1998) is used to pay premiums to com-panies performing specific activities related to the dismantling and recycling of ELVs. In 1997, Germany adopted a regulation on the treatment of ELVs,[17] which has been in effect since April 1998. In 1998, the Flanders region of Belgium adopted a decree which, *inter alia*, sets out rules for ELVs.[18] Both the Dutch and German measures are part of a set of measures which also include voluntary agreements or self-commitment by some of the economic operators concerned (similar measures are being prepared in Flanders). It should be noted that there are other voluntary initiatives that have been initiated by eco-nomic operators in France (1993), Spain (1996), Italy (1997, amended in 1998), Austria (1992, amended in 1996), and the United Kingdom (UK)(1997). These voluntary commitments, whose effect is often unclear as they are not subject to any binding objectives or compulsory monitoring measures, are also quite different in their nature and contents. For example, it may be useful to identify the quantified targets for recovery and recycling as well as the rules on the take-back of ELVs.

Table IV reveals that no two initiatives are identical. Assuming that "maxi-mum generation of final waste" in the French and Spanish agreements corre-sponds to "maximum disposal", the targets in these countries would be similar to those set by the German agreement (although the French agreement does not indicate any date for the accomplishment of the long-term target). Yet, the targets in the UK are not comparable to those in France, Spain, and Germany since the term "disposal" is wider than "landfilling" (disposal also includes incineration without energy recovery). Whilst there may be some overlap between the German and Swedish targets, it can be argued that the nature of their measures (legislation versus agreement) is so completely different as to invalidate the alleged similarity. It should be noted also that in three countries the take-back follows market conditions. The table reflects that for five

---

[15] SFS 1997:788, published 11 Nov. 1997.   [16] Staatscourant No. 246, 21 Dec. 1994.
[17] *Verordnung über die Entsorgung von Altautos und die Anpassung straßenverkehrs-Zulassungs-Ordnung,* in Bundesgesetzblatt No. 46 of 10 July 1997.
[18] *Vlaamse Reglement inzake afvalvoorkoming en beheer* ("VLAREA"), Belgisch Staatsblad, 16 Apr. 1998, 11281.

Table IV: Summary of the quantified targets of national initiatives and of "take-back" rules.

Country	Short-term target	Long-term target	Take-back conditions
France[a]	Max. generation of final waste: 15% by 2002	Max. generation of final waste: 5% (no year specified)	Not addressed (market conditions)
Spain[a]	Max. generation of final waste: 15% by 2002	Max. generation of final waste: 5% by 2015	Not addressed (market conditions)
The Netherlands[b]	86% recycling by 2000		Free of charge + scrap fee
Germany[b]	Max. 15% disposal by 2002	Max. 5% disposal by 2015	Free of charge only for vehicles less than twelve years old and if marketed after 1 April 1998
Austria[a]	80% recovery (no year indicated)		Voluntary free of charge and only if a new vehicle is purchased
Italy[a]	85% recovery 80% recycling by 2002	95% recovery 85% recycling by 2010	Some producers promote free of charge take-back when a new vehicle is purchased
UK[a]	Max 15% landfilling by 2002	Max. 5% landfilling by 2015	Not addressed (market conditions)
Sweden[c]	85% recovery by 2002	95% recovery by 2015	Free of charge for vehicles marketed after 1998. Scrap premium for all vehicles
Flanders[c]	85% recovery 80% reuse by 2005	95% recovery 85% recycling by 2015	From July 1998, free of charge when a new vehicle is purchased. From July 2004, free of charge in all cases.

[a] = voluntary commitment
[b] = voluntary commitment plus legislation
[c] = legislation

countries (and part of Belgium) it is possible to discard the ELV free of charge, but the conditions are different, ranging from a free of charge in all cases (Netherlands), to a conditional free of charge (Germany, Italy, Sweden, Austria, and Flanders). Finally, more doubts about the comparability of the national initiatives arise if the conditions included in the agreements are studied closely.

ii. Subsidiarity

It must be acknowledged that the above-described national initiatives indicate that we are a long way off from arriving at a fully coherent approach to ELVs. In practice, the existence of diverse regulatory regimes has a negative impact on both an effective protection of the environment and the internal market, resulting in competition distortions both in the dismantling and recycling sectors, as well as in the export of ELVs to countries with lower environmental requirement. The upshot is that investment in countries with higher environmental standards may well be jeopardized.[19] Probably action at EC level is required to ensure a coherent approach within the EU. To this end, the harmonization of requirements for the management of ELVs is fully in line with the objective of the Treaty on non-distorted competition within the internal market (Article 3g EC). It should be noted that the economic interests at stake are substantial. Not only does the vehicle industry represent the main industrial sector in several Member States, but also dismantling and recycling activities involve a large number of companies.[20]

Yet, it should be noted that harmonization of regulations concerning ELVs has occurred at the product phase of vehicles. Vehicles are in fact subject to several pieces of international and Community legislation. An advanced level of harmonization has been reached through the "Type-Approval" Directive (Directive 70/156/EEC as last amended by Directive 98/14/EC[21]). This Directive harmonizes the requirements related to the manufacturing of passenger vehicles in view of the placing of those vehicles on the EU market. Accordingly, since 1 January 1996, type-approval conditions are identical in all Member States, and vehicles type-approved in one Member State can then be put on the market in any other Member State. After that date, Member States cannot adopt any national legislation relating to the construction of vehicles. The process is rather detailed: some fifty-two so-called "daughter directives" harmonize a wide range of requirements (e.g. sound levels, rear visibility, seat belts, lamps, power, tyres, emissions, etcetera).

The objective of regulating the product phase of vehicles is twofold: first, improving safety and environmental performance; and secondly, reducing overall industrial costs by creating a functioning single market. Similar objectives can be said to operate at the waste phase. Legislation serves on the one hand to protect the environment, and on the other hand to create an internal market for the management of waste vehicles. Although the actors involved, particularly the manufacturing industry, strongly push for regulating the

---

[19] This kind of problem has been documented (presentations by G. M. Eggink, Director of Auto Recycling Nederland, on 24 Nov. 1997 at the Economic and Social Committee of the EU and on 3 Dec. 1997 at the Intergroup for Automobile Users of the European Parliament; Communications to the Commission by German associations of vehicle dismantlers and recyclers).

[20] Car production represents about 10% of European employment. The number of vehicle dismantlers in the largest EU countries (Germany, France, Italy, UK) varies between 3,000 and 5,000, employing some 15,000 to 20,000 people per country (precise figures do not exist due to the substantial number of dismantlers operating illegally—about 60% in Italy and 20% in the UK).

[21] [1970] OJ L42/1; [1998] OJ L091/1.

product phase as much as possible at international and EU level, no such pressure exists for the waste phase, mainly because the main actor involved in this phase, the environment, has no voice. But a functioning internal market for the waste phase is also in the interest of economic operators. In the absence of an EU legislative framework, certain Member States would adopt national rules to protect their environment (some are already acting in this respect), and in the long run this would affect the internal market. If a Member State imposes a tax on new vehicles to cover the impact of ELVs on the environment, or if it imposes conditions relating to the discarding, collection, and treatment of vehicles, this would undoubtedly affect the internal market. For this reason, it makes little sense to regulate products (all products) until a certain phase in their life-cycle (the placing on the market) is reached; and once this stage has been reached, to leave the waste phase in the hands of Member States. Ideally a functioning internal market should encompass all phases of a product's life cycle.[22]

In this sense, the case of the Waste Packaging Directive is a good illustration of this form of regulation. When the Commission first began to consider regulating the packaging waste phase in the early 1980s, most economic operators were opposed to the proposed action. As a consequence of these objections, the Commission promulgated Directive 85/339/EEC on Containers of Liquids for Human Consumption,[23] which obliged Member States to "draw up programmes for reducing the tonnage and/or volume of containers of liquids for human consumption in household waste to be finally disposed of" (Article 3(1) of the Directive). Interestingly, the Directive failed to stimulate any serious harmonization, but rather provoked the emergence of different, and often incompatible, national legislation, with the result of endangering the internal market. As a consequence, economic operators demanded a new EU directive based on Article 95 (formerly Article 100a) EC. In response a directive was adopted, with the full support of the industries concerned, on 31 December 1994 (Directive 94/62/EC on Packaging and Packaging Waste). However, the existence of diverging national legislation made it very difficult to adopt a European directive and the well-known weaknesses of this Directive (now fully in force) are largely due to a text which is a clear political compromise between already-existing legislation.

iii. The Economic Impact

An appraisal of all advantages of and changes in Community action must be carried out pursuant to the Treaty (Article 174(3) (formerly Article 130r(3)) EC), in order to assess the potential effectiveness of the measure. However, it is important to note that, should doubts about this effectiveness arise, other principles would also play a role, in particular the preventive action principle and the task of improving the quality of the environment. Hence, a clear

---

[22] L. Krämer, *E.C. Treaty and Environmental Law* (2nd edn., London: Sweet & Maxwell, 1995), 22–3.

[23] [1985] OJ L176/18.

balance in favour of the advantages over the costs is not a necessary condition for taking action at EU level.[24]

It is very difficult to quantify precisely the economic impact, in terms of both cost and benefits, of a proposal that could have an impact on several industrial sectors. Correspondingly, it is also problematic to quantify with precision the long-term economic benefits of a functioning internal market for vehicles and ELVs. But it is evident that a more integrated Europe, be it for products or waste, can only bring net advantages in the longer term. Similarly, it is almost impossible to quantify in monetary terms the benefits for the environment of reduced pollution by ELVs, apart from the short-term saving of disposal costs.

To be sure, better organization within the collection, dismantling, and recycling sectors is likely to generate higher profits and create new jobs only if the environmental externalities are internalized in the price of the new vehicles. An interesting question relates to the quantification of these externalities. One way of calculating it consists of estimating the resources needed in order to comply with the treatment requirements and the recovery/recycling targets of the Proposal. This can only be accomplished in a static way (i.e. based on the present costs, the market situation, and the price of recyclates). It is obvious that the cost of complying with the Directive will decrease over time, when vehicles will be produced with a view to being recycled. In addition, increasing the volume of the recycling business will generate economies of scale and reduce overall costs. It is estimated that the amount of money required to satisfy the Proposal's short-term targets (80 per cent recycling, 85 per cent recovery) is equivalent to 20–130 Euros per vehicle, in other words to less than 1 per cent of the average price of a new vehicle.[25] The investment cost required for dismantlers to comply with the requirements of the Proposal has been estimated at around 100,000 Euros where infrastructure is very inadequate, to much less where national requirements already exist.

The cost of producing new vehicles in line with the Proposal is far more difficult to quantify, mainly because it will depend on future market developments. It has, however, been estimated that the replacement of many materials which today make recycling difficult and expensive (e.g. lead, PVC) is not a great problem since alternative materials, with better environmental performances, already exist at an acceptable cost. Interestingly, the Department of Trade and Industry (DTI) in the UK has produced a memorandum quantifying the cost of compliance with the ELV Directive. The cost of achieving the quantified targets is, according to DTI, 28 Euros per vehicle for 2005 and 101 Euros per vehicle for 2015. The total cost indicated by DTI for compliance with the Proposal equals approximately 273–428 Euros per vehicle for 2005 and

---

24 L. Krämer, *E.C. Treaty and Environmental Law* (3rd edn., London: Sweet & Maxwell, 1998), 80.

25 Sources: "Current Basic Data Reflecting the Overall Ecological and Economic Context of the ELV Issue", Institute for European Environmental Policy, Final Report (Paris: IEEP, 1996); "Explanatory Memorandum on the ELV Proposal", Department of Trade and Industry, 28 Oct. 1997; most of the information on costs has been obtained in the form of verbal communications by vehicle producers and recyclers and is not available in writing.

341–496 Euros per vehicle for 2015. It should be pointed out that there are a number of inconsistencies in these calculations. First, it seems that certain costs have been taken into consideration twice.[26] Secondly, it should be noted that costs for 2015 are probably over-estimated. The DTI estimations are in fact based on static assumptions and do not take into account the fact that new vehicles will also be designed with a view to their dismantling and recycling, significantly reducing the compliance costs. Thirdly, even the cost of bringing illegal scrapyards up to legal standards have been considered costs of compliance with the Directive, whereas these costs should obviously not be attributed to the Directive. Fourthly, some basis for the calculation of the costs do not appear to be fully correct (e.g. £35 per hour of administrative work is clearly too much).

A Dutch source[27] has calculated the number of new jobs created in the entire EU, taking a recycling target of 85 per cent, to be between 10,000 and 15,000. A German source[28] indicates that around 30,000 new jobs (in Germany) will be created if achieving a recovery target of 95 per cent. This would correspond to about 120,000 jobs for the entire EU. Although all estimations are to be taken with some precaution, they are based on the fact that recycling is still a mostly labour-intensive activity. Obviously there is some dispute regarding the number of jobs that will be created as a result of the new dismantling and recycling activities. However, should we decide to compare the estimated cost per vehicle necessary to achieve the Proposal targets (i.e. dividing the quantifiable costs of implementation of the proposal by the number of vehicles which will be covered by the Proposal), it becomes clear that the benefits appear to outweigh the costs. It should be noted that while the "cost per vehicle" of implementing the Proposal does not seem to be significant compared to a vehicle's price, these costs, overall, are likely to generate significant competition distortions if the requirements for managing the ELV problem are not sufficiently harmonized in the EU.

B.   WHAT KIND OF EC INITIATIVE IS BEST?

Now that we have reviewed the reasons for taking action at EC level, the next step is to determine what kind of initiative is likely to be the most appropriate.

---

[26] DTI mentions that Art. 5 will generate a cost corresponding to 187–282 Euros per vehicle, in addition to the cost of compliance with Art. 7, while it is obvious that this cost will appear only once. The aim of Art. 5(4) is in fact to avoid the cost of complying with the Proposal target being borne by the last user of the vehicle, so as not to generate extra costs. Therefore, the total cost of compliance should be 86–138 Euros per vehicle for 2005 (these figures would be fully in line with the estimations gathered by the Commission in other countries) and 153–214 Euros per vehicle for 2015—the result obtained not taking into account costs corresponding to Art. 5, or 239–394 Euros per vehicle—the result obtained not taking into account costs corresponding to Art. 7. This double-counting is probably due to the fact that the memorandum looks only at costs to industry and does not take into account that to certain industrial costs correspond equal benefits to the consumer and consequently no net costs to society as a whole arise.
[27] Auto Recycling Nederland BV.
[28] Arbeitsgemeinschaft Deutscher Auto-Recyclingbetriebe GMBH.

Article 249 (formerly Article 189) EC provides for three types of initiatives, i.e. directive, regulation, or recommendation. We now turn to evaluate the effectiveness of the respective approaches.

i. Directives and Regulations

It is plain that a non-binding recommendation is unlikely to be the preferred course of action. Generally, environmental legislation is characterized by a low level of implementation and enforcement and therefore a non-binding measure will have little effect on behaviour. It should be noted that at least one recommendation in the waste sector exists. Council Recommendation 81/972/EEC concerns the re-use of used paper and the use of recycled paper.[29] It must be stated that while the recycling rate of paper has increased over time, the contents of this Recommendation remains practically unknown in most Member States. In this regard, it is very difficult to assume that the Recommendation has played any significant role in changing the conditions of use.

In contrast with a non-binding recommendation, a regulation has many advantages. In particular, it offers greater enforcement potential while avoiding the risk of divergent national measures. Despite these clear benefits, it would probably be very difficult to reach the necessary consensus on a regulation in the Council, in light of the fact that certain Member States have already taken national measures, and these measures differ in terms of their contents. Thus, a qualified majority in the Council is unlikely to be reached on many substantial aspects of a regulation on ELVs. It can also be argued that a regulation leaves too little space for adapting the general framework to different economic and social conditions in Member States. However, it may be that certain aspects, such as authorization requirements and the certificate of destruction, could constitute part of an EC regulation. The same might be said for provisions of a simple nature such as prohibitions (e.g. the prohibition on putting components containing heavy metals into shredders). To be sure, it should be noted that a regulation would be less than ideal in relation to quantified targets, given that some discretion is left to Member States to determine how to achieve these targets.[30] It may be that resort to the use of a directive would be the single best option since it allows for the precise wording of specific requirements and the general objectives, for which Member States can decide which are the instruments best designed to realize these objectives.[31]

---

[29] [1981] OJ L355/56.

[30] During the preparatory work within the Commission prior to the adoption of the Proposal on ELVs, it was clear that Member States considered a Directive to be the appropriate instrument, particularly in light of the fact that some of them had already taken measures and would not be willing to change them completely, as would most likely be the case if a regulation was adopted at EC level.

[31] It should also be added that, except for the control of the transport of waste (for which a Regulation exists), the Community has always opted for directives in order to regulate waste-related issues. A number of decisions have also been adopted, but always in the framework of existing directives (examples are Commission Decision 94/3/EC establishing the European waste catalogue as required by Art. 1a of Council Dir. 75/442/EEC on waste [1994] OJ L5/15; Council Decision 94/904/EC establishing a list of hazardous waste (n. 14 above); Commission Decisions 97/129/EC

ii. Voluntary Agreements

Interestingly, the EC, in its preparatory work on the ELV Proposal, considered yet another possible option for EC action, notably a voluntary agreement signed by economic operators and recognized by public authorities. It was decided, after analysing the positive and negative aspects of all the possible options, that the voluntary approach was inappropriate for this segment of the industry. Before commencing our analysis of voluntary agreements, it is essential to ascertain the conditions when an agreement may be considered for use. Voluntary agreements may be considered in the context of the following situations: (a) when adopted to replace (or avoid the adoption of) Community legislation; or (b) when adopted by a Member State to implement Community directives. This initial distinction should nonetheless be supplemented by a further distinction within case (a) between agreements that operate at different levels:

(a1) a national approach (nothing is done at EC level. Member States may resort to agreements with economic operators);

(a2) a Community approach (agreement between the Commission and European associations of economic operators).

It should be noted that both distinctions are rather theoretical. Turning to the situation of ELVs, the voluntary approach at national level (case a1) was rejected for reasons described earlier. That is, the perception was that there existed little evidence that voluntary agreements would be reached and implemented throughout the Member States. Separate from this problem, there was an additional concern that the existing agreements (in seven Member States) did not adequately fulfil the objectives of the EU Proposal but also varied considerably in both their nature and content.

Yet the voluntary approach suffers from another, more serious problem. For the most part, these agreements are, by their very nature, unable to force powerful economic operators to participate in these agreements. Moreover, there are very few economic partners who would agree to take part in an agreement aimed at realizing the objectives proposed at Community level. Part of the problem stems from the widespread disagreement among economic partners regarding the voluntary approach. In the instant case, vehicle manufacturers, as well as many producers of materials, were initially in favour of voluntary agreements being implemented just at national level ("national implementation groups").[32] However, it soon became apparent that leaving the matter

[1997] OJ L50/28 and 97/138 [1997] OJ L52/22 complementing Dir. 94/62/EC on packaging and packaging waste; Commission Decision 96/350/EC adapting Annexes IIA and IIB of Dir. 75/442/EEC [1996] OJ L135/32).

[32] In July 1996, 16 industrial associations, representing mostly material and vehicle manufacturers, signed a commitment "to improve the environmentally sound treatment of end of life vehicles" which called for action to be taken by industry in each Member State in view of "common landfill targets, the sharing of responsibilities between the parties and building on present free-market conditions". Such general and vague declared objectives could not, and in fact did not, give

entirely to national voluntary agreements would have produced a less than adequate solution. As a result, certain economic operators (particularly vehicle producers) tended to prefer either a voluntary agreement at EC level or a directive (though significantly weaker than the one proposed by the Commission).[33]

At the same time, there are other economic operators, such as dismantlers and recycling associations, who tend to prefer, for economic and political reasons, the introduction of a mandatory instrument at EC level.[34] It is plain that dismantlers and recyclers are, to a certain extent, suffering due to the low level of recyclability of vehicles across the EU. Indeed, the very fact that their business becomes gradually more expensive and less profitable, due to environmental requirements, suggests that these groups may be less willing to continue their support of the *status quo*. It is evident that they face serious problems on the economic front since they are unable to alter significantly the production process so as to make their businesses more profitable. More problematic and more far-reaching is the fact that these businesses, which are smaller and not as well organized as vehicle and material manufacturers, have little influence over the policy-making process. This lack of influence is, no doubt, caused by the fact there are few large companies operating in this sector. Thus, it is not surprising that dismantlers and recyclers groups tend to reject voluntary agreements and believe that they might be more protected by legislative measures.

It should be noted that the idea of a voluntary agreement between economic operators and the Commission (case a2) was also not pursued. In this context, there was another serious problem, besides the issues described with regard to case a1, that made it difficult to pursue this course of action. More specifically, whilst the Commission could endorse the commitments made by industry (through a recommendation), it did not have confidence that there would be sufficient monitoring and adequate implementation of the agreement in Member States. Clearly, the only way to ensure the appropriate level of monitoring and enforcement would have been to involve national administrations in the negotiation and drafting of the agreement. Yet, including the Member

rise to compatible approaches in all fifteen Member States, particularly because they were stated in the context of a declaration gathering only some of the economic actors of the automotive chain (excluding dismantler associations as well as many recycling associations). The intention of these industries was to leave only the establishment of a certificate of destruction, the necessary licensing procedures, and "implementation groups to develop recovery actions and monitor progress" to national legislators. It is interesting that after this commitment was made only one new agreement at national level was reached (in Italy). (The remaining agreements, including those signed after that date, had already been proposed and were under discussion on the date when the industry commitment was made public). Sources: Communication by the European Automobile Manufacturers Association (ACEA) to the Commission of 30 July 1996, communications to the Commission by the European Plastic Converters (EUPC), 31 May 1996, and by the Association of Plastics Manufacturers in Europe (APME), 4 Oct. 1996.

[33] Communication of ACEA to the Commission (9 Sept. 1996).

[34] e.g. European Group of Automotive Recycling Associations (EGARA), *Arbeitsgemeinschaft Deutscher Auto-Recyclingbetriebe GmbH* (ADA), *Bundesverband Sekundärrohstoffe und Entsorgung eV* (Bvse), *Auto Recycling Nederland BV* (ARN).

States (the Council) in the negotiation process, would practically mean using one of the acts provided for by the EC Treaty in Article 249 (formerly Article 189) which, in the Commission's view, excludes voluntary agreements.

One possible way of overcoming these difficulties could be to adopt a binding Community instrument and subsequently to suspend its effect only if economic operators are able to demonstrate adequately that they have established voluntary measures consistent with objectives envisaged in the binding instrument. More specifically, a directive could have a suspense clause, and its entry into force could be triggered by a Commission decision where economic operators are unable to prove that the objectives are being achieved. In this regard, mandatory legislation could be used as the "stick" if the "carrot" approach failed.

To be sure, this approach to regulation would require the introduction of intermediate targets and a verification process that would provide a yardstick for evaluating the progress of the parties at regular intervals (for instance, every two years). It must be acknowledged that this approach is not without problems. For example, if the Commission wishes to formulate a proposal for a decision revoking or confirming the validity of the suspension clause, there must exist an adequate monitoring procedure at national level.[35] Yet the parties to the agreement may be unable to supply the requisite monitoring services. Thus, it may be necessary to contract with an independent third party for the supply of the monitoring services. Under this scheme, it is crucial that the parties to the agreement agree upon the substantive terms of the monitoring instrument or the independent third party. Yet, under certain conditions it may not be possible for strategic parties to make such decisions. Hence, in the absence of a common view on the objectives, it is difficult to keep alive the idea of an EC voluntary agreement. Indeed this is perhaps the main reason this idea was not pursued for ELVs. That is, it was clear that the material and vehicle producers could not agree with the key objectives proposed by the Commission. Given the lack of consensus, it would be difficult to imagine how a transparent monitoring system could have been established to support the terms of the agreement. Ironically, it might even have been necessary to introduce a binding regulation for monitoring the agreement, in which case the benefits of the self-regulatory approach would have been substantially reduced.

One could also say that, with an agreement in the ELV sector, it is difficult to believe that economic operators would commit themselves to achieve more than what these economic operators would do anyway under normal market forces.[36]

---

[35] It is useful to recall the case-study carried out by the European Environmental Agency on the French agreement on ELVs ("Environmental Agreements—Environmental Effectiveness", Environmental Issues Series 3, 1997), which concludes that "quantitative assessment of environmental effectiveness is not possible because of a lack of monitoring data", "monitoring arrangements are being improved", "it is not possible, however, to determine whether it is more cost-effective than alternative policy measures".

[36] This is also the conclusion reached by Rennings, Brockmann, and Bergmann, of the Zentrum für Europäische Wirtschaftsforschung (ZEW) in their "Möglichkeiten und Grenzen von freiwilligen Umweltschutzmaßnahmen der Wirtschaft unter ordnungspolitischen Aspekten", study carried out for the German Ministry of Economics (Mannheim, 1996).

Despite these limitations, it is important to point out that the Commission is not, in principle, against the use of voluntary agreements. On 27 November 1996, the Commission adopted a Communication on Environmental Agreements[37] (which touches on the question of agreements at EU level and national level). The Communication states that agreements at EU level (case a2) can be used as effective environmental measures, provided that a number of conditions are complied with (conditions which, in the ELV case were not, or could not be, complied with).

Turning to the subject of the implementation of a Community directive by agreements (case b), this issue was also addressed in the Commission Communication of 27 November 1997, where a number of precise conditions were listed. On that same date, the Commission adopted Recommendation 96/773/EC[38] on environmental agreements implementing Community directives. In that Recommendation, the Commission recognized that agreements "can cost-effectively contribute to achieving environmental objectives by encouraging a pro-active approach from industry" and "might in certain circumstances complement legislation or replace otherwise more detailed legislation". The Recommendation lists the guidelines that agreements should comply with, and a number of complementary conditions, and invites the listing in each relevant directive of the provisions that should be implemented by environmental agreements. In any case, it is submitted that agreements should take the form of an enforceable contract. Typically an agreement will provide both quantifiable and intermediary targets and will be published in the national Official Journal or equivalent document. Such agreements will also provide for appropriate monitoring of the results, and the information will be transmitted to the public. At the same time, such contracts must be open to all parties who are to satisfy the conditions of the agreement. Unsurprisingly, none of the existing agreements on ELVs comply with these conditions.[39]

By way of conclusion, the Community (Commission, Council of Ministers, and European Parliament) has clearly taken a position in favour of agreements as a means of implementing legislative provisions when certain conditions are complied with. It seems clear that the main condition relates to the "degree of bindingness" of the agreements. In any case, agreements must not be used as a means of "escaping" from legislation, whatever the economic burden of the legislation may be.[40] The existing agreements on ELVs have yet to evolve to

---

[37] COM(96)561.   [38] [1996] OJ L333/59.

[39] Pocklington (D. Pocklington, "An Assessment of the Proposed European Legislation for End-of-life Vehicles" (1998) 5 *European Environmental Law Review* 138–45) concludes that, in the light of the existing voluntary initiatives, there is little added value in the proposed EU Directive on ELVs. However, the same author recognizes the legal inconveniences of the voluntary approach, and in particular that "a useful definition of environmental agreements is given in Commission Recommendation 96/773" (*ibid.*, 141). Given that existing national agreements are far from complying with this definition, one cannot but see some contradiction between this recognition and the conclusion concerning the alleged "little added value" of the EU Directive.

[40] Council Resolution on environmental agreements of 7 Oct. 1997 [1997] OJ C 321/6; European Parliament Resolution A4–0224/97 [1997] OJ C286/254. The Council is particularly explicit in quoting "the normal transposition of Directives . . . the requirement of legal certainty and the need

such a degree that it would be possible to make an inference that they are not employed as a means of escaping legislation.

C.   THE LEGAL BASIS

We have seen that a number of considerations justified the preparation of a Community directive on ELVs. Naturally, these interests relate to environmental protection and the internal market. Both Articles 95 (formerly Article 100a) and 175 (formerly Article 130s) EC are the principal legal bases in support of this directive. Article 95 EC is the legal basis used for measures adopted with a view to achieving the objectives set out in Article 14 (formerly Article 7a) EC (internal market). Article 175 EC is referred to for measures aimed at fulfilling the objectives set out in Article 174 (formerly Article 130r) EC. The Commission also based the ELV Proposal on Article 175 EC.

The choice of the legal basis for measures dealing with environmental issues has proved to be rather complex in the past. There are a number of cases on the theme which have been decided by the European Court of Justice (ECJ).[41] The demarcation line between Articles 95 and 175 EC is all but clear. Without wishing to enter into this long-debated legal issue,[42] it may be useful to recall the following technical points. First, the ECJ has stated that the legal basis shall depend on the aim and contents of the legislative act. Where more than one aim co-exists, a "centre of gravity" shall be identified, according to the preambles and the contents of the measure, and the legal basis chosen accordingly. Secondly, the Council's general practice is to base waste directives on Article 175 EC, except where they regulate specific types of waste (e.g. batteries, packaging waste). Hence, directives dealing with waste in general as well as directives on waste disposal installations are based on Article 175 EC. The Court has accepted this viewpoint.

On the first point, it can be observed that the use of the theory of the centre of gravity can be problematic[43] in the waste sector, as in any other product-related legislation where environmental protection and trade are inextricably linked. Almost any waste-related measure has two centres of gravity:

---

to ensure that the rights and obligations of individuals are not prejudiced" (point 5) and stating that "environmental agreements must have specified objectives, be transparent, reliable and enforceable". The European Parliament Resolution is also along the same wavelength (points 5, 6, 10, 16, and 17).

[41] Cases C–300/89 *EC Commission* v. *Council* [1991] ECR I–2867; C–155/91 *EC Commission* v. *Council* [1993] ECR I–939; C–187/93 *European Parliament* v. *Council* [1994] ECR I–2857.

[42] For a detailed analysis of this matter, cf Krämer (n. 25 above), 86–91. For an analysis of the jurisprudence, cf L. Krämer, *European Environmental Law. Casebook* (London: Sweet & Maxwell, 1993), 21–36 and 291–301; H. Somsen, "Legal Basis of Environmental Law" [1993] *European Environmental Law Review*, 121; H. Somsen, case note in (1992) 29 *Common Market Law Review* 140; J. Robinson, "The Legal Basis of EC Environmental Law" (1992) I *Journal of Environmental Law* 112–20; N. De Sadeleer, "La question du choix de la base juridique des actes communautaires ayant trait à la protection de l'environnement . . ." [1993] *Revue Juridique de l'Environnement* 593; A. Wachsmann, case note in (1993) 30 *Common Market Law Review* 1051.

[43] L. Krämer, *Focus on European Environmental Law* (1st edn., London: Sweet & Maxwell, 1992), 79–85.

protection of the environment and functioning of the internal market. To be sure, the fact that one prevails (51 per cent) over the other (49 per cent) does not allow it to be said that the measure has only one centre of gravity. Environmental protection is the centre of gravity for Directives 94/62/EC (Packaging and Packaging Waste) and 91/157/EEC (Batteries). At the same time, they are based on Article 95 EC, since they affect products, and the free circulation of products is a key element in the internal market. Also the ELV Proposal's centre of gravity is environmental protection. Yet, this does not mean that the objective articulated in Article 14 EC is not pursued.

Concerning the second point, the fact that the ELV Proposal not only deals with a specific type of waste but also addresses installations for collection and treatment suggests that the line of demarcation is not evident. The mixed character of the Directive, affecting at the same time products (vehicles) and installations for waste recovery or disposal, is a recent development in Community waste legislation. Neither the Packaging and Packaging Waste Directive nor the Batteries Directive (both based on Article 95 EC) contains measures that directly affect waste recovery or disposal installations, only measures which relate either to the product or to its handling once it has become waste (e.g. collection, marking). Directive 96/59/EC on the Disposal of PCB/PCT[44] (based on Article 175 EC) lays down measures for the collection, handling, and disposal of PCBs but does not contain measures affecting the products. Similarly, Directives 78/176/EEC[45] and 92/112/EC[46] on waste from the Titanium Dioxide Industry (based on Article 94 (formerly Article 100) EC and 308 (formerly Article 235) EC and 95 EC respectively) also contain no measures which directly affect the product, only measures on the disposal of waste. Hitherto, however, the Council has made clear its intention not to change Article 175 EC as the legal basis of the ELV Proposal.

As a consequence of (a) the practical difficulties in using the theory of the centre of gravity and (b) the difficulties in establishing a clear demarcation line between product- and installation-related measures, the criteria upon which the choice of the legal basis should be based should be carefully considered. Thus, rather than applying the theory of the centre of gravity or making a choice depending on the nature of the provision (product-related or installation-related), the key question should be "what is the legal basis which best allows the objectives of the Directive to be attained?" In other words, in the absence of a clear demarcation line based on the "traditional" criteria, the choice should rely not so much on theoretical considerations relating to the main focus or contents of the Proposal, but rather on functional and practical elements.

At this point, special attention should be given to the general consequences of the choice of the legal basis for Community acts, the meaning of which relates to the following points: first, the legislative procedure to be followed; secondly, the conditions to be taken into account in the drafting of the mea-

---

[44] [1996] OJ L243/31.   [45] [1978] OJ L54/19.   [46] [1992] OJ L409/11.

sure; and thirdly, the possibility for Member States to derogate from the harmonization measure. At the end of the day, point (a) more directly concerns the Council and the European Parliament than the Commission. Indeed, proposals based on Article 95 EC are adopted jointly by the Parliament and the Council, in accordance with the co-decision procedure set out in Article 251 (formerly Article 189b) EC. Proposals based on Article 175 EC are adopted by the Council, in co-operation with the European Parliament, in line with the procedure set out in Article 252 (formerly Article 189c) EC. The co-decision procedure, allowing for greater involvement by the Parliament, must certainly be viewed as a more democratic procedure than the co-operation procedure. However, the Amsterdam Treaty has aligned the decision-making procedures under Articles 95 and 175 EC. Therefore, this aspect has lost practical importance now that the new Treaty is in force.

The second point relates to the conditions laid down in Articles 95 and 174 EC respectively. Article 95 EC refers to a "high level of [environmental] protection" of proposals. This is a condition applying to the Commission proposals. Article 174 EC mentions the "high level of environmental protection" to be aimed at by Community policy. This condition applies to the Council and to environmental policy in general, not to each specific measure.[47] Article 174 EC refers to a number of principles: precaution, preventive action, rectifying damage at the source, as well as the "polluter pays" principle. These are not mentioned in Article 95 EC. However, since environmental protection requirements must be integrated into the definition and implementation of other Community policies (Article 174 EC, last sentence), they are of relevance also when the chosen legal basis is Article 95 EC.

The third point appears to be the main reason the Council has hitherto favoured Article 175 EC as the legal basis for most of the waste-related legislation, in spite of the fact that this could endanger the internal market. Under the former EC Treaty, the conditions for diverting from a harmonization measure, based on Article 95 EC, were quite restrictive. Only the fourth paragraph of Article 95 EC allowed more stringent measures to be maintained, and only on restrictive conditions which must be verified in each case by the Commission.[48] By contrast, Member States may, on the basis of Article 176 EC, maintain or introduce more stringent protective measures as long as the Commission is notified and they are compatible with the Treaty. This clause made the Council favour Article 175 EC as a legal basis, since it makes it easier to agree on a minimum harmonization level. Those countries which aim at a higher level of protection may resort to Article 176 EC. This approach has negative consequences for Community policy, in that Member States which aim for a high level of environmental protection will prefer to "go it on their own" rather than pull the whole Community together. Furthermore, Member States wishing to "go it on their own" may become reluctant to go "very far" so as not to put their economic operators at a competitive disadvantage. Therefore, all

---

[47] Cf Krämer (n. 24 above), 59–63.   [48] *Ibid.*, 61–2 and 129–37.

Member States are "winners" with just one loser—the level of environmental protection. The Amsterdam Treaty has made some substantial changes to the EC Treaty by making the possibility of derogating from harmonization measures adopted under Article 95 EC more accessible.[49] In this context, one may wonder whether the Amsterdam Treaty has brought about an improvement or, rather, will be detrimental for raising the overall level of environmental protection in the EU.

Let us now return to the question which legal basis allows us best to fulfil the objectives of the ELV Proposal? This question may lose its significance in light of the new Treaty (particularly because Article 95 EC has been revised). In this regard, it could be that Article 95 EC is still the most appropriate legal basis. The following elements favour Article 95 EC:

— One of the main arguments put forward by economic operators in favour of the Directive is the need to avoid further competitive distortions.

— Several provisions of the Proposal will strongly affect new vehicles. Furthermore, although the Proposal focuses more on treatment installations than on products, both the free circulation of services and non-distorted competition among installations are fundamental aspects of the internal market.

— The ELV Proposal recognizes the potential impact of product-related standards on the internal market, and for this reason makes direct reference to the need to adopt fully harmonized rules on recyclability requirements for new vehicles in the context of Directive 70/156/EEC (Article 7(4)).[50] Rather than proposing recyclability requirements within the ELV Proposal, the Commission makes reference to an *ad hoc* instrument based on Article 95 EC. We may wonder why the Commission has not simply chosen to base the ELV Directive on Article 95 EC. One answer could be that, as far as product-related standards are concerned, the Commission reverts to Article 95 EC (by means of the reference to

[49] Art. 95 EC establishes, *inter alia*, that if, after the adoption of a harmonization measure, a Member State deems it necessary to maintain national provisions on the grounds of major needs referred to in Art. 28 (formerly Art. 30) EC or relating to the protection of the environment or the working environment, it shall notify the Commission of these provisions as well as of the grounds for maintaining them (para. 4). This procedure applies also if a Member State, after the adoption of a harmonization measure, deems it necessary to introduce national provisions based on new scientific evidence relating, *inter alia*, to the protection of the environment (para. 5). The Commission shall, within six months of the notification, approve or reject the national provisions after having verified that they are not a means of arbitrary discrimination or a disguised restriction on trade and that they shall not constitute an obstacle to the functioning of the internal market (para. 6). In the absence of a decision by the Commission within this period, the national provisions shall be deemed to have been approved. The Commission may, when justified by the complexity of the matter and in the absence of danger for human health, extend the "standstill" period for a further period of up to six months. When a Member State is authorized to maintain or introduce national provisions derogating from a harmonization measure, the Commission shall immediately examine whether or not to propose an adaptation to that measure (para. 7).

[50] Art. 7(4) of the Directive states: "the Council . . . shall amend Dir. 70/156/EEC so that vehicles . . . put on the market after 1 Jan. 2005 are re-usable and or recyclable to a minimum of 85 per cent by weight per vehicle and are re-usable and/or recoverable to a minimum of 95 per cent by weight per vehicle".

Directive 70/156/EEC), whereas for all other provisions it makes use of Article 175 EC. But then the other product-related provisions contained in the Proposal (such as rules on the presence of heavy metals in vehicles and on marking of components), should also be based on Article 95 EC, which is not the case in the ELV Proposal.

Notwithstanding the potential impact of product standards on the internal market, it may appear to be unnecessary to base the ELV Directive on Article 95 EC since placing vehicles on the market is regulated by Directive 70/156/EEC, which expressly forbids any new national product-related standards being introduced. However, the ELV Directive will prevail over Directive 70/156/EEC, given that *lex posterior abrogat legem anteriorem,* and therefore national product-related standards, adopted on the basis of Article 176 EC, would be permitted. To avoid this risk, the ELV Proposal probably should have been based on Article 95 EC. However, this also depends on how the new version of Article 95 EC will be applied in practice. It should be noted that the risk of adoption of more stringent measures by Member States is increased by the possibility that the adopted ELV Directive will be based on a lower level of environmental protection than the Commission Proposal. It is quite common that the Council adopts environmental directives where the level of protection is significantly lower than that initially proposed by the Commission.

IV.   The Legal Issues

A.   PRODUCT OR WASTE?

This section discusses two important issues relating to the specific legal nature of waste in the context of the ELV Proposal.

i.   *Definition of ELVs*

Any sound legislative act should be based on clear definitions. In this regard, ELVs require clear identification. The most logical way of proceeding is to define an ELV as any object that satisfies both the definition of a vehicle and the definition of waste. It should be noted that both definitions already exist in Community legislation. The definition of a vehicle is provided in Article 2, third indent, of Directive 70/156/EEC on the Type-Approval of Vehicles and their Trailers.[51] The definition of waste is contained in Article 1 of Directive 75/442/EEC on Waste[52] as amended by Directive 91/156/EEC.[53] According to this definition, waste is any substance or object which the holder discards or

---

[51] "Vehicle means any motor vehicle intended for use on the road, being complete or incomplete, having at least four wheels and a maximum design speed exceeding 25 km/h, and its trailers, with the exception of vehicles which run on rails and of agricultural and forestry tractors and all mobile machinery." This definition is completed by Annex II to the same Directive (n. 21 above), which also contains the classification of vehicles into different categories (M1, N1, etc.).

[52] [1975] OJ L194/39.   [53] [1991] OJ L78/32.

intends or is required to discard.[54] The intention of the holder is decisive: should a vehicle comply with the technical and fiscal provisions that regulate the circulation of vehicles in the national territory, the holder may freely decide to retain this vehicle for as long as he desires. However, if for any reason the vehicle is no longer allowed to remain in circulation (for instance because it does not comply with minimum safety requirements), then it may become waste *ex lege*, unless it undergoes the necessary repairs.

In light of the foregoing analysis two observations can be made. First, there are no fully harmonized Community rules regarding the technical requirements which vehicles must satisfy in order to continue to be used. The Type-approval Directive in fact relates to the technical requirements for placing a new vehicle on the market. Directive 96/96/EC Relating to Roadworthiness Tests for Motor Vehicles and their Trailers[55] sets out minimum requirements and leaves Member States free to adopt stricter rules (in particular pertaining to safety aspects). The upshot is that this Directive creates certain discrepancies between Member States, in that a vehicle which can no longer be used in one Member State may still be eligible to be used in another Member State.

The following examples may prove useful in further clarifying the scope of the definition of ELVs. In France and the Netherlands, the distinction between used vehicles (products) and ELVs (waste) is based on cost (vehicle value and repair cost). If the repair cost does not exceed the vehicle's value, the vehicle is not considered waste and can be sold or exported as a second-hand product. The decision is made on a case-by-case basis. In France, even when the repair cost exceeds the vehicle's price, and therefore the vehicle is considered to be waste, the owner can still obtain a certification of "economically non-repairable vehicle", in which case the vehicle can still be sold or exported as a second-hand vehicle. In contrast, the rule in Austria is that the ratio between the repair cost and the value of the vehicle may not be used as the only criterion to define end of life vehicles. Accordingly, a vehicle becomes waste only when it is deemed to be destined for dismantling or shredding. This requires a degree of subjectiveness. As a consequence of the subjectiveness aspects of the definition and of the different national rules which make vehicles become waste *ex lege*, the definition of ELVs is not identical across the EU.

Our second observation relates to possible abuses in defining ELVs. For example, a used vehicle that is discarded by its owner may be considered worth driving by another person. In this context the vehicle which is likely to become waste continues to be a product because, instead of being discarded, it is sold as a second-hand product.[56] This decision, seen beyond the frontiers

[54] The reference, in this definition, to the categories set out in Annex I to Dir. 75/442/EEC is of no relevance since the last entry in this Annex (Q16) refers to any materials, substances, or products which are not contained in the other categories listed in the Annex. The function of this part of the definition of waste is only to facilitate its application by listing some examples of categories of waste.

[55] [1997] OJ L46/1.

[56] Cf L. Giesberts and J. Hilf, *Kreislaufwirtschaft Altauto: Altautoverordnung und freiwillige Selbstverpflichtung, Abfallwirtschafts in Forschung und Praxis* (Berlin: Erich Schmidt Verlag GmbH, 1998), CV, 60.

of one country, can have significant implications. That is, a vehicle which may be scrapped in one country might still find a new owner in another country (typically an economically less developed one). It is not easy to assess to what extent this situation is desirable. On the one hand, it could be argued that the flow of used vehicles from more to less developed countries is positive since consumers in less developed countries could not afford new vehicles. On the other hand, there is little justification for the sale of waste disguised as second-hand vehicles since it is clear that this waste will place a significant burden on the environment of the importing country.[57] It should be noted that these difficulties with the definition of ELVs will probably remain unchanged after the adoption of the ELV Proposal, in that the Proposal does not include any new definition of waste which could solve this problem.[58]

From a legal point of view, the export of waste vehicles is subject to Regulation (EC) No. 259/93 concerning the Supervision and Control of Shipments of Waste Within, Into, and Out of the EC. This Regulation prohibits the export of waste for disposal from the EC except to EFTA member countries. The export of waste for recovery from the EC to third countries is subject to a number of procedures and controls that vary according to the classification of the waste. For example, "motor vehicle wrecks drained of liquids" feature in the "green list" (Annex II to the Regulation)[59] and, as a consequence, can be exported without any control. Nevertheless, certain control procedures apply to the export of this waste to a number of non-OECD countries which have explicitly requested this. Vehicles which contain liquids are not mentioned in the Regulation and therefore fall under the "red list" procedure (Annex IV), which requires prior notification as well as written authorization by the competent authorities in all the countries involved in the shipment.[60] In addition, this Regulation allows certain restrictions on the export of some components contained in ELVs (e.g. brake fluids, lead acid batteries, hydraulic fluids, antifreeze fluids), as well as on the light fraction from automobile shredding. However, these restrictions (notably the "amber list" procedure—Annex III) do not apply to ELVs that contain such components so as long as the vehicles in question are drained of liquids.

It is important to remember that these procedures apply only to vehicles that fall within the definition of waste. It is therefore possible that the export of

[57] In Sept. 1996, the NGO "EURAFRIC" reported to the European Commission that the import of large quantities of "moving wrecks", on average older than 10 years, into West Africa started to be widely recognized as a major form of environmental pollution.

[58] This issue was discussed between the Commission and the Member States, but a better definition of ELV could not be found. Denmark proposed to consider unroadworthy vehicles (meaning vehicles not complying with roadworthiness rules)—including repairable vehicles—as waste until they are repaired. This would mean that the export of vehicles before their repair takes place would be considered as export of waste, thus allowing authorities to control it. However, for many other Member States, this solution would go "too far"!

[59] Code GC 040.

[60] Austria has submitted an application to the Commission to include "non-depolluted discarded vehicles" in the Community hazardous waste list. By virtue of Commission Reg. (EC) No. 2408/98 [1998] OJ L298/19 amending Annex V to Council Reg. (EC) No. 259/93, this would result in an automatic ban on the export of these vehicles to non-OECD countries.

ELVs takes place without control. Authorities in exporting countries have little choice in avoiding this state of affairs which is due mainly to the subjectiveness of the definition of waste. Naturally these regulators could ensure that a vehicle which becomes waste *ex lege* shall not be exported. But this may not be enough to solve the problem since many low-value vehicles could still be exported as second-hand products. Authorities in importing countries could possibly play a larger role. This is more likely to occur in jurisdictions in which the legislation of importing countries is equivalent to the rules of exporting countries, ensuring that a vehicle will not be allowed to circulate in the importing country.

Poland provides a good example of an importing country attempting to raise standards in order to avoid the import of less environmentally friendly vehicles. Whilst a member of the OECD, Poland does not apply the OECD Decision on transboundary movements of waste for recovery. As a consequence, pursuant to Commission Decision 94/575/EC,[61] exports of all types of waste listed on the "green list" are subject to the "amber list" procedure (prior notification and tacit consent). In addition, Polish authorities have prohibited the import of cars older than ten years and have established that all cars registered for the first time in Poland (including second-hand imported cars) must be equipped with a catalytic converter. This is clearly an attempt to protect the environment by prohibiting the import of technologically old products. However, the fact that old Polish cars not equipped with a catalytic converter could still continue to circulate raises the question of violation of the principle of non-discrimination towards imported products. To avoid such a risk, Poland should have imposed the same requirements on cars already in circulation in Poland. Leaving aside this question, what is important in this instance is that these regulations clearly try to deal with the serious environmental threat arising from the import of old vehicles into Poland.

ii. *Reduction of Hazardous Substances (Qualitative Prevention)*

We now turn to consider the question of the effectiveness of the EC hazardous waste and products regime. We shall begin with a consideration of what the prevention of waste means. It is argued that it means, *inter alia*, the generation of waste that is less harmful for the environment (qualitative prevention).

Vehicles contain a wide range of materials and substances, some of them hazardous. As a consequence, they generate waste that is harmful to the environment. For example, shredder residues are classified as waste whose movement needs to be controlled by Regulation (EC) No. 259/93 ("amber list" procedure) and by the Basel Convention on the Control of Transboundary Movements of Hazardous Waste and its Disposal.[62] For the moment, this waste is not considered hazardous by EC legislation although a request to include it

---

[61] [1994] OJ L220/15. Note that this Decision is to be repealed by a Regulation, covering more countries, presently under the adoption procedure.

[62] Ratified by the EC by Council Decisions 93/98/EC [1993] OJ L39/1, corrigendum in [1994] OJ L74/52 and 97/640/EC [1997] OJ L272/45.

in the EC list of hazardous waste (Council Decision 94/904/EC) has recently been tabled and a decision possibly amending this list accordingly is awaited.

When addressing the question of how to achieve qualitative prevention, it is useful to analyse, briefly, the current instruments at EC level which concern the hazardous nature of products. Waste essentially are products which have reached a particular phase in their life cycle. In general, a product becomes waste following a decision or an act by its owner, but this does not mean that the product has undergone any physical change in order to become, legally speaking, waste. Viewed from an environmental perspective, there is no difference between a product and waste, since both may have the same environmental impact. To be sure, there are objective conditions that make waste a greater environmental concern than other products. But this does not mean that the same object, before becoming waste, cannot have the same impact on the environment. As a consequence, the environmental impact of any object, be it a product or waste, should be subject to the same kind of control. Legislation on hazards caused by products should be devised with a view to the entire life cycle of the object, from cradle to grave.

In practice this has not, and does not happen. It appears that existing EC product legislation fails to take into account the waste phases of products. For example, there are several pieces of EC legislation on waste that focus exclusively on products which have become waste (e.g. Directive 91/157/EEC on Batteries—which includes a ban on batteries exceeding a maximum content of mercury; Article 11 of Directive 94/62/EC Laying Down Maximum Concentration Limits for Heavy Metals in Packaging), while avoiding the subject of waste-treatment installations. These examples are evidence that, in certain cases, in order to ensure a high level of environmental protection in relation to waste, the product must be banned or its marketing restricted by specific conditions.

It is true that EC legislation on dangerous substances and preparations contains waste-management elements. Annex VI of Directive 67/548/EEC,[63] listing the general classification and labelling requirements for dangerous substances and preparations, includes some "safety advice phrases" which relate to waste management (e.g. S60: "to be disposed of as hazardous waste"). Also, Annex VII to this Directive, listing the information required for notifying a substance to the competent authorities, includes, among the "possibilities for rendering the substance harmless", the option of "recycling" and "destruction", including discharge and incineration. However, this attempt to include aspects of waste management in product legislation is not sufficient to ensure a high level of protection in relation to the waste phase of the products. There are no requirements on *how* the product must be treated (collected, transported, recovered, disposed of). Legislation on dangerous products is in fact limited to notification, classification, packaging, and labelling, and this by

---

[63] [1967] OJ L196/1, last amendment by Commission Dir. 98/73/EC [1998] OJ L305/1. See nn. 3 and 4 above.

definition is not sufficient for proper waste management.[64] If a substance or preparation is classified as dangerous, that means that it must be properly labelled and packaged. This, however, does not mean that dangerous products will not end up as waste and thus undergo inappropriate waste treatment operations. Supplementary rules for this waste are therefore necessary. The Community legislator has recognized the importance of promulgating these rules.

We should point out that Directive 76/769/EEC,[65] concerning Restrictions to Marketing and Use of Certain Dangerous Substances and Preparations, is an advance when compared to Directives 67/548/EEC and 88/379/EEC. That is, the Directive attempts to regulate dangerous products by supplying restrictions on their marketing and use.[66] But in order to determine which products are subject to restrictions, this Directive uses the same "tools" provided for by Directives 67/548/EEC and 88/379/EEC (test methods, risk assessment, etc.). It is submitted that these "tools" are often inadequate fully to take into account the waste phase of products and, in general, focus mainly on the need to protect human health rather than on environmental issues.[67] In addition, each restriction on a product requires a modification of Directive 76/769/EEC by the Council, involving a significant amount of time. For all these reasons, this Directive cannot be considered a satisfactory tool for ensuring a high level of protection in relation to waste. Marketing restrictions are sometimes implemented by the EC in response to national measures, so that internal market distortions are avoided, but very seldom is a ban on a substance decided on the basis of a Community initiative.

By way of summary, legislation on products should ideally cover all phases of a product's life cycle, including the waste phase. In practice, however, this is not usually the case, due in part to peculiarities of product legislation and the influence of economic pressures (e.g. product market demands). Since waste often has a negative value, there is little or no demand for it. This generates the risk of waste being more easily spread in the environment than products. In addition, there are other factors that make waste a specific issue compared to products. For example, two non-dangerous substances could become hazardous waste if mixed. This risk can be controlled relatively easily for products (for instance, by a proper warning on the label). But for waste, controlling this risk is far more difficult, since the mixing of waste with other wastes is generally unintentional. Moreover, a product can be safe during its normal use but might generate toxic emissions if incinerated (e.g. hard PVC). Or it can cause an environmental concern both during its lifetime as a product and as waste albeit for completely different reasons (e.g. soft PVC).

---

[64] It is also doubtful to what extent this Directive promotes environmentally friendly products, cf L. Krämer, "Products and Sustainable Development at Community Level" in L. Krämer, *Focus on European Environmental Law* (2nd edn., London: Sweet & Maxwell, 1997), 215.

[65] [1976] OJ L262/10; last amended by Commission Dir. 97/64/EC [1997] OJ L315/13.

[66] e.g. asbestos, benzene, cadmium (used in certain applications, such as pigments and PVC).

[67] Cf Krämer (n. 24 above), 23.

iii. General EC Waste Legislation and Qualitative Prevention

So far we have talked of product legislation in relation to waste. A few words on the role of general EC waste legislation in contributing to qualitative prevention are also necessary. The effects of Directive 91/689/EEC on Hazardous Waste *de facto* are limited to the environmentally sound management of waste already generated. The need to prevent the generation of hazardous waste is not mentioned either in the preamble to Directive 91/689/EEC or in its Articles. The explicit aim of this Directive is to approximate the laws of Member States on the controlled management of hazardous waste. In fact all provisions relating to this Directive refer to labelling, packaging, disposal, recovery, transport, and handling of hazardous waste and there are no specific provisions aimed at reducing the generation of hazardous waste. This may seem surprising if considered in light of the first aim of Directive 75/442/EEC on Waste, which is to "prevent or reduce waste prevention and its harmfulness".[68] But, in reality, this Directive also, apart from Article 3, does not contain any binding provision on concrete measures to be taken in order to reduce the hazardous nature of waste.

The fact that a specific waste is classified as hazardous waste (e.g. some of the heavy metals contained in an ELV) should promote its reduction, since the management of hazardous waste is more expensive than that of non-hazardous waste. However, in practice this does not happen because there is no direct relationship between the actors who choose the materials for manufacturing a product (usually private economic actors) and those who pay for the disposal of the waste generated by that product (usually the public sector).

Having reached the conclusion that neither existing EC product legislation nor general EC waste legislation is sufficient to ensure that the objective of qualitative prevention in relation to ELV is achieved, let us spend a few words on the solution proposed by the Commission in the ELV Proposal. Two combined elements are envisaged:

— The first consists of applying the "extended producer responsibility principle" (EPR), in order to establish an economic link between the actors who put on the market materials which then become waste, and the costs to be paid to treat such waste. In practice this means making vehicle producers responsible for the disposal costs of ELVs. From a theoretical point of view this seems to be an appropriate solution, although in practice there are some difficulties to overcome, mainly relating to the difficulty in quantifying environmental costs. Disposal costs do not always reflect the real impact of disposal operations and installations on the environment.[69]

---

[68] Art. 3 (a), first indent.
[69] For instance, the cost of incineration in Italy is artificially low since a law obliges the National Electrical Energy Company to buy energy from waste incinerators carrying out energy recovery at a politically fixed price.

— The second element is based on the assumption that the impact of several kinds of waste on the environment can somehow be controlled as long as they are clearly identifiable and recyclable. Lead batteries can be collected after use and recycled. But lead in steel alloys cannot be collected separately and recycled, thus requiring the setting up of expensive end-of-pipe monitoring and control technologies, less effective than preventive measures such as the replacement of lead with other substances.[70]

As a consequence, the Commission came to the conclusion that one way of avoiding environmental contamination by heavy metals may be by prohibiting their introduction into certain treatment operations where they would no longer be controllable. This means that the substances are not prohibited and that they can be used in vehicles. If they are used, they must be separable from the vehicles before the vehicles are shredded, and they cannot be incinerated or landfilled. Substances that cannot be separated from ELVs would *de facto* be banned from the market, although there is no legal requirement which prohibits their placing on the market. They would *de facto* be banned because their presence in the vehicles would make it impossible to achieve the recovery and recycling targets set by the Directive. This solution could help to overcome the strong resistance of industries which oppose bans on the marketing of the substances they produce or use. It could also encourage the development of a new industrial mentality. In the presence of substances whose impact on the environment can be reduced only by fully recycling them after use, it would be possible to market these substances only in a form which makes them suitable for recycling.

From a legal perspective this option is not entirely new. There are already many examples of national requirements prohibiting specific recovery and disposal methods for certain kinds of waste. In the Netherlands used tyres cannot be landfilled. In many Member States hazardous waste cannot be incinerated or landfilled in installations for non-hazardous waste. These measures always have the effect of channelling the waste towards other waste-management methods. The aim of the Commission's Proposal is to channel heavy metals used in vehicles towards recycling. In this specific case, however, one may wonder whether channelling polluting substances towards recycling represents, from the environmental point of view, the best option or whether the use of polluting substances should not simply be prohibited.

B.   THE COLLECTION AND RECOVERY OF ELVS

The Commission Proposal addresses the question of ELV collection and recycling/recovery by means of several complementary provisions. We now turn to address the specific terms of these provisions.

---

[70] Cf Nordic Council of Ministers, "Costs of Lead Related to Waste Products" (1994) 639 *TemaNord* 11.

An initial provision requires that vehicles be deregistered from public registers only after the owner has received a certificate of destruction, which can only be issued by authorized dismantlers. In order to be authorized to issue certificates of destruction, a dismantler must comply with a number of technical requirements, mainly related to the necessary equipment and operations to avoid environmental contamination during the dismantling process. This very simple provision, by linking together environmental requirements, permits, and certificates of destruction, is intended to ensure that all vehicles reaching the end of their life will be channelled towards the appropriate waste management schemes and are no longer abandoned in the environment.

A second provision for collection of an economic nature establishes that owners of ELVs will no longer have to pay for discarding their vehicles. This means that if the ELV has a negative market value (and as a consequence the dismantler demands money for issuing a certificate of destruction) this money would be reimbursed to the vehicle owner by the producer (through the dealer). This provision is considered necessary for several reasons. First, there is no reason why end-users should bear the financial consequences of products which, when they become waste, have a negative value since they were not produced with a view to recovery. If in fact these costs are borne by end-users, there is no incentive for producers to invest in cleaner products. We will return to this issue below. Secondly, if vehicle owners do not incur any expense to get rid of their vehicles, it is less likely that vehicles will be exported, though in practice this could still happen.

i. Extended Producer Responsibility

In the past, ELVs almost always had a positive value. This was in part due to the presence of externalities. Where environmental requirements have been introduced, profits from recycling ELVs have decreased, with the consequence that in several countries ELVs now have a negative value. This situation is typical for many types of waste. As long as objects are products, they (usually) have a market. When they become waste, collection and recovery costs often make these objects marketless and taxpayers must subsidize the cost for their eventual disposal.

This phenomenon was first identified in the packaging sector, where "extended producer responsibility (EPR) schemes", aimed at also incorporating product manufacturers in the waste phase, were first introduced. The idea behind that was that if a manufacturer would pay for the cost imposed by waste on society, he would produce the product in such a way that such costs would be as low as possible. Although in fact any cost borne by producers is ultimately passed on to consumers, for competitive reasons producers have an interest in keeping the price of their products as low as possible. Consumer choices will more likely be directed towards products which, under an EPR scheme, are more easy to recycle, simply because these products are cheaper than others. In order for such schemes to function properly, a competitive mechanism must also be set in motion. This can be done by differentiating the prices paid by consumers in relation to the burden that the products cause once they become waste.

Examples of "extended producer responsibility" in the waste sector appeared first in some Member States. The first and most famous case is the German Packaging Ordinance of 12 June 1991. Today, EPR schemes exist also in the area of vehicles, tyres, paper, electric "white" goods, and construction waste.[71] However, so far EPR measures have only appeared in national legislation, whereas there are no examples yet in Community legislation. Directive 94/62/EC on Packaging and Packaging Waste in fact does not contain binding measures on EPR.

In legal terms, extended producer responsibility is not a clearly-defined concept. It is rather a policy concept which can take different forms in practice, in order to switch from public costs to private costs and apply the "polluter pays" principle (a vaguely defined economic principle)[72] by "internalising" certain costs and reducing "externalities". EPR programmes are still a novelty, and their impact on policy as well as their economic and environmental implications is not fully understood.[73] However, the beneficial effects of waste generation from EPR schemes in the packaging sector is certain. There is no reason such effects should not also occur in other sectors.

It is important to note that the existing deposit-refund schemes (e.g. refilling systems for bottles existing in many countries, fee-premium scheme for ELVs in Sweden from 1975[74]) are not forms of EPR. Their aim is limited to the collection phase and there is no incentive to change the product design. EPR schemes go one step further: they incorporate an incentive for collection and an incentive to change the design of products. Therefore, the effects of EPR schemes are much more marked than those concerning collection schemes. A key issue is how an EPR scheme can be set up in the vehicle sector. This question was discussed both at national level and within the Commission.[75]

There remain two basic questions. The first relates to how to establish EPR schemes so that producers are involved in the post-consumption phase of their products and pushed to make new vehicles more recyclable. We will call this "organizational" EPR. The second relates to how to avoid externalities, in particular before changes in the design of new vehicles occur, being paid for by the environment or by society, i.e. how to shift financial responsibility from the public to the private sector. We will call this financial EPR.

---

[71] OECD, "Extended Producer Responsibility in the OECD Area", Appendix 1, *Environment Monograph* (issue 114, 1996), 42–59.

[72] H. Smets, *"Examen critique du principe-pollueur-payeur", Mankind and the Environment, what rights for the twenty-first century? en hommage à Alexandre Kiss* (Paris: Editions Frison-Roche, 1998), 79–95; Krämer (n. 24 above), 69–70.

[73] J. Salzman, "Extended Producer Responsibility: Take-back Programmes and International Trade Law", internal OECD paper (1997).

[74] Cf n. 16 above.

[75] For a more detailed analysis of various economic options, see E. Rydén, "Car Scrap: Throw It Away? Or Make It Pay?", Research report 2, International Institute for Industrial Environmental Economics, Lund University (Lund: Lund University Press, 1995).

Concerning organizational EPR, the following alternatives have been considered. Let us begin with "pure" organizational EPR schemes. They have been implemented in Sweden in 1998. Under these schemes, producers are responsible for take-back and for recycling of "their" vehicles. The main advantage of these schemes is that they strongly incite producers to modify the design of products. The disadvantage is that, since there is a relatively small number of vehicle producers, there would be no guarantee that a competitive mechanism is set in motion. Producers could increase the price of all vehicles uniformly. Consumers would not play any active selection role and there is a risk that design changes may not occur at all. In addition, unlike in the packaging area, in the vehicle sector there is no direct economic relationship between producers on the one hand and dismantlers and recyclers on the other.

Vehicle recycling has not so far been a significant worry for producers. It can be argued that making vehicle producers fully responsible for the take-back and recovery of ELVs could push producers to set up their own collection and recycling infrastructures, cutting off the business of existing dismantlers and recyclers. In practice, this is very unlikely to happen because it would require massive investment in a sector already characterized by large overcapacities. Still, one could argue that producers would enter into agreements with existing dismantling and recycling companies, leading to the former controlling the latter. Indeed, this is the reason why many dismantler associations have been so strongly against "pure" EPR schemes. In any case, nothing would stop producers from taking control of the dismantling and recycling business also in absence of EPR schemes.

We next consider "soft" organizational EPR schemes. Under this procedure, the responsibility for the take-back and recovery of ELVs is shared by producers and all other economic actors (dismantlers, recyclers) or public authorities. The main advantages are that there is less resistance on the part of vehicle producers, in addition to the fact that "dismantlers'" independence over producers seems to be preserved better. The disadvantages relate to the difficulty in organizing the collection and recovery of ELVs without knowing in advance who is responsible for each aspect of the procedure. One may also wonder whether these schemes can really be classified as EPR schemes since they may in practice imply that producers do not do anything more than they would have done anyway in the absence of any intervention by the public sector. Finally, since "shared responsibility" schemes seem to call for the establishment of co-operative implementation systems, the need to avoid undesirable anti-competitive effects should also be carefully taken into consideration.

The EU Proposal has opted for a "soft" organizational scheme and places responsibility for the allocation of tasks with the various economic operators in Member States. In this respect, there is no strong organizational EPR principle applied in the ELV Proposal. The essence of the EPR principle applied by the ELV Proposal is to be found in the financial responsibility mechanism.

As regards the financial EPR, an initial option considered consisted of a fee to be paid by consumers when they purchase a new vehicle, which would be channelled as a "scrap premium" into the dismantling and recycling sector. This was the solution chosen by the Netherlands. One major advantage of this approach is that it allows the recycling of already existing ELVs to be financed. For example, the fee paid in 1998 can immediately be used for financing the recycling of vehicles which have become waste in 1998 but which were produced long before then. The difficulties in applying this scheme reside in the need to handle the fee properly, so as to ensure that it reflects real costs and that premiums are given where they are really needed and not to subsidize activities which do not make economic sense. The key question seems to be the way the fee/premium is managed. The risk of anti-competitive behaviour also depends largely on this. Over-compensation of recycling activities, for instance, would be difficult to justify under Articles 87 (formerly Article 92) and 88 (formerly Article 93) EC, on state aids. A major disadvantage is the lack of proper incentives aimed at changing a vehicle's design, if a fee of the exact same amount has to be paid by all purchasers of new vehicles. The fee could then be differentiated in order to reflect the actual state of recyclability of the model of the new vehicle, so that the competitive mechanism is set in motion. Yet, given that the fee would probably not be very significant as compared to the price of a new vehicle, this would need to be made very visible to consumers in order to trigger a competitive mechanism.

The "scrap fee" can be paid as a lump sum when a new vehicle is purchased or otherwise annually (for example with the vehicle insurance). It can immediately be put into a premium fund (as is the case in the Netherlands) or set aside to cover the possible negative value of the ELV (as an insurance fee). An annual payment would have the advantage that, the more the vehicle ages and therefore the higher the risk becomes, it will have a negative value, the more the fund set aside will increase. It would be a form of "insurance" against the vehicle having negative value when it becomes an ELV. If the ELV then does not have a negative value, the vehicle owner can be reimbursed for the payments made. The annual payment could be proportional to the "recycling performance" of the corresponding vehicle model (which will be an indicator of the vehicle recyclability). A disadvantage would be that if the annual fee were not perceived by consumers as part of the vehicle's price, there would be no competitive mechanism in operation and producers would not have any incentive to change the design of new vehicles.

The scrap-fee model can be applied both at national level (each country managing its own fund) and at Community level (by setting up a European fund). However, in order to apply it at Community level, a European organization dealing with the collection and re-allocation of the fee would need to be set up. This would therefore require an *ad hoc* measure (possibly a regulation) and would need to be agreed upon by most Member States. It would also probably require that measures of a fiscal nature be adopted at EU level. Since fiscal measures require unanimity in the Council, it would be very difficult to arrive at a solution. Moreover, recyclability also depends on dynamic market conditions, and it is a difficult concept to measure *ex ante* in monetary terms. Any pre-set fee therefore runs the risk of being arbitrary. For this reason, the Commission proposes a model which relies more on market forces than other models.

Article 5(4) of the ELV Proposal establishes that:

> any costs incurred by the last holder and/or owner at delivery of the vehicle to an authorized treatment facility . . . as a result of the vehicle's having a negative market value, shall be reimbursable by the vehicle dealer acting on behalf of the producer, unless the dealer decides to take back the end of life vehicle at no cost to the last holder and/or owner.

If the vehicle is designed in such a way as not to have a negative market value when it becomes waste, normal market forces apply: the consumer receives the money corresponding to the value of the vehicle from the dismantler. However, if the vehicle has a negative market value, the producer has to bear the corresponding cost unless it agrees to take back the ELV free of charge from the consumer. This is the method in which the Commission intends to apply the EPR principle to ELVs, not by "organizational" responsibility but by placing "financial" responsibility on producers.

This approach has certain advantages. For example, it is expected to have a strong effect on prevention. Producers, to avoid running the risk of having to pay for dismantling and recycling costs, are pressurized into changing the design of new vehicles so that recycling becomes profitable. A second benefit is that it can also be used to finance the recycling of vehicles which are already on the market. We should note the view of vehicle producers that they are not responsible for the negative market value of vehicles produced before waste-management considerations were included in the design of new vehicles.

The main limitation of the Commission Proposal resides in practical difficulties relating to its implementation. Knowing that the last owner of the vehicle would be reimbursed by the producer, dismantlers would, in the absence of a control mechanism, charge whatever price they wished to the last users of vehicles. One way of overcoming this problem is by establishing reference value lists referring to the various models on the market. Value lists for second-hand vehicles already exist. It should not be difficult to adapt them to ELVs. The year the vehicle was constructed, as well as a number of other parameters (physical state, presence of valuable parts), could be taken into consideration in drawing up these lists. A second disadvantage is the fact that ideally there should be competition among dismantlers to obtain ELVs so that the consumer can choose the one offering the best price—in case of negative value, the lowest cost. But if the last owner knows that he will be reimbursed by the producer, he will not be encouraged, where his vehicle has negative value, to seek the best deal. This may ultimately limit the efficiency of the system. However, some loss of economic efficiency has to be tolerated in view of the environmental advantages of the system. After all, if the market itself could ensure optimum protection of the environment there would be little need for regulatory intervention. Unfortunately market failures emerge too often in the context of waste management.

Finally, a potential problem concerns ELVs whose producer no longer exists, or which are not represented by any dealer in the country where the vehicle becomes waste. Both cases are possible in practice, although they are certainly not likely to be common occurrences. In the first instance, a fund, financed by vehicle users (via insurance fees or circulation taxes) could be set up. Given that this situation is very unlikely, contributions to the fund would only need to be very small. The second problem is a more complex one. A possible solution could be that whenever a vehicle is imported directly (without the presence of a representative of the corresponding producer on the market of import) a scrap fee covering the possible negative value of the vehicle at a later date would have to be paid.

ii. Setting and Measuring Targets

Another important matter relates to the setting of quantitative targets for the re-use, recycling, and recovery of ELVs. This section offers insights into how the targets set forth in the Proposal were chosen. In setting quantitative targets, the Commission pursues two parallel objectives: first, to divert waste from disposal operations (landfilling, incineration), i.e. diverting waste towards recovery operations; and secondly to apply, within the recovery methods, the hierarchy which favours material recycling over energy recovery operations. This hierarchy reflects a number of environmental, energetic, social, and economic considerations.[76] The issue we address concerns how targets are set.

Recovery targets have been proposed by economic operators, particularly by vehicle producers. They had proposed 85 per cent by the year 2002 and 95 per cent by 2015. The Commission agreed with this suggestion, except that, in the political compromise which gave rise to its Proposal, it changed the date from 2002 to 2005.

Recycling targets have been set by taking the best current situations in the EU market into consideration. In certain areas (for example, the Netherlands, certain regions in Italy, and Spain), a recycling target of 82 per cent is already being achieved. By relying on a number of technological, environmental, and economic considerations, the Commission concluded that 80 per cent recycling would certainly be feasible in the entire EU territory by 2005. In view of the changes made to the design of new vehicles, a recycling target of 85 per cent is also considered feasible by 2015.

What needs to be stressed is that any quantitative target, is by definition, arbitrary. But the meaning of setting quantitative targets is not only to apply solutions which appear to be best from an economic standpoint. It also means giving precise political signals to economic operators so that they will invest in technologies which, from an environmental point of view, are considered preferable by the public sector. It is practically impossible, given the failure of economic instruments to measure environmental benefits, to prove from an

---

[76] See the Review of the Community Strategy for Waste Management, n. 11 above.

economic point of view that the targets chosen will lead to Paretian out-comes.[77] On the other hand, it is reasonable to imagine that the chosen targets can be achieved without dramatic interference in the market, since they have already been achieved in some parts of the EU.

The recycling targets of the EU Proposal have been strongly criticized by some industrial associations as being unacceptable "market interference". However, the same industrial associations fully support the quantitative targets for recovery. Therefore, either all kinds of targets are considered to be unacceptable market interference or none of them are. The principles behind the recovery and the recycling targets are, in fact, exactly the same. Leaving theory aside for a moment, the best proof that the chosen targets are feasible appears in the voluntary commitment of 16 April 1998 between FIAT and the Italian Ministry for the Environment, in which FIAT commits itself to achieve the targets of the EU Proposal in advance of the deadlines specified in the EU Proposal. It is clear that in order to monitor the achievement of the targets, specific statistical tools will have to be set up and common terminology fully adopted by the Member States. To this end, the Proposal calls for the Commission to set up an appropriate database and adopt formats which can be used by Member States for providing data on the progress made towards meeting the targets. Without common language, no sound monitoring would be possible.

V. The Future of the Proposal

Despite the advantages of Article 95 EC described above, the Commission has decided, on the basis of the centre of gravity approach, to base the Proposal on Article 175 (formerly Article 130s) EC, and accordingly the legislative procedure set forth in Article 252 (formerly Article 189c) EC applies. Under the Amsterdam Treaty, the legislative acts based on Article 175 EC are required to undergo a co-decision procedure set forth in Article 252 EC. This latter procedure is designed in part to equalize the decision-making power of Council and Parliament, by giving the European Parliament more scope for influencing the contents of the act.

Turning to other institutions, the opinion of the Economic and Social Committee (ESC) was delivered on 25 February 1998. This opinion is obligatory and not binding on the other institutions. Generally speaking it is supportive of the Proposal. It demands stricter measures to be adopted for qualitative prevention (heavy metals) and PVC. (The Commission proposal does not contain any measure on PVC, but recognizes that there is a need further to investigate the environmental impact of this material, and it calls for a "horizontal approach", covering all waste streams.)

Under the Austrian Presidency (July–December 1998), the Council made substantial progress towards a possible agreement in view of a common

[77] This concept indicates a situation in which it is not possible to improve the state of one variable without necessarily worsening that of another variable.

position. The Proposal was discussed by the Ministers for the Environment during the Council meeting of 21 December 1998. A consensus was expressed on the essential elements of the Proposal (extended producer responsibility (EPR), quantitative targets, restrictions on heavy metals), although, pending the opinion of the Parliament, a definitive stand could not be taken. However, the Council seemed determined to leave the organizational and financial details of EPR systems to Member States, rather than fixing them at Community level. In addition, the Council would consider allowing for the implementation of certain Articles of the Proposal by environmental agreements, subject to a number of conditions, particularly concerning their enforceability under contractual law. The first reading by Parliament occurred in February 1999. This opinion is also supportive of the essential elements of the Proposal.

The common position should have been adopted by the Council in March 1999. However, following pressure from vehicle producers, particularly against the provisions on EPR, the German Presidency requested and obtained a postponement of its adoption. Yet, the ministers pledged to adopt the common position, without changes, during the June Council. Surprisingly, the Council did not honour its commitment. Subsequently, Germany, the UK, and Spain formed a blocking minority. It is unprecedented that the Environment Council fails to honour a political agreement following direct intervention by a branch industry, setting an alarming institutional precedent which may undermine the credibility of the Council. Yet the Finnish Presidency managed, by changing the implementation date of the EPR provision from 2003 to 2006, to attract sufficient consensus for a qualified majority so that the Common Position was eventually adopted on 29 July 1999.

It is worth noting that the main difficulties which have arisen during discussions in the Council relate to resistance from certain Member States to accept European rules which would force them to adapt the initiatives taken at national level. This confirms the urgent need for a Community legislative framework, before the diverging national initiatives make any European solution impossible. The stalemate that has arisen following the Environment Council of June 1999 shows that this concern is fully justified.

VI. Conclusion

There are two broad visions of waste management. The first is the classical "end-of-pipe" strategy, consisting mainly of measures aimed at controlling the impact of the waste already generated on the environment. This strategy focuses necessarily on the disposal phase (landfilling, incineration) and does not affect the generation of waste. The second vision is based on the full recognition of the close inter-relationship between waste management and product policy. Wastes are products, in the sense that any goods manufactured one day will become waste. Therefore, preventing or reducing the impact of waste on the environment means focusing on what is produced and put on the market. This vision attempts to build on the concept of sustainability. Many of the problems discussed in this article are the result of the equivalence between products and waste. The extended producer responsibility principle is the consequence of political society becoming gradually aware of this equivalence and reacting accordingly.

The success of a legislative measure in the field of waste, in terms of compliance by the actors concerned as well as environmental results, also depends greatly on the recognition of the integration of waste management and industrial policy. Also, the essence of the impact of any waste management measure on the internal market lies in this integration.

In parallel with the strategies of Member States, the EC is also moving in this direction. The Proposal on ELVs is an example of (future) waste management legislation which integrates the end-of-pipe dimension with industrial policy considerations. Regulating the impact of waste vehicles on the environment means focusing at the same time on the choice of materials, design of vehicles and on the organization and control of the collection, recovery, and disposal phases. Therefore, several complex legal, technical, economic, and political elements underpin a proposal of this kind.

Like any other proposal, it is probable that the ELV Proposal will undergo a number of changes (by the Council and the European Parliament) before it becomes law. But, regardless of these changes, the principle of fully integrating waste management into industrial policy will remain. In this sense, this Proposal could be a model for regulating other waste streams (such as electrical and electronic goods) or for orienting the future modifications of existing legislation (such as the Directive on Packaging and Packaging Waste).

The Environmental Guarantee After Amsterdam: Does The Emperor Have New Clothes?

HANNA SEVENSTER*

I. Introduction

This article examines the amendments to the former Article 100a EC agreed at the 1997 Intergovernmental Conference (IGC) by the fifteen Member States of the EU in the so-called Treaty of Amsterdam. The former Article 100a EC, inserted into the EC Treaty by the Single European Act (1987), contained a paragraph (4) permitting Member States, under certain conditions, to apply more stringent national provisions after adoption of a European harmonization measure.[1]

The possibility of derogation after harmonization is considered very important in the environmental sphere. It was introduced at the insistence of the Danish government with a view specifically to environmental imperatives, and it is hence popularly referred to as the "environmental guarantee". Not only do environmental conditions within the European Union differ widely, necessitating discrimination between national environmental laws, the same must be presumed to apply to the relative importance which individual Member States attach to environmental objectives *vis-à-vis*, in particular, economic goals.[2] Whilst EC environmental policy has paid lip-service to these concerns in policy documents,[3] secondary legislation, and the EC

---

* Professor of European Environmental Law, Centre of Environmental Law, University of Amsterdam, attorney admitted to the Dutch Bar for De Brauw Blackstone Westbroek Linklaters & Alliance, The Hague.

[1] It has rightly been pointed out that Art. 95(4)(g) (formerly Art. 100a(4)) EC is not to be applied where a harmonization measure does not apply or when the harmonization measure itself pursues minimum harmonization or allows for other possibilities for derogation. Cf Case C–127/97, *Burstein* v. *Freistaat Bayern (Burstein)* [1998] ECR I–6005, in which a preliminary reference was made about the application of Art. 100a(4) EC. The ECJ, however, concluded that the national legislation in question was not covered by the Directive concerned, thereby rendering further treatment of Art. 100a(4) EC superfluous. Cf A. Middeke, "Nationale Alleingänge, in H-W. Rengeling, *Handbuch zum europäischen und deutschen Umweltrecht* (Cologne–Berlin–Bonn–Munich: Carl Heymanns Verlag KG, 1998), 954.

[2] On the wider issue of the desirability of "federal" (EU) regulation of the environment see the challenging article by R. Revesz at p. 1 of this volume.

[3] See, e.g., Resolution 93/C138/01 of the Council and the Representatives of the Governments of the Member States, meeting within the Council of 1 Feb. 1993 on a Community programme of policy and action in relation to the environment and sustainable development (Fifth Environmental Action Programme) [1993] OJ C287/27.

Treaty,[4] the realities of the internal market in practice severely constrain any potential for national variations on a Communitarian theme.[5] Thus, although evidence of a more sympathetic attitude towards the notion of flexibility in environmental regulation may be found in particular in recent secondary environmental law harmonizing processes,[6] the scope for national variety in product regulation remains much more contentious. Yet, with the prospect of an ever increasing number of Member States with environmental protection relatively low on their political agenda adopting legislation by a qualified majority, and notwithstanding an explicit Treaty commitment that the Community is to pursue "high" levels of environmental protection,[7] the case for Member State autonomy in choosing to apply or introduce more stringent environmental (product) standards after harmonization appears more compelling than ever before. It is against this background that the ensuing detailed analysis of the degree of discretion left to Member States in the context of Article 95 EC should be appreciated.

Despite the considerable body of literature dedicated to the environmental guarantee, the conditions for its application are still contentious and may remain so. It has been unclear, in particular, whether this provision could only be invoked to justify national legislation that was already in existence before a directive was adopted, or could also justify legislation adopted subsequent to the harmonization measure. Nor was it clear whether it was necessary for the Member State in question to have voted against the harmonization measure for it to invoke Article 100a(4) EC.

The Treaty of Amsterdam has introduced amendments and additions to the former Article 100a, now numbered Article 95 EC. First of all, Article 95(4)–(9) explicitly creates scope for introducing new measures following harmonization. It also includes common conditions governing the application of the provisions to existing and new measures, e.g. with regard to the examination of the legislation by the European Commission.

This contribution aims to analyse the significance of the new provisions from the perspective of the national environmental legislature, both in isolation and in relation to the former Article 100a(4) EC. At first glance, the scope for derogation contained in Article 95 EC seems to be more generous than that under the former Article 100a EC.[8] A closer look, however, reveals that the provision (although removing some of the presumed restrictions and uncertainties) imposes additional conditions to the application of the derogation as well.

For the purpose of this analysis, this contribution will first briefly outline the situation regarding the former Article 100a(4) EC, which will serve as an inter-

---

[4] In particular Arts. 5 (formerly Art. 3b) EC and 174 (formerly Art. 130r) EC.

[5] See the Commission Communication Concerning Single Market and Environment of 9 June 1999, COM(99)263 final.

[6] An illustrative case study is provided by J. Scott at p. 37 of this volume.

[7] Arts. 95(3) (formerly Art. 100a(3)) EC and 174(2) (formerly Art. 130r(2)) EC.

[8] Cf S. Langrish, "The Treaty of Amsterdam: Selected Highlights" (1998) 23 *European Law Review* 3.

pretative guide to Article 95 EC.[9] This will be followed, in section III, by a detailed analysis of the various individual paragraphs in Article 95 EC, on the basis of which conclusions will be explicated in section IV.

II. The Former Article 100a(4) EC

Article 100a(4) EC read as follows:

If, after the adoption of a harmonisation measure by the Council acting by a qualified majority, a Member State deems it necessary to apply national provisions on grounds of major needs referred to in Article 36, or relating to protection of the environment or the working environment, it shall notify the Commission of these provisions. The Commission shall confirm the provisions involved after having verified that they are not a means of arbitrary discrimination or a disguised restriction on trade between Member States.

By way of derogation from the procedure laid down in Articles 169 and 170, the Commission or any Member State may bring the matter directly before the Court of Justice if it considers that another Member State is making improper use of the powers provided for in this Article.

Since its inclusion in the EC Treaty in 1987, Article 100a(4) EC has given rise to a good deal of debate,[10] owing mainly to the fact that the system provided for (derogation after harmonization based on a Treaty Article) did not fit the established case law of the Court of Justice. According to this settled case law, once harmonization has taken place, there are no other ways of derogating from the harmonization measure (directive or regulation) other than those included in the measure itself.[11] The proper application and interpretation of the provision (a narrow one, in the view of many commentators) is therefore considered extremely important for the unity and cohesion of European law.

Paradoxically, the provision has been applied rarely in practice.[12] So far, the Commission has issued two decisions on specific cases, both in relation to Directive 91/173/EEC (the PCP-Directive).[13] It should be noted, however, that

[9] For more details, the reader is referred to the extensive body of literature concerning Art. 100a(4) EC, incorporated in the notes below.

[10] Cf C. D. Ehlermann, "The Internal Market following the Single European Act" (1987) 24 *Common Market Law Review* 361; L. Krämer, "The Single European Act and Environmental Protection: Reflections on Several New Provisions in Community Law" (1987) 24 *Common Market Law Review* 659; B. Langeheine, "Rechtsangleichung under Artikel 100a EWGV: Harmonisierung vs national Schutzinteressen" [1989] *Europarecht* 235; C. Gulmann, "The Single European Act—Some Remarks from a Danish Perspective" (1987) 24 *Common Market Law Review* 31; J. Flynn, "How will Art. 100a(4) EC Work? A Comparison to Art. 93" (1987) 24 *Common Market Law Review* 689; P. Pescatore, "Some Critical Remarks on the 'Single European Act'" (1987) 24 *Common Market Law Review* 9; J. H. Jans, *European Environmental Law* (The Hague–Boston, Mass.–London: Kluwer Law International, 1995), 106; Middeke, n. 1 above, 954; H. G. Sevenster, *Milieubeleid en Gemeenschapsrecht* (Deventer: Kluwer, 1992), 242.

[11] See, e.g., Case C-1/96, *The Queen* v. *Minister for Agriculture, Fisheries and Food, ex parte Compassion in World Farming Ltd.* (*Compassion*) [1998] ECR I–1251.

[12] Cf R. Barents, "Het Verdrag van Amsterdam en het Europees Gemeenschapsrecht" (1997) 45 *Sociaal Economische Wetgeving* 351.

[13] See n. 22 below.

several[14] other requests for application of Article 100a(4) EC have been made by Member States, which have so far not been dealt with by the Commission.[15] The German PCP case provided the Court of Justice with an opportunity to shed light on the provision in a procedure under Article 230 (formerly Article 173) EC.[16] In the recent *Kortas* case the ECJ gave its second ruling in a preliminary reference which, however, did not answer all the questions about the derogation clause.[17] Yet, not only does Article 95(4) EC not remove these uncertainties, it even introduces new ones.[18] For example, it is not clear whether Article 100(a)(4) EC could be invoked by a Member State which voted in favour of the Community measure.[19] Similar ambiguities arise if the harmonization measure is a Commission act rather than a Council measure. Crucial, too, is the question whether it can be invoked to justify national provisions brought in after the adoption of the harmonization measure, or only if national law is already in force at that time.[20] The nature of the procedure for notification and "confirmation" by the Commission, the time limits for notification and for the Commission's decision, and, more specifically, whether the national measure may be applied before the Commission has approved it are far from clear. Of vital importance, too, is the question whether the national measure must be non-discriminatory and proportionate. Although of crucial significance, the literature remains divided on these questions.[21]

A.   CASE LAW

Since coming into force in 1987, Article 100a(4) EC has been applied twice. Both cases related to Directive 91/173/EEC Amending for the Ninth Time Directive 76/769/EEC on the Approximation of the Laws, Regulations, and

[14] According to Dutch government officials, 10 requests in total have been submitted.

[15] See also Case C–319/97, *Antoine Kortas*, of 1 June 1999, not yet reported.

[16] Case C–41/93, *French Republic* v. *Commission* [1994] ECR I–1829.

[17] *Kortas*, n. 15 above.

[18] Cf Jans, n. 10 above, 167. One question which is not considered here is whether the term "confirm" means that the Commission can only approve the measure or whether it can also reject it: nobody has seriously called this latter power into question. Moreover, the Court made this clear in Case C–41/93 (n. 16 above) commented on, *inter alia*, by R. Hayder (1994) 5 *Europäische Zeitschrift für Wirtschaftsrecht* 407; H. Somsen (1994) 3 *European Environmental Law Review* 238; J. Schnutenhaus, (1994) 13 *Neue Zeitschrift für Verwaltungsrecht* 875; S. Breier, (1994) 10 *Zeitschrift für Umwelrecht* 249; K. J. M. Mortelmans (1994) 42 *Sociaal Economische Wetgeving* 823; N. Reich, (1994) 47 *Neue Juristische Wochenschrift* 3334.

[19] This question arises partly because the provision explicitly referred to "acting by a qualified majority". It has been answered in the negative by G. van Calster and K. Deketelaere, "Amsterdam, the IGC and the EU Treaty" (1998) 7 *European Environmental Law Review* 12; see also Jans, n. 10 above, 110; and Middeke, n. 1 above, 961–2.

[20] In contrast to Art. 176 (formerly Art. 130t) EC, which refers to "maintaining or introducing" measures, Art. 100a EC refers only to "apply[ing]". It is thus unclear what is meant is both maintaining existing measures and introducing new measures, or only the former. See Jans, n. 10 above, 109. This question is often—although not predominantly—answered in the negative. It should be noted that the writers in favour of the inclusion of new measures are mainly German (and Danish) who, undeniably, have a tendency towards a broad, "environment-friendly" interpretation.

[21] See the debate initiated by the writers mentioned in n. 10 above. Only the last question is answered in the affirmative by most commentators.

Administrative Provisions of the Member States relating to Restrictions on the Marketing and Use of Certain Dangerous Substances and Preparations (PCP Directive).[22] The countries concerned were Germany and Denmark[23] and in both cases the Commission accepted their plea and in the process shed light on some of the above questions.

France appealed to the Court of Justice against the original decision in the German case,[24] but the Court confined itself to formal aspects, as it considered that the Commission's decision did not satisfy the requirement to state reasons under Article 253 (formerly Article 190) EC. The Court therefore quashed the first German decision on procedural grounds and did not deal with any of the substantive aspects. No appeal was lodged against the second German decision (for which the Commission gave more detailed reasons) or the Danish decision.

In *Kortas*, the ECJ was provided with an opportunity to clarify the status of national legislation after notification to the Commission but prior to its approval. Commission decisions on the requests still pending and appeals to the ECJ may take away some further uncertainties. However, it appears unlikely that the ECJ will be in a position to rule on the issue of new national measures after harmonization under the former Article 100a(4) EC because all requests pending concern legislation already in existence before the adoption of the harmonization measure.[25] In the remainder of this section, attention will be afforded to these cases with a view to clarifying some of the more contentious issues.

i.   *The European Commission: The PCP Decisions*

Both requests for application of the former Article 100a(4) EC related to derogations from the PCP Directive, a so-called "daughter" directive of the Framework Directive 76/769/EEC on Dangerous Substances. The PCP Directive lays down a general ban on trade in PCPs, with four exceptions. Since the Directive pursues total harmonization, these exceptions are compulsory and legislation that does not incorporate these derogations contravenes the system laid down by the Directive. Germany invoked Article 100a(4) EC because German legislation did not authorize exemptions to the ban and hence was more stringent than the Directive. The Commission's first decision for which insufficient reasons were given was annulled by the ECJ, and it was followed by the second PCP decision, which reflects the Commission's views on certain questions. The Commission explicitly noted that Germany had voted against the PCP Directive and that the German provision was already in existence when the PCP Directive was adopted. The Commission also observed that notification took place on 2 August 1991, whereas the Directive dated from 21 March 1991 and had to be implemented by 1 July 1992.

---

[22] [1991] OJ L085/34.

[23] See Decision in *PCP-Germany I* [1992] OJ L334/8; Decision 94/783/EC, *PCP-Germany II* [1994] OJ L316/43; and Decision 96/211/EC, *PCP-Denmark* [1996] OJ L68/32.

[24] Case C–41/93, n. 16 above.   [25] According to Dutch government sources.

Finally, the Commission examined in detail whether the measure was non-discriminatory and did not involve disguised protectionism; it gauged the proportionality of the measure, however, from the seriousness of the PCP problem in Germany.

It may be deduced that the Commission regarded these circumstances as a condition for the application of the former Article 100a(4) EC. It also follows that the Commission deemed the German derogation from the Directive to be justified by the fact that PCPs pose problems to health and the environment specific to Germany due to its high population density, degree of industrialization, and local (climatological) factors. Thus, the Commission argued that Germany's derogation from the Directive was necessary and proportional.

The third decision related to Denmark's policy on PCPs.[26] The Commission noted that the Danish measure existed before the Directive was adopted, that Denmark had voted against the Directive and had a specific problem with PCPs, and that the legislation was non-discriminatory and did not involve disguised protectionism. This seems to confirm that the Commission regards these circumstances as conditions for applying Article 100a(4) EC. The Commission justified the Danish derogation (i.e. its proportionality) by the fact that ground water is the main source of drinking water in Denmark, PCPs are not readily absorbed by the alkaline soil, and that they break down slowly because of low temperatures. On the question of dioxin pollution, the Commission referred to the German decision (the need to protect certain at-risk sections of the population). Thus, rather than examining in detail whether the more stringent measures are proportional to the environmental and health hazards in question, it appears that the Commission considers whether a specific environmental and health problem actually exists. If the answer is in the affirmative, it concludes that a more stringent policy is justified.

ii.   *The Court of Justice: The* PCP *judgment and the* Kortas *case*

As noted, the Court did not rule on any of the substantive aspects of France's appeal against the approval of the German legislation. However, on the notification procedure, the Court ruled that it follows from Article 100a(4) EC that Member States may not apply their legislation until the Commission has approved it.[27] According to the Court, therefore, there is a "standstill period" during which the legislation under examination may not be applied. The Court did not substantiate its ruling, which is remarkable given that Article 100a(4) EC itself does not contain an explicit standstill requirement. However,

---

[26] This Decision raises some questions on the Commission's statement that the national provisions are in fact to be considered more stringent. The Commission argues that although Danish law provides for more exemptions from the PCP ban than the Directive, such exemptions are never granted in practice. Thus the Danish legislation is "more restrictive" than the Directive. This interpretation is in conflict with the case law of the ECJ on implementation. See, e.g., Case C–339/87, *Commission* v. *The Netherlands* [1990] ECR I–851, in which the ECJ ruled that the fact that conflicting national provisions are not implemented in practice cannot justify the incorrect formal implementation of a directive.

[27] Ground 30 of the judgment.

the ECJ added that non-application is obligatory only after expiry of the deadline for implementation, since prior to that date no Member State is obliged to bring its legislation into line with a directive.[28]

In *Kortas*, the ECJ was more explicit and elaborate on this issue. The case concerned a preliminary reference from a Swedish penal court concerning Swedish legislation banning certain food additives from sweets because of alleged health risks. Although the relevant EC Directive[29] allows the additive concerned in sweets, Mr Kortas was facing criminal charges following sales of sweets, before expiry of the implementation period, containing the additive. He was prosecuted, however, after the deadline for implementation had expired. In the event of changes in the legislation, Swedish criminal law prescribes application of the less stringent law. Swedish authorities had notified their legislation under Article 100a(4) EC, following an unsuccessful attempt to negotiate a derogation during the accession negotiations. At the time of the ECJ judgment, the Commission had not yet decided the application. Therefore, the Swedish court asked the ECJ whether, after expiry of the implementation period, national or EC law had to be applied. Advocate General Saggio, drawing parallels with the procedure under Article 88 (formerly Article 93) EC and the *PCP* judgment, opined that in the absence of Commission approval, the Directive will indeed be directly effective as from the date of implementation.[30] Insensitive to the argument of the Swedish government that the Commission had forgone its rights to decide the case because of the unreasonable delay, the Advocate General referred to the procedures of Articles 232, 242, and 243 (formerly Articles 175, 185, and 186) EC enabling Member States to request a Court ruling against the Commission, compelling it to act. The Court followed the Advocate General, and ruled that the Directive was directly effective after expiry of the implementation period. Unlike the Advocate General, the ECJ did not refer to Article 88 EC, but merely to its *PCP* judgment. In respect of the arguments concerning the time limits for the Commission, the ECJ clearly stated that Article 100a(4) EC, unlike its Amsterdam successor, Article 95 EC, does not contain such time limits. The Swedish government was thus left with legislation which, at least until approval by the Commission, was invalid.

Interestingly, the French government argued in *Kortas* that Sweden could not invoke the derogation at all, because at the time of the adoption of the Directive concerned it had yet to join the Community.[31] This argument seems to rest on the premise that Member States must vote against the harmonization measure in order to be able to invoke the environmental guarantee. The Court rejected this reasoning, simply stating that nothing in the wording of Article 100a(4) EC suggests that Member States who joined the Community

---

[28] The Commission observed in the Danish *PCP* decision (point 5) that reliance on Art. 100a(4) EC is in effect a request to apply the offending national legislation after the time limit for implementation has expired.

[29] Dir. 94/36/EC on colours for use in foodstuffs [1994] OJ L237/13.

[30] Opinion of 28 Jan. 1999; cf also his opinion in *Burstein*, n. 1 above.

[31] *Kortas*, n. 15 above, para. 18.

after the adoption of a Directive may not invoke the derogation with regard to that Directive.[32] This would seem to suggest that reliance on the clause is not dependent on any voting requirement. Yet, the ruling must be read in its context, and its relevance may be limited to the specific situation of a Member State having joined the EC after adoption of a directive from which derogation is sought. *Kortas* hence does not definitively tackle the issue of voting requirements.

III.   The Present Article 95 EC

Article 95 (4)–(9) EC reads as follows:[33]

4. If, after the adoption by the Council or by the Commission of a harmonisation measure, a Member State deems it necessary to maintain national provisions on grounds of major needs referred to in Article 30, or relating to the protection of the environment or the working environment, it shall notify the Commission of these provisions as well as the grounds for maintaining them.

5. Moreover, without prejudice to paragraph 4, if, after the adoption by the Council or by the Commission of a harmonisation measure, a Member State deems it necessary to introduce national provisions based on new scientific evidence relating to the protection of the environment or the working environment on grounds of a problem specific to that Member State arising after the adoption of the harmonisation measure, it shall notify the Commission of the envisaged provisions as well as the grounds for introducing them.

6. The Commission shall, within six months of the notifications as referred to in paragraphs 4 and 5, approve or reject the national provisions involved after having verified whether or not they are a means of arbitrary discrimination or a disguised restriction on trade between Member States and whether or not they shall constitute an obstacle to the functioning of the internal market.

In the absence of a decision by the Commission within this period the national provisions referred to in paragraphs 4 and 5 shall be deemed to have been approved.

When justified by the complexity of the matter and in the absence of danger for human health, the Commission may notify the Member State concerned that the period referred to in this paragraph may be extended for a further period of up to six months.

7. When, pursuant to paragraph 6, a Member State is authorised to maintain or introduce national provisions derogating from a harmonisation measure, the Commission shall immediately examine whether to propose an adaptation to that measure.

8. When a Member State raises a specific problem on public health in a field which has been the subject of prior harmonisation measures, it shall bring it to the attention of the Commission which shall immediately examine whether to propose appropriate measures to the Council.

---

[32] *Kortas*, n. 15 above, para. 19.
[33] Consolidated text based on the Treaty of Amsterdam as signed by the Heads of State of the Member States on 2 Oct. 1997 [1997] OJ C340/145.

9. By way of derogation from the procedure laid down in Articles 226 and 227, the Commission or any Member State may bring the matter directly before the Court of Justice if it considers that another Member State is making improper use of the powers provided for in this Article.[34]

As a general starting point for our analysis of Article 95 EC, we assume that the changes introduced by Amsterdam in the area of environmental protection were generally intended to strengthen Community (and national) environmental policy. This may be deduced from the inclusion of the objective of "sustainable development" in Article 2 EC and the elevation of the principle of integration from the Environment Title to the new Article 6 EC. Additional indications may be found in the strengthening of environmental decision-making in the new Article 175 EC (co-decision procedure),[35] and the amended paragraph 3 of Article 95 EC. The latter stipulates that the Commission shall take as a base in its harmonization proposals in the environmental sphere a high level of protection, "taking account in particular of any new development based on scientific facts. Within their respective powers, the European Parliament and the Council will also seek to achieve this objective." Although the first of these additions in particular remains somewhat ambiguous, it may be assumed that the additions are designed to add further weight to environmental imperatives.[36] Whilst a "green" interpretation of Article 95 EC thus seems appropriate, obviously a proper balance between the ecological goals and the other goals of the Community, notably the establishment of the internal market, needs to be maintained.

A.   EXISTING NATIONAL MEASURES: ARTICLE 95(4) EC

Paragraph 4 differs in important respects from the former Article 100a(4) EC. First, it unambiguously states that it is permissible to derogate from harmonization measures introduced by the Commission. The qualification, "acting by a qualified majority", has been removed, so that "voting against" no longer appears to be required in the case of measures introduced by the Council.[37] Finally, the word "apply" has been changed to "maintain" analogous to Article

---

[34] This paragraph will not be discussed further here, since no changes were made in relation to the last sentence of the former Art. 100a(4) EC.

[35] It is generally felt that the European Parliament is the "greenest" institution, so that more influence by the Parliament is likewise generally thought to enhance environmental protection within the Community.

[36] Given the precautionary principle in Art. 174(2) (formerly Art. 130r(2)) EC, which also applies to Art. 95 EC by way of the integration principle (new Art. 6 EC). Cf also S. Bär and R. A. Krämer, "European Environmental Policy after Amsterdam" (1998) 10 *Journal of Environmental Law* 315; see also van Calster and Deketelaere, n. 19 above, 15. Barents, however, takes a different view: Barents, n. 12 above, 353. He supports the right of the Community legislature (i.e. the Council) to put up a fight if it is forced by public opinion or the European Parliament to introduce measures based on insufficiently verified or even unfounded hypotheses. Examples are the issues of synthetic hormones in meat and the patenting of biotechnological inventions.

[37] Cf van Calster and Deketelaere, n. 19 above, 17.

176 (formerly Article 130t) EC, putting it beyond doubt that paragraph (4) applies only to existing measures.[38]

The combined effect of these changes and clarifications is to increase the degree of discretion of national legislators.[39] The most important change is the removal of the qualification "qualified majority". This suggested that derogation from a measure adopted unanimously was not permitted,[40] forcing a Member State to vote against the measure so as to be able to invoke Article 100a(4) EC, an interpretation further supported by the premise that Article 100a(4) EC was intended to compensate for the transition to qualified majority voting. The clause was hence thought to be designed for Member States which maintained higher levels of protection than pursued by a proposed directive, the aim being to prevent outvoted Member States from having to lower their levels in order to comply with a directive.[41] However, such a "requirement to vote against" compels Member States sympathetic to a harmonization measure but which favour still higher national levels to vote against the measure, thus obstructing harmonization. As the phrase "acting by a qualified majority" has been deleted voting against is not (or no longer[42]) required.[43]

B. NEW NATIONAL MEASURES: ARTICLE 95(5) EC

The insertion of paragraph 5 has created explicit authority to justify more stringent new national provisions to protect the environment or the working environment adopted after harmonization. The phrase "[m]oreover, without prejudice to paragraph 4" is presumably intended to indicate that paragraphs (4) and (5) concern different scenarios. Although the word "moreover" may appear to suggest otherwise, teleological interpretation also points in this direction.[44]

---

[38] Further changes of minor importance are that the order of "environment" and "working environment" has been reversed (this is probably without significance) and that the text now makes clear what must be notified to the Commission; the measures and the grounds for wishing to maintain them. The latter was not entirely clear in the previous text. Logically, however, the Member State must give notification of the fact that it wishes to maintain certain measures, the reasons, and the substance of the measures.

[39] Cf Bär and Kraemer, n. 36 above, 319.   [40] See n. 19 above.

[41] Cf the Commission in *PCP-Germany I* (n. 23 above) and Case C–41/93 (n. 16 above). The same compensating function may also be advanced as an argument for restricting Art. 100a(4) EC to existing national provisions.

[42] As explained above, the ECJ has stated that a Member State having joined the EC after the adoption of a directive is not barred from invoking the former Art. 100a(4) EC: *Kortas*, n. 15 above, para. 19.

[43] See also C. W. A. Timmermans, "Het Verdrag van Amsterdam" (1997) 45 *Sociaal Economische Wetgeving* 344; and H. G. von Meijenfeldt, "Vergroening van het Verdrag van Amsterdam" (1997) 24 *Tijdschrift voor Milieu & Recht* 174. Jans further notes that the principle of estoppel could obstruct recourse by a Member State to voting against (J. H. Jans, "Environmental Protection and the Amsterdam Treaty", as yet unpublished contribution to 1997 Groningen Conference).

[44] However, it might be argued that the provisions may be applied simultaneously, in situations in which neither paragraph is strictly speaking applicable.

i. Grounds for Justification

It is striking that for new measures the scope is restricted to provisions designed to protect the environment or the working environment. The omission in paragraph 5 of Article 30 (formerly Article 36) EC is regrettable, since the grounds in Article 30 EC ("major needs") now can only be invoked in order to uphold existing provisions (paragraph (4)). Among the grounds listed in Article 30 EC, the most relevant for our purposes are "the protection of health and life of humans, animals or plants",[45] which is usually viewed as distinct from the broader notion of "protection of the environment".[46] Hence, the two classes of interest do not fully coincide, which explains why the Commission cited both the interests of environmental protection and (public) human[47] health in the Danish and German *PCP* cases. From the case law of the Court of Justice on the free movement of goods,[48] it also follows that the applicability of Article 30 EC is restricted to serious dangers to the environment (hazardous waste, dangerous substances such as pesticides, endangered species) and does not comprise environmental problems not directly posing a danger to humans, flora, and fauna (non-hazardous waste, recycling of packaging). Restrictions on trade motivated by this latter category of environmental problems may only be justified by the "rule of reason", the conditions for which are more stringent than Article 30 EC.[49] A crucial difference between the two categories is that restrictions on trade designed to protect the environment in the narrow sense of Article 30 EC may be discriminatory (although not arbitrarily so), whereas measures to protect the broader environmental interest not covered by Article 30 EC must be strictly neutral.[50]

It is curious that human (public) health is not a ground justifying new measures after harmonization,[51] as it implies that there is no room for national initiatives to counter a threat to public (human) health once harmonization has taken place. This may explain paragraph 8, which implies that in such a case the Commission may merely be asked to propose "appropriate measures". If the rationale for the omission of human health was to restrict the scope for new environmental measures to those that are absolutely necessary, it is difficult to understand why the narrower definition (reflected in the exhaustive list in Article 30 EC) was not chosen instead of the broader one. Thus, although

---

[45] The other grounds listed in Art. 30 EC are public morality, public policy, public security, the protection of the national artistic, historic, and archaeological heritage, and the protection of industrial and commercial property.

[46] See also Art. 174(1) (formerly Art. 130r(1)) EC: "Community policy on the environment shall contribute to pursuit of the following objectives: protecting human health".

[47] Barents (albeit in a different context) notes that there is a "complex distinction" between *santé humaine* and *santé publique*: Barents, n. 12 above, 356.

[48] See in particular Case C–2/90, *Wallonian Waste* [1992] ECR I–4431.

[49] See, e.g., Jans n. 15 above, 237–51.

[50] This was the background to a proposal made in the "preliminary rounds" of the IGC (but not adopted) to include the broader term "protection of the environment" in Art. 30 (formerly Art. 36) EC: see van Calster and Deketelaere, n. 19 above, 16.

[51] Cf Bär and Kraemer, n. 36 above, 323, who wonder whether the exclusion has taken place on purpose.

high priority has been afforded to environmental policy, this has been achieved at the expense of national policy on public health since, if a danger to public health does not simultaneously entail a danger to the environment, Article 95(5) EC cannot be invoked. Consider the situation where, following harmonization of health standards of a product, fresh scientific evidence indicates that a particular substance in the product is carcinogenic. Assuming the product poses no danger to the environment, the national government would not be able to take action other than notifying the Commission under paragraph 8. As already observed, it is for this reason that in both *PCP* decisions the Commission relied on grounds of both environmental protection and human health. This suggests that future cases under paragraph 5 will be harder to justify on environmental grounds only.

ii. Problems Specific to Particular Member States

If Article 95(5) EC is to be successfully invoked, the environmental problem must be specific to the Member State in question. This requirement would seem to be reflected in the Commission's current practice.[52] When it comes to justifying derogations, it is only logical that a Member State should demonstrate why its specific need requires it to depart from the Community standard. It should be emphasized, however, that Member States may desire to depart from the Community measure, simply because they are convinced that a higher level of protection is more desirable. Yet, this option now seems to be excluded by Article 95(5) EC, since a desire for a higher level of protection does not in itself constitute an environmental problem specific to a Member State.[53] Still, it appears not strictly necessary for the problem to arise exclusively in the Member State in question.[54] This is confirmed by two *PCP* decisions, in which the Commission accepted that both countries in question (Germany and Denmark) had a specific PCP problem, albeit each for its own "local" reasons.[55] It seems sufficient for the Member State invoking Article 95(5) EC to demonstrate that an individual derogation is necessary (justified), which may also apply to several other Member States faced with the same problem. Any other interpretation would lead to the absurd result that the more Member States are faced with a given problem after harmonization, the smaller the chance that their individual counter-measures will be autho-

---

[52] See von Meijenfeldt, n. 43 above, 176; and Jans, n. 43 above. Meanwhile, no Court guidance on the interpretation of the former Art. 100a(4) EC by the Commission exists on this particular issue. Given that the new Art. 95(5) EC lays down this requirement only in the case of new measures, it may be anticipated that the Court will rule that a specific problem is, *a contrario*, not required under para. (4) or under the former Art. 100a(4) EC. A parallel may be drawn with *Kortas*, n. 15 above, in which the Court argued that the express inclusion of a time limit for decisions by the Commission in the new Art. 95(6) EC indicates that Art. 100a(4) EC, *a contrario*, does not contain any time limits: para. 33 of the judgment.

[53] It may be asked, at this point, whether the precautionary principle and the principle of a high level of protection provide arguments in favour of higher national standards in the absence of a specific (environmental) problem. Given the explicit text of para. 5 and the subsequent requirement that the specific problem must have arisen after harmonization, the answer to this question should probably be in the negative.

[54] See also Bär and Kraemer, n. 36 above, 322.   [55] See Section II(A)(i) above.

rized.[56] Such an interpretation therefore must be rejected, as it is incompatible with the principle of a high level of environmental protection. This conclusion is in no way affected by the fact that the principles and objectives of Community environmental policy apply to the institutions and are not directly binding on Member States.[57] The Commission itself is required to take these principles into account when scrutinizing national provisions under Article 95(5) EC.

iii. Problems Arising after Harmonization

Article 95(5) EC requires that the specific environmental problem has arisen after adoption of the harmonization measure. This would seem to preclude the application of this paragraph to a mere change in policy[58] as well as to cases in which the Member State concerned simply considers the Community level of protection to be too low. Also evidently excluded are national provisions that reflect measures already drafted at the time of the harmonization measure, since the environmental problem in that case did not arise after harmonization. It must be assumed that, once more, in the light of the precautionary principle a common sense (i.e. not too narrow) interpretation is called for. Although, according to the Court, exceptions to general doctrines and fundamental Treaty provisions must be interpreted restrictively,[59] the *effet utile* of the provision must also be taken into account. This certainly applies to situations where provisions of different Member States that are substantively the same would be permitted in one case but not in another for purely temporal reasons.[60] It seems all the more reasonable to interpret this requirement purposively in the case of environmental problems, as the most serious threats to the environment often manifest themselves gradually.

The situation where an environmental problem is recognized before harmonization, but the necessary national provisions are not (or cannot be) adopted until afterwards also deserves consideration. A literal interpretation would not allow application of paragraph (4) (since there are no existing national provisions at the time of harmonization) or paragraph (5) (since this is a problem preceding harmonization). This certainly seems an undesirable result. In my opinion, it is conceivable that the Member State in question could notify the proposed provisions under both paragraphs (4) and (5).[61] Procedurally the requirements for new provisions (in particular the standstill period) could apply, substantively, the broader requirements of paragraph (4).

---

[56] Cf W. T. Douma, "Het Verdrag van Amsterdam en het milieu: twee stappen vooruit, een stap terug?" (1997) 24 *Tijdschrift voor Milieu & Recht* 179.

[57] Case C–379/92, *Peralta* [1994] ECR I–3453.   [58] See Barents, n. 12 above, 353–4.

[59] See, e.g., Case C–228/87, *Pretura di Torino* [1988] ECR I–5099.

[60] In effect, the same arguments against a narrow interpretation apply (to some extent) as those informing the view that the former Art. 100a(4) EC should also permit new measures. See Sevenster, n. 10 above, 254–6.

[61] I have already referred to the potential of the phrase "without prejudice to" in this respect: cf III(B) above.

iv. New Scientific Evidence

Most writers interpret this phrase in paragraph (5) as restricting the national scope for environmental measures. Not only must the measures be based on scientific data, the data must also be new. "New" in this context, read in conjunction with the remainder of paragraph (5), probably means "subsequent to harmonization". Again, a strictly literal interpretation would imply that an environmental problem that can scientifically be demonstrated already to have existed before harmonization cannot be exempted. Here again, I would argue in favour of a purposive interpretation. The requirement that the data must be new must not lead to the exclusion from paragraphs (4) and (5) of measures and scientific knowledge in progress. Indeed, it may be wondered how realistic it is to exclude "old data" since environmental problems often evolve gradually,[62] to conclude that the use of existing data rules out new measures would be incompatible with the purpose of paragraphs (4) and (5) in the light of the precautionary principle.

The English version of paragraph (5) refers to scientific "evidence". The other language versions of the new Article 95(5) EC use terms that also tilt towards "evidence" more than "proof" (*belagg, belaeg, prove, provas, novedades, gegevens, Erkentnisse, preuves*).[63] By contrast, earlier versions of the draft Treaty are said to have used the term "proof". This indicates that, indeed, proof is not required. Irrespective of the outcome of literal and historical interpretation, the requirement must in any event always be interpreted consistently with the precautionary principle.[64] This means that real "proof" (as opposed to "evidence") is not required and that it must be sufficient for the Member State to demonstrate on the basis of current scientific knowledge that there could be an environmental problem.[65] It should be recalled in this context that Article 100a(3) EC was also amended: the Commission must in its harmonization proposals take as a base a high level of protection "taking account in particular of any new development based on scientific facts". The phrase relating to scientific data hence would seem to refer to "any new developments", including those which are more speculative.[66]

In summary, it is often claimed that Article 95(5) EC has put an end to the "ambiguity" of its predecessor, Article 100a(4) EC, as regards the scope for new

[62] An illustrative example of these problems is the deterioration of the ozone layer, which probably started many years ago and on which scientific data have long been available: measures were not introduced until much later, however.

[63] See also Bär and Kraemer, n. 36 above, 322.

[64] Von Meijenfeldt, n. 43 above, 176, mentions the Rio Declaration here; see Art. 130r(2) EC. See also Douma, n. 56 above, 183.

[65] Douma refers to "acceptable indications", n. 56 above, 183.

[66] Jans therefore argues that the requirement under Art. 95(3) EC for the Commission is more stringent than the corresponding provision for measures on the basis of Art. 175 (formerly Art. 130s) EC (Jans, n. 43 above). This interpretation does not, however, necessarily follow from the text, as shown by the fact that Barents views the new formula in para. (3) as increasing the "objectivity of proposals and decision-making on the sensitive subject of . . . environmental protection". "In particular, this change places a limit on the unbridled use of the so-called 'precautionary principle'", Barents, n. 12 above, 353.

national provisions,[67] the criteria for which are now said to be "extremely strict".[68] Yet, the requirements for new measures may appear more stringent in the text than they are likely to be in practice. In particular, the requirements that the problem be specific and backed up by new scientific data cannot be interpreted as restrictively as some commentators believe, given the principles of Community environmental law. Undoubtedly, however, for reasons of economic integration, the intention was to make the criteria for new derogations stricter than those for existing measures.

C. SCRUTINY BY THE COMMISSION: ARTICLE 95(6) EC

Compared to Article 100a(4) EC, several changes have occurred in respect of the supervisory role of the Commission. First, the change from "confirm" to "approve or reject" makes it unequivocal that the Commission can also reject national provisions. However, this had already been decided by the ECJ in respect of Article 100a(4) EC.[69] Consequently, it now also provides that the Commission shall examine "whether" the provisions comply with certain requirements, and not "that" it will do so. In addition to the two previous criteria (arbitrary discrimination, disguised restriction on trade) Article 95(5) EC requires the Commission to examine whether the national provisions do not "constitute an obstacle to the functioning of the internal market", a requirement which will be examined more extensively below. Finally, in contrast to Article 100a(4) EC, the Commission is required to reach a decision within six months, or the provisions are deemed to have been approved. This is a major improvement from the perspective of national environmental legislators.[70] This six-month time limit may be extended by a maximum of a further six months if the case is complex, provided human health is not at risk (rather than any threat to the environment).[71]

The wording of paragraph (6) does not make clear whether the Commission enjoys the power to impose conditions on the Member State concerned in its (positive) decision, such as geographical restrictions or time-limits on the application of the national law. However, the explicit authority of the Commission to reject a Member State's application seems to imply such power to attach conditions.

i. *Obstacles to the Functioning of the Internal Market*

The Commission must examine whether the national provisions constitute arbitrary discrimination, a disguised restriction on trade, or an obstacle to the

---

[67] Timmermans, n. 43 above, 349; and Barents, n. 12 above, 353, noting that Art. 100a(4) EC is unclear on this point, but that the possibility is not ruled out.

[68] Timmermans, n. 43 above, 349. Barents refers to "much more stringent requirements": Barents, n. 12 above, 353.

[69] See n. 18 above. See also Middeke, n. 1 above, 972, who recognizes full competence by the Commission in this regard under the former Art. 100a(4) EC.

[70] Several writers rightly point to the fact that, e.g., the Dutch Cadmium Decree has been in abeyance since 1993 pending the Commission's decision: see, e.g., Douma, n. 56 above, 181.

[71] Cf Bär and Kraemer, n. 36 above, 325.

functioning of the internal market. The first two requirements were already contained in Article 100a(4) EC (as well as in Article 30 (formerly Article 36) EC). It is generally assumed that these requirements, based on their interpretation in the context of Article 30 EC, involve an examination of the national provision in terms of protectionism and proportionality.[72] The proportionality test revolves around the questions whether the selected measure (or measures) is commensurate with the environmental objective and whether there is a means of achieving the same environmental objective with less restrictive effects on trade. It is sometimes inferred from *Danish Bottles* that the Court regards the balancing of environmental objectives against the interest of the free movement of goods as part of the proportionality test,[73] but this interpretation is contentious.[74] In the German *PCP* case the Advocate General noted that the proportionality test is more onerous in the context of the former Article 100a(4) EC than the former Article 36 EC, "as it is not possible not to take account of the levels of protection already laid down by the harmonized measure". It would hence appear that merely demonstrating that the national provisions assure a higher level of protection provides insufficient justification.[75]

It may be wondered what this additional requirement adds to past practice. By way of a preliminary observation, it should be pointed out that any national derogation after harmonization, by definition, constitutes an "obstacle to the functioning of the internal market". Under prevailing European law "obstacle" is synonymous with "restriction to trade".[76] This is precisely why provisions are examined in terms of discrimination, protectionism, and proportionality. A literal interpretation, in any event, is of little use. It has been said that the background to this provision is a "somewhat unfortunate" attempt to incorporate an explicit proportionality requirement,[77] in which case the "new" requirement does not add anything to the previous regime, which already incorporated the proportionality test.[78] Others maintain that the requirement must be intended to add something (although precisely what is not clear), in any event making the test for national measures a tougher one.[79] Although probably superfluous, the most workable interpretation would seem to be that the condition operates as a "proportionality test".[80] It was already noted that in the two *PCP* decisions the Commission did not examine the proportionality of the

[72] See Sevenster, n. 10 above, 316–17, and Jans, n. 15 above, 245–6.

[73] Case 302/86, *Commission* v. *Denmark* [1988] ECR I–4607.

[74] See Jans, n. 15 above, 240–4.   [75] Opinion of Tesauro AG of 26 Jan. 1994, point 6.

[76] Cf the goal in Art. 3(c) EC: "an internal market characterised by the abolition, as between Member States, of obstacles to the free movement of goods, persons, services and capital". See also Case C–128/89, *Commission* v. *Italy* [1990] ECR I–3239, ground 16: Here the Court refers to "obstacles" that could result from national legislation in accordance with Art. 30 EC: i.e. even after they have been scrutinized in line with Art. 30 EC (arbitrary discrimination and disguised restrictions on trade) they remain "obstacles".

[77] Von Meijenfeldt, n. 43 above, 176.

[78] Douma argues that the requirement clarifies the two other criteria and concludes that it would have been better to omit the new requirement: Douma, n. 56 above, 183.

[79] Jans, n. 43 above; and Barents, n. 12 above, 354. See also Bär and Kraemer, n. 36 above, 39 and 326.

[80] Cf *Ibid.*, 38–9.

national legislation as such. Having accepted the specific environmental problem in the countries concerned, the Commission considered that more stringent measures were necessary and proportionate, and therefore justified. As a result of the new requirement, the Commission may have to go into more detail in its decisions on the necessity, appropriateness, and proportionality of the measure selected to address the environmental problem.

ii. The Effects of Notification

A first question surrounding the notification requirement concerns the consequences of a failure to notify national measures. It is unambiguous that, prior to notification, national measures qualifying under Article 95(4) and (5) EC may not be applied after expiry of the implementation period for the Community measure.[81] Another important question concerns the legal status of national measures that have been notified. Are we to deduce an implicit standstill obligation from the combination of notification to the Commission, the six-month time limit, and substantive examination, in the sense that national measures notified to the Commission for approval may not be applied before approval is granted?

As already noted, in the German *PCP* case the Court ruled under the former Article 100a(4) EC that, once notified, national provisions may not be applied until the Commission has approved them. This was surprising in view of its far-reaching consequences: suspension of existing legislation pending the Commission's decision, without the Commission being subject to a time limit, without the Treaty explicitly requiring such a standstill.[82] In this regard it should be borne in mind that until the implementation period has expired (normally considerably longer than six months) no Member State is required to adapt its legislation.[83]

Yet, when confirming the direct effect of the Directive from which derogation was sought in *Kortas*, the ECJ observed that Member States are only barred from applying national legislation *after* expiry of the implementation period.[84] While *Kortas* concerned existing national measures under Article 100a(4) EC, the same *a fortiori* holds true for newly introduced measures. Although new measures may not be applied after expiry of the implementation period, the question remains to what extent Member States may apply new measures *before* expiry of this period. In principle Member States enjoy complete freedom during this period and the outer-limit of this freedom is only exceeded when (legislative) measures are taken which may endanger the eventual correct and timely implementation of the Community measure.[85]

---

[81] See *Kortas*, n. 15 above, para. 28. See also Middeke, n. 1 above, 971.

[82] Unlike Art. 88(3) EC, in particular, regarding notified intentions to introduce new aid measures, and unlike, e.g., the Notification Dir., which gave rise to the ECJ's judgment in Case C–194/94, *CIA Security* [1996] ECR I–2230. In my view, the AG was therefore wrong to draw such comparison with state aids in his Opinion in *Kortas*, n. 15 above, para. 25, and *Burstein*, n. 1 above, para. 23.

[83] See Middeke, n. 1 above, 959.   [84] *Kortas*, n. 15 above, paras. 24–38.

[85] Case C–129/96, *Inter-Environnement* [1997] ECR I–741/1.

However, it seems to follow from the obligation of prior notification that Member States are indeed barred from the application of new measures in the absence of approval by the Commission, irrespective of whether the time limit for implementation has expired. Hence, in respect of the legal effects of notification of national measures to the Commission, a further distinction needs to be made here between existing and new provisions.[86] In summary, Member States (and their national courts) have to refrain from applying any national legislation that has not been notified, from applying any legislation that has been notified after expiry of the implementation period without approval by the Commission, as well as from applying new legislation before approval by the Commission, even before expiry of the implementation deadline.

D.   ARTICLE 95(7) EC

This novel provision requires the Commission, once national provisions have been approved, to examine whether the harmonization measure from which these provisions derogate needs to be adapted (or at least whether an amendment needs to be proposed). The clause has no direct impact on the discretion of national environmental legislators and is unlikely to have much significance in practice. If the provision approved concerns existing national legislation, the fact that the Member State in question applies a more stringent policy than required by the harmonization measure will have become apparent during negotiations on the harmonization measure. It therefore appears pointless for the Commission "immediately" to examine whether the harmonization measure needs to be adapted. Such action would be more appropriate in the case of new legislation, but since paragraph (5) restricts the scope for adopting new national provisions to problems specific to a particular Member State, an across-the-board amendment of the harmonization measure for all Member States will not always be appropriate.

E.   ARTICLE 95(8) EC

This new provision would seem to be a variation on paragraph (7), relating specifically to public health. As was seen, under paragraph (5), public (human) health grounds do not justify more stringent measures unless they coincide with the more general jurisprudential notion of "protection of the environment". Public health (in the narrow sense), on the other hand, is a ground listed in Article 30 EC ("the protection of health and life of humans, animals or plants"). Paragraph (8) stipulates that if a specific problem occurs in a Member State after harmonization, that state has the right to require the Commission to examine whether it should propose "appropriate measures" to the Council.[87] The wording is highly ambiguous. It is not clear, for instance, why

---

[86] In a similar vein see Barents, n. 12 above, 354, and von Meijenfeldt, n. 43 above, 176.

[87] It is striking that amendment of Commission measures is not mentioned here. This is probably due to the sloppy drafting of para. 8, rather than a deliberate omission.

the term "raises" is used (where?), or whether "appropriate measures" refers merely to adaptation of the previous harmonization measure, or to other action as well. This is all the more unsatisfactory since, unlike environmental imperatives, Member States are unable to introduce measures unilaterally for reasons of public health. It is bizarre that the environment and even the working environment should enjoy preferential status over public health. The provision is even more peculiar considering that, under paragraph (6), extension of the time limit is subject to the condition that there is no danger to human health (i.e. public health). Since this probably applies to proposed national measures (paragraph (5)), these measures could not relate to public (human) health in any event.

IV. Conclusions

This article has shown that several questions surrounding the application of the environmental guarantee have been tackled by the Amsterdam amendments, which at the same time give rise to fresh controversy.[88] This holds true for the restrictions to the derogation clause in particular. While some amendments seem to widen the scope of application of the derogation clause, thus strengthening the position of Member States, other requirements (notably those applicable to newly introduced national measures) apparently aim to narrow its scope. Especially significant is the fact that under paragraph (5) Member States will most likely not be able to introduce higher standards in the absence of a proven environmental problem, which seemed to be allowed under the former Article 100a(4) EC for existing measures.[89] Also, the limitation of the potential justification grounds to environmental protection and protection of the working environment represents a considerable restriction, compared to the former Article 100a(4) EC.

In summary, it may be concluded that from the perspective of national legislators, Amsterdam constitutes an improvement only if it is assumed that under the former provision Member States did not enjoy the power to introduce new measures. Since under the previous regime only existing national measures have been notified to the Commission, this will probably never be clarified. Even possible future Court cases about the notifications presently pending will therefore not shed any light on the issue of new measures. It remains to be seen how the notifications pending will be dealt with under the new regime. In the absence of a transitional regime, it may be expected that the Commission will have to apply the new rules with immediate effect. This means that the additional "obstacle" test will be applied, as well as the time limits of paragraph (6).

In an apparent effort to strike a balance between, *inter alia*, environmental interests and the requirements of the internal market, the IGC has drafted

[88] See also Bär and Kraemer, n. 36 above, 319–20.
[89] Although the Commission's decisions may suggest otherwise.

provisions which are certainly interesting in many respects. It will be even more interesting to see the interpretation by the ECJ of the new provisions, should Member States contest the decisions of the Commission in individual cases. The recent *Kortas* case concerning the old Article 100a(4) EC seems to suggest that the Court is hesitant to expand the environmental guarantee beyond its primary function as an exception to the rule. The Court's reluctance to broaden the scope for national environmental initiatives after harmonization may not be fully in harmony with the political tide of the day which, partly forced by impending accessions, appears more sympathetic towards incursions into the domain of the internal market for the sake of increased environmental quality in selective cases. The foregoing analysis has shown that a strictly legal approach to Article 95 EC does not necessarily result in such a conservative attitude towards Member States' reserved powers following harmonization. In numerous respects, the precautionary principle in particular could serve to tilt the balance in favour of Member States' powers to take the measures they deem most suited to serve their unique environments. Special mention, too, deserves the much-applauded principle of integration,[90] the legal significance of which was enhanced considerably by the Treaty of Amsterdam which ranked it amongst other general principles of Community law such as subsidiarity[91] and solidarity.[92] Perversely, whereas the principle of integration rests on the premise that the pursuit of the Community's environmental ambitions should not be inhibited by virtue of the fact that it takes place in contexts extraneous from environmental policy *strictu sensu*, the Court's restrictive approach towards the environmental guarantee in Article 95 EC merely serves to reinforce the old and problematic dichotomy between "internal market" and "environmental" policy. One probable consequence of this is that, in spite of the increased consistency between the decision-making procedures in Articles 95 and 175 EC, the Court is likely to continue to be faced with Member States challenging the legal basis of EC environmental legislation.

[90] Art. 6 EC.   [91] Art. 5 EC.   [92] Art. 10 EC.

The Private Enforcement of Member State Compliance with EC Environmental Law: an Unfulfilled Promise?

HAN SOMSEN*

I. Introduction

The effectiveness of Community ("direct")[1] enforcement of Member State compliance with EC environmental law pursuant to Article 226 (formerly Article 169) EC has become a matter of concern for academics,[2] environmental interest groups and also the Commission itself.[3] In view of its ongoing relationship with Member States at different stages of the policy process, the Commission will frequently not be in a position (or prepared) to draw a line in the sand. This may be so even where Member States' breaches of EC environmental law are known to be serious and persistent.[4] In addition, and irrespective of any

---

* University of Nijmegen. The author is indebted to Gavin Anderson, Joseph Fleuren and Gerard van Solinge for their comments on earlier versions of this chapter. The responsibility for any errors remains exclusively the author's.

[1] The European Court of Justice (ECJ) derives jurisdiction to enforce Member State compliance with EC environmental law from different provisions of the EC Treaty. Most importantly, it may do so on the Commission's instigation acting under Art. 226 (formerly Art. 169) EC. A similar provision, but of much lesser practical significance, is found in Art. 227 (formerly Art. 170) EC, pursuant to which Member States may bring alleged breaches of EC environmental law committed by fellow Member States to the attention of the ECJ.

[2] See in particular R. Williams, "The European Commission and the Enforcement of Environmental Law; an Invidious Position" (1995) 14 *Yearbook of European Law*, 351–99.

[3] In its 15th Annual Report on monitoring the application of Community law, the Commission concedes:

> In its scrutiny of individual cases, the Commission must analyze, from a factual and legal standpoint, problems that are very tangible and are of direct concern to the public. This can give rise to certain practical difficulties, since proper scrutiny demands detailed knowledge of the case in point, but the Commission is both geographically remote and ill-equipped to conduct investigations, having no resources to carry out inspections in the environmental field. Yet scrutiny is a vital task, because what matters most to individual citizens is that the law is effectively applied to their own particular circumstances, and because there is a danger that Community law may be formally transposed without any changes in actual behaviour to the extent required by Community rules.

COM(98) 317, [1998] OJ C250/1.

[4] Despite the secrecy surrounding the infringement procedure, occasionally cases where the Commission chooses to tolerate breaches of environmental law become public, invariably causing considerable academic and public dismay. See, e.g., P. Kuznlik, "Environmental Impact Assessment: the British Cases" (1995) 4 *European Environmental Law Review*, 336–44.

enforcement policy it may pursue,[5] the Commission is severely handicapped in its efforts to ensure Member State compliance with EC environmental law through its lack of resources and investigative powers.[6] Beyond a whistle-blowing role, individuals exert little or no influence over the crucial question whether and how any infringement procedure is subsequently to proceed.[7]

And yet, as they are single-issue players, individuals or groups of individuals are unlikely to be discouraged by any possible reverberations of their actions beyond the narrow issue that concerns them. Nor are they susceptible to political pressure emanating from Member States in the way that the Commission so clearly is. Also, their factual know-how and (financial) resourcefulness in their areas of expertise are, as a rule, far superior to those of the Commission which enjoys little or no fact-finding powers enabling it to ascertain practical breaches of EC environmental law.[8]

It is accordingly of crucial importance that, together with direct recourse, the European Court of Justice (ECJ) may be seised indirectly by individuals. Indirect enforcement occurs when a national court, in the context of national proceedings before it, submits a request for a preliminary ruling pursuant to Article 234 (formerly Article 177) EC. Such a request may concern issues of interpretation or the validity of Community environmental law. Since private actors rather than public authorities take legal action, this type of indirect enforcement in effect amounts to "private enforcement" of Member State compliance with EC environmental law.[9] For the purpose of conceptualizing private enforcement, in this chapter it will be viewed as a process set in motion by private actors acting upon principles of both Community and national law and consisting of discrete but interlocking stages designed to secure a previously agreed result in law. Borrowing the ECJ's own well-worn phrase:

---

[5] An analysis of the evolution of the Commission's priorities as regards the enforcement of Member State compliance with EC environmental law is provided by H. Somsen, "Subsidiarity and the Enforcement of EC Environmental Law", in U. Collier, J. Golub and A. Kreher (eds.), *Subsidiarity and Shared Responsibility: New Challenges for EU Environmental Policy* (Baden Baden: Nomos Verlagsgesellschaft, 1997), 57–75.

[6] See Williams, n. 2 above.

[7] The Commission communication implementing Community environmental law (COM(96)500 final) suggests measures to increase private participation in the enforcement of Member State compliance with EC environmental law. First, national procedures for receiving and examining public complaints on the application of relevant legislation should be established. In addition, the Commission argues for broader access to national courts—in connection with the application of Community environmental law—for members of the public and representative organizations.

[8] In respect of Dir. 79/409/EEC on the conservation of wild birds ([1979] OJ L103), e.g., the Royal Society for the Protection of Birds, which has 880,000 members, is a more effective force in securing compliance in the United Kingdom than the Commission could ever aspire to be. See J. Faulks and L. Rose, "Common Interest Groups and the Enforcement of European Environmental Law", in H. Somsen (ed.), *Protecting the European Environment: Enforcing EC Environmental Law*, (London: Blackstone, 1996), 195–208.

[9] See G. Betlem, "Cross-border Private Enforcement of Community Law", in J. Vervaele (ed.), *Compliance and Enforcement of European Community Law*, (The Hague–London–Boston: Kluwer, 1999), 391–418.

The vigilance of individuals concerned to protect their rights amounts to an effective supervision in addition to the supervision entrusted by Articles 169 and 170 to the diligence of the Commission and of the Member States.

One of the most widely quoted passages of the case law of the ECJ, it embodies two implied but central claims affecting the private enforcement of EC environmental law. First, Article 234 EC is construed as an instrument serving to protect individual "rights". As will be seen, however, the question whether the existence of such rights is *a conditio sine qua non* for private enforcement is as vital as it is contentious.[10] Secondly, the process of enforcing individual environmental rights at national level is perceived as a complement to Articles 226 and 227 EC. Legal literature and the case law of the ECJ[11] indeed now regard private enforcement as an established, realistic and potent alternative to direct enforcement pursuant to the infringement procedure of Article 226 EC, compensating for any of the latter's well documented shortcomings in the process.

Political scientists have only more recently turned their attention to the preliminary reference procedure, not infrequently with a specific focus on the environment. Locked in a seemingly perpetual clash of neo-functionalist,[12] inter-governmental/national[13] or transaction-based approaches to legal integration,[14] the role of the ECJ in private enforcement consistently primarily serves to support one theory at the expense of others.

Yet, notwithstanding the vigour of the opinions expressed, no attempts are undertaken to verify whether private enforcement in practice really is a significant force in securing Member State compliance with EC environmental law. Although a considerable and growing body of literature exists exploring constitutive elements of private enforcement, no holistic perspective encompassing the interaction of these elements yet exists. This contribution represents a first attempt to fill this gap. As its aim is to provide a rather more panoramic analysis of the most important variables impacting on the private enforcement of EC environmental law, it does not aspire to be exhaustive.

Since this contribution predominantly concerns the enforcement of *Member State* compliance with EC environmental law, beyond some observations of a general nature, the judicial review of Community acts will not be

---

[10] See M. Ruffert, "Rights and Remedies in European Community Law: a Comparative View", (1997) 34 *Common Market Law Review*, 307–36; S. Prechal, *Directives in European Community Law* (Oxford: Clarendon Press, 1995).

[11] Most notably Case 26/62, *Van Gend & Loos* [1963] ECR 1. The ECJ also insists that national environmental legislation implementing EC environmental directives should be of a nature as to allow private individuals to enforce it (n. 60 below).

[12] R. A. Cichowsky, "Integrating the Environment: The European Court and the Construction of Supranational Policy", (1998) 5 *Journal of European Public Policy*, 387–405.

[13] P. M. Haas, "Compliance with EU Directives: Insights from International Relations and Comparative Politics", (1998) 5 *Journal of European Public Policy* 17–37; J. Golub, "The Politics of Judicial Discretion: Rethinking the Interaction between National Courts and the European Court of Justice", (1996) 19 *West European Politics*, 360–85.

[14] A. Stone Sweet and T. L. Brunell, "The European Court and the National Courts: A Statistical Analysis of Preliminary References, 1961–95", (1998) 5 *Journal of European Public Policy*, 66–97.

analysed in any detail.[15] It will be seen that Community law (such as the nature of the preliminary ruling procedure and the doctrines of direct effect, indirect effect and non-contractual state liability) governs some of these variables. Others, however, are embedded in a national law context, albeit within the confines of increasingly pervasive minimum standards elaborated in the case law of the ECJ. Following a brief exploration of the nature of private enforcement of EC environmental law (section II), these variables will be conceptualized in the form of a "private enforcement chain" (section III). The separate links of this chain will be explored in sections IV–IX. Finally, conclusions and recommendations will be summarized in section X.

II. The Nature of Private Enforcement Pursuant to Article 234 EC

A first and vital characteristic of private enforcement pursuant to Article 234 EC is that, while it is based on an assumption of co-operation between national courts and the ECJ, at least conceptually, it also seems to presume a strict division of responsibilities between the two.[16] This division of responsibilities resides in the fact that it is the national court which, within the confines of its discretion, decides whether a reference is necessary and ultimately resolves the case for which the reference was deemed necessary. Also, at its present stage of development, Community law departs from the principle of national procedural autonomy.[17]

The ECJ's responsibility in the process is limited to pronouncing on the interpretation or validity of any Community provision at stake. Most important, the private enforcement process does not allow the ECJ to rule on the conformity of national law with provisions of EC environmental law, which is a conclusion only the national court may reach. Simply put, and presuming that alleged breaches of EC environmental law are put before national courts, the effectiveness of the procedure depends on national courts' preparedness to refer questions to the ECJ and subsequently faithfully to apply its rulings.

---

[15] For recent developments as regards the use of Art. 230 EC in the sphere of the environment, see the contribution of A. Ward at p. 137.

[16] Case 6/64, *Costa ENEL* [1964] ECR 585; Case 244/80, *Foglia* v. *Novello* [1981] ECR 3045.

[17] See, e.g., D. Curtin, "The Decentralized Enforcement of Community Law Rights. Judicial Snakes and Ladders", in D. Curtin and D. O'Keeffe (eds.), *Consitutional Adjudication in European Community and National Law: Essays for the Honourable Mr. Justice T.F.O. Higgins*, (London: Butterworths, 1992); D. Curtin and T. Heukels (eds.), *International Dynamics of European Integration: Liber Amicorum for Henry G. Schermers*, (Dordrecht: Martinus Nijhoff, 1994); C. M. H. Himsworth, "Things Fall Apart: The Harmonisation of Community Judicial Procedural Protection Revisited", (1997) 22 European Law Review, 291–311; M. Hoskins, "Tilting the Balance: Supremacy and National Procedural Rules" (1996) 21 *European Law Review*, 365–77; C. N. Kakouris, "Do the Member States Possess Judicial Procedural 'Autonomy'?" (1997) 34 *Common Market Law Review*, 1389–1412; S. Prechal, "Community Law in National Courts: The Lessons from *Van Schijndel*" (1998) 35 *Common Market Law Review*, 681–706; M. Ruffert, "Rights and Remedies in European Community Law: A Comparative View", (1997) 34 *Common Market Law Review*, 307–36; E. Szyszczak and J. Delicostopolous, "Intrusions into National Procedural Autonomy: The French Paradigm" (1997) 22 *European Law Review*, 141–9.

Because the spirit of co-operation is so vital for the success of the private enforcement process, the ECJ in practice is determined to avoid transgressing into spheres of competence reserved to national courts, if necessary by declining jurisdiction. The relationship between national courts and the ECJ in this context is therefore intended to be predominantly horizontal/equal rather than vertical/hierarchical, a model which, however, has become increasingly strained.[18]

Compared to Article 226 EC, pursuant to which the ECJ can pronounce directly on the compatibility of national law with EC environmental law, the effectiveness of private enforcement pursuant to Article 234 EC is dependent on the co-operation of both individuals and national courts. However, rather than having played a subordinate role, in general terms it is correct to say that the landmark cases clarifying the relationship between national and EC law, almost without exception, arose out of preliminary references, in turn more often than not submitted by lower and intermediate national courts.[19] In many areas of Community law, such as the free movement of goods and equal treatment, compliance has been secured more as a result of private enforcement in lower and intermediate courts than the diligence of the Commission in its use of the infringement procedure of Article 226 EC.

This key role occupied by lower national courts may appear striking. However, for lower national courts the preliminary reference probably is not merely a tool to guide them in their application of Community environmental law. Rather, it represents a sometimes irresistible escape from the rigid hierarchy imposed upon them by national constitutional law, introducing added prestige and innovation into their daily routines. Because in many legal systems the power to invalidate national laws is strictly reserved to constitutional courts, the prospect of setting aside provisions of national law must surely at times be an attractive one for the solitary judge struggling with provincial tedium in, say, the *Uudenmaan Lääninoikeu*r in Finland.[20] Against this background, the disproportionate share of preliminary references originating from lower or medium-ranked courts becomes more understandable.

The preliminary procedure has become by far the most important tool for the ECJ's judicial activism, which of course explains political scientists' interest in the procedure. Indeed, the infringement procedure does not fulfil this function to the same extent. This difference is explained in part by the nature of Article 234 EC itself which, at least in theory, compels the ECJ to limit itself to abstract issues of interpretation. In the context of the infringement procedure, on the other hand, it is the sole and final arbiter in concrete disputes, and hence less likely to stray into general constitutional issues.

---

[18] P. Craig and G. de Búrca, *EU Law*, 2nd edn. (Oxford: Oxford University Press, 1998), 407.

[19] For comprehensive statistics regarding various aspects of the preliminary reference procedure see Stone Sweet and Brunell, n. 14 above.

[20] This is the Uusiman Provincial Administrative Court, which recently referred a question in Case C–213/96, *Outokumpu Oy* [1998] ECR I–1777.

Also, by enlisting national courts as "agents" which ultimately pronounce on the compatibility of national law with EC law and hence identifying with individuals in a given dispute, rather than the Commission, the ECJ has been able to divert attention from its judicial activism. Compared with the confrontational infringement procedure, which culminates in a clash of titans between Member States and the Community, when the ECJ acts under the guise of private enforcement it does so as the protector of individual rights and is therefore politically correct rather than politically engaged. It also appears likely that, once assured of the co-operation of national courts which of their own accord have brought a matter to the attention of the ECJ, there exists a momentum in favour of compliance.[21]

However, notwithstanding the merits of private enforcement, this should not obscure the fact that, unlike Article 226 EC, which has as its clear and sole objective to secure Member State compliance with Community law, the rationale behind Article 234 EC is not solely or even primarily to secure Member State compliance. Rather, its aim first and foremost is to ensure the uniform and coherent interpretation throughout the fifteen Member States. In a system where both "supreme"[22] and subordinate courts must apply and interpret common rules, such a mechanism clearly is indispensable.[23] In this respect, it must be remembered that it is Member States that are to implement and enforce EC environmental law and that national courts therefore simultaneously serve as Community courts. Against implementing measures taken at national level, individuals must turn to the competent national courts, which for this purpose interpret and apply the relevant Community provisions.[24] Article 234 EC primarily serves to guarantee the uniformity and

---

[21] Weiler refers to "compliance pull" in this context. See J. H. H. Weiler, "Journey to an Unknown Destination: A Retrospective and Prospective of the European Court of Justice in the Arena of Political Integration", (1993) 31 *Journal of Common Market Studies* 417–46 at 422.

[22] Art. 234 EC does not presume any hierarchy between the ECJ and national courts. However, a *de iure* hierarchy exists as regards the final authority to interpret Community law, which resides with the ECJ. Recent developments also point in the direction of a hierarchy, in that rulings by the ECJ under Art. 234 EC are increasingly producing *de facto erga omnes* effects.

[23] For a comparison with the system of US Supreme Court review of state court judgments (where a similar problem of concurrent jurisdiction exists) see J. C. Cohen, "The European Preliminary Reference and U.S. Supreme Court Review of State Court Judgments: A Study in Comparative Judicial Federalism", (1996) XLIV *The American Journal of Comparative Law*, 421–61.

[24] An interesting situation recently arose in Case CN–321/95, *Stichting Greenpeace* v. *Commission* [1988] I–1651. This was an appeal against an order of the CFI in Case T–585/93, *Greenpeace and Others* v. *Commission* [1995] ECR II–205. The applicants, which sought annulment of a decision of the Commission to release structural funds under Reg. (EC) No. 2052/88 to construct power stations in the Canary Islands, failed as a result of the restrictive criteria relating to access under Art. 230 EC. The ECJ notes, however, that the individuals could challenge the fact that no environmental impact assessment had been carried out in respect of the project in Spanish courts. Hence, implementation of the principle that any decisions by virtue of Reg. (EC) No. 2052/88 must be "in keeping with the provisions of the Treaties, with the instruments adopted pursuant thereto and with Community policies, including those concerning environmental protection" is *de facto* to be realized by the national authorities which are to carry out the assessment. (Council Reg. (EC) No 2052/88 on the tasks of the structural funds and their effectiveness and on coordination of their activities between themselves and with the operations of the EIB and the other existing financial instruments, [1988] OJ L185/9.)

consistency of this process. The ECJ has emphasized that the uniform interpretation of Community law is a fundamental principle of Community law,
which must not be undermined by provisions of national law, irrespective of
their status.[25]

However, the mere fact that EC environmental law is interpreted uniformly
and consistently is no guarantee for uniform and coherent compliance. It is
the national courts which are to secure *de facto* compliance, in which they are
aided by authoritative interpretations delivered by the ECJ. It is true that a ruling pursuant to Article 226 EC by itself does not secure compliance either,
since that judgment itself needs to be complied with. However, at the very least
it can be said that what will be termed "the private enforcement chain" is a
longer one (as it involves the co-operation of national courts), increasing the
potential for disorientation and what will be termed "enforcement leakage".

As was pointed out in section I, the private enforcement of EC environmental law appears to depend on the empowerment of individuals to uphold their
rights. Private enforcement of EC environmental law therefore cannot be
properly understood with a mere reference to Article 234 EC. Rather, it
acquires significance and meaning by virtue of the doctrines of supremacy,
direct effect, indirect effect and non-contractual state liability, which the ECJ
has enunciated in a long line of case law, in turn made possible by the preliminary ruling procedure. It is this interplay between the preliminary reference
and the doctrines of direct effect, supremacy, indirect and non-contractual
state liability which allows national courts, in response to individuals seeking
to uphold their environmental rights, to review Member State compliance
with provisions of EC environmental law. Whereas the primary function of
Article 234 EC is to secure uniform interpretation of EC law, a secondary function is to serve as a vehicle affording individuals judicial protection. If the preliminary ruling procedure is the engine of this vehicle, the doctrines of
supremacy, direct effect, indirect effect and non-contractual state liability are
commonly viewed as its four wheels. The extent to which private enforcement
may complement the infringement procedure depends as much on the operation of these doctrines in Member States' legal orders as it does on the peculiarities of the preliminary ruling procedure.

Although they are perhaps intrinsically linked, it remains important to
acknowledge the respective spheres of operation of these doctrines and the
preliminary reference. Thus, for a question to be submitted to the ECJ the environmental provision at stake does not need to be directly effective and, *vice
versa*, the direct effect of directives is by no means a necessary corollary of
Article 234 EC.

It has been seen that private enforcement of EC environmental law may
occur in one of two scenarios. First, individuals may challenge the compatibility of rules of national environmental law with (directly effective) provisions of
Community environmental law. This is not an avenue open to individuals

---

[25] Case 1/58, *Stork* [1959] ECR 43.

under any of the provisions authorizing the direct enforcement of Community environmental law. Evidently, in such a case it is not the ECJ itself which will pronounce on the validity of national law. However, the final result should be that any provisions of national environmental law incompatible with Community environmental law as interpreted by the ECJ will have either to be set aside or to be reinterpreted in a way fully consistent with the relevant Community provisions. In its earliest case law the ECJ already emphasized that the existence of a procedure to challenge the legality of Member States' acts in the form of Articles 226 and 227 EC does not rule out that similar questions may be referred to it under Article 234 EC.[26]

Second, whereas individuals cannot challenge the validity of generic Community acts on the basis of Article 230 EC, the ECJ may pronounce on the validity of environmental regulations or directives by virtue of Article 234(1)(b) EC.

In sum, private enforcement could serve to compensate for the lack of individual involvement in the direct enforcement of European Community environmental law (manifest in both Articles 226 and 230 EC) as well as any shortcomings in the infringement procedure generally. Clearly, given the remarkable contribution of private enforcement to the effectiveness of Community law in so many areas, it becomes interesting to see whether it performs or may perform a similar function to the benefit of the environment.

III. The Private Enforcement Chain

Having briefly discussed the nature of the preliminary reference procedure as a tool for the enforcement of EC environmental law, it is now necessary to assess its actual workings in somewhat more detail. However, we should first acknowledge a number of important limitations that bear upon the scope of this endeavour.

The process of private enforcement is particularly complex and protracted, as it involves multiple interrelating actors with diverging aspirations and powers at both national and European levels. Its effectiveness depends on numerous socio-legal factors, most importantly the attitudes of private individuals and national courts or administrative authorities in which judicial discretion is vested. Although certainly something that needs to be considered for future research, no systematic interviews could be conducted, as this would have extended well beyond what is practically feasible.

Instead, this article focuses on the references that have been made to the ECJ which, it is anticipated, will provide valuable clues about the role played by private enforcement in the arena of EC environmental law. Of course, this approach has a number of inherent limitations. For example, no data are available on the number of instances where courts fail to refer questions relating to

---

[26] Case 26/62, *Van Gend & Loos*, n. 11 above.

EC environmental law to the ECJ and, consequently, the reasons for such omissions remain unclear. In some instances, national courts may—appropriately or not—decide that EC environmental law is not of decisive importance to the outcome of a case, and comply with other (national) rules. In other cases, they may judge the provisions of EC environmental law at stake to be unambiguous and apply them directly without the intervention of the ECJ. They may be reluctant to refer for other reasons too, such as the urgent need to resolve a case or even a psychological barrier to becoming involved in a procedure not necessarily familiar to them. The impact of private enforcement action that will be revealed as a result of the ensuing analysis therefore necessarily represents the tip of an iceberg, the precise dimension of which will remain largely obscure.

Yet, despite these reservations, a simple model depicting the totality of the legal factors impacting on the preliminary reference as a tool for the effective enforcement of EC environmental law will considerably aid our understanding of the current state of private environmental enforcement. In addition, such a model could serve as a possible basis for future research, which is undoubtedly necessary for a fuller grasp of the dynamics of private enforcement of EC environmental law.

We may take the metaphor of a water supply system by way of illustration. Consisting of individual pipes joined with the simple purpose of supplying water where it is needed, it resembles our image of private enforcement. As with leaks in water supply systems, enforcement leakage may occur anywhere in the private enforcement process. Leaks may result from sudden and unexpected cracks in individual pipes. Such leaks are spectacular and are therefore usually addressed as a matter of immediate priority. Yet, ultimately, the most serious wastage is caused by the steadily dripping tap, or by tiny leaks where different pipes are joined and water escapes as a matter of routine, albeit perhaps at a relatively modest pace. Likewise, academics tend to focus on spectacular but rare incidents where courts of final appeal refuse to refer a question to the ECJ, or question the supremacy of Community law. However, the most serious threats to the effectiveness of private enforcement are posed by less eye-catching but more structural tensions in the co-operation between the ECJ and national courts, or the synergy between Community law and national law more generally. Although cracks in the system may be repaired, as long as these are not all addressed simultaneously, leakage is likely merely to be redirected to other parts of the system. In summary, the private enforcement chain may usefully be illustrated as follows in Figure 1.

More concretely, the private enforcement chain consists of six interlocking links. First, private enforcement of Member State compliance with EC environmental law presumes that (1) individuals will involve national courts. This, in turn, (2) is one of the ways in which national courts may identify relevant issues, although they may also do so *ex proprio motu*. The third link in the chain consists of the phase where (3) national courts decide whether the issues thus identified call for a preliminary reference. The way in which the

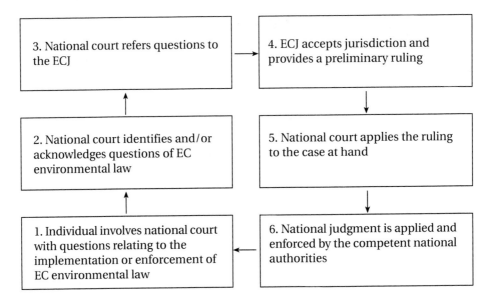

Figure 1: The private enforcement chain

question is eventually phrased determines to an important extent what occurs in the next link, where (4) the ECJ must decide whether or not it enjoys jurisdiction to deliver a preliminary judgment. Presuming that the ECJ accepts jurisdiction and provides a preliminary ruling, (5) the national court then is required to apply the ruling to the particular case before it. The final link in the chain comes into play after (6) the national court has passed a final judgment. Where this is done incorrectly, or where national authorities fail to take the requisite measures, novel questions may be referred to the ECJ with a view to addressing such a failure.

In analysing the factors that may account for enforcement leakage in this process, these six phases will be discussed individually. Obviously, some of these factors may be of simultaneous importance in more than one phase, and it is not suggested that the division of the private enforcement process into these six phases should be rigidly adhered to.

IV. Vigilance in upholding Individual Environmental Rights

Individuals asking national courts questions relating to EC environmental law set the private enforcement process in motion. Although the initiative to refer a question to the ECJ resides exclusively with national courts, it is obviously only after individuals have seised those courts that the opportunity to initiate the enforcement process will arise. Individuals thus play a pivotal role in enforcing EC environmental law in national courts. By way of a preliminary analysis, it is first necessary to examine what kind of issues of EC environmental law individuals in theory may raise in the context of national proceedings.

A. ISSUES OF EC ENVIRONMENTAL LAW WHICH MAY BE REFERRED

Article 234 EC provides as follows:

> The Court of Justice shall have jurisdiction to give preliminary rulings concerning:
> a) the interpretation of this Treaty:
> b) the validity and interpretation of acts of the institutions of the Community and of the ECB;
> c) The interpretation of the statutes of bodies established by an act of the Council, where those statutes so provide.
> Where such a question is raised before any court or tribunal of a Member State, that court or tribunal may, if it considers that a decision is necessary to enable it to give judgment, request the Court of Justice to give a ruling thereon.
> Where any such question is raised in a case pending before a court or tribunal of a Member State against whose decisions there is no judicial remedy under national law, that court or tribunal shall bring the matter before the Court of Justice.

The term "this Treaty" comprises all treaties, their protocols and declarations, as well as the Treaties amending or supplementing the EC Treaty. General principles of law, too, may be subsumed under this category and so form the subject of a preliminary question.[27] Relatively few references have been made relating to the interpretation of the environmental provisions of the Treaty. This may be explained in part by the fact that it is highly doubtful whether either Article 95 (formerly Article100a) EC or Articles 174–176 (formerly Articles 130r–t) EC are directly effective, which evidently reduces the likelihood of them becoming the subject of a reference.[28] Consequently, unlike directly effective Treaty provisions securing market access or equal treatment, the ECJ has not had the opportunity to promote EC environmental law in response to private enforcement initiatives. Nor would it be appropriate if it were to assume such a role in respect of Treaty provisions which, because they are conditional upon further Community action, lack direct effect. As the ECJ itself pointed out in *Peralta*: "Article 130r (now Article 174) EC is confined to defining the general objectives of the Community in the matter of the environment. Responsibility for what action is to be taken is conferred on the Council by Article 130s EC" (now Article 175 EC).

Still, the mere fact that the environmental provisions lack direct effect in itself poses no insurmountable obstacle to the national judge in referring a question to the ECJ. Thus, in *Peralta* the Pretura Circondale di Ravenna

---

[27] See H. Krück, "Artikel 177" in H von der Gruben, *Kommentar zum EU-/EG-Vertrag* (5th edn., Baden Baden: Nomos, 1997), 4/614.
[28] For detailed analyses of the direct effect of primary and secondary Community environmental law see Somsen, n. 8 above.

referred a question relating to the interpretation of, *inter alia*, Article 174 EC with a view to assessing the compatibility of the *Codice di Navigazione* with that provision.[29]

Much more important for our purposes is the category of acts mentioned in Article 234(1)(b) EC, which includes all acts enumerated in Article 249 (formerly Article 189) EC; regulations, directives, decisions, and recommendations. "Soft" law instruments are relevant in this context too, as the ECJ has declared itself competent to receive preliminary questions related to the interpretation or validity of soft law.[30] As far as provisions of directives are concerned, these obviously need not be directly effective in order to become subject to private enforcement action. For example, a national court may simply seek guidance on the question whether national environmental law is in conformity with the provisions of Community environmental law it is designed to implement.[31] For past environmental action programmes, which were adopted in the form of acts *sui generis*, the situation is ambiguous.[32] Krück argues that, in so as far as acts *sui generis* relate to the realization of Community objectives and are published in the Official Journal, the answer should be in the affirmative.[33] Since future environmental action programmes are to be adopted by virtue of Article 251 (formerly Article 189b) EC, there remains no doubt that they may also become subject of a preliminary reference.

Another important group of acts not explicitly mentioned in Article 234(1)(b) EC consists of international environmental treaties to which the Community is a party, or by which it is bound. The ECJ is competent to give preliminary rulings on the interpretation of such treaties, irrespective of whether the Community's competence is "exclusive" or, as is invariably the case in the sphere of the environment, "mixed". In respect of mixed international agreements (i.e. where Member States enjoy competence in respect of some of the subjects it regulates and the Community in respect of others), the ECJ's competence to interpret the Treaty nevertheless relates to the totality of the agreement.[34] Less clear is the question whether the ECJ may also pro-

---

[29] Case C–379/92, *Matteo Peralta* [1994] ECR I–3453, with case report by H. Somsen (1995) 4 *European Environmental Law Review*, 245–51.

[30] Case 322/88, *Grimaldi* [1989] ECR 4407. On the significance of soft law for the Community's environmental policy, see H. Somsen, "Dynamics, Process and Instruments of Environmental Decision-Making in the European Union", in T. Jewell and J. Steele (eds.), *Law in Environmental Decision-Making* (Oxford: Clarendon Press, 1998), 190.

[31] Some recent cases illustrating the point include Joined Cases C–304/94, C–330/94, C–342/94 and C–224/95, *Euro Tombesi* [1997] ECR I-3561, Case C–129/96, *Inter-Environnement Wallonie* [1997] ECR I–7411, Case C–321/96, *Mecklenburg* [1998] ECR I–3809, Case C–81/96, *Haarlemmerliede* [1998] ECR I–3923, Case C–203/96, *Dusseldorp* [1998] ECR I–4075 and Case C–192/96, *Beside* [1998] ECR I–4029.

[32] The first environmental action programme, e.g., was adopted as a "Declaration of the Council of the European Communities, and of the representatives of the Governments of the Member State meeting in the Council [1973] OJ C12/1. Subsequent programmes are equally ambiguous about their legal status: see [1977] OJ C139/1 (second), [1983] OJC 46/1 (third), [1987] OJ C328/1 (fourth) and [1993] OJ C138/1 (fifth).

[33] See Krück, n. 27 above, 4/614.

[34] Case 104/87, *Hauptzollamt Mainz* v. *Kupferberg* [1982] ECR 3641.

nounce on the *validity* of environmental treaties. Since the legal effects of such a ruling would not extend beyond the Community itself and so not affect the binding effect of the treaty *vis-à-vis* third countries, there would appear to be few objections to an affirmative answer to this question.[35]

Finally, the question arises whether acts emanating from the European Parliament and the ECJ itself can be referred to the ECJ under Article 234 EC. As to the former, since it is accepted that decisions of the European Parliament may form the subject of a challenge under Article 230 EC, as a corollary it appears that such acts may also form the substance of a preliminary reference.[36] Similarly, acts of the ECJ may also be referred to it.[37] Although the ECJ's judgments under Article 234 EC themselves are final and binding and thus fall outside the scope of Article 234 EC, this obviously does not preclude a national court from referring a second question when it deems this appropriate.[38]

Article 234(1)(c) EC is devoid of any practical significance and hence little attention needs to be afforded to "the interpretation of the statues of bodies established by an act of the Council, where the statutes so provide". Since such acts of the Council (such as statutes governing operation of the institution) would normally be presumed to fall within the ambit of Article 234(1)(a) EC, the purpose of this provision is conceivably to restrict the scope of application of the latter.[39]

B. ISSUES CONCERNING THE INTERPRETATION OF EC ENVIRONMENTAL LAW

Since Article 234 EC does not define the term "interpretation", the ECJ has been able to develop its own distinctive, teleological interpretation style as a tool for its judicial activism. Questions relating to the interpretation of Community environmental law may relate simply to the content or scope of a particular provision or act, or gaps in the law which need to be addressed, or seek guidance on general principles of law. Although the notion of interpretation is a broad one, it does not extend to "application" within the meaning of Article 220 (formerly Article 164) EC, which refers to both interpretation and application. Whereas the application of Community environmental law to the main case remains the preserve of the referring court, in practice it is not possible to adhere rigidly to the distinction between "application" and "interpretation". This is because the question itself is often phrased in such a way that

---

[35] See Krück, n. 27, 4/616.

[36] Case 294/83, *Parti Ecologiste Les Verts* v. *European Parliament* [1986] ECR 1339.

[37] Case 62/72, *Bollmann* v. *Hauptzollamt Hamburg* [1973] ECR 269.

[38] See Case 14/86, *Pretore di Salò* v. *Persons Unknown* [1987] ECR 2545, where the ECJ held: "The fact that judgments delivered on the basis of references for a preliminary ruling are binding on the national courts does not preclude the national court to which such a judgment is addressed from making a further reference if it considers it necessary in order to give judgment in the main proceedings." On this issue, see section IX below.

[39] See T. C. Hartley, *The Foundations of European Community Law* (3rd edn., Oxford: Clarendon Press, 1994), 271–4.

any answer is bound to leave little or no leeway to the national court as to its application to the dispute. Moreover, the ECJ's reference must be sufficiently precise for the national court to apply it to the case.

C. CHALLENGING THE VALIDITY OF EC ENVIRONMENTAL LAW

Individuals seeking annulment of an environmental measure will obviously have to show incompatibility of such an act with some higher principle in the Community's hierarchy of norms, in which primary Community law features at the top. However, in view of their programmatic character, in practice it is troublesome to challenge the legality of a Community environmental directive on the basis of its incompatibility with, for example, the polluter pays principle of Article 174 EC.[40] *Armand Mondiet* and more recently *Bettati*[41] show that the ECJ will primarily engage in a formal review of the Community environmental measure.

The question could be posed whether, among the provisions of primary Community law *inter se*, a further hierarchy exists. This question is a particularly pertinent one since Community environmental policy is "horizontal" and hence regularly conflicts with other Community policies. It has been argued, for example, that Directive 75/439 EEC on the Disposal of Waste Oils infringed provisions relating to the free movement of goods and competition.[42] Although it is correct that secondary Community law must respect primary Community law, the ECJ in that case ruled that environmental protection belonged to the fundamental objectives of the Treaty, which warranted exceptions to the free movement of goods. At the time of the ruling, the Treaty did not even contain any provisions relating to the environment which implies, a *fortiori*, that the present Articles 174–176 EC do not occupy a position inferior to provisions such as Article 28 (formerly Article EC 30).

Next in the hierarchy come the general principles of law, including fundamental human rights. It is a well-established principle of Community law that fundamental rights form an integral part of general principles of law, the observance of which the ECJ ensures. For that purpose, the ECJ draws inspiration from the constitutional traditions common to the Member States and from guidelines supplied by international treaties for the protection of human rights on which Member States have collaborated or of which they are signatory.[43] Consequently, where national legislation falls within the scope of Community law, the ECJ, in a reference for a preliminary ruling, must give the national court the guidance necessary to enable it to assess the compatibility

---

[40] See H. G. Sevenster, *Milieubeleid en Gemeenschapsrecht* (Deventer: Kluwer, 1992).

[41] Case C–341/95, *Gianni Bettati* [1998] ECR I–4355, where the ECJ formally assessed the validity of Reg. (EC) No. 3093/94 on ozone depleting substances ([1994] OJ L333/1) in the light of the criteria of Art. 231 (formerly Art. 174) EC.

[42] Case 240/83, *Procureur de la République* v. *Association de Défense des Bruleurs de l'Huiles Usagées* [1985] ECR 531.

[43] See Opinion 2/94 [1996] ECR I–1759.

of that legislation with the fundamental rights.[44] In *Annibaldi*, the ECJ had to assess the compatibility of national provisions which prohibited undertakings incorporated within a nature and archaeological park to undertake any activity whatsoever in the area concerned with the fundamental right to property, to carry out business and to equal treatment by the national authorities.[45] After examination of, in particular Article 34(3) (formerly Article 40(3)) EC relating to the Common Agricultural Policy, the ECJ concluded that the national measure in question fell outside the scope of Community law, and hence that it did not enjoy jurisdiction to rule on the question. More recently, in *Standley* the ECJ ruled that the action programmes to be drawn up in the context of Directive 91/676/EEC on the Protection of Waters Against Pollution Caused by Nitrates from Agricultural Sources did not infringe the right to property.[46]

A principle that is particularly relevant in proceedings relating to the validity of EC environmental law is that of proportionality, also found in Article 5 (formerly Article 3b) EC. The preventive and precautionary rationale underpinning environmental measures, the tenuous scientific evidence on which some parameters have been based, as well as the technical nature of environmental directives, invites challenges based on the principle of proportionality. As exemplified by *Armand Mondiet*, wisely, the ECJ is reluctant to test substantively the institutions' environmental decision-making against the principle of proportionality and, instead, engages in a more formal review of the decision-making process.[47]

Secondary environmental law must also conform with any international environmental conventions to which the Community is a party. In *Peralta*, the ECJ ruled that it does not have jurisdiction to interpret environmental conventions to which the Community is not a party and which deal with an area the powers of which have not been assumed by the Community.

Whereas, as observed, there exists no hierarchy amongst rules of primary law *inter se*, there may be such a hierarchy amongst rules of secondary environmental law. In particular, it is conceivable that the many environmental framework directives occupy a status superior to subsequent implementing rules, and that individuals may challenge the validity of implementing directives in the light of earlier framework directives. For example, the Community could attempt to adopt limit values for dangerous substances in water without simultaneously elaborating quality objectives for the same substance. However, this legislation could then be challenged on the basis of its

---

[44] See in particular Case C–299/95, *Kremzow* v. *Austrian State* [1997] ECR I–2629, para. 15.

[45] Case C–309/96, *Annibaldi* [1997] ECR I–7493.

[46] Case C–293/97, *Standley* judgment of 29 Apr. 1999 (not yet reported).

[47] Case C–405/92, *Etablissements Armand Mondiet* [1993] ECR I–6133, where the Court ruled: "As regards the Council's duty to take scientific data into account, the Court has already ruled that judicial review must, having regard to the discretionary power conferred on the Council ... be limited to examining whether the measure in question is vitiated by a manifest error or misuse of powers, or whether the authority in question has manifestly exceeded the limits of its discretion" (para. 32).

incompatibility with the dual approach enshrined in framework Directive 76/464/EEC on Pollution Caused by Certain Dangerous Substances Discharged Into the Aquatic Environment and the implementing directives subsequently adopted.[48]

D THE IMPACT OF PRIVATE ENFORCEMENT: AN INITIAL ANALYSIS

Until mid-1999, the ECJ issued just forty-six preliminary judgments that for the present purposes may be termed "environmental".[49] This number is striking, particularly if compared with the abundance of provisions of secondary environmental law currently in force.[50]

By way of explanation, the Commission in the past has noted that, unlike in other areas of Community law such as the free movement of goods or equal

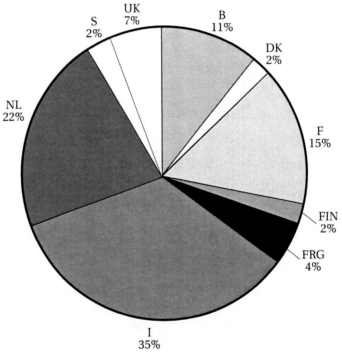

Figure 2: Origin of Preliminary Environmental Rulings

---

[48] [1976] OJ L108/41. The dual approach was formalized in Dir. 86/280/EEC on limit values and quality objectives included in List I of the Annex to Dir. 76/464/EEC [1986] OJ L181/16.

[49] See Table I. Cases concerning the Euratom Treaty have not been included. It should be noted that, due to the horizontal character of EC environmental law, in practice it is difficult categorically to distinguish cases which are "environmental" from those which are not.

[50] For details, see *Directory of EC Legislation in Force and Other Acts of the Community Institutions* (Luxembourg: Office for Official Publications of the EC, 1998).

pay, individuals lack self-interest to initiate national proceedings. Indeed, in the absence of private (market) interests in the proper enforcement of environmental directives, the privatization of the enforcement of Member State compliance with the law is bound to be problematic.

An examination of the cases that have hitherto been decided by the ECJ pursuant to Article 234 EC appears to bear out this hypothesis. Of the cases that were referred, more than half concerned internal market and/or waste issues —where market forces are predominant (see Table I). Moreover, twenty-four cases arose in the context of criminal proceedings where, as will be seen, rather than securing Member State compliance with EC environmental law, individuals invoke EC environmental law by way of defence against criminal sanctions based on national law.

The remaining references related to the general issue concerning the effects of directives, environmental impact assessment, access to information, and nature conservation. Even within this more promising category, the issues are mostly related to narrow individual interests. Examples are the right to hunt birds in relation to Directive 79/409/EEC on the Conservation of Wild Birds,[51] or access to navigable waterways in the context of Directive 85/337/EEC on the Assessment of the Effects of Certain Public and Private Projects on the Environment.[52]

Yet, there are also other important factors that may account for the failure of private enforcement to take off in the environment field. Of primary importance amongst these may be the problem of the detection of infringements of EC environmental law. The bulk of environmental directives fix emission standards or quality objectives for air, noise or water, the breach of which may be suspected but not readily shown by private individuals.

It is not self-evident that current moves to secure wider access to environmental information will serve to change this pattern. Much will depend on the extent to which Member States will comply with the obligation of Article 7 of Directive 90/313/EEC on Freedom of Access to Environmental Information *actively* to disseminate information relating to the environment.[53]

It is particularly striking that, traditionally, an overwhelming proportion of individual complaints in the context of Article 226 EC (and also Article 194 (formerly Article138d) EC) in fact relates to alleged breaches of environmental law, which is in stark contrast to the meagre number of environmental references.[54] A plausible explanation for this contrast is that individuals, in so far as they suspect any infringements, may prefer the safe and inexpensive route of Article 226 EC. This would make particular sense in respect of breaches of directives fixing limit values and quality objectives, where they could justifiably prefer to leave the difficult matter of proving breaches of the values to the Commission.

---

[51] [1979] OJ L103/1.   [52] [1985] OJ L175/40.   [53] [1990] OJ L158/56.
[54] For analyses of trends in individual complaints see R. Macrory, "Community Supervision in the Field of the Environment" in Somsen, n. 8 above, 9–21.

Table 1: Breakdown of Preliminary Environmental references

Case	Name	ECR	No.	Court	I/V	MS	Substance
1	148/78	Ratti	1979	1629	Crim.	I	I	Free movement-labelling-effect directives
2	272/80	Biological Products	1981	3277	Crim	I	NL	Free movement (of biological products)
3	172/82	Inter-Huiles	1983	555	Civil	I	F	Free movement (of waste oils)—Directive 75/439/EEC
4	94/83	Albert Heijn	1984	3263	Crim	I	NL	Free movement (of foodstuffs containing residues of pesticides)
5	240/83	ABDHU	1985	531	Crim	I/V	F	Free movement (of waste oils)—validity Directive 75/439/EEC
6	54/85	Mirepoix	1986	1067	Crim	I	F	Free movement (of foodstuffs containing residues of pesticides)
7	372–374/85	Oscar Traen	1987	2141	Crim	I	B	Scope Directive 75/442/EEC—effect directives
8	14/86	Salo	1987	2545	Crim	I	I	Nature Article 234 EC—effect directives
9	118/86	Nertsvoederfabriek	1987	3883	Crim	I	NL	Free movement (of poultry offal)
10	228/87	Pretura Unificata	1988	5099	Crim	I	I	Scope of derogations in Article 10 of Directive 80/778/EEC
11	380/87	Balsamo	1989	2491	Adm	I	I	Scope Directive 75/442/EEC—consequences of breach to notify draft legislation
12	125/88	Nijman	1989	3533	Crim	I	NL	Free movement (of plant protection products)—indirect effect Directive 79/117/EEC
13	C-169/89	Vd Burg	1990	I-2143	Crim	I	NL	Free movement (of dead red grouse)—effect directives (i.e. Directive 79/409/EEC)
14	C-206 and 207/88	Vessoso and Zanetti	1990	I-1461	Crim	I	NL	Scope of concept of 'waste' in Directive 75/442/EEC
15	C-359/88	Zanetti	1990	I-1509	Crim	I	I	Scope of Directive 75/442/EEC—concept of "waste"—export of waste
16	C-37/92	Vanacker	1993	I-4947	Crim	I	F	Free movement (of waste oils)—scope Directive 75/439/EEC
17	C-405/92	Mondiet	1993	I-6133	Civil	V	F	Validity Regulation (EEC) No. 345/92—Articles 33 and 175 EC
18	C-435/92	APAS	1994	I-67	Adm	I	F	Legality staggered closing date hunting season in light Directive 79/409/EEC

19	C-236/92	Difesa della Cava	1994	I-483	Adm	I	I	Direct effect Article 4 Directive 75/442/EEC
20	C-379/92	Peralta	1994	I-3453	Crim	I	I	Compatibility criminal sanctions for discharging chemicals at sea Arts. 3, 7 (old), 28, 39, 43, 49 62 (old), 80, and 174 EC
21	C-396/92	Bund	1994	I-3717	Adm	I	FRG	Temporal scope Article 12(1) of Directive 85/337/EEC
22	C-54 and 74/94	Cacchiarelli	1995	I-391	Crim	I	I	Free movement, scope Directive 90/462/EEC on maximum levels for pesticide residues
23	C-202/94	Vd Feesten	1996	I-355	Crim	I	I	Scope Directive 79/409/EEC—application to subspecies not occurring naturally in the wild
24	C-149/94	Vergy	1996	I-299	Crim	I	F	Scope Directive 79/409/EEC—application to specimens born and reared in captivity
25	C-118/94	WWF	1996	I-1223	Adm	I	I	Jurisdiction of ECJ under Art. 234 EC—scope of derogation in Directive 79/409/EEC
26	C-293/94	Brandsma	1996	I-3159	Crim	I	B	Free movement (of biocides)
27	C-44/95	RSPB	1996	I-3805	Adm	I	UK	Scope Directive 79/409/EEC and Directive 92/43/EEC—delimitation of Special Protection Areas
28	C-58/95 et al	Gallotti	1996	I-4345	Crim	I	I	Jurisdiction of ECJ under Art 234 EC—power of Member State to impose criminal sanctions for breaches of EC law
29	C-168/95	Arcaro	1996	I-4705	Crim	I	I	Jurisdiction of ECJ under Art 234 EC—water pollution—effect directives
30	C-72/95	Kraaijeveld	1996	I-5403	Adm	I	NL	Scope Directive 85/337/EEC—direct effect Article 4(2)—examination *ex officio*
31	C-10/96	Ligue Royal Belge	1996	I-6775	Adm	I	B	Scope Directive 79/409/EEC—derogation from the prohibition of killing or capturing protected species
32	C-343/95	Diego Cali	1997	I-1547	Civil	I	I	Abuse of a dominant position—pollution control
33	C-13/96	Bic	1997	I-1753	Adm	I	B	Notification of technical standards and regulations—environmental tax—included
34	C-304/94 et al.	Euro Tombesi	1997	I-3561	Crim	I	I	Jurisdiction of the ECJ under Art. 234 EC—Article 75/442/EEC—definition of "waste"
35	309/96	Annibaldi	1997	I-7493	Adm	I	I	Expropriations in national park—legality under Community law—jurisdiction of the ECJ under Article 234 EC
36	C-129/96	Inter-Environne-ment	1997	I-7411	Adm	I	B	Effect of Directive 91/156/EEC prior to expiry deadline for implementation—definition of waste

Table 1: cont.

Case	Name	ECR	No.	Court	I/V	MS	Substance
37	C-329/95	*VAG Sverige*	1997	I-2675	Adm	I	S	Free movement (of type-approved vehicles)—national exhaust emission certificate—compatibility with Directive 70/156/EEC
38	C-1/96	*Compassion*	1998	I-1251	Adm	I/V	UK	Free movement (of calves)—exhaustive harmonization—extra-territorial scope of Article 30 EC—validity Directive 91/629/EEC
39	C-213/96	*Outokumpu Oy*	1998	I-1777	Adm	I	FIN	Discriminatory environmental tax—compatibility with Article 90 EC
40	C-321/96	*Mecklenburg*	1998	I-3809	Adm	I	FRG	Scope Directive 90/313/EEC
41	C-81/96	*Haarlem-merliede*	1998	I-3923	Adm	I	NL	Scope Directive 85/337/EEC—new consent for a zoning plan
42	C-192/96	*Beside*	1998	I-4029	Adm	I	NL	Scope "municipal waste" Regulation (EEC) No. 259/93—scope—storage of materials—Directive 75/442/EEC—scope
43	C-203/96	*Dusseldorp*	1998	I-4075	Adm	I	NL	Scope Directive 75/442/EEC and Regulation (EEC) No. 259/93—self-sufficiency and proximity—applicability to shipments of waste for recovery—exclusive right to incinerate waste—compatibility with Art 82 and 86 EC
44	C-341/95	*Betatti*	1998	I-4355	Crim	V	I	Validity of Regulation (EC) No. 3093/94 (Ozone)
45	C-67/97	*Ditlev Bluhme*	1998	I-8033	Crim	I	DK	Compatibility of restrictions on the importation of bees with Articles 28 and 30 EC
46	C-293/97	*Standley*	1999	I-0000	Adm	I/V	UK	Scope Directive 91/676/EEC—identification of waters affected by pollution—designation of vulnerable zones—criteria—validity

Case = case number
Name = summary name
Year = volume ECR
No. = page number ECR
Court = type of procedure (administrative, civil, criminal)
I/V = questions concerning interpretation and/or validity
Substance = subject matter of the reference

On the other hand, environmental interest groups are often extremely well informed and usually do not suffer from these handicaps. Indeed, on a few occasions environmental interest groups have been instrumental in referring a preliminary question to the ECJ. The preliminary route may be the only appropriate one where environmental harm should and can be addressed as a matter of relative urgency, such as was the case with French legislation allowing the closing dates of the hunting season to be staggered.[55] In this regard it should be noted that, for the period between 1995 and 1997, the average length of an "environmental" preliminary procedure was sixteen months, with a maximum of twenty-two months and a minimum of eleven months.[56] Again, this contrasts sharply with the length of infringement procedures in the same period. Even if measured from the time when the reasoned opinion was delivered, for simple issues relating to formal implementation this averaged from forty-four months (for cases dealing with a complete failure to adopt legislation), to sixty-three months (for cases dealing with erroneous transposition) up to sixty-six months (for cases dealing with issues of practical implementation). Moreover, some cases lasted close to ninety months, and this is even without taking into account the period preceding the issue of the reasoned opinion, which on occasion may amount to well over a year and which, realistically, should be taken into account when assessing the effectiveness of the procedure.[57]

In the light of this information, it may appear surprising that environmental interest groups have not more frequently made use of the preliminary reference procedure, and instead have often opted to file complaints with the Commission with a view to initiating infringement proceedings under Article 226 EC. However, as has already been noted, compared to judgments pursuant to Article 226 EC, preliminary rulings are relatively low-profile in political terms. Whereas this has been gratefully exploited by the ECJ to pursue judicial policy, the interests of environmental interest groups may sometimes be quite the opposite. Their wish to seek maximum political exposure for breaches of environmental law may often have tilted the balance in favour of infringement proceedings, even if private enforcement may have been a realistic and perhaps more efficient alternative.

In addition, national procedural law may limit access to the courts or judicial review,[58] for example to those who can show they have a (private) interest in the issues at stake and may limit or even rule out group actions. The extent to which such national limits to access are compatible with the recent case law of the ECJ will be briefly assessed elsewhere. However, it remains true that

---

[55] L. Krämer, "Die Rechtsprechung der EG-Gerichte zum Umweltrecht 1995 bis 1997" (1998) 25 *Europäische Grundrechte Zeitschrift* 309–20. See also J. D. C. Harte, "The Rule of Law in European Community Environmental Protection (1997) 9 *Journal of Environmental Law* 168–80. In a "practical postscript" the author draws explicit attention to the fact that, pending the ECJ's preliminary judgment, Lappel Bank was allowed to be destroyed and underlines national courts' responsibilities to halt development for the sake of environmental protection.

[56] Krämer, n. 55 above.   [57] *Ibid.*

[58] See n. 17 above. See also *Implementing Community Environmental Law*, n. 7 above.

such restrictive national rules, even where they may not be fully compatible with the minimum standards the ECJ has elaborated, may at least *de facto* have discouraged individuals to seise their courts.

Equally important are national provisions relating to legal aid, which are far from uniform in the Union, and which have a profound impact on the extent to which individuals, in the absence of any private interests, can be expected to serve as a private police force in addition to the Commission.

Finally, the (perceived) lack of direct effect of relevant provisions of EC environmental law may conceivably also play a role in individuals' reluctance to seise national courts. Although for lawyers the issue of the direct effect of environmental directives has sometimes become a fulcrum for technical discourse and legal construction, it is a doctrine designed first and foremost for ordinary individuals to enforce their (environmental) rights. In order for the private enforcement of Member State compliance with EC environmental law to be fully exploited, individuals must have the conviction that the direct effect of environmental directives is an important arrow to their bow. In this area, as in others, there exists a gap between the culture of the legal elite, which by now may hold such a conviction, and the legal culture of ordinary citizens, which does not appear to have kept up with developments stimulated by the former.[59] Although the Commission is pursuing an active policy designed to bridge this divide, for example by organizing regular seminars targeted in particular at judges, prosecutors and environmental administrators, this may not be sufficient to address the problem. The same holds true, it is submitted, for the doctrines of indirect effect and non-contractual liability.

All this would perhaps merely appear to confirm that private enforcement of EC environmental law will be limited to areas where individual (economic) interests are at stake. Arguing *a contrario*, this conclusion may come as little surprise to the domestic lawyer living by the adage *ubi ius, ibi remedium*. However, on numerous occasions the ECJ has explicitly ruled that secondary EC environmental law creates "rights" for individuals, which they should be in a position to uphold in their national courts.[60] In any event, whereas national procedural autonomy may be the starting point, Community law increasingly imposes itself where the protection of these Community rights is concerned. In summary, EC law may have given rise to a new notion of "rights", the observance of which, as a matter of Community law, may require national remedies even where these do not exist for similar national "rights".

---

[59] See F. Snyder, "Preconditions for the Effectiveness of EU Law: Reflections on Constitutionalism and EMU" in J. A. E. Vervaele (ed.), *Compliance and Enforcement of European Community Law* (The Hague: Kluwer, 1999), 3–26.

[60] e.g. see Case 131/88, *Commission* v. *Germany* [1991] ECR I–825 and Case 361/88, *Commission* v. *Germany* [1991] ECR I–2567 (in respect of Dir. 80/68/EEC on the protection of groundwater against pollution caused by certain dangerous substances and Dir. 80/779/EEC on air quality limit value and guide values for sulphur dioxide and suspended particles). On the notion of environmental rights see further H. Somsen, "Francovich and its Application to EC Environmental Law" in Somsen, n. 8 above, 135–50. Regarding the relationship between rights and remedies more generally, see Ruffert, n. 17 above.

The disappointing number and range of environmental cases which have arisen in private enforcement actions should therefore not discourage further examination of the private enforcement chain. For this purpose, it first becomes necessary to conceptualize the kind of breaches of EC environmental law which, in theory, could become the subject of private enforcement action. At the most basic level, such breaches have been distinguished as those relating to the duty to provide information, formal implementation (i.e. relating to the proper transposition of EC environmental law) and practical implementation.[61]

Member States' (almost routinely flouted) duty to provide information to the Commission is not normally of a nature to allow individuals to enforce its compliance in national courts. Thus, in *Balsamo* the ECJ ruled in respect of Article 3(2) of Directive 75/442/EEC on Waste:

It follows from the foregoing that [Article 3(2) of Directive 75/442/EEC] concerns relations between the Member States and does not give rise to any right of individuals which might be infringed by a Member State's breach of its obligation to inform the Commission in advance of draft rules.[62]

In this context, special mention should also be made of Directive 91/692/EEC Standardizing and Rationalizing Reports on the Implementation of Certain Directives Relating to the Environment. The Directive, which spells out the required frequency of reports to be submitted to the Commission in various sectors, likewise does not appear to give rise to any "rights" which individuals may enforce before their national courts. Only where Member States' duty to provide information somehow involves individuals, as was the case in *CIA Securitel*, may the latter enforce those rights in national courts.[63] In the field of the environment, this is illustated by *BIC*[64] where, following action in a Belgian court, the ECJ ruled that an environmental tax fell within the scope of Directive 83/189/EEC Laying Down a Procedure for the Provision of Information in the Field of Technical Standards and Regulations.[65] For the widespread breaches of the duty to inform the Commission of the transposition of environmental directives, Article 226 EC hence remains the appropriate and only instrument.

The situation in respect of issues of formal and practical implementation is much more complex. Where no national implementing environmental rules exist, individuals will have to resort to the doctrines of direct effect or non-contractual state liability to enforce Member State compliance.[66] To the extent that national implementing rules do exist and afford the national court a degree of flexibility, individuals may also seek to obtain the desired result (i.e.

---

[61] Case 96/81, *Commission v. Netherlands* [1982] ECR 1791.

[62] Case 380/87, *Cinsello Balsamo* [1989] ECR 2491

[63] Case C–194/94, *CIA Security International v. Signalson SA and Securitel SPRL* [1995] ECR I–2201.

[64] Case C–13/96, *Bic Benelux SA v. Belgium State* [1997] ECR I–1753.

[65] [1983] OJ L109/8, as amended by Dir. 88/182 EEC, [1988] OJ L81/75.

[66] For extensive analyses of the operation of these doctrines in the sphere of the environment, see Somsen, n. 8 above.

one which complies with Community environmental law) through interpretation which conforms to the relevant directives (indirect effect).

However, closer scrutiny of the wide array of regulatory instruments most commonly found in environmental directives is required in order to obtain a more precise idea about the extent to which individuals may realistically be expected to contribute to their enforcement in national courts. Sevenster's inventory may usefully serve as a starting point for this purpose, of which only the most important examples need to be examined.[67]

i Organizational instruments

Some EC environmental legislation (mostly decisions) pursues *information exchange* as its primary or secondary objective.[68] Such is the case, for example, with Decision 77/795/EEC Establishing a Common Procedure for the Exchange of Information on the Quality of Surface Fresh Water in the Community.[69] The Decision requires Member States to designate a central agency which is to forward the information as specified in the decision. The decision also circumscribes the nature of the information to be provided and the way in which it is to be collated (frequency of sampling and analysis). Similarly, Article 3 of Decision 82/795/EEC on the Consolidation of Precautionary Measures Concerning Chlorofluorocarbons in the Environment obliges Member States, subject to commercial confidentiality, to provide the Commission with the results of any study or research available to them.[70] Applying the principle of *Balsamo*, it appears *prima facie* impossible for individuals to enforce these provisions in the context of national proceedings. Only in cases where commercial confidentiality is at issue may individuals have a role to play, although this would be to *restrict* the impact of the Community measure at national level.

The potential for private enforcement in respect of Community provisions setting up forms of *co-operation between Member States*, manifest in many environmental directives, appears similarly limited. For example, Article 11 of Directive 80/779/EEC on Air Quality Limit Values and Guide Values for Sulphur Dioxide and Suspended Particulates[71] provides that, where Member States fix values for concentrations in border regions of sulphur dioxide and suspended particulates in the atmosphere, they shall hold prior consultations. Once more, it is very difficult to think of situations where individuals might be in a position privately to enforce this obligation. Similar provisions are found, *inter alia*, in Article 4(4) of Directive 76/160/EEC on the Quality of Bathing Waters, Article 10 of Directive

---

[67] Sevenster, n. 40 above, 75–85.

[68] See also Decision 75/441/EEC establishing a common procedure for the exchange of information between the surveillance and monitoring networks based on data relating to atmospheric pollution caused by certain compounds and suspended particulates [1975] OJ L194/32; Decision 81/971/EEC establishing a community information system for the control and reduction of pollution caused by hydrocarbons discharged at sea [1981] OJ L355/52, and Decision 86/85/EEC establishing a community information system for the control and reduction of pollution caused by the spillage of hydrocarbons and other harmful substances at sea [1986] OJ 77/33; Decision 82/459/EEC establishing a reciprocal exchange of information and data from networks and individual stations measuring air pollution within member states [1982] OJ L210/1.

[69] [1977] OJ L334/29.   [70] [1982] OJ L329/29.   [71] [1980] OJ L229/30.

78/659/EEC concerning Freshwater Fish, Article 10 of Directive 79/923/EEC on the Quality Required of Shellfish Waters, and Article 17 of Directive 80/68/EEC on the Protection of Ground Water Against Pollution by Dangerous Substances, implementing directives adopted in the context of Directive 76/464/EEC on Dangerous Substances Discharged into the Aquatic Environment as well as Directive 86/280/EEC on Limit Values and Quality Objectives for Discharges of Black-List Substances. In all these cases, the provisions at issue are designed to impose obligations on Member States *inter se* or between Member States and the Commission and so cannot be privately enforced. Once more, Article 226 EC becomes the exclusive tool for the enforcement of these provisions.[72]

Usually, Member States are required to *designate a competent authority*, for example in the context of Decision 77/795/EEC Establishing a Common Procedure for the Exchange of Information on the Quality of Surface Fresh Water in the Community.[73] Once more, in respect of these obligations individuals have only a marginal role to play in respect of their enforcement. Thus, it would appear to follow from the *Balsamo* doctrine that only when the designation of the competent authority is a *conditio sine qua non* for the exercise of any individual rights created by secondary Community law that private enforcement becomes a prospect. One such example is provided by Regulation (EC) No. 259/93 on the Supervision and Control of Shipments of Waste Within Into and Out of the European Community. According to Article 36 of this Regulation, a competent authority must be designated for the purpose of the implementation of the Regulation. Since individuals enjoy the right to transport waste, subject only to certain procedures to be verified by these competent authorities, private enforcement of Article 36 is clearly possible. In the vast majority of cases, no individual rights are intrinsically associated with the designation of competent authorities, however. It therefore would seem that, realistically, the Commission is the sole authority that may enforce compliance with this type of obligation. This is true, for example, with regard to Decision 77/795/EEC Establishing a Common Procedure for the Exchange of Information on the Quality of Surface Fresh Water in the Community.[74]

Some environmental directives explicitly require a system of *judicial and/or administrative review* to be provided for.[75] The most important example is Directive 90/313/EEC on the Freedom of Access to Information on the Environment.[76] In Article 4 it provides that a person who considers that his request for information has been unreasonably refused or ignored, or has been inadequately answered by a public authority, may seek judicial or

---

[72] Art. 226 EC was used once in this context, in Case C–186/91, *Commission* v. *Belgium* [1993] ECR I–851. On the subject of co-operation between Member States in the context of the implementation of environmental directives see also the commentary on this case by H. Somsen (1993) 2 *European Environmental Law Review*, 178–93.

[73] [1977] OJ L334/29.

[74] Art. 3 of the Decision requires that each Member State shall designate a central agency and inform the Commission thereof within 15 days of the notification of the Decision.

[75] See Dir. 84/532/EEC on the approximation of the laws of the Member States relating to common provisions for construction plant and equipment [1984] OJ L300/111.

[76] [1990] OJ L158/56.

administrative review of the decision in accordance with the relevant national legal system. There can be little doubt that this provision, which gives rise to clearly defined individual rights, may form the subject of a preliminary reference with a view to its enforcement.

Organizational provisions are also those relating to *supervision, control and testing*, examples of which are found in numerous environmental directives. Directive 76/160/EEC Concerning the Quality of Bathing Waters, for example, contains elaborate provisions relating to the sampling frequency as well as the method of analysis and inspection for its parameters.[77] Although it may appear unlikely that individuals should wish to invoke provisions of this nature in national courts, they are a necessary corollary to the operational values (emission values, quality objectives or otherwise) which, according to the ECJ, *can* be invoked by individuals.[78] It is accordingly submitted that if national authorities can be shown to fail to adhere to minimum sampling frequencies, yet grant authorizations for discharges in water, such individuals may invoke and privately enforce provisions concerning sampling.

In general, however, organizational instruments and private enforcement are not natural bedfellows. Since the chief business of environmental law is to anticipate and prevent environmental harm or to make arrangements for the eventuality of environmental calamities, for which organization instruments are suitable *par excellence*, the ramifications of this conclusion can hardly be overestimated. Only if organizational arrangements have an individual dimension may these in theory be enforced privately. This may be the case both if they concern individuals directly (e.g. Article 4 of Directive 90/313/EEC) or indirectly (e.g. the sampling provisions in the context of Directive 76/160/EEC).

ii Physical Instruments

A second important category of instruments which, in many respects, forms the operational backbone of EC environmental law consists of what has been termed "physical instruments".[79] The most important physical instruments employed in EC environmental law are limit values and emission standards, quality objectives, obligations to act, prohibitions, product standards, programmes and permit systems.

Examples of directives containing *limit values and/or quality objectives* are numerous and still form the core of much of the EC environmental law in force. According to the ECJ, these directives have endowed individuals with rights which they are in a position to enforce in national courts.[80] However, it is far from clear how such private enforcement of limit values or quality objectives is to be realized. Different types of situations may be distinguished. When harmonization is total, individuals compelled to comply with more stringent national standards obviously may invoke the Community standards in the context of national proceedings. Total harmonization, however, is exceptional in the field of the environment and in the majority of cases, where minimum

---

[77] [1976] OJ L31/1.

[78] See the case law in n. 60 above.

[79] Sevenster, n. 67 above.

[80] See the case law in n. 60 above.

harmonization is used, reliance on the directive will therefore not be possible.[81] It should be noted that, although private enforcement in those cases does serve to protect individual rights, it once more results in lower, rather than higher, levels of environmental protection.

It is also conceivable that national legislation does not contain the (appropriate) emission standards or quality objectives required by the directive. The issue being purely one of formal implementation, the most likely scenario that could enforce proper compliance is for environmental interest groups to question the compatibility of the national provisions with the relevant environmental directive. This indeed was what occurred in *Inter Environnement*.[82]

If administered by means of a system of permits and authorizations, and it can be shown that these have been granted in breach of uniform EC *limit values*, individuals may simply oppose the granting of those permits. If EC *quality objectives* are used, however (which is the United Kingdom's preferred option in the context of Directive 76/464/EEC on the Discharge of Dangerous Substances into the Aquatic Environment) such uniform EC limit values do not come to the aid of individuals. Instead, the obligation resting with Member States is to adhere to the quality objectives applying to the receiving aquatic or ambient environment. Consequently, quality objectives appear much more difficult to enforce privately. This may usefully be illustrated by the example of cadmium concentrations in water. Instead of simply showing that the emission standards specified in UK consents do not coincide with the uniform EC limit value (which involves a simple and purely formal comparison of standards on paper), UK citizens have to show that total cadmium concentration in inland surface waters affected by discharges exceeds five μg/litre.[83]

Similar obstacles exist for all other directives that are not based on a system of prior authorizations with reference to uniform limit values, but instead fix quality objectives. It does not appear terribly realistic to expect that the "vigilance of individuals to uphold their rights" will amount to an effective enforcement of values for total coliforms in bathing water, or pesticides and related products in drinking water. The statistics relating to the subjects of the preliminary references decided by the ECJ bear out that, indeed, little or no private enforcement of substantive environmental law standards is taking place.

Often, environmental directives oblige Member States to establish *improvement* programmes.[84] A consistent concern voiced in the Commission's annual reports relating to the application of Community law is Member States' blatant disregard for these obligations.[85] Although, ideally, interest groups would fulfil

---

[81] See Art. 176 (formerly Art. 130t) EC.

[82] Case C–129/96, *Inter Environnement* [1997] ECR I–7411.

[83] Dir. 83/513/EEC on limit values and quality objectives for cadmium discharges, Annex II 1.1 [1983] OJ L291/1.

[84] Directives containing such obligations are conveniently listed in Dir. 91/692/EEC standardizing and rationalizing reports on the implementation of certain directives relating to the environment [1991] OJ L377/48.

[85] Most recently in the 15th Report on Monitoring the Application of EC Law, COM(98)317 [1998] OJ C250/1.

an important role by enforcing such provisions in their national courts, as far as the author is aware, to date not a single case relating to Member States' failure to draw up programmes has found its way to the ECJ pursuant to Article 234 EC. In contrast, farmers directly and adversely affected by programmes on nitrate in water were quick to challenge the UK Secretary of State's decision to designate certain waters as vulnerable zones (and hence subject such waters to a regime contained in special action programmes to be adopted for this purpose).[86]

Quality objectives, uniform limit values and improvement programmes thus become enforceable by virtue of *systems of prior authorization* (permits). If directives contain limit values for dangerous substances in water, it is by virtue of the fact that individuals may oppose the grant of a permit that does not comply with the directive's limit values that the latter may be privately enforced. Obversely, individuals may enforce any right to discharge such substances by demanding a permit (provided they comply with the emission standards contained in national implementing legislation).[87] A system of prior authorization may hence be said to disentangle bundled and predominantly abstract interests into individual, concretely challengeable acts, and consequently to invite a process of private enforcement.[88] By comparison, where no permit system is used (as is the case with Directive 91/676/EEC Concerning the Protection of Waters Against Pollution Caused by Nitrates from Agricultural Sources) the range of participants will necessarily be more limited. Thus, it is conceivable that environmental interest groups may challenge failures to designate certain areas of land as vulnerable zones.[89] However, since the action programmes which need to be drawn up for these zones do not require prior authorizations (for example in respect of the use of fertilizers) it is doubtful whether the action programmes themselves could become the issue of private enforcement.

Packaging or labelling requirements gave rise to the first proper preliminary reference in the sphere of the environment.[90] Just as limit values or quality objectives become enforceable by virtue of a system of prior authorization, packaging or labelling requirements are individualized by virtue of their internal market orientation, which is sometimes given expression by a "free movement clause".[91] Leaving aside the numerous criminal cases where labelling requirements have been at issue, they are therefore most likely to be invoked by individuals with cross-jurisdictional trading aspirations. If national law

[86] Case C–293/97, *H.A. Standley and Others* judgment of 29 Apr. 1999 (not yet reported).

[87] Since minimum harmonization is used, these emission standards may be more stringent than the uniform limit values contained in the directive.

[88] Enforcement of limit values hence does not take place horizontally (against the discharger) but vertically (against the national authority vested with the authority to grant or refuse permits).

[89] This obligation to designate vulnerable zones is analogous to the obligation to designate Special Protection Areas in the context of Dir. 79/409/EEC on the conservation of wild birds, [1979] OJ L103/1. It would hence appear that, likewise, this obligation may be privately enforced (see Case C–44/94, *Royal Society for the Protection of Birds* [1996] ECR I–3805).

[90] Case 148/78, *Ratti* [1979] ECR 1629.

[91] Such directives are usually based on the former Art. 100 or 100a (presently Arts. 94 or 95) EC.

flouts EC labelling requirements in a way not hindering private traders, once more it appears that private enforcement will depend on the vigilance of consumer or environmental groups. As yet, there are no practical examples of such instances. Identical observations apply *a fortiori* to the related category of *product standards* again often accompanied by "free circulation clauses".[92]

Important examples of what *prima facie* appear more discretionary *obligations to act* are found in the fields of environmental impact assessment and nature conservation.[93] Article 4 of Directive 85/337/EEC requires an environmental impact assessment to be undertaken for projects listed in Annexes I and II, in the latter case only when Member States consider that *their characteristics so require*.[94] Article 4(1) of Directive 79/409/EEC obliges Member States to classify the *most suitable* territories in number and size as special protection areas for the conservation of Annex I species taking into account their protection requirements in the geographical sea and land area where the Directive applies.[95]

It is precisely in view of the considerable discretion vested in national public authorities in the implementation of this type of provision that one might be forgiven for holding out little hope for private individuals to play a constructive role in their enforcement. After all, any discretion on the part of national implementing authorities has long been regarded an insurmountable hurdle for the direct effect of provisions of directives and consequently their private enforcement. Yet, this black-and-white perspective of private enforcement simply does not accord with the much more subtle case law of the ECJ.

Thus, on the basis of the relevant provisions of Directive 79/409/EEC the ECJ has judicially reviewed failures to designate Special Protection Areas in specific cases,[96] as well as the combined area of Special Protection Areas in a single Member State.[97] Consequently, there is no reason why national courts seised by private individuals should not similarly, with or without a prior preliminary reference to the ECJ, judicially review Member States' compliance with the obligation to classify Special Protection Areas. Indeed, the Royal Society for the Protection of Birds has successfully challenged the UK Secretary of State's decision to exclude Lappel Bank from the Medway Special Protection Area, after the House of Lords referred a question to the ECJ.[98]

---

[92] e.g. Art. 2 of Dir. 70/220/EEC on the approximation of the laws of the Member States on measures to be taken against air pollution by emissions from motor vehicles [1970] OJ L76/1: "No Member State may refuse to grant EEC type approval or national type-approval of a vehicle on grounds relating to air pollution by gases from positive-ignition engines of motor vehicles where that vehicle satisfies."

[93] Other examples fitting into this category are Art. 1(2)(a) of Dir. 76/160/EEC (designation of bathing waters), Art. 3(2) of Dir. 91/676 (designation of nitrate sensitive zones), Art. 4 of Dir. 79/923/EEC (designation of shellfish waters) and Art. 4 of Dir. 78/659/EEC (designation of fresh water fish waters).

[94] Dir. 85/337/EEC on the assessment of the effects of certain public and private projects on the environment [1985] OJ L176/18, as amended by Dir. 97/11/EEC [1997] OJ L73/5 (emphasis added).

[95] Dir. 79/409/EEC on the conservation of wild birds [1979] OJ L103/1 (emphasis added).

[96] Case C–355/90, *Commission v. Spain* [1993] ECR I–4221 (concerning the Santoña Marshes) and Case C–44/95, *Regina v. Secretary of State for the Environment, ex parte: Royal Society for the Protection of Birds* [1996] ECR I–3805 (concerning the classification of Lappel Bank).

[97] Case C–3/96, *Commission v. Netherlands* [1998] ECR I–3031.   [98] *Ibid.*

Meanwhile, although the ECJ has checked Member State autonomy as regards its implementation, this does not imply that Article 4(1) of Directive 79/409/EEC is directly effective *in toto*. Rather, it has identified the precise extent to which the Directive affords national authorities any discretion and consequently enables individuals judicially to review the proper exercise of that discretion. Put simply, in the context of Directive 79/409/EEC this means that individuals may enforce the obligation to designate certain areas as Special Protection Areas for Annex I species, but not the detailed arrangements for such a designation. In this latter respect, Member States continue to enjoy considerable freedom.[99]

Kraaijeveld shows that similar conclusions apply to environmental impact assessment. In respect of Articles 2(1) and 4(2) of Directive 85/337/EEC on the Assessment of the Effects of Certain Public and Private Projects on the environment the *Nederlandse Raad van State* asked:

does that obligation have direct effect, that is to say, may it be relied upon by an individual before a national court and must it be applied by the national court even if it was not invoked in the matter pending before that court? [100]

The Raad van State referred two questions; as it equates the right to rely on Article 4(2) with the question of its direct effect and submits a second question on the duty of national courts to raise Community law *ex proprio motu*. Crucially, the ECJ distills three questions by severing the issue of the direct effect of Article 4(2) from its private enforcement. As for the direct effect of Article 4(2), the ECJ strongly suggests that, due to the discretion it affords, the provision gives rise to no such effect. However, this conclusion has no impact on the right of individuals to invoke a directive or of the national courts to take it into consideration:

it would be incompatible with the binding effect attributed to a directive by Article 189 to exclude, in principle, the possibility that the obligation which it imposes may be invoked by those concerned. In particular, where the Community authorities have, by directive, imposed on Member States the obligation to pursue a particular course of conduct, the useful effect of such an act would be weakened if individuals were prevented from relying on it before national courts, and if the latter were prevented from taking it into consideration as an element of Community law in order to rule whether the national legislature, in exercising in the choice open to it as to the form and methods of implementation, has kept within the limits of its discretion set out in the directive.[101]

National courts may or must examine whether national authorities have remained within the limits of their discretion in implementing a directive. In respect of Articles 2(1) and 4(2) of the Directive, the limits of this discretion would be exceeded if, in practice, all projects (*in casu* relating to dykes) were exempted in advance from the requirement of an impact assessment, unless

---

[99] See H. Somsen, (1998) 7 *European Environmental Law Review* 117–23.
[100] Case C–72/95, *Aannemersbedrijf Kraaijeveld BV e.a.* v. *Gedeputeeerde Staten van Zuid Holland* [1996] ECR I–5403, para. 20.
[101] *Ibid.*, para. 56.

all projects excluded could, when viewed as a whole, be regarded as not being likely to have significant effects on the environment.[102]

As the ECJ pointed out in *Van Gend en Loos*, where it first introduced the notion of private enforcement, *prohibitions* are ideally suited for this purpose.[103] The prohibition on discharging dangerous substances directly into groundwater, for example, is one which, according to the ECJ, private individuals may enforce in their national court.[104] By contrast, in respect of Article 4 of Directive 75/442/EEC on Waste the ECJ explicitly denied individuals the right to enforce the prohibition it contains.[105] The provision at issue provided as follows:

Member States shall take the necessary measures to ensure that waste is removed or disposed of without endangering human health and without using processes or methods which could harm the environment, and in particular:
— without risk to water, air, soil and plants and animals;
— without causing a nuisance through noise or odours;
— without adversely affecting the countryside or places of special interest. Member States shall also take the necessary measure to prohibit the abandonment, dumping or uncontrolled disposal of waste.

The ECJ ruled that the provision was 'neither unconditional, nor sufficiently precise and thus not capable of conferring rights on which individuals may rely as against the State'. In fact, as Krämer points out, the ECJ suggests that none of the various elements of Article 4 are amenable to private enforcement.[106] This outcome is in stark and not altogether comprehensible contrast to the *Kraaijeveld* doctrine. There appears no reason why individuals should not ascertain whether national authorities exceeded the limits of discretion afforded to them by Article 4 of Directive 75/442/EEC on Waste. Even the most superficial reading of Article 4 suggests that national authorities' discretion is clearly defined in that, whatever form of waste management is preferred, waste must be disposed of without harm to human health and the environment. Also, the abandonment, dumping or uncontrolled disposal of waste should be simply prohibited.

Neither does *Difesa della Cava* sit easily with *Leybucht Dykes*, where a prohibition analogous to that of Article 4 of Directive 75/442 on waste was at stake.[107] In respect of Special Protection Areas established by Member States pursuant to Article 4(1) of Directive 79/409/EEC on the Conservation of Wild Birds, Article 4(4) obliges Member States to:

take all appropriate steps to avoid pollution or deterioration of habitats or any disturbances affecting the birds, in so far as these would be significant having regard to the objectives of this Article.

---

[102] *Ibid.*, para. 53. [103] Case 26/62, *Van Gend en Loos*, n. 11 above.

[104] Case 131/88, *Commission* v. *Germany* [1991] ECR 825.

[105] Case C–236/92, *Difesa della Cava* [1994] ECR I–485.

[106] See L. Krämer, "Direct Effect of EC Environmental Law", in Somsen, n. 8 above, 99–134.

[107] Case C–57/89, *Commission* v. *Germany* [1991] ECR I–883. For a full analysis of the nature of the provisions concerning the obligation to designate and prevent subsequent deterioration of Special Protection Areas see D. A. C. Freestone, "The Enforcement of the Wild Birds Directive: A Case Study" in Somsen, n. 8 above.

The ECJ in this case ruled that Member States were not at liberty to reduce the size and extent of Special Protection Areas in the absence of exceptional interests superior to the general interests represented by the ecological objectives of the Directive. Although this case arose in the context of infringement proceedings, again it is submitted that it necessarily implies that individuals may privately enforce Article 4(4) of the Directive.

There is no obvious explanation for the contrasting outcomes in the two cases. Most likely, however, the ECJ in *Kraaijeveld* introduced a nuance to the private enforcement of EC environmental law, albeit one consistent with previous but somewhat forgotten case law.[108] It is significant that in *Difesa della Cava* the ECJ still equated private enforcement with the conventional notion of direct effect. Following *Kraaijeveld*, however, the issue of direct effect has become little more than the extreme end of a scale according to which Member States have been afforded discretion in the implementation of EC environmental law. Directly effective provisions allow national courts to substitute their decisions for those of public authorities in charge of implementing EC environmental law, since those authorities enjoy no substantive discretion. In the absence of direct effect, however, those courts may still pronounce on the question whether the authorities have honoured the limits of their discretion.

iii New Instruments

In the pursuit of its environmental policy, the Community is committed to the use of a wider range of instruments.[109] The new instruments that are considered for this purpose in particular include soft law, taxes, subsidies and environmental agreements. It is not viable to assess the extent to which compliance with all these instruments may be enforced privately here. However, private enforceability is a concern which should be of decisive importance for any decision to resort to such new instruments in concrete instances. If the *acquis communautaire* is to be preserved, new instruments should only be used in instances where this does not disadvantage individuals wishing to invoke EC environmental law in their national courts. It has already been observed that, in fact, there already exist numerous clear, precise and unconditional provisions of environmental directives that cannot be invoked by individuals. In these instances, alternatives to command and control types of regulation appear unproblematic and, given their poor implementation rate, may even be desirable. For example, in respect of the duty to furnish the Commission with information on the quality of the aquatic environment, environmental agreements between the Commission and (privatized) authorities responsible for monitoring and testing appear an attractive alternative to the *status quo*. After all, at present this obligation is routinely flouted and

---

[108] Case 51/76, *Vereniging Nederlandse Ondernemingen* [1977] ECR 113; C.W.A. Timmermans, "Directives: Their Effect Within the National Legal Systems" (1979) 16 *Common Market Law Review* 533–55.

[109] See Fifth Environmental Action Programme, *Towards Sustainability* [1993] OJ C138/1.

private individuals cannot aid in its enforcement. Alternative instruments could therefore be considered.

Since the alternative to the agreement with the European automobile industry[110] would be a directive fixing CO_2 emission limit values for passenger cars, this environmental agreement is less unambiguous in this respect. Presumably, a system analogous to Directive 70/156/EEC on the Approximation of the Laws of the Member States to the Type Approval of Motor Vehicles and their Trailers would have come to apply.[111] Under this system, manufacturers may apply with the national authorities for an approval valid in all Member States ("Community type-approval") for a model ("vehicle type") if it complies with the specifications of the more than forty so-called "separate" directives harmonizing the technical rules. It is the grant or refusal of this Community type-approval that is instrumental in affording individuals an opportunity to enforce Member State compliance with the Directive. This has occurred in practice although, not surprisingly, in response to a refusal rather than a grant of a type approval.[112] The agreement between the Commission and the European automobile industry, on the other hand, does not allow individuals to play any such role.

The case law of the ECJ[113] and the Commission's Communication on Environmental Agreements[114] suggest that these reservations concerning new instruments also apply to their use at national level.

V. Identifying questions of EC environmental law

Although Article 234 EC is crucial for the participation of individuals in the enforcement of EC environmental law, it is not individuals involved in a dispute before a national court who have a right to refer questions to the ECJ. Instead, the initiative to refer must emanate from the national court. Neither are the institutions of the Community,[115] administrative authorities in Member States,[116] courts in third states[117] or international tribunals[118] entitled to refer. That administrative authorities do not enjoy the right to refer a question to the ECJ is not wholly satisfactory since these authorities *are* under an obligation to apply directly effective provisions of EC environmental law in the same way as national courts do.[119] Since questions relating to the direct

---

[110] COM (88)495 final. [111] [1970] OJ Spec. Ed. (I) 96.

[112] Case C–329/95, *VAG Sverige AB* [1997] ECR I–2675.   [113] See the case law at n. 60 above.

[114] COM(96)561. See in particular the contribution by J. Verschuuren at p. 103.

[115] But see the new Title H of the Treaty of Amsterdam.

[116] Case C–24/92, *Corbiau* v. *Administration des contributions* [1993] ECR I–1277.

[117] This is with the exception of courts of the EFTA countries (see Art. 107 of the EEA agreement).

[118] See Krück, n. 27 above, 4/620.

[119] See Case 103/88, *Fratelli Costanzo* [1988] ECR 339, where in respect of Dir. 71/305/EEC on award procedures for public construction projects [1971] OJ L185/5, it was held that: "An authority, including a local authority, has the same duty as a national court to apply Article 29(5) of Council Directive 71/305/EEC and not to apply those provisions of national law that are incompatible with it."

effect of environmental directives are questions of interpretation, and thus ultimately for the ECJ to decide, the denial of a right to refer questions for these authorities amounts to something of a paradox. However, as has already been observed, the preliminary ruling procedure and the doctrine of direct effect have distinct spheres of operation and so, purely conceptually, this paradox is understandable, albeit perhaps undesirable from the perspective of the uniform application and interpretation of Community environmental law.

Since the very object of Article 234 EC is to ensure the uniform interpretation of Community law, not surprisingly, the meaning of the term "court" in Article 234 EC is determined by Community law and has itself been the subject of numerous preliminary questions. Because, from the perspective of the uniform interpretation of Community law, it is desirable that all those national judicial bodies which apply and interpret Community law have access to the ECJ's interpretative guidance, the ECJ has embraced a functional and wide interpretation of the concept.[120] In summary, for a request from a judicial body for a preliminary ruling to be admissible, such a body must be independent, its jurisdiction obligatory and founded on law, have a permanent character, and its judgments based on legal norms.[121]

Thus, although for the private enforcement of EC environmental law the mobilization of individuals' vigilance to protect their rights is a necessary precondition, it is the national court that decides whether and which questions of Community environmental law are at issue. Evidently, before this question arises, the national court must first identify and/or acknowledge that issues of EC environmental law *prima facie* exist.

In this regard, two scenarios must be distinguished. The first and most obvious way in which an issue of EC environmental law may become the subject of national proceedings is by the initiative of the parties themselves. However, perhaps a more interesting scenario arises where the parties themselves fail to bring up the relevant issues of EC environmental law. Such was the case in *Kraaijeveld*, where the Dutch Raad van State asked whether, where an obligation of, *in casu*, the environmental impact assessment directive is directly effective, it must be applied by national courts even if it was not in fact invoked in the matter pending before that court. The ECJ answered this question in the affirmative. If under national law a court must or may raise of its own motion pleas in law based on a binding national rule which have not been put forward by the parties, it must, for matters within its jurisdiction, examine of its own

---

[120] In Case 14/86, *Pretore Salò* v. *X* [1987] ECR 2545, which dealt with Dir. 78/659/EEC on the quality of fresh waters needing protection in order to support fish life, the Italian Government questioned the jurisdiction of the Pretore to refer questions. The ECJ, however, noted that: "the Court has jurisdiction to reply to a request for a preliminary ruling if that request emanates from a court or tribunal which has acted in the general framework of its task of judging, independently and in accordance with the law, cases coming within the jurisdiction conferred on it by law, even though certain functions of that court or tribunal in the proceedings which gave rise to the reference for a preliminary ruling are not strictly speaking, of a judicial nature."

[121] See Krück, n. 27 above, 4/621.

motion whether the legislative or administrative authorities of the Member State have remained within the limits of their discretion.[122]

Whereas *Kraaijeveld* concerned administrative proceedings—as will be seen by far the most fruitful option for the private enforcement of Member State compliance—*Van Schijndel*[123] arose in civil proceedings and shows that the extent to which such an obligation exists depends on the nature of the proceedings in which the issue of EC environmental law arises. Thus, in adversarial proceedings such as the civil proceedings in *Van Schijndel*, where the judge's role is a passive one, the obligation to raise points *ex proprio motu* does not exist save for reasons of the public interest.[124] This in turn implies that contentious proceedings may be expected to be a more promising source of preliminary references than adversary proceedings. Whereas, for example, the Dutch judge in criminal courts occupies an active role (contentious proceedings), English judges preside over adversarial proceedings and so, as a matter of Community law, are not expected to raise points on their own motion to the same extent. Despite these limits to the obligation to raise points *ex proprio motu*, it is clear that it considerably increases the effectiveness of private enforcement of EC environmental law. Private enforcement is no longer a direct function of the interests of private individuals, but extends beyond the narrow subject matter of a given dispute, at least in contentious administrative proceedings.

Since national courts, and particularly those presiding over contentious proceedings, may be faced with an obligation to raise issues of EC environmental law on their own motion—and thus to identify them on their own motion—it becomes difficult to deny the *erga omnes* effect of preliminary rulings. This, in turn, calls into question the perceived bilateral/horizontal nature of the procedure. It is through preliminary rulings that the direct effect of provisions of EC environmental law is established which, according to *Kraaijeveld*, national courts may subsequently be under an obligation to raise *ex proprio motu*. In other words, *erga omnes* effects of preliminary rulings are a necessary corollary of the duty of national courts to raise issues of EC environmental law in national proceedings.

VI. To Refer or Not to Refer: Is There a Question?

That it is not a matter for the litigants to initiate a preliminary procedure was already noted above. Although they may obviously request that a reference be made, ultimately it is the national judge alone who has the sole power to decide whether and what to refer to the ECJ. The ECJ will also not in any way review the subjective necessity of the question; if the *national court* deems a question necessary (provided the question concerns the interpretation or

---

[122] Case C–72/95, *Kraaijeveld* [1996] ECR I–5403.
[123] Joined Cases C–430-431/93 [1995] ECR I–4705.
[124] On the viability of such a "procedural rule of reason" see Prechal, n. 17 above, 690.

validity of Community law) the ECJ will pass a preliminary judgment.[125] As a corollary, national law cannot restrict the competence of national courts to request a preliminary reference.[126]

Whereas lower courts enjoy complete discretion, the third paragraph of Article 234 EC imposes an obligation on courts or tribunals of Member States "against whose decisions there is no judicial remedy under national law", to make a referral to the ECJ where a question is raised.[127]

The scope of the obligation to refer and, more generally, the *erga omnes* effect of preliminary rulings is crucial for the purposes of determining the potential of Article 234 EC as an enforcement mechanism in addition to that contained in Article 226 EC. In theory, two extreme positions may be distinguished. The first is that courts are obliged to refer even if the ECJ in a previous reference gave a clear answer to an identical question of Community environmental law or, in other words, if there is no "question" in the opinion of the referring court. The attraction of this approach resides in the fact that it secures the widest possible uniformity of EC environmental law and minimizes any risks of judicial error. The disadvantages of this approach, however, are as numerous as they are compelling. Quite apart from inevitable capacity problems—with which the ECJ is already faced—national procedures would often unnecessarily be delayed, in turn leading to needless environmental degradation. Another even more dangerous side effect is that the authority of the ECJ's references (since they merely generate *ad hoc* effects) and the cognitive function of preliminary rulings will be reduced to a bare minimum. An absolute obligation to refer stifles any incentives on the part of national courts to learn EC environmental law from previous preliminary rulings. This is a clearly unacceptable consequence of the obligation to refer. It may be said that there is an inverse relationship between the extent to which national courts are compelled to refer questions against their own better instincts and the value of preliminary references for enforcement purposes.

The second approach is to accept the doctrine of precedent for preliminary rulings, which bind other national courts. This could imply that national

---

[125] This was demonstrated recently in Joined Cases C–304, 330, 342/194, and 224/95, *Euro Tombesi*, [1997] ECR I–3561, where the ECJ ruled that under the procedure provided for in Art. 234 EC: "it is solely for the national courts before which actions are brought, and which must bear the responsibility for the subsequent judicial decision, to determine in the light of the special features of each case both the need for a preliminary ruling in order to enable them to deliver judgment and the relevance of the questions which they submit to the Court" (para. 38).

[126] See, e.g., Case 176/73, *Rheinmühlen Düsseldorf v. Einfuhr und Vorratsstelle für Getreide und Futtermittel* [1974] ECR 33. In this case the issue was whether national law could limit the competence of lower national courts to refer a question where according to national law they were merely to follow the instructions of a higher court.

[127] Some commentators interpret this obligation to mean that in all cases where *de facto* no further judicial remedies are possible, such an obligation exists ("concrete theory"), whilst others argue that this obligation relates only to the highest courts of the Member State ("abstract theory"). From Case 6/64, *Costa v. ENEL* [1964] ECR 1253, it has been inferred that the ECJ itself is inclined towards the concrete theory. In summary proceedings, even when they are final, such an obligation does not exist (Case 107/76, *Hofmann-La Roche* [1977] ECR 972; Case 35/82, *Morson* [1982] ECR 3723).

courts, which are confronted with an identical or even similar question to one that has been previously decided by the ECJ, should apply that previous ruling and must not refer a question. Obviously, the authority of the ECJ's rulings would increase dramatically, far fewer cases would be submitted to it and national proceedings would not be unnecessarily delayed by pointless references. Most important, national courts are delegated crucial enforcement powers which they can exercise freely and to some extent independently from the ECJ.[128] Clearly, however, it would open the door for judicial error and could, at least occasionally, undermine the uniformity of EC environmental law. At the same time, the relationship between the ECJ and national courts would become vertical/multilateral; a fundamental departure from its present horizontal/bilateral character. Ultimately, this might adversely affect the preparedness of national courts to refer even in those instances where they should.

Neither of the two approaches are therefore fully acceptable in their purest forms. The ECJ indeed pursues a middle course, the net effect of which, it is submitted, is largely positive for the private enforcement of EC environmental law and which may be summarized as follows.

First, the ECJ has clarified the significance of prior preliminary references. Where an *identical* question has been referred, there is no obligation to refer.[129] In the same case, the ECJ also ruled that this equally applies if previous ECJ judgments have already dealt with the point of law in question, irrespective of the nature of those proceedings (criminal, administrative or civil), even though the questions at issue are *not strictly identical*. However, in both cases, national courts and tribunals remain entirely at liberty to refer questions if they consider it appropriate to do so. Whereas these observations apply to questions relating to interpretation, they apply *a fortiori* to questions relating to the validity of Community environmental law,[130] and a national court cannot pronounce on the validity of a measure of EC environmental law without a prior reference to the ECJ.[131]

Secondly, the ECJ has also provided guidance on the issue as to what extent there is an obligation to refer if there are no prior ECJ rulings on a particular issue, more commonly known as the doctrine of *acte clair*. In short, this doctrine stipulates that courts are under no obligation to refer if "it has established that the question raised is irrelevant or that the Community provision in question has already been interpreted by the ECJ or that the correct application of Community law is so obvious as to leave no scope for any reasonable doubt".[132] However, the ECJ advocates reserve on the part of national courts in the light of the specific characteristics of Community law, in particular

---

[128] See Craig and De Búrca, n. 18 above, 498–552.
[129] Cases 28–30/62, *Da Costa* [1963] ECR 31.
[130] Case 66/80, *International Chemical Corporation* [1981] ECR 1191.
[131] Case 314/85, *Foto Frost* [1987] ECR 4199.
[132] Case 281/81, *Srl CILFIT* [1982] ECR 3415.

differences to which its interpretation gives rise and the risk of divergences in judicial decisions within the Community.[133]

Even where a national court is not obliged to refer according to the ECJ's guidelines, it will answer any reference which the national court deems desirable. It has also been seen that, if questions are framed imprecisely or little factual information is provided, the ECJ has developed a practice of rephrasing the questions or distilling relevant issues so as to assist the national court as far as possible. However, as is exemplified by numerous cases, the ECJ has become increasingly inclined to decline jurisdiction where it feels that the reference arose out of a dispute which was not genuine or has hypothetical or that the question was not relevant to the outcome of the national case.[134]

Yet, Community law does not in any way condition the kind of procedures in which a preliminary question may be referred and in practice issues of EC environmental law have arisen in criminal, civil and administrative proceedings.[135] The nature of these proceedings being different, the function which (directly effective) provisions of EC environmental law perform varies accordingly. In assessing the impact of private enforcement on securing Member State compliance with EC environmental law, apart from the subject matter of any preliminary reference, the type of proceedings which has given rise to the reference is therefore also an important factor. An initial insight into the distribution of instances of private enforcement over administrative, civil and criminal proceedings may be obtained from Figure 1.

A. CRIMINAL PROCEEDINGS

A considerable proportion of the environmental preliminary references which have hitherto reached the ECJ, arose in the context of national criminal proceedings.[136] Such cases necessarily arise at the stage of the imposition of sanctions as a result of breaches of national environmental law. In some Member States, notably Italy and to a lesser extent the Netherlands, criminal sanctions are commonly used for breaches of environmental law, something that the administrative nature of EC environmental law does not rule out.[137] In these instances, EC environmental law is not advanced in order to enforce Member State compliance or to protect environmental rights. Rather, it is used as a protective shield against criminal sanctions embedded in national environmen-

---

[133] Case 281/81, *Srl CILFIT* [1982] ECR 3415.

[134] See Cases 297/88 and 197/89, *Dzodzi* v. *Belgium* [1990] ECR I-3763, paras 35 and 39. See also Case C-118/94, *Associazone Italiana per il World Wildlife Fund* [1996] ECR I-1223 paras. 14 and 15.

[135] Between 30 Nov. 1976 and 29 Apr. 1999 a total of 46 preliminary references, which for the purpose of this study can be said to deal with environmental issues, were made to the ECJ. Of these, 19 arose in proceedings of an administrative nature, 24 in proceedings of a criminal nature, and 3 were in civil cases.

[136] *Ibid.*

[137] In joined Cases C-58, 75, 112, 123, 135, 140, 141, 154, and 157/95, *Gallotti* [1996] ECR I-4345 the question was asked whether Dir. 91/156/EEC amending Dir. 75/442/EEC on waste ([1991] OJ L78/32) allowed Member States to impose criminal penalties for its breach. The ECJ answered this question in the affirmative.

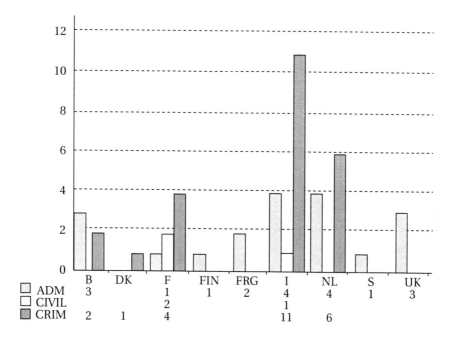

	B	DK	F	FIN	FRG	I	NL	S	UK
☐ ADM	3	1	1	1	2	4	4	1	3
☐ CIVIL			2			1			
▉ CRIM	2	1	4			11	6		

Figure 1. EC Environmental Law in National Courts

tal law. This immediately puts the number of references emanating from Italian and Dutch courts in a different perspective, as well as their contribution to enforcing Member State compliance with EC environmental law.

Sometimes, the defendant will have complied with national provisions of environmental law which, if interpreted in accordance with EC law or set aside in favour of directly effective provisions of EC environmental law, would aggravate the defendant's criminal responsibility. The ECJ has consistently emphasized that EC environmental law cannot have such effects *vis-à-vis* individuals.[138]

Conversely, criminal sanctions may be applied for breaches of national environmental laws with which the defendant did *not* comply, but which are

---

[138] See Case C–168/95, *Arcaro* [1996] ECR I–4705. See also Case C–14/86, *Pretore di Salò* v. *Persons Unknown* [1987] ECR 2545. An interesting, if somewhat curious question arose in the context of Case 228/87, *Pretura unificata di Torino* v. *X.* [1988] ECR 5099. In this case, the criminal proceedings in question concerned the offence of failing to fulfil official duties provided for in Art. 328 of the Italian Criminal Code inasmuch as the authorities in question had not prohibited the consumption by humans of waters which did not satisfy the conditions laid down in an Italian decree. According to the Pretore, the authorities would not be criminally liable if the derogations from the decree were in conformity with the derogations permitted under Dir. 80/778 [1980] OJ L229/11. The curiosity of the case resides in the fact that it is difficult to see how, in view of the doctrine that EC environmental law cannot aggravate individuals' criminal responsibility, the ECJ's interpretation could have made any difference to the outcome of the national case. A similar observation applies to Case C–224/94, *Euro Tombesi* [1997] ECR I–3561. The ECJ in this latter case actually did draw attention to this principle, but nevertheless proceeded to answer the Italian court's questions.

not in conformity with secondary or primary EC (environmental) law. In the latter case, the ECJ may be asked to determine whether certain activities carried out by a defendant ought to have been subject to a prior authorization or are prohibited. For this purpose, it may have to interpret, for example, the concept of "waste" or "species". Depending on the outcome of such a question, a breach may have occurred which may be punishable by some form of criminal sanction, or the activities may fall outside the scope of the directive, in which case prior authorization could not be required.[139]

A final class of related cases arose in criminal proceedings where national environmental law was alleged to be in breach of provisions of primary Community law, notably those relating to the free movement of goods and provisions relating to competition.[140]

The effect of the reference in criminal cases therefore is usually not that Community environmental law prevails over conflicting national provisions. Rather, the reverse is often true in that private enforcement ensures that a failure of a Member State to comply with Community environmental law does *not*

---

[139] See Joined Cases C–394, 330, 342/194, and 224/95, *Euro Tombesi* [1997] ECR I–3561; Case 359/88 *Zanetti* [1990] ECR I–1509; Joined Cases C–206 and 207/88, *Vessoso and Zanetti* [1990] ECR I–1461; Joined Cases 372–374/85, *Oscar Traen* [1987] ECR 2141, where criminal responsibility of the defendants hinged on the question whether the concept of waste comprised the activities in which they were involved.

Similarly, Dir. 79/409/EEC on the conservation of wild birds ([1979] OJ L103/1) was successfully invoked in Case C–149/94 when criminal proceedings were instituted against Mr Vergy for keeping specimens of birds protected under the Directive which were born and reared in captivity [1996] ECR I–299. Directive 79/409/EEC provided no successful defence in Case C–202/94, *van der Feesten* [1996] ECR I–355, where it was decided that the concept of "species" included all subdivisions, such as breeds of subspecies.

The scope of Dir. 90/642/EEC ([1990] OJ L350/71) was at issue in Joined Cases C–54 and 74/94, *Cacchiarelli* [1995] ECR 391, where the ECJ held that the Dir. allowed Member States scope to regulate certain substances not covered by the Directive.

Case C–379/92, *Peralta* [1994] ECR I–3453 revolved around the compatibility of Italian criminal provisions on the discharge of hydrocarbons into the sea with primary and secondary Community law.

[140] Where criminal sanctions are imposed on the illegal marketing of certain products which are harmful to human health or the environment, issues have arisen as regards the compatibility of such legislation with Arts. 28–30 (formerly Arts. 30–36) EC, where such products are lawfully marketed in another Member State (see Case C–293/94, *Brandsma* [1996] ECR I–3159). The compatibility of national criminal sanctions with the provisions on the free movement of goods and secondary waste legislation was also at stake in Case C–37/92, *Vanacker* [1993] ECR I–4947 which dealt with the French system of waste oil collection. Also fitting into this category is Case C–169/89, *Gourmetterie Van den Burg* [1990] ECR I–2143 dealing with the compatibility of more stringent Dutch conservation measures in respect of the red grouse with Arts. 28 and 30 EC. Case 125/88, *Nijman* [1989] ECR 3533, too, dealt with the compatibility of more extensive national rules than those contained in Dir. 79/117/EEC on plant-production products ([1979] OJ L33/36) with Arts. 28 and 30 EC. See also Case C–118/86, *Openbaar Ministerie* v. *Nertsvoederfabriek* [1987] ECR 3883, concerning the compatibility of Dutch rules requiring poultry offal to be delivered to approved rendering plants only with, *inter alia*, Arts. 28, 29, and 30 EC. See also Case C–240/83, *ADBHU* [1985] ECR 531 and Case C–172/82, *Inter Huiles* [1983] ECR 555, on the compatibility of Dir. 75/439/EEC on the disposal of waste oils ([1975] OJ L194/23) with Arts. 3, 29, 30, and 81 EC. In Case C–148/78, *Ratti* [1979] ECR 1629, the question was, *inter alia*, whether a Member State could regulate certain substances after the adoption of harmonizing measures pursuant to Art. 94 (formerly Art. 100) EC and enforce such rules with criminal sanctions.

have effects in the national legal order in so far as it could aggravate the criminal responsibility of individuals.

Whereas these criminal cases on occasion give rise to clarification of certain concepts such as "waste" or "species", they may restrict the impact of (EC) environmental law at the national level. This occurs either by virtue of the principle that the criminal responsibility of individuals cannot be aggravated as a result of the (in)direct effect of provisions of EC environmental law, or because the national provisions which attract the criminal sanctions under national law breach directly effective provisions of EC (environmental) law.

B. CIVIL PROCEEDINGS

On only three occasions civil proceedings have given rise to private enforcement of EC environmental law. This is partly because directives lack horizontal direct effect, partly because at present there is little private European environmental law other than the judicially established doctrine of non-contractual state liability.[141]

Where civil proceedings give rise to a preliminary reference their enforcement function is restricted. In civil proceedings, parties will usually not argue the incompatibility of national law with EC environmental law. Instead, they will often seek to challenge the validity of a Community act that forms an obstacle to the performance of a contractual obligation tying the parties. For example, recently the validity of Regulation (EC) No. 3093/94 on Substances which Deplete the Ozone Layer[142] was challenged on the basis of its alleged compatibility with Articles 3, 10, 28, 82, 87, and 231 of the Treaty (formerly Articles 3, 5, 30, 86, 92, and 174). The preliminary question arose in the context of civil proceedings after one of the parties refused payment on the basis that the product it had purchased could no longer be legally marketed after entry into force of Article 5 of the Regulation.[143] Similarly, in *Etablissements Armand Mondiet*, the legality of Regulation (EC) No. 345/92,[144] which outlawed driftnets with a length exceeding 2.5 kilometres, was challenged in civil proceedings by a party seeking performance of contractual obligations arising out of the sale of driftnets which were seven kilometres long.[145]

In these civil cases, private enforcement at present frequently concerns the adverse effects resulting from the unlawful exercise of EC legislative powers in the field of the environment and primarily serves as an alternative to Article 230 EC. Questions concerning the compatibility of national environmental law with EC environmental law rarely arise, and the civil cases where issues of EC environmental law are at stake do not appear to complement Article 226 EC in any significant way.

---

[141] In the Netherlands, claims based on the non-contractual liability of the state for breaches of EC environmental law will normally arise in the context of civil proceedings. Meanwhile, this does not apply to all jurisdictions.

[142] [1994] OJ L333/1. [143] Case C–341/95, *Gianni Bettati* [1998] ECR I–4355.

[144] [1992] OJ L42/15.

[145] Case C–405/92, *Etablissements Armand Mondiet* [1993] ECR I–6133.

C. ADMINISTRATIVE PROCEEDINGS

The most fertile ground for private enforcement of Member State compliance with EC environmental law is represented by administrative proceedings. In the course of administrative proceedings, national courts may judicially review the role of the state as legislator (formal implementation), the exercise of public authority discretion by virtue of environmental legislation (practical implementation), and the way in which compliance with environmental laws is secured (enforcement).[146] As Table I shows, by far the most interesting cases indeed have arisen in the context of administrative proceedings.

As illustrated by cases such as *Kraaijeveld*[147] and *RSPB*,[148] it is because environmental directives oblige national authorities to exercise discretion in particular circumscribed ways that private individuals acquire a role in the enforcement process. Thus, if a directive requires prior authorizations for the discharge of certain dangerous substances in water which are to satisfy certain limit values or quality objectives, individuals may challenge the grant of permits which do not meet those minimum standards. National courts thus become arenas for a tripartite enforcement process. This process involves the relevant competent national authority (e.g. responsible for granting or refusing authorizations to discharge dangerous substances in water), the addressees of any decision (e.g. those applying for a permit) and parties who may be indirectly affected by the exercise of discretion vested with the national competent authorities, such as downstream riparian owners of land or environmental interest groups.

D. ANALYSIS

It has already been observed that preliminary references play a crucial role in the development of the Community legal order and the enforcement of its rules. This is true in qualitative terms (the importance of the issues decided by way of a preliminary ruling) but also in quantitative terms (the number of preliminary rulings as compared to, in particular, judgments pursuant to Article 226 EC).

Yet practice in the sphere of the environment is not consistent with this pattern. For Community law *in toto*, the total number of preliminary references consistently outnumbers the total number of direct actions, by approximately a factor of 4.[149] Strikingly, the mirror image emerges in the sphere of the environment; infringement proceedings outnumber preliminary rulings, again by

---

[146] During the period assessed, 19 preliminary references were referred in the course of administrative proceedings.

[147] Case C–72/95, *Aannemersbedrijf Kraaijeveld BV* [1996] ECR I–3805.

[148] Case C–44/95, *Royal Society for the Protection of Birds* [1996] ECR I–3805.

[149] For 1997, the total number of judgments pursuant to Art. 226 EC amounted to 43, whilst the ECJ delivered 161 preliminary references. Source: statistical information of the Court of Justice, on the Internet at: *http://curia.eu.int/en/stat/index.htm*.

approximately a factor of 4.[150] In good part, this is explained by the "leakage" in the preceding two links of the private enforcement chain. It might be suggested that discrete factors related to the subject matter and/or the attitude of national courts also impact on the number of references actually made in the field of the environment.

However, there are no *prima facie* grounds for suspecting that national courts are inherently less prepared to refer questions relating to EC environmental law than other issues of Community law. Unless national courts have a much clearer grasp of issues of EC environmental law than the present writer, it is also unlikely that the doctrine of *acte clair* explains the low number of questions referred. There are simply too many fundamental issues of EC environmental law which remain unresolved. In any event, *acte clair* must be presumed equally to affect other areas of EC law, and hence does not explain comparative differences in numbers of preliminary references.

It could also be suggested that some of the most controversial provisions of EC environmental law likely to give rise to private enforcement action are perceived to lack direct effect, ruling out a reference to the ECJ. Once more, and for obvious reasons, this explanation lacks force. First, questions concerning the effect of provisions of EC environmental law are questions of interpretation and therefore ideally suited to being referred to the ECJ. Secondly, as has already been sufficiently shown, direct effect is not a precondition for a preliminary reference. Moreover, in view of the doctrine of indirect effect, which is designed partly to compensate for the effects caused by the absence of (horizontal) direct effect of environmental directives, a flood of references relating to the interpretation of provisions of environmental directives might have been anticipated.

VII. The Jurisdiction of the ECJ Pursuant to Article 234 EC

Article 234 EC empowers the ECJ both to "interpret" Community law and to rule on the "validity" of acts of the institutions of the Community and the ECB. Obviously, the ECJ cannot pronounce on the validity of primary Community environmental law. The ECJ is not in any way constrained in respect of the grounds for review of the validity of Community environmental law and, in particular, all the grounds for review contained in Article 230 EC may feature similarly in the procedure of Article 234 EC.[151]

Whereas it is essentially for the national court to decide whether a referral to the ECJ is opportune, the nature of the preliminary procedure requires a number of elementary conditions to be satisfied. The fact that pursuant to Article 234 the ECJ may not pronounce on the validity of national environmental law has already been alluded to. It is somewhat surprising that national courts

---

[150] In 1997, under the subject heading "environment and consumers" 34 direct actions were initiated against 8 preliminary rulings.

[151] Case 74/63, *Internationale Crediet en Handelsvereniging* [1964] ECR 1.

continue so frequently to ask the ECJ to pronounce on the validity of national environmental law. The ECJ in such cases will not decline to provide a judgment. Rather, it will "supply the national court with an interpretation of Community law on all such points as may enable that court to determine that issue of compatibility for the purpose of the case before it".[152] Similarly, even if the question does not concern the validity of national law but is simply vaguely formulated, the ECJ will not shy away from "rephrasing" the question. In *Arcaro*, the question referred by the Italian court was ambiguously formulated and also concerned the interpretation of countless Community environmental directives which an Italian Decree was intended to implement. Nevertheless, the ECJ focused on Directive 76/464/EEC on Pollution Caused by Certain Dangerous Substances Discharged Into the Aquatic Environment and Directive 83/513/EEC on Limit Values and Quality Objectives for Cadmium Discharges.[153]

In addition, the ECJ will not pronounce on questions that did not arise out of a genuine dispute.[154] In *Associazone Italiana per il World Wildlife Fund*, where a number of environmental groups challenged the granting of hunting permits on the basis of Directive 79/409/EEC on the Conservation of Wild Birds, the Italian hunting federation questioned the ECJ's jurisdiction on this ground. The ECJ replied that it would refuse to provide a reference only if it were apparent either that the procedure provided for in Article 234 EC had been diverted from its true purpose and was being used in fact to lead the ECJ to give a ruling by means of a contrived dispute, or that the provision of Community law referred to the ECJ for interpretation was manifestly incapable of applying.[155]

Nor will the ECJ accept jurisdiction to rule on questions by a national court if those questions bear no relation to the facts of the subject matter of the main action and are not objectively required in order to settle the dispute in the main action.[156] Such was the case, for example, in *Corsica Ferries*, which dealt with a system of compulsory piloting services operated in the port of Genoa.[157] The ECJ in this case sifted out the questions that were related to the facts of the main action, and did not accept jurisdiction in respect of the other questions.

Evidently, for the ECJ to be able to make such a judgement, it needs to have a minimum degree of insight into the factual situation that gave rise to the national dispute. In *Pretore di Salò*, the ECJ merely noted that "it might be *convenient* in certain circumstances for the facts of the case to be established and for questions of purely national law to be settled at the time when the reference is made".[158] In a number of more recent instances, not in the sphere of the

---

[152] See Joined Cases C–304, 330, 342/94, and 224/95, *Euro Tombesi* [1997] ECR I–3561 (para. 36).
[153] Case C–168/95, *Arcaro* [1996] ECR I–4705, para. 20.
[154] See Joined Cases 297/88 and 197/89, *Dzodzi* v. *Belgium* [1990] ECR I–3763, paras. 35 and 39. See also Cases 104/79 and 244/80, *Foglia* v. *Novello* [1980] ECR 745 and [1981] ECR 3045.
[155] Case C–118/94, *Associazone per il World Wildlife Fund* [1996] ECR I–1223, para 15.
[156] See Joined Cases C–304, 330, 342/94, and 224/95, *Euro Tombesi* [1997] ECR I–3561, para. 38.
[157] Case C–18/93, *Corsica Ferries* [1994] ECR I–1783.
[158] Case 14/86, *Pretore di Salò* v. *X* [1986] ECR 2525, para. 10, emphasis added.

environment, the ECJ has refused jurisdiction to provide a reference on the basis that it did not have the necessary minimum factual information.[159] In *Gallotti*, for example, an Italian court referred a question relating to the power of Member States to impose criminal sanctions for breaches of EC waste legislation. The Commission and the French government invited the ECJ to decline jurisdiction on the basis of the absence of the required factual context, but the ECJ felt that it had sufficient information to provide a helpful answer to those questions.[160] In a recent study, it has been suggested that the ECJ appears more lenient in "interesting" cases allowing it to expand the scope of Community law or to clarify fundamental questions than it is in cases of lesser importance.[161]

The instances in which the ECJ has actually declined jurisdiction have been severely criticized. It is argued that a judgment on the genuineness of a dispute requires the ECJ to engage in an appreciation of the facts giving rise to the case, a responsibility which, under Article 234 EC, is reserved to national courts. Consequently, the spirit of cooperation and the strict separation of responsibilities on which the preliminary procedure is based and which at the same time explains its success may be undermined, in turn threatening the continued effectiveness of the preliminary reference process.

Yet, an examination of practice in the sphere of the environment does not reveal any systematic pattern giving rise to serious concern. Critics of the ECJ's (occasional) reserve point in particular at the purpose and spirit of the preliminary reference procedure. Yet, in doing so they fail to recognize that the spirit and purpose of the procedure might equally and more seriously be undermined were it to become a true substitute for Article 226 EC. This would be the case if the ECJ allowed questions of a general or even contrived nature, unrelated to specific issues forming part of a genuine dispute, to be referred to it in the context of a preliminary reference.

It is therefore important to respect the distinct spheres of operation of the infringement procedure and the preliminary reference procedure. Also, the ECJ may have a more practical, arguably less legitimate, interest in the control of the number of preliminary references submitted to it. The steady rise of preliminary references, which in the light of recent and future enlargements can only be expected to continue, potentially threatens the effectiveness of the ECJ, something it will obviously seek to prevent.

Indeed, some commentators have advanced docket-control as the single most important factor explaining the ECJ's case law relating to its jurisdiction under Article 234.[162] Ever since Rasmussen published his much acclaimed *On*

---

[159] See, e.g., Case C–378/93, *La Pyramide* [1994] ECR I–3999, para 15, Case C–257/95, *Bresle* [1996] ECR I–233 paras. 15–17.

[160] Joined Cases C–58, 75, 112, 123, 135, 140, 141, 154, and 157/95, *Gallotti* [1996] ECR I–4345 para. 9.

[161] C. Barnhard and E. Sharpston, "The Changing Face of Article 177 References" (1997) 34 *Common Market Law Review*, 1113–71. Examples of cases where the ECJ, had it applied the strict approach it employed in some other cases, could have declined jurisdiction, according to the authors, include the seminal cases *Costa* v. *ENEL*, *Faccini Dori* and *Bosman*.

[162] See Barnhard and Sharpston, *Ibid*.

Law and Policy in the European Court of Justice,[163] such policy-oriented analyses of the ECJ's activities have become common ground. Yet, it is most doubtful whether the ECJ's "guidelines", even if it were to adhere to them more systematically than at present appears to be the case, could serve as an effective instrument of docket control. The number of cases where the ECJ has refused to provide a reference is insignificant in relative terms and may be expected to diminish further as a result of judicial learning. Such a cognitive process is in fact stimulated by the ECJ itself, not only through its case law laying down minimum standards for preliminary references, but also more proactively by issuing a "Note for Guidance on References by National Courts for Preliminary Rulings".[164] Far from discouraging national courts from referring questions to the ECJ, it seeks to encourage national courts to comply with, in particular, the minimum standards relating to the information to be provided.

A more effective (and, it is submitted, more appropriate) mechanism impacting on the number of Article 234 references is the more established doctrine of *acte clair*.

VIII. National Court Compliance with the Preliminary Ruling

After the ECJ has accepted jurisdiction and delivered its judgment, its role in the private enforcement process should normally come to an end. As the ECJ's role does not extend beyond interpretation, the application of the ruling to the concrete national case remains the exclusive preserve of the referring national court. Little systematic information is available in respect of the extent to which national courts apply preliminary judgments faithfully. Although it appears that compliance rates with preliminary judgments are generally good,[165] national courts may obviously apply the judgment erroneously. The question thus arises to what extent such misapplication gives rise to enforcement leaks.

In assessing the potential for erroneous application of preliminary judgments by national courts, a useful distinction may be made between courts which refer a question and subsequently apply the ECJ's ruling to the case, and courts other than the one which made the reference.[166] As for the former, a further distinction appears appropriate. Lower and intermediate courts—under no obligation to refer—may generally be expected to be favourably disposed towards the preliminary judgment which, after all, they voluntarily requested. In addition, it is by applying a preliminary ruling (e.g. by setting aside national provisions of environmental law) more than by requesting it that these courts

---

[163] H. Rasmussen, *On Law and Policy in the European Court of Justice* (Dordrecht: Martinus Nijhoff, 1986).

[164] These were published as part of the analysis by Barnhard and Sharpston, n. 161 above.

[165] J. A. Usher, "Compliance with Judgments of the Court of Justice of the European Communities" in M. K. Bulterman and M. Kuijer (eds.), *Compliance with Judgments of International Courts* (The Hague: Martinus Nijhoff, 1996), 106–10.

[166] *Ibid.*

may increase their status and powers in the national judicial hierarchy. By the same token, courts of final appeal, which perhaps were compelled to refer a question, may be the most likely candidates for resisting the implications of a preliminary judgment. Not only may these be less than fully convinced of the necessity of the reference; by ignoring its implications they may seek to reaffirm their predominance and status in the judicial hierarchy. However, although the little empirical data that are available do provide *some* evidence that indeed it is the highest courts which are most likely to stray,[167] this leakage is comparatively insignificant. It may be presumed that, because the doctrine of *acte clair* has minimized the cases where courts of final instance are compelled to refer a question, courts of final appeal in general will be prepared faithfully to apply the preliminary judgment.

It has been seen that comparatively few preliminary questions concerning EC environmental law have been submitted to the ECJ. For the private enforcement of EC environmental law, as important as faithful application by the referring court is therefore the extent to which courts follow preliminary judgments delivered in response to questions referred by other courts. The fact that so few environmental preliminary questions have been referred to the ECJ may in part be explained by the circumstance that, indeed, national courts *do* follow previous preliminary rulings by way of "precedent". However, it is impossible to obtain reliable data on whether specific environmental references are actually followed by national courts in the other Member States. It is likely that different patterns prevail in different jurisdictions. For example, whereas United Kingdom courts traditionally follow precedent (and hence may be expected to feel equally bound by preliminary judgments initiated by other courts) continental courts may be less inclined to do so. Indeed, compared to the Conseil d'Etat or the German Constitutional Court, the House of Lords has generally been more compliant.

Ideally, of course, national courts do not merely follow environmental preliminary judgments delivered at the request of courts in their own jurisdiction, but are also aware of and follow preliminary rulings delivered in foreign courts. Again, whether such cross-jurisdictional learning actually takes place is difficult to ascertain. However, private discussions with national judges have left the distinct impression that these often tend to take national implementing legislation as their point of departure and take heed only of preliminary rulings that bear specifically upon their interpretation and validity. If this is indeed the case, national courts will take into account past preliminary rulings only if these directly concern the national rules with which they are faced in the course of subsequent proceedings. However, they are much less likely to take into account rulings that arose in the context of proceedings before foreign courts, even though from the perspective of Community law these are equally authoritative. By way of example, national judges appear to register a preliminary ruling as one relating to the *Vogelwet* (Dutch implementing

---

[167] *Ibid.*, 106–10.

legislation relating to Directive 79/409/EEC on the Conservation of Wild Birds) rather than one concerning Directive 79/409/EEC. This national perspective of preliminary rulings obviously forms an obstacle to their *erga omnes* application.

IX. Compliance with the National Judgment

The final phase in the private enforcement chain, crucially, concerns compliance with the national court's final judgment. It is well known that non-compliance with the ECJ's judgments pursuant to Article 226 EC is a widespread phenomenon[168] and it would be naïve to presume that similar problems do not also occur in a private enforcement setting.

When a judgment by a national court is not complied with, the ECJ may be asked to deliver a second judgment. If the same or a higher national court feels that issues of interpretation remain unresolved that are crucial for the outcome of the national case,[169] this could materialize in the context of a second preliminary procedure. The ECJ's preliminary ruling may also provide authority for a (private) action in damages against a defaulting Member State, should the latter prove unwilling to comply with the national court's judgment. In such cases, too, the national court may feel it requires a second preliminary judgment, this time perhaps concerning questions more directly related to the Member States' non-contractual liability.[170]

The ECJ's renewed involvement could also occur at the instigation of the Commission or Member State pursuant to Articles 226–227 EC. This is quite strikingly illustrated by *Belgium* v. *Spain*.[171] In this case, Belgium has taken the highly unusual step of challenging Spain pursuant to Article 227 EC for its failure to comply with *Delhaize Frères*,[172] which was delivered after a Spanish court had referred a question to the ECJ concerning Article 34 EC.[173] In support of its arguments, the Belgian government has invoked Article 10 EC (formerly Article 5) EC.

The same provision featured centrally in *Spanish Strawberries*, which further suggests that, under special circumstances, breaches of Community environmental law (and, *a fortiori*, non-compliance with ECJ judgments) per-

---

[168] In 1997, approximately 15 cases reached the Art. 228 EC letter or reasoned opinion stage, for failure to notify national implementing measures, incorrect transposal or incorrect application: Source: Statistical Information of the Court of Justice 1997, n. 149 above. See also J. Diez-Hochleitner, "Le Traité et l'Inexécution des Arrêts de la Cour de Justice par les États Membres" (1994) 2 *Revue du Marché Unique Européen* 111–59.

[169] See Case 14/86, *Pretore di Salò* v. *Persons Unknown* [1987] ECR 2545, n. 38 above.

[170] See H. Somsen, "Francovich and its Application to EC Environmental Law" in Somsen, n. 8 above.

[171] Case C–388/95 [1996] OJ C46/5 (case pending).

[172] Case C–47/90, *Delhaize Frères* [1992] ECR I–3669.

[173] This is only the second time that an action has been brought pursuant to Art. 227 EC. The first, and thus far only, case which the ECJ decided on this basis was Case 141/68, *France* v. *United Kingdom* [1979] ECR 2923.

petrated by private individuals may nevertheless be attributed to Member States.[174] Private breaches of national judgments involving EC environmental law thus could become the subject of an infringement procedure. Should a Member State continue to fail to comply with the ECJ's judgment in such cases, Article 228 (formerly Article 171) EC could eventually be resorted to.

The ECJ in all these cases exercises control over (Member State) compliance with national judgments delivered following a preliminary ruling. It is perhaps consistent with the increasingly "federal" character of the Union that the ECJ should become the final arbiter in cases where private national enforcement has failed. That such Community involvement is of more than mere symbolic significance is illustrated by the fact that in 1997 the Commission for the first time referred five environmental cases to the ECJ in accordance with Article 228 EC. Under the second subparagraph of this provision, the Commission may bring a case before the ECJ requesting that financial penalties (fines or penalty payments) be imposed which in practice appear to range from ECU 26,000 to ECU 30,000 per day. According to the Commission, Article 228 EC has already proved its effectiveness, since four of the five cases were settled by the end of 1997.[175]

X. Conclusions

This article has attempted to offer an impressionistic perspective of the most important factors impacting on the effectiveness of the private enforcement of Member State compliance with EC environmental law. For reasons of practical feasibility, the preliminary judgments delivered by the ECJ have informed this analysis. Little of the equally vital national socio-legal context of the private enforcement process could be explored which, it is submitted, calls for urgent future research. However, on the basis of our analysis an attempt may already be undertaken to draw a number of general conclusions.

A first, relatively safe, conclusion concerns the number and significance of cases brought to the attention of the ECJ by private enforcement action. Forty-six cases over twenty years are hardly impressive considering the wealth and breadth of environmental regulation. If we entertain the ambition for private enforcement significantly to contribute to protecting the European environment for future generations, any optimism will have been dealt a further blow by the subjects at issue. When the cases revolving around exclusively commercial/personal interests are not taken into consideration (e.g. the free movement of pesticides, or many of the criminal cases), in effect only a handful of cases remains that may be said to contribute to realizing this goal. The claim that private enforcement has had "a direct impact on the construction of supranational [environmental] policy and the deepening of integration"

---

[174] Case C–265/95, *Commission* v. *French Republic* [1997] ECR I–6959.
[175] 15th Annual Report on Monitoring the Application of Community Law, COM(98)317 [1998] OJ C250/1, para. 12.1.

becomes difficult to sustain, at least if environmental policy is viewed as distinct from internal market policy.[176]

Since the objective of environmental law in essence is to prevent future environmental harm, organizational instruments play a role of predominant importance. Indeed, frequently as their primary objective environmental directives require Member States to set up certain administrative structures, supply the Commission with information or improvement reports, or to engage in regular consultations with other Member States. Whereas in other contexts such organizational instruments may have been termed "ancillary" with some justification, not infrequently they constitute the "hard core" of environmental directives.[177] Despite their importance, according to the *Balsamo* doctrine, Member State compliance with these obligations in the main cannot be enforced privately.

Even in respect of substantive EC environmental law, however, private enforcement of Member State compliance is far from straightforward. The troublesome enforceability of quality objectives clearly not only adversely affects the Commission in its capacity of guardian of the Treaty:[178] it similarly complicates the private enforcement of substantive environmental standards to the extent that it may be virtually impossible. Indeed, the ECJ has yet to rule on any reference concerning alleged breaches of quality objectives. The same applies to uniform limit values, even though the latter appear to offer much better prospects for their private enforcement.[179]

By contrast, the importance of the direct effect of environmental directives, often regarded as the most important stumbling block to the private enforcement of Member State compliance with EC environmental law, may have been exaggerated. Quite apart from the perspectives offered by the indirect effect of environmental directives and, to a lesser extent, non-contractual liability of Member States, even in the absence of direct effect individuals may review the exercise of public authority discretion in the implementation or enforcement of EC environmental law. *Kraaijeveld* and *RSPB* demonstrate that the promise of private enforcement of Member State compliance with EC environmental law may yet be fulfilled. They also provide strong arguments in favour of Community action guaranteeing access to national courts for the purpose of such private enforcement initiatives.[180]

---

[176] R. A. Cichowski, "Integrating the Environment: the European Court and the Construction of Supranational Policy", n. 12 above, 403.

[177] Prechal, *Directives in European Community Law*, n. 10 above, 45–53.

[178] See H. Somsen and A. Sprokkereef, "Making Subsidiarity Work for the Environmental Policy of the European Community: The Role of Science" (1995) 1 *International Journal of Biosciences and the Law*, 37–67.

[179] Case C-168/95, *Arcaro* [1996] ECR I–4705 is not such an example since, although the issue was raised by the referring court, the ECJ merely underlined that individuals' criminal responsibility could not be aggravated by the environmental directive at issue.

[180] See E. Rehbinder, "*Locus Standi*, Community Law and the Case for Harmonization", in Somsen, n. 8 above, 151–66.

CURRENT SURVEY

Substantive European Community Environmental Law

I. Atmospheric Pollution

JÜRGEN LEFEVERE*

A. INTRODUCTION

The European Environment Agency (EEA) concluded in its 1997 report on Air Pollution in Europe that:

Europe, and in particular the European Union, is making progress in reducing some air pollution and its impact on human health and ecosystems. The main improvements have been in acidification and urban air quality, due to the reduction of sulphur emissions from point sources and the introduction of unleaded petrol for passenger cars. However, these improvements have not been sufficient to achieve acceptable levels of sulphur and lead in the environment in many parts of Europe. For other environmental problems related to air pollution (climate change and tropospheric ozone) there has been no improvement, or only stabilisation, in recent years. For all air related environmental problems, the policies and measures to abate emissions have been largely offset by an increase in the driving forces behind the pressures, particularly in the transport sector. Further substantial reductions of all atmospheric emissions are needed to reach target levels for air quality and for exceedances of critical loads on ecosystems.[1]

This section gives an overview of the development of the European Community's (EC) policy and legislation concerning atmospheric pollution. Atmospheric pollution has topped Europe's environmental agenda in 1998. The Community's unprecedented activity in the field of atmospheric pollution-related issues can be explained by the fact that several large dossiers entered key stages in their adoption process. Of these dossiers, the two most important and controversial concern climate change and the adoption of

* Staff Lawyer, Foundation for International Environmental Law and Development (FIELD), London, UK.

[1] European Environment Agency, *Air Pollution in Europe, Executive summary*, EEA Environmental Monograph No. 4 (Copenhagen: EEA, 1997), 3.

measures under the Auto/Oil I programme. In addition, some other dossiers have been subject to much discussion during 1998. These dossiers include the measures on acidification, the protection of the ozone layer, the adoption of daughter directives to the Ambient Air Quality Directive, and the Community's response to some developments under the 1979 Convention on Long-Range Transboundary Airborne Pollution (LRTAP).

B.   CLIMATE CHANGE

A major part of the 1998 Environment Council's agenda was taken up by the discussions on the EC's climate change strategy. The adoption of the Kyoto Protocol to the United Nations Framework Convention on Climate Change (UNFCCC) in December 1997 was a landmark in both the international and the European Community's climate discussions. Whereas in 1997, a considerable part of the Environment Council's time was taken up by preparations for the negotiations, 1998 was marked by discussions on the Community's measures to implement the Kyoto targets and the international negotiations filling the gaps of issues left undecided in Kyoto.

i.   A Leadership Role for the Community

The EC's flurry of activities can be explained by its pledge to act as one of the driving forces behind international action to tackle the issue of climate change. Already in 1990, the EC agreed, in a joint Council meeting of the Energy and Environment Ministers of the Member States, to a non-binding declaration, requiring the Community as a whole to stabilize its total CO_2 emissions at 1990 levels by the year 2000.[2] This commitment played an important role in the UNFCCC negotiations. The UNFCCC was finally signed at the United Nations Conference on Environment and Development (UNCED) in 1992, and entered into force on 21 March 1994.[3]

The Commission prepared a comprehensive package of measures in order to guarantee compliance with its self-proclaimed 1990 stabilization target, a goal that was also laid down in non-binding terms in the UNFCCC. Compromise on these measures, however, proved more difficult to reach. The main reason for this was the fact that the backbone of the package consisted of a proposal for the adoption of a Community-wide tax on carbon dioxide (CO_2).[4] Due to the controversial nature of EC harmonization of taxation, no agreement could be reached on this proposal. In addition, most of the other proposals were seriously watered down during their negotiation. The result was that none of the EC instruments adopted under the first package contained obligations more binding than commitments to set up research pro-

---

[2] Joint Council meeting of the Energy and Environment Ministers, 29 Oct. 1990 [1990] EC Bull., point 1.3.77.
[3] On 15 Dec. 1993, the EC ratified Council Decision 94/69/EC concerning the conclusion of the United Nations framework convention on climate change [1994] OJ L33/11.
[4] COM(92)226 [1992] OJ C196/1.

grammes, giving financial aid and monitoring and reporting the emissions in the Member States.[5]

ii. Preparing for Kyoto

Although the Community did not succeed in implementing the measures originally proposed, important action was undertaken in the Community's preparation for Kyoto. Under the Dutch Presidency, on 2 March 1997, the Council managed to reach agreement on a Community position for the international climate change talks. At the Environment Council, ministers agreed to adopt a 15 per cent cut in EU emissions of a basket of three greenhouse gases (carbon dioxide (CO_2), methane (CH_4), and nitrous oxide (N_2O)) by 2010, as the EC negotiation position in the talks under the UNFCCC. Three more gases (the hydrofluorocarbons (HFCs), perfluorocarbons (PFCs), and sulphur hexafluoride (SF_6)) that were originally included in the proposals were not included in the final reduction goal. A victory for the Dutch Presidency was that it managed to get the burden-sharing agreement adopted. The burden-sharing agreement, the adoption of which initially seemed impossible, set specific post-2000 emission targets for each Member State.[6] This victory was overshadowed by the fact that the total emissions on the basis of the agreed burden sharing amounted to only two-thirds of the 15 per cent reduction agreed for the Community as a whole. Also, the agreement did not entail a unilateral commitment, but was dependent on what states would agree upon at the meeting in Kyoto in December 1997.

In the course of 1997, the Community discussed its strategy for negotiations in Kyoto. The key points of the strategy were set out in the conclusions of the three Environment Council meetings preceding Kyoto,[7] and in the Commission Communication on Climate Change—The EU Approach for Kyoto.[8] The Community's goal was to adopt a protocol under the UNFCCC, containing, on the one hand, specific emission-reduction objectives and, on the other hand, a set of policies and measures to achieve these objectives. Regarding the emission reduction objectives, the Community aimed at the inclusion of a 15 per cent emissions reduction for CO_2, CH_4, and N_2O, by 2010 (with the reference year 1990). In addition, an interim reduction target of 7.5 per cent needed to be set for 2005. Although initially only three gases were to be included, the

---

[5] The three main measures which were adopted are Council Decision 91/565/EEC of 29 Oct. 1991 concerning the promotion of energy efficiency in the Community (the SAVE: specific actions for vigorous energy efficiency programme) [1991] OJ L307/34; Decision 93/500/EEC concerning the promotion of renewable energy sources in the Community (the ALTENER: alternative energy programme) [1993] OJ L235/41; Council Decision 93/389/EC of 24 June 1993 for a monitoring mechanism of Community CO_2 and other greenhouse gas emissions [1993] OJ L167/31. A list of instruments adopted before Dec. 1993 can be found in Annex B to the ratification decision.

[6] Agreed was: Austria: −25%; Belgium: −10%; Denmark: −25%; Finland: 0%; France: 0%; Germany: −25%; Greece: +30%; Ireland: +15%; Italy: −7%; Luxembourg: −30%; the Netherlands: −10%; Portugal: +40%; Spain: +17%; Sweden: +5%; the United Kingdom: −10%.

[7] Conclusions of the 1990th Council meeting, Brussels, 3 Mar. 1997; Conclusions of the 2017th Council meeting, Luxembourg, 19–20 June 1997 and the Conclusions of the 2033rd Council meeting, Luxembourg, 16 Oct. 1997.

[8] COM(97)481, 1 Oct. 1997.

Community aimed at adding HFC, PFC, and SF_6 to the basket of gases no later than 2000. In addition, the Community was to be allowed to reach the reduction targets with the Community as a whole (the "bubble" concept), allowing the Community to set emission reduction objectives among its Member States.

iii. The Kyoto Protocol

The Kyoto Protocol to the UNFCCC was negotiated at the third conference of the parties (COP3) of the UNFCCC, which took place in Kyoto, Japan, from 1–10 December 1997.[9] The result of the intense negotiations was a unique document, containing binding targets for the reduction or limitation of the emission of greenhouse gases by developed countries, as listed in its Annex B, by the "first commitment period" of 2008–2012. The results of the Kyoto conference were significantly different from those the EC had hoped to obtain. Other than the EC's position, which aimed at reduction targets for only three gases, the protocol commits developed states to reducing their collective emissions of six key greenhouse gases, adding HFCs, PFCs, and SF_6. The protocol requires the reductions in the emissions of the six gases to be measured as reductions in the "basket" of gases, with reductions in individual gases translated into CO_2 equivalents, which are added up to produce a single figure.

Not only did the EC not manage to maintain its position on the gases to be included, it also failed to find international agreement on its ambitious goal to reduce emissions by 15 per cent by 2010. Instead, different quantified emission limitation and reduction commitments (QELRCs) were negotiated for developed countries,[10] within a general obligation that the global reduction in emissions should be 5 per cent within the commitment period 2008–2012. Rather than setting an interim target, which the EC proposed, the Kyoto Protocol requires that "demonstrable progress" must be made by 2005.

The Community's insistence on the adoption of legally binding policies and measures (PAMs) did not hold during the negotiations. Rather than focussing on the PAMs, the protocol introduced three so-called Kyoto mechanisms (often also referred to as the flexibility mechanisms). These three mechanisms are joint implementation (JI), the clean development mechanism (CDM), and international emissions trading (IET).[11] None of the three mechanisms, how-

---

[9] A good overview of the negotiations and results of COP3 can be found in F. Yamin, "The Kyoto Protocol: Origins, Assessment and Future Challenges" (1998) 7 *Review of European Community and International Environmental Law* 113–27.

[10] The QELRCs includes reductions of 7% for the USA, 8% for the EC, and 6% for Japan. Three countries were allowed increases: Australia (8%), Norway (1%) and Iceland (10%). Russia, the Ukraine, and New Zealand were allowed to stabilize. Hungary and Poland are required to reduce by 6%, Croatia by 5%, and all remaining developed countries by 8%.

[11] See for an in-depth discussion of the different flexibility mechanisms: F. Missfeldt, "Flexibility Mechanisms: Which Path to Take after Kyoto?" (1998) 7 *Review of European Community and International Environmental Law* 128–39; M. Grubb, "International Emissions Trading under the Kyoto Protocol: Core Issues in Implementation" (1998) 7 *Review of European Community and International Environmental Law* 140–6; and J. Werksman, "The Clean Development Mechanism: Unwrapping the 'Kyoto Surprise'" (1998) 7 *Review of European Community and International Environmental Law* 147–58.

ever, contained sufficiently elaborated rules to allow their functioning on the basis of the Kyoto Protocol. Instead, development of these rules was left to a later COP. The EC did succeed in including its bubble concept into the text of the protocol, allowing the Community to reach its 8 per cent reduction target with the Community as a whole.

iv. The Community's Reaction to Kyoto

At its meeting on 23 March 1998, the EU Environment Council showed its satisfaction with the results achieved, calling it a major step forwards in the fight against climate change. It agreed on signing the protocol, jointly with all the Member States.[12] At the time of signature, the Community submitted a statement to the effect that the Community was going to make use of the option to reach the 8 per cent QELRC with the Community as a whole.[13] At this same meeting in March 1998, the Council agreed upon swift ratification of the protocol by both the EC and its Member States. The Council expressly held that, before ratification, satisfactory progress on a number of outstanding issues is necessary, in particular with regard to the operation of the Kyoto mechanisms.

To allow the Community to use the "bubble" possibility, it had to renegotiate its initial burden-sharing agreement of 23 March 1997, adapting it to requirements of the Kyoto Protocol. On the Environment Council meeting, on 16 and 17 June 1998, the Member States agreed to divide the 8 per cent emission reduction for the European Community as a whole over the Member States:

Table V: Member State targets under the "bubble" agreement

Austria	−13%
Belgium	−7.5%
Denmark	−21%
Finland	0%
France	0%
Germany	−21%
Greece	+25%
Ireland	+13%
Italy	−6.5%
Luxembourg	−28%
The Netherlands	−6%
Portugal	+27%
Spain	+15%
Sweden	+4%
United Kingdom	−12.5%

---

[12] This was done by Environment Commissioner Bjerregaard in New York on 29 Apr. 1998.

[13] The European Community and its Member States will fulfil their respective commitments under Art. 31 of the Protocol jointly in accordance with the provisions of Art. 4 of the Protocol.

v. Common and Co-ordinated Policies and Measures

The Community now needs to decide upon action to be undertaken to implement the burden-sharing agreement, agreed upon by the Council. In its meeting in March 1997, the Environment Council gave a list with examples of common and co-ordinated policies and measures (CCPMs) for reaching the target, at that time still to be agreed in Kyoto. A first move by the Commission to elaborate a comprehensive strategy for the development of a post-Kyoto strategy was made on 3 June 1998, when it presented its Communication on Climate Change—Towards a Post-Kyoto Strategy.[14] In this Communication, the Commission proposed, *inter alia*, adopting indicative sectoral targets for the sectors of transport, energy, industry, agriculture and domestic and tertiary sectors. In addition, it pleaded for the step-by-step introduction of the Kyoto mechanisms in the Community. The Commission report is now being discussed by the Member States. These have to provide information on their strategies and what they expect from the Community by the end of 1998. This information will be the basis for a second report by the Commission in the first half of 1999.

As early as 1990, a number of Community measures were developed to tackle the problem of climate change. The development and adoption of these measures continued during 1998.

vi. Renewable Energy Funding

The two main programmes for the implementation of the Community's climate commitment through the promotion of renewable energy are the SAVE (Specific Actions for Vigorous Energy Efficiency) and ALTENER (Alternative Energy) programmes. These programmes are designed to provide funding for research and actions combating climate change. Both programmes were adopted in 1993, and had a time-span of five years. In December 1996, SAVE was extended to 2000, with a budget of 45 million Euros.[15] The purpose of ALTENER is to make an essential contribution to the increased use of environment-friendly renewable energy sources, as part of the Community strategy to reduce the emission of CO_2. The extension of the programme to 2000 by ALTENER II, was initially held up by a conflict on its budget.[16] Agreement was reached in May 1998,[17] allowing its adoption.[18]

Essential in reaching this agreement was the new framework programme for actions in the energy sector, proposed by the Commission on 18 November 1997.[19] This new programme aims to bring together a number of existing EU energy programmes, including the ALTENER and SAVE programmes, as well as programmes such as Synergy (international co-operation) and Carnot (clean and efficient use of solid fuels). Severely cutting the originally proposed budget,[20]

---

[14] COM(98)353.   [15] Adopted on 16 Dec. 1996, 96/737/EC [1996] OJ L335/50.
[16] Commission proposal COM(97)87 of 18 Nov. 1997.
[17] *ENDS Environment Daily*, 8 May 1998.   [18] On 18 May [1998] OJ L159/53.
[19] COM(97)550 [1998] OJ C46/7.   [20] *ENDS Environment Daily*, 12 May 1998.

the current Council agreement allows ALTENER II and SAVE II, the two main components of the framework, to have five-year budgets of respectively 74 and 64 million Euros.[21] After Parliament's first reading in October 1998, the Commission has issued a revised proposal,[22] which is now awaiting the Council's common position.

vii. CO_2 Monitoring Mechanism

The CO_2 monitoring mechanism was another important Community instrument for the implementation of the UNFCCC. A revised mechanism was proposed by the Commission in September 1996, in the Proposal for a Council Decision amending Decision 93/389/EC for a Monitoring Mechanism of Community CO_2 and other Greenhouse Gas Emissions.[23] The Proposal was more recently amended to bring it into line with the results of Kyoto.[24] At its meeting on 23 March 1998, the Environment Council reached political agreement on a common position, which was formally adopted at the Environment Council meeting in June 1998.[25] The proposal aligns the monitoring mechanism with the Kyoto requirements, extending monitoring to the six greenhouse gases covered by the protocol. More importantly, the proposal requires the Member States to devise, publish, and implement national programmes for limiting greenhouse gas emissions, in order to fulfil the obligations of the Kyoto Protocol. The proposal is currently awaiting second reading in the European Parliament.

viii. CO_2 Emissions from Passenger Cars

One of the main sources of emission of the most important greenhouse gas, CO_2, is transport. In December 1995, the Commission published its Communication on the Community's Strategy to reduce CO_2 emissions from passenger cars and improve fuel efficiency.[26] The Community proposed four actions to reach this double goal:

— an agreement with the car industry;
— the adoption of tax incentives in order to persuade consumers to buy fuel-efficient cars;
— providing better information to the consumers on the CO_2 emissions of car-types through a labelling system;
— increasing research efforts into cleaner engine technologies.

The objective of these combined efforts is to reach CO_2 emissions, of 120 g/km by 2005 (2010 at the latest), expressed as an average for the new car fleet. This equals a fuel consumption of 5 l/100 km for petrol driven cars and 4.5 l/100km for diesel vehicles. This target amounts to a 35 per cent reduction compared to 1995 emissions.

---

[21] *ENDS Environment Daily*, 16 Nov. 1998. [22] COM(98)607.
[23] COM(96)369 of 4 Sept. 1996 [1996] OJ C314/11.
[24] COM(98)108 of 2 Mar. 1998 [1998] OJ C120/22. [25] [1998] OJ C333/38.
[26] COM(95)689 of 20 Dec. 1995.

Parliament rejected the idea of negotiating an agreement with car manufacturers, and instead argued for legislation and increased taxes on petrol and diesel.[27] However, the Commission, supported by the Council, did go ahead with the negotiations. The European Automobile Manufacturers Association (ACEA), representing the European Automotive industry, initially rejected the Commission's target as totally unrealistic, instead proposing a target of 150–160 g/km by 2005.[28] The Environment Council, at its meeting on 16 December 1997, in line with the Commission's point of view, rejected this proposal as "quite inadequate". In order to put pressure on ACEA to go further, the Environment Council asked the Commission to report on the outcome of the negotiations before the Environment Council meeting in March 1998 and, in absence of a satisfactory result, to submit a proposal for a directive containing binding restrictions. Under the threat of legislation, ACEA presented a new proposal, offering 140g/km by 2008 rather than 2005, corresponding to an average fuel efficiency of 6 l/100 km for petrol cars, and 5.3 l/100 km for diesel cars.[29] The Commission accepted the proposal, mainly because it felt that the remaining 20g/km could be overcome by additional measures. In addition, it was felt that adopting legislation would be difficult, as Member States producing large cars would object to too stringent targets. Following the Commission, the Environment Council, at its meeting on 23 March, also accepted ACEA's proposal as a basis for further negotiations. Although initially the negotiations appeared stranded on the availability of low sulphur fuel, an issue discussed under the Auto/Oil programme[30] (discussed below), the Commission managed to reach agreement with ACEA on 29 July 1998.

The agreement requires car manufacturers to reduce CO_2 emissions from new cars by 25 per cent by 2008. Cars produced in 2008 should emit an average of 140 g/km CO_2, equivalent to a fuel consumption of 5.71 l/100 km. In addition, ACEA has agreed to introduce some vehicles that emit 120 g/km by 2000. ACEA is also to review the situation in 2003, with the aim of proposing further reductions in order to reach the target of 120g/km by 2012. The Commission endorsed the agreement in a Communication to the Council and the European Parliament.[31]

The negotiated agreements received mixed reactions. Various industry associations hailed it as an example for agreements in other areas.[32] Environmental NGOs, on the other hand, condemned the targets in the agreement as too weak, in fact allowing an increase in emissions from passenger cars.[33] The European Parliament discussed the agreement with ACEA together

[27] Discussion in the Parliament on 10 Apr. 1997 [1997] OJ C132/210.
[28] *ENDS Environment Daily*, 16 Oct. 1997 and 18 Nov. 1997.
[29] *ENDS Environment Daily*, 11 Mar. 1998.
[30] *ENDS Environment Daily*, 3 June and 2 July 1998.
[31] Commission Communication on a voluntary agreement with the automobile industry concerning the reduction of CO_2 emissions, COM(98)495 of 29 July 1998. The text of the agreement is reproduced in the documents section of this volume.
[32] *ENDS Environment Daily*, 9 Oct. 1998.
[33] Letter from the European Environment Bureau to the EU environment ministers from 11 June 1998.

with the Commission's proposal for a post-Kyoto strategy.[34] In its resolution, adopted on the subject, Parliament criticized the agreement as lacking some vital components, such as provisions in case ACEA members fail to comply, the absence of a binding interim target for 2003[35] and the lack of a procedure for revision of the agreement in 2003. In addition, the Parliament repeated its doubts about the effectiveness of negotiated agreements.

The Council, at its meeting in October 1998, approved the agreement with ACEA, with reservations from Denmark and Greece.[36] The agreement has now been notified under Article 81 (formerly Article 85) EC, in order to allow the Commission to examine competition aspects.

Concerning the other measures proposed in the Community strategy paper, on 12 June 1998, the Commission published its Proposal for a Decision Establishing a Scheme to Monitor the Average Specific Emissions of Carbon Dioxide from New Passenger Cars.[37] The aim of this proposal is to allow independent monitoring of the progress in reaching the target of 120 g/km CO_2 by 2005. The monitoring scheme requires Member States to report annually on a range of data concerning the CO_2 emissions by passenger cars, the first report to be submitted by 1 July 2001. The proposal is currently in its first reading with the European Parliament. The Environment Committee from Parliament, on 8 December 1998, adopted its report on the proposal in first reading.[38] Amendments adopted by the Committee include the addition of light commercial vehicles (a significant source of CO_2 emissions in urban areas) to the scope of the proposal, as well as bringing forward various deadlines. It is very likely that at the December 1998 meeting of the Environment Council political agreement on a common position will be reached.

The monitoring proposal was followed by a Proposal for a Directive on the Availability of Consumer Information on Fuel Economy in Respect of the Marketing of New Passenger Cars, which was published on 3 September 1998.[39] The consumer information on fuel economy labelling Proposal contains four essential elements. First, a fuel economy label needs to be introduced for all new cars. Secondly, Member States must produce a fuel economy guide. Thirdly, the proposal requires a list to be displayed in the form of a poster at all car-dealers, containing the fuel efficiency and CO_2 emissions of all new passenger cars. Finally, the proposal will require the inclusion of official fuel-consumption data in promotional literature. The proposal was the subject of an open policy debate, together with the monitoring proposal, at the Environment Council meeting in October 1998. During this discussion Finland, supported by Italy, suggested that the Directive should be extended to cover used cars as well. The Commission proposal was discussed by the

[34] Climate Change—Towards a Post-Kyoto Strategy, COM(98)353, discussed above in the text to n. 14.

[35] Parliament minutes of 17 Sept. 1998.

[36] *ENDS Environment Daily*, 6 Oct. 1998, see the text of the Council conclusions of 6 Oct. 1998.

[37] COM(98)348 of 12 June 1998 [1998] OJ C231/6.

[38] Report A4–0492/98 by L. Gonzalez Alvarez, 8 Dec. 1998.

[39] COM(98)489 of 3 Sept. 1998, [1998] OJ C305/2.

Environment Committee of the European Parliament.[40] The Committee's report suggests various amendments, including requiring the provision of specific information on CO_2 emissions and the deletion of the need to provide information on estimated fuel costs (which could unfairly favour diesel). In addition, it suggests including the obligation to remind consumers that extra equipment, such as air conditioning, may increase fuel consumption substantially.

ix.   Integration into other Policy Sectors

The Community's climate policy is increasingly challenged by the need to integrate climate change considerations into other policy areas. The new Article 6 EC reinforces the requirement of integration of environmental considerations in other policy areas. The process of far-reaching integration was started by the Luxembourg European Council in December 1997, and after the publication of a Communication on integration by the Commission in June 1998,[41] the Cardiff European Council in June 1998 decided to invite the transport, energy, and agriculture sectors to start the process.[42] The Commission, in its Integration Communication, proposed climate change and Agenda 2000 (the preparation for the accession of new Member States) as two priority areas for integration into these sectors. At the Vienna European Council meeting of December 1998, the heads of state and government decided to add the internal market, industry and development to the integration list.[43]

Apart from the transport sector,[44] particularly important is the energy sector. Several programmes aimed at increasing the use of renewables and energy efficiency have already been discussed. In order to promote the integration of climate change considerations in the Community's energy policy on 14 May 1997, the Commission issued its Communication on the energy dimension of climate change.[45] In November 1997, the Commission presented a White Paper entitled "Energy for the Future—Renewable Sources of Energy".[46] In this White Paper, the Commission lays down the target of doubling the use of renewable energy, to a total of 12 per cent by 2010. The Council endorsed the Commission's position in a resolution, adopted on 8 June 1998.[47] The European Parliament, in its resolution of 18 June 1998, urged the Commission to use this target as a minimum and to undertake the necessary steps to reach this goal, including adoption of an energy-related taxation model.[48]

---

[40] Report A4–0489/98 by M. P. Kestelijn-Sierens, 8 Dec. 1998.
[41] Partnership for Integration—A Strategy for Integrating Environment into EU Policies, COM(98)333.
[42] *ENDS Environment Daily*, 17 June 1998.   [43] *ENDS Environment Daily*, 14 Dec. 1998.
[44] See in addition to this also the Commission Communication of 31 Mar. 1998 on Transport and CO_2—Developing a Community Approach, COM(98)204.
[45] COM(97)196.   [46] COM(97)599 of 26 Nov. 1997.
[47] [1998] OJ C198/1.   [48] [1998] OJ C315/5.

x.   The Kyoto follow-up: Buenos Aires

The Kyoto Climate Conference in December 1997 left many important issues unresolved. These issues were put forward to the next Conference of the Parties, COP4, which took place in Buenos Aires, from 2–13 November 1998. At the centre of the discussions in Buenos Aires was the elaboration of a workplan for resolving the issues left undecided by Kyoto. An important part of the discussion on the workplan concerned the elaboration of rules for the operation of the flexibility mechanisms. The result of the Buenos Aires meeting was disappointing, with states only agreeing on a meagre Buenos Aires plan of action, laying down a very rudimentary workplan, listing issues to be decided over the next few years.[49] On the basis of this plan of action, a number of key issues will need to be resolved by COP6, which is to take place in 2000.

C.   THE AUTO/OIL PROGRAMME

The Auto/Oil I programme was initiated by the Commission in 1992. The programme aimed at controlling the atmospheric emissions from road transport. Its goal was to identify cost-effective measures reducing vehicle emissions, in order to allow the Community to reach its air quality targets. In order to reach these goals, the Commission engaged in a tripartite discussion with the motor industry and oil industry, identifying technical possibilities. The scientific basis of the programme was an analysis of the present ambient air quality data in the Community. On the basis of an extensive analysis of air quality in several major European cities, the Commission had calculated necessary emission reduction rates. With these emission reduction rates in mind, the Commission proposed a package of three types of measures. First, it proposed to improve vehicle technology to reduce emissions. Secondly, it aimed at improving fuel quality, allowing better vehicle technology, but also reducing pollution in itself. Thirdly, the Commission proposed several non-technical measures.

The Auto/Oil Programme was published on 18 June 1996, in the Commission Communication concerning a future strategy on the reduction of emissions of road transport taking into account the results of the Auto/Oil programme.[50] The Communication proposed to bring out five legislative measures:

— the tightening of emission standards for passenger cars and light commercial vehicles by modifying Directive 70/220/EEC;[51]

---

[49] The decisions taken at COP 4 are contained in document FCCC/CP/1998/16/Add.1, a copy of which can be found on the Internet at http://www.unfccc.de.

[50] COM(96)248 [1997] OJ C77/1.

[51] Council Dir. 70/220/EEC on the approximation of the laws of the Member States relating to measures to be taken against air pollution by gases from positive-ignition engines of motor vehicles [1970] OJ L 76/1.

— the amendment of Directive 88/77/EEC[52] in order to tighten the standards for engines used principally in heavy duty vehicles;
— the improvement of fuel quality by proposing for a Directive on the quality of petrol and diesel fuel and amending Directive 93/12/EC,[53] reducing the emission of benzene, volatile organic compounds (VOCs), nitrogen oxides (NOx), carbon monoxide (CO), and particulate matter;
— increasing research on alternative propulsion systems;
— submission of proposals in order to strengthen the requirements laid down in Directive 92/55/EC[54] on Requirements Concerning Technical Approval and Maintenance of Vehicles.

The Commission initially focussed on the emissions from private cars and fuel quality. It published two proposals, together with the Commission Communication on the Auto/Oil Programme. The first was the Proposal for a Directive on the Quality of Petrol and Diesel Fuels and amending Council Directive 93/12/EC.[55] The second was the Proposal for a Directive Relating to Measures to be Taken Against Air Pollution by Emissions from Motor Vehicles and Amending Council Directives 70/156/EEC and 70/220/EEC.[56] The Fuel Quality Proposal harmonized limit values for various parameters and regulated the gradual elimination of leaded petrol by 2000. The Vehicle Emissions Proposal contained a reduction in the emission of various pollutants between 20 and 40 per cent by 2000, as well as indicative limit values for new vehicles by 2005.

i.　Vehicle Emissions and the Quality of Fuels: The Auto/Oil Controversy

The Communication and the two proposals received severe criticism. The European Parliament discussed both the programme and the two proposals on 10 April 1997,[57] on the basis of three reports from the environment committee.[58] The critique of the European Parliament focussed on several main points. First, the Parliament found that additional fiscal incentives were necessary to promote the use of cleaner vehicles and cleaner fuels. Secondly, the Parliament found that the targets in the various proposals were too lax and

---

[52] Council Dir. 88/77/EEC on the approximation of the laws of the Member States relating to the measures to be taken against the emission of gaseous pollutants from diesel engines for use in vehicles [1988] OJ L36/33.
[53] Council Dir. 93/12/EEC relating to the sulphur content of certain liquid fuels [1993] OJ L74/81.
[54] [1992] OJ L225/68.　　　　　　　　　　　　　　　[55] COM(96)248 [1997] OJ C77/1.
[56] COM(96)248, amended by COM(97)77 [1997] OJ C106/11.
[57] See the Parliament's resolution adopted on 10 Apr. 1997 [1997] OJ C132/125.
[58] Report A4–0099/97 of 20 Mar. 1997 on the communication from the Commission to the European Parliament and the Council on a future strategy for the control of atmospheric emissions from road transport taking into account the results from the Auto/Oil Programme (COM(96)0248), *rapporteur* D. Eisma: Report A4–0096/97 of 20 Mar. 1997 on the proposal for a European Parliament and Council Directive on the quality of petrol and diesel fuels and amending Council Dir. 93/12/EEC, *rapporteur* Mr Mamère; and report A4–0116/97 of 20 Mar. 1997 on the proposal and the amended proposal for a European Parliament and Council Directive relating to measures to be taken against air pollution by emissions from motor vehicles and amending Council Dir. 70/156/EEC and Council Dir. 70/220/EEC, *rapporteur* B. Lange.

criticized the fact that too much focus had been put on the improvement of technology of the car manufacturers and too little attention had been given to the oil industry. As cleaner fuels were needed to improve car technology, Parliament considered this a serious gap. Thirdly, Parliament criticized the fact that discussions on the proposals involved only three parties; the Commission, the oil industry, and car manufacturers, whereas other interest groups had been left out. Finally, the Parliament criticized the proposals for lack of integration with other air pollution programmes and legislation. As both proposals are based on Article 95 (formerly Article 100a) EC, their adoption follows the co-decision procedure, giving considerable weight to the Parliament's objections.

In reaction to the amendments proposed by the Parliament, the Commission adopted its amended proposals on 5 June 1997,[59] taking over only very few of the Parliament's proposed amendments. The subsequent discussion on a common position in the Council left the Commission's proposal on vehicle emissions virtually unamended. A heated discussion ensued, however, on the fuel quality proposal. On this proposal, the Council found itself split between the North and the South.[60] The result of the discussions was that the Council adopted a common position, which on certain points went considerably further than the original Commission proposal. In order to satisfy the southern Member States, several derogations were included for countries which could indicate that the standards would cause severe socio-economic problems.[61] With these changes the Council reached a common position in its meeting on 19 and 20 June 1997.[62]

The auto/oil controversy had just started. Not only was there a North/South divide between Member States and a difference of opinion between Community institutions, but it also became increasingly apparent that a rift between the parties negotiating the original Commission proposals existed. The difference of opinion in the Council on the sulphur content of fuel also divided the European Petroleum Industry Association (EUROPIA) and the Association of European Car Manufacturers (ACEA). According to ACEA, lower sulphur levels were necessary in order to allow more advanced catalytic converter technology.[63] EUROPIA, on the other hand, argued that new catalytic converters were getting more, rather than less, sulphur tolerant, and that therefore these lower sulphur levels were not necessary.[64] Parliament and environmental NGOs supported the car manufacturers in their drive to focus more attention on obligations for the oil producers. It was found that the oil lobby had been much stronger than the manufacturers' lobby during the

---

[59] COM(97)271 [1997] OJ C209/25 (fuels); and COM(97)255 [1997] OJ C257/6 (vehicles).

[60] A. Friedrich, M. Tappe, and R. Wurzel, "The Auto Oil Programme: An Interim Critical Assessment" (1998) 7(4) *European Environmental Law Review* 104–11.

[61] *ENDS Environment Daily*, 20 June 1997.

[62] The Common position was adopted by the Council on 7 Oct. 1997 [1997] OJ C351/1 (fuels); and [1997] OJ C351/13 (vehicles).

[63] See also text to n. 26, the discussion on CO_2 emissions by passenger cars, above.

[64] *ENDS Environment Daily*, 6 Jan. 1998.

negotiations of the proposals, leading to an unbalanced result.[65] In addition, the NGOs were increasingly supporting the European Parliament, as this held the "greenest" opinion on the proposals.[66]

During these increasingly polarized discussions, the Commission introduced a third proposal; the Proposal for a Directive Relating to Measures to be taken against air pollution by emissions from motor vehicles, and amending Directive 70/220/EEC in relation to light commercial vehicles.[67] Although originally a separate proposal, the Environment Council indicated at its meeting on 16 October 1997 that the discussion of this proposal was to be joined with the discussion of the other two proposals. The Parliament therefore agreed to speed up its discussion. The contents of the proposal followed the same line as the Passenger Cars Proposal. It contains emission standards and requirements for on-board diagnostics for commercial vehicles up to 3.5 tonnes, for 2000. It was discussed for the first time by the European Parliament in its first reading on 18 February 1998.[68]

During the second reading of the proposals in the Parliament, on 18 February 1998, it became apparent, once more, how polarized the debate had become.[69] The Parliament, ignoring explicit appeals from the Commission to follow the Council's common position, re-adopted most of the amendments which it had proposed in the first reading.[70] The large majority by which these amendments were re-adopted (400–450 in favour out of 550 members present) sent a clear signal to the Council and the Commission that the Parliament intended to play hard.[71]

In the meantime, the Proposal on light commercial vehicles[72] was rushed through the Council, and a common position was adopted on 23 March 1998.[73] The approach in the common position was similar to that on passenger cars, setting binding limits for 2000 and indicative targets for 2005. The proposal went through the Parliament's second reading on 30 April 1998.[74] The

---

[65] Friedrich *et al.* (n. 60 above), 106.

[66] European Environment Bureau press release 10 Mar. 1998, European Environment Bureau launching campaign to support European Parliament on fuel and emissions standards. See also Friedrich *et al.* (n. 60 above), 105.

[67] COM(97)61 [1997] OJ C106/6.

[68] Report A4–0043/98, Recommendation for a first reading on the amended proposal for a European Parliament and Council directive relating to measures to be taken against air pollution by emissions from motor vehicles and amending Council Dirs. 70/156/EEC and 70/220/EEC, *rapporteur* B. Lange. The Parliament proposed only one amendment: [1998] OJ C80/128.

[69] Report A4–0038/98, Recommendation for a second reading on the common position established by the Council with a view to the adoption of a European Parliament and Council directive on the quality of petrols and diesel fuels and amending Dir. 93/12/EC *rapporteur* Ms. Hautala; Report A4–0044/98, Recommendation for a second reading on the common position established by the Council with a view to adopting a European Parliament and Council directive relating to measures to be taken against air pollution by emissions from motor vehicles and amending Dir. 70/220/EEC, *rapporteur* B. Lange.

[70] Friedrich *et al.* (n. 60 above), 105.   [71] *ENDS Environment Daily*, 18 Feb. 1998.

[72] COM(97)61 [1997] OJ C106/6.

[73] [1998] OJ C152/141, see also *ENDS Environment Daily*, 24 Mar. 1998.

[74] Report A4–0126/98, Decision on the common position adopted by the Council with a view to adopting a European Parliament and Council directive relating to measures to be taken against air

Parliament once more made clear that it was not going to give in to pressure from the Commission and Council. The stage was hence set for conciliation negotiations on all three proposals.

The Conciliation Committee convened in April 1998, and held various meetings, resulting in a compromise on 29 June 1998, one day before the end of the UK's Council presidency. The main elements of the compromise were, first, that the Council accepted the Parliament's position on making the limit values for vehicle emissions in 2005 mandatory, rather than indicative, for both passenger cars and light commercial vehicles. Secondly, in exchange for this, the Parliament accepted the limit values adopted by the Council in its common position for 2000 and for 2005. Finally, the Council accepted the Parliament's amendments that provided for the earlier phasing in of cleaner diesel and petrol.[75] The Parliament discussed and adopted the Conciliation Committee reports on 15 September 1998.

ii.   Heavy Goods Vehicle Emissions and Roadside Inspections

The success in the three difficult dossiers allowed the continuation of work on the two remaining proposals under Auto/Oil I; the Heavy Goods Vehicle Emissions Proposal and the Roadside Inspections Proposal.

On 3 December 1997, the Commission published the Proposal for a directive amending Council Directive 88/77/EEC on the Approximation of the Laws of the Member States Relating to the Measures to be Taken Against the Emission of Gaseous and Particulate Pollutants from Diesel Engines for Use in Vehicles.[76] The proposal met with the same critique as the previous Auto/Oil Proposals during its first reading in Parliament on 21 October 1998.[77] The Parliament approved the Commission proposal on first reading, subject to 23 amendments. A modified Commission proposal is now awaited. The Council already held two initial debates at its meetings in June and October 1998. At these preliminary discussions it became clear that the main points of discussion will be the use of tax incentives and the introduction of mandatory limit values for 2005. The Environment Council is expected to come up with a common position at its meeting in December 1998.

pollution by emissions from motor vehicles and amending Dir. 70/220/EEC with regard to light commercial vehicles. See also *ENDS Environment Daily*, 16 Apr. 1998.

[75] See for the results of the negotiations: Report A4–313/98, Report of 10 Sept. 1998 on the joint text, approved by the Conciliation Committee, for a European Parliament and Council directive. relating to the quality of petrol and diesel fuels and amending Council Dir. 93/12/EEC, *rapporteur* H. Hautala; and Report A4–314/98, of 10 Sept. 1998 on the joint text, approved by the Conciliation Committee, for a European Parliament and Council directive relating to (1) measures to be taken against air pollution by emissions from motor vehicles and amending Directive 70/220/EEC and (2) measures to be taken agains air pollution by emissions from motor vehicles and amending Directive 70/220/EEC with regard to light commercial vehicles, *rapporteur* B. Lange. See also *ENDS Environment Daily*, 30 June 1998.

[76] COM(97)627 of 3 Dec. 1997 [1997] OJ C173/1.

[77] Report A4–364/98 of 15 Oct. 1998 on the proposal for a European Parliament and Council directive on the approximation of the laws of the Member States relating to the measures to be taken against the emissions of gaseous and particulate pollutants from diesel engines for use in vehicles, *rapporteur* B. Lange.

The Commission published the Proposal for the roadside inspection of commercial vehicles circulating in the Community on 11 March 1998.[78] The proposed inspection system consists of inspection of the most visible aspects of the safety and environmental protection systems and equipment fitted to vehicles. The Commission's draft is currently pending before the Parliament for its first reading, which is expected by the end of January 1999.

During the discussions on the adoption of the measures under the Auto/Oil I programme, negotiations have begun for the Auto/Oil II package. The aim of these negotiations is to agree upon a package of legislative proposals for post-2005 standards. The focus of these legislative proposals should be non-technical measures rather than the technical measures proposed under Auto/Oil I. Originally, Auto/Oil II was to set standards for 2005, but since the Parliament's success in the inclusion of mandatory standards for 2005 in the Auto/Oil I measures, the scope of the Auto/Oil II negotiations was changed. Apart from the parties which negotiated the Auto/Oil II package, environmental NGOs are also involved in the Auto/Oil II negotiations. The Commission is expected to present concrete proposals in mid-1999.[79]

D.   ACIDIFICATION

In March 1997, the Commission, in reaction to a request by the Environment Council of 18 December 1995, presented its Proposal for a Community strategy to combat acidification.[80] The Community strategy is intended to implement the Community's obligations under the 1994 Oslo Protocol on further reduction of sulphur,[81] which was negotiated under the Convention on Long-Range Transboundary Airborne Pollution (LRTAP). The aim of the proposed strategy is to ensure that the critical loads are not exceeded anywhere in the EU. The Commission's proposal lays down a strategy for a first phase of reduction of critical load. During the first phase, which ends in 2010, the areas of sensitive ecosystems in which critical loads are exceeded need to be reduced by 50 per cent. In order to reach this goal, the Commission proposed in its strategy to undertake a number of actions. First, the Commission proposed the ratification by the EU and all Member States of the 1994 Sulphur Protocol. Secondly, the Commission proposed the adoption of a directive limiting the sulphur content of fuel oils. Thirdly, it proposed a revision of the Directive on the Limitation of Emissions from Large Combustion Plants.[82] Finally, action was to be undertaken by the IMO to reduce emissions from shipping. Both the

---

[78] COM(98)0117 of 11 Mar. 1998 [1998] OJ C190/10.

[79] *ENDS Environment Daily* of 24 Oct. 1997, 8 Apr. 1998 and 2 July 1998.

[80] COM(97)88 of 12 Mar. 1997.

[81] The Community ratified the 1994 Protocol on 24 Apr. 1998, Council Decision 98/686/EC on the conclusion by the European Community of the Protocol to the 1979 Convention on long-range transboundary air pollution on further reductions of sulphur emissions [1998] OJ L326/34. The Protocol entered into force on 5 Aug. 1998.

[82] Council Dir. 88/609/EEC on the limitation of emissions of certain pollutants into the air from large combustion plants [1988] OJ L336/1.

Parliament and the Environment Council, in its December 1997 meeting, gave ample support to the Commission's proposal.[83]

Shortly after bringing out the acidification strategy, the Commission published its Proposal for a Council Directive Relating to a Reduction of the Sulphur Content of Certain Liquid Fuels in March 1997.[84] The proposal requires the sulphur content of heavy fuel oil to be limited to 1 per cent by 2003.[85] In addition, the proposal contains a sulphur content limit of 0.2 per cent for gas oil upon entry into force of the Directive, as well as a 0.1 per cent limit by 2008. The Commission proposal was discussed in the Parliament in May 1998.[86] The Parliament criticized the proposal for not covering bunker fuel oils and marine diesel oils, as well as for not setting sufficiently stringent standards. The Parliament proposed to bring the 1 per cent target forward to 1 January 1999 (the original proposal stated 1 January 2000), as well as to halve the gas oil limit to 0.1 per cent. The Council, in June 1998, did not agree to bring all maritime emissions under the proposal, but limited it to specific categories. In addition, the Council brought forward the reduction date for heavy fuel oil from 2000 to 2003, as proposed by the Commission, rather than 1999, as proposed by the Parliament.[87] The proposal is currently awaiting its second reading in Parliament.

The Commission Proposal for a directive amending Directive 88/609/EEC on the Limitation of Emissions of Certain Pollutants Into the Air from Large Combustion Plants, was published only on 13 August 1998.[88] This proposal aims to amend the existing Directive on Emissions of Combustion Plants on several important points. First, it sets new emission limit values for new installations put into service after 1 January 2000. Secondly, it aims to cover gas-turbine combustion plants. Finally, it promotes the development of combined heat and electricity production and reinforces the verification provisions. The proposal is currently with the European Parliament for a first reading.

E.   OZONE

On 17 August 1998, the Commission published a Proposal for a new Council Regulation on Substances that Deplete the Ozone Layer.[89] This proposal is to replace Council Regulation (EC) No. 3093/94,[90] which implemented the Montreal Protocol on Substances that Deplete the Ozone Layer and the amendments to that protocol adopted in Copenhagen in 1992. The reason for the new proposal is a number of amendments and adjustments that have

---

[83] Report A4–0162/98 of 28 Apr. 1998, *rapporteur* Mrs. Hulthén.

[84] COM(97)88 of 12 Mar. 1997 [1997] OJ C190/9.

[85] This limit is however subject to the exception that Member States can move the limit up to 3% if they can demonstrate that their burning of heavy fuel oil does not contribute to acidification.

[86] Report A4–0174/98, by H. Hautala, 23 Apr. 1998. EP opinion 1st reading on 13 May 1998 [1998] OJ C167/79 and 117.

[87] The Commission amended the proposal after the Parliament's first reading: COM(98)385 of 8 July 1998 [1998] OJ C259/5: Council common position of 6 Oct. 1998 [1998] OJ C364/20.

[88] COM(98)415 of 8 July 1998 [1998] OJ C300/6.

[89] COM(98)398 of 14 Aug. 1998 [1998] OJ C286/6.   [90] [1994] OJ L333/1.

taken place under the Montreal regime, relating in particular to the phasing out of methyl bromide and the placing on the market of methyl bromide within the Community, as well as relating to the licensing of imports and exports of ozone-depleting substances. The proposal does not, however, limit itself to the implementation of the changes in the Montreal regime, but adopts a number of stricter measures than required by this protocol. A preliminary discussion on the proposal was held in the Environment Council meeting in October 1998. During this meeting it became clear that the proposal's provisions concerning the early phasing out of HCFCs and methyl bromide are likely to cause lively discussions. Fears have been expressed that the phasing out of the HCFC production in the EC, which is mainly aimed at export to developing countries, will give a competitive advantage to the United States of America (USA) and Japan. Similar arguments were raised by Spain, Greece, Italy, Portugal and France, on the issue of methyl bromide, especially as the USA has decided not to enforce its phase-out by 2001,[91] and the Montreal phase-out deadline is 2005. The proposal is currently awaiting its first reading in the European Parliament.[92]

From 23 to 24 November 1998, the tenth meeting of the parties to the Montreal Protocol took place in Cairo. At this meeting it was decided to ask an expert panel to examine how the use of hydrofluorocarbons (HFCs) and perfluorocarbons (PFCs), as substitutes for ozone-depleting substances, could be minimized. HFCs and PFCs are powerful greenhouse gases, the increased use of which as the result of the Montreal Protocol has an important effect on global warming. This decision creates an important direct link between the Montreal Protocol and the Climate Change Convention.

Related to the issue of ozone is the Commission's Proposal for a Directive on the Reduction of Emissions of Volatile Organic Compounds (VOCs) Caused by the Use of Organic Solutives in Certain Industrial Processes.[93] The original proposal was published in November 1996. The proposal intends to implement the 1991 Geneva Protocol to the 1979 LRTAP. The Geneva Protocol concerns the control of emissions of volatile organic compounds or their transboundary fluxes. The protocol entered into force on 29 September 1997, requiring the Member States to reach a 30 per cent reduction in emissions of VOCs by 1999, using a year between 1984 and 1990 as a basis. The Directive goes a step further than the protocol, by requiring a reduction of at least 50 per cent by 2010, compared to 1990 levels. The Directive covers the main types of solvent-using installations, defining reduction targets by means of emission limit values. The Directive also allows Member States to use national plans tailored to national circumstances, rather than using emission limit values for every single installation. On 25 March 1998, the Commission published a modified proposal.[94] The

[91] *ENDS Environment Daily*, 8 Dec. 1998 and 17 Nov. 1998.

[92] The Environment Committee has adopted its report on the proposal on 27 Nov. 1998, A4–0465/98, *rapporteur* I. Graenitz.

[93] COM(96)538 of 6 Nov. 1996 [1997] OJ C99/32.

[94] COM(98)190 of 25 Mar. 1998, [1998] OJ C126/8, which takes into account some of the Parliament's amendments adopted on 14 Jan. 1998 [1998] OJ C034/83.

Council adopted its common position in June 1998, after having discussed the details at its March Environment Council meeting.[95] The proposal, discussed in second reading in the Parliament,[96] is now awaiting final adoption by the Council.

F.　AIR QUALITY: DAUGHTER DIRECTIVES

In 1996, the Council adopted a new Directive on Ambient Air Quality Assessment and Management.[97] This directive revised a number of older air quality directives into a new Framework Directive.[98] The Framework Directive did not, however, contain any limit values, alert thresholds or target values for the substances listed in its Annex I. Instead, these values were to be adopted on the basis of daughter directives.[99]

On 8 October 1997, almost a year behind schedule,[100] the Commission published the proposal for the first daughter directive, relating to limit values for sulphur dioxide, oxides of nitrogen, particulate matter, and lead in ambient air.[101] The proposal is, for a large part, based on recent World Health Organization guidelines, and in some cases goes further. The standards for lead and sulphur dioxide are supposed to be easily met. The standards for nitrogen dioxide and particulate matter will be more difficult to meet, as they require strict action against the main emitters; cars. The Council having adopted a common position,[102] the proposal is currently awaiting its second reading in the European Parliament.[103]

On 2 December 1998, the Commission published the proposal for the second daughter directive, the directive on benzene and carbon monoxide (CO),[104] again almost a year behind schedule. The proposal sets a limit value for benzene of $5\mu g/m^3$ to be met by 1 January 2010 and $10\mu g/m^3$ to be met on 1 January 2005. Reaching these limits will require reductions of up to 70 per cent of total benzene emissions and up to 30 per cent of CO emissions. The

---

[95]　On 16 June 1998 [1998] OJ C248/1.

[96]　On 21 Oct. 1998. For the Parliament's objections see report A4–358/98 by C. Cabrol of 13 Oct. 1998.

[97]　Dir. 96/62/EC on ambient air quality assessment and management [1996] OJ L296/55.

[98]　More elaborately on the Ambient Air Quality Directive see J. Lefevere, "The New Directive on Ambient Air Quality Assessment and Management" (1997) 6(7) *European Environmental Law Review* 210–14.

[99]　Art. 4 of the Directive gives the following timetable: no later than 31 Dec. 1996 for sulphur dioxide, nitrogen dioxide, fine particulate matter such as soot, suspended particulate matter, and lead; no later than 21 Mar. 1998 for ozone; no later than 31 Dec. 1997 for benzene and carbon monoxide; and as soon as possible, and no later than 31 Dec. 1999, for poly-aromatic hydrocarbons, cadmium, arsenic, nickel, and mercury.

[100]　This was mainly due to the unusually inclusive consultation of all involved actors, which was praised by the European Parliament in its first reading: see report A4–0161/98, *rapporteur* A. Pollack.

[101]　COM(97)500 [1998] OJ C9/6.

[102]　On 24 Sept. 1998 [1998] OJ C360/99. The common position incorporates 21 out of 28 amendments proposed by the Parliament.

[103]　The Parliament's comments are contained in report A4–0483/98 of 25 Nov. 1998.

[104]　See Commission press release IP/98/1049.

proposal is currently awaiting its first reading in the European Parliament. The Proposal on Ozone, which was due to be published in March 1998, is now expected in early 1999.[105]

G.   INTERNATIONAL DEVELOPMENTS

Various Community measures serving to implement international agreements have already been discussed earlier in this text, including the developments under the Climate Change Convention and the Montreal Protocol, as well as the implementation of the Sulphur Protocol and the VOC Protocol. In addition, several other important developments have taken place over 1998.

Two other important protocols were adopted, which were elaborated under the United Nations Economic Commission for Europe (UN-ECE) Convention on Long Range Transboundary Airborne Pollution (LRTAP), to which the Community is a party.[106] On 24 June 1998, at the fourth Pan-European conference of environment ministers for Europe, the LRTAP's executive body adopted the Protocol on persistent organic pollutants (POPs) and the Protocol on heavy metals. The two protocols form an important addition to the Convention and the five protocols already adopted under it.

The POPs Protocol covers a list of sixteen substances, comprising eleven pesticides, two industrial chemicals, and three by-products/contaminants. The aim of the protocol is to eliminate all emissions of these POPS into the atmosphere. In order to do so, it bans the production and use of aldrin, chlordane, chlordecone, dieldrin, endrin, hexabromobiphenyl, mirex, and toxaphene. In addition it schedules DDT, heptachlor, hexabromobiphenyl and PCBs for elimination at a later stage. Furthermore it severely restricts the use of DDT, HCH (including lindane), and PCBs. The protocol also requires parties to reduce the emissions of dioxins, furans, PAHs, and HCD below their 1990 emission levels (or an alternative year between 1985 and 1990). Finally, the protocol addresses the problem of waste of banned products and incineration of municipal, hazardous, and medical waste.

The Heavy Metals Protocol addresses atmospheric emissions of three heavy metals: cadmium, lead, and mercury. The protocol requires states to reduce their emissions of these metals below 1990 levels (or an alternative year between 1985 and 1990). In order to do so, the protocol addresses both stationary and other sources. For stationary sources, it lays down specific emission values and suggests the use of BAT (Best Available Techniques). Concerning the other sources, it addresses the problems of the lead content of petrol and mercury in batteries, as well as other products containing heavy metals, such as thermometers, pesticides, and paints.

Apart from the adoption of the two protocols, an eighth protocol is currently being negotiated within the framework of the LRTAP. This International Multi-

---

[105] *ENDS Environment Daily*, 10 Sept. 1998.
[106] Decision 81/462/EEC concluding the Convention by the Community [1981] OJ L171.

effects and Multi-pollutant Protocol is to address the interdependence of various environmental problems, in particular those related to ground level ozone, acidification, and eutrophication. The aim is to have it ready for adoption in 1999.

H.   OTHER ISSUES

Several other Community actions in the field of the environment need to be mentioned. First, the Commission published two proposals concerning incineration of waste. The first of these, the Proposal for a Directive on the Incineration of Hazardous Waste, amending Directive 94/67/EC, was published at the end of November 1997.[107] This proposal was followed by the Proposal for a Directive on the Incineration of Non-Hazardous Wastes and Wastes Excluded from Directive 94/67/EC, in October 1998.[108] Both proposals are discussed more extensively in the waste section of this volume.

In the field of air pollution by aviation, in February 1998, the Commission published a Proposal for a Directive on the Emission of Oxides of Nitrogen Oxide from Civil Subsonic Jet Aeroplanes.[109] This proposal requires a 16 per cent reduction in emissions for new aircraft by 2000. In addition, it requires existing aircraft to meet the new limit from 2008. The proposal, based on Article 80(2) (formerly Article 84(2)) EC, is currently under discussion in the Transport Council after it was approved without amendment by the Parliament on 1 April 1998.[110]

Mention should also be made of the adoption of the Directive on Emissions by Non-Road Mobile Machinery.[111] This Directive was drawn up with the aim of reducing emissions of nitrogen oxides, hydrocarbons, and particulates from off-road equipment such as construction, agricultural, and forestry vehicles. The proposal was finally adopted in December 1997, after a long discussion on committee procedures.[112] Complementing this Directive, in September 1998, the Commission published a Proposal for the emission of gaseous pollutants and particulate matters, from agricultural tractors.[113]

I.   CONCLUSION

The many issues under discussion during 1998, although in principle treated as separate dossiers, have increasingly become linked. This has forced the Community to develop a more integrated approach to the problem of atmospheric pollution, which has given rise to complicated discussions, and made

---

[107] COM(97)604, 21 Nov. 1997 [1998] OJ C13/6.

[108] COM(98)558, 29 Oct. 1998 [1998] OJ C372/11.

[109] COM(97)629, 3 Feb. 1998 [1998] OJ C108/14.   [110] [1998] OJ C138/84.

[111] Dir. 97/68/EC concerning measures against the emissions of gaseous and particulate pollutants from internal combustion engines to be installed in non-road mobile machinery [1998] OJ L059/1.

[112] *ENDS Environment Daily*, 18 Dec. 1997.

[113] COM(98)472, 3 Sept. 1998 [1998] OJ C303/9.

progress on one issue dependent on progress in another dossier. Increasing inter-dependence exists between the issue of CO_2 emissions by cars and the Auto/Oil discussions. In these discussions, a clear link was shown between the quality of fuels and the car manufacturer's ability to introduce technology reducing CO_2 emissions. An interesting development is also that the tenth meeting of the parties to the Montreal Protocol, held in Cairo from 23–24 November 1998, for the first time took up the issue of powerful greenhouse gases being used as substitutes for substances that deplete the ozone layer. Finally, an overlap could be seen between the acidification dossier and discussions on standards under the ambient air quality daughter directives. In the future, the Community will see itself increasingly confronted with these inter-relationships, which are very likely to force a more general approach to the issue of atmospheric pollution than currently is the case.

II. Chemicals and Biotechnology

ELIZABETH VOGELEZANG-STOUTE*

A. LEGISLATION ADOPTED

i. Major-accident Hazards

One of the requirements of Council Directive 96/82/EC on the control of major-accident hazards involving dangerous substances (Seveso II)[1] is that a safety report has to be produced by the establishments to which the Directive applies. When, however, an establishment is incapable of creating a major-accident hazard, a Member State may limit the information required in the report. For that purpose, the Commission, in 1998, established criteria in Decision 98/433/EC on Harmonized Criteria for Dispensations according to Article 9 of Council Directive 96/82/EC.[2] In short, these criteria relate to the form, containment and quantities, location and quantities, and classification of the substance. If at least one of the criteria is fulfilled, a Member State may limit the required information in the safety reports. The establishment of these criteria was necessary before bringing this Directive into application.

ii. Biocides Directive

Council Directive 98/8/EC of the European Parliament and of the Council Concerning the Placing of Biocidal Products on the Market (Biocides Directive)[3] entered into force in 1998. This Directive aims at removing trade barriers for biocidal products, and at the same time ensuring a high level of protection for humans, animals and the environment.[4] To accomplish this, a dual authorization system is established. The Directive provides for criteria and procedures for the authorization of biocidal products at the national level. It also establishes an authorization system for active substances of the products at Community level.[5] The active substance has to be approved by inclusion in an Annex of the Directive. This inclusion is a requirement for the authorization at the national level of the biocide in question.

The Directive also creates a system of mutual recognition, which means that the authorization of a product in one Member State must be recognized by another Member State, provided certain conditions are comparable.

The system of the Biocides Directive resembles that of Directive 91/414/EEC Concerning the Placing of Plant Protection Products on the Market.[6] There are,

---

* Researcher at the Centre for Environmental Law, University of Amsterdam.

[1] [1997] OJ L10/13.　　　　　　[2] [1998] OJ L192/19.　　　　　　[3] [1998] OJ L123/1.

[4] Biocides are non-agricultural pesticides, used mainly in industry or by households, such as wood preservatives, anti-fouling paints, and certain disinfectants.

[5] An active substance is the essential ingredient of the biocidal product. It gives the product its biocidal effect. From one active substance many different biocidal products can be made.

[6] [1991] OJ L230/1.

however, several differences, such as a comparative assessment for the active substance and a simplified procedure for the "low-risk" biocides, which the Biocides Directive introduces.[7]

Implementation of the Biocides Directive must take place before 14 May 2000.[8] Because of transitional measures it may take several years before the requirements of the Directive apply to biocides containing existing substances. For new substances the requirements apply immediately.[9]

iii. Genetically Modified Organisms

In the field of genetically modified organisms (GMOs) and genetically modified micro-organisms (GMMs), far-reaching developments are taking place. Hence, legislation is developing rapidly.[10] Community legislation on GMOs and GMMs covers the following aspects:

— contained use of GMMs in the manufacturing process in laboratories and research centres (Directive 90/219/EEC on the Contained Use of Genetically Modified Micro-organisms);[11]
— intentional introduction into the environment of GMOs (Directive 90/220/EEC on the Deliberate Release Into the Environment of Genetically Modified Organisms);[12]
— sectoral legislation for products resulting from genetic modification (e.g. European Parliament and Council Regulation (EC) No. 258/97 on Novel Foods);[13]
— specific regulations on genetically modified maize and soya (Council Regulation (EC) No. 1139/98 providing for labelling for products containing genetically modified soya or maize).[14]

In 1998, a number of measures and decisions were taken.

Council Directive 90/219/EEC on the Contained Use of Genetically Modified Micro-organisms[15] was amended by Council Directive 98/81/EC.[16] The Directive has been brought into line with technical progress and new knowledge in the area of risk assessment. Administrative procedures, notification requirements and protection measures are linked to risks.

The Commission proposed an amendment of Council Directive 90/220/EEC on the Deliberate Release Into the Environment of Genetically

---

[7] The comparative assessment allows refusal or removal of an active substance from the list if another (similar) substance presents significantly less risk to health or the environment. The Directive requires a thorough assessment and lays down certain conditions for the assessment in Art. 10(5). Low-risk biocides contain certain active substances, listed in Annex IA.

[8] Art. 34 of Dir. 98/8/EC.

[9] Art. 16(1) of ibid. Substances not yet on the market on 14 May 2000 are new substances.

[10] The Appendix to the opinion of the Economic and Social Committee on genetically modified organisms in agriculture—impact on the Common Agricultural Policy [1998] OJ C284/39, gives a good overview of the development of this legislation.

[11] [1990] OJ L117/1, as last amended [1998] OJ L330/13.

[12] [1990] OJ L117/15, as last amended [1997] OJ L169/72.   [13] [1997] OJ L43/1.

[14] [1998] OJ L159/4.   [15] [1990] OJ L 117/1.

[16] Council Dir. 98/81/EC amending Dir. 90/219 [1998] OJ L330/13.

Modified Organisms.[17] This proposal, *inter alia*, aims to introduce simplified and more transparent authorization procedures for the placing on the market of GMOs, and to restrict the use of the safeguard clause (Article 16 of the Directive) by the Member States. It also seeks to establish labelling requirements, through obligations for the notifier and it sets out common principles for risk assessment.[18]

The Commission took several decisions concerning the placing on the market of genetically modified maize and spring swede rape, pursuant to Directive 90/220/EEC on the Deliberate Release Into the Environment of Genetically Modified Organisms.[19] Favourable decisions were given for the marketing in the UK of these grains, which are modified either to produce their own toxin against pests or to develop an increased tolerance against pesticides.[20]

Subsequently, Austria and Luxembourg, by using the safeguard clause of the Directive, banned the marketing of genetically modified maize. The Regulatory Committee of Directive 90/220/EEC failed to deliver an opinion, and the Commission adopted proposals for Council decisions forcing withdrawals of the national bans.[21]

For products containing soya beans or maize, specific labelling requirements were established in Council Regulation (EC) No. 1139/98 concerning the compulsory indication of the labelling of certain foodstuffs produced from genetically modified organisms of particulars other than those provided for in Directive 79/112/EEC.[22]

B.   LEGISLATION IN PROGRESS

The Commission forwarded a proposal to amend for the 18th time Directive 76/769/EEC Concerning Restrictions on the Marketing and Use of Certain Dangerous Substances and Preparations.[23] The proposal adds to Annex I[24] sixteen substances classified as carcinogenic, mutagenic, or toxic to reproduction of category 1 or 2 (c/m/r). Substances included in points 29, 30, and 31 of this Annex should not be placed on the market for use by the general public.

The substances in question were already classified as c/m/r in1996 under Directive 67/548/EEC.[25] Because of the time that has passed, the Economic and Social Committee concluded that it would be better if the restriction on the sale of these substances would follow automatically after the classification under Directive 67/548/EEC.[26]

[17] [1998] OJ C139/1.

[18] See W. Douma and M. Matthee, "Towards New EC Rules on Genetically Modified Organisms" (1999) 8 *Review of European Community and International Environmental Law* 152–159.

[19] [1990] OJ L117/15, as last amended [1997] OJ L169/72.

[20] Commission Decisions 98/291/EC, 98/292/EC, 98/293/EC, and 98/294/EC [1998] OJ L131/26, 28, 30, and 33.

[21] "Eurobrief" (1998) 7 *European Environmental Law Review* 252; COM(1998)339–340.

[22] [1998] OJ L159/4.   [23] [1976] OJ L262/201, as amended [1997] OJ L333/1.

[24] COM(97)738, 7 Jan. 1998 [1998] OJ C59/5.

[25] [1967] OJ L196/1, as amended [1996] at L278/1.

[26] Opinion of the Economic and Social Committee on the Proposal for a European Parliament and Council Directive amending for the 18th time Dir. 76/769/EEC [1998] OJ C214/73.

C. POLICY DOCUMENTS

The informal transport and environment Council meeting, held in Chester (United Kingdom) on 24–26 April 1998, was the starting point for a review of existing legislation of chemicals. In November, the Commission published a Working Document on the evaluation of three directives and one regulation: Directive 67/548/EEC, Directive 76/769/EEC, Directive 88/379/EEC, and Regulation (EEC) No. 793/93.[27] The limited progress that has been made in assessing chemicals has led the Commission to conclude that a more effective and efficient use of these instruments and more stringent enforcement are needed. New problems, such as the effects of substances on endocrine systems, need to be addressed, and the precautionary principle has to be taken into consideration.[28] In December 1998, the Council approved these conclusions of the Commission.[29]

D. CASE LAW

i. Chemicals

In a preliminary ruling in the *Burstein* case,[30] the European Court of Justice (ECJ) held that Directive 76/769/EEC Relating to the Restrictions on the Marketing and Use of Certain Dangerous Substances and Preparations,[31] as amended by Council Directive 91/173/EEC,[32] is applicable to PCP (pentachlorophenol), its salts and esters, and to preparations produced from those substances, but not to products treated with those substances or preparations.

The Commission commenced many proceedings against Member States for not implementing one or more directives on chemicals.[33] In *Commission* v. *Belgium*,[34] the ECJ ruled that Belgium failed to adopt laws to comply with Directive 94/69/EC,[35] adapting to technical progress Directive 67/548/EEC on the Approximation of the Laws, Regulations and Administrative Provisions Relating to the Classification, Packaging, and Labelling of Dangerous Substances.[36]

In a preliminary ruling regarding the authorization of pesticides, the *Harpegnies* case, the ECJ held that Directive 91/414/EEC[37] requires prior authorization of a plant protection product from the competent authority of each Member State in which such a product is placed on the market. With regard to biocidal products, the ECJ held that national legislation must be

---

[27] [1967] OJ L196/1, [1976] OJ L262/201, [1988] OJ L187/14, [1993] OJ L84/1.

[28] COM(98)587, 18 Nov. 1998; EC Bull 11–1998, at 50/51; "Eurobrief (1999) *European Environmental Law Review* 50.

[29] EC Bull 12–1998, 83.   [30] Case C–127/97, *Burstein* v. *Freistaat Bayern* [1998] ECR I–6005.

[31] [1976] OJ L262/201.   [32] [1991] OJ L85/34.

[33] *Inter alia*, Case C–66/98, *Commission* v. *Italy* [1998] OJ C137/12; Case C–308/98, *Commission* v. *Ireland* [1998] OJ C299/29; Case C–328/98, *Commission* v. *Belgium* [1998] OJ C327/12; Case C–346/98, *Commission* v. *Ireland* [1998] OJ C340/12.

[34] Case C–79/98, *Commission* v. *Belgium* [1998] ECR I–6039.

[35] [1994] OJ L381/1.   [36] [1967] OJ L196/1.   [37] Above, n. 6.

assessed by reference to Article 28 (formerly Article 30) EC, while the Biocides Directive[38] had not been adopted at the time the facts arose. The authorization requirement for a biocide is a quantitative restriction, justified under Article 30 (formerly Article 36) EC, even if that product has already been authorized in another Member State, provided that analyses or tests are not unnecessarily required when these have already been carried out in the other Member State and when results are available or can be made available to the competent authority of the importing Member State.[39]

ii.   Genetically Modified Organisms

In several cases,[40] the ECJ ruled that Member States failed to transpose Directives 90/219/EEC and 90/220/EEC and/or the directives adapting to technical progress Directives 90/219/EEC[41] and/or 90/220/EEC.[42]

E.   INTERNATIONAL CO-OPERATION

i.   Transboundary Effects of Industrial Accidents

On behalf of the Community, the UN Convention on the Transboundary Effects of Industrial Accidents was approved by the Council in March 1998. The Council formulates its reservations about certain threshold quantities for substances in Annex I to the Convention, as these differ from the threshold quantities set out in Directive 98/82/EEC[43] on the control of major-accident hazards.[44]

The UN Convention on Transboundary Effects aims at the protection of human beings and the environment against industrial accidents capable of causing such transboundary effects. Furthermore, it aims at promoting active international co-operation between contracting parties, before, during, and after such accidents. The parties shall take appropriate measures for the prevention of, preparedness for, and response to industrial accidents. Mutual assistance, research and development, and exchange of information and technology are required. The Convention also requires policies and strategies for reducing risks. The parties must designate a competent authority and a Conference of parties must be held to review the implementation of the Convention at least every year. In the Convention, procedures are laid down for, *inter alia*, dispute settlement.[45]

---

[38] Above, n. 3.   [39] Case C–400/96, *Harpegnies* [1998] ECR I–5121.

[40] Case C–285/97, *Commission* v. *Portugal* [1998] ECR I–4895; Case C–339/97, *Commission* v. *Luxembourg* [1998] ECR I–4903; Case C–343/97, *Commission* v. *Belgium* [1998] ECR I–4291.

[41] Dir. 90/219/EEC on the contained use of genetically modified micro-organisms [1991] OJ L117/1, as amended by Dir. 94/51/EC [1994] OJ L297/29.

[42] Dir. 90/220/EEC on the deliberate release into the environment of genetically modified organisms [1991] OJ L117/15, as amended by Dir. 94/15/EC [1994] OJ L103/20.

[43] Directive 98/82/EC amending the Annexes to Council Directives 86/362/EEC and 90/642/EEC on the fixing of maximum levels for pesticide residues in and on cereals, foodstuffs of animal origin and certain procedures of plant origin, including fruit and vegetables respectively Official Journal [1999] OJ L175/83.

[44] Council Decision 98/685/EC concerning the conclusion of the Convention on the Transboundary Effects of Industrial Accidents [1998] OJ L326/1.

[45] The text of the Convention, signed in 1992 in Helsinki, was published in [1998] OJ L326/6.

ii. Prior Informed Consent

In September 1998 the Rotterdam Convention on Trade in Certain Hazardous Chemicals and Pesticides was signed on behalf of the Community. This Convention establishes the principle of prior informed consent (PIC) in international law. The PIC principle, currently a voluntary code, implemented by FAO and UNEP, requires that certain banned or severely restricted chemicals and pesticides not be exported unless explicitly agreed by the importing country participating in the procedure. The Convention initially covers five chemicals and twenty-two pesticides. It will enter into force upon the fiftieth ratification.[46] For EU Member States, the PIC regime is already mandatory through Regulation (EEC) No. 2455/92 on the import and export of certain dangerous chemicals.[47]

F.   MISCELLANEOUS

i. Chemicals

Household Laundry Detergents

The Commission published a Recommendation for household laundry detergents. This Recommendation is based on an agreement with the Association Internationale de la Savonnerie de la Détergence et des Produits d'Entretien (AISE). AISE, which represents over 90 per cent of the detergent and cleaning product industries in the Community, has committed itself to ensure compliance with the Recommendation. Targets are set for the year 2002. Compared to 1996, certain reductions per wash cycle should be reached in energy used, detergents, packaging, and poorly biodegradable organic ingredients.[48]

Hexachloroethane

Council Decision 98/241/EC approves, on behalf of the Community, the phasing-out of the use of hexachloroethane in the non-ferrous metal industry, as laid down in PARCOM Decision 96/1.[49] Hexachloroethane is one of the dangerous substances listed in Annex I to Directive 76/769/EEC Relating to Restrictions on the Marketing and Use of Certain Dangerous Substances and Preparations.[50]

---

[46] Final Act of the Conference of Plenipotentiaries on the Convention on the Prior Informed Consent Procedure for Certain Hazardous Chemicals and Pesticides in International Trade, 10–11 Sept. 1998, Rotterdam.

[47] [1992] OJ L251/13, as amended [1998] OJ L282/12.

[48] Commission Recommendation 98/480/EC concerning good environmental practice for household laundry detergents [1998] OJ L215/73.

[49] Council Decision 98/241/EC concerning the approval, on behalf of the Community, of PARCOM Decision 96/1 [1998] OJ L96/41. PARCOM (the Paris Commission) is the executive body of the Paris Convention on the Prevention of Marine Pollution from Land-Based Sources.

[50] [1976] OJ L262/201, as last amended [1997] OJ L315/13.

Directive on Plant Protection Products

In May 1998, the Commission organized a workshop on the sustainable use of plant protection products in the European Union. The background to this initiative was the Fifth Environmental Action Programme 1992, which pledged the development of proposals for progressive replacement of harmful pesticides and progressive use limitations. There was consensus among participants on the need for additional risk-reduction policy instruments for plant protection products and on the need to speed up the review of active substances under Directive 91/414/EEC.[51]

The inclusion of active substances in Annex I of Directive 91/414/EEC is continuing very slowly. In 1998, the Commission took approximately twenty so-called completeness decisions[52] and several withdrawal decisions.[53] Only one decision on inclusion was taken in this year: the second substance was included in Annex I by Directive 98/47/EC.[54] Given the fact that half of the twelve year transition period of this Directive has passed and that there are approximately 800 existing active substances, one can conclude that even this twelve year period will not suffice. According to Article 8(2) of Directive 91/414/EC[55], the Commission must present a progress report to the European Parliament in 2000.

ii. Genetically Modified Organisms

Regarding the legislation on genetically modified organisms (GMOs), many questions remain, especially concerning environmental and agricultural aspects of marketing and use of these products. One of these questions concerns the applicability of pesticide legislation to a product, such as maize, mentioned before, that is genetically modified to produce a toxin, for use as a pesticide. Non-governmental organizations consider this product to be a pesticide, to which pesticide legislation should apply, especially because one of the possible effects is the resistance of the target organism.[56] Another question that remains is the applicability of the precautionary principle, which would appear to be of particular importance in this field of legislation because of the unknown long-term effects of many developments in this area.

---

[51] Procceedings of the Second Workshop on a framework for the sustainable use of plant protection products in the European Union, Brussels, 12–14 May 1998. Information can be found on the internet at: http://europa.eu.int/comm/dg11/ppps.

[52] A completeness decision recognizes in principle the completeness of the submitted dossiers. An example is the decision on BAS 620H (tepraloxydim), S-metolachlor and SZX 0722 [1998] OJ L228/35.

[53] A withdrawal decision requires withdrawal by Member States of authorizations for plant protection products based on a certain active substance. E.g. Commission Decision 98/269/EC concerning the withdrawal of authorisations for plant protection products containing dinoterb as an active substance [1998] OJ L117/13 and Commission Decision 98/270/EC concerning the withdrawal of authorizations for plant protection products containing fenvalerate as an active substance [1998] OJ L117/15.

[54] Commission Dir. 98/47/EC Including an active substance (Azoxystrobin) in Annex I to Council Dir. 91/414/EEC [1998] OJ L191/50.

[55] Council Directive 91/414/EEC concerning the placing of plant protection products on the market [1992] OJ L170/40.

[56] R. Jenkins, "Biopesticides Join the Pesticide Treadmill" (1998) 42 *Pesticides News*, 6–7.

III.   Nature Conservation

CHRIS BACKES*

A.   INTRODUCTION

In the field of nature conservation the main EC instruments are:

— Council Directive 79/409/EEC on the Conservation of Wild Birds (Wild Birds Directive);[1]
— Council Directive 92/43/EC on the Conservation of Natural Habitats and of Wild Fauna and Flora (Habitats Directive);[2] and
— Council Regulation (EC) No. 338/97 on the Protection of Species of Wild Fauna and Flora by Regulating Trade Therein (CITES Regulation).[3]

In addition, a range of other subjects are dealt with in EC nature conservation law, for example humane trapping standards, principles of sustainable forest management, protection of juveniles of marine organisms, etc. Therefore, this overview of EC nature conservation law in 1998 covers legislation, case law and policy documents, relating to the Wild Birds Directive, the Habitats Directive, the CITES Regulation and miscellaneous measures.

As this is the first annual overview of this kind, some events of the second half of 1997 are included.

B.   LEGISLATION

i.   Wild Birds Directive

There was only one minor adaptation of the Wild Birds Directive in 1997. On 29 July 1997, Commission Directive 97/49/EC amending Annex I to the Wild Birds Directive was published.[4] This Annex lists the species of birds which need special protection. One specific subspecies was deleted from the list because, according to the latest information, this subspecies had reached a favourable conservation status.

ii.   Habitats Directive

Annex I of the Habitats Directive was changed also, although one of these changes concerned a purely technical matter. In 1996, the Commission had published a new interpretation manual with new Natura 2000 codes for the identification of each category of natural habitat. These codes replaced the codes of the former Corine programme. Council Directive 97/62/EC[5] adopted

---

* Professor of Environmental Law, University of Utrecht.
[1] [1979] OJ L103/1.   [2] [1992] OJ L206/7.   [3] [1997] OJ L61/1.
[4] [1997] OJ L223/9.
[5] Council Dir. 97/62/EC adapting to technical and scientific progress Dir. 92/43/EEC on the conservation of natural habitats and of natural fauna and flora [1997] OJ L305/42.

a new Annex I to the Habitats Directive with these new codes. The Member States had to comply with this Directive by the end of 1997. They will now have to take the new Annex into account when finishing the process of site selection.

In 1997 and 1998, members of the European Parliament asked numerous questions concerning the application and enforcement of the Habitats Directive. From a legal point of view some of these questions, and the answers thereto, are interesting as they reveal the Commission's interpretation of some objectives of the Directive.

In Finland, some problems arose with the interpretation of Articles 4(5) and 6 of the Habitats Directive. In early 1997, some changes had already been introduced to the Finnish text of the Directive.[6] On 1 September 1997, a Finnish Member of the European Parliament asked a question which seemed typical of the discussions taking place in many Member States. Although the designation as a Natura 2000 area in the future may entail restrictions for land use, the Directive does not provide for a procedure of consultation of owners and land-users in the first stage of the process of designating sites. This has caused irritation in many Member States. The Finnish MEP enquired what the Member States are expected to do in this first stage of the site-selection procedure. The Commission pointed out that it is up to each Member State to decide this in detail. In any case, the introduction of such management measures should not slow down this stage of the procedure, which must be based exclusively on scientific criteria.[7]

A similar question was asked by a German Member of the European Parliament. The Commission was asked how "social groups" and NGOs should participate in the process of site selection, namely in the compilation of a national list as mentioned in Article 4(1) of the Habitats Directive. The Commission again stressed that this first stage falls completely within the competence of Member States and that the list must be composed on the basis of scientific criteria only. In the second stage, the European Habitat Forum will take part in the meetings of the biogeographical regions as a qualified umbrella NGO.[8]

Another Finnish question concerned whether and how Member States can change any part of the Natura 2000 programme once the areas have been designated. The Commission answered that, if a Member State intends to reduce a protected area, the situation has to be assessed in the light of Article 6 of the Directive.[9] In other words, there is no special provision or procedure concerning the reduction of special protected areas.

Another Finnish Member of the Parliament asked questions about the regime of Article 6(4) of the Habitats Directive. The Commission clarified that

[6] See Written Question 2061/97 of 9 June 1997 [1997] OJ C060/87.

[7] Written Question 2751/97 of 1 Sept. 1997 [1997] OJ C102/110 on the interpretation of Arts. 4(5) and 6 of the Habitats Dir.

[8] Written Question 3577/97 of 13 Nov. 1997 [1997] OJ C158/153 on the interpretation of Arts. 3 and 4 of the Habitats Dir.

[9] Written Question 1676/97 of 9 Dec. 1997 [1997] OJ C373/155.

no economic activity is either authorized or prohibited *per se* by the Directive.[10] The other questions were less interesting from a legal point of view.[11] Some of these questions dealt with Regulation (EC) No. 1973/92 Establishing a Financial Instrument for the Environment (Life Regulation).[12]

iii. CITES Regulation

After the old CITES Regulation had been replaced by Council Regulation (EC) No. 338/97 of 9 December 1996 on the Protection of Species of Wild Fauna and Flora by Regulating Trade Therein,[13] some further changes were necessary in 1998. These changes were mainly the result of the tenth meeting of the Conference of Parties to the UN Convention on International Trade in Endangered Species of Wild Fauna and Flora (CITES Convention), held in Harare (Zimbabwe) in June 1997. Although the Member States are party to the Convention, the EU itself is not. At the tenth meeting, the Conference of Parties adopted a number of resolutions and decisions. As a result, certain provisions of the CITES Regulation had to be amended. Commission Regulation (EC) No. 767/98[14] entailed an adaptation of Article 24 of the CITES Regulation, and some of the definitions included in Article 1 of the CITES Regulation, both Articles concerning specimens of animal species bred in captivity. The same goes for various other provisions of the Regulation, in particular for Article 26, concerning timber taken from trees grown in monoculture.

Annexes A, B, C, and D to the CITES Regulation were changed by Commission Regulation (EC) No. 2307/97[15] of 18 November 1997, amending Council Regulation (EC) No. 338/97 on the Protection of Species of Wild Fauna and Flora by Regulating Trade Therein, as a result of the amendments to Appendices I, II, and III to the CITES Convention. Another amendment to the

---

[10] Written Question 2775/97 of 1 Sept. 1997 [1997] OJ C082/140 on the interpretation of Art. 6 of the Habitats Directive.

[11] Written Questions: 693/97 [1997] OJ C319/162 about the French blockade of implementation of the Directive; 1413/97 [1997] OJ C391/83 about a rocket launch site (island of El Hierro); 1490/97 [1997] OJ C82/8 about the protection of Cetacea in Tenerife (Spain); 1526/97 [1997] OJ C391/97 about wolves in Northern Italy; 1726/97 [1997] OJ C21/86 about Southport sea wall; 1950/97 [1997] OJ C45/128 about a composting plant at Castiglione del Lago (Italy); 2478/97 [1197] OJ C117/19 about Natura 2000 and the CEECs; 2506/97 [1997] OJ C102/51 about environmental damage in the Picos de Europa national park (Spain); 2543/97 [1997] OJ C117/23 about pollution of the lake Koroneia; 2667/97 [1997] OJ C102/86 about survival of the "Cretan tracker dog" 2683/97 [1997] OJ C117/44 about deterioration of the river Segura; 2741/97 [1997] OJ C82/135 about protection of the Akamas peninsula (Cyprus); 2834/97 [1997] OJ C134/23 about protecting the Pego Oliva marshes (Spain); 2953/97 [1997] OJ C102/152 about protection of Montana Tindaya (Canary Islands); 2990/97 [1997] OJ C134/48 about sand extraction on Majorca; 2991/97 [1997] OJ C134/49 about the protection of the Marjal del Moro (Spain); 3009/97 [1997] OJ C134/57 about Lake Kerkinis (Greece); 3189/97 [1997] OJ C158/52 about "De Damervallei" (Belgium); 3442 and 3443/97 [1997] OJ C158/113 and 114 about hamsters in the south of the Netherlands; 3580/97 [1997] OJ C158/55 about the Wetlands of Nea Fokaia (Greece).

[12] [1992] OJ L206/1 as modified by Council Regulation (EC) No. 1404/96 [1996] OJ L1818/1.

[13] [1996] OJ L61/1.

[14] Commission Reg. (EC) No. 767/98 of 7 Apr. amending Reg. (EC) No. 939/97 laying down detailed rules concerning the implementation of Council Reg. (EC) No. 338/97 on the protection of species of wild fauna and flora by regulating trade therein [1998] OJ L109/7.

[15] [1997] OJ L325/1.

CITES Regulation is not directly the result of the Conference of Parties to the Convention, but is a reaction to abuse of Article 7(3) of the CITES Regulation. Article 7(3) allows derogation from the prohibitions of Article 5 of the Regulation as far as personal or household effects are concerned. In a new sub-paragraph of Article 28(1) of the Regulation it is now made clear that goods exported or re-exported from the Community in order to be used for commercial gain, can never be considered to be for personal or household purposes.[16]

Finally, Commission Regulation (EC) No. 2551/97 of 15 December 1997, Suspending the Introduction Into the Community of Specimens of Certain Species of Wild Fauna and Flora,[17] added two new species to Annex B. The introduction of live specimens listed in Annex B into the natural habitat of the Community is restricted because these species could constitute an ecological threat to wild species of fauna and flora indigenous to the Community.

iv. Miscellaneous

On 25 February 1998, a proposal for a Council Decision was submitted concerning the approval of an amendment to Appendices II and III of the Bern Convention on the Conservation of European Wildlife and Natural Habitats.[18] At the seventeenth meeting of the Bern Convention Standing Committee in December 1997, four endangered species were added to Appendix II and twenty-two species to Appendix III. Within the Community the Birds Directive and the Habitats Directive already cover some of these species. The Commission took the opportunity to comment on the fact that the amendment of the Appendices by the Standing Committee was possible thanks to the decisive support from the Community.

The Community is a contracting party not only to the Bern Convention, but also to the Convention on the Conservation of Migratory Species of Wild Animals (Bonn Convention). Council Decision 98/145/EC[19] contains the approval of the decisions of the fifth meeting of the Conference of Parties, held in Geneva in April 1996. The meeting of the Parties decided to add twenty-one species to Appendix I and twenty-two species to Appendix II to the Bonn Convention. Eleven of those species were already covered by the Birds Directive. A good example of the integration of environmental protection requirements into other Community policies is Council Regulation (EC) No. 850/98 of 30 March 1998,[20] on the Conservation of Fishery Resources Through Technical Measures for the Protection of Juveniles of Marine Organisms. This Regulation, based on Article 37 (formerly Article 43) EC, replaces an earlier regulation on the same subject.[21] The new Regulation was necessary due to

---

[16] The new subpara. was inserted by Commission Reg. (EC) No. 1006/98 of 14 May 1998 amending Reg. (EC) No. 939/97 laying down detailed rules concerning the implementation of Council Reg. (EC) No. 338/97 on the protection of species of wild fauna and flora by regulating trade therein [1997] OJ L145/3.

[17] [1997] OJ L349/4. [18] [1997] OJ C116/24. [19] [1997] OJ L46/6.

[20] [1997] OJ L125/1.

[21] Reg. (EC) No. 894/97 laying down certain technical measures for the conservation of fishery resources [1997] OJ L132/1.

problems with the application and enforcement of earlier regulations, which, due to frequent and substantial amendments, had become too complex. In the new Regulation, the number of different specifications of mesh-sizes is reduced, the number of different mesh-sizes that may be kept on board is restricted, and the concept of protected species is dispensed with. However, it is submitted that the new Regulation is also rather complicated and very detailed. It is to be hoped that the problems of enforcement will at least in part be solved by the new Regulation.

Finally, a number of legislative documents in the second half of 1997 and in 1998 dealt with Council Regulation (EEC) No. 3254/91 of 4 November 1991 prohibiting the use of leghold traps in the Community and the introduction into the Community of pelts and manufactured goods of certain wild animal species originating in countries where they are caught by means of leghold traps or other trapping methods which do not meet international humane trapping standards. According to Article 3(1) of Regulation (EEC) No. 3254/91, pelts and goods may (only) be imported from states listed in an Annex to the Regulation. These states have an agreement on humane trapping standards. Council Decision 97/602/EC of 22 July 1997[22] introduces such a list.

Early in 1996, no such international agreement existed and no country could export furs into the European Union. Third countries had no way of guaranteeing that the methods used on their territories complied with internationally agreed humane trapping standards. From June 1996 onwards, the Commission tried to negotiate bilateral agreements on humane trapping standards with Canada, Russia, and the United States of America (USA).[23] The texts of the agreements are attached to the Proposals for the Council Decision concerning the international agreements mentioned above.[24]

C. CASE LAW

i. Wild Birds Directive

On 19 May 1998, the Netherlands were found guilty of not having fulfilled their obligations under Article 4(1) of the Wild Birds Directive, by classifying fewer special protection areas (SPAs) than necessary.[25] The decision of the Court mainly follows the line set out in earlier decisions, in particular in the *Lappel Bank* case.[26] Hence, the obligation to classify SPAs is purely an ecological or ornithological one. If an area belongs to the most suitable territories in num-

---

[22] [1997] OJ L242/64.

[23] Council Decision 98/142/EC of 26 Jan. 1998, concerning the conclusion of an agreement on international humane trapping standards between the European Community, Canada and the Russian Federation [1998] OJ L42/40; Council Decision 98/487/EC of 14 July 1998, concerning the conclusion of an agreement on international humane trapping standards between the European Community, Canada, and the United States of America [1998] OJ L219/24.

[24] Proposal for a Council Decision concerning the signing and conclusion of an international agreement in the form of an agreed minute between the European Community and the United States of America [1998] OJ C32/8.

[25] Case C–3/96, *EC Commission v. Kingdom of the Netherlands* [1998] ECR I–3031.

[26] Case C–44/95, *EC Commission v. Secretary of State for the Environment* [1996] ECR I–3805.

ber of birds and size for the conservation of the species mentioned in Annex I, the area therefore has to be designated as a SPA. In those circumstances Member States are then not allowed to circumvent this obligation by adopting other special conservation methods or to balance the ecological interest of conservation against other economic or social interests. Member States' margin of discretion in choosing the most suitable territories hence concerns only the application of the ecological criteria.

The Dutch case differs from earlier cases because in this instance the infringement was not related to a certain area, but to the overall number and total size of the areas that should have been designated. In 1989, an ornithological report "Inventory of Important Bird Areas in the European Community" (IBA 89)[27] was published. The Court considers that the IBA 89 list "has proved to be the only document containing scientific evidence" of what areas are the ornithologically most suitable ones. "This situation would be different if the Netherlands had produced scientific evidence, in particular to show that the obligation in question could be fulfilled by classifying as SPAs territories whose number and total area were less than those resulting from IBA 89."[28]

It would hence seem that all areas mentioned in IBA 89 should have been classified as SPAs by the Netherlands. The only way to reduce the number or total size of the areas compared to IBA 89 is to prove, on ornithological grounds, why a certain area does not (any longer) belong to the most suitable areas for the protection of Annex I birds. In the Netherlands, this means that about 2.5 times as much acreage should be classified as SPAs than is presently the case. In many other Member States, the situation will probably not be very different.

According to *Lappel Bank* and earlier cases, Article 4(4) of the Wild Birds Directive (which is now replaced by Article 6(2), (3), and (4) of the Habitats Directive) has to be applied directly to areas which for ornithological reasons should have been classified as SPAs, but were not. The impact of the decision therefore may be considerable.

In the meantime, IBA 89 has been updated as far as the Netherlands is concerned. According to the revised IBA 94,[29] the Netherlands count about 30 per cent more areas (in size) than IBA 89. The Court of Justice could not, on procedural grounds, decide whether IBA 94 is also a document of scientific evidence. However, a Dutch court has already decided that IBA 94 can be regarded as such a scientific document which can serve as a basis of reference.[30] This means that, if an area mentioned in IBA 94 is not classified, convincing ornithological justifications have to be put forward. This outcome

[27] R. F. A. Grimmett and T. A. Jones (eds.), *Important Bird Areas in Europe* (Cambridge: BirdLife International, 1989).
[28] See n. 26 above at para. 69.
[29] R. Van den Tempel and E. R. Osieck, *Belangrijke Vogelgebieden in Nederland* (Zeist: Vogelbescherming Nederland, 1994).
[30] Rechtbank Leeuwarden 17 July 1998 (1998) 45 Administratiefrechtelijke Beslissingen 405.

appears somewhat dubious since the procedure for the drafting of IBA 94 was clearly less thorough than the procedure for IBA 89.

ii. Habitats Directive

There have been two Court of Justice judgments concerning the Habitats Directive within the period covered. On 26 June 1997, Greece was found guilty of failing to transpose the provisions of the Directive into national law.[31] Greece had not replied to formal notices of the Commission and did not deny that the Directive was not transposed within the prescribed period. The decision of the Court was therefore a formal one.

The same applies to the judgment against Germany.[32] Germany did not deny the absence of transposing measures either, but defended itself with the argument that while German authorities were drafting the provisions necessary to comply with the Directive, the Directive was applied directly by the competent authorities. It was not difficult to foresee that the Court would not accept this defence.

D. POLICY DOCUMENTS

i. CITES

In June 1997, the European Parliament discussed a resolution on the CITES Convention.[33] The resolution was mainly a reaction to the tenth meeting of the Conference of Parties, that had been held in Harare (Zimbabwe) some days before. The CITES Secretariat had submitted a "highly critical report on the implementation of the convention within the European Union". The resolution stressed the need for more collaboration for the implementation, increased exchange of know-how between the parties, and more effective sanctions. The protection of elephants and tigers was addressed in particular.

ii. Miscellaneous

The Committee of the Regions adopted a common opinion on management, use, and protection of forests in the EU.[34] This lengthy document exhaustively covers nature conservation aspects, and all aspects of forestry. It partly constitutes a reaction to the European Parliament's Resolution on the European Union's forest strategy of 18 December 1996. In Chapter 5.4 of the opinion the committee spells out what conservation measures it deems necessary. An important document that does not concern nature conservation in a broad sense is the Information of the Commission to the Council about the strategy of the European Union in the field of biodiversity.[35] This Information should be reviewed as a report on the strategy of the Commission in a broader field,

---

[31] Case C–329/96, *EC Commission* v. *Hellenic Republic* [1997] ECR I–3749.
[32] Case C–83/97, *EC Commission* v. *Federal Republic of Germany* [1997] ECR I–7191.
[33] [1998] OJ C200/181.   [34] [1998] OJ C64/04.
[35] Commission of the European Community, Information of the Commission to the Council about the strategy of the European Union in the field of biodiversity, COM(1998)42 final.

where nature conservation and nature conservation law have an important part to play. In Chapter II, four topics are addressed:

— conservation and sustainable use of biological diversity;
— sharing of benefits arising out of the utilization of genetic resources;
— research, identification, monitoring and exchange of information;
— education, training and awareness.

Chapter III shows, in accordance with Article 157 (formerly Article 130(2)) EC, in what policy fields the aim of conservation of biodiversity has to be integrated and how that should take place.

IV. Waste

Geert van Calster*

A. LEGISLATION ADOPTED

i. Shipments of Waste

The Fourth Conference of the Parties to the Basel Convention[1] has adopted the (non-exhaustive) lists of hazardous wastes, which makes the agreed export ban to non-OECD countries operational.[2] The Commission has adopted a proposal for the Council formally to adopt Annexes VIII and IX to the Basel Convention.[3] In accordance with its competence to adapt Annex V to the Waste Shipments Regulation,[4] the Commission has already adapted Annex V to the Regulation.[5] Annex V prohibits export to non-OECD countries of wastes listed and now comprises three classification systems:

— Annexes VIII and IX to the Basel Convention (Annex IX, listing those wastes which are considered non-hazardous for the purposes of the Basel Convention, and thus not covered by the export ban under the Basel Convention, is included for clarification purposes only);
— the EU list of hazardous wastes,[6] and
— the amber and red lists of wastes annexed to the Shipments Regulation.

The latter two classes are an application of the Basel Convention's authorization for parties to take measures that go further than the Convention's provisions. However, Annex V provides that in the event of conflict or discrepancy between the classification under the Basel Convention, and the classification under EU legislation, the former prevails. This provision is not to prevent

* Research Fellow, Institute of Environmental and Energy Law, Collegium Falconis, KU Leuven; Caestecker & Partners, Brussels. Given the publication of the up-to-date overview of EC waste legislation and policy elsewhere in this volume, this review of the year offers a quick reference to 1998 developments. For a full account readers are referred to the chapter by G. van Calster, at p. 161 of this volume.

[1] Basel Convention of 22 Mar. 1989 on the Control of Transboundary Movements of Hazardous Wastes and their Disposal (1989) 28 International Legal materials 649.

[2] Report of the Fourth Meeting of the Conference of the Parties to the Basel Convention, Malaysia, 23–27 Feb. 1998, UNEP/CHW.4/35.

[3] Commission Proposal of 6 Nov. 1998 for a Council Decision on the approval, on behalf of the Community, of the amendment of Annex I and the adoption of new Annexes VIII and IX to the Convention on the Control of Transboundary Movements of Hazardous Wastes and their Disposal (Basel Convention), as laid down in Decision IV/9 of the Conference of the Parties, COM(98)634.

[4] Council Reg. (EC) No. 259/93/EC of 1 Feb. 1993 on the supervision and control of shipments of waste within, into, and out of the European Community [1993] OJ L30/1.

[5] Commission Reg. (EC) No. 2408/98/EC of 6 Nov. 1998 amending Annex V to Council Reg. (EC) No. 259/93/EC on the supervision and control of shipments of waste within, into, and out of the European Community [1998] OJ L298/19.

[6] Laid down in Decision 94/904/EC of 22 Dec. 1994 establishing a list of hazardous waste pursuant to Art. 1,4° of Council Dir. 91/689/EEC on hazardous waste [1994] OJ L356/14.

Annex IX from taking effect, and is motivated by the consideration that the lists of the Basel Convention reflect the most recent work on the issue. The Regulation expressly considers that in the future, further measures may indeed be taken.

Commission Decision 98/368/EC[7] integrates the modifications adopted by the OECD Council Decision of 10 December 1996, Concerning the green and amber lists of waste.[8]

B. LEGISLATION IN PROGRESS

i. *Exports of "Green Waste" to Non-OECD Countries*

The Commission has presented an amended proposal for the exports of green list wastes to non-OECD states.[9] Under the previous proposal,[10] for countries that clearly indicate they wish one of the control procedures which are provided for in the Regulation to apply to some or all types of green list wastes, Commission decisions would lay down specific procedures. For those countries that have either not responded, or indicated that they do not wish to receive some or all types of green list wastes, the Commission proposed to apply the red list-procedure (prior authorization of the authorities of destination required). This would have allowed non-OECD countries flexibility in dealing with import requests, whilst at the same time establishing strict monitoring. The proposal received fierce criticism. The Commission amended its proposal; for those countries that indicate they do not wish to receive some or all types of green list waste, the Commission now proposes not to allow the exports concerned. For countries that have not responded, the proposal maintains the red list-route.[11]

The Council has adopted its common position, and follows the Commission proposal.[12]

ii. *Landfill of Waste*

The first version of the current initiatives on landfill of waste was submitted by the Commission on 5 March 1997.[13] The new elements of the proposal, when compared to a 1991 proposal, are:

[7] Commission Decision (EC) No. 98/368/EEC of 18 May 1998 adapting, pursuant to Art. 42(3) Annexes II and III to Council Reg. (EC) No. 259/93 on the supervision and control of shipments of waste within, into, and out of the European Community [1998] OJ L165/20.   [8] COM(96)231.

[9] Amended Commission Proposal of 26 Jan. 1998 for a Council Regulation establishing common rules and procedures to apply to shipments to certain non-OECD countries of certain types of waste COM(97)685.

[10] Commission Proposal of 8 Feb. 1995 for a Council Regulation establishing common rules and procedures to apply to shipments to certain non-OECD countries of certain shipments of waste, COM(94)678.

[11] Amended Commission Proposal of 26 Jan. 1998 for a Council Regulation establishing common rules and procedures to apply to shipments to certain non-OECD countries of certain types of waste, COM(97)685.

[12] Common Position 48/98 of 4 June 1998 with a view to adopting Council Reg. No. .../98, establishing common rules and procedures to apply to shipments to certain non-OECD countries of certain types of waste [1998] OJ C333/1.

[13] Commission Proposal of 5 Mar. 1997 for a Council Directive on the landfill of waste, COM(97)105.

— the reduction of the landfill of biodegradable waste;
— the requirement that waste be pre-treated before it is landfilled;
— a ban on the disposal of used tyres;
— the requirement that the costs of landfill be increased;
— a prohibition of co-disposal of (non-)hazardous waste;
— an improvement of the general requirements for all classes of landfills and stricter conditions for existing landfills; and,
— more restricted exemptions for remote areas.

In February 1998, the Parliament adopted a number of amendments, which closely followed the report of the EP's environment committee on the matter.[14] The Commission subsequently adapted its proposal, taking some of the Parliament's suggestions on board.[15] The Council formally reached an agreement on the Commission's proposal.[16] The provisions of the common position are based on the principle of classification of landfills according to the types of waste which they accept: non-hazardous, hazardous, and inert waste. The classification is coupled with a differentiation in the procedures for issuing acceptance permits, and for control and monitoring of the site during the operational and the closure phase. Hazardous waste which has been rendered non-hazardous would also be subject to specific requirements.

Certain types of wastes would as such be excluded from acceptance in landfills: liquid waste; explosive, combustible or flammable wastes; hospital wastes and other infectious clinical wastes; and any other type of waste which does not fulfil the acceptance criteria defined in the Directive. The proposal introduces a quantified reduction strategy for the landfill of biodegradable municipal waste. A reduction would have to be realized of this type of waste accepted for landfill to 75 per cent (2006), 50 per cent (2009) and 35 per cent (2016) of the tonnage produced in 1995. The Directive would enter into force in 1999, and the figures would be reviewed in 2014, when an extra four years might be granted to those Member States which rely heavily on landfill sites. All waste would have to undergo treatment before going to landfill, except where this would not further the objectives of the Directive or, in the case of inert waste, would not be technically feasible. Member States are being urged to levy a waste disposal and landfill dumping charge. The charge should at least cover the costs involved in the setting up and operation of the site. Exemptions may be granted to landfill sites for non-hazardous or inert waste, serving small islands which have only a single landfill site with a total capacity of less than 15,000 tonnes, or serving isolated settlements (no more than 500 inhabitants and with difficult access). The text is to grind its way through the legislative process during the course of 1999.

---

[14] Report on the proposal for a Directive on the landfill of waste, A4–0026/98, 30 Jan. 1998 (*Rapporteur* Caroline Jackson MEP).
[15] Amended Commission proposal for a Directive on the landfill of waste, COM(98)189 [1998] OJ C126/11.
[16] Council Common Position 49/98 of 4 June 1998 with a view to adopting Council Dir. 98/... of ... on the landfill of waste [1998] OJ C333/15.

iii. End-of-life Vehicles

The Council has initiated the debate on the 1997 Commission Proposal for a Directive on the Disposal of End-of-life Vehicles.[17] Ministers generally welcomed the priority which the proposal gives to re-use and recycling of car components. The general feeling, however, was that the proposed targets are over-ambitious.[18] The emphasis on producer responsibility, including the principle that the last owner of the vehicle should be able to dispose of it in an environmentally friendly way, with no cost for him/her involved, led to theoretic approval, but also to a feeling of caution. Delegations expressed serious doubts about the feasibility of voluntary agreements in this context.[19]

iv. Incineration of Waste

After calls from the Council, the Commission has put forward a proposal to streamline the EC's regime on the incineration of waste, and to strengthen existing provisions.[20] Almost all waste which is not caught by the Hazardous Waste Incineration Directive[21] is to fall under the new initiative. The two existing directives on municipal waste[22] are to be abolished and stricter emission limits will be put in place (dioxin and furan emissions are targeted in particular). Both new and existing plants will have to conform with these new limits. As in the Hazardous Waste Incineration Directive, the proposed Directive introduces specific provisions for co-incineration.

v. Port Waste Facilities

A Commission Proposal for a Directive on Port Waste Reception Facilities is to complement international rules on the discharge of waste at sea. The proposed regime lays down specific standards covering the requirements for ports and port states to provide adequate reception facilities (including proper waste reception and handling planning, clear notification guidelines, and adequate final treatment). It improves and specifies the obligations of ships to use these facilities (as a general rule, all ships have to deliver all ship-generated

---

[17] Commission Proposal of 9 July 1997 for a Council Directive on end-of-life vehicles, COM(97)358 [1997] OJ C337.

[18] By 1 Jan. 2005, for all end of life vehicles, the re-use and recovery should be increased to a minimum of 85% by weight per vehicle whereas the re-use and recycling target should be increased to a minimum of 80% by weight per vehicle. No later than 1 Jan. 2015, the re-use and recovery targets will be increased to a minimum of 95% by weight per vehicle whereas the re-use and recycling limit will then be increased to a minimum of 85% by weight per vehicle. After the year 2015, these targets should be further increased by the Council.

[19] 2121st Council meeting—Environment—Luxembourg, 6 Oct. 1998, PRES/98/323. For a full account, see M. Onida at p. 253 this volume.

[20] Commission Proposal of 7 Oct. 1998 for a Council Directive on the Incineration of Waste [1998] OJ C372/11.

[21] Dir. 94/67/EC on the incineration of hazardous waste [1994] OJ L365/34. See also Commission proposal of 21 Nov. 1997 for a Council Directive amending Dir. 94/67 on incineration of hazardous waste, COM(97)604 [1998] OJ C13/6 (which strengthens certain requirements).

[22] Dir. 89/369/EEC on the prevention of air pollution from new municipal waste incineration plants [1989] OJ L163/32, and Dir. 89/429/EEC on existing plants [1989] OJ L203/50.

waste to a port reception facility, unless there is proof of adequate on-board storage facilities) and installs a monitoring regime.[23]

vi. Proposal for the Management of Waste from Electric and Electronical Equipment

The management of waste from electric and electronic equipment is high on the Commission's environmental agenda. It is expected to issue a proposal on the subject in the near future (probably by autumn 1999). Reportedly, the focus of the expected proposal is very much on prioritizing re-use. Commission drafts have suggested a 80 to 90 per cent take-back rate for large household goods, office equipment, and dispensing machines, such as freezers, refrigerators, washing machines, computers, etc. Figures of 40 per cent to 60 per cent are proposed for smaller household goods (including televisions and lamps). Crucially, between 70 per cent and 90 per cent of large household goods, IT equipment, and some other goods would have to be recycled into new equipment. A recycling figure of between 40 per cent and 60 per cent is proposed for smaller household goods such as televisions. The use of, *inter alia*, lead, would be banned.

C.   CASE LAW

i. Euro Tombesi *and* Inter-Environnement

Both *Euro Tombesi*[24] and *Inter-Environnement*[25] concern the EC definition of waste, as found in Council Directive 75/442/EEC on waste (the Framework Waste Directive).[26] Currently, in order to assess whether a certain substance is to be considered "waste" under EC waste law, the following elements need to be taken into account:

— the definition of the Directive, with its emphasis on "to discard". Using the term "to discard" was intended to eradicate all doubts about the inclusion in the definition of waste which has economic value.
— Annex I to the Directive contains the "categories of waste". The annex, however, is exemplary rather than definitive.
— The case law of the Court of Justice, which underlines that products with a negative economic value are not *per se* excluded from the definition.

The best route for practitioners and lawyers to obtain some guidance on the EC definition of waste is to read the opinions of Advocate General Jacobs, who

---

[23] Commission proposal of 17 July 1998 for a Council Directive on port reception facilities for ship-generated waste and cargo residues, COM(98)452.

[24] Judgment of 25 June 1997 in Joined Cases C–304/94, C–330/94, C–342/94, and C–224/95, *Criminal Proceedings against Euro Tombesi et al.* [1997] ECR I–3561.

[25] Judgment of 18 Dec. 1997 in Case C–129/96, *Inter-Environnement Wallonie ASBL* v. *Région-Wallonne* [1997] ECR I–7411.

[26] [1975] OJ L194/39, amended by Council Dir. 91/156/EC. 1991 [1991] OJ L78/32.

has set out a rather consistent line. It is uncertain, however, to what extent he is followed by the Court. The core of Mr Jacobs' approach is that the term "discard" encompasses both disposal and recovery, and that the scope of the term waste therefore depends on what is meant by "disposal operation" and "recovery operation". He suggests that a substance should be made subject to Community waste legislation if its holder discards it or intends or is required to discard it (that is the definition of Article 1), and that a substance is discarded if it is disposed of or is subject to a recovery operation listed in Annex II(B) of Directive 75/442/EEC (a non-exhaustive list), or to an analogous operation.

In *Euro Tombesi*, the Court implicitly adopted the approach of the Advocate General, by focusing attention on the concepts of "recovery" and "disposal", rather than on the issue of "to discard". *Inter-Environnement* could have provided guidance in one of the EC's definition's most contested applications: residues and by-products of production processes. Practice shows that a lot of these products are re-used by the same manufacturer and/or by other manufacturers, often within one and the same economic grouping. Are they waste?

In *Euro Tombesi*, Advocate General Jacobs took the view that where a residue cannot be used in a normal industrial process without undergoing a recovery operation such as those listed in Annex IIB, it must be regarded as waste, until such time as it is recovered. He reiterates this view in *Inter-Environnement*, suggesting that a by-product or a residual product would not constitute waste if it was destined for direct use in a further process in its existing form, in other words if it was not destined for disposal or consignment to a recovery operation prior to its continued use. Aware of its limitations, the Advocate General, for the notion of "recovery operation", refers to Annex II(B) of the Directive. A particular problem concerns the distinction between direct use and recovery.

It appears from a recent OECD survey that there is general consensus among OECD countries that it is relevant to consider whether the use of a residual product or by-product as a substitute for another material or ingredient is as environmentally sound as that of the material or ingredient which it is replacing.[27] This led the Advocate General to conclude that where, owing to the fact that it is a residue, by-product, secondary raw material, or other material resulting from an industrial process, a substance—or the process which it undergoes—does not meet normal health or environmental requirements or standards, it must be regarded as waste. In so far as a substance is wholly interchangeable with another product and requires no additional regulation or supervision beyond that applicable to the product it is replacing it is, in the Advocate-General's view, unnecessary for it to be classified as waste.

The Court limited itself in *Inter-Environnement* to giving the national court the guidance which was strictly necessary: that substances forming part of an industrial process may constitute "waste" within the meaning of the Directive. It added however the important *obiter* that its conclusion does not undermine

---

[27] Discussion Paper on guidance for distinguishing waste from non-waste, issued by the OECD Waste Management Policy Group, ENV/EPOC/WMP(96)1.

the distinction which must be drawn between waste recovery and normal industrial treatment of products which are not waste.

Thus, the case law on the definition of waste may be summarized as follows. In *Euro Tombesi*, the Court implicitly agreed with the Advocate General, that one should devote less time to the meaning of "to discard", focusing instead on the meaning of "disposal" and "recovery". In *Inter-Environnement*, it recognizes a distinction between waste recovery and normal industrial treatment of products which are not waste, whereas Advocate General Jacobs set out the guidelines which should be followed in making this distinction, the Court did not. In other words, there is plenty of contentious potential left.

ii. Dusseldorp

Dusseldorp concerned the application of the abovementioned Waste Shipments Regulation, and has limited the application of the principles of self-sufficiency and proximity to waste destined for disposal.[28]

In *Dusseldorp*, the Court of Justice rebuked the Dutch government for over-enthusiastically restricting waste exports. It found that the principles of self-sufficiency and proximity, laid down in the Framework Waste Directive and in the Waste Shipments Regulation, do not apply to shipments of waste for recovery. The Dutch invocation of Article 176 (formerly Article 130t) EC[29] failed, as the Court did not accept imperative reasons for derogating from Article 29 (formerly Article 34) EC.[30] Finally, the existence of a waste agency with exclusive rights to handle certain waste management operations was held to be incompatible with Article 86(1) (formerly Article 90(1)) EC.

Dusseldorp highlights the dichotomy between the protection of the environment and the internal market. The facts underline that, in the waste management sector, increasing use is being made of restrictions to exports, and of exclusive rights.

iii. Beside BV

Beside BV also interpreted the Waste Shipments Regulation, pursuant to which the classification of mixed types of wastes remains problematic. The judgment does not seem to have solved the issue. In *Beside*, the Court held that a small quantity of materials not included in the green list does not alter the classification of the complete batch as belonging to the green list. It did not, however, indicate how the qualification "small" should be interpreted, as it left this to national courts.[31]

---

[28] See the author's note "Court rebukes restrictions to free movement of waste", in [1999] *European Law Review* 178–184; on Case C–203/96, *Chemische Afvalstoffen Dusseldorp and Others* v. *VROM* [1998] ECR I–4075.

[29] Allowing for stricter national measures after Community harmonizing legislation has been introduced.

[30] That prohibits export restrictions.

[31] More details in A. Van Rossem and H. G. Sevenster, "Hof beantwoordt vragen Afdeling over afvalregime" [1998] *Nederlands Tijdschrift voor Europees Recht* 196–201.

D. INTERNATIONAL CO-OPERATION

Under the strong influence of the EC, the parties to the Basel Convention on Shipments of Hazardous Wastes[32] have adopted the list of hazardous wastes.[33] The Convention foresees in a ban on the export of hazardous wastes for recovery to non-OECD states.

In an Annex to the Convention, the Hazardous Waste List (List A) bans the export of wastes containing arsenic, lead, mercury, asbestos, and dozens of other chemicals and substances. The non-hazardous waste list (List B) exempts from the ban those wastes that can be safely recycled or re-used, including scrap iron, steel or copper, certain electronic assemblies, non-hazardous chemical catalysts, paper, and textile wastes. The ban and the Annexes need further ratification by a minimum number of parties, in order for them to enter into force. For the EC, however, the Annexes have already entered into force (see above).

E. POLICY DOCUMENTS

i. *Disused Offshore Oil and Gas Installations*

As a preparation for the OSPAR meeting in July, the Commission adopted in February a Communication on the removal and disposal of disused offshore oil and gas installations.[34] Following the controversy surrounding Shell's disposal plans with its Brent Spar platform, the Commission suggests that all but a few of the approximately 600 platforms currently in use in EC waters can be safely and efficiently taken to land for recycling and partial disposal. The Commission suggests that exception should be made for concrete platforms and for individual cases only.

ii. *Competitiveness of Recycling Industries*

A Commission review of the competitiveness of the EC's recycling industries,[35] has resulted in the creation of a forum for recycling which, in a concerted effort by industry and authorities, will focus on identifying weaknesses in structures and in the functioning of markets; on formulating proposals to remedy these shortcomings; on promoting intangible investment and co-ordinating strategies for innovation; on strengthening industrial co-operation in the various recycling industries; and on improving the existing business framework, including, where appropriate, economic instruments and/or voluntary and/or negotiated agreements between industrial actors, consumer organizations, and/or public authorities.

Moreover, the Commission has pledged to devise its own actions, focusing in particular on transparency at the economic level, encouraging the development of markets for recyclable and secondary materials, by co-ordinated

---

[32] See no. 1 above.   [33] See n. 2 above.   [34] COM(98)49.
[35] Commission Communication of 22 July 1998 on the competitiveness of the recycling industries, COM(98)463.

action regarding standardization and quality assurance (in particular through research) and the smooth functioning of the internal market, in particular by seeking to harmonize implementation by Member States of existing legislation and, where appropriate, by new regulatory measures. Interesting aspects of the Communication include, in particular, the apparent lack of overall data for the industries concerned throughout the EC.

F.   MISCELLANEOUS

i.   Danish Cans

1998 saw a further instalment of the Danish cans saga. Denmark stands accused of not properly implementing the Packaging and Packaging Waste Directive.[36] The Danish packaging regulations include a ban on the sale of canned beer and soft drinks. The Commission has now decided to step up legal action against the Danish regime.

The Danish government is defiant, and in its reply to the Commission submitted that the Packaging Waste Directive authorizes the use of packaging return system which it employs. Denmark's case would seem to be weakened by the environmental experience in other states, such as Sweden, where successful and environmentally-friendly systems for collecting and recycling cans have been set in place. No time limit is imposed on the Commission to reply to the Danish defence, and there are no guarantees as to the Commission's determination to pursue the issue.

---

[36] Dir. 94/62/EC on packaging and packaging waste [1994] OJ L365/10.

V. Water

Annemarie Sprokkereef*

A. LEGISLATION ADOPTED

i. Port State Control

In the enforcement of international standards for ship safety, pollution prevention, and shipboard living and working conditions, Directive 95/21/EC on Port State Control[1] has now been amended by Directive 98/42/EC[2] bearing the same name, so as to introduce criteria for selecting ships for inspection under the 1995 Directive.

ii. Urban Waste Water

The collection, treatment, and discharge of urban waste water from certain industrial sectors is regulated by Directive 91/171/EEC concerning Urban Waste Water Treatment (Urban Waste Water Directive).[3] In order to clarify the interpretation of Table 2 of Annex I to this Directive, an amending directive was adopted in 1998.[4] Thus, Directive 98/15/EC amending Council Directive 91/171/EEC with respect to certain requirements, established in Annex I thereof, specifies requirements for discharges from urban waste water treatment plants to sensitive areas which are subject to eutrophication. The Directive had to be implemented by 30 September 1998.

iii. Vessels Carrying Dangerous or Polluting Goods

Directive 93/75/EC concerning the Minimum Requirements for Vessels Bound for or Leaving Community Ports and Carrying Dangerous or Polluting Goods[5] has been amended so as to apply to certain radioactive materials. The amended Directive introduces a simplified procedure for updating Annexes I and II, taking account of amendments to the MARPOL Convention and the IBC (International Bulk Chemical) and IGC (International Gas Carrier) Codes.[6]

---

* Associate fellow, CEDAR, University of Warwick.

[1] Dir. 95/21/EC concerning the enforcement, in respect of shipping using Community ports and sailing in the waters under the jurisdiction of the Member States, of international standards for ship safety, pollution prevention and shipboard living and working conditions (Port State Control) [1995] OJ L157/1.

[2] Dir. 98/42/EC amending Council Dir. 95/21/EC concerning the enforcement, in respect of shipping using Community ports and sailing in the waters under the jurisdiction of the Member States, of international standards for ship safety, pollution prevention and shipboard living and working conditions (Port State Control) [1998] OJ L184/40.

[3] [1991] OJ L135/40.   [4] [1998] OJ L67/29.   [5] [1993] OJ L247/19.

[6] Dir. 98/55/EC amending Dir. 93/75/EC concerning minimum requirements for vessels bound for or leaving Community ports and carrying dangerous or polluting goods [1998] OJ L215/65.

B. LEGISLATION IN PROGRESS

i. *Water for Human Consumption*

It has taken some time for methods to be worked out for water sampling and for measuring the parameters defining the physical, chemical, and microbiological values corresponding to the different uses of water and in particular water for human consumption. Directive 80/778/EEC relating to the Quality of Water Intended for Human Consumption (Drinking Water Directive)[7] needed adapting to new scientific techniques and methods, as well as new scientific insights into health hazards. In 1988, the Commission first proposed such an amending directive. After a drawn-out legislative process, the Commission has now submitted its re-examined proposal for a Council Directive on the Quality of Water Intended for Human Consumption.[8] The purpose of the proposed directive is to reduce the number of parameters to be complied with, by maintaining only those parameters considered to be essential to protect health at Community level, leaving it to Member States to define additional parameters if they so wish. Whilst new parameters have been added to take account of scientific progress, the total number of parameters to be complied with will be reduced and some parameter values will be adjusted.

ii. *Bathing Water Directive*

Directive 76/160/EEC on the Quality of Bathing Waters (Bathing Water Directive)[9] was one of the first directives in the field of water. Although its updating was considered necessary, this has been a slow process and it was only in 1998 that the Commission amended its 1994 Proposal.[10] Apart from important revisions to Article 5 (circumstances under which water is deemed to be of good quality or deemed to comply with the Directive), Article 6 (sampling and analysis), Article 7 (prohibition of bathing where pollution constitutes a threat to public health), and Article 11 (reporting on implementation) of the Directive, the revised proposal includes amended definitions of "bathing season" and "competent authority".

iii. *Framework Directive*

An important recent development in EC water law has been the attempt to review current legislation to develop a legislative framework with strategic coherence. The Commission set itself the goal of proposing a directive which would replace prescriptive and *ad hoc* measures with broad environmental objectives and a flexible approach to standard-setting.[11] The proposed

---

[7] [1980] OJ L299/11.

[8] COM(98)388. See also Council Common Position (EC) 13/98 [1998] OJ C91/1.

[9] [1976] OJ L30/1.

[10] COM(94)36, Proposal for a Council Directive on the quality of bathing water [1994] OJC 12/3; COM(97)585, Amended Proposal for a Council Directive on the quality of bathing water [1998] OJ C6/9.

[11] COM(97)49, Council Directive establishing a framework for Community action in the field of water policy [1997] OJ C148/20.

Framework Directive is aimed at building on progress made in the context of Community water legislation, whilst repealing some earlier, now less suitable, legislation. The four main objectives of the Directive are:

— the provision of drinking water;
— the provision of water for other activities;
— the protection of the environment;
— the alleviation of the impact of floods and droughts.

An amended proposal for a Council Directive,[12] adopted by the Commission in early 1998, comprises the further development of the proposed contents of Annex V of this Directive,[13] and proposes a scheme for the identification of surface water status and groundwater status.[14]

The effort to develop a fully integrated approach in the Framework Directive has been welcomed by the European Parliament. At the same time, critics have voiced concern that the current proposal fails to resolve some of the existing troublesome contradictions. In particular, the ambiguous relationship between the emission limit approach and quality standards remains unresolved. Yet, adoption of the Framework Directive is anticipated, an event which will bring about a major change in the Community's policy for the protection of the aquatic environment. Once the Framework Directive is adopted, it is anticipated that Directive 75/440/EEC on the Quality of Surface Water Intended for the Abstraction of Drinking Water (Surface Water Directive),[15] Directive 80/68/EEC on the Protection of Groundwater Against Certain Dangerous Substances (Groundwater Directive)[16] and Directive 79/923/EEC on the Quality Required of Shellfish Waters (Shellfish Directive)[17] will be repealed and the Proposal for a Directive on the Ecological Quality of Water withdrawn. However, earlier legislation, such as the Bathing Water Directive and the Urban Waste Water Directive, will continue to exist as discrete pieces of Community water legislation. This has led to some scepticism about the feasibility of a fully integrated approach in practice.

iv.　Port Facilities

The Commission has adopted the Proposal for a Council Directive on port reception facilities for ship-generated waste and cargo residues.[18] The purpose of this Directive is to reduce discharges of ship-generated waste and

---

[12] COM(98)76, amended Proposal establishing a framework Directive for water policy [1998] OJ C16/14.

[13] Annex V of the Directive is a general outline for technical specification for the definition, classification, and monitoring of the ecological and chemical status of groundwaters.

[14] The scheme for the identification of surface water status consists of five elements: parameters to be considered in determining ecological status; normative definitions based on the former; a set of criteria for the division of surface water bodies into ecotypes; a set of monitoring requirements; and a system for common presentation of results according to a harmonized classification system. Concerning groundwater status, the revised proposal sets out basic provisions on the identification, mapping, and characteristics of groundwater bodies, split into assessment of the characteristics of the body itself, and of the impact on its human activity.

[15] [1975] OJ L194/26.　　[16] [1980] OJ L20/43.

[17] [1979] OJ L281/47.　　[18] COM(98)452 [1998] OJ C271/79.

cargo residues into the sea, by improving the availability and use of port reception facilities, thereby enhancing the protection of the marine environment. The Directive is aimed especially at combatting illegal discharges.

C.   CASE LAW

i. Judgments

In a number of cases, the European Court of Justice (ECJ) has ruled that Member States have failed to fulfil obligations pursuant to water directives. In *Commission* v. *Portugal*,[19] Portugal was found not to have adopted laws implementing the Ground Water Directive.

Similarly, implementation of the Directive 76/464/EEC on Pollution Caused by Certain Dangerous Substances Discharged Into the Aquatic Environment (Dangerous Substances Directive)[20] has also been the subject of cases brought by the Commission. In *Commission* v. *Luxembourg*,[21] the ECJ ruled that Luxembourg had failed to adopt programmes to reduce pollution in respect of ninety-nine substances of List I in the Annex of the Directive. In fact, several cases concerned the failure to establish programmes, including quality objectives, and setting deadlines for their implementation as required under Article 7 of the Directive,[22] or failure to identify a programme for the reduction of pollution by substances in List II of the Directive's Annex.[23]

As regards the Surface Water Directive, the ECJ ruled in *Commission* v. *Portugal* that the latter had failed to adopt a systematic plan of action, including a timetable for the improvement of surface water.[24] In another case concerning Directive 76/869/EEC on Methods of Measurement and Frequencies of Sampling and Analysis of Surface Waters Intended for the Abstraction of Drinking Water in the Member States,[25] Portugal was also found to have failed to adopt the laws necessary to implement this Directive.[26]

In a case which resembles *Commission* v. *United Kingdom*,[27] where the United Kingdom (UK) unsuccessfully attempted to justify non-compliance with the Bathing Water Directive, Spain put forward several circumstances (notably the occurrence of prolonged droughts) to justify non-compliance with the same Directive in a case before the ECJ this year.[28] As was already made clear in *Commission* v. *United Kingdom*, the Court does not appear to

---

[19] Case C–183/97 of 18 June 1998 (not yet reported).   [20] [1976] OJ L129/33.

[21] Case C–206/96 [1998] ECR I–3401.

[22] Case C–214/96, *Commission* v. *Spain* of 25 Nov. 1998 (not yet reported); Case C–285/96, *Commission* v. *Italy* of 1 Oct. 1998 (not yet reported); Joined Cases C–232/95 and C–233/9, *Commission* v. *Greece* [1998] ECR I–3343.

[23] Case C–384/97, *Commission* v. *Greece* [1998] OJ C26/2. In addition, three cases are pending regarding failure to take adequate steps as required by this Dir.: Case C–152/98, *Commission* v. *Netherlands*; Case C–261/98, *Commission* v. *Portugal*; and Case C–274/98, *Commission* v. *Spain*, now pending.

[24] Case C–214/98, *Commission* v. *Portugal* [1998] ECR I–3839.   [25] [1979] OJ L271/26.

[26] Case C–229/97, *Commission* v. *Portugal* [1998] ECR I–6059.

[27] Case C–56/90 [1993] ECR I–4109.

[28] Case C–92/96, *Commission* v. *Spain* [1998] ECR I–505.

accept any justifications for non-compliance other than those explicitly provided for in the Directive. Spain was therefore found to be in breach of the
Directive by having failed to designate areas and to have breached quality
objectives as laid down in the Directive.

Finally, in *Commission* v. *Italy*, the ECJ ruled that Italy had failed, first, to designate waters needing protection or improvement to support shellfish life and
growth in accordance with Article 4 of the Shellfish Directive;[29] secondly, to
establish programmes to reduce pollution in accordance with Article 5; and,
finally, to set values for the parameters listed in points 8 and 9 of the Annex.
The Italian government argued that the obligation to designate waters according to Article 4(2) of the Directive may be gradual and in proportion to the total
area of relevant waters. This view was rejected by the Court, holding that there
is nothing in the wording of the Directive to support an interpretation which
would allow Member States not to designate all shellfish waters.[30] In addition,
although Member States may make additional designations, that option does
not imply that they are not *obliged* to do so where the conditions laid down by
the Directive are met.[31]

ii.   Cases Pending

Cases alleging use of incorrect legal bases for Community environmental legislation continue to come before the ECJ. For example, in a case currently
pending, *Commission* v. *Spain*,[32] the Spanish government has claimed that the
Commission should annul Decision 97/825/EC concerning the Conclusion of
the Convention on Co-operation for the Protection and Sustainable Use of the
River Danube,[33] because it should have been adopted pursuant to Article
175(2) (formerly Article 130s(2)) EC.[34]

In 1998, the Commission brought several cases before the ECJ concerning
failure of Member States to comply with water directives. In September 1998,
the Commission allowed the UK three months in which to adopt the necessary
legislation to give effect to the Groundwater Directive, in particular with
regard to the problem of the disposal of sheep-dip, before it would apply to the
ECJ for non-compliance.[35]

The Commission also started infringement procedures regarding the implementation of Directive 91/676/EEC on Pollution Caused by Nitrates from
Agricultural Sources (Nitrates Directive)[36] against most Member States. This
includes a case against Italy, for its alleged failure to establish action programmes, to monitor water quality correctly, and to provide an adequate monitoring report.[37] The Commission issued numerous reasoned opinions
concerning non-compliance with EC water legislation. These opinions range
from failure to ensure the control of pollution from one particular industrial

---

[29] Case C–225/96 [1997] ECR I–6887.   [30] Para. 26.   [31] Para. 27.
[32] Case C–36/98, now pending.   [33] [1997] OJ L342/18.
[34] Case C–36/98 [1998] OJ C113/7.
[35] This information was not only brought to the attention of the UK government, but also
released to the press: Press release IP/98/875, 9 Sept. 1998.
[36] [1991] OJ L375/1.   [37] Press release IP/98/883, 12 Oct. 1998.

plant[38] to failure to identify pollution sensitive areas.[39] In the case of the Nitrates Directive, problems occur in terms of alleged defective implementing legislation concerning monitoring systems, and incomplete rules for identifying vulnerable zones,[40] and also failure to monitor water quality to assess nitrate levels properly.[41]

In respect of the Bathing Water Directive,[42] reasoned opinions have been issued to Austria (failure to give full effect) and the Netherlands (failure to comply with quality standards and sufficiently to monitor inland waters).[43] Finally, problems persist with the obligation to draw up implementation reports as required by the 1991 Directive on Standardization and Rationalization of Implementation Reports.[44] In 1998, Luxembourg and Ireland have been issued with reasoned opinions concerning failure to draw up reports on the implementation of directives on water. The reports in question should have been submitted by the end of 1996.[45]

D. INTERNATIONAL CO-OPERATION

i. UN Convention on the Law of the Sea

The UN Convention on the Law of the Sea and the implementation of part XI thereof[46] have been approved on behalf of the EU in the form of the adoption of Decision 98/392/EC.[47]

Some other minor legislation has been adopted, or is in the process of being adopted, to fulfil obligations flowing from the Community's involvement in international agreements.[48]

---

[38] A reasoned opinion addressed to Portugal for failure to comply with Dir. 76/466/EEC concerning pollution caused by certain dangerous substances discharged into the aquatic environment [1976] OJ L129/23(Commission Press Release IP/98/1, 7 Jan. 1998).

[39] This concerns Dir. 91/271/EEC [1991] OJ L135/40; Commission Press Release IP/98/1, 7 Jan. 1998.

[40] Reasoned opinion to Portugal: Press Release IP/98/883 of 12 Oct.1998.

[41] Reasoned opinion concerning Dir. 91/676/EEC on pollution caused by nitrates from agricultural sources [1991] OJ L375/1; notified to the Netherlands (Commission Press Release IP/98/1, 7 Jan. 1998). Belgium, Germany, and Luxembourg have also been notified reasoned opinions concerning failure to comply with this Dir.; (Commission Press Release IP/98/637, 7 July 1998).

[42] [1976] OJ L31/1.   [43] Commission Press Release IP/98/634, 7 July 1998.

[44] [1991] OJ L377/48.   [45] Press Release IP/98/881, 12 Oct. 1998.

[46] United Nations Convention on the Law of the Sea. Implementation of part XI thereof was effected by the agreement of 28 July 1994.

[47] Council Decision 98/392/EC concerning the conclusion by the European Community of the UN Convention of 10 Dec. 1982 on the Law of the Sea and the Agreement of 28 July 1994 relating to the implementation of part XI thereof [1998] OJ L179/1.

[48] E.g. COM(98)540, Parcom Decision [1998] OJ C364/13. Also Dir. 98/74/EC amending Council Dir. 93/75/EC on vessels carrying dangerous or polluting goods [1993] OJ L247/19 to take account of the MARPOL Convention (International Convention for the Prevention of Pollution from Ships) and the IBG and IGC Codes [1998] OJ L276/7. The Commission has also proposed a Council Decision on the Convention on the International Commission for the Protection of the Oder: COM(98)528 [1998] OJ C316/5.

E.   POLICY AND IMPLEMENTATION REPORTS

i.   Removal and Disposal of Disused Offshore Installations

In response to the problems surrounding the disposal of the Brent Spar in 1996, the Commission has issued a Communication on the removal and disposal of disused offshore oil and gas installations.[49] The Communication states that almost all of the 600 installations in European waters can be completely, economically, and safely taken to land for recycling and safe disposal. According to the Commission, Community rules should be based on the principle of prohibiting the disposal of platforms, and only limited exceptions to this general prohibition are envisaged. The recommended approach is that of Community negotiations of multilateral agreements in international fora such as OSPAR.[50]

ii.   Implementation of the Nitrates Directive

In its report on the implementation of the Nitrates Directive,[51] the Commission observes that there is significant lack of progress in respect of the implementation of the Directive by Member States. At the moment of issuing the report, the Commission had begun enforcement procedures against thirteen out of the fifteen Member States.[52] The report concludes that, because implementation is so unsatisfactory, any revision of the Directive would be inappropriate. The Directive itself is the subject of a reference originating from a UK court, in a case supported by the National Farmers' Union, in which the validity of the Directive is challenged in the light of the polluter pays principle, the principle of proportionality, and the right to property.[53]

iii.   Court of Auditors' Report on Implementation of Water Policy and Action

The implementation of Community policy and action concerning water pollution has been the subject of a Court of Auditors' report.[54] The report highlights the Commission's difficulty in securing implementation of an

---

[49] Communication on the removal and disposal of disused oil and gas installations: COM(98)49.

[50] OSPAR—the Convention for the Prevention of Marine Pollution by Dumping from Ships and Aircraft. It was signed on 22 Sept. 1992 in Paris, and awaits ratification.

[51] Communication on the implementation of Council Dir. 91/676/EEC: COM(97)473; Council Dir. 91/676/EEC concerning the protection of waters against pollution caused by nitrates from agricultural sources [1991] OJ L375/1.

[52] Commission Press Release IP 97/843, 2 Oct. 1997.

[53] Case C–293/97, *The Queen* v. *Secretary of State for the Environment and Minister of Agriculture, Fisheries and Food ex parte H. A. Standley and others and D. G. D. Metson and others,* now pending. See the opinion of 8 Oct. 1998 of the AG, who considers that Art. 5 of the Directive must be interpreted as requiring the Member States to impose on farmers only the cost of plant for the reduction or avoidance of the pollution caused by nitrates for which farmers are responsible, to the exclusion of any other cost. That interpretation complies strictly with the polluter pays principle (para. 98). In conclusion, the AG holds that examination of the questions raised has disclosed no factor of such kind as to affect the validity of Dir. 91/676/EEC (para. 100).

[54] Court of Auditors' (EC) Special Report 3/98 on the implementation of EU policy and action concerning water pollution [1998] OJ C191/2.

effective policy against water pollution, and also stresses that insufficient progress has been made in reducing contributions to water pollution arising from intensive methods of agricultural production. The report makes a strong case for improved co-ordination within the Commission. Furthermore, the Court of Auditors is concerned about imcompatibilities between the structure by which EU projects are financed and the polluter pays principle. In particular, in order to qualify for maximum EU assistance, this may discourage Member States from ensuring that the principal polluters bear their proper share of the costs.

VI. Horizontal Instruments

JANE HOLDER, JONATHAN VERSCHUUREN, and JOS JANSSEN*

A. LEGISLATION IN PROGRESS

i. *Environmental Impact Assessment*

Council Directive 85/337/EEC on the Assessment of the Effects of Certain Public and Private Projects on the Environment (EIA Directive)[1] is, *par excellence*, a horizontal instrument. The requirement that all development projects likely to significantly affect the environment be subject to an assessment process of sorts cuts across administrative and institutional boundaries and, most importantly, concerns the effects of developments not merely on all environmental media but also flora, fauna, the "cultural" environment and humans. As such, the Directive is an agent for integration and, theoretically then, the prevention of harm. Debate about the effectiveness of environmental assessment as a preventive and, indeed, precautionary measure has focused on the further need to extend the law and practice of environmental assessment, to include *strategic* environmental assessment, or "forward planning".[2] During 1998, some progress was made on refining the proposed Directive on Strategic Environmental Assessment,[3] although there was some slippage in the legislative timetable for its adoption. However, fundamentally, the proposed Directive falls short of extending the current regime for environmental assessment into a more comprehensive assessment of policies, plans, and programmes.

The background to the proposed Directive on Strategic Environmental Assessment lies in the limited nature of the EIA Directive. The adoption of this Directive was delayed due to Member States' concerns that it would encourage litigation, as in the United States of America (USA), and hamper economic development. This in part accounts for the weak nature of its provisions, particularly the fact that it applies only to development projects and not to policies, as included in early drafts of the Directive. The Commission has, however, long recommended extending environmental assessment to include the effects of policies, plans, and programmes on the environment. This is seen as logical, given that individual development consents for projects at a local level are inevitably decided in the context of wider regional and national objectives, set out for example in highways, energy, and land-use plans. Decisions taken

---

* Jane Holder, Faculty of Laws, University College London (environmental impact assessment); Professor Jonathan Verschuuren, University of Tilburg (eco-management and audit scheme); Jos Janssen, University of Nijmegen (access to information).

[1] [1985] OJ L175/40.

[2] On this, see A. Sifakis, "Precaution, Prevention and the Environmental Impact Assessment Directive" (1998) 12 *European Environmental Law Review* 349–52.

[3] COM(96)511 final [1997] OJ C129/14. Most recently COM(99)73 def. [1999] OJ C83/13.

at these higher levels can hamper environmentally sound decision-making. This was borne out by research commissioned by the European Commission, which concluded that the evaluation of projects too late in the development planning process and at a local level has the result of removing from consideration the possible adoption of alternatives both to the individual project under consideration as well as its particular location or route.[4] As a consequence of such concerns, the Commission began consultation on an instrument for strategic environmental assessment in 1990.[5] Early drafts of a directive were discussed but abandoned, following a veto by the United Kingdom (UK) government. In 1997, Commission initiatives on strategic environmental assessment were resurrected in the form of a proposed Directive on the Assessment of the Effects of Certain Plans and Programmes on the Environment.[6] The scope of this is limited: it sets rules for assessment of the effects of certain plans and programmes on the environment, not policies. Therefore, there is some doubt whether without this dimension the proposal can properly provide for strategic environmental assessment in any event.[7] This limitation, again, reflects the narrowing down of the proposed Directive in the face of Member States' resistance to a broad strategic environmental assessment instrument.

The preamble to the proposed Directive states that land-use plans or programmes are to be assessed for their likely effects upon the environment. This assessment sets the framework for subsequent development consent decisions on tangible projects in the energy, waste, water, industry, telecommunications, tourist, and transport sectors (i.e. those sectors already subject to assessment under the EIA Directive). By its very nature, the draft Directive applies only to the actions of competent authorities. Otherwise, the provisions of the proposed Strategic Environmental Assessment Directive mirror those of the EIA Directive. The competent authority must prepare an environmental statement containing the types of information referred to in the Annex (Article 5(1) of the Directive) and those which may reasonably be required in order to assess the significant direct and indirect effects of implementation of plans and programmes upon human beings, fauna, flora, soil, water, air, climate, landscape, material assets, and cultural heritage, taking into account the level of detail in the plan or programme, its stage in the decision making process and the extent to which certain matters can be more appropriately assessed at different levels in that process (Article 5(2)). Inevitably, the precision with

---

[4] Report from the Commission on the implementation of Dir. 85/337/EEC on the assessment of certain public and private projects on the environment COM(93) 28, 2 Feb. 1993.

[5] Draft Proposal for a Directive on the environmental assessment of policies, plans and programmes, XI/194/90-EN-REV, 4 June 1990. Note, however, that a form of strategic environmental assessment has been in operation in the context of the Community's regional development policy: see J. Scott, *EC Environmental Law* (London: Longman, 1998), chap. 7.

[6] See n. 3 above.

[7] See D. Vaughan, *Law of the European Communities Service* (London: Butterworths, looseleaf, updated, Part 8). See also S. Tromans and C. Roger-Machart, "Strategic Environmental Assessment: Early Evaluation Equals Efficiency?" [1997] *Journal of Planning and Environmental Law* 993.

which effects on the environment can be predicted is less than is the case with project-based environmental assessment. The competent authorities must consult environmental authorities, designated by Member States, when deciding the scope and level of detail of this information (Article 5(3)) and provide a non-technical summary (Article 5(4)). The draft plan or programme and environmental statement are to be made available both to the environmental authorities and the "public concerned", the exact meaning of the latter to be decided by Member States. Both the environmental authorities and public concerned are to be given an opportunity to express their opinions on the draft plan or programme and the accompanying environmental statement, before adoption or submission. The central provision is that the competent authority responsible for the plan or programme shall consider, before it is adopted, the environmental statement, any opinions expressed, and the results of consultations concerning transboundary effects detailed under Article 7 (Article 8 of the Directive).

The legislative timetable set for the proposal suggested that the draft Directive be adopted in October 1998, with compliance by the Member States by October 2000. However, the European Parliament had given only a first reading to the draft by the first deadline. The delay has been attributed to discussion about the Directive's legal base.[8] In the event MEPs voted on the Directive without calling for a change of legal base from the Commission's proposal. This means that the Council of Ministers may pass the Directive by qualified majority vote rather than requiring unanimity.[9] Parliament passed several amendments including an amendment to extend the Directive's scope to cover plans and programmes in agriculture, forestry, and fishing. Parliament also voted to strengthen public participation rights.[10] Notwithstanding such progress, the chances of the Council adopting the draft Directive remain slim, given that none of the Member States which hold the presidency for the next few turns appear to consider it to be a high priority.

It remains the case that the proposed Directive, if adopted, will not lead to the extension of environmental assessment into strategic environmental assessment: its scope is too narrow to accomplish this, although, if adopted, the European Parliament's amendments to the proposed Directive will ensure that the measure applies to key areas beyond those originally envisaged. The form of strategic environmental assessment proposed is likely to operate as an "add on" to existing land-use decision-making procedures. That the proposed Directive is incapable of significantly affecting the future development of project-based environmental assessment may be seen by the fact that the current proposals are poorly integrated into the existing law on environmental assessment. A more integrated approach would have been to have extended the scope of environmental assessment at the time of the amendment of Directive

[8] *ENDS Daily*, 18 Sept. 1998.
[9] As with a town and country planning provision, unanimity within the Council is required unless otherwise waived: Art. 175(2) (formerly Article 130s(2)) EC.
[10] *ENDS Daily*, 23 Oct. 1998.

85/337/EEC by Directive 97/11/EC.[11] The limited form of environmental assessment envisaged in the draft Directive may usefully be compared with its counterpart in the USA, which sanctions a more comprehensive assessment of a wide range of policies, such as defence policies.[12]

ii.   Eco-management and Audit Scheme

Regulation (EC) No. 1836/93 of 29 June 1993, Allowing Voluntary Participation by Companies in the Industrial Sector in a Community Eco-management and Audit Scheme (EMAS), which entered into force in 1995, is currently being revised, as a result, *inter alia*, of a large assessment study on the implementation status of the Regulation in the Member States.[13] On 30 October 1998, a proposal was published to amend Regulation (EC) No. 1836/93.[14] One of the central aims of the amendments is to attract more companies to participate in the EMAS, especially by improving the relationship between EMAS and international environmental norms, such as ISO 14001, and by enhancing the visibility of the participants to EMAS. Under the new regulation, it will be made easier for companies registered under the popular ISO 14001 to have verification made under EMAS as well. Although ISO 14001 was already recognized under Article 12 of the Regulation in 1997,[15] important differences between the two still remain. Not only is ISO 14001 far less outspoken on the aim of "continuous improvement of the environmental performance", which is a central aim of EMAS (see Article 3), ISO 14001 neither explicitly requires an external verification, nor publication of the audit and of the results of the environmental analysis.[16] Notwithstanding these differences, the 1998 proposal stipulates that the environmental management system should be carried out according to ISO 14001, thus replacing the requirements included in Annex A of Regulation (EC) No. 1836/93. Companies already certified under ISO 14001 therefore do not have to change anything in their management systems to be verified under EMAS. The environmental statement (including a report on the audit results), however, remains accessible to the public. As far as openness and publicity is concerned, the new Regulation keeps its additional value *vis-à-vis* ISO 14001. Another new feature in the proposal for a revised regulation on EMAS is the introduction of the possibility for other than industrial com-

---

[11] [1997] OJ L73/5.

[12] On the National Environmental Policy Act 1969, see S. Taylor, *Making Bureaucracies Think: The Environmental Impact Statement Strategy of Administrative Reform* (Stanford: Stanford University Press, 1984).

[13] R. Hillary, M. Gelber, V. Bondi, and M. Tamborra, *An Assessment of the Implementation Status of Council Regulation (EC) No. 1836/93 Eco-management and Audit Scheme in the Member States (AIMS-EMAS), Final Report* (London: Centre for Environmental Technology, 1998).

[14] COM(98)622 [1998] OJ C400/7.

[15] Commission Decision 97/265/EC of 16 Apr. 1997 [1997] OJ L104/37.

[16] See for a comparison between EMAS and ISO 14001, K. Deketelaere (ed.), *European Environmental Law, International Encyclopaedia of Laws* (The Hague/London/Boston: Kluwer Law International, 1998), 123–6, and (in German) G. Feldhaus, "Wettbewerb zwischen EMAS und ISO 14001" (1998) 2 *Umwelt- und Planungsrecht* 41–3. For a comparison between EMAS and British Standard BS 7750 see A. R. Zito and M. Egan, "Environmental Management Standards, Corporate Strategies, and Policy Networks" (1998) 7(3) *Environmental Politics* 94–117.

panies to be verified under EMAS. Small and medium-sized enterprises (SMEs) will fall explicitly under the scope of EMAS. Member States will be urged to stimulate these companies to participate in EMAS. The scheme will remain voluntary, although some Member States suggested making it obligatory.[17] When the proposal is accepted, Regulation (EC) No. 1836/93 will be withdrawn.

On the subject of small and medium-sized enterprises, it is worthwhile noting that in 1998 the plan of the Commission to extend the scope of Directive 96/61/EC on Integrated Pollution Prevention and Control (IPPC) to SMEs, as announced in the Commission's Working Plan for 1997,[18] was dropped because of limited support by the Member States. The reasons are threefold. According to some, the principle of subsidiarity prohibits environmental legislation at EU level, as far as SMEs are concerned. Also, it is argued that existing environmental legislation should first be more efficiently enforced. Finally, it was held to be appropriate to await the results of a study on the nature and scale of the environmental problems caused by SMEs.[19]

B. CASE LAW

i. Environmental Impact Assessment

The most significant case heard in 1998, in terms of the interpretation and future development of environmental assessment, is *Burgemeester en Wethouders van Haarlemmerliede en Spaarnwoude and Others* v. *Gedeputeerde Staten van Noord-Holland*.[20] This preliminary ruling arose out of proceedings brought by several people challenging an authority's decision to approve a zoning plan without having conducted an environmental assessment as, arguably, required by the EIA Directive.[21] The projects granted planning consent by the zoning plan (a port and an industrial zone in Amsterdam) had also been the subject of zoning plans in 1968, 1979, and 1987, but little progress had been made on their construction. The national law transposing the EIA Directive states that such projects require environmental assessment, but not where a project has already been incorporated in a current zoning plan. The question therefore arose whether the provisions of the Directive could be waived in such a way where the projects had already been the subject of consent granted before 3 July 1988 (the deadline for implementation of the Directive), no environmental assessment was conducted, but little work on the projects was done and a fresh consent procedure was initiated after 3 July 1988.

In its judgment, the European Court of Justice confirmed its previous ruling in *Bund Naturschutz in Bayern and Others*[22] that the Directive does not authorize Member States to exempt projects in respect of which the consent procedures were initiated after the deadline of 3 July 1988 from the obligation

[17] Deketelaere (ed.), n. 16 above, 127.
[19] Deketelaere (ed.), n. 16 above, 103.
[21] See n. 1 above.

[18] COM(96)507.
[20] Case C-81/96 [1998] ECR I-3923.
[22] Case C-396/92 [1994] ECR I-3717, para. 18.

to carry out an environmental assessment. The principle contained in Article 2(1) of the Directive, that projects likely to have significant effects on the environment must be subject to an environmental assessment, applies. It also confirmed that, as was held in *Commission v. Germany*,[23] since the Directive makes no provision for transitional rules covering projects in which the consent procedure was initiated before 3 July 1988 but were still in progress on that date, that principle does not apply where the application for consent was *formally* lodged before the 3 July 1988 deadline. The Court distinguished these cases from the facts of the present case—an application made after 3 July 1988 seeking fresh consent for a project listed in Annex I of the Directive—but, as with its previous case law, based its judgment on the need to secure the effectiveness of the Directive and to give effect to the principle contained in Article 2 of the Directive. It concluded that:

where . . . a fresh procedure is formally initiated after 3 July 1988, that procedure is subject to the obligations regarding environmental assessment imposed by the Directive. Any other solution would run counter to the principle that an environmental assessment must be made of certain major projects, set out in Article 2 of the Directive, and would compromise its effectiveness.[24]

In so ruling, the Court of Justice offers a common sense and expansive reading of the Directive which has the effect of limiting Member States' ability to waive its requirements. When considering the possible expansion of environmental assessment to include policies, plans, and programmes, it is interesting that the national law of concern in *Haarlemmerliede*, by allowing development consent by plans rather than by requiring individual consent, effectively brought development planning within the scope of the EIA Directive.

Commission v. Germany[25] is the latest case in a long line of cases brought for a declaration that a Member State has infringed Directive 85/337/EEC.[26] The case primarily concerns Germany's exclusion in advance of the whole class of projects listed in Annex II to the Directive from the national law, the *Gesetz über die Umweltverträglichkeitsprüfung*. These projects might be said to be discretionary, since whether an environmental assessment is to be conducted is to be decided on the basis of, *inter alia*, the "nature, size, and location" of the project (Article 2(1) of the Directive). The prior exclusion of Annex II projects has been a common interpretation of the discretion conferred on Member States by Article 4(2) of the Directive.[27] In addition, the Commission alleged a delay in transposing the Directive, and a failure to transpose correctly Article 5(2), which specifies the information which a developer must supply concern-

---

[23] Case C–431/92 [1995] ECR I–2189, para. 32.   [24] Ibid., at para. 27.

[25] Case C–30/95, not yet reported, judgment of 22 Oct. 1998.

[26] See, e.g., Case C–313/93, *Commission* v. *Luxembourg* [1994] ECR I–2179, Case 431/92, *Commission* v. *Germany*, n. 16 above; and Case C–133/94, *Commission* v. *Belgium* [1996] ECR I–2323.

[27] Member States may specify certain types or projects for which environmental assessment will be required, or may establish criteria and/or thresholds for determining which projects falling within the Annex II categories will be subject to environmental assessment. See Scott, n. 6 above, chap. 6.

ing a project subject to environmental assessment. Closely following an Opinion by Advocate General Mischo,[28] the Court declared that Germany had, by excluding *a priori* from the environmental assessment requirements whole classes of projects listed in Annex II to that Directive, failed to fulfil its obligations under Articles 2(1) and 4(2) of that Directive. The Court relied on this point on its earlier judgment in *Commission v. Belgium*[29] that "Article 4(2) does not empower Member States to exclude generally and definitively from possible assessment one or more classes mentioned in Annex II".[30] The Court also found a failure to communicate to the Commission the measures which it had taken to comply with the Directive. The Commission did not, however, succeed on the Article 5(2) allegation; this was dismissed because the Directive allows stricter rules to be laid down. Two of the issues raised in this case, the exact nature of the duty under Article 2 of the Directive concerning Annex II projects and the status and extent of information to be supplied by developers under Article 5(2), serve to emphasize the ambiguities which are a feature of the original EIA Directive and a product of its lengthy and acrimonious gestation. A central objective of the amending Directive 97/11/EC is to clarify these issues.

The shortcomings of the original EIA Directive are also exemplified in *Commission v. Ireland*, currently pending. The main concern is that the Annex II thresholds set in Irish law fail to take adequate account of the incremental or cumulative effects of a number of separate projects, especially in "sensitive areas", in terms of nature conservation. This is because areas where nature conservation is important are often small in relation to the thresholds set and may therefore be excluded from prior environmental impact assessment, for failing to reach a quantitative threshold. But, taken together, several small projects may cause considerable damage to the environment. At issue are the extent and nature of the discretion Member States may exercise in determining whether a project should be subject to environmental impact assessment. In adopting the measures in question, Ireland, arguably, exceeded its discretion under the Directive. Of particular concern was the environmental consequence of the use of uncultivated land or semi-natural areas for intensive agricultural purposes, initial afforestation and land reclamation, and the extraction of peat. *Commission v. Ireland* is therefore concerned with whether legislative thresholds are unlawful because they are set in disregard of the criterion of the project's location.

Advocate General La Pergola recounted that the Court of Justice has consistently held that the discretion which Article 4(2) of the Directive confers on Member States is subject to the limitations imposed by Article 2(1) of the Directive, which provides that "Member States shall adopt all measures necessary to ensure that, before consent is given, projects likely to have significant effects on the environment by virtue, *inter alia*, of their nature, size or location

---

[28] 12 Mar. 1998.   [29] See n. 26 above.
[30] Ibid., para. 43. See also Case C–72/95, *Aannemersbedrijf P.K. Kraaijeveld BV and Others v. Gedeputeerde Staten van Zuid-Holland ("Dutch Dykes")* [1996] ECR I–5403.

are made subject to an assessment with regard to their effect".[31] In *Kraaijeveld*,[32] the Court decided that Article 4(2) entails the need to take account of not only the characteristics of a single project, but the characteristics as a whole of projects planned which fall within the category under consideration. Advocate General La Pergola considered that the location of a project must also be considered because Article 2(1) expressly identifies this as a characteristic to be taken into account. The discretion enjoyed by Member States under Article 4(2) to set thresholds or criteria must therefore be consistent with the wording and *purpose* of Article 2(1). Following this reasoning, he found that the Commission succeeded in providing evidence to show that several projects, which are likely to have a significant environmental impact, concern sensitive areas, and that the application of thresholds which exclude them from assessment amounts to a failure to comply with the Directive. It is particularly significant that, respecting the preventive nature of environmental impact assessment as a regulatory instrument, the only evidence which the Commission may be required to show is that there are areas in which development projects may have adverse repercussions on the environment; it is not necessary to show that the impact envisaged by the Directive actually has occurred.[33]

The Advocate General's approach is forthright and purposive and builds upon the Court's previous judgment in *Kraaijeveld*. The Opinion is in line with the approach adopted in Directive 97/11/EC,[34] which lists in an Annex a series of selection criteria focusing on the characteristics of projects and their potential impact, of which the cumulation of effects on the environment is listed as one such characteristic. There is also some clarification on the possible direct effect of the Directive, a point sidestepped by the Court in *Kraaijeveld*.[35] In addition, Advocate General La Pergola states that the fact that an assessment must be carried out when the characteristics of projects as defined in Article 2(1) of the Directive so require means that this is an obligation as to the result to be achieved.[36] Elsewhere he states that the rule in Article 2(1) is akin to a regulation:

In many respects, the Directive in question is comparable to a regulation in view of the direct effect of its key provision (Article 2(1)) and the exhaustive nature of its legislative content.[37]

This is particularly telling, given that the Court of Justice appears to be limiting Member States' discretion in transposing the Directive, the instrument's main legal characteristic.

---

[31] In his opinion of 17 Dec. 1998.   [32] See n. 30 above.   [33] Para. 26.
[34] Dir. 97/11/EC amending Dir. 85/337/EEC on the assessment of the effects of certain public or private projects on the environment [1997] OJ L73/5.
[35] The Court held that the Directive imposes a duty on national courts to determine whether the boundaries of any discretionary power have been exceeded and set aside inconsistent national legislation (public law effect), but fell short of determining the issue of the Directive's direct effect.
[36] *Kraaijeveld*, n. 30 above, at para. 18.   [37] Ibid., at para 61.

ii. Access to Information

In the period under consideration, the Court delivered the first judgment on Directive 90/313/EEC on the Freedom of Access to Information on the Environment (Environmental Information Directive),[38] in *Wilhelm Mecklenburg v. Kreis Pinneberg—Der Landrat*.[39] The *Oberverwaltungsgericht Schleswig-Holstein* (Germany) submitted preliminary questions to the Court, concerning the interpretation of the concept of "information relating to the environment" and the scope of one of the grounds justifying refusal to grant access. From this judgment, two general points of interpretation concerning the Directive can be derived. First, the Court acknowledged that the wording of Article 2(a) of the Directive makes it clear that the Community legislature intended the concept of "information relating to the environment" to be a broad one. According to that provision, environmental information includes any information on the state of various aspects of the environment (i.e. the state of water, air, soil, fauna, flora, land, and natural sites), as well as on activities or measures which may adversely affect or protect those aspects, including administrative measures and environmental management programmes. In addition, the Court stated that the Community legislature expressly avoided giving any definition of "information relating to the environment", in order to avoid exclusion of any of the activities engaged by public authorities. In reply to the first question put forward by the national court, the Court of Justice held that a statement of views given by a countryside protection authority in development consent proceedings comes within the ambit of "information relating to the environment", if that statement is capable of influencing the outcome of those proceedings as regards interests pertaining to the protection of the environment.

A second general conclusion which can be drawn from this judgment is that derogations from the freedom of access to environmental information should be construed narrowly. Here, the Court applies a proportionality test in stating that the derogations may not be interpreted in such a way as to extend its effects beyond what is necessary to safeguard the interest. Moreover, the scope of the derogations should be determined in the light of the aims pursued by the Directive.[40] As the seventh recital in the preamble to the Directive indicates, refusal to comply with a request for information relating to the environment may be justified in certain specific and clearly defined cases. Such a narrow interpretation of the derogations is illustrated in this case. Accordingly, a grammatical interpretation in the other official EU languages of the term "preliminary investigation proceedings", as referred to in the derogation under Article 3(2), third indent, of the Directive, leads the Court to the conclusion that an administrative procedure, such as that referred to by the German *Umweltinformationsgesetz*, constitutes preliminary investigation proceedings only if it immediately precedes a contentious or quasi-contentious procedure and arises from the need to obtain proof or to investigate a matter prior to the opening of the actual procedure.

[38] [1990] OJ L158/56.   [39] Case C–321/96 [1998] ECR I–3809.
[40] Case C–335/94, *Mrozek and Jäger* [1996] ECR I–1573, para. 9.

Another case on the Environmental Information Directive is pending before the Court and involves infringement proceedings against Germany. The Commission brought an action against Germany for not complying with a reasoned opinion stating that certain provisions of the *Umweltinformationsgesetz* were not compatible with the Directive.[41]

C.   INTERNATIONAL CO-OPERATION

i.   *Access to Information*

The legal framework establishing a right of access to environmental information is laid down in the Environmental Information Directive. The Directive obliges Member States to ensure public access to environmental information held by national public authorities, subject to certain conditions outlined in the Directive.[42] The freedom of access to environmental information puts national public authorities under an obligation both to disclose environmental information on request and to disseminate such information in an active manner. Whereas environmental information may be requested without the applicant having to prove any interest, public authorities may refuse access on limited grounds set out in the Directive. As the Directive was adopted on the basis of Article 175 (formerly Article 130s) EC, Member States are allowed to maintain or introduce more stringent measures by virtue of Article 176 (formerly Article 130t) EC. The Directive should have been complied with at the end of 1992.

The Community institutions themselves, however, are not bound by the Directive. Nevertheless, an obligation exists, at least for the Council and the Commission, to grant access to the documents and information held by them, including environmental information, as laid down in the Code of Conduct on Public Access to Council and Commission Documents.[43] That is, the decisions implementing the Code of Conduct are capable of conferring rights to individuals.[44] Meanwhile, the European Parliament has adopted similar general rules on access to its documents.[45] In accordance with these measures, a new provision, Article 255 EC, was inserted by the Treaty of Amsterdam, which establishes a Treaty-based right of access to information held by the European Parliament, the Council, and the Commission. Furthermore, the European Ombudsman recommended that the other institutions and EU organs estab-

---

[41] Meanwhile, the Court ruled that Germany had failed to fulfil its obligations under the Directive on 3 grounds. See Case C–217/97, *Commission* v. *Germany*, judgment of 9 Sept. 1999, not yet reported.

[42] On the origins of the Directive see L. Krämer, *Focus on European Environmental Law* (London: Sweet & Maxwell, 1992), 290. For a critical analysis of the Directive and its implementation by some Member States see C. Kimber, "Understanding Access to Environmental Information: the European Experience", in T. Jewell and J. Steele (eds.), *Law in Environmental Decision-Making* (Oxford: Oxford University Press, 1998), 139–60.

[43] Decision 93/730/EC [1993] OJ C340/41 as implemented in Council Decision 93/731/EC [1993] OJ L340/43, and Commission Decision 94/90/ECSC/EC/Euratom [1994] OJ L46/58.

[44] See Case T–105/95, *WWF UK* v. *Commission* [1997] ECR II–313, para. 55.

[45] Decision 97/362/ECSC/EC/Euratom [1997] OJ L262/27.

lish rules on public access to their documents, for failure to do so would constitute a case of maladministration.[46]

Consequently, the European Environment Agency, among some fifteen other EU organs, is now subjected to rules on access to its documents.[47]

In this context, the most important event in the field of access to information took place at the international level, where the United Nations Economic Commission for Europe (UN/ECE) Convention on Access to Information, Public Participation and Access to Justice in Environmental Matters (hereinafter: Århus Convention) was concluded in June 1998 in Århus (Denmark).[48] The objective of the Århus Convention is to raise public awareness of environmental concerns by promoting access to information and participation in the decision-making process.

The Commission, on behalf of the European Communities, took part in the negotiating process, as far as the areas of access to information and public participation in decisions on specific activities were concerned, since the Community has competence in these areas.[49] In a declaration on the Proposal for a Council Decision on the signature of the Århus Convention,[50] the Community declares that it intends to apply the Convention to its institutions too, since the Community itself is actively involved in protecting the environment and, consequently, the definition of "public authority" in the Århus Convention should be held to be applicable also to the Community institutions.[51] As the Commission submits in the abovementioned Proposal, it is in fact the first time that an international convention has been applied to the Community institutions as such. Accordingly, the signing of the Århus Convention will put an end to the unsatisfactory situation that Member States are bound by specific rules on access to environmental information, whereas the Community institutions themselves are not.

The provisions on access to information laid down in Article 4 of the Århus Convention for a large part coincide with Directive 90/313/EEC. A substantial difference, however, is to be found in Article 4(5) of this Convention, which requires public authorities not in possession of the information requested either to inform the applicant of the public authority to which it believes it is possible to apply for the information, or to transfer the request to that

---

[46] See Special Report from the European Ombudsman to the European Parliament following the own-initiative inquiry into public access to documents, 616/PUBAC/F/IJH [1998] OJ C44/9.

[47] Decision of 21 Mar. 1997 on public access to European Environment Agency documents [1997] OJ C282/5.

[48] The text of the Århus Convention is annexed to the Proposal for a Council decision on the signature by the European Community of the UN/ECE Convention on Access to Information, Public Participation and Access to Justice in Environmental Matters, COM(1998)344 final.

[49] Dir. 85/337/EEC on the assessment of the effects of certain public and private projects on the environment [1985] OJ L175/40; and Dir. 96/61/EC concerning integrated pollution prevention and control (IPPC) [1996] OJ L257/26.

[50] Proposal for a Council Decision on the signature by the European Communities of the UN/ECE Convention on Access to Information, Public Participation and Access to Justice in Environment Matters, COM(98)344 final.

[51] COM(1998)344 final.

authority. Hence, at least from a practical point of view, this provision makes the citizen's right to obtain the information demanded much more effective.

In addition, in Article 5 of the Århus Convention the issue of active dissemination of environmental information by public authorities is dealt with in a very extensive fashion, whereas this aspect is hardly elaborated in Article 7 of the Directive. For example, Article 5 of the Convention requires the establishment of electronic databases on environmental information, easily accessible to the public, which should include, *inter alia*, reports on the state of the environment, texts of environmental legislation, and plans and programmes on the environment. In any event, the Directive will have to be reviewed in order to comply with the Århus Convention, notably with regard to the provisions on the dissemination of environmental information.

VII. Miscellaneous Instruments

DIANE RYLAND*

A. LEGISLATION ADOPTED

i. Action Programmes

Council Decision 97/872/EC of 16 December 1997 establishes a Community Action Programme promoting non-governmental organizations (NGOs) primarily active in the field of environmental protection.[1] For the purposes of this Decision, environmental NGOs are independent and non-profit-making organizations, primarily active in the field of environmental protection with an environmental objective aimed at the public good (Article 1 of the Decision).

The areas of activity eligible for Community financial assistance are defined under the headings of:

— information on the environment;
— analysis of environmental activities;
— co-operation between actors in the environment and NGOs active at European level (Article 2(1), Annex of the Decision).

Community financial assistance may be provided for activities which are of Community interest, contribute significantly to the further development and implementation of Community environmental policy and legislation, and meet the principles underlying the fifth action programme (Article 2(1) of the Decision).

The programme has a four-year duration, from 1 January 1998 to 31 December 2001. The financial reference amount for the implementation of the programme is 10.6 million Euros (Article 6(1) of the Decision).

A Community Action Programme in the field of civil protection is established by Council Decision 98/22/EC, of 19 December 1997, in order to contribute to the protection of persons, the environment, and property in the event of a natural or technological disaster, without prejudice to the internal division of competences in Member States (Article 1 of the Decision).[2] The legal basis for this Decision is Article 308 (formerly Article 235) EC.

The programme is intended to support and supplement Member States' efforts within the framework of their action on national, regional, and local levels in matters of civil protection, and to facilitate co-operation between Member States in this field. It excludes any measures aimed at the harmonization of the laws and regulations of Member States, or organization of national preparedness of Member States (Article 1 of the Decision). The duration of the

* Senior Lecturer, Department of Law, University of Lincolnshire and Humberside.
[1] [1998] OJ L354/25.   [2] [1998] OJ L8/20.

programme is two years, from 1 January 1998 to 31 December 1999. The financial reference amount for the programme's implementation is 3 million Euros. (Article 2(1), (2) of the Decision).

Individual actions shall be selected primarily on the basis of the following criteria:

— contribution to lessening the risk and damage to persons, the environment, and property in the event of a natural or technological disaster;
— contribution to increasing the degree of preparedness of those involved in civil protection in Member States, in order to increase their ability to respond to an emergency;
— pilot projects: contribution to improving techniques and methods of response;
— contribution to public information, education,. and awareness, so as to help citizens to protect themselves more effectively (Article 3(2) of the Decision).

In European Parliament and Council Decision 2179/98/EC of 24 September 1998 on the review of the European Community programme of policy and action in relation to the environment and sustainable development "Towards Sustainability",[3] the Community confirms its commitment to the general approach and strategy of that European Community action programme. Member States, enterprises, and citizens are encouraged to accept their respective responsibilities and play their full part in the continuing implementation of the programme and to speed up progress. For its part, in order to accelerate the achievement of the programme's objectives and to ensure more efficient implementation of its approach, the Community will step up its efforts on five key priorities and five other issues (Article 1 of the Decision).

The five priorities are identified as:

— the integration of environmental requirements into other policies;
— broadening the range of instruments;
— the implementation and enforcement of legislation;
— awareness raising;
— international co-operation (Articles 2–5 of the Decision).

In recognition of the cross-border nature of environmental problems and the Community's prospects of becoming the driving force in the further development of international environmental rules, the Community will seek to strengthen its role and take the lead, in particular as regards the international obligations which it has entered into under conventions and protocols. This implies, in particular, strengthening its approach to co-operation with the countries of Central and Eastern Europe and the Mediterranean, and enhancing its role in relation to environmental issues as identified in Agenda 21 and

---

[3] [1998] OJ L275/1.

in relation to bilateral and multilateral co-operation on sustainable development issues (Article 6 of the Decision).[4]

In addition, the Commission issued statements relating to the Common
Agricultural Policy, environmental liability, enforcement, and waste management.

ii. Energy

In its Resolution of 18 December 1997, the Council endorses a Community
strategy to promote combined heat and power.[5] The Council considers that
the efficient use of energy from combined heat and power can contribute
positively both to the environmental policies of the European Union and the
competitive situation of the Union and its Member States, as well as to the
security of energy supply. It is noted that the situations in Member States,
regarding combined heat and power, vary significantly. Taking this into
account, the Council confirms the indicative target proposed by the
Commission, i.e. to double the overall share of combined heat and power in
the Community by 2010.

The main responsibility for promoting combined heat and power, it is
stressed, lies with Member States. However, the Council underlines the fact
that Member States and the Community, within their respective competences,
need actively to promote the use of combined heat and power by stimulating,
where appropriate, the market for combined heat and power and by removing
the barriers to this market.

The Council agrees in another Resolution, of 8 June 1998 on renewable
sources of energy,[6] that there is a need to promote sustained and substantially
increased use of renewable sources of energy throughout the Community. This
is in the light of the valuable contribution renewables can make to environmental protection and the implementation of the commitments under the
Kyoto Protocol, to security of supply and the preservation of finite energy
resources, and to economic and social development in general. In this
Resolution, the Council urges Member States to continue to develop, in conformity with national procedures, national strategies, and structures for the
promotion of renewables throughout the Community. The Council considers
that the relative costs of renewables must be reduced to allow them to compete with other energy sources. It is noted that Member States choose the most
appropriate means of promoting the use of renewables from, *inter alia*, fiscal
measures, subsidies, preferential tariffs, levies on energy consumption
designed to promote sustainable energy systems, and voluntary agreements
with industry.

The role of the Community as a complement is confirmed. The Council
stresses the important role of the ALTENER programme, which will become an

---

[4] Other issues to which particular attention will be given include: improving the basis for environmental policy, sustainable production and consumption patterns, shared responsibility and
partnership, promotion of local and regional initiatives, environmental themes (Art. 11 of the
Decision).

[5] [1998] OJ C4/1.   [6] [1998] OJ C198/1.

integral part of the Energy Framework Programme, to develop and promote support measures at Community level.

The belief is held in the Council that it is highly desirable to build renewables into other Community policies, where it is appropriate to do so, and that full account must be taken of renewables in the development of Community policies on agriculture and waste management. The Council recognizes that other Community policies, including regional, rural development, research and technology, external, competition, and state aid policies, could make a significant contribution to the promotion of renewables. It is agreed that interest must be raised among industry, investors, and the public. The Council also recognizes that this will require the mobilization of private-sector as well as public-sector funds in Member States and the Community, and invites the Commission to bring forward proposals on how this is to be done, in particular in relation to financing. Member States are encouraged to co-operate and co-ordinate policy, to be complemented by Community action, in line with the principle of subsidiarity. In this context, the Council is resolute that Member States and the Commission should regularly exchange information on progress made at national level.

iii.   Financial Instruments

The Council has adopted Decision 98/352/EC of 18 May 1998, establishing a multi-annual programme for the promotion of renewable energy sources in the Community (ALTENER II).[7] The legal basis for this Decision is Article 175(1) (formerly Article 130s(1)) EC. The programme's two specific objectives are:

— to help create the necessary conditions for the implementation of a Community action plan for renewable energy sources and, in particular, the legal, socio-economic, and administrative conditions;
— to encourage private and public investments in the production and use of energy from renewable sources (Article 1(1)(a) and (b) of the Decision).

Community financial support will be granted under the programme for actions meeting the programme's specific objectives. The financial reference amount for the implementation of the programme is 22 million Euros (Article 1(2) and (3)).

Provisions are included in the Decision for participation in the ALTENER II programme by the associated countries of Central and Eastern Europe, and by Cyprus, respectively (Article 7 of the Decision). The Decision applies from 1 January 1998 until the entry into force of the Multi-Annual Framework Programme for measures in the energy sector, and until 31 December 1999 at the latest (Article 8 of the Decision).

---

[7] [1998] OJ L159/53.

iv. Research and Development Programmes

The European Parliament and the Council, acting jointly, have decided upon an increase of 115 million Euros in the maximum overall amount for Community financial participation in the fourth framework programme (Decision 2535/97/EC of the European Parliament and Council of 1 December 1997, adapting for the second time Decision 1110/94/EC concerning the Fourth Framework Programme of the European Community activities in the field of research and technological development and demonstration).[8] This is to be allocated to certain specific programmes of the first activity of the fourth framework programme. Indicative allocations of the financial supplement for the specific programmes of industrial and material technologies, environment and climate, transport, and energy, are given as 15 million Euros, 7 million Euros, 7 million Euros, and 9 million Euros respectively (Annex I of the Directive). Decision 1110/94/EC is amended. The maximum overall amount for Community financial participation in the fourth framework programme shall be 11,879 million Euros. Of this, 5,449 million Euros shall be for the period 1994 to 1996 and 6,430 million Euros for the period 1997 to 1998. Annex I in the former Decision is replaced by Annex II to this Decision. In the latter Annex, an indicative breakdown of the themes and subjects in the first activity (research, technological development, and demonstration programmes), for the period 1994 to 1998 includes 1,157 million Euros in respect of the environment, broken down into 914 million Euros for environment and climate, and 243 million Euros for marine sciences and technologies. It is noted that environment-related research projects will also be conducted within several other lines of the first activity, in particular in the fields of industrial technologies, energy, and transport, for which total indicative allocations for the period 1994 to 1998 are 2,140 million Euros, 1,076 million Euros, and 263 million Euros, respectively.

v. State Aids

The Council has adopted Regulation (EC) No. 994/98, on the Application of Articles 87 and 88 (formerly Articles 92 and 93) of the Treaty Establishing the European Community to Certain Categories of Horizontal State Aid, with effect from 15 May 1998.[9] This Regulation enables the Commission, acting in accordance both with the procedures laid down therein and Article 87 (formerly Article 92) EC, to adopt a group exemption in respect of aid in favour of, *inter alia*, environmental protection by means of a regulation (Article 1(a)(iii) of the Regulation). Aid for such purposes will be deemed compatible with the common market and will not be subject to the notification requirements of Article 88(3) (formerly Article 93(3)) EC, subject to a *de minimis* rule, and provided that aid granted to the same undertaking over a given period of time does not exceed a certain fixed amount (Articles 1(1) and 2(1) of the Regulation). An exemption regulation is required to specify:

[8] [1997] OJ L347/1.   [9] [1998] OJ L142/1.

— the purpose of the aid; the categories of beneficiaries;
— thresholds expressed either in terms of aid intensities in relation to a set of eligible costs or in terms of maximum amounts;
— the conditions governing the cumulation of aid;
— monitoring conditions (Article 1(2) of the Regulation).

The exemption regulation may also set thresholds or other conditions for the notification of awards of individual aid, exclude certain sectors from their scope, and attach further conditions for the compatibility of aid exempted under such regulations (Article 1(3) of the Regulation).

A group exemption regulation will apply for a specific period, and aid exempted thereunder will be exempted for the period of validity of that regulation or any adjustment period set in accordance with Regulation (EC) No. 994/98 (Article 4(1) of the Regulation).

A published draft regulation will precede the adoption of an exemption regulation, to enable all interested parties to submit their comments within a reasonable time, of not less than one month, to be determined by the Commission. The Commission is required to consult the Advisory Committee on State Aid before publishing any regulation (Articles 7 and 8 of the Regulation).

B.   POLICY DOCUMENTS

According to the Communication on energy efficiency in the European Community—towards a strategy for the rational use of energy of 29 April 1998,[10] the Commission is of the opinion that there is an urgent need to reinvigorate commitment by both the Community and Member States to promote energy efficiency more actively.

The underlying objective of another Communication by the Commission in the field of energy policy (Commission Communication strengthening environmental integration within Community energy policy, of 14 October 1998)[11] is the development and implementation of a sustainable energy policy. Accordingly, a range of actions is proposed towards reinforcing greater integration of environmental objectives within Community energy policy. Member States have the primary responsibility for energy policy, and the necessity for national, local, and regional authorities to integrate the environmental dimension into energy policy is therefore emphasized. The Commission undertakes to strengthen its own contribution in environmental integration and invites the Council and the European Parliament to endorse or adopt a number of key energy proposals.

The Communication underlines the necessity of implementing the integration of environmental objectives within energy policy in a flexible and balanced way. It is deemed particularly important to take into account energy policy priority objectives of security of supply and competitiveness in pro-

---

[10] COM(98)246.   [11] COM(98)571.

moting sustainability. The Council and the European Parliament are invited to support environmental integration with energy policy in decisions affecting energy taken in the framework of other policies, for example, framework programmes for research, technology and development, and international cooperation. In this context, it is stated that particular attention needs to be given to the objectives of internalization of external cost and fiscal measures. The Communication also draws attention to the need to monitor progress in environmental integration on the basis of suitable indicators.

C.   CASE LAW

Windpark Groothusen GmbH & Co. Betriebs KG v. *Commission*,[12] the European Court of Justice dismissed the appeal brought by Windpark Groothusen GmbH against a judgment of the Court of First Instance, of 13 December 1995.[13] In that case, the Court of First Instance rejected the application for the annulment of the Commission's Decision of 13 January 1994, refusing to grant Windpark Groothusen funding under the Thermie programme for 1993.[14]

In support of its appeal, Windpark pleaded, *inter alia*, breach of the duty to state reasons. In its judgment, rejecting this plea in law, the European Court of Justice ruled that participation in a financial support programme does not give rise to any right on the part of an applicant for funding, whose legal position remains unchanged in the event of rejection, and whose sole entitlement is to the objective examination of the application in the course of the selection procedure. The Court stated that the Thermie Regulation lays down the essential criteria on the basis of which the various projects are assessed, thus enabling the candidates to gauge to what extent their projects meet those criteria. Furthermore, in view of the special features of the selection procedure in question (i.e. publication of the criteria for eligibility and the participation of committees in the selection of projects) there is no need for an individual, detailed statement of reasons. It follows that, in a procedure such as in the present case, where the number of participants is high, the parties concerned are aware in advance of the criteria laid down by the Regulation for selecting the various projects, provision is made for the participation of committees and the results are published, there can be no duty to provide a detailed statement of the reasons for a decision rejecting an application for financial support, including comparative information on the projects selected. The Court of First Instance was therefore correct in holding that the statement of reasons accompanying the Decision of 13 January 1994 was sufficient and proper, namely exhaustion of the funds available at that time, so that Windpark's project could not be awarded financial support.

---

[12] Case C–48/96P, judgment of the European Court of Justice, 14 May 1998 (not yet reported).
[13] Case T–109/94 [1995] ECR II–3007 (not yet reported).
[14] Council Reg. (EC) No. 2008/90 concerning the promotion of energy technology in Europe [1990] OJ L185/1.

D. INTERNATIONAL CO-OPERATION

The Council and the Commission have approved the Energy Charter Treaty and the Energy Charter Protocol on energy efficiency and related environmental aspects, on behalf of the European Communities, with effect from 16 April 1998.[15] The Commission has adopted a Proposal for a Council Decision on the position to be adopted by the European Community within the energy conference and the international conference of the signatories of the Energy Charter Treaty on the amendment to the trade-related provisions of the Energy Charter Treaty and its provisional application.[16]

E. MISCELLANEOUS

i. Cohesion Fund

The Commission has issued its Annual Report on the Cohesion Fund for 1997.[17] The Cohesion Fund fully implemented all its commitment and payment appropriations, 2748.7 million Euros, for the year 1997.

Between 1993 and 1997, transport accounted for 50.8 per cent of commitments and the environment sector for 49.2 per cent. Almost a third (32 per cent) of overall commitments under the transport budget went to rail projects in 1997.

In 1997, the Fund continued to concentrate resources on the abstraction and distribution of drinking water, waste-water treatment, and the handling and treatment of solid waste.

The Cohesion Fund initiated a major study to demonstrate the environmental dimension of the transport and environmental projects it assists.

In 1995, the Fund commissioned the London School of Economics to estimate the socio-economic impact of the Fund, the result of which became available in 1997. The study shows a strong positive relationship between public and private investment, resulting in significant long-term employment effects, and also important economic spillovers between regions and between the cohesion countries and their neighbours.

During 1997, the Commission agreed on the detailed terms of reference for a programme to be commissioned, concerning the *ex post* evaluation of the Cohesion Fund, which will run until the end of 2000, for the present generation of the Cohesion Fund.

The process of monitoring and following up on decisions from previous years has gradually been gaining in importance over the appraisal and approval of new applications. The Monitoring Committees in the four countries met eleven times in 1997. In autumn 1997, the Cohesion Fund negotiated

---

[15] Council and Commission Decision 98/181/EC, ECSC, Euratom of 23 Sept. 1997 on the conclusion by the European Communities, of the Energy Charter Treaty and the Energy Charter Protocol on energy efficiency and related environmental aspects [1998] OJ L69/1.

[16] COM(98)267, 6 May 1998.

[17] Annual Report of the Cohesion Fund, COM(98)543, 7 Oct. 1998.

a simplified consultation procedure for amendments, which concern only minor adjustments to the initial Commission decision.

The Cohesion Fund, in 1997, undertook an exercise in order to establish principles governing the eligibility of expenditure using part-financing with Cohesion Fund assistance. The final version of this document will be appended to all grant decisions from the Fund as a supplement to the financial implementing provisions.

Greece received 493.5 million Euros in assistance from the Cohesion Fund in 1997. Twenty-seven environmental projects were approved during 1997 and a total of 210.5 million Euros (42.65 per cent of the total 1997 allocation) was committed to the environment. In 1997, transport infrastructure accounted for 283 million Euros (57.35 per cent of the total) of Cohesion Fund support.

Spain received 1,514.6 million Euros, with 853.1 million Euros (56 per cent of the total) going to environmental projects and 661.5 million Euros (44 per cent of the total) to transport infrastructure. 1997 saw an increased emphasis on environment projects.

Ireland received 245.5 million Euros in 1997, with 134.1 million Euros (54.6 per cent of the total) going to environmental projects. Transport infrastructure accounted for 111.4 million Euros (45.4 per cent of the total).

Portugal received 493.2 million Euros in 1997, with 302 million Euros (61.2 per cent of the total) going to environmental projects and 191.2 million Euros (38.8 per cent of the total) to transport infrastructure.

The annual general government deficit target for Greece for 1997 was set at 4.2 per cent of GDP. The general government deficit for that year was 4 per cent of GDP. In view of assurances from the government and the inherent uncertainty of forecast figures, the Commission decided not to suspend Cohesion Fund financing for Greece. On 1 May 1998, the Council decided that Spain and Portugal each no longer had an excessive deficit. Since Ireland was not in an excessive deficit position, no decision was required.

In 1997, the Commission gave its agreement to a range of internal measures concerning integration. These are intended to ensure that greater account is taken of environmental considerations when policy and administrative decisions are taken. The European Parliament planned and adopted increased appropriations for the environment. As part of its policy on the dissemination of information, Parliament established the new budget heading B2–1600 ("Greening of the Budget"), and the cohesion countries are invited to submit new projects to spread good environmental practices resulting from investment by the Cohesion Fund in that country.

ii.   Implementation

The Commission has presented its fifteenth Annual Report on Monitoring the Application of Community Law for 1997.[18]

Following an own-initiative inquiry, the Ombudsman concluded that there was a general need to review the position of complainants in Article 226

---

[18]   COM(98)317, 19 May 1998 [1998] OJ C250/1.

(formerly Article 169) EC proceedings. The Ombudsman proposed, *inter alia*, that the Commission should seek the complainant's opinion before closing a case. In 1997, in response to this recommendation, the Commission stated:

Leaving aside cases where the complaint is obviously without foundation and cases where nothing further is heard from the complainant, the Commission will ensure that a complainant is informed of its intention to close a case.

The sector of environmental law gave rise to 18 per cent of the total number of infringement proceedings against Member States in 1997.[19] With particular regard to monitoring the implementation of environmental law, the Commission, in 1997, referred thirty-seven cases to the European Court of Justice and sent sixty-nine reasoned opinions to Member States, concerning the environmental sector.

The Commission set out its first requests for daily financial penalties under Article 228 (formerly Article 171) EC, in January 1997, which range from 26,000 Euros to 30,000 Euros per day. In 1997, approximately fifteen cases reached the Article 228 (formerly Article 171) EC letter or reasoned opinion stage, for failure to notify national implementing measures, incorrect transposition, or incorrect application.

The Commission notes that the delays in transposition can sometimes be attributed to the institutional and administrative structures of Member States. Also, in extremely technical fields, such as chemicals and biotechnology, some Member States clearly have problems keeping up the transposition rate for successive adaptations to technical progress. The Commission states that some proceedings for incorrect transposition could easily be avoided if other Member States would follow the example of Denmark, Germany, Finland, and Sweden, and would take the trouble to attach detailed explanations and concordance tables matching national provisions with the corresponding Community provisions, whenever they notified the Commission of legislation and regulations designed to transpose directives. The Commission's monitoring tasks are further complicated by the choice of certain legislative techniques for transposition (e.g. the use of several legal instruments). The Commission concludes, therefore, that there is a particular need to work more closely with Member States which choose such methods, in order to explain the details of transposition. Except in rare cases, complaints are concerned with problems in the application of Community law rather than the conformity of implementing measures or compliance with transposition deadlines. After having fallen for two years in succession, the number of complaints has now risen again. On analysing the complaints registered in 1997, the Commission has found that one in every two complaints was concerned with nature conservation and one in every four with environmental impact, while waste-related problems were raised in one in ten cases, as were air pollution and water pollution.

[19] Commission Press Release IP 98/519.

The Commission is of the opinion that the application of Community law might improve if national civil servants, in particular, were better informed about Community law and received better training.

Among the most common subjects of complaint are the refusal by national authorities to respond to requests for information, the time taken for replies, a tendency by national government departments to adopt an excessively broad interpretation when allowing exceptions to the principle of disclosure, and demands for payment of unreasonably high fees.

Complaints and petitions are also often primarily concerned with the quality of impact assessments (especially the lack of adequate assessment of the indirect effects of the project), and the lack of weight given to recommendations arising from the evaluation of the impact assessment (particularly following public enquiries) in the final decision. This last objection, in part, covers cases where work is started before the impact assessment has been completed, one of the other most common complaints.

There has been a significant drop in the number of infringement proceedings in the sector of air, mainly because implementing measures were notified for a number of directives, albeit late and often after the Commission had commenced proceedings. Problems persist in the application of directives dating from the 1980s, which are now being revised, and in respect of ozone and the incineration of waste.

Delays in the transposition of directives concerning chemicals and biotechnology adopting measures to new knowledge are all too frequent. In such cases, the Commission automatically commences proceedings.

Around a quarter of all current environmental infringement proceedings concern water.

The complaints about noise received by the Commission concerned ambient noise, which cannot be addressed as there is no overall Community policy regarding health and the quality of life. Nevertheless, proceedings were initiated in respect of an infringement of Council Directive 92/14/EEC on the Limitation of the Operation of Aeroplanes Covered by Part II, Chapter 2, Volume I of Annex 16 to the Convention on International Civil Aviation, Second Edition (1988).[20]

Several Member States have yet to comply fully with the Directive 75/442/EEC on Waste.[21] The related complaints were primarily concerned with the dumping of waste. Finally, the Commission is still receiving large numbers of complaints about infringements of Community legislation on nature. National laws still do not comply with Community law in the areas of hunting, regulation of species, trade, designation of areas fulfilling the objective ornithological criteria as Special Protection Areas, and projects affecting SPAs.

---

[20] [1992] OJ L76/21.
[21] [1975] OJ L194/39, as amended by Dir. 91/156/EEC [1991] OJ L78/32.

iii. Information

The European Environment Agency has issued its Annual Report for 1997, detailing its main achievements during the year.[22]

The installation phase of the telematics network of the European Environment Information and Observation Network (EIONET), began in March 1997. The final scheduled installation test for the entire network was undertaken in June 1997. The first phase, that of connecting the national focal points in Member States, was thus made operational. Significant progress was made during the year in developing each of the main elements of EIONET, e.g. the designation of national focal points by all Member States, and the designation of national reference centres by most Member States to help co-ordinate national activity with the various European topic centres.

A new European topic centre on Waste was established on 30 October 1997, bringing the number of topic centres supporting the Agency's network to nine. Co-operation with Eurostat and the European Community's joint research centre continued in 1997. A memorandum of understanding was signed between the European Environment Agency and the United Nations Environment Programme (UNEP) on 23 October 1997, in order to further develop mutually supportive reporting and networking activities.

The Agency's main achievements in 1997 in the area of monitoring and reporting include a first annual joint statement with UNEP on water stress in Europe, a report on air pollution in Europe; a pamphlet on air and health (with the WHO), a guidebook on sustainable development for local authorities, a report on voluntary environmental agreements; an expert's report on public access to environmental information, an educational package derived from the Dobris assessment; and the publication of various topic reports. In addition, much development and preparatory work was carried out in 1997 towards the state of the environment report entitled *Europe's Environment: The Second Assessment*, which the Agency was asked to prepare for the fourth Pan-European Conference of Environment Ministers, from 23 to 25 June 1998, in Århus (Denmark). Co-operation between the European Environment Agency and the European Green Spider Communication Network started in 1997.

The General European Multi-lingual Environmental Thesaurus (GEMET) was finalized in seven languages (including English) in 1997. The Thesaurus will be a major tool in the multi-lingual search for specialized environmental information, in providing a classification and description of information.

[22] European Environment Agency Annual Report 1997.

VIII.   Case Law of the European Court of Justice

KIERAN ST. C. BRADLEY*

A.   INTRODUCTION

April was indeed the cruellest month; the Court saw no reason to admit Greenpeace's challenge to a Commission financing decision alleged to contravene the Community's environmental policy. True, on the same day as Greenpeace got the red light, the Court acknowledged the legality of environmentally-driven differential rates of excise duty on national electricity production. However, by requiring that, in the circumstances, the lowest rate be applied to imported electricity, the Court in effect exempted an important source of energy from the whole scheme.

Various aspects of intra-state trade in, and management of, waste occupied the Court throughout the year, which also saw the usual sorry stream of Member States which had failed to comply with the Community's water protection legislation. A brace of judgments on the interpretation and validity of prohibition on hydrochlorofluorocarbons (HCFCs) provide a striking illustration of how effective regulations can be, as a means of ensuring environmental protection, as compared with directives. A number of judgments clarify the temporal and material scope of the Member States' obligations regarding environmental impact assessment. Nature conservation got a boost with the Court's upholding the Commission's complaint against the Netherlands for failing to classify sufficient habitats for endangered bird species, while in the first of what promises to be a large number of judgments on the interpretation of Directive 90/313/EEC on the Freedom of Access to Information on the Environment,[1] the Court was keen to keep the derogations allowed within reasonable bounds.

B.   AIR POLLUTION

The validity of the HCFC prohibition laid down by Regulation (EC) 3093/94[2] was upheld by the Court in July 1998, in two preliminary rulings arising from the delivery by the same Italian company of consignments of HCFCs for firefighting equipment.[3] The first question concerned the scope of the

---

* Distinguished lecturer on European law, Harvard University. (Spring 2000), and *Référendaire* at the Court of Justice, Luxembourg. The views expressed are personal to the author, and may not be attributed to the institution or to any member thereof. Please note that some of the cases referred to are afforded more detailed attention in the relevant sectoral reports of this survey.

[1] [1990] OJ L158/56.

[2] Council Reg. (EC) No. 3093/94 on substances that deplete the ozone layer [1994] OJ L333/1.

[3] Cases C–284/95, *Safety Hi-Tech* [1998] ECR I–4301 and C–341/95, *Bettati* [1998] ECR I–4355; for convenience, references are given to the former judgment only.

prohibition. As is its wont, the Court interpreted the Regulation in the light of the Community's international obligations, here the Vienna Convention and Montreal Protocol on the Protection of the Ozone Layer, before concluding that the use of HCFCs for firefighting was not amongst the exceptions exhaustively listed in Article 5(1) of the Regulation. The Court added that, though not expressly mentioned, the prohibition on use included a marketing prohibition.

On the main question, the applicant argued that the Regulation infringed Article 174 (formerly Article 130r) EC. The Council had based its decision only on the ozone depletion potential (ODP) of HCFCs, without taking account of their global warming potential (GWP) and atmospheric lifetime (ALT); by not banning more damaging substances, such as halons, the Council had failed to ensure the protection of the environment as a whole. Noting that its review was limited to a manifest error of appraisal, the Court held that the absence of a ban on halons could not affect the validity of a ban on HCFCs, and that Article 174 EC allowed the Community legislature to deal with specific aspects of environmental protection in a given measure. Though Article 174(2) EC required a high level of environmental protection,[4] this need not be the highest technically possible; otherwise Article 176 (formerly Article 130t) EC, allowing more stringent national measures, would be rendered nugatory. On its terms, the Regulation, contrary to Hi-Tech's claim, took account of the scientific and technical data available at the time of adoption and allowed for subsequent developments. The non-prohibition of halons was nonetheless considered relevant to the issue of proportionality; the Court noted that halons were irreplaceable substitutes for HCFCs for certain specific uses, such as firefighting in small spaces, and are of extremely low toxicity compared to the equivalent use of HCFCs. The prohibition did not therefore breach the principle of proportionality. Nor was it found to infringe the principle of the free movement of goods, environmental protection having long been recognized as "an imperative requirement which may limit the application of Article 28 [formerly Article 30] EC", which had already been held to be proportional to the stated aim of the Regulation.

C.   BIOTECHNOLOGY

A number of Member States were condemned for not transposing into their national law the Directives implementing the 1990 Directives on the contained use and the deliberate release of genetically modified (micro)organ-

---

[4] Léger AG took the view that this was merely a recommendation to the Community legislator (para. 67). However, this approach puts the bar too low; what if the legislator could be shown to have aimed at a demonstrably low level of protection? The Court's "manifest error" test is clearly preferable. The AG's affirmation (para. 55) that the environment is the only policy which benefits from an integration principle is misleading, in that similar principles are found in other areas of Community activity (see, e.g., Art. 151(4) (formerly Art. 128(4)), Art. 152(1) (formerly Art. 129(1)) EC third indent, Art. 157(3) (formerly Art. 130(3)) EC, Art. 159 (formerly Art. 130b) EC 1st subpara., and Art. 178 (formerly Art. 130v) EC).

isms.[5] The most extreme case was Luxembourg, which explained its failure to transpose the amending Directives by the fact that it had only transposed the two basic Directives in January 1997.[6] The major event of the year in this area, however, was undoubtedly the adoption of, and subsequent legal challenge to, Directive 98/44/EC on the Patent Protection of Biotechnological Inventions.[7]

D.   CHEMICALS

The proceedings in *Burstein* promised rather more than they ultimately delivered, which may explain why observations were submitted by no fewer than six governments, as well as the parties and the Commission.[8] The questions referred by the Administrative Court in Regensburg were infinitely more interesting than the answers supplied. In December 1992, the Commission authorized Germany to apply its Pentachlorophenol (PCP) Regulation,[9] rather than Directive 91/173/EEC[10] under the derogation allowed by Article 95(4) (formerly Article 100a(4)) EC. Two weeks later, the applicant was ordered to dispose of 120,000 boxes of army surplus ammunition, on the ground that, under the national provisions, this was a product treated with PCP. The Commission Decision was subsequently annulled for an insufficient statement of reasons, and re-adopted in September 1994.[11] However, as no authorization was in force at the time of the order to dispose of the ammunition, Mr Burstein challenged the compatibility with the Directive of the disposal order. Apart from an interpretation of its scope, the national court asked whether the Directive prohibited the application of a more stringent national provision pending the adoption of a Commission decision, whether the Community provision could be applied notwithstanding its annulment, and whether the ground for annulment was relevant in this regard, or whether the Directive could have direct effect. The Court held simply that the Directive does not apply to products treated with PCP, and hence that the Member States were free in principle to fix limit values for such products independently. It did not, therefore, reach the other questions referred.

In May 1998, Spain was found to have failed to adopt or communicate the programmes prescribed by Article 6 of Directive 91/157/EEC on Batteries and Accumulators Containing Certain Dangerous Substances.[12] Its defence that

---

[5] Dir. 94/15/EC concerning the adaptation to technical progress of Dir. 90/220/EEC on the deliberate release into the environment of genetically modified organisms [1994] OJ L103/20, and Dir. 94/51/EC concerning the adaptation to technical progress of Dir. 90/219/EEC on the contained use of genetically modified micro-organisms [1994] OJ L297/29.

[6] Case C–339/97, *Commission* v. *Luxembourg* [1998] ECR I–4903; see also Case C–285/97 *Commission* v. *Portugal* [1998] ECR I–4895.

[7] [1998] OJ L213/13; Case C–377/98, *Netherlands* v. *Parliament and Council* [1998] OJ C378/13.

[8] Case C–127/97 [1998] ECR I–6005.

[9] *Pentachlorphenolverbotsverordnung* [1989] *Bundesgesetzblatt* 2235.

[10] [1991] OJ L85/34.

[11] Case C–41/93, *France* v. *Commission* [1994] ECR I–1829; Commission Decision (EC) 94/783 [1994] OJ L316/43.

[12] [1991] L78/38; Case C–298/97 [1998] ECR I–3301.

programmes were not sufficient, that this provision required specific action to attain its objectives, and that gradual fulfilment was being achieved by initiatives taken by the autonomous communities, cut little ice with the Court, which noted the undisputed absence of the necessary programme, and added that "incomplete practical measures and fragmentary legislation cannot discharge [the] obligation . . . to draw up a comprehensive programme". In Case C–208/97, Portugal was found not to have complied with Directive 84/156/EEC on Limit Values and Quality Objectives for Mercury Discharges by Sectors Other Than the Chlor-alkali Electrolysis Industry.[13]

The Court's ruling in *Harpegnies* is of incidental interest, given the environmental protection content of the conditions under which pesticides may be marketed.[14] In this case a farmer had been charged with marketing unapproved plant protection products and trading in such products without authorization, though the order for reference failed to specify whether these were pesticides or biocides. As regards the former, the Court confirmed that a prior authorization was mandatory for marketing in a given Member State, notwithstanding that such authorization had already been granted in another Member State. For biocides, not subject to Community legislation at the time of the facts giving rise to the main proceedings, the Court held that a prior authorization was a restriction on trade between Member States, but that this was justified under Article 30 (formerly Article 36) EC.[15]

E.   NATURE CONSERVATION

The infringement proceedings in *Commission* v. *Netherlands*[16] were the first in which the Commission sought a declaration that a Member State had failed in its obligation under Article 4 of Directive 79/409/EEC (the Wild Birds Directive)[17] to classify special protections areas (SPAs) generally, rather than in relation to a particular site.[18] In essence, the Commission's claim was that the Netherlands had not classified sufficient sites, in number or in area. Its related complaint that the SPAs which had been classified were qualitatively insufficient, particularly as regards the protection of freshwater lakes and marshes, was ruled inadmissible by the Court, as it had not been raised at the pre-litigation stage. Though holding that under Article 4(1) of the Directive "Member States must classify as SPAs sufficient territories, in terms of quantity and quality, to ensure conservation of the species listed in Annex I", a mere

[13] [1984] OJ L74/49; [1998] ECR I–4017.

[14] Case C–400/96 [1998] ECR I–5121; see also Case C–303/94, *Parliament* v. *Council* [1996] ECR I–2943, on the Court's willingness to enforce these conditions in implementing legislation. It is, incidentally, rather anomalous that pesticides should be treated as an agricultural product under Art. 37 (formerly Art. 43) EC.

[15] See also Case C–293/94, *Brandsma* [1996] ECR I–3159.

[16] Case C–3/96 [1998] ECR I–3031.

[17] [1979] OJ L103/1, as amended; the amendments were not material to these proceedings.

[18] See Case C–355/90, *Commission* v. *Spain* ('*Santoña Marshes*') [1993] ECR I–4221; the matter can also arise in requests for preliminary rulings: Case C–44/95, *Royal Society for the Protection of Birds* [1996] ECR I–3805.

allegation of a breach of this provision did not necessarily cover the qualitative aspects.[19] The Court also dealt with two other admissibility points of note. It held that the Commission was entitled to refer in its application to the failure to classify two particular sites, in order to illustrate the general claim of insufficient classification, without these being considered allegations of specific breaches. On the other hand, the Commission was not permitted to rely on an ornithological study which had been drawn up after the expiry of the deadline for compliance with the reasoned opinion.

In ruling on the merits of the complaint the Court held as follows:

— a Member State may not avoid its obligation to classify SPAs by resorting to other conservation methods, such as the adoption of a nature conservation law, the sale of sites to nature conservation organizations and the adoption of bird conservation plans;

— "if [endangered] species occur on the territory of a Member State, it is obliged to define, *inter alia*, SPAs for them";

— Article 4 of the Directive requires "a system of specifically targeted and reinforced protection" for endangered species, *a fortiori*, since Article 3 of the Directive already provides for the creation of protected areas for all wild birds species covered by the Directive.

The Court added that the classification of SPAs was required to ensure that a coherent networks of such areas, as provided for in Article 4(3) of the Directive, could be created. Recalling that the classification of SPAs was subject to ornithological criteria to the exclusion of economic requirements,[20] the Court went on to hold that the Member States' margin of discretion was restricted to the application of those criteria for identifying the most suitable territories for the conservation of the species listed in Annex I. Once so identified, the obligation to classify the particular site as an SPA is automatic.[21] It therefore rejected the Netherlands' argument that the Commission must establish a series of breaches in relation to specific sites, in circumstances in which the number and total area of the sites are "manifestly less" than required. The Netherlands' slightly erratic attack[22] on the probative value of the much-quoted 1989 ornithological survey *Inventory of Important Bird Areas in the European Community* (IBA 89) fared no better, as it failed to produce the criteria its rival national survey was based on. While holding that "IBA 89 has proved to be the only document containing scientific evidence making it possible to assess whether the defendant state has fulfilled its obligation to classify SPAs", the Court indicated that it would be willing to consider such other

---

[19] Ibid., para. 31.

[20] This arises from *Santoña Marshes*, and was reaffirmed with particular clarity in *RSPB* (see n. 18 above).

[21] In his Opinion, Fennelly AG makes an analogy with the limited discretion Member States enjoy in deciding on whether Annex II projects should be subject to an environmental impact assessment (Opinion, para. 42, n. 23). This analogy was suggested by the referring court in Case C–72/95 *Kraaijeveld* [1996] ECR I–5403, paras. 44, 49, and 50; see also Case C–225/96, discussed below.

[22] Judgment, paras. 65–73; Opinion, paras. 47–57.

scientific evidence as was produced. The Court concluded that "by classifying as SPAs territories whose number and total area are clearly smaller that the number and total area of the territories suitable for classification as SPAs" the Netherlands had failed in its obligations under Article 4(1) of the Directive.

A request for access to the opinions of the legal services of the Council and the Commission, on the adequacy of Article 308 (formerly Article 235) EC as the legal basis of the Directive was at the origin of the annulment proceedings in *Carlsen and Others*, in which the president of the Court of First Instance rejected a request for interim measures in March 1998.[23] The Court of Justice has never ruled on the matter, though Advocate General Fennelly proffered some helpful observations justifying the reliance on this legal basis in rejecting a United Kingdom argument seeking to put an economic slant on the interpretation of the Directive in *RSBP*.[24]

Germany's long-standing failure to transpose Directive 92/43/EEC on the Conservation of Natural Habitats and of Wild Fauna and Flora (the Habitats Directive),[25] was condemned by the Court in December 1997.[26]

While perhaps not directly relevant to the Wild Birds or Habitats Directives, the Court's judgment in *Annibaldi* illustrates some of the problems to which the classification of sites for environmental protection purposes can give rise at the national level.[27] Just over half an agricultural holding owned by the applicant farmer lay within a park created, *inter alia*, to protect the value of the local environment. Refused permission to plant a three-hectare orchard, he claimed the regional law designating the park breached his fundamental right to property and to carry on a business. While noting that Member States are bound to respect such rights when implementing Community policy, the Court held that nothing in the contested law suggested that it was implementing provisions on either agriculture or the environment; the regional law was found to apply to a situation which does not fall within the scope of Community law as it stands at present. The matter could arise in relation to SPAs or SACs (special areas of conservation), particularly where the latter are classified by the Council under Article 5(3) of the Habitats Directive.[28]

F. NOISE EMISSIONS

The applicant in *Aher-Waggon GmbH*[29] was refused permission in 1992 to register in Germany a Piper PA 28–140 aircraft, registered in Denmark since 1974. The relevant provisions applied stricter noise limits for non-German aircraft first registered prior to the implementation of Directive 80/51/EEC on the Limitations of Noise Emissions from Subsonic Aircraft[30] than either those laid

---

[23] Case T–610/97, *Carlsen and Others* v. *Council* [1998] ECR II–485; the main action was subsequently withdrawn.

[24] Case C–44/95, *Royal Society for the Protection of Birds* [1996] ECR I–3805, 3823–6 (paras. 42–49); these were in turn quoted with approval by Jacobs AG in *Outokumpu Oy* (see section J(i) below).

[25] [1992] OJ L206/7.

[26] Case C–83/97 [1997] ECR I–7191.

[27] Case C–309/96 [1997] ECR I–7493.

[28] [1992] OJ L206/7.

[29] Case C–389/96 [1998] ECR I–4473.

[30] [1980] OJ L18/26.

down by the Directive or those applied to old domestic aircraft, which were exempted from compliance with the Directive. The national court referred a question concerning the compatibility of this scheme with the principle of the free movement of goods.

Though noting that the Directive allowed Member States to lay down stricter standards, the Court found the national provisions to restrict intra-Community trade. The restriction was nonetheless held to be justified by considerations of public health and environmental protection. On the question of the proportional character of the scheme, the Court accepted Germany's contention that limiting aircraft noise emissions is the most effective and convenient means of combating the noise pollution they generate, and that, as old domestic aircraft were required to comply with the stricter standards whenever subject to technical modification of any kind or a temporary withdrawal from service, their numbers would necessarily fall, bringing overall noise pollution levels down gradually. The effectiveness of this policy would, the Court held, be undermined if the fleet could be increased by aircraft from other Member States, whose numbers the national authorities could not control.

Belgium and Italy were both condemned during 1998 for failing to transpose Directive 95/271/EC amending Directive 86/662/EEC on the Limitation of Noise Emitted by Hydraulic Excavators, Rope-operated Excavators, Dozers, Loaders and Excavator-loaders.[31]

G.   WASTE

The ruling requested by the Belgian Conseil d'Etat in *Inter-Environnement Wallonie*[32] threw up two questions, one more limited, on the scope of the notion of "waste" in Directive 75/442/EEC on Waste (Waste Framework Directive),[33] and one of major constitutional significance, both in the field of environmental legislation and beyond. The first question was whether a substance is excluded from the definition of "waste" because it directly or indirectly forms an integral part of an industrial production process. On the interpretation of this term, which had exercised the Court some months before in *Tombesi*,[34] the Court held that its meaning turned on the meaning of "discard", and that discard included both disposal and recovery of a substance or object. Nothing in the Directive excluded, in principle, "any kind of residue, industrial by-product or other substance arising from production processes", and therefore held that these were "waste", notwithstanding the difficulty which may arise in distinguishing recovery of waste from the normal

---

[31] [1986] OJ L384/1; Cases C–326/97, *Commission v. Belgium* [1998] ECR I–6107 and C–324/97, *Commission v. Italy* [1998] ECR I–6099.

[32] 1997] ECR I–7411; see H. Somsen (1998) 7 *European Environmental Law Review* 88.

[33] [1975] OJ L194/39 as amended by Dir. 91/156/EEC [1991] OJ L78/32.

[34] Joined Cases C–304/94, *Tombesi et al.* [1997] ECR I–3561; see also M. Purdue, "The Distinction between Using Raw Materials and the Recovery of Waste", and the comment by A. van Rossem (1998) 10 *Journal of Environmental Law* 136.

industrial treatment of non-waste products, such as residues and secondary
raw materials.

The second question was whether Community law precluded a Member
State from adopting a provision contrary to a Directive (*in casu*, the
Framework Waste Directive), in the period between the adoption of the
Directive and the expiry of the deadline for compliance. The Court's balanced
but unequivocal answer was as follows: all the authorities of a Member State,
including the courts, are bound to take the measures necessary to achieve the
result prescribed by a Directive, which has legal effect from the moment of its
notification; though not obliged to transpose a Directive before the date fixed,
the Member States must, during that period, "refrain from taking any measure
liable seriously to compromise the result prescribed"; it is for the national
court in each case to assess the validity of such national provisions, taking
account in particular of whether these purport to constitute full and definitive
transposition, or are merely transitional measures which can be replaced or
amended before the date for compliance.

The judgment in *Chemische Afvalstoffen Dusseldorp*[35] addresses a number
of issues concerning the movement of waste between Member States, the regulation of which, despite indications to the contrary,[36] emerges as the real *rai-
son d'être* of Title II of Regulation (EEC) No. 259/93 on the Supervision and
Control of Shipments of Waste Within, Into and Out of the European
Community (Waste Shipments Regulation).[37] The applicant company was
refused authorization to export two consignments of oil filters and related
waste to Germany, under Dutch provisions, which restricted such export
where disposal in the state of import was not considered to be at an equivalent
level; it therefore challenged the compatibility of these provisions with
Community law.

On a close reading of the text and legislative history of the Waste Shipments
Regulation and the Framework Waste Directive, the Court concluded that
these did not provide for the application of the principles of self-sufficiency
and proximity to waste for recovery. The Court held that the difference in the
treatment of such waste and of waste for disposal reflects the different roles
played by each type of waste in the development of the Community's environmental policy. By definition, only waste for recovery can contribute towards

---

[35] Case C–203/96 [1998] ECR I–4075.

[36] In Case C–187/93, *Parliament* v. *Council* [1995] ECR I–2857, though acknowledging that Title
II sets out the conditions governing shipments of waste between Member States, the Court held
that these provisions were not of an internal market character, largely on the ground that Member
States were permitted to prevent such shipments. By so doing, the Court appears to have ignored
its own warning against defining the objective of a measure on the basis of a single element taken
in isolation (recently reaffirmed in Case C–180/96, *United Kingdom* v. *Commission* [1998] ECR
I–2265, para. 66). The fact that trade in waste could legitimately be impeded reflects the integration principle of Art. 174(2) (formerly Art. 130r(2)) EC, but does not change the character of the
Regulation; Member States could have implemented self-sufficiency and proximity, but not
traded in waste, without it.

[37] [1993] OJ L30/1.

implementation of the principle of priority for recovery laid down in Article 4(3) of the Regulation.[38]

The Court went on to note that the Regulation had provided for the free movement of waste for recovery, in order to encourage recovery in the Community as a whole, which precluded the application of self-sufficiency and proximity. Nor could the application of these principles be justified by reference to either Article 176 (formerly Article 130t) EC or Article 30 (formerly Article 36) EC in the present case, as the national provisions were motivated by essentially economic concerns and the export of the waste in question had not been shown to pose a threat to the environment or human health.[39]

The classification of waste in the green, amber, and red lists annexed to the Waste Shipments Regulation, and the interpretation of the term "storage", were examined in the judgment in *Beside*, delivered the same day.[40] The applicants in the main proceedings had shipped waste, which they argued should be considered "green", from Germany to the Netherlands without notification, and had stored it prior to sale to the Far East. The consignments were found to be non-homogenous, being plastic mixed with paper, cardboard, metals, wood, glass, textiles, and, in one bale, six rounds of live ammunition. As the Netherlands authorities took the view that the waste was "municipal/household waste" on the amber list, and that the shipment was hence illegal, the applicants were ordered to return the waste to Germany.

The first question was whether a consignment comprising mainly waste classified in the green list should be classified in the Amber List, where mixed either with other green waste or with small quantities of materials not on the green list. The intervening governments suggested a variety of classification tests: origin of the waste, homogeneity of the batch, separate collection and sorting. Recalling that the Waste Shipments Regulation had laid down a common definition of waste,[41] the Court rejected the origin test, and held that "municipal/household waste" remains on the amber list, unless it has been collected separately or properly sorted. Waste may not be moved as green waste if so contaminated by other materials as to present a risk justifying inclusion on the amber or red lists or as to prevent recovery in an environmentally sound manner.

On a reading of the relevant provisions of the Regulation and the Framework Waste Directive, the Court held that "storage is expressly included in the definitions of both disposal and recovery operations". As both recovery and disposal of the waste and its shipment give rise to a risk to the environment, "it is of no importance whether a particular batch of waste is stored at the place where it is finally subjected to a recovery operation, or at some other place", or whether the recovery takes place inside or outside the Community. The Court also held that, in order to establish that "green waste" not subject to

---

[38] Ibid., para. 33.
[39] The Court also dealt with the competition aspects of the Netherlands' scheme, which are not directly relevant in the present context.
[40] Case C–192/96 [1998] ECR I–4029.   [41] Case C–304/94, *Tombesi et al.* [1997] ECR I–3561.

notification is intended for recovery, the competent authorities must, as a minimum, be able to require the information specified in Article 11 of the Regulation.

H. WATER

The implementation of Directive 76/464/EEC on Pollution Caused by Certain Dangerous Substances Discharged into the Aquatic Environment of the Community[42] continues to cause the Member States problems. In *Commission* v. *Greece*,[43] the defendant Member State was condemned for failing to adopt specific programmes for the reduction of pollution from List II substances, in Lake Vegorrítis, the River Soulos, and the Gulf of Pagasaí. A separate plea, regarding the failure to make discharges of industrial waste containing List II substances conditional on an authorization, was deemed to be subsumed into that concerning the establishment of programmes, as such authorizations could only contain emission standards calculated in accordance with quality objectives previously laid down in a water protection programme. A further complaint regarding Greece's alleged failure to adopt measures for the control of urban waste water discharges into Lake Vegorrítis and the River Soulos was rejected, as one water purification plant was already in operation, and a second was under construction.

Luxembourg was also in the dock for not implementing the abovementioned Directive, though the breach was of a more general character, concerning the failure to adopt programmes to reduce pollution in respect of ninety-nine List I substances which, pending the fixing of limit values, are to be treated as List II substances.[44] The Court did not accept Luxembourg's initial defence, that there are no waste-producing industrial or commercial sectors in the Grand Duchy which process any of these substances and, indeed, at the hearing the government conceded that some of the substances covered by the Directive were discharged into the aquatic environment. Italy and Spain were also condemned for failing to transpose the same Directive,[45] while Portugal was condemned for failing to transpose Directive 86/280/EEC on Limit Values and Quality Objectives of Certain Dangerous Substances included in the Annex I list[46] and Directive 88/347/EEC which implement Directive 76/464/EEC in respect of certain substances.[47]

Spain put up a stout but ultimately unsuccessful defence in proceedings for failure to comply with Directive 76/160/EEC Concerning the Quality of Bathing Water,[48] in respect of inshore bathing waters.[49] The Court rejected the suggested justifications, based on the facts that modifications to the Directive

---

[42] [1976] OJ L129/33.   [43] Joined Cases C–232/95 and 233/95 [1998] ECR I–3343.
[44] Case C–206/96, *Commission* v. *Luxembourg* [1998] ECR I–3401.
[45] Cases C–285/96, *Commission* v. *Italy* [1998] ECR I–5935 and C–214/96, *Commission* v. *Spain* [1998] ECR I–7661.
[46] [1986] OJ L181/16.   [47] Case C–213/97, *Commission* v. *Portugal* [1998] ECR I–3298.
[48] [1976] OJ L31/1.
[49] Case C–92/96, *Commission* v. *Spain* [1998] ECR I–505; see Somsen, n. 32 above, at 121.

were envisaged, that a related Directive allowed a longer deadline for compliance, and that bathers had abandoned a large number of the bathing areas in question in favour of swimming pools.[50] While Article 5(2) of the Directive, allowing derogations in case of abnormal weather conditions, could in principle include drought, Spain had failed to prove either that the drought on which it relied was abnormal, or that the drought had prevented compliance with the standards set by the Directive.

Italy sought to argue that it had implemented Directive 79/923/EEC on the Quality Required of Shellfish Waters[51] by designating waters in number and surface area which were "reasonably proportionate" to the total coast and brackish waters, and contended that the fact that only three out of the fifteen regions with access to the sea had not designated waters was insufficient to constitute a breach.[52] Using language strongly reminiscent of that which it employs in relation to the classification of SPAs (see section E above), the Court acknowledged a discretion for the Member States to determine whether particular shellfish waters need protection or improvement in order to support shellfish. However, should those conditions obtain, then the Member States are obliged to designate, and nothing in the Directive allows gradual implementation.

Portugal was condemned by the Court, in uncontested infringement actions, for its failure to properly transpose into national law three further directives concerning water protection measures: Directive 75/440/EEC on the Quality Required of Surface Water Intended for the Abstraction of Drinking Water,[53] Directive 79/869/EEC Concerning the Methods of Measurement and Frequencies of Sampling and Analysis of Surface Water Intended for the Abstraction of Drinking Water,[54] and Directive 80/68/EEC on the Protection of Groundwater Against Pollution Caused by Certain Dangerous Substances.[55] Spain was also condemned for failing to designate vulnerable zones, to establish codes of good agricultural practice, and to notify these to the Commission, under Directive 91/676/EEC on the protection of water against pollution caused by nitrates from agricultural sources.[56]

I. HORIZONTAL INSTRUMENTS

i. *Environmental Impact Assessment*

The Court had an opportunity during the year to clarify and explain the temporal application of Directive 85/337/EEC on the Assessment of the Effects of Certain Public and Private Projects on the Environment (EIA Directive),[57] as it

---

[50] On this last point, Lenz AG pointed out that the abandonment of such haunts could be due to the low quality of the water rather than a change of social habits (n. 49 above, para. 38, 518; para. 43, 519).

[51] [1979] OJ L281/47.

[52] Case C-225/96, *Commission* v. *Italy* [1997] ECR I-6887; see Somsen, n. 32 above, at 119.

[53] [1975] OJ L194/26; Case C-214/97 [1998] ECR I-3839.

[54] [1979] OJ L271/44; Case C-229/97 [1998] ECR I-6059.

[55] [1980] OJ L20/43; Case C-183/97 [1998] ECR I-4005.

[56] [1991] OJ L375/1; Case C-71/97 [1998] ECR I-5991.   [57] [1985] OJ L175/40.

arises from *Bund Naturschutz* and *Commission* v. *Germany*.[58] In *Haarlemmerliede en Spaarnwoude*,[59] the Dutch Council of State asked the Court whether the EIA Directive applied to projects for which consent had been given, without any environmental assessment, before the transposition date (3 July 1988), but where the consent had not been acted upon and where a fresh consent procedure had been initiated after 3 July 1988. *In limine*, the Court noted that the question whether an approval procedure constitued "consent" for the purposes of Article 1(2) of the Directive was within the purview of the national court. Here the referring court had established that it was. Recalling that nothing in the Directive allowed exemptions for consent procedures initiated after the transposition date (*Bund Naturschutz*), the Court explained the exclusion of projects initiated before, and still in progress on, that date as follows:

the Directive is primarily designed to cover large-scale projects which will often require a long time to complete. It would therefore not be appropriate for the relevant procedures, which are already complex at the national level . . . to be made more cumbersome and time-consuming by the specific requirements imposed by the Directive, and for situations already established to be affected by it.[60]

The Court found this not to be the case here, as the proceedings concerned a fresh application for consent, and the considerations which had justified its decision in *Commission* v. *Germany* did not apply. Any other solution would run counter to the wording of Article 2 of the Directive, and compromise its effectiveness.

Meanwhile, Germany was in trouble again for its implementation of the Directive in October 1998.[61] The Commission's complaint was upheld on four grounds:

— late transposition: the fact that the Court had already ruled on this in *Bund Naturschutz* was irrelevant, as only infringement proceedings allowed the Court to reach a formal finding that a Member State had failed in its obligations. The Court added ominously that a "formal finding is a prerequisite for the initiation, where appropriate, of the procedure provided for in Article 228 [formerly Article 171] EC", to wit the possibility of the imposition of a fine or penalty payment;
— failure to communicate the relevant provisions adopted by the *Länder*: the scope of the obligation applies to all provisions transposing the Directive, regardless of the federal or unitary structure of the state; the fact that the federal provisions may take precedence does not obviate the need to communicate those of the *Länder*;
— failure to apply the Directive to all projects for which consent was given after 3 July 1988: the national implementing law, the UVPG, came into

---

[58] Case C–396/92 [1994] ECR I–3717, and Case C–431/92, [1995] ECR I–2189, respectively.
[59] Case C–81/96 [1998] ECR I–3923.   [60] Ibid., para. 24.
[61] Case C–301/95 [1998] ECR I–6135.

force only on 1 August 1990, and the finding in *Bund Naturschutz* is again not relevant;

— incomplete transposition, as regards Annex II projects: Article 4(2) of the Directive is designed to facilitate the examination of particular projects, in order to determine whether they are subject to the assessment requirement. Each of the sub-headings indicated by a number and a letter in Annex II is a class of project, and Member States may not exempt in advance of whole classes of projects.

ii. Access to Environmental Information

The implications of the Court's approach to the interpretation of Directive 90/313/EEC on the Freedom of Access to Information on the Environment,[62] and particularly of the restrictions on access, in *Mecklenburg*[63] may well extend beyond the confines of the environmental policy to that of transparency in general.[64] In the absence of any transposition measure at the time, the applicant relied directly on the Directive in requesting access to the statement of views of the competent countryside protection authority on a road construction project. The applicant was refused on the dual grounds that the statement was not environmental information, but merely an assessment of such information, and that the development consent procedure was a "preliminary investigation proceeding", regarding which access could be refused under Article 3(2) of the Directive.

Noting that the concept of "information relating to the environment" was broadly defined to embrace "both information and activities relating to the state of [various] aspects of the environment", the Court held that this phrase included any "act capable of adversely affecting or protecting the state of one of the sectors of the environment covered by the directive".[65] On the scope of "investigation proceeeding", the Court held:

as a derogation from the general rules laid down by the Directive, Article 3(2), third indent, may not be interpreted in such a way as to extend its effects beyond what is necessary to safeguard the interests which it seeks to secure. Furthermore, the scope of [such] derogations . . . must be determined in the light of the aims pursued by the Directive.[66]

Referring to both the legislative history of the Directive and all the language versions of this provision, the Court concluded that the exemption covered an investigation only where this "immediately precedes a contentious or quasi-contentious procedure and arises from the need to obtain proof or to investigate a matter prior to the opening of the actual procedure".[67] Following the ruling in this case, a second request for a preliminary ruling from the German courts was withdrawn.[68] Germany is still not out of the woods in this regard;

[62] [1990] OJ L158/56. [63] Case C–321/96 [1998] ECR I–3809.
[64] See K. Bradley, "La Transparence de l'Union européenne: une évidence ou un trompe l'oeil?" (1999) 35 *Cahiers de droit européen*, 283.
[65] Ibid., para. 21. [66] Ibid., para. 25. [67] Ibid., para. 30.
[68] Case C–296/97, *Gloger* v. *Bergamt Kamen*, unpublished order of 7 Oct. 1998.

the Court gave judgment on an infringement action in respect of certain aspects of the *Umweltinformationsgesetz* in September 1999.[69]

J. MISCELLANEOUS

i. Differentiated Environmental Taxes

In *Outokumpu Oy*, apparently the first ruling requested by a Finnish court to come to judgment, the Court was asked to assess the compatibility with Article 90 (formerly Article 95) EC of a flat-rate duty on the import of electricity, which was higher than the duty imposed on certain forms of national electricity production and lower than others.[70] Under the relevant national provisions, nuclear electricity was subject to an excise duty of 2.4 p/kWh, hydroelectric power 0.4 p/kWh, and imported electricity 2.2 p/kWh. In a potentially significant statement of principle, the Court held:

Article 90 [formerly Article 95] EC . . . does not preclude the rate of an internal tax on electricity from varying according to the manner in which the electricity is produced and the raw material used for its production, in so far as that differentiation is based . . . on environmental considerations.[71]

On the facts of the case, despite an eloquent plea by Advocate General Jacobs, the Court found that the Finnish scheme fell foul of Article 90 (formerly Article 95) EC, and could not be justified by the practical difficulties in applying differential rates to imported electricity; in particular, the importer could not benefit from the lower rate, even if he could show his electricity were produced in the more environmentally friendly fashion.

ii. Risk Assessment, Prevention and Integration

Amongst the issues dealt with by the Court, in ruling on the validity of the Commission's 1996 ban on the export of British beef,[72] were those of risk assessment and prevention. In answering the UK's argument that the Commission was not empowered by the relevant legislation to impose the ban, the Court noted that the significant alteration of the perception of the risk to human health, which resulted from the announcement of the link between BSE and Creutzfeldt-Jakob disease, authorized the Commission to adopt the contested safeguard measures. In these circumstances, the Commission had not therefore clearly exceeded the bounds of its discretion. On the question of the proportionality of imposing such a ban, the Court held:

---

[69] Case C–217/97, *Commission v. Germany*, judgment of 9 Sept. 1999, not yet reported; the major point at issue is the interpretation of Art. 5 of the Directive, regarding the "reasonable costs" which may be charged.

[70] Case C–213/96 [1998] ECR I–1777.   [71] *Ibid.*, para. 31.

[72] Case C–180/96, *United Kingdom v. Commission* [1998] ECR I–2265; see also Case C–157/96, *National Farmers' Union* [1998] ECR I–2211; for convenience, citations are given from the former judgment only.

[where] there is uncertainty as to the existence or extent of risks to human health, the institutions may take protective measures without having to wait until the reality and seriousness of those risks become fully apparent.[73]

The Court based this latter statement on the inclusion of public health in the Community's environmental policy, and the principle of preventive action and the integration principle contained in Article 157 (formerly Article 130(2)) EC.

iii.   *VAT and Premiums for Less Intensive Farming*

In *Landboden-Agrardienste GmbH*,[74] the Court held that the extensification of potato production under a public scheme is not the supply of services, and that VAT is not therefore payable on the compensation awarded to the producer.

iv.   Locus standi

The proceedings in *Stichting Greenpeace International* were initiated before the Court of First Instance in 1993 by fifteen individuals and three environmental associations to challenge a Commission decision granting financial assistance of some 12 million ECU to Spain for the construction of two power stations in the Canary Islands. The application was dismissed by a three-judge chamber of that court, for want of individual concern.[75] The decision of the Court of Justice to hear the appeal in a full plenary formation (few enough appeals even make it to judgment, and full plenary consideration is almost unheard of) might have been read in some quarters[76] as indicating a willingness, at least, to consider relaxing the traditional interpretation of *locus standi* under Article 230 (formerly Article 173) EC in the untraditional area of environmental protection. If so, those hopes were to be dashed. In a brief judgment, following the conclusions of the much more expansive opinion of Advocate General Cosmas, the Court held that the only rights on which the applicants relied were those arising under the Environmental Impact Assessment Directive, that the contested financing decision affected those rights only indirectly and that effective judicial protection could be secured by the national proceedings Greenpeace had initiated before the Spanish courts "which may, if need be, refer a question to [the] Court for a preliminary ruling under Article 234 [formerly Article 177] EC".[77]

That "direct and individual concern", as interpreted heretofore, was likely to prove an obstacle to the admissibility of annulment actions seeking to vindicate environmental rights is hardly news. It is in the nature of environmental law that protection claims for breach can generally not be squeezed into the straitjacket of Article 230 (formerly Article 173) EC, which was designed, as regards non-privileged parties, to allow the defence of discrete economic interests, not diffuse ecological values. In giving judgment, the Court was of

---

[73] Ibid., para. 99.
[74] Case C–384/95 [1997] ECR I–7387.   [75] Case T–585/93 [1995] ECR II–2205.
[76] Though a number of cases were dealt with the plenary Court around this period for organizational reasons, in the run-up to the partial renewal of the Court in Oct. 1997.
[77] Case C–321/95P [1998] ECR I–1651.

course conscious that attempts at Amsterdam, if any, to broaden the *locus standi* of individuals by amending this provision had failed, and indeed the narrowness of its current jurisdiction in this regard was one of the few substantive points raised by the Court itself in its May 1995 Report on certain aspects of the application of the Treaty on European Union, albeit in another context.[78] Of course, interpreting the "sounds of silence", if this indeed formed any part of the Court's unspoken reasoning, is a notoriously dangerous exercise, one which has already served the Court badly on at least one previous occasion where it was considering the scope of Article 230 (formerly Article 173) EC, *ratione personae*.[79]

It is easy in reading the judgment to forget the basis of the *Greenpeace* challenge. In assessing the necessity to review the existing case law on *locus standi* in the light of the specificity of environmental interests, the Court expressly held that the decision to build the power stations was "liable to affect the environmental rights, arising under the Environmental Impact Assessment Directive, that the appellants [sought] to invoke". However, in these proceedings the appellants were neither challenging the construction of the power stations (the action was against the Commission, and no-one contended that the Commission was in the construction business) nor relying directly upon the Directive, which is addressed to the Member States, not the Community institutions. Their complaint was instead that the Commission had failed to respect Article 7 of Council Regulation (EEC) No. 2052/88,[80] to wit, to comply with "the provisions of the Treaties, with the instruments adopted pursuant thereto and with Community policies, including . . . those concerning environmental protection";[81] the alleged breach of Article 7 of the Regulation by the Commission would not necessarily depend on an infringement of the Environmental Impact Assessment Directive by Spain, and vice versa.[82] The question facing the Court was therefore how such an obligation, which is much broader than that found in the Directive, could be enforced, when the Member States (and, hence, the Council) would not, and the European Parliament could not, challenge the disbursement of large amounts of regional funds to the Member States. Was the Court forgetting its grand declaration that:

[78] The matter was raised in relation to the protection of fundamental rights (Court of Justice, Luxembourg, 1995), 10, para. 20.

[79] Amongst the considerations which influenced the Court to refuse the European Parliament even a limited *locus standi* to initiate annulment proceedings in the so-called *Comitology* judgment was the fact that its prerogatives "[had] been augmented by the Single European Act . . . without any changes having been made to Art. 230 [formerly Art. 173] EC" (Case 302/87, *Parliament* v. *Council* [1988] ECR 5615, 5644, para. 26). The Court was forced to backtrack from this ill-advised stance just twenty-two months later (Case C–70/88, *Parliament* v. *Council* [1990] ECR I–2041).

[80] Council Reg. (EEC) 2052/88 on the tasks of the structural funds and their effectiveness and on coordination of their activities between themselves and with the operations of the European Investment Bank and the other existing financial instruments [1988] OJ L185/9.

[81] Though cited correctly by the AG at para. 6 of his Opinion, by para. 63 this had shrunk to "Community policies" and, by para. 66, to "Community environmental legislation".

[82] If the two were not related, the Court's analysis of the "effective judicial protection" guaranteed by the national proceedings initiated by *Greenpeace* would be rather undermined.

the . . . Community is a Community based on the rule of law, in as much as neither its Member States nor its institutions can avoid a review of the question whether the measures adopted by them are in conformity with the basic constitutional charter, the Treaty?[83]

An order of 7 May 1998, in proceedings by Ireland against the Commission, indirectly provides a footnote to the related case of *An Taisce*.[84] It appears that in 1997 the Commission reduced the regional funding for Ireland's 1989–93 tourism programme, in respect, *inter alia*, of the Burren National Park, the development of which had given rise to proceedings in both the national and the Community courts and questions and debates, even a proposed motion of censure, which was subsequently withdrawn, in the European Parliament.[85] The row at the Community level ended (if end it did) not with a bang, but a whimper; Ireland's application to annul the Commission's decision was submitted three days late, owing to a delayed aircraft arrival in Brussels and an intervening weekend, and was ruled out of time.

---

[83] Case 294/83, *Les Verts* v. *European Parliament* [1986] ECR 1339, 1365, para. 23.

[84] Case T–461/93, *An Taisce and WWF* v. *Commission* [1994] ECR II–733, and, on appeal, C–325/94P [1996] ECR I–3727; see also Case T–105/95, *WWF UK* v. *Commission* [1997] ECR II–313, on access to Commission documents on the matter.

[85] For the national proceedings, see in particular *Howard* v. *Commissioners of Public Works in Ireland* [1994] 1 IR 101 and 123; for details of the proceedings in the European Parliament, see comment by K. Bradley and A. Feeney (1994) 13 *Yearbook of European Law* 383, 409–10.

Environmental Law in the Member States

I. Austria

Karl Weber*

A. INTRODUCTION

Recent reforms of and developments in Austrian environmental law were partly inspired by the development of EC law, which in turn necessitated changes to national law. At the same time, the legislation tried to streamline and simplify the complicated *ad hoc* body of environmental law and to enrich this branch of law with modern instruments and procedures. Because of global competition, the legislature's priorities were to keep economic operators in Austria, ruling out an over-progressive protection policy.

A central problem with the development of environmental law is the rather obscure system of allocation of competences in the federal structure of Austria, which is extremely complex. It is based on the constitutional law of the Austro-Hungarian Monarchy, as expressed in the federal Constitution of 1920.[1] Environmental protection being a "cross-section-matter" (*Querschnittsmaterie*), almost every measure first needs to negotiate the legal hurdle of allocation of competences. As a result, comprehensive measures for environmental protection can be realized only after tenacious negotiations and compromises between the federation and the states (*Länder*).

The following account of developments of Austrian environmental law concerns 1998, although some acts of 1997 which became effective the following year are sometimes taken into consideration.

B. AIR POLLUTION

One of the most important environmental protection acts is the "Emission Protection Law—Air"(hereafter, IG-L).[2] Its aim is the protection of human health, flora and fauna, eco-systems, as well as cultural property against the effects of air pollution and the precautionary reduction of air pollution. To achieve this goal, the law contains a variety of measures and procedures for the reduction of pollution.

* Professor of Law, University of Innsbruck.
[1] P. Pernthaler, *Kompetenzverteilung in der Krise* (Wien: Institut für Föderalismusforschung—Innsbruck, 1989).
[2] *Immissionsschutzgesetz-Luft*, BGBl I 1997/115.

The IG-L lays down limits for emissions of air pollutants and ozone, which are fixed in accordance with EC air pollution laws. To guarantee adherence to these limits, a statistical survey of all important data in the whole federal territory is carried out.

On the basis of a comprehensive data analysis, a range of measures needs to be realized. This includes a step-by-step reduction of emissions in polluted areas according to strict environmental standards. For example, the authorities can order the use of low emission engines and clean fuels, prohibit use of specific engines, procedures, or techniques, enact traffic limits, speed reductions, etc. Severely polluting plants have to present ecological development plans for fixed periods of time. Although the IG-L is a very stringent environmental law, it includes numerous exceptions for industry and, therefore, expectations regarding the efficiency of these measures should not be exaggerated.

The IG-L covers traffic as such, rather than individual cars. The law only very vaguely specifies emission reducing traffic-specific measures (*verkehrsspezifische Maßnahmen*). For example, it lists optimization of the traffic infrastructure (for example combined traffic, integrated traffic routes) and ecological optimization of traffic routes as potential subjects for general orders of the federal government.

Because of the allocation of competences, heating systems are not covered by the IG-L, which instead belongs to the competences of the states. The federation and the states will conclude a treaty according to Article 15a of the *Bundesverwaltungsgesetz*, to ensure that the rules of the IG-L will also be applicable to heating systems.

The IG-L also reforms other air pollution laws, especially laws concerning industrial plants. Industrial plants, boiler plants, waste plants, and mines must be improved in conformity with the IG-L. The law came into force on 1 April 1998 and, with regard to specific air polluters, will progressively come into force until 2003.

Many general acts on the basis of different laws relating to industrial installations contain measures concerning air quality.[3] The *Feuerungsanlagenverordnung 1997*,[4] which came into force on 1 June 1998, contains obligations for installations for burning solid, liquid, and gaseous substances as well as emission limits and inspection procedures.

Other general acts, based on state construction laws, also contribute to clean air, containing rules on the use of isolation materials and other measures to reduce energy use.[5]

---

[3] e.g. the *Verordnung zur Begrenzung der Emission von luftverunreinigenden Stoffen*, BGBl II 1997/160 und 1998/1; *die Luftreinhalteverordnung für Kesselanlagen*, BGBl II 1997/324.

[4] BGBl II 1997/331.

[5] See S. Ebensperger, I. Wallnöfer, K. Weber, and Th. Walzel von Wiesentreu, *Ecology of the Rehabilitation of Old Buildings. Guidelines for Subsidization with Regard to Energy Consumption, Emissions and Optical Aspects*, SAVE-Project No SA/35/95/AU, Part I: Legal and financial considerations (St. Pölten: NÖ-Landesakademie, 1998).

C.   BIOTECHNOLOGY AND CHEMICALS

The *Gentechnikgesetz-Novelle 1998*[6] regulates the release of genetically modified plants. Impairments to the environment now also attract civil liability.

The *Chemikaliengesetz*,[7] which has come gradually into force since 1997, is much more orientated towards environmental protection than its predecessors. The law combines self-regulation and individual responsibility with state control. It includes an extensive chapter on the assessment of environmental effects of consumer goods. The law will be implemented by several general acts. In 1998 only one such general act was passed.[8]

D.   NATURE CONSERVATION

With one exception, the state nature conservation laws changed only marginally. Vienna passed a new Nature Conservation Law and integrated elements of city ecology into the traditional system of nature protection and landscape conservation.

The (small) reforms of the other states[9] concerned a streamlining of procedures and the establishment of compensatory areas for ecologically precious areas that were sacrificed for economic reasons. State nature conservation laws are reformed periodically on the basis of experience with the administration of the laws. As a result, the reforms are very specific and difficult to assess for outsiders.

E.   WASTE AND WATER

As a result of the allocation of competences in the Austrian Constitution, legislation on the administration of dangerous waste is the responsibility of the Federation, whereas non-dangerous waste is regulated by the states.[10]

The Federation's *Abfallwirtschaftsgesetz 1990*[11] was marginally reformed during 1997/8.[12] Beside terminological clarifications, competences of the authorities to enact general orders were extended.

Several general acts amended the limit values for the quality of ground water and water from waste water purification plants.[13]

---

[6] BGBl I 1998/73.   [7] BGBl I 1997/53.   [8] BGBl II 1998/65.
[9] Niederösterreich: LGBl 1998/34; Salzburg: LGBl 1998/2, 43; Tirol: LGBl 1998/78.
[10] Art. 10(1) Z 12 B-VG.   [11] BGBl 1990/325.   [12] BGBl I 1997/115.
[13] *Grundwassersch wellenwertverordnung*, BGBl II 1997/213; which will be complemented with several wastewater emission regulations (*Abwasseremissionsverordnungen*: BGBl II 1997/344–50).

F.   HORIZONTAL INSTRUMENTS

i.   Eco-audit

The EC Eco-audit Regulation[14] was widely welcomed by trade and industry and is implemented by the *Umweltgutachter- und Standorteverzeichnisgesetz*.[15] When an environmental audit takes place according to the Eco-audit Regulation, the periodical inspections of factories and installations by the authorities cease to be required.[16] Consequently, more and more installations will be supervised this way.

ii.   Environmental Information

The *Umweltinformationsgesetz 1993*[17] is derived from the Environmental Information Directive.[18] According to Article 5(4) of this law, the authorities may charge flat-rate fees for information when its dissemination causes higher costs. As a result of criticisms by the Commission, this system will be replaced, and information will be distributed free of charge; only the costs for sending the information to the applicant will be charged.[19]

iii.   IPPC

The Directive Concerning Integrated Pollution Prevention and Control (IPPC Directive) of 10 October 1996[20] has not yet been fully implemented. However, during 1997/8 Austrian legislation introduced important initiatives towards a uniform law applicable to installations.

The 1997 addition to the *Gewerbeordnung*[21] introduced an integrated procedure for permits applicable to installations. The permit, according to the *Gewerbeordnung*, includes all other necessary permits according to federal law. However, permits falling outside the scope of the *Gewerbeordnung* are still granted according to several specific procedures.

The implementation of the IPPC Directive is to be realized by a uniform law concerning installations. The government will introduce a bill into the parliament in 1999, which will codify the law relating to installations. The central point of this reform is the concentration of the procedures and permits of all kinds of installations in one administrative body ("one-stop-shop"). The use of Best Available Technology (BAT) and the consideration of economic principles when setting environmental standards are other important features of this bill.

The scope of the bill comprises every installation that is designed for recurrent economic activity. Traffic facilities, pipelines, and arable areas are

---

[14] Council Reg. (EC) No. 1836/93 allowing voluntary participation by companies in the industrial sector in a community eco-management and audit scheme [1993] OJ L168/1.

[15] BGBl I 1995/622.   [16] Art. 82b(5) of the *Gewerbeordnung*.   [17] BGBl 1993/495.

[18] Council Dir. 90/313/EEC on the freedom of access to information on the environment [1990] OJ L158/56.

[19] See the proposal by the *Bundesministerium für Umwelt, Jugend und Familie* of 12 Nov. 1998, Zl. 224735/27-II/2/98.

[20] [1996] OJ L257/26.   [21] BGBl I 1997/63.

excluded. The environmental impact procedure will become part of the new law.

Decisions concerning individual installations follow procedures comprising public hearings. The scope of participation depends on the nature of the pollution caused by the installation. The system of control and supervision of existing installations and the adaptation of existing installations to the best available techniques will be improved.

The implementation of the IPPC Directive has to be completed before 31 October 1999. Before that date, the bill is likely to be amended in some respects, but its overarching principles will probably survive.

G. MISCELLANEOUS/GENERAL INSTRUMENTS

i. Taxes

During 1998, intensive discussions took place about an ecological tax reform at different levels. The aim was to ease labour cost and to provide incentives for "green" behaviour. In particular higher taxation of electricity, gas, oil, and fossil fuels was at the centre of the discussions. Meanwhile the government shelved plans for an energy tax in anticipation of EU initiatives.

ii. Subsidies

According to Article 17 of the Austrian Constitution, subsidies fall outside the regular allocation of competences. This means that the Federation and the states can employ instruments of private law in areas in which they enjoy no competences. Furthermore, both can grant subsidies without any legal basis. This high degree of discretion stands at the basis of a very complicated and opaque system of subsidies. The subsidies are based partly on laws, partly on guidelines. Furthermore, the Federation and the states increase EC subsidies of different European programmes. This heterogeneous practice of subsidies can be summarized as follows:

— Subsidies based on the *Umweltförderungsgesetz* (UFG):[22] after an addition to the UFG,[23] the Federation grants additional subsidies of Sch. 3000 million for municipal waste water management for the years 1996–2000.
— Subsidies for National Parks: federal government requires a share of state government expenditure to be allocated to the National Parks Hohe Tauern, Kalkalpen, Donau-Auen, and Neusiedler See. The base finance is guaranteed by the states.
— Subsidies for non-governmental organisations (NGOs): the Ministry of Environment, Youth and Family sponsors activities of NGOs with periodical payments. There is no legal basis for these subsidies and the NGOs hence have no legal title to the subsidies.

---

[22] UFG, BGBl 1993/185.   [23] BGBl I 1998/79.

— Subsidies for the support of scientific environmental projects: the Federation and the states in practice support these initiatives without legal basis and without legal title of the scientific community.
— Contract nature conservation: the states and the owners of ecological areas make contracts through which they bind themselves to renounce the use of these areas or to enact special conservation measures.
— Subsidies for measures to reduce the consumption of energy: the states spend about Sch. 35 million (2,541,169 Euros) to support the living environment. The granting of subsidies depends on different ecological measures and are also given for the rehabilitation of old buildings.[24]

iii. Energy Policy

The *Elektrizitätswirtschaftsorganisationsgesetz*[25] liberalized and deregulated the electricity industry and adapted the existing laws to EC directives. The Ministry of Environment and some NGOs called for rules to improve environmental policy in this branch, but ultimately economic interests seem to have prevailed.

In the residential laws of the states, many reforms are aimed at reducing energy consumption.[26] New buildings must comply with maximum levels of energy consumption they may not be erected.

---

[24] See n. 3 above.   [25] ElWOG—BGBl I 1998/143.   [26] See n. 3 above.

II. Belgium

KURT DEKETELAERE*

A. AIR POLLUTION

A decision of the Brussels capital government of 28 May 1998 amends a decision of 31 May 1991 on the reduction of air pollution from existing installations for the incineration of domestic waste, by deleting the last sentence of Article 3(a) of the old decision,[1] so as to make it conform with Council Directive 89/429/EEC on the Reduction of Air Pollution from Existing Municipal Waste Incineration Plants.[2]

B. BIOTECHNOLOGY

i. Federal Government

A co-operation agreement between the different regions regarding bio-safety, and the Law of 3 March 1998 approving it, was published in the *Moniteur Belge* of 14 July 1998. The co-operation agreement aims to secure the safety of man, the environment, and biodiversity when genetically modified organisms are used. It transposes into national law Council Directives 90/220/EEC on the Deliberate Release Into the Environment of Genetically Modified Organisms[3] and Council Directive 90/219/EEC on the Contained Use of Genetically Modified Micro-organisms[4] and establishes a common system for scientific evaluation. The approval of the co-operation agreement by Walloon decree and Brussels ordinance was published in the same issue of the *Moniteur Belge.*[5] A decree of the Flemish parliament of 17 December 1997 approves the co-operation agreement on bio-safety concluded between the federal state and the regions on 25 April 1997.[6]

ii. Brussels Capital Region

By Ministerial Decision of 22 September 1998, the annexes to the decision of the Brussels capital government of 9 December 1993, concerning installations where genetically modified organisms are used, were modified.[7]

C. CHEMICALS

A Royal Decision of 13 November 1997 amends the Royal Decision of 24 May 1982 on trade in substances harmful to man or the environment. It is the

* Professor of Law, Director Institute for Environmental and Energy Law, University of Leuven, Belgium.

[1] *Moniteur Belge/Belgisch Staatsblad*, 16 June 1998.   [2] [1989] OJ L203/1.
[3] [1990] OJ L117/15.   [4] [1990] OJ L117/1.   [5] *Moniteur Belge*, 14 July 1998.
[6] *Moniteur Belge*, 31 Jan. 1998.   [7] *Moniteur Belge*, 20 Nov. 1998.

transposition into Belgian law of a number of European directives. It regulates various aspects of trade involving dangerous substances (notifications, characteristics of the substances, a monitoring commission, packaging, etc.) and replaces and amends the annexes to the 1982 Royal Decision.[8]

D.   NATURE CONSERVATION

i. Flemish Region

On 21 October 1997, the Flemish parliament adopted the Decree on nature conservation and the natural environment.[9] This Decree regulates territorial demarcation, structures, and procedures under the Flemish nature conservation policy. Chapter II of the Decree establishes the structures (the Flemish High Council for Nature Conservation and the Nature Conservation Institute). Chapter III determines objectives and planning (nature report, nature policy plan (general and specific)). In Chapter IV the Flemish government is empowered to take all necessary measures for the conservation of nature (for example by prohibiting certain activities). Following these general rules, Chapter V lays down the basis for a territory-oriented policy. It provides for the creation of different categories of territories grouped together in networks. Finally, the Decree contains provisions on education, local government, exceptions, and sanctions.[10]

A Decree of the Flemish parliament of 14 July 1998 gives legal force to the following international instruments in the Flemish region: the protocol to amend the Convention on Wetlands of International Importance, particularly Waterfowl Habitats, agreed in Paris on 3 December 1982, and the amendments to the Convention adopted in Regina on 28 May 1987.[11]

The Decision of the Flemish government of 23 July 1998 establishes specific rules implementing the Flemish Decree of 21 October 1997 on nature conservation and the natural environment. It contains procedural rules on the demarcation of the so-called Flemish Ecological Network and the Integral Network for Acquisition and Support, the acquisition of land by the authorities and the modification of vegetation and nature planning projects.[12]

ii. Walloon Region

A Decree of the Walloon Council of 22 January 1998 inserts a new provision into the Law of 12 July 1973 on nature conservation, establishing a system compensating those working in agriculture, forestry, horticulture, or fisheries who suffer damage caused by endangered species. They will be eligible for compensation if they meet specified requirements.[13]

---

[8] *Moniteur Belge*, 26 Mar. 1998.
[10] *Moniteur Belge*, 10 Jan. 1998.
[12] *Moniteur Belge*, 10 Sept. 1998.

[9] *Moniteur Belge*, 10 Jan.1998.
[11] *Moniteur Belge*, 22 Aug.1998.
[13] *Moniteur Belge*, 26 Feb. 1998.

E. WASTE

i. Flemish Region

By decision of the inter-regional packaging commission of 18 December 1997, the non-profit-making association FOST Plus was approved as the organization for household packaging waste. FOST Plus had applied for recognition to the inter-regional packaging commission (a commission established by a co-operation agreement on the prevention and control of packaging waste, of 30 May 1996, made up between the three regions). Since FOST Plus met all the requirements, it was granted approval for the period from 18 December 1997 to 31 December 1998. The Decision also lays down concrete rules for the operation of FOST Plus (percentages of materials to be recycled, standard agreements, insurance, contributions, etc.).[14]

On 17 April 1998, an environmental policy agreement[15] was concluded between the Flemish government and organizations representing the pharmaceutical sector. It contains detailed provisions aiming at the selective collection of old and expired pharmaceuticals. A similar agreement was concluded (on the same date) with the sector comprising large paper consumers. It contains recycling percentages and other practical provisions. Further practical arrangements are contained in a protocol to the agreement.[16]

The Flemish land company has published data on the usage and production of phosphorus per municipality in accordance with the decree of the Flemish parliament of 23 January 1991 (and the corresponding decision of 20 December 1995) on the protection of the environment against contamination by manure.[17] A decision of the Flemish government of 16 December 1997 allows for derogations in respect of certain sites falling within the framework of the Decree of the Flemish parliament of 23 January 1991. In some areas, and under certain conditions, the use of manure is allowed by way of derogation from the provisions of the Decree.[18]

By decision of the Flemish government of 20 January 1998 (a decision amending the decision of the Flemish government of 4 March 1997 which, in accordance with Article 30(2) of the Decree of the Flemish parliament of 22 February 1995 on soil sanitation, determined which soils have to be treated), the list of contaminated soils was complemented and certain sites were removed from that list.[19]

ii. Brussels Capital Region

An ordinance of the Brussels capital council of 18 December 1997 completes the ordinance of 19 July 1990 establishing the "Regional Agency for Tidiness". It regulates the powers of the officials who control (illegal) waste disposal.[20]

---

[14] *Moniteur Belge*, 10 Feb. 1998.
[15] On the use of environmental agreements, see J. Verschuuren in this volume.
[16] *Moniteur Belge*, 24 Apr. 1998.   [17] *Moniteur Belge*, 18 June 1998.
[18] *Moniteur Belge*, 6 Feb. 1998.   [19] *Moniteur Belge*, 6 Mar. 1998.
[20] *Moniteur Belge*, 24 Feb. 1998.

iii. Walloon Region

A decision of the Walloon government of 27 November 1997 concerning the storage and sorting of scrap metal and used cars regulates the conditions under which such facilities should operate. A decision of the same date amends the provisions of the General Regulation on protection at work in respect of the same facilities.[21]

A decision of the Walloon government of 15 January 1998 approved the Walloon waste plan "2010" and repealed the plan for the period 1991–5.[22] The Walloon waste plan "2010" was published in the *Moniteur Belge* of 29 April 1998. It contains a variety of measures (aiming at prevention, recycling, etc.), quotas (for dumping, incineration, etc.) and procedures, and designates the competent institution or authority.[23]

A decision of the Walloon government of 30 April 1998 regulates premiums for waste prevention and waste management payable to local authorities. One chapter deals specifically with waste-processing operations. It determines which facilities qualify for a subsidy and which experimental projects are eligible for support. Other provisions deal with obligations of the beneficiary, the amount of the subsidy, procedure etc. Another chapter concerns subsidies to municipalities for prevention, selective collection etc.[24]

F.   WATER

The Walloon Budget Decree of 17 December 1997 contains (in Title IV) various provisions relating to environmental matters. A fund for water protection is established and certain legal instruments are amended (the Decree of 7 October 1985 on surface water, the Decree of 30 April 1990, concerning a levy on discharging waste water and the Decree of the same date on drinking water).[25]

G.   HORIZONTAL INSTRUMENTS

i. Environmental Impact Assessment

a. Flemish Government

A decision of the Flemish government of 10 March 1998 complements a decision of 23 March 1989 on environmental impact assessment of certain categories of classified installations. In Case C–133/94 of 2 May 1996,[26] the European Court of Justice found that Belgium had failed fully to transpose into national law Council Directive 85/337/EEC on the Assessment of the Effects of Certain Public and Private Projects on the Environment (EIA Directive).[27] A

---

[21] *Moniteur Belge*, 15 Jan. 1998; *erratum, Moniteur Belge*, 3 Mar. 1998. See further the chapter by M. Onida in this volume.

[22] *Moniteur Belge*, 21 Apr. 1998.

[23] *Moniteur Belge*, 29 Apr. 1998.

[24] *Moniteur Belge*, 19 June 1998.

[25] *Moniteur Belge*, 27 Jan. 1998.

[26] *European Commission* v. *Belgium* [1996] ECR I–2323.

[27] [1985] OJ L175/40.

letter of 8 September 1997 from the European Commission had urged Belgium (and more specifically the Flemish region) to execute the Court's decision.[28] For similar reasons the decision determining the categories of activities that need an EIA was also amended.[29]

b. Walloon Region

By decision of the Walloon government of 8 October 1998, the decision of 31 October 1991 on Environmental Impact Assessment was modified.[30]

ii. IPPC

a. Flemish Region

The decision of the Flemish government of 1 June 1995, containing general and sectoral conditions for classified installations (Title II of "VLAREM"), was amended by a decision of the Flemish government of 24 March 1998. The purpose is to adapt VLAREM II to Council Directive 96/61/EC Concerning Integrated Pollution Prevention and Control (IPPC Directive),[31] Council Directive 96/62/EC on ambient air quality assessment and management[32] and other directives.[33]

b. Brussels Capital Region

A decision of the Brussels capital government of 22 January 1998 amends the decision of 10 June 1993, to refer to the new ordinance of the Brussels capital council of 5 June 1997 on environmental permits. The same change is made (by a decision of the Brussels capital government of 22 January 1998) to a decision of the Brussels capital government of 17 March 1994 on subsidies for municipalities for tasks concerning environmental permits.[34]

---

[28] *Moniteur Belge*, 30 Apr. 1998 (2nd edn.). [29] Ibid.
[30] Decision of the Walloon government of 8 Oct. 1998 modifying the decision of the Walloon government of 31 Oct. 1991, implementing the decree of 11 Sept. 1985, organizing the environmental impact assessment in the Walloon region: *Moniteur Belge*, 23 Oct. 1998.
[31] [1996] OJ L257/26. [32] [1996] OJ L296/55.
[33] *Moniteur Belge*, 30 Apr. 1998 (2nd edn.). [34] *Moniteur Belge*, 24 Feb. 1998.

III. Denmark

PETER PAGH*

A. AIR POLLUTION AND CHEMICALS

Besides green taxes on fuel, the only legislative effort in 1998 has been the implementation of Directive 97/68/EC on the Approximation of the Laws of the Member States Relating to Measures Against the Emission of Gaseous and Particulate Pollutants from Internal Combustion Engines to be Installed in Non-road Mobile Machinery[1] by Statutory Order No 667 of 14 September 1998.[2]

In order to limit the use of pesticides and biocides, taxes on these products have been increased by Act no 417 of 26 June 1998.[3] Under the auspices of the Environment Minister, a preparatory committee is drafting legislation to ban or limit the use of pesticides in farming and elsewhere. No final report has been submitted by the committee. However, under Directive 83/189/EEC Laying Down a Procedure for the Provision of Information in the Field of Technical Standards and Regulations[4] the Environment Minister has notified the Commission of a draft Act banning the use of pesticides in private gardens.

By Statutory Order No. 692 of 22 September 1998 the Minister of Environment has banned the sale and export of mercury and products containing mercury.[5] The Statutory Order exempted certain types of use from the ban and the Commission has been notified under Directive 83/189/EEC.

B. NATURE CONSERVATION

In 1998, the National Forest and Nature Agency completed the designation of habitats under Directive 92/43/EC on the Conservation of Natural Habitats and of Wild Fauna and Flora (Habitat Directive)[6] and the Minister of the Environment has submitted Statutory Order No 782 of 1 November 1998 on the designation and administration of international habitats.[7] The designated habitats cover more than 7 per cent of the land and the sea-territory of Denmark and in this respect appear to comply with the Habitat Directive. However, the Statutory Order includes derogations which may not in all respect comply with Articles 6 and 7 of the Habitat Directive.

---

* Professor of Environmental Law, Law Faculty, University of Copenhagen.

[1] [1998] OJ L059/1.

[2] Statutory Order on the limitation of air pollution from mobile sources (not vehicles).

[3] Act amending the Act on taxation of pesticides.

[4] [1983] OJ L109/8.

[5] Statutory Order on the prohibition of the marketing and export of mercury and products containing mercury.

[6] [1992] OJ L206/7.

[7] Statutory Order on the designation and administration of international habitats.

C.   WASTE

Under the Environmental Protection Act, the 275 local councils (municipalities) are responsible for waste management. Each local council has its own waste law (regulations) and waste management plan, which it also enforces. Most local councils are economically engaged in the waste business (collection, treatment, incineration, and waste recovery). During the last decade, this public engagement was extended to industrial waste and waste for recovery—activities which in the past have been left to private business. In view of the competing tasks of local councils as legislators, enforcers, and economic actors, private business have argued that this amounts to unfair competition, contrary to national and EU competition law as well as the free trade provisions of the Treaty. Litigation has focused on two questions: the public involvement in waste recovery and the public procurement (tender) of waste management services under Directive 92/50/EEC.[8]

One case is pending before the Østne Landsnet (Eastern High Court) concerning market access for the recovery of non-dangerous construction waste. According to regulations of the City of Copenhagen, construction waste may be managed only by selected companies—one of which was partly established by the city council. The limitation of access to this market is said to be justified by interests of the efficient use of capacity, self-sufficiency, and environmental protection. Due to the regulation, a privately owned installation situated in an industrial zone in the city was prevented from receiving any of the capital's construction waste. In May, the High Court submitted preliminary questions to the European Court of Justice on the interpretation of Directive 75/442/EEC[9] on Waste and on Articles 29, 82, and 86 (formerly Articles 34, 86, and 90) EC.[10]

Over the past five years, it has been highly controversial whether the local councils' collection and treatment of waste should be subject to the public procurement procedure as prescribed by Directive 92/50/EEC. In February 1998, a report from the Ministry of Justice concluded that there was no such obligation when the Council enjoys ownership of the inter-municipal company. This appears in accordance with the ECJ ruling in the *Arnhem/BFI* case.[11] That there are situations which do require a tender under Directive 92/50/EEC is illustrated by a recent case brought before the Administrative Board of Appeal on Public Procurement, established under Directive 89/665/EEC.[12] In that case, the Administrative Board ruled that the contract between the city of

[8] Council Dir. 92/50/EEC relating to the co-ordination of procedures for the award of public service contracts [1992] OJ L209/1.

[9] [1975] OJ L194/39.

[10] See Case C–209/98, *Contractors Association, Waste Section* v. *City Council of Copenhagen* on whether building materials waste for recovery is subject to the principle of self-sufficiency.

[11] Case C–360/96, *Gemeente Arnhem en Gemeente Rheden* v. *BFI Holding BV* [1998] ECR I–6821.

[12] Council Dir. 89/665/EEC on the co-ordination of the laws, regulations and administrative provisions relating to the application of review procedures to the award of public supply and public works contracts [1989] OJ L395/33.

Copenhagen and the private foundation R–98 should have been subject to a public tender under Directive 92/50/EEC, and that the Commission should have been notified under Article 88(3) (formerly Article 93(3)) EC on state aids.[13]

In 1998, the Commission took the final step in infringement proceedings against Denmark concerning the Danish ban on the marketing of canned beer. The Commission claims that the Danish ban breaches the free trade clause in Article 18 of Directive 94/62/EC on Packaging and Packaging Waste[14] and Article 28 (formerly Article 30) EC. It argues that derogations based on Article 30 (formerly Article 36) EC or mandatory requirements are not available. By contrast, the Danish government argues that the Packaging Waste Directive is not exhaustive and the Danish ban can be justified by environmental imperatives.[15]

To ensure the efficient and environmentally sound disposal of waste, new provisions were inserted into the Environmental Protection Act concerning subsidies for cleaner technology.[16] The Act has been notified to the Commission under the Packaging Waste Directive and under Directive 83/189/EEC,[17] but there is no information suggesting notification under Article 88(3) (formerly Article 93(3)) EC.

D.   WATER

During 1998, the implementation of EU directives on water quality and water pollution gave rise to political and legal controversy. After the Commission found Danish implementation of Directive 91/676/EEC on the Protection of Waters from Pollution by Nitrates from Agricultural Sources[18] to be deficient, the parliament adopted a new action plan for water protection. As part of the action plan, Act No 479 of 1 July 1998 was adopted, granting the regional councils and the Minister of the Environment the power to designate farming areas as sensitive for the protection of water resources. In the designated areas the use of fertilisers and manure is subject to limitations, and the land can be expropriated.

In 1997, Greenpeace complained to the Commission about the deposit of 400,000 m³ of slightly contaminated soil on a man-made peninsula at the coast of Öresund, without a prior environmental impact assessment. Although the Commission did not find any conflict with Directive 85/337/EEC on the Assessment of the Effects of Certain Public and Private Projects on the Environment (EIA Directive),[19] it concluded that the deposit was in conflict with Directive 76/464/EEC on Pollution Caused by Certain Dangerous Substances Discharged Into the Aquatic Environment of the Community.[20]

[13] *Farum Industrial Renovation v. City of Copenhagen*, ruling of 21 Oct. 1998, KFE.1999.69.
[14] [1994] OJ L365/10.
[15] On Art. 26 (formerely Art. 28) EC and environmental protection, see H. Temmink at p. 61 of this volume.
[16] Act No 408 of 26 June 1998.   [17] [1983] OJ L109/8.   [18] [1993] OJ L375/1.
[19] [1985] OJ L175/40.   [20] [1976] OJ L129/23.

Although it is unclear whether the Commission will initiate infringement proceedings before the ECJ on this matter, the statement of the Commission might have an impact on future Danish waste disposal strategy which has been to place landfills close to the coast.

E.   HORIZONTAL INSTRUMENTS

i. Environmental Impact Assessment

An increasing number of disputes regarding Danish implementation of the EIA Directive have been reported. The majority of these cases were brought before the (administrative) Nature Protection Board of Appeal and concerned the quality of the EIA, the screening criteria of Annex II projects, or the question whether deposits of contaminated soil were within the scope of annex I(9). In 1998, two cases were decided by national courts. The first, *Danish Biking Association v. Council of Roskilde*, concerned a road connection between two main roads. The Council had not performed an EIA because of the size of the project. By contrast, the Biking Association claimed an EIA was required because of the major environmental impact of the road connection. The Eastern High Court, in its ruling of 25 June, found that an EIA was not required.[21] The Biking Association has appealed to the Supreme Court.

The other case, *Greenpeace v. Minister of Traffic*, concerning the Öresund bridge, was finally decided by the Supreme Court on 2 December 1998.[22] The dispute focused on four questions of interpretation of the EIA Directive:

(a) is the 1991 Act concerning the Öresund bridge to Sweden covered by the exception in Article 1(5) of the Directive (projects adopted in detail by national legislator)?;
(b) must the public hearing mentioned in Article 6(2) of the Directive be carried out *after* the developer's application for a consent under Article 5(2);
(c) must the public hearing under Article 6(2) of the Directive be carried out *before* the consent is granted in the light of Article 8?; and
(d) how is the date of consent influenced by the national division of responsibilities for consents concerning construction of the bridge and the excavation of raw materials under Öresund?

Greenpeace claimed that the procedure followed was contrary to the EIA Directive. Parliament had first decided to build the bridge, leaving it to the state-owned consortium to define the project and to the Minister of Traffic to hold public hearings before the application for consent to the project. After the first consent was granted by the Minister of Traffic in July 1994, the project was changed without further public hearings and a new consent was granted in 1995. In response, the Minister of Traffic claimed that the whole project was

---

[21] *Danish Biking Association v. City of Roskilde*, MAD.1998.585.
[22] *Greenpeace v. Minister of Traffic*, EfR.1999.367 H.

excluded from the EIA Directive and that, in any event, the procedure followed had been in accordance with the EIA Directive. The Eastern Higher Court ruled in November 1996 that only the procedure followed after the Act had been in accordance with the EIA Directive.[23] However, the Supreme Court found the Act complied with the requirements of the derogation clause in Article 1(5) of the EIA Directive. The substantial changes to the project after 1991 were, according to the Supreme Court, subject to the mandatory EIA procedure only to the extent that this was required for Annex II projects. The Supreme Court did not decide whether an EIA procedure was required but concluded that, "in any event", the two hearings in 1993 had been sufficient to satisfy the requirements concerning public hearings under Article 6(2). Because of the highly controversial political issues involved, Greenpeace on several occasions unsuccessfully asked the High Court and the Supreme Court to refer questions on the interpretation of the EIA Directive to the European Court of Justice (ECJ). It is doubtful whether this refusal accords with the spirit of Article 234(3) (formerly Article 177(3)) EC, considering the difficult questions of interpretation of the EIA Directive involved in the case. Moreover, the outcome regarding the derogation clause of Article 1(5) is surprising, because the Supreme Court in an earlier ruling on injunctions in 1995 did not find that the Act was excluded under Article 1(5).[24]

ii. IPPC

The discussion on how properly to implement Directive 96/61/EC Concerning Integrated Pollution Prevention and Control (IPPC Directive)[25] in the Environmental Protection Act continues. One of the issues concerns the definition of the holder of an IPPC licence. In the current Environmental Protection Act, it is the *plant* "which" is the holder. The Act does not identify or require that the licence is granted to any physical or legal person. In contrast to the transport and restaurant sectors, there are no requirements regarding the financial or technical capacity of the operator of a strongly polluting plant. This has caused confusion regarding criminal, administrative, and civil liability in various cases where the installation had been taken over. In a highly disputed ruling, a lower court concluded that an owner cannot be held criminally liable for deposits of waste caused by a previous owner. The fact that the new undertaking was owned by two sons of the "old" bankrupted firm was immaterial.[26]

iii. General Instruments

In 1998, so-called "green taxes" were used in new areas and existing rates of taxation have been increased. Green taxes apply to waste for disposal, waste used for heating, waste water, drinking water, packaging, CO_2 emission, sulphur dioxide emission, pesticides and biocides, CFC-gases and Halons,

---

[23] MAD.1996.984.   [24] U.1995.634H.   [25] [1996] OJ L257/26.
[26] *The State v. H. & C. Prom Kemi ApS* (bankrupt estate), Vordingborg Lower Court ruling of 4 Dec. 1998, SS 522/97.

chlorinated preparations, batteries, and certain fuels. New green taxes are levied on fertilisers and soft polyvinylchloride. The well-known confusion surrounding the definition of waste has also led to problems in the field of taxation. Whereas tax authorities hold that all deposits of even slightly contaminated soil must be taxed as disposal of waste, many local councils consider the use of slightly contaminated soil in dykes utilization and recovery of waste, which is exempt from taxation. The use of wood chips for heating is also a subject of controversy. Local councils claim it is fuel, while tax authorities claim it is waste and therefore subject to taxation.

IV. Finland

PEKKA VIHERVUORI*

A. INTRODUCTION

Finnish environmental law has traditionally been divided into different sectors such as water, air, waste, public health, and neighbourhood relations. Until 1992, this held true both substantively and procedurally. In a 1991 reform, the majority of the various permit procedures were consolidated in the Environmental Permit Procedure Act.[1]

Since developments regarding the combined permit have been by far the most important, they will be treated relatively extensively. However, it should be noted that other sectors of environmental law have also witnessed important events.

B. NATURE CONSERVATION

Legislation on nature conservation was substantially reformed in 1996. The new Nature Conservation Act[2] came into force on 1 January 1997, and replaced its predecessor of 1923 bearing a similar title. The overhaul was necessitated by domestic needs and EC legislation, in particular Directive 79/409/EEC on the Conservation of Wild Birds (Wild Birds Directive)[3] and Directive 92/43/EEC on the Conservation of Natural Habitats and of Wild Fauna and Flora (Habitats Directive).[4] The two Directives bound Finland from the beginning of its EU membership, 1 January 1995. Due to legal and political problems with the implementation of previous National Conservation Programmes, national provisions concerning the Natura 2000 network have become rather detailed. During 1997 and 1998, a programme was prepared by the environmental administration. The work, particularly the way of dissemination of information, has been criticized in parts of the media and by farmers' interest organizations. Also, the alleged vagueness of the legal effects of the network resulted in political difficulties. The proposal includes 1,457 designated areas (439 special protection areas (SPAs)) relating to the Wild Birds Directive and 1,325 sites of Community importance (SCAs) relating to the Habitats Directive, with a total area of 4.77 million hectares corresponding to 12 per cent of the total area of the country. Approximately 97 per cent of these areas were also protected in some way prior to the programme.

---

* Professor of Law, Justice at the Supreme Administrative Court, Helsinki, Finland.
[1] Official Legislation Journal No. 735/1991.
[2] Official Legislation Journal No. 1096/1996.   [3] [1979] OJ L103/1.   [4] [1992] OJ L206/7.

C.   HORIZONTAL INSTRUMENTS

i. IPPC

Depending on the characteristics of the actual project, present combined environmental permits may comprise a location consent pursuant to the Neighbourhood Relations Act, a location consent pursuant to the Public Health Act of 1994, a waste permit pursuant to the Waste Act, and an air emission permit pursuant to the Air Pollution Prevention Act. The combined permit is required where any of these activities forms part of the total activity at the site. Water pollution aspects are subject to the combined environmental permit decisions only when necessitated by the Public Health Act. The combined environmental permits are administered either by regional environmental centres or by municipal environmental authorities. Appeal to an administrative court, up to the Supreme Administrative Court, is always possible.

A far more ambitious reform of environmental law[5] has been prepared for several years. The reasons are two-fold, but inter-related. On the one hand, there is domestic pressure to create a uniform substantive and procedural legislative regime for all regulation on pollution and nuisances. On the other hand, Directive 96/61/EC Concerning Integrated Pollution Prevention and Control (IPPC Directive) has created an obligation to adjust Finnish legislation to new European requirements, which poses challenges of in particular an administrative and judicial nature.[6] An integrated Environmental Protection Act was jointly proposed by two governmental committees in 1995 in order to satisfy these domestic and EC needs. The proposal was developed further during 1996–8 by a working group under auspices of the Ministries of Justice and the Environment. The final proposal was published by the end of September 1998.

The new Environmental Protection Act replaces the Environmental Permit Procedure Act, the Air Pollution Prevention Act, the Noise Abatement Act, and the pollution-related parts of the Water Act, the Waste Act, the Public Health Act, and the Neighbourhood Relations Act. Due to the integrated approach, the new legislation clearly represents more than just the sum of the present sectoral provisions.

In the IPPC Directive, the principle of Best Available Technology (BAT) occupies a central position. However, there are many situations in which a permit's conditions could and should go beyond BAT, for example, in order to avoid significant harmful effects to the physical environment or to protect a nature reserve water supply.

In order to safeguard the existing level of pollution control, a permit would be necessary in far more cases than required by the IPPC Directive. In addition to a list of installations and activities, a permit would be required for all activ-

---

[5] This is now Bill 84/1999, introduced into the parliament in Sept. 1999.
[6] [1996] OJ L257/26.

ities posing a risk of surface water pollution and for all activities likely to cause unlawful nuisance to neighbours. This is a consequence of the fact that the Finnish permit system is also an instrument for the protection of private subjects and a framework for participation, rather than merely a vertical tool for "command and control". Section 14a of the Constitution provides that it is the duty of government to ensure that participation in environmental decision-making is possible. The permit system also functions as a safeguard for the protection of ownership of affected areas, including the aquatic environment. These constitutional requirements are one reason why ideas of environmental agreements or tradable emission rights have not been developed in Finland. Apart from substantive changes, organizational changes initiated by the IPPC Directive are also significant. Here, the main impulse is Article 7 of the Directive, requiring the Member States to:

take the measures necessary to ensure that the conditions of, and procedure for the grant of, the permit are fully co-ordinated where more than one competent authority is involved, in order to guarantee an effective integrated approach by all authorities competent for this procedure.

Of course, there are various ways of implementing Article 7. It is recognized that one single permit authority is not the only legitimate solution. On the other hand, the status of an independent court could be problematic if the activities of that court would be co-ordinated by an administrative body (and the same holds true if the court co-ordinates administrative bodies). The issue has been widely debated. According to the proposal, the three water courts would be abolished, irrespective of their merits, and three regional environmental permit authorities would be created instead, by a specific Act.

First, the environmental permit authorities would deal with permit applications regarding the most important activities and installations under the Environmental Protection Act. Secondly, they would have a similar task within the remaining parts of the Water Act (construction in water bodies, hydro-electric plants, water regulation, water abstraction, man-made lakes, waterways, drainage, sea-bed gravel abstraction, embankment, timber floating etc.). The regional environment centres and the municipal environmental authorities would also be permit (and supervision) authorities under the Environmental Protection Act. In all cases, the Regional Administrative Courts would be the appellate bodies of first instance. However, one of the Regional Administrative Courts, into which the Superior Water Court would be merged, would be vested with the main competence under both the Environmental Protection Act and the Water Act. The Supreme Administrative Court would remain the final court of appeal.

ii. EIA Legislation

The present Environmental Impact Assessment Act (EIA Act),[7] with the associated amendment acts, was adopted to meet the requirements of the

---

[7] Official Legislation Journal No. 468/1994.

Directive 85/337/EEC on the Assessment of the Effects of Certain Public and Private Projects on the Environment (EIA Directive)[8] and of the Convention on Environmental Impact Assessment in a Transboundary Context (signed at Espoo, Finland, in 1991). Moreover, many of the Commission's plans to develop the Directive further were already anticipated. Consequently, Directive 97/11/EC[9] necessitated only few amendments in EIA legislation.

Presently, a Bill[10] on the amendments of the EIA Act is being introduced into the parliament. More specific provisions regarding the necessity of EIA in individual cases will be inserted. In addition, some definitions, the relation between the EIA Act and certain other acts, and the rules on the EIA procedure will be clarified. The proposed amendments are intended to become effective by 14 March 1999, which is the deadline for implementation of Directive 97/11/EC.

D.   MISCELLANEOUS INSTRUMENTS

i. Compulsory Environmental Insurance

The provisions concerning compensation for environmental damage were, with certain exceptions such as the Water Act mentioned above, codified in the Environmental Damages Act.[11] This Act imposes strict liability for damage covered by it, aiming to provide judicial protection to victims of pollution and nuisance. The model is in many respects similar to that adopted in Sweden and Norway. For example, the provisions on proving causality are more favourable to the victim than is common in tort law. The Environmental Damages Act covers in principle all non-contractual damage caused by a stationary activity. The scope of application of the Act is not limited by a positive list of fixed activities or chemical substances. Consequently, strict liability is general, and the provisions are far more comprehensive than the 1993 Lugano Convention on Environmental Liability—a convention signed but not yet ratified by Finland.

However, civil liability for environmental damage is useless to the victim if the polluter remains unidentified or is insolvent. In view of these problems and also to meet the requirements of Article 12 of the Lugano Convention, a specific secondary liability mechanism has been prepared. As a result, the Environmental Insurance Act was enacted in January 1998, entering into force 1 January 1999.[12]

Environmental insurance is different from any existing domestic or foreign form of insurance. Insurance is required, from 1 January 1999, for all major industrial and commercial activities involving a risk of environmental dam-

---

[8] [1985] OJ L175/40.

[9] Council Dir. 97/11/EC amending Dir. 85/337 on the assessment of the effects of certain public and private projects on the environment [1997] OJ L73/5.

[10] Bill 182/1998. This came into force on 1 Apr. 1999 (Official Legislation Journal No. 267/1999).

[11] Official Legislation Journal No. 737/1994.   [12] Official Legislation Journal No. 81/1998.

age, as specified by the Environmental Insurance Decree.[13] The main rule is that all permit holders pursuant to the Environmental Permit Procedure Act (or its predecessors), the water pollution prevention provisions of the Water Act or the Chemicals Act[14] fall under the insurance regime. Compliance is enforced by regional environmental centres.

Unlike traditional liability insurance, environmental insurance does not cover all instances of environmental damages, but only those when individual polluters, liable pursuant to the Environmental Damages Act, are insolvent. Additionally, the insurance covers damage which would fall within the scope of the Environmental Damages Act if the polluter had been detected.

Unlike compensation for damages caused by air or soil pollution, which belongs to the jurisdiction of general courts pursuant to the Environmental Damages Act, compensation for damages caused by authorized waste water discharges is decided *ex officio* and, where possible, in advance by water courts.

ii. *Reform of the Legislation on Planning and Building*

An overall reform of the Planning and Building Act[15] has been discussed and prepared for years. Just before the parliamentary elections of 1995, the previous Bill was withdrawn, due to political disagreements regarding, *inter alia*, the division of powers between municipalities and state environmental administration.

The proposed Land Use and Building Act[16] is environmentally relevant in many ways. Equilibrium between municipal self-government and wider public interests has been achieved in a sophisticated way. Municipal land use plans will no longer be submitted to the regional environmental centres or the Ministry of the Environment for approval. Neither will state authorities any longer function as appellate authorities. Instead, appeal will be possible to regional administrative courts and the Supreme Administrative court against all municipal planning decisions. These arrangements also grant a right of appeal to the regional environmental centres.

The proposed legislation is in many ways relevant to EU legislation, for example concerning birds and natural habitats, EIA, major industrial hazards, and construction products.

---

[13] Official Legislation Journal No. 717/1998. [14] Official Legislation Journal No. 744/1989.
[15] Official Legislation Journal No. 370/1958. [16] This comes into force on 1 Jan. 2000.

V. France

MICHEL PRIEUR*

A. INTRODUCTION

The most important environmental decisions taken by the current coalition government of socialists, communists, and ecologists (greens) can be summarized as follows: to cease the operation of the "Superphénix" rapid breed-reactor at Creys Malaville, to cancel the construction of a large canal linking the Rhine and the Rhône, and to resume implementation of Directive 92/43/EC on the Conservation of Natural Habitats and of Wild Fauna and Flora,[1] the transposition of which was suspended in 1996 by former Prime Minister Alain Juppé after pressure from various lobbying groups (farmers, landowners, hunters, etc.).

B. AIR POLLUTION

Several decrees have been adopted for the implementation of the Air Pollution Law,[2] which contributes to the transposition of Directive 96/62/EC on Ambient Air Quality Assessment and Management.[3] To attain the goals set by the Directive, a sophisticated system has been put in place, which comprises three levels of plans: regional air quality plans, local air quality plans (for towns with a population exceeding 250,000 and specified polluted areas), and urban traffic plans. In connection with these plans, several decrees have been adopted specifying, *inter alia*, the monitoring of air quality.

C. HORIZONTAL INSTRUMENTS

i. IPPC

French environmental law governing industrial installations appears to be in conformity with Council Directive 96/61/EC Concerning Integrated Pollution Prevention and Control (IPPC Directive).[4] The implementation of that Directive should therefore not present any problems. In fact, the French model of "classified installations" served as a model for the IPPC Directive. By requiring prior examination of the effects of an industrial activity on the environment, it seeks to achieve a high level of protection for the environment as a whole. In 1993, the French minister for the environment issued an administrative regulation aimed at an "integrated regulation", but the Conseil d'Etat

---

* Professor of Environmental Law, University of Limoges, Director of the CRIDEAU-CNRS.
[1] Council Dir. 92/43/EC [1992] OJ L206/7.
[2] Air Pollution Law No. 96–1236, 30 Dec. 1996, Journal Officiel, 1 Jan. 1997.
[3] [1996] OJ L296/55.   [4] [1996] OJ L257/26.

annulled this on the grounds that the ministry of the Environment lacked competence and that the regulation should have been enacted by the Prime Minister. At that time, the powers of the Minister of the Environment were confined to technical measures applicable to a limited number of classified installations. In order fully to empower the minister for the environment, the law was modified by Article 45 of the Air Pollution Law.[5] This allows the minister to intervene by administrative regulation to control all matters relating to classified installations and to establish new regulations. In accordance with this additional right, the order of 2 February 1998[6] implements the Directive for all classified installations.

ii. Environmental Information and Public Participation

For environmental decision-making, it is appropriate to stress the importance of the signature of the Århus Convention of June 1998 concerning Access to Information, Public Participation in Decision-Making and Access to Justice in Environmental Matters and Directive 90/313/EEC on the Freedom of Access to Information on the Environment (Environmental Information Directive).[7] According to Article 6 of the Convention, the process of public information and participation should be carried out well in advance of the realization of any project. An interesting experiment took place in France in 1997 and 1998 in the holding of a public debate on large-scale national projects that have important socio-economic effects or a significant impact on the environment.

The National Commission for Public Debate (the Commission) intervenes before any public inquiry is set up and the main elements of the project are published in the French Official Journal. The Commission is composed of two members of the parliament and four locally elected representatives, three members of the Conseil d'Etat, three members of administrative and judicial authorities, two members representing nationally recognized associations for the protection of the environment, two members representing private interests, and two "experts".

Projects may be brought before the Commission by the ministers concerned, by twenty delegates or twenty senators, by regional councils, or by authorized national associations for the protection of the environment. However, the possibility of referring a project to the Commission could be limited as a result of the restrictive interpretation of section 4 of the 1996 implementing legislation.[8] Pursuant to section 4, a request must be made by a regional council whose territory is affected, and include the corresponding deliberation of the regional council. The Commission is not required to explain its decision and, since there is no judicial control, any public debate remains optional.

Initially, it was recommended that the National Commission should be an independent administrative authority. This proposal was rejected, however. During the parliamentary debates, the parliament ensured that the

---

[5] N° 96.1236.   [6] Journal Officiel, 7 Feb. 1998.   [7] [1990] OJ L158/56.
[8] S. 4 of decree No. 96–388, 10 May 1996, Journal Officiel, 11 May 1996.

Commission could not begin an inquiry on its own. Furthermore, the Commission is not permitted to organize debates directly; each project needs to be assigned to a specific committee presided over by one of the Commission members.

D.   MISCELLANEOUS DEVELOPMENTS

French environmental law has always been and still is profoundly influenced by court decisions. There are three sectors of judicial activity that are most interesting: state liability, state liability for administrative faults, and the elaboration of the precautionary principle.

i.   State Liability

As regards administrative liability, an important issue remains whether a farmer or landowner can claim compensation for damage caused by certain protected animal species. Since the protection of certain species is a state obligation pursuant to the Bonn Convention,[9] the question arises whether the state is liable for damage caused by protected species. Following a lower court decision allowing compensation for damage to a rice plantation by pink flamingos,[10] the Council of State refused to allow compensation on the grounds that the protection of flamingos was of general interest and that the law excluded state liability.[11] French legal doctrine to the effect that the state is responsible for damages caused by its laws could not be applied in this case.

ii.   State Liability for Administrative Faults

State responsibility for administrative fault may similarly arise. For example, regarding damage caused to a fish farm by cormorants, an administrative tribunal (lower court) considered that the proliferation of the protected cormorants at that time required counter-measures by the state and that the inaction was a fault justifying compensation.[12] A subsequent French request to the European Commission resulted in the deletion of cormorants from the European protected species list.[13]

iii.   The Precautionary Principle

The Council of State has also made important contributions to the legal development of the precautionary principle. The principle was introduced into French law in 1995[14] and was considered a general policy without any specific legal effect. An administrative order of the Ministry of Agriculture authorized

---

[9] The 1979 Bonn Convention on the Conservation of Migratory Species of Wild Animals [1982] OJ L210/11.

[10] Administrative Court of Appeal Lyon 1 Feb. 1994. Plan [1994] RJE 263.

[11] CE 24 Jan. 1998, Min. of Environment/ Plan (1998) RFDA 568.

[12] T. A. Nantes, "Droit de l'Environnement" (1998) 55 *Revue Juridique de l'Environnement* 10 and 95.

[13] Dir. 97/49/EC of 29 July 1997 modifiying Dir. 79/409/EEC [1991] OJ L223/9.

[14] No. 95–101, 2 Feb. 1995, Art. L.200.1, Rural Code.

a company, Novartis, to introduce and cultivate three species of genetically modified corn. The French Greenpeace Association sued the state and requested the immediate suspension of the permit in order to stop the importation of the corn into France. In a first decision, the Council of State granted the suspension with a reference to the precautionary principle.[15] In a second decision, the Council of State decided to ask the European Court of Justice for a preliminary ruling on the interpretation of Directive 90/220/EEC on the Deliberate Release into the Environment of Genetically Modified Organisms.[16] If the Commission gives its consent, is the national authority which transmitted the request to the Commission and obtained its consent obliged to give a written consent or has that national authority the power to refuse the introduction of the GMO?[17]

[15] CE, 25 Sept. 1998, *Assoc. Greenpeace.*   [16] [1990] OJ L117/15.
[17] CE, 11 Dec. 1998, *Assoc. Greenpeace.*

VI. Germany

MICHAEL RODI*

A. INTRODUCTION

Environmental law is likely to become increasingly important in Germany, as the newly elected federal government emphasized environmental protection as one of its main goals.[1] The consolidation of environmental law, which now consists of many separate legal acts, into one single Environmental Code (UGB) is being pursued further.[2] The main items of current environmental policy are the abolition of nuclear energy and ecological tax reform.

The importance of these eco-taxes is exemplified by the fact that the revenue of increased taxes on mineral oil as well as on electricity shall finance the reduction of social security contributions.[3]

B. NATURE CONSERVATION

The evolution, fuelled by Community law, of nature protection law towards biodiversity law remains problematic in Germany. After Germany was condemned by the European Court of Justice,[4] Directive 79/409/EEC on the Conservation of Wild Birds (Wild Birds Directive)[5] and Directive 92/43/EEC on the Conservation of Natural Habitats and of Wild Fauna and Flora (Habitats Directive)[6] were recently implemented into national law,[7] amending the Protection of Nature and Conservation of Landscape Act.[8] Since the states are still competent for the designation of special protection areas (SPAs), two judgments of the Federal Administrative Court of 19 May 1998 concerning the legal status of SPAs will remain important.

In a decision regarding the construction of the so-called *Ostsee-Autobahn* (Baltic Sea inter-state highway)[9] the court *assumed* the existence of an actual SPA in the context of the Habitats Directive.[10] Because the court assumed the existence of potential protected areas in the sense of Article 4(1) of the

---

* Professor of Law, University of Greifswald.

[1] See Coalition Agreement between the Social Democratic Party of Germany and Bündnis 90/Die Grünen, 20 Oct. 1998, especially part IV, "Ecological Modernization".

[2] See Ministry for the Environment, Nature Conservation and Nuclear Safety of the Federal Republic of Germany (ed.), *Environmental Code (Umweltgesetzbuch-UGB)*, draft prepared by the Independent Expert Commission, Berlin, 1998.

[3] See Act for the Beginning of an Ecological Tax Reform (*Gesetz zum Einstieg in die ökologische Steuerreform*) of 24 Mar. 1999, BGBl. 1999 I 378, especially Art. 1 of the Electricity Tax Act.

[4] Case C–83/97, *Commission* v. *Germany* [1997] ECR I–7191.

[5] [1979] OJ L103/1. [6] [1992] OJ L206/7. [7] BGBl. 1998 I 2994.

[8] Bundesnaturschutzgesetz, BGBl. 1987 I 889.

[9] Bundesverwaltungsgericht, 19 May 1998, published in (1998) 18 Umwelt- und Planungsrecht 384.

[10] Art. 4(1), (2) of the Wild Birds Directive'; Art. 6(3), (4) of the Habitats Directive.

Habitats Directive, a submission to the European Court of Justice was not considered necessary. The court presumed that Germany would not be able to fulfil the obligation of Article 4(2) of the Habitats Directive. Nevertheless, the project could be carried out because of compelling reasons of public interest.[11]

In a second decision,[12] the Federal Administrative Court annulled a decision of a lower court, because the possible implications on the SPA, as specified in Article 4(4) of the Wild Birds Directive, were insufficiently examined. Limitations of the regime of protection were only allowed on the grounds of health, public safety, and the protection of the environment and nature. Economical considerations were irrelevant. The direct effect of the Directive created a right in favour of citizens affected by the plan.

C.   WASTE

The Waste Management and Product Recycling Act,[13] in force since 1996, obliges private individuals to prevent, safely dispose of, or recycle waste. A special regime of product liability for producers (Articles 22 *et seq.*) is introduced by the Ordinance on the prevention and recycling of packaging waste.[14] The individual obligation to take back packaging waste can be avoided by joining a sufficiently successful collecting and recycling system ("dual system"). Several new requirements, especially with regard to recycling quotas, are put in place to implement Directive 94/62/EC on Packaging and Packaging Waste.[15] The provisions on recycling systems, which are based on a system of obligations which the Commission in the past considered a violation of Article 28 (formerly Article 30) EC,[16] were kept essentially unaltered.

Directive 92/3/Euratom on the Supervision and Control of Shipments of Radioactive Waste Between Member States and Into and Out of the Community[17] was implemented by the Ordinance on Shipments of Radioactive Waste into or out of Germany of 27 July 1998.[18]

D.   HORIZONTAL INSTRUMENTS

i. Environmental Impact Assessment

German environmental law excludes public participation in the planning procedure of federal motorways. According to a ruling of the Federal

---

[11] Art. 6(4), (1) of the Habitats Directive.

[12] Bundesverwaltungsgericht, 19 May 1998, published in (1998) 18 Umwelt- und Planungsrecht 389.

[13] *Kreislaufwirtschafts- und Abfallgesetz* (KrW-AbfG), BGBl. 1994 I 1354.

[14] *Verpackungsverordnung* (VerpackV). The Ordinance of 1991 is now replaced by the Ordinance of 21 Aug. 1998, BGBl. 1998 I 2379; see H. J. Koch, "Die neue Verpackungsverordnung" (1998) 17 *Neue Zeitschrift für Verwaltungsrecht* 1155.

[15] [1994] OJ L365/10.

[16] Letter of formal notice No. 91–4489 of the Commission of 12 Dec. 1995.

[17] [1992] OJ L35/24.   [18] BGBl. 1998 I 1918.

Administrative Court, this does not violate obligations arising from Directive 85/337/EEC on the Assessment of the Effects of Certain Public and Private Projects on the Environment (EIA Directive).[19] A preliminary reference to the European Court of Justice was not considered necessary.[20] According to Article 6(3) of the EIA Directive, the Member States can determine in which way the affected public may participate. Because the licensing authority may still decide about the project, this would not infringe the principle that an assessment of the project must occur before consent is given (Article 2(1) of the EIA Directive).

In the same decision, the court ruled that an obligation of the body responsible for the project to conduct an independent environmental assessment can be derived neither from Article 6 of the Environmental Impact Assessment Act (UVPG)[21] nor from Article 5 of the EIA Directive. These rules merely contain minimum standards concerning the duty to provide information. According to the Federal Administrative Court, the fact that no evaluation of the project's effects has been conducted does not lead to substantive invalidity of the licence. This is because environmental impact assessment is not a discrete procedure, but one that is integrated into the planning procedure. According to German planning law, a lawsuit may only be based on an error in the procedure that affected the planning decision in a legally relevant way. The ability to take legal action independently is not required by the EIA Directive.[22]

ii.   *Environmental Information*

The Environmental Information Act,[23] which came into force in 1994, not only involved German courts[24] but also the European Court of Justice, which had to answer some preliminary questions from the Higher Administrative Court, Schleswig.[25] The notion of "preliminary investigation proceedings" in Article 3(2) of Directive 90/313 on the Freedom of Access to Information on the Environment[26] means that the ground for derogation, contained in Article 7(1) No. 2 UIG for "administrative procedures", does not apply to normal permit procedures. It is assumed that the internal administrative procedure (*Widerspruchsverfahren*) according to Article 68 of the Code governing administrative courts (VwGO) has no direct relation to a court procedure because it serves as an internal administrative review of legality.[27]

---

[19] [1985] OJ L175/40.

[20] Bundesverwaltungsgericht, 17 Feb. 1997, published in (1998) 20 Natur und Recht 305; Bundesverwaltungsgericht, 19 May 1998, published in (1998) 18 Umwelt- und Planungsrecht 389.

[21] *Gesetz über die Umweltverträglichkeitsprüfung* (UVPG), BGBl. 1990 I 205.

[22] Bundesverwaltungsgericht, 17 Feb. 1997, published in (1997) 20 Natur und Recht 305.

[23] *Umweltinformationsgesetz* (UIG), BGBl. 1994 I 1490.

[24] See F. Stollmann, "Recent Jurisdiction on Environmental Information Law" (1998) 20 *Natur und Recht* 78.

[25] Case C–321/96, *Wilhelm Mecklenburg v. Kreis Pinneberg* [1998] ECR I–3809.

[26] [1990] OJ L158/56.

[27] See A. Turiaux, "Das Deutsche Umweltinformationsgesetz auf den Prüfstand de EG-Rechts" (1998) 9 *Europäische Zeitschrift für Wirtschaftsrecht* 717.

According to the European Court of Justice, the right of access to environmental information found in Article 3(2) of the UIG is to be interpreted widely on the basis of Article 2a of the Environmental Information Directive. According to the Higher Administrative Court, Lüneburg, however, the term "measures for the protection of the relevant environmental areas" in Article 3(2) No. 3 of the UIG is to be interpreted restrictively and only concerns measures which aim at a direct improvement of the environment.[28] Measures that contribute to the protection of the environment only indirectly, such as financial programmes promoting measures for the improvement of the environment, are not included in this definition.

The same line of thought is found in a judgment of the Higher Administrative Court, Mannheim.[29] Information on closed proceedings regarding a criminal or regulatory offence cannot be the object of a claim for information. This information does not contribute to the protection of environment in the sense of Article 3(2) No. 3 of the UIG. Like the European Court of Justice, the Administrative Court, Mannheim, also had to deal with the reasons for derogation during, *inter alia*, court proceedings or preliminary investigations.[30] It was held that a total derogation was not intended. Any other interpretation would mean that the German legislator would infringe Article 3(2) third dash of the EIA Directive.

E.   MISCELLANEOUS DEVELOPMENTS

i.   Environmental Taxes and Levies

Environmental taxes and levies are increasingly favoured by the new federal government as well as by states (*Länder*) and local authorities as an instrument of environmental policy. The use of environmental taxes by a state may lead to conflicts between the (formal) legislative competence for taxes and substantive legislation (*Sachgesetzgebung*).

Since the legislative competence for environmental law is to a large extent federal, the Federal Administrative Court, in two spectacular decisions of 7 May 1998, declared environmental levies demanded by states and local authorities unconstitutional because of lack of competence. These decisions concerned state taxes on wastes threatening the environment and wastes requiring supervision and local packaging taxes on disposable containers. The court avoided questions concerning the division of competences.[31] Instead, it found a breach of the constitutional rule of non-contradiction (*Widerspruchsfreiheit*) of the legal system. Under this rule, direct effects of law on behaviour regulated by substantive law may interfere neither with the general concep-

---

[28] Oberverwaltungsgericht Lüneburg, 19 Nov. 1997, published in (1998) 18 Umwelt- und Planungsrecht 155.

[29] Verwaltungsgerichtshof Mannheim, 10 June 1998, published in (1998) 17 Neue Zeitschrift für Verwaltungsrecht 987.

[30] Art. 7(1) no. 2 of the UIG.

[31] In particular, whether a substantial legislative competence is required for incentive taxes besides the formal tax competence.

tion of the substantive regulation, nor with a special rule. According to the Federal Court, the problem of avoiding waste by reducing the use of disposables is regulated by the federal Waste Act as well as the federal Packaging Ordinance. Even if the purposes of the levies and the federal waste law are identical, the levy is inconsistent with the principle of co-operation. Legal literature has criticized the fact that a competence problem was solved on grounds of the constitutional principle of non-contradiction and the assumption that federal waste law is based on the principle of co-operation.[32]

ii. Environmental Liability

In exceptional cases, environmental damages caused by private individuals may generate constitutional claims against the state. The Federal Constitutional Court[33] ruled that damage to forests is predominantly caused by private conduct and consequently the state is normally not liable. The lack of rules permitting compensation would be unconstitutional in light of the constitutional property right only if there were an evident violation of constitutional protective duties of the state. In the case of damage to forests this was not the case. On the one hand, the state takes extensive measures to protect the atmosphere, on the other hand, damage which still takes place is limited because of public support for forest management measures.

---

[32] M. Rodi, "Bundesstaatliche Kompetenzausübungsschranken für Lenkungssteuern" (1999) 26 *Steuer und Wirtschaft* 105.

[33] Bundesverwaltungsgericht, 26 May 1998, published in (1998) 20 Natur und Recht 597.

VII.   Greece

JOANNA KOUFAKIS*

A.   BIOTECHNOLOGY

Greece has yet to adopt legislative measures to transpose into national law Commission Directive 97/35/EC[1] of 18 June 1997 adapting Council Directive 90/220/EEC[2] on the Deliberate Release Into the Environment of Genetically Modified Organisms. The Directive was to be implemented by Member States before 31 July 1997. The European Commission decided to send a reasoned opinion to Greece, since Greece had failed to notify the Commission of any legislative measures[3] for its transposition.

B.   CHEMICALS

i.   Dangerous Substances and Preparations

On 8 April 1998, Decree 54/1998[4] of the Minister of National Economy and Economics amended Presidential Decree 445/83 in accordance with the new requirements set out by Commission Directives 96/55/EC,[5] 97/10/EC[6] and 97/16/EC,[7] Amending for the Fifteenth Time Directive 76/769/EEC[8] on Restrictions on the Marketing and Use of Certain Dangerous Substances and Preparations.

ii.   Dangerous Substances Classification, Packaging and Labelling

Decree 590/1997[9] of the Minister of National Economy and Economics transposed Commission Directive 96/54/EC[10] into Greek law. This Directive adapts Council Directive 67/548/EEC[11] on the Approximation of the Laws, Regulations, and Administrative Provisions Relating to the Classification, Packaging, and Labelling of Dangerous Substances.

iii.   Plant Protection Products

Council Directive 97/57/EC[12] Establishing Annex IV to Directive 91/414/EC Concerning the Placing of Plant Protection Products on the Market[13] was transposed into Greek law by Presidential Decree 290/1998,[14] which amended Presidential Decree 115/97. The Presidential Decree was adopted in order to

---

* Advocate, LL.M., member of the Athens Bar Association.
1   [1997] OJ L169/72.   2   [1990] OJ L117/15.
3   Press Release, IP/98/622, 3 July 1998.   4   Official Gazette, Vol. B, No. 387, 29 Apr. 1998.
5   [1996] OJ L231/201.   6   [1997] OJ L68/24.   7   [1997] OJ L116/31.
8   [1967] OJ L262/201.   9   Official Gazette, Vol. B, No. 294, 26 Mar. 1998.
10   [1996] OJ L248/1.   11   [1967] OJ L196/1.   12   [1997] OJ L265/48.
13   [1991] OJ L230/1.   14   Official Gazette, Vol. A, No. 209, 9 Sept. 1998.

comply with the new requirements of Annex VI to Directive 91/414/EEC which had to be implemented before October 1997.

Presidential Decree 141/1998[15] implemented Commission Directives 95/44/EC[16] and 97/46/EC[17] amending Directive 95/44/EC establishing the conditions under which certain harmful organisms, plants, plant products, and other objects listed in Annexes I to V to Council Directive 77/93/EC may be introduced into or moved within the Community or certain protected zones thereof, for trial or scientific purposes and for work on varietal selections.[18]

C. NATURE CONSERVATION

i. *Special Protection Areas, Wetlands*

On 30 March 1998, a Joint Ministerial Decree, No 8586/1838[19] on the protection of wetlands in the area of the Evros river, was adopted. Through this decision, 95,000 square kilometres are registered on the list of wetlands of international importance of the Ramsar Convention and designated as special protected areas according to the provisions of Article 4 of Directive 79/409/EEC on the Conservation of Wild Birds.[20]

ii. *Habitats Directive*

On 26 June 1997, the European Court of Justice[21] ruled that Greece had failed to adopt the necessary legislative measures to transpose Council Directive 92/43/EC on the Conservation of Natural Habitats and of Wild Fauna and Flora (Habitats Directive)[22] into Greek law. Greece still has not adopted the measures necessary to comply with the provisions of the Habitats Directive.

In spite of the fact that Greece has already proposed an extensive list of sites for inclusion in the Natura 2000 network, as foreseen by the Directive, the European Commission has decided to take further steps against it within the framework of Article 228 (formerly Article 171) EC, since Greece has failed to comply with the above judgment.[23]

In addition, the European Commission decided to issue a letter of formal notice for failure to protect the rare Mediterranean sea turtle.[24] The Commission considers the failure to provide for undisturbed nesting beaches for these turtles to be a violation of the Habitats Directive.

iii. *Wild Fauna and Flora*

Regulation (EC) No. 338/97 on the Protection of Species of Wild Fauna and Flora by Regulating Trade Therein (Regulation on Trade in Endangered Species)[25]

---

[15] Official Gazette, Vol. A, No. 108, 22 May 1998. [16] [1995] OJ L184/34.
[17] [1997] OJ L204/43. [18] [1977] OJ L26/20.
[19] Official Gazette, Vol. B, No. 376 , 27 Apr. 1998. [20] [1979] OJ L103/1.
[21] Case C–329/96, *European Commission* v. *Greece* [1997] ECR I–3749. [22] [1992] OJ L206/7.
[23] Press Release, IP/98/737, 30 July 1998. [24] Press Release, IP/98/872, 9 Oct. 1998.
[25] [1997] OJ L61/1.

provides for stringent controls on trade in some species of wild fauna and flora and requires Member States to back up these protective measures with effective sanctions. The European Commission has decided to apply to the European Court of Justice against Greece for failure to respect its obligations under this Regulation on Trade in Endangered Species.[26]

D. WASTE

i. Waste Management Plans

Waste strategy in Greece is almost non-existent, which is exemplified by the fact that over 90 per cent of all waste is still dumped illegally. Directive 75/442/EEC on Waste[27] and Directive 91/689/EEC on Hazardous Waste[28] were transposed into national law only after a great delay and a Court ruling against Greece for failure to comply with their provisions.

As yet, Greek waste-management plans have not taken any account of the provisions of the relevant Community waste legislation, and the European Commission decided to send a reasoned opinion on the subject.[29]

ii. Batteries and Accumulators

Council Directive 91/157/EEC on Batteries and Accumulators Containing certain Dangerous Substances[30] requires Member States to introduce the necessary legislative measures to promote the recovery and controlled disposal of spent batteries and accumulators containing dangerous substances, thereby reducing the impact of battery waste on the environment. In so doing, Member States are required to introduce and apply waste reduction programmes and notify these to the Commission.

Greece transposed the Directive, as amended by Council Directive 93/86/EC adapting to technical progress Council Directive 91/157/EEC,[31] into national law by Joint Ministerial Decree 73537/1438/1995.[32] However, it has not yet adopted waste reduction programmes, as required by Article 6 of the Directive.

In 1998, the European Commission brought an action under Article 226 (formerly Article 169) EC for a declaration that, by not adopting and notifying to the Commission the waste reduction plans necessary to comply with the provisions of Article 6 of Directive 91/157/EEC, Greece has failed to fulfil its obligations under the EC Treaty and that Directive.[33]

iii. Hazardous Waste Incineration

Greece has not yet adopted any legislative measures to transpose into national law Council Directive 94/67/EC[34] on the Incineration of Hazardous Waste. The

---

[26] Press Release, IP/98/872, 9 Oct. 1998.   [27] [1975] OJ L194/47.
[28] [1991] OJ L377/20.   [29] Press Release, IP/98/580, 30 June 1998.
[30] [1991] OJ L78/38.   [31] [1993] OJ L264/51.
[32] Official Gazette, Vol. B, No. 781, 12 Sept. 1995.
[33] Case C–215/98, *European Commission* v. *Greece*, pending.   [34] [1994] OJ L365/34.

Directive was to be implemented by 31 December 1996. The European Commission decided to send a reasoned opinion to the Greek government.[35]

iv. *Packaging and Packaging Waste Directive*

Greece has yet to adopt legislative measures in order to transpose into national law Directive 94/62/EC[36] on Packaging and Packaging Waste, even though the deadline for compliance was 30 June 1996. The European Commission has decided to bring a case before the European Court of Justice for its failure to adopt the necessary national legislation to implement this Directive.[37]

E.   WATER

Under Council Directive 76/464/EEC on pollution caused by certain dangerous substances discharged into the aquatic environment of the Community, Member States are obliged to enact pollution reduction programmes for these substances with binding quality objectives.[38] Greece transposed the Directive into national law by Joint Ministerial Decree 55648/2210/1991,[39] but has not yet fixed any quality objectives set by the Directive. The European Commission decided to bring a case against Greece before the European Court of Justice for failure to give proper effect to the Directive.[40]

Concerning transport of dangerous substances over water, Presidential Decree 174/1998[41] amended Presidential Decree 346/1994 in line with Directive 97/26/EC[42] amending Council Directive 93/75/EC Concerning Minimum Requirements for Vessels Bound For or Leaving Community Ports and Carrying Dangerous or Polluting Goods.[43]

F.   HORIZONTAL INSTRUMENTS

i. *Eco-audit*

The Eco-Audit Regulation,[44] which aims at promoting continuous improvements in the environmental performance of industrial activities, requires Member States to appoint a competent body with responsibility for registering sites that participate in the scheme and to establish a system for the accreditation of the independent environmental verifiers.

From 1997, the prefectures of South Attika, Thessaloniki, and Kozani, within the framework of the earlier Eco-audit Regulation, have run pilot projects concerning the application of the eco-audit scheme to enterprises in the public sector.

---

[35] Press Release, IP/98/578, 30 June 1998.
[36] [1994] OJ L365/10.
[37] Press Release, IP/98/579, 30 June 1998.
[38] [1976] OJ L129/43.
[39] Official Gazette, Vol. B, No. 323, 13 May 1991.
[40] Press Release, IP/97/577, 30 June 1998.
[41] Official Gazette, Vol. A, No. 129, 16 June 1998.
[42] [1997] OJ L158/40.
[43] [1993] OJ L247/19.
[44] Council Reg. (EEC) No. 1836/93 allowing voluntary participation by companies in the industrial sector in a Community eco-management and audit scheme [1993] OJ L168/1.

On 12 November 1998, the Ministers of National Economy, Economics, Development, the Environment, Physical Planning, and Public Works adopted a Joint Ministerial Decree No. 28489/2669/1998[45] taking the necessary measures for the application of the Regulation. According to Article 6 of the Regulation, the competent body is the Accreditation National Council, which was founded by Law 2231/1994.[46]

ii. Eco-label

By Joint Ministerial Decree 86644/2482/1993[47] the competent body for awarding the eco-label was appointed, according to the relevant provisions of Regulation (EC) No. 880/92.[48] The Supreme Board for Awarding the Ecological Label, ASAOS, provides information to the business community and consumers, organizes international meetings, and establishes criteria for several areas within the framework of the Regulation. On 9 April 1998 the first eco-label was awarded.

G.   MISCELLANEOUS DEVELOPMENTS

i. Energy Policy in General

The Hellenic Action Programme to reduce CO_2 and other greenhouse gas emissions is based on a drastic energy-conservation policy in all sectors of final consumption (industry, transport, commercial, and the domestic sector), as well as on the use of natural gas and the promotion of renewable resources.

The energy programme (1994–9), launched by the Ministry for Development, promotes energy efficiency, rational use of renewable energy sources, and the use of natural gas.

The National Action Plan of Energy Conservation in the Developed Environment, Energy 2001, carried out by the Ministry for the Environment, Physical Planning, and Public Works, intends to change existing production and consumption patterns through the promotion of building construction techniques and services aiming at energy conservation and the integration of renewable energy technologies. The Action Plan is to be applied through specific legislation, concerning an incentive policy for energy-saving measures in existing buildings as well as policies, policy instruments, measures, and new standards concerning new buildings.

ii. SAVE Directive

Despite the promising energy programmes of the Ministry for Development and of the Ministry for the Environment, Physical Planning and Public Works, mentioned above, Greece only recently transposed into national law Council Directive 93/76/EC to Limit Carbon Dioxide Emissions by Improving Energy Efficiency (SAVE).[49] Joint Ministerial

---

[45] Official Gazette, Vol. B, No. 1177, 12 Nov. 1998.   [46] Official Journal, Vol. A, No. 139, 1994.
[47] Official Gazette, Vol. B, No. 763, 30 Sept. 1993.   [48] [1992] OJ L99/1.
[49] [1993] OJ L37/28.

Decree 214/75/4704[50] was signed on 30 July 1998, although the Directive was
to be implemented by Member States before 31 December 1994.

iii.   Household Washing Machines

By Joint Ministerial Decree Δ6/B/10.200/1998,[51] Greece transposed into
national law Commission Directive 97/17/EC[52] implementing Council
Directive 92/75/EC[53] with regard to Energy Labelling of Household
Dishwashers.[54] The Directive had to be implemented before 15 June 1998, subject to a transitional provision.

iv.   LIFE

The European Commission has decided to co-fund four Greek demonstration
projects within the framework of the LIFE programme for the year 1998. These
projects concern, for example, research on hazardous waste treatment, more
effective recycling methods, and water purification techniques.

---

[50] Official Gazette, Vol. B, No. 880, 19 Aug. 1998.
[51] Official Gazette, Vol. B, No. 591, 16 June 1998.   [52] [1997] OJ L118/1.
[53] Dir. 92/75/EEC on the indication by labelling and standard product information of the consumption of energy and other resources by household appliances, [1992] OJ L297/16.
[54] Official Gazette, Vol. B, No. 591, 16 June 1998.

VIII.   Ireland

Yvonne Scannell*

A.   AIR POLLUTION

The European Communities Regulations 1998[1] implement Council Directive 94/67/EEC on the Incineration of Hazardous Waste.[2] The Directive will be implemented through the licensing system established under the Environmental Protection Agency Act 1992 and operated and enforced by the Environmental Protection Agency which authorizes and regulates activities subject to integrated pollution control.

The Air Pollution Act Regulations 1998[3] ban the marketing, sale, and distribution of non-smokeless solid fuels in specified urban areas. The regulations were necessary to secure compliance with Council Directive 80/779/EEC on Air Quality Limit Values and Guide Values for Sulphur Dioxide and Suspended Particles.[4]

To comply with the Kyoto Protocol to the Convention on Long-Range Transboundary Air Pollution, Ireland is preparing a national greenhouse gas strategy that will limit its increase in the emission of greenhouse gases to 13 per cent above 1990 levels.

B.   CHEMICALS

The European Communities (Introduction of Organisms Harmful to Plants or Plant Products) Regulations 1998[5] implement Council Directive 97/3/EC amending Council Directive 77/93/EEC on Protective Measures Against the Introduction Into the Community of Organisms Harmful to Plants or Plant Products and Against their Spread Within the Community.[6] The European Communities (Pesticide Residues) (Cereals) (Amendment) Regulations 1998,[7] the European Communities (Pesticide Residues) (Foodstuffs of Animal Origin) (Amendment) Regulations 1998[8] and the European Communities (Pesticide Residues) (Products of Plant Origin, including Fruit and Vegetables) (Amendment) Regulations 1998[9] implement Council Directive 97/71/EC.[10]

The European Communities (Introduction of Organisms Harmful to Plants or Plant Products) (Prohibition) (Amendment) (1998/2) Regulations 1998[11] implement the provisions of Commission Directives 98/1, 98/2 and 98/17/EC Containing Protective Measures Against the Introduction and Spread of

---

* Professor of Law, Trinity College Law School, Dublin; Arthur Cox, Solicitors.

[1] SI 1998/64.   [2] [1994] OJ L263/34.   [3] SI 1998/118.
[4] [1980] OJ L229/30.   [5] SI 1998/78.   [6] [1997] OJ L27/30.
[7] SI 1998/72.   [8] SI 1998/70.   [9] SI 1998/71.
[10] [1997] OJ L347/42.   [11] SI 1998/120.

Organisms Harmful to Plants and Plant Products.[12] The European Communities (Introduction of Organisms Harmful to Plants or Plant Products) (Prohibition) (Amendment) (1998/3) Regulations 1998[13] implement the provisions of Commission Decision 98/105/EEC.[14]

C. NATURE CONSERVATION

The European Communities (Conservation of Wild Birds) (Amendment) Regulations 1998[15] classify Wexford Harbour as a Special Protection Area for the purposes of Council Directive 79/409/EEC on the Conservation of Wild Birds.[16] The European Commission has initiated proceedings against Ireland for failure to provide reports required under the Directive 92/43/EEC[17] on the Conservation of Natural Habitats and of Wild Fauna and Flora (Habitats Directive).[18] The European Communities (Natural Habitats) (Amendment) Regulations 1998[19] amend the European Communities Habitats Regulations 1997 to give effect to Council Directive 97/62[20] adapting the Habitats Directive to technical and scientific progress.[21]

D. WASTE

The law relating to waste management was reformed and largely codified by the Waste Management Act 1996, which also established a structure for implementing all EC directives on waste. The Act itself is framework legislation and had to be supplemented by subordinate legislation giving effect to the principles and policies it enunciated. A series of regulations was enacted in 1997 and 1998 to do this. This report deals only with the 1998 regulations. The Waste Management (Amendment of the Waste Management Act 1996) Regulations 1998[22] amended the Act in order to enable better effect to be given to Directive 86/278 on the protection of the environment and in particular of the soil, when sewage sludge is used in agriculture.[23]

The Waste Management (Permit) Regulations 1998[24] provide for the granting of waste permits and for the registration of the storage of hazardous waste by local authorities and were enacted, *inter alia*, to implement Council Directive 91/689 on Hazardous Waste.[25] Further amendments of the Act were made by the Waste Management (Amendment of the Waste Management Act 1996) Regulations 1998[26] in order, *inter alia*, to give effect to Council Directive 75/442 on Waste[27] as amended by Council Directive 91/156/EEC.[28] They empower local

[12] Respectively: [1998] OJ L15/26, [1998] OJ L15/34, and [1998] OJ L85/28.

[13] SI 1998/167.   [14] [1998] OJ L25/101.   [15] SI 1998/154.

[16] [1979] OJ L103/1.   [17] [1992] OJ L206/7.

[18] Press Release IP/98/872, 9 Oct. 1998.   [19] SI 1998/233.   [20] [1997] OJ L305/42.

[21] The implementation of the Habitats Directive has been severely criticized in Y. Scannell, R. Cannon, D. Clarke, and A. Doyle, *The Habitats Directive in Ireland* (Dublin: Centre for European Law and Policy, 1999).

[22] SI 1998/146 and 1998/148.   [23] [1986] OJ L181/6.   [24] SI 1998/165.

[25] [1991] OJ L377/20.   [26] SI 1998/166.   [27] [1975] OJ L194/47.

[28] Council Dir. 91/156/EEC amending Dir. 75/442/EEC on waste [1991] OJ L78/2.

authorities to operate a permit system for certain waste recovery and disposal activities and make miscellaneous amendments to the 1996 Act.

The Waste Management (Movement of Hazardous Waste) Regulations 1998[29] were enacted, *inter alia*, to implement Council Directive 91/689/EEC on Hazardous Waste[30] and to supplement Council Regulation (EC) No. 259/93 on the Supervision and Control of Shipments of Waste Within, Into and Out of the European Community[31] as amended. Similarly, the Waste Management (Transfrontier Shipment of Waste) Regulations 1998[32] were made to give effect to Council Regulation (EC) No. 259/93, as amended, by providing for adminis-trative details and enforcement matters.

Furthermore, Waste Management (Miscellaneous Provisions) Regulations 1998[33] were enacted partly to give effect to Council Directive 75/439 on the Disposal of Waste Oils,[34] as amended by Council Directive 87/101/EEC.[35]

Effect was given to Council Directive 94/67/EC on the Incineration of Hazardous Waste[36] by the European Communities (Licensing of Incinerators of Hazardous Waste) Regulations 1998.[37] Hazardous waste incinerators are subject to integrated pollution control under the Environmental Protection Agency Act 1992.

E. WATER

The Environmental Protection Agency published a discussion document on "Environmental Quality Objectives and Environmental Quality Standards for the Aquatic Environment" in late 1997 and invited comments from the public in early 1998. This document goes further than EC directives in that it proposes the promulgation of environmental quality objectives for *all* waters in the state and its territorial waters. It advocated that the use category of fishery water should be applied to all surface waters in the state and that associated envi-ronmental quality standards (EQSs) should be applied as general overall crite-ria for the satisfactory environmental quality of such waters. All surface waters would thus have to meet the appropriate quality requirements for fisheries unless particular local circumstances make such a goal unattainable "without inordinate effort". (This is the *de facto* situation in Ireland where discharges to waters are licensed by most local authorities and the EPA itself but not where policies for non-point discharges to waters are implemented.) Additional envi-ronmental quality objectives and standards are proposed in certain locations for particular uses such as water abstraction. Further EQSs are proposed for substances covered by List II of Council Directive 76/464/EEC on Pollution Caused by Certain Dangerous Substances Discharged Into the Aquatic Environment of the Community,[38] but particular emphasis is placed on selected metals and organo-halogenated compounds, primarily organo-chlorine

---

[29] SI 1998/147.   [30] [1991] OJ L377/20.   [31] [1993] OJ L30/1.
[32] SI 1998/149.   [33] SI 1998/164.   [34] [1975] OJ L194/31.
[35] Council Dir. 87/101/EEC amending Council Dir. 75/439/EEC [1987] OJ L42/43.
[36] [1994] OJ L365/34.   [37] SI 1998/64.   [38] [1976] OJ L129/23.

compounds, which are largely pesticides. EQS values, proposed by the EU expert committee on biotoxicology, are adopted as the values to form the basis of national EQSs where possible.

The Local Government (Water Pollution) Act 1977 (Water Quality Standards for Phosphorus) Regulations 1998[39] were enacted, *inter alia*, to ensure further compliance with Council Directive 76/464/EEC. The regulations require specified improvements in water quality conditions in rivers and lakes based on phosphorus concentrations or related water quality classifications within given time-frames, and contain a standstill clause whereby waters that already meet required standards must be maintained. Local authorities are required to submit a report to the EPA by 31 July 1999 containing their action plans for achieving the objectives in the regulations and progress reports must be submitted at stated intervals.

The Local Government (Water Pollution) Act 1977 (Nutrient Management Planning Consultation) Regulations 1998[40] require local authorities to consult the EPA before serving notices under section 21A of the Local Government (Water Pollution) Act 1977,[41] requiring owners or occupiers of land to prepare nutrient management plans. There have been jurisdictional difficulties concerning the question whether the EPA has power to regulate activities carried on outside the area defined in the licence application for the carrying on of the activity subjected to IPC licensing.

The Quality of Bathing Waters (Amendment) Regulations 1998[42] amend the Quality of Bathing Waters (Amendment) Regulations 1992 which implement Council Directive 76/160/EEC Concerning the Quality of Bathing Water.[43] New bathing areas were added to the extensive list in the 1992 Regulations.

The Department of the Marine has won the administrative battle to secure jurisdiction for the management of the environmental effects of aquaculture. (It was anticipated that aquaculture might be subjected to integrated pollution control and hence controlled by the EPA.) Aquaculture licences must be obtained under the Fisheries (Amendment) Act 1997. The Aquaculture Licence Regulations 1998[44] prescribe the application procedures for obtaining a licence from the Minister for the Marine. The Aquaculture Licences Appeal Board (Establishment) Order 1998[45] established an Aquaculture Licences Appeals Board to which appeals against decisions on licences may be made.

F. HORIZONTAL INSTRUMENTS

i. Environmental Information

The European Communities (Access to Environmental Information) Regulations 1998[46] implement Council Directive 90/313/EEC on the Freedom of Access to Information on the Environment.[47] While the regulations define

---

[39] SI 1998/248.   [40] SI 1998/257.
[41] As substituted by the Waste Management Act 1996, 66.   [42] SI 1998/177.
[43] [1976] OJ L31/1.   [44] SI 1998/236.   [45] SI 1998/204.
[46] SI 1998/125.   [47] [1990] OJ L158/56.

public authorities subject to the obligation to provide environmental information widely, some rights available under them are less extensive that those available under the Freedom of Information Act 1997, which is of more general application.[48] The regulations adhere closely to the Directive and they provide detailed procedures and time limits for complying with requests for information.

ii. Environmental Impact Assessment, IPPC

The European Communities (Environmental Impact Assessment) Regulations 1998[49] give effect to Council Directive 97/11/EC amending Council Directive 85/337 on the Assessment of the Effects of Certain Public and Private Projects on the Environment.[50] All activities listed in the second schedule to the Environmental Protection Agency Act 1992 have now been subjected to integrated pollution control. Taking together Council Directive 96/61/EC Concerning Integrated Pollution Prevention and Control (IPPC Directive)[51] and the Eco Audit Regulation,[52] the National Accreditation Board and the EPA are considering developing a common audit for Eco Audit and integrated pollution control. The EPA is also considering whether an ISO 14000 audit would suffice for the purposes of integrated pollution control.

G. MISCELLANEOUS DEVELOPMENTS

A large number environmental cases featured in the court lists in 1998. Most consisted of applications for judicial review of decisions on various authorizations for potentially polluting activities and planning permissions. All major challenges based on the quality or merits of decisions made were successfully resisted by decision-makers as the Irish courts have set a very high threshold for disturbing administrative decisions, more especially in environmental cases.[53] Some judicial challenges alleging procedural irregularities or that decisions were *ultra vires* because they exceeded the scope of powers conferred in legislation were successful. This commentary will deal only with cases that raise issues of general interest to an international readership.

i. Locus standi

The most interesting decision was the majority supreme court decision in *Lancefort* v. *An Bord Pleanala*,[54] which addressed the question whether

---

[48] See A. Ryall, "Access to Information on the Environment" [1998] *Irish Journal of Planning and Environmental Law* 48.

[49] SI 1998/351.   [50] [1997] OJ L73/5.   [51] [1996] OJ L257/26.

[52] Council Reg. (EC) No. 1836/93 allowing voluntary participation by companies in the industrial sector in a Community eco-management and audit scheme [1993] OJ L168/1.

[53] Since *O'Keeffe* v. *An Bord Pleanala* [1993] 1 IR 39, [1992] *Irish Law Reports Monthly* 237, the courts will not overturn a decision on the merits unless there were no grounds on which the decision-maker could have based its decision.

[54] [1998] Irish Law Reports Monthly 401. An Bord Pleanala (translated as the Planning Appeals Board) is a statutory appeal tribunal which hears appeals against decisions on, *inter alia*, planning permissions and air and water pollution licences.

companies expressly incorporated to litigate should have *locus standi* to bring judicial review proceedings. Although a majority of the court[55] ultimately denied *locus standi* to the applicant who challenged the *vires* of a decision permitting a commercial development on the site of listed buildings because, *inter alia*, of alleged non-compliance with the EIA Directive, the entire court held that the fact that a company was incorporated for the express purposes of bringing proceedings to challenge an environmental decision and to avoid liability for costs in the event of losing, would not necessarily deprive it of *locus standi* to bring the challenge. *Locus standi* in environmental cases is therefore very wide indeed in Ireland. Individuals will be deemed to have a "sufficient interest" to bring judicial review proceedings, even if their personal or proprietary interests are not affected, as long as they are not abusing the judicial process. The rationale for this is based on the theory that judicial remedies in these cases are granted to uphold the rule of law, not to vindicate private interests.[56] *Lancefort* is also interesting because the Supreme Court, citing *Aannemersbedrijf PK Kraaijeveld BV* v. *Gedeputeerde Staten Van Zuid-Holland*,[57] stated that the obligation on the courts to implement Community law may justify a generous approach to permitting access to the courts by those alleging infringements of Community law.

[55] Denham J dissenting.

[56] See *ESB* v. *Gormley* [1985] IR129, [1985] Irish Law Report Monthly 494; *Chambers* v. *An Bord Pleanala* [1992] 1 IR 134, [1992] Irish Law Report Monthly 296; *Fallon* v. *An Bord Pleanala* [1992] 2 IR 380, [1991] ILRM 799; *Lancefort Ltd* v. *An Bord Pleanala* [1998] Irish Law Report Monthly 401; *Ni h-Eili* v. *Environmental Protection Agency*, High Court, 20 Feb. 1998. In *Fallon* the applicant was identified as someone who had been "specifically chosen from a number of people to take the action, in that he was not a mark for costs and had no special material interest in the result of the action or any very special aesthetic or general interest". He was in fact a 28-year-old telephonist and receptionist who could not possibly afford to pay the high costs of litigating. In another recent case, *McBride* v. *Galway Corporation* (1998) 5 Irish Journal of Planning and Environmental Law 175. the Supreme Court accepted the *locus stand* of an unemployed actor alleging that a decision to locate a waste water treatment plant in Galway violated Council Dir. 85/337 on environmental impact assessment and Dir. 92/43/EC on the conservation of natural habitats and of wild fauna and flora although the applicant lost the case on the merits.

[57] Case C–72/95 [1996] ECR 1–5403.

IX. Italy

FRANCESCO FRANCIONI and MASSIMILIANO MONTINI*

A. AIR POLLUTION

The so-called "Auto-Oil" Directives[1] aim at the reduction of emissions from new cars and the improvement in the quality of petrol and other fuels. This coincides with Italian policy in this sector. Italy is promoting new cars with ever lower emissions. As part of this policy, the Italian government has already adopted various acts consisting of, *inter alia*, voluntary agreements, such as with the car manufacturer Fiat and with the oil refining and distribution company, Agip. The aim of both agreements is to reduce emissions from the transport sector.[2]

In July 1998, the Ministry of Public Works, in co-operation with the Ministry of Environment and the Ministry of Health, issued a decree aimed at strengthening monitoring of emissions from cars in the biggest cities (the "blue label" rule). The decree determines procedures and modalities to give effect to Article 7(1)(b) of the Road Traffic Code, which allows mayors of cities with more than 150,000 inhabitants to suspend traffic in city centres when particularly high levels of pollution are reached.

During 1998, the Italian government made considerable efforts to define the Italian climate programme, prepared by a inter-ministerial committee of experts which was finally approved by CIPE (Inter-ministerial Committee for Economic Planning) in November 1998. The programme defines six main areas in which action is required in order to satisfy the target agreed for reduction in greenhouse gases agreed in the Kyoto Protocol on Climate Change.

B. NATURE CONSERVATION

Several new parks and protected areas have been created pursuant to framework law No 394/91.[3] A new incentive towards a better management of natural parks could come from the decentralization of administrative powers in the field of nature conservation and natural parks. These powers are increasingly transferred from state to the local public authorities.

Through the Decreto del Presidente della Repubblica (DPR) of 8 August 1997,[4] Italy has finally implemented Council Directive 92/43/EC on the Conservation of National Habitats and of Wild Fauna and Flora.[5]

---

* Both Professor and Researcher, at the Faculty of Law of the University of Siena.

[1] Commission Proposal for a European Parliament and Council dir. relating to the quality of petrol and diesel fuels and amending Council Dir. 93/12, COM(96)248 [1997] OJ C77/1.

[2] See further the contribution of M. Onida in this volume.

[3] Law of 6 Dec. 1991 No. 394, Gazzetta Ufficiale della Repubblica Italiana (GURI) 13 Dec. 1991 no. 292.

[4] GURI 23 Oct. 1997 No. 248.   [5] [1992] OJ L206/7.

C.   WASTE

The decrees designed to implement the new framework law on waste have been the main focus of attention from the Ministry of Environment in this sector during the last year.[6] The CONAI, the super-consortium of all producers of waste, finally began its activities in November 1998. The CONAI is empowered to organize and co-ordinate the re-use, recycling and recovery of waste in the whole country.

Decreto Legislativo (D.Lgs.) No. 22/97 also contains new provisions on soil cleansing and remedial action to prevent or minimize environmental damage due to soil pollution or contamination. Unfortunately, the full operation of Article 22 of the Decree, which contains framework provisions on soil cleansing, has been hindered by the failure of the Ministry of Environment to enact the necessary implementation Decree.

Regarding nuclear waste, Italy's most important electricity undertaking, ENEL, recently published a plan that concerns the costs of dismantling nuclear power plants and dealing with nuclear waste.

D.   HORIZONTAL INSTRUMENTS

i.   Eco-audit, Eco-label

In order to implement the Eco Audit[7] and the Eco-label Regulations,[8] ANPA, the National Agency for the Protection of the Environment, responsible for the administration of the eco-audit and eco-label schemes, has effectively begun its work.

With regard to eco-audit, just eight industrial sites have been granted the EMAS award. The eco-label, however, has not been awarded even once, which is in line with the disappointing results seen throughout Europe.

ii.   Environmental Impact Assessment, IPPC

The new draft framework act on environmental impact assessment was approved in June 1998 by the Senate and now awaits final approval by the Chamber of Deputies. It intends comprehensively to transpose Directive 85/337/EEC on the Assessment of the Effects of Certain Public and Private Projects on the Environment (EIA Directive)[9] as amended by Directives 97/11/EC[10] and 96/61/EC Concerning Integrated Pollution Prevention and Control (IPPC Directive)[11] into the Italian legal system. The new framework law defines the principles and procedures for identifying and assessing the direct as well as indirect effects of projects, plans and programmes regarding

---

[6] The so-called *Ronchi* Decree; D.Lgs. No. 22/97, as amended by D.Lgs. No. 389/97, GURI 28 Nov. 1997 No. 278.

[7] Council Reg. (EC) No. 1836/93 allowing voluntary participation by companies in the industrial sector in a Community eco-management and audit scheme [1993] OJ L168/1.

[8] Council Reg. (EC) No. 880/92 on a Community eco-label award scheme [1992] OJ L99/1.

[9] [1985] OJ L175/40.   [10] Dir. 97/11/EC amending the EIA Directive [1997] OJ L73/5.

[11] [1996] OJ L257/26.

national resources and the national heritage. According to the framework law, the EIA procedure will accomplish two fundamental functions: evaluation of the impacts and informing the public.

In the meantime, the DPR of 11 February 1998[12] amended the list of projects of "national interest" contained in the Decree of the President of the Council of Ministers (DPCM) of 10 August 1988 No. 377, for which competence with regard to the environmental impact of which is reserved to the state. The DPCM of 10 August 1988 No. 377 (as amended) now lists all the projects contained in Annex I of the EIA Directive and some of projects contained in Annex II. Furthermore, it takes into account Directive 97/11/EC amending the EIA Directive[13] although Italy has not yet formally implemented it. It is understood that, awaiting the adoption of the new framework act on EIA, the competence of the regions in the EIA sphere remain confined pursuant the DPR of 12 April 1996[14] to the projects listed in Annex II of the EIA Directive, in so far they are not expressly reserved to the state.

iii. Environmental Information

Following intense debate, Council Directive 90/313/EEC on the Freedom of Access to Information on the Environment[15] was at last formally implemented in Italy by decree D.Lgs. 39/1997.[16] In order to evaluate its practical impact, the Ministry of the Environment's first Annual Report to the Parliament on the implementation of the right of access to environmental information is still awaited.

E. MISCELLANEOUS DEVELOPMENTS

i. Eco-incentives

The first set of incentives for the acquisition of new cars with lower levels of emission was put in place in 1997 and lasted until 31 January 1998. This scheme provided for an incentive for purchasing all new cars, irrespective of their polluting potential.

More interesting is the second set of incentives, which related to fuel consumption of cars, thus granting true eco-incentives for the acquisition of cleaner cars. This second set of incentives expired on 31 July 1998 and has not been replaced by any new scheme. Only some limited incentives remain in place with reference to electrically-powered and gas-powered cars. Apart from eco-incentives for the acquisition of new and less polluting cars, the government is now planning the launch of some new ecological incentives to accompany and facilitate the implementation of the Italian climate programme, which implements the Kyoto Protocol.

The first sector to benefit from these new eco-incentives would be the electric household appliances sector. The scheme provides for incentives for the

---

[12] GURI 27 Mar. 1998 No. 72.   [13] [1997] OJ L73/5.   [14] GURI 7 Sept. 1996 No. 210.
[15] [1990] OJ L158/56.   [16] GURI 6 Mar. 1997 No. 54.

acquisition of new appliances with lower energy consumption, in order to promote and enhance energy efficiency.

ii. Eco-taxes

Apart from the example of the tax on landfills of waste introduced by the 1996 budget law, the 1998 budget law can be seen as the first move towards the "greening" of the Italian fiscal system.

In this respect, the most interesting feature of the 1998 budget law is the introduction of a tax on sulphuride and nitrogenide emissions from large industrial combustion plants. As an example of further "greening", the 1999 budget law introduces a carbon tax into Italian fiscal laws. The newly established carbon tax, which aims at reducing CO_2 emissions in the atmosphere, will take the form of a progressive remodulation of the excise duties levied on different fossil fuels (carbon, crude oil, oil, gas) according to their relative greenhouse gas potential.

X. The Netherlands

JONATHAN VERSCHUUREN*

A. AIR POLLUTION

In March 1998, new provisions were added to the Environmental Management Act (EMA)[1] and the Air Pollution Act in order to implement fully Council Directive 96/62/EC on Ambient Air Quality Assessment and Management.[2] These new rules comprise, *inter alia*, the power to fix alert thresholds for ambient air and the drafting of lists with information for the air quality in certain zones and agglomerations.[3]

B. CHEMICALS

The Decree on the implementation of the EC Chemical Substances Directive[4] was modified on 4 February 1998[5] to implement Directive 97/16/EC[6] and the 15th amendment of Directive 76/769.[7] Furthermore, a new ministerial Regulation on the disposal of PCBs was issued on 30 July 1998[8] to implement Council Directive 96/59/EC on the Disposal of PCBs and PCTs.[9]

A proposal to amend the EMA, the Disasters Act, and the Working Conditions Act to implement Council Directive 96/82/EC of 9 December 1996 on the Control of Major-Accident Hazards Involving Dangerous Substances (Seveso II Directive)[10] was sent to parliament in April 1998.[11] Most of the substantive norms found in the Seveso II Directive will be implemented through the Major Accident Hazards Decree.[12] An important new feature of the implementing legislation will be the introduction of a new integral safety report, which replaces the existing reports on working conditions and on external safety. This constitutes an important improvement compared to the existing situation, where there are different reports from various governmental authorities.

---

* Professor of European and International Environmental Law at the Centre for Legislative Studies, Tilburg University.

[1] *Wet milieubeheer.*   [2] [1996] OJ L296/55.

[3] Act of 26 Mar. 1998, Bulletin of Acts and Decrees 1998, 221.

[4] *Besluit implementatie EEG-stoffenrichtlijn Wet milieugevaarlijke stoffen*, Stb. 1998, 260.

[5] The new version of this Decree was republished in the Bulletin of Acts and Decrees 1998, No. 260.

[6] [1997] OJ L116/31.

[7] Dir. 76/769/EEC on the approximation of the laws, regulations and administrative provisions of the Member States relating to restrictions on the marketing and use of certain dangerous substances and preparations [1976] OJ L262/201.

[8] Government Gazette No. 154.   [9] [1996] OJ L243/31.

[10] [1996] OJ L10/13.   [11] Parliamentary Documents II, 1997–1998, 25 972, Nos. 1–3.

[12] *Besluit risico's zware ongevallen.*

In a case between some environmental organizations and the Minister of Agriculture, Nature Management and Fisheries,[13] the trade and industry appeals tribunal has reviewed several decisions on the admission of pesticides in the Netherlands in the light of Directive 91/414/EEC Concerning the Placing of Plant Protection Products on the Market.[14] It is interesting to note that the tribunal found that decisions on the admission of pesticides made before the national legislation implementing Directive 91/414/EEC had come into effect can be tested by the tribunal against this implementing legislation, especially since the legislation entered into force on 1 February 1995, while the Directive had to be implemented on 25 July 1993.

C. NATURE CONSERVATION

In several cases at both European and national level, courts ruled that Directive 79/409/EEC on the Conservation of Wild Birds (Wild Birds Directive)[15] and Directive 92/43/EEC on the Conservation of Natural Habitats and of Wild Fauna and Flora (Habitats Directive)[16] have been inadequately implemented in the Netherlands. The European Court of Justice ruled that the Netherlands did not classify a sufficient number of special protection areas (SPAs) under the Wild Birds Directive.[17] According to the Court, Member States are obliged to classify as SPAs all sites which, applying ornithological criteria, appear to be the most suitable for conservation of the species in question. This is the fifth case in which the Netherlands has been found by the ECJ to have inadequately implemented the Wild Birds Directive.

A very important national decision with regard to the Habitats and the Wild Birds Directives was the *Waddensea* case from the District Court of Leeuwarden on 17 July 1998.[18] Four out of five decisions allowing exploratory drilling in the Waddensea were quashed by the district court because of non-compliance with the Wild Birds and Habitats Directives.

D. WASTE

Two important preliminary questions from the Council of State, on the application in the Netherlands of Regulation (EC) No. 259/93 on the Supervision and Control of Shipments of Waste Within, Into, and Out of the European Community[19] were answered by the European Court of Justice on 25 June

---

[13] Trade and Industry Appeals Tribunal, *Stichting Zuidhollandse Milieufederatie* v. *Minister of Agriculture, Nature Management and Fisheries*, 29 Jan. 1998, comment by Vogelenzang published at (1998) 33 *Milieu&Recht* 97; comment by Van der Veen published at (1998) 111 *Administratiefrechtelijke Beslissingen* 501. See also H. G. Sevenster, "Succes voor milieu-organisaties met behulp van de gewasbeschermingsmiddelenrichtlijn" (1998) 6 *Nederlands Tijdschrift voor Europees Recht* 120–1.

[14] [1991] OJ L230/1.   [15] [1979] OJ L103/1.   [16] [1992] OJ L206/7.

[17] Case C–3/96, *Commission* v. *the Netherlands* [1998] ECR I–3031.

[18] District Court of Leeuwarden, *Waddenvereniging* v. *Minister of Economic Affairs*, 17 July 1998, comment by Backes published at (1998) 89 *Milieu&Recht* 250.

[19] [1993] OJ L30/1.

1998.[20] In the *Beside* case, the Court ruled (*inter alia*) that in the case of mixed categories of waste (i.e. household waste and green list waste), not the origin (i.e. from households or industry), but the composition is decisive for the purpose of identifying it as red, amber or green-list waste.[21] The *Dusseldorp* case is more interesting for Dutch policy and law on waste.[22] In this case, the ECJ ruled that Dutch policy to apply the principles of self-sufficiency and proximity, not only to the shipment of waste for disposal but also for recovery, is in violation of Community law. Secondly, the Court held the exclusive rights conferred upon AVR Chemie, as the sole end-processor for the incineration of dangerous waste in a high-performance rotary furnace, to be contrary to Article 30 (formerly Article 36) EC. Thirdly, the same exclusive rights are contrary to Article 86 (formerly Article 90)EC in conjunction with Article 82 (formerly Article 86) EC.

Despite the fact that it was amended in 1997 in order to prevent further problems like *Dusseldorp*, the Long-Term Plan for the Disposal of Dangerous Waste is still troublesome as far as compliance with Regulation (EC) No. 259/93 is concerned.[23]

To implement Council Directive 94/67/EC on the Incineration of Hazardous Waste[24] ministerial rules on the incineration of dangerous wastes have been published in the Government Gazette.[25] These rules have to be followed by all competent authorities dealing with installations for the incineration of wastes. Apart from these rules for competent authorities, the regulation also imposes several obligations on persons operating waste incinerators, such as the duty to take samples and analyse all wastes that are offered for incineration.

E. WATER

In December 1997, the competent ministers issued an "action programme" to combat the consequences of high levels of nitrates in surface and ground waters caused by large-scale bio-industry in several parts of the country.[26] This was necessary to comply with Article 12(1) of Directive 91/676/EEC Concerning the Protection of Waters Against Pollution Caused by Nitrates from Agricultural Sources.[27] The Commission had already sent a letter of formal notice because of non-compliance with this provision on 13 June 1997.

[20] See A. van Rossem, "Nieuwe ontwikkelingen in het Europese afvalstoffenrecht?" (1998) 3 *Nederlands Tijdschrift voor Europees Recht* 20–3; and A. van Rossem and H. G. Sevenster, "Hof beantwoordt vragen Afdeling over afvalregime" (1998) 9 *Nederlands Tijdschrift voor Europees Recht* 196–201.

[21] Case C–192/96, *Beside and Besselsen* v. *Minister van Housing, Spatial Planning and the Environment* [1998] ECR I–4029, comment by Backes published at (1998) 339 *Administratiefrechtelijke Beslissingen* 1636.

[22] Case C–203/96, *Chemische Afvalstoffen Dusseldorp and others* v. *Minister of Housing, Spatial Planning and the Environment* [1998] ECR I–4075, comment by Backes published at (1998) 340 *Administratiefrechtelijke Beslissingen* 1641.

[23] *Scoribel* v. *Minister of Housing, Spatial Planning and the Environment* (1998) 341 *Administratiefrechtelijke Beslissingen* 1651.

[24] [1994] OJ L365/34.

[25] 27 Apr. 1998, No. 79.

[26] Parliamentary Documents I, 1997–1998, 25 389, No. 312, 2.

[27] [1991] OJ L375/1.

The Commission discontinued the procedure of Article 226 (formerly Article 169) EC, but in October initiated a new procedure because the programme did not meet the requirements of the Directive. According to the Commission, the Dutch system of specifying nitrate standards for individual businesses rather than standards per hectare is insufficient. A number of environmental and consumer organizations have requested a Dutch court to force national authorities to implement Directive 91/676/EEC.

In two cases published in 1998, a preliminary ruling has been requested concerning the application of Directive 76/464/EEC on Pollution Caused by Certain Dangerous Substances Discharged Into the Aquatic Environment of the Community.[28] The Council of State asked, *inter alia*, whether the placing of wood impregnated with creosote oil in water can be considered a "discharge" pursuant to Directive 76/464/EEC. In the second case, the same kind of question arose in respect of the precipitation of polluted steam.[29] Advocate-General Saggio has already delivered his opinion in both cases.[30]

Meanwhile, the Court has in both cases concluded that these emissions can be considered to be discharged pursuant to the Directive.

F.   HORIZONTAL INSTRUMENTS

i. *Environmental Information*

In March 1998, Directive 90/313/EEC on the Freedom of Access to Information on the Environment[31] was finally implemented in the Netherlands by amending the Government Information Act. In its former version, the Public Information Act offered public authorities too many opportunities to refuse to provide information relating to the environment. These grounds for exception have therefore been changed as far as environmental information is concerned.[32] Courts have been reviewing refusals to provide information related to the environment directly against the Environmental Information Directive.[33] It is anticipated that the *Guerra* case of the European Court of Human Rights[34] may again necessitate new legislation with regard to providing information related to the environment.[35]

---

[28] [1976] OJ L129/23.

[29] Administrative Law Division of the Council of State, *Van Rooij* v. *District Water Control Board*, 17 June 1997, comment by Backes published at (1998) 296 *Administratiefrechtelijke Beslissingen* 1447.

[30] Case C–232/97, *Nederhoff* v. *District Water Control Board* and Case C–231/97, *Van Rooij* v. *District Water Control Board*, Judgments of 29 Sept. 1999, not yet reported.

[31] [1990] OJ L158/56.   [32] Bulletin of Acts and Decrees 1998, No. 180.

[33] E.g. District Court Roermond, *Vereniging voor Cultuur- en Milieubehoud "De Kring"* v. *Municipal Executive of Weert*, 20 Jan. 1997, comment by Koning published at (1997) 3 *Jurisprudentie Bestuursrecht* 232–7; see also M. Klijnstra and H. G. Sevenster, "Directe toetsing aan richtlijn milieu-informatie" (1997) 11 *Nederlands Tijdschrift voor Europees Recht* 264–6.

[34] ECHR, 19 Feb. 1998, comment by Verschuuren published at (1998) 66 *Milieu&Recht* 183.

[35] H. Koning, "Artikel 10 lid 1 sub c WOB in strijd met EVRM?" (1998) 25 *Nederlands Juristenblad* 1107.

ii. Environmental Impact Assessment

Directive 85/337/EEC on the Assessment of the Effects of Certain Public and Private Projects on the Environment (EIA Directive)[36] still generates a lot of case law in the Netherlands. In the *Ruigoord* case, the ECJ ruled that a project initiated before the date on which the EIA Directive came into effect (3 July 1988) still needs to undergo an environmental impact assessment (EIA) if (as was the case in *Ruigoord*) the project was granted a permit before the transposition date, but without the project being carried out and, for reasons inherent in the applicable national rules, a new procedure was formally initiated after 3 July 1988.[37]

In several decisions by the Council of State, national legislation was set aside due to incompatibility with the Directive. If, for example, a project listed in Annex II has considerable effects on the environment in view of its size and location, the competent authorities must make a decision on the question whether or not an EIA procedure must be followed, even if national legislation does not require this.[38] The national decision on the *Kraaijeveld* case[39] was also published in 1998. The Council of State ruled that Dutch law, according to which certain projects concerning reinforcing of dykes are exempted from the duty to undergo an EIA, is not contrary to the EIA Directive. The exemption of an entire category of projects from the duty to undergo an EIA, which would be contrary to the Directive as a result of the ECJ's ruling in *Kraaijeveld*, will not occur, according to the Dutch administrative court.[40]

Adaptation of the EMA and the Decree on Environmental Impact Assessment to the revised EIA Directive 97/11/EC[41] is presently undertaken at the Ministry of the Environment and is not expected to be complete before 1999.

G. MISCELLANEOUS DEVELOPMENTS

i. Implementation

In April 1998, a draft of new rules on compliance with EC regulations and directives was submitted to Parliament to simplify and quicken the compliance with regulations.[42] In Chapter three of the EMA, the chapter on international affairs, the proposed Article 3.1 grants the competent minister the power to issue any rules to protect the environment, as long as these are

---

[36] [1985] OJ L175/40.

[37] Case C–81/96, *Municipal Executive of Haarlemmerliede en Spaarnwoude and others* v. *Provincial Executive of Noord-Holland* [1998] ECR I–3923.

[38] President of the Administrative Law Division of the Council of State, *Vughts Deelnemingen* v. *Municipal Executive of Delfzijl*, 11 Sept. 1997, comment by Verschuuren published at (1998) 72 *Milieu&Recht* 200.

[39] Case C–72/95, *Kraaijeveld* v. *Gedeputeerde Staten van Zuid-Holland* [1996] ECR I–5403.

[40] Administrative Law Division of the Council of State, *Kraaijeveld* v. *Provincial Executive of Zuid-Holland*, 20 Oct. 1997, comment by Jesse published at (1998) 57 *Milieu&Recht* 57; comment by Soppe published in (1998) 62 *Administratiefrechtelijke Beslissingen* 297.

[41] Dir. 97/11/EC amending Dir. 85/337/EEC [1997] OJ L73/5.

[42] Parliamentary Documents II, 1997–1998, 25 991, Nos. 1–3.

exclusively necessary to give effect to EC regulations. These ministerial rules may even suspend existing statutory rules (Acts and Orders in Council), if such existing rules are in conflict with EC regulations. This provision is a direct consequence of Case 168/85,[43] and its first application will be necessary to enable the correct implementation of Regulation (EC) No. 793/93 on the Evaluation and Control of the Risks of Existing Substances.[44] As far as directives are concerned, the minister's powers are less far-reaching. The minister is allowed to issue ministerial rules only where national legislation states that an Order in Council is necessary.[45] These rules may not suspend existing legislation.[46]

ii. *Financial Instruments*

Several tax laws were changed to serve environmental policy goals in the so-called Act on Fiscal Reinforcement of the Environment.[47] Among these was the Environmental Taxation Act, in which rules on "green electricity" were introduced prescribing that no taxes will be imposed on sustainably produced electricity. On 17 June 1998 the European Commission informed the Dutch minister that there were no objections to this "zero-levy", after which the new rules came into force.[48]

---

[43] *Commission* v. *Italy* [1986] ECR 2945.   [44] [1993] OJ L84/1.

[45] Art. 3.2, the former Art. 21.6(6) EMA.

[46] See further B. M. Veltkamp, *Implementatie van EG-milieurichtlijnen in Nederland* (Deventer: Kluwer, 1998), with a summary in English.

[47] Act of 18 Dec. 1997, Bulletin of Acts and Decrees 1997, 732.

[48] Bulletin of Acts and Decrees 1998, No. 323.

XI.   Portugal

Luís Caeiro Pitta*

A.   BIOTECHNOLOGY

Commission Directive 94/51/EC[1] adapting to technical progress Council Directive 90/219/EEC on the Contained Use of Genetically Modified Micro-organisms[2] has been transposed by Decree-Law 119/98, of 7 May 1998. This Decree-Law amends Regulation (EC) No. 602/94, of 13 July 1994 on the Notification of the Deliberate Release Into the Environment of Genetically Modified Organisms by the substitution of Annex II.

Furthermore, the amendment of Council Directive 90/220/EEC[3] on the Deliberate Release Into the Environment of Genetically Modified Organisms by Council Directive 97/35/EC[4] was brought into effect in Portugal through Decree-Law 172/98 of 25 June 1998 that has modified Regulation (EC) No. 751/94, Concerning the Notification on the Deliberate Release Into the Environment of Genetically Modified Organisms.

In the process of implementing these amendments to the Directives, several gaps were also addressed so that a failure to comply with Community directives could be prevented.

B.   NATURE CONSERVATION

The main event in this field of environmental law was the adoption of Decree-Law 227/98 concerning the national network of protected areas.[5] Through this amendment, the marine reserves and the marine parks were also included in the National Network of Protected Areas.

Furthermore, the Regulation on the Application of the National System of Agro-environmental Measures, as defined in Council Regulation (EEC) No. 2078/92[6] was adopted. This Regulation defines the agricultural production methods that are compatible with the requirements of environmental protection and the maintenance of the countryside.

---

* Associate Professor, Managing Director, AMBIFORUM, Centre for Environmental Studies, Lisbon.

   [1] [1994] OJ L297/29.   [2] [1990] OJ L117/1.   [3] [1990] OJ L117/15.
   [4] [1997] OJ L169/72.   [5] Of 17 July 1998, amending Decree-Law 13/93 of 23 Jan. 1993.
   [6] Council Reg. (EEC) No. 2078/92 on agricultural production methods compatible with the requirements of the protection of the environment and the maintenance of the countryside [1992] OJ L215/85, as amended by Reg. (EC) No. 2772/95 [1995] OJ L288/35.

C.   WASTE

Since the presentation of the Strategic Plan for Solid Urban Waste in November 1996 and the approval of the management strategy for industrial waste,[7] a great number of measures have been implemented, with the purpose of ensuring adequate treatment of the different categories of wastes existing in the country.

Most significantly, Regulation 29–B/98, of 15 January 1998, establishing rules for the functioning of the consigned system of waste, was adopted. The rules contained in this Regulation are applied to recycled as well as non-recycled packaging materials.

Primarily, the Regulation serves to implement Directive 94/62/EC on Packaging and Packaging Waste.[8] To transpose the provisions of this Directive, it has replaced Regulation 313/96 of 29 June 1996 which, like Decree-Laws 322/95 and 366–A/97, were aimed at implementing the Packaging Directive but were considered inadequate by the Commission.

This new legislation should solve the problems spelled out by the Commission, in that it corrects some technical aspects and allows for the organization of systems of consignation or special systems of selective collection.

Council Directive 94/67/EC on the Incineration of Hazardous Waste[9] was transposed by Decree-Law 273/98 of 2 September 1998. Despite this transposition, the issue of incineration of hazardous waste remains problematic in Portugal. The abovementioned Council of Ministers Resolution 98/97 on the management strategy for industrial waste lists co-incineration in cement plants as the preferred treatment of industrial hazardous waste. Contrary to this, Ministry of Health Regulation 242/96 of 5 July 1996 prescribes that hazardous hospital waste is merely to be incinerated. At the time of writing, public discussion is taking place on a national plan for the treatment of hospital waste and a national plan on health and the environment.

To bring Portuguese practice into line with the European Waste Catalogue,[10] Regulation 792/98 of 22 September 1998 on the model of mapping and registration of industrial waste was adopted and the previous Regulation 189/95 of 1995 was revoked.

D.   WATER

As regards the protection of the aquatic environment, the most important legislative event was the publication of Decree-Law 236/98 of 1 August 1998. This Decree-Law establishes rules, criteria and quality objectives to protect the aquatic environment and, generally, to improve the quality of waters. The new

---

[7] Council of Ministers Resolution 98/97/EC of 5 June 1997 approving the management strategy for industrial waste.

[8] [1994] OJ L365/10.   [9] [1994] OJ L365/34.

[10] Commission Decision 94/3/EC [1993] OJ L5/15 establishing a list of waste pursuant to Art. 1 of Council Dir. 75/442.EEC on waste.

Decree also replaces the old Decree-Law that was considered an incorrect and inadequate transposition of the relevant Community directives.

In particular, Directives 79/869/EEC,[11] 80/778/EEC,[12] 78/659/EEC,[13] 79/923/EEC,[14] 76/464/EEC[15] and 80/68/EEC[16] were inadequately implemented.

Despite the last Decree-Law, the legislation on water is still inadequate from the perspective of the recent Council Directive 98/83/EC on the Quality of Water Intended for Human Consumption.[17]

Decree-law 348/98 of 9 November 1998 which amended Decree-Law 152/97, of 19 June 1997, transposing Council Directive 91/271/EEC Concerning Urban Waste Water Treatment,[18] should also be mentioned. This Decree-Law implemented the new requirements for discharges of urban wastewater in sensitive areas subject to eutrophication.

E. MISCELLANEOUS DEVELOPMENTS

During 1998 the European Court of Justice declared that Portugal had failed to fulfil its obligations in a number of cases. In Case C–213/97,[19] the Court ruled that Portugal had failed to comply with Council Directives 86/280/EEC[20] and 88/347/EEC[21] on Limit Values and Quality Objectives for Discharges of Certain Dangerous Substances Included in List I of the Annex to Council Directive 76/464/EEC.[22]

In Case C–214/97,[23] the Court decided that Portugal had failed to comply with Council Directive 75/440/EEC Concerning the Quality Required of Surface Water Intended for the Abstraction of Drinking Water in the Member States.[24]

The Court decided in Case C–208/97,[25] that Portugal had failed to comply with Council Directive 84/156/EEC on Limit Values and Quality Objectives for Mercury Discharges by Sectors Other than the Chlor-alkali Electrolysis Industry.[26]

In Case C–183/97[27] the Court decided Portugal had failed to transpose Council Directive 80/68/EEC on the Protection of Groundwater Against Pollution Caused by Certain Dangerous Substances.[28]

---

[11] Dir. 79/869/EEC concerning the methods of measurement and frequencies of sampling and analysis of surface water intended for the abstraction of drinking water in the Member States [1979] OJ L271/44.

[12] Dir. 80/778/EEC relating to the quality of water intended for human consumption [1980] OJ L229/11.

[13] Dir. 78/659/EEC on the quality of fresh waters needing protection or improvement in order to support fish life [1978] OJ L222/1.

[14] Dir. 79/923/EEC on the quality required of shellfish waters [1979] OJ L281/47.

[15] Dir. 76/464/EEC on pollution caused by certain dangerous substances discharged into the aquatic environment of the community [1976] OJ L129/23.

[16] Dir. 80/68/EEC on the protection of groundwater against pollution caused by certain dangerous substances [1980] OJ L20/43.

[17] [1998] OJ L330/2.

[18] [1991] OJ L135/40.

[19] [1998] ECR I–3289.

[20] [1986] OJ L181/16.

[21] [1988] OJ L158/35.

[22] [1976] OJ L129/23.

[23] [1998] ECR I–3839.

[24] [1975] OJ L194/34.

[25] [1998] ECR I–4017.

[26] [1984] OJ L75/49.

[27] [1998] ECR I–4005.

[28] [1979] OJ L20/43.

The Court decided, in Case C–285/97,[29] that Portugal failed to implement Commission Directive 94/51/EC on the Contained Use of Genetically Modified Micro organisms.[30]

In Case C–229/97[31] the Court decided once more that Portugal had failed to implement Community legislation. The case concerned the implementation of Council Directive 79/869/EEC Concerning the Methods of Measurement and Frequencies of Sampling and Analysis of Surface Water Intended for the Abstraction of Drinking Water in the Member States.[32]

During 1998 the Commission initiated proceedings, claiming that Portugal had infringed or had failed to take all necessary national measures to comply with several Community provisions:

— Council Directive 90/313/EEC on the Freedom of Access to Information on the Environment.[33]
— Council Directive 75/439/EEC on the Disposal of Waste Oils.[34]
— Council Directive 91/692/EEC Standardizing and Rationalizing Reports on the Implementation of Certain Directives Relating to the Environment.[35]
— Council Directive 91/271/EEC Concerning Urban Waste Water Treatment.[36]
— Council Directive 91/676/EEC Concerning the Protection of Waters Against Pollution Caused by Nitrates from Agricultural Sources.[37]
— Council Regulation (EC) No. 1836/93 allowing voluntary participation by companies in the industrial sector in a Community eco-management and audit scheme.[38]

[29] [1998] ECR I–4895.   [30] [1994] OJ L297/29.   [31] 15 Oct. 1998, not yet reported.
[32] [1979] OJ L271/44.   [33] [1990] OJ L158/56.   [34] [1975] OJ L194/31.
[35] [1991] OJ L377/48.   [36] [1991] OJ L135/40.   [37] [1991] OJ L375/1.
[38] [1993] OJ L168/1.

XII. Spain

CARMEN PLAZA*

A. INTRODUCTION

Following the creation in 1996 of a Ministry of the Environment,[1] Spain has attempted to speed up the transposition of EC directives whose incorporation into Spanish law had been delayed at the state level. In 1998, the most significant improvements took place in the field of waste legislation. Several Autonomous Communities have also exercised their normative powers, giving rise to some interesting issues, a selection of which will be referred to below. Furthermore, the Constitutional Court has delivered some important judgments.[2]

B. AIR POLLUTION

According to Article 19 of Regulation (EC) No. 3093/94 on Substances that Deplete the Ozone Layer,[3] Member States must provide for a system of sanctions to enforce the obligations enshrined in this piece of EC legislation. Whereas the effectiveness of EC environmental regulations depends to a great extent on national enforcement mechanisms and the designation of competent public authorities, this aspect has traditionally been neglected, since most of Community and Member States' attention has instead focused on the transposition of EC directives. By Law 4/1998,[4] Parliament enacted a regime of administrative sanctions for breaches of Regulation (EC) No. 3093/94 as required by the aforementioned provision. Prior to the enactment of Law

---

* Lecturer in EC Administrative Law, Universidad Complutense, Madrid.

[1] See Royal Decree 758/1996 on the structure of the ministerial departments, Official State Gazette (hereafter BOE) No. 110, of 6 May 1996; Royal Decree 839/1996 and Royal Decree 1894/1996 on the basic organic structure of the Ministry of Environment, BOE No.115 of 11 May 1996 and BOE No. 189 of 6 Aug. 1996. One of its core tasks is to draft governmental proposals for the Parliament to enact state basic laws, and itself to adopt basic statutes for the protection of the environment.

[2] As regards the distribution of environmental powers between the state and the Autonomous Communities, the state has powers to pass basic legislation and the Autonomous Communities have powers to pass laws both to implement the basic national laws and to establish additional protective norms, as well as the executive powers to implement environmental policy and law (Art. 149.1.23 and Art. 148.1.9 of the Spanish constitution and the Organic Laws regulating self-government for each Autonomous Community). The concept of "basic environmental laws" has been interpreted by the Constitutional Court as those rules which establish minimum standards of environmental protection that have to be complied with across the country (see STC 102/1995, 26 June 1995, BOE No. 181, 31 July 1995). However, other constitutional rules regarding the allocation of power also interact with Art. 149.1.23.

[3] [1994] OJ L333/1.

[4] *Ley 4/1998 por la que se establece el régimen sancionador previsto en el Reglamento 3093/1994 relativo a las sustancias que agotan la capa de ozono*, BOE No. 54, 4 Mar. 1998, 7393.

4/1998, several infringements of the Ozone Regulation could be punished by means of other pieces of legislation.[5] There existed, however, no comprehensive system of administrative sanctions to ensure the effectiveness of Regulation (EC) No. 3093/94 until Law 4/1998 was passed. It establishes that infringements can be punished with fines of up to 200,000,000 ptas. (1,202,024 Euros) as well as closure of the premises.

In the field of climate change, however, Spain has been struggling to define a coherent strategy in 1998, as evidenced by Royal Decree 177/1998.[6] Its objective is to establish guidelines for the design of a national strategy on climate change and to create a National Climate Council in charge of designing it. According to this statute the national strategy, which will be subject to approval by the government, is to establish national plans and programmes, and sector-orientated measures in order to comply with Spanish international commitments on climate change. The National Council replaces the former National Climate Commission, which was created in 1992 but which proved ineffective.

C. NATURE CONSERVATION

On 2 August 1993 the European Court of Justice delivered its landmark decision in Case C–355/90[7] declaring that, by not classifying Marismas de Santoña as a special protection area and by not taking the appropriate steps to avoid pollution or deterioration of habitats in that area, contrary to the provisions of Article 4 of Directive 79/409/EEC on the Conservation of Wild Birds (Wild Birds Directive)[8] Spain had failed to fulfil its Community obligations. More than five years later, the Constitutional Court stated in its Ruling 195/1998[9] that Law 6/1992, which declared the core part of Marismas de Santoña a Natural Reserve,[10] was unconstitutional and hence void. When Law 6 of 1992 was passed by the state Parliament, the government of the Cantabrian Autonomous Community challenged its constitutionality before the Spanish Constitutional Court. It argued that the fact that the coastal public domain was state-owned did not lead to the conclusion that the competence to designate and manage nature protection areas also belonged to the state. The Constitutional Court stated that the designation of a nature protection area and the delimitation of its spatial boundaries is an executive activity, and according to the Constitution hence belongs to the Autonomous Community. Following Ruling 102/1995,[11] it declared that the fact that the area at issue is placed within the state-owned public domain does not alter the division of

---

[5] For instance penal law on smuggling (*Ley Orgánica* 12/1995, BOE No. 297, 13 Dec. 1995, 35701) or Law 21/1992 on industry (BOE No. 176, 23 July 1992).

[6] BOE No. 42, 18 Feb. 1998.

[7] Case C–355/90, *European Commission* v. *Spain* (Marsimas de Santoña) [1993] ECR I–4241. See case report by H. Somsen (1993) 2 *European Environmental Law Review* 268–74.

[8] [1979] OJ L103/1.   [9] STC 195/1998, of 1 Oct. 1998, BOE No. 260 of 30 Oct. 1998.

[10] BOE No. 77, 30 Mar. 1992, 10681.

[11] STC 102/1995, 26 June 1995, BOE No. 181, 31 July 1995, 3.

competences between the state and the Autonomous Communities. Therefore, the designation and management of a nature protection area are within the realm of the Autonomous Communities, and consequently Law 6/1992 was unconstitutional as it was passed by the national parliament. Since, according to Article 39 of the Organic Law of the Constitutional Court, a ruling which declares the unconstitutionality of a legal provision also means it is void, it seemed that the Constitutional decision could create a legal vacuum regarding the protection of Santoña's marshes. The decision came at a critical moment as the Commission was closely following Spain's compliance with the ECJ judgment under Article 228 (formerly Article 171) EC. Therefore, the Constitutional Court considered that, in this case, it was necessary to limit the scope of its decision. It argued that annulling every provision of Law 6/1992 could result in serious damage to Santoña's natural resources. The Court noted that the Cantabrian government had already approved a plan for nature resources management,[12] and stated that this is a prior step for the designation of the whole area as a Regional Park, Natural Reserve, or any other form of nature protection enshrined in the Law. However, it considered that:

as long as the Autonomous Autonomy does not exercise such a power, the immediate annulment of Law No. 6/1996 could entail serious damages to the area, prejudicing not only the national interest, but also interests which go beyond the national boundaries, as is shown by the European Court of Justice's judgment of 2 August 1993.

For this reason the Constitutional Court decided to declare Law 6/1992 unconstitutional but, for the first time in its case law, postponed the declaration of nullity. Thus, Law 6/1992 would continue to be applied until the Autonomous Community decided to declare the area a Nature Regional Park, or any other designation as formally set out in Basic Law 4/1989 or the Autonomous Community's own rules on nature protection. This decision of the Constitutional Court reflects not only the court's environmental awareness, but also a commitment to guarantee implementation of the Birds Directive and compliance with the ECJ judgment.[13]

D. WASTE

During the past months, Spanish legislation on waste was given fresh impetus, mainly by the implementation of Directive 91/156/EEC amending Directive 75/442/EEC on Waste[14] and Directive 94/62/EC on Packaging and Packaging Waste.[15]

---

[12] *Plan de ordenación de los recursos de las Marismas de Santoña*, approved by Cantabrian governmental Decree of 24 Apr. 1997. In order to comply with the ECJ decision, it protects a much larger area than that to which Law 6/1992 applies, and it is legally binding according to state basic Law 4/1989 on the conservation of natural habitats and wild fauna and flora (BOE No. 181, 20 July 1988).

[13] For an analysis and critical appraisal of this ruling see R. Alonso Garcia, B. Lozano and C. Plaza, "El medio ambiente ante el Tribunal Constitucional: problemas competenciales y ultraeficacia protectora" (1999) 148 *Revista de Administración Pública* 99.

[14] [1991] OJ L78/32.   [15] [1994] OJ L365/10.

i. General Waste Legislation

On 5 June 1997, the ECJ declared that Spain had infringed its obligations to adopt the legal, regulatory and administrative measures to implement Directive 91/156/EEC.[16] On 21 April 1998, based on a governmental draft proposal, the parliament finally enacted Law 10/1998, which establishes the basic state legislation on waste. Following the approach of Directive 75/442/EEC on Waste,[17] it applies to all categories of waste (with the exception of radioactive waste and emissions to the atmosphere and water). It also attempts to co-ordinate waste policy with economic, industrial, and land planning policies.

Law 10/1998 provides for the establishment of national plans on waste which integrate the Autonomous Communities' and "local authorities' plans",[18] and follow an integral approach to waste policy, regulating not only waste management, but also waste production activities, trade and importation of waste. In line with the polluter pays principle, it places the cost of waste management on the product which will become waste at the end of its life.

Regarding movements of waste, the law regulates the implementation by the Autonomous Communities and the state authorities of Regulation (EC) No. 259/93 on the Supervision and Control of Shipment of Waste Within, Into and Out of the European Community[19] and also sets the conditions under which the Autonomous Communities may restrict waste movements within Spanish territory according to the principle of proximity. With regard to local authorities' powers waste management, Law 7/1985 on the bases of the local regime[20] has been amended so that every local authority is obliged to ensure the collection, transport, and disposal of urban waste, whilst Law 7/1985 had created that obligation only for municipal districts with more than 50,000 inhabitants. Furthermore, in such districts, local authorities must now establish selective waste collection systems.

Implementation Law 10/1998 allows for new instruments, such as voluntary agreements and contracts between the economic actors and public authorities. Furthermore, economic incentives and eco-taxes are also provided for as mechanisms to achieve reduction, re-use, recovery, and recycling targets. Finally, it includes provisions on polluted land and clean-up programmes, environmental liability, monitoring and inspection mechanisms, and a sanctions system.

ii. Packaging and Packaging Waste

More specifically with regard to packaging and packaging waste, Law 11/1997 implemented those provisions of Directive 94/62/EC on Packaging and

---

[16] Case C–107/96, *Commission* v. *Spain* [1997] ECR I–3193.   [17] [1975] OJ L194/47.

[18] It remains to be seen whether this approach would help to achieve a timely and correct compliance with the ECJ decision in case C–298/97, *Commission* v. *Spain* (not yet reported) in which the Court declared that Spain had failed to fulfil the obligation to establish programmes according to Dir. 91/157/EEC on batteries and accumulators containing certain dangerous substances [1991] OJ L78/1.

[19] [1993] OJ L30/1, later amended.

[20] *Ley/71985 reguladora de las Bases del Régimen Local*, BOE No. 80, 3 Apr. 1985.

Packaging Waste which, according to the Spanish legal system, were reserved for enactment by Parliament. As provided for by Law 11/1997, in 1998 the Ministry of Environment has adopted two statutes to implement the Directive. First, Royal Decree 782/1998 approved the Regulation for the development and implementation of Law 11/1997.[21] Particularly important are the provisions that establish the obligation for enterprises to adopt packaging waste prevention plans, as they constitute the main mechanism for guaranteeing the realization of the waste packaging prevention and reduction targets set in Law 11/1997. The plans must take into account the programmes on packaging and waste packaging established by the state and the Autonomous Communities, and include quantified prevention targets, measures to achieve them, and monitoring mechanisms. The statute also foresees public authorities' use of economic incentives, eco-taxes, and other economic instruments of incentives for the re-use and recycling of packaging. Furthermore, there are provisions detailing the obligations and the working procedures of the two alternative systems for packaging and waste packaging return and management established by Law 11/1997:

   i) the deposit, devolution and return system, and
   ii) the integral management system.

The Ministry of Environment Order of 20 May 1998[22] has established the prices to be paid by those placing packaging materials on the market under the deposit and return system for used packaging and/or packaging waste, as well as the identification symbol to be used.

E.   WATER

The most important event of the last decades in Spanish water law has been the approval by the government, after more than 10 years of fruitless attempts, of the hydrologic river basin plans by Royal Decree 1664/1998.[23] The enactment and implementation of these legally binding plans was provided for by Law 29/1985 on water[24] as the main instrument for achieving better management of water resources.[25] These plans were eventually approved after long and difficult negotiations in which the Ministry of Environment played a leading role, together with other Departments and Autonomous Communities. In anticipation of the new Framework Directive on Water,[26] it is uncertain whether these national plans will constitute correct implementation of the plans and programmes which this forthcoming piece of EC legislation will demand of the Member States.[27] More importantly, it also remains to be seen

---

[21] BOE No. 104, 1 May 1998, 14701.   [22] BOE No. 120, 1 May 1998, 14716.
[23] BOE 11 Aug. 1998.   [24] BOE No. 189, 8 Aug. 1985.
[25] Art. 3 of Law 29/1985.
[26] See Commission proposal for a Framework Water Directive, COM(97)49 final.
[27] Taking into account the ECJ case law regarding compliance with obligation to adopt environmental plans and programmes, it does not seem very likely that these plans will fulfil all the requirements for correct implementation, see Case C–298/95, *Commission* v. *Germany* [1996] ECR I–6747.

whether these plans are an effective mechanism for overcoming deficiencies in Spanish water policy with regard to the implementation of EC water quality standards, as well as specific zoning or planning obligations; deficiencies which gave rise in 1998 to three ECJ judgments pursuant Article 226 (formerly Article 169) EC.[28]

F.   HORIZONTAL INSTRUMENTS

Traditionally, environmental law in Spain has pursued a sectoral approach resulting in a complex cluster of rules concerning air, water, soil, nature, classified activities, chemicals, and waste management. The need to adopt an overarching environmental protection act, establishing a common foundation and providing for an integrated approach to environmental protection, has been discussed since the birth of environmental legislation in Spain. However, as yet, no such initiative has been taken by the state.

In this context, the General Law on Environmental Protection in the Basque Country Autonomous Community is noteworthy.[29] Basque Law 3/1998 on the protection of the environment[30] has attempted to lay the foundations for "a clear, stable and workable legal framework for the protection of the environment" in this Autonomous Community, following the classical principles of precaution, prevention, and restoration, the polluter pays, shared liability, and public participation and information. It enshrines the right to use and enjoy a healthy environment and to be informed and to participate in environmental decision-making. It also establishes an *actio popularis* to request compliance with the provisions of this general law and provides for the use of alternative dispute resolutions to environmental conflicts between citizens and the administration.

Law 3/1998 also lays down the general rules on the protection of bio-diversity, waters and coasts, land, atmosphere, environmental impact assessment, classified activities, waste, and polluted land. Furthermore, it comprises general rules on environmental law and policy instruments, such as environmental planning, economic instruments (especially funds to finance environmental protection measures, economic incentives, eco-taxes, and

---

[28] Case C–92/96 [1998] ECR I–505, in which the Court declared the infringement of Dir. 76/160/EEC on bathing waters with regard to compliance of the quality standards on inshore bathing waters; Case C–71/97, judgment of 1 Oct. 1998, not yet reported, in which it declared that Spain had failed to implement Dir. 91/676/EEC concerning the protection of waters against pollution caused by nitrates from agriculture sources ([1991] OJ L375/1) as it neither designated vulnerable zones in compliance nor communicated to the Commission codes of good agricultural practice, as required by Arts. 3 and 4; Case C–214/96, judgment of 25 Nov. 1998, in which the Court declared that it infringed Art, 7 of Council Dir. 76/464/EEC on pollution caused by certain dangerous substances discharged into the aquatic environment of the Community as it did not establish programmes for reducing pollution of surface waters and territorial waters by substances falling within List II.

[29] Art. 11. 1 of *Ley Orgánica* 3/1979 *del Estatuto de Autonomía para el País Vasco* (Organic Law on the Basque Country Autonomy Regime) establishes that it has competence for legislative and administrative implementation of the state basic environmental legislation, BOE No. 306, 22 Dec. 1979.

[30] Official Gazette of the Basque Country No. 59, 27 Mar. 1998.

environmental risk insurance), voluntary instruments (eco-label and eco-audit), education, etc. Thirdly, it specifies the principles of environmental liability, monitoring, and inspection, and the regime of administrative sanctions. However, several provisions of the Law regarding environmental impact assessment have been challenged by the state government before the Constitutional Court on the ground that the distribution of powers between the state and the Autonomous Community has been infringed. This has suspended the entry into force of these provisions.[31]

With regard to integrated pollution control, the state government is drafting a proposal to incorporate the integral approach to pollution prevention and control into basic state legislation as required by Council Directive 96/61/EC Concerning Integrated Pollution Prevention and Control (IPPC Directive).[32] This task has proved to be particularly complex, given the Spanish traditional sector-by-sector approach to environmental law and the decentralized distribution of competences. The Catalan Autonomous Community has already passed its Law 3/1998 on the integral action of environmental administration which, *inter alia*, seeks to integrate the different authorization systems to control emissions and dumping of polluting substances into the air, water and land within Catalonia.[33]

---

[31] BOE No. 162, 8 July 1998. Constitutional Court Ruling 13/1998 is relevant to this conflict of competence, as it settled a former conflict between the Basque country government and the state with regard to similar issues of the environmental impact assessment procedure (BOE No. 47, 24 Feb. 1998). In this case, the Basque government had challenged the provisions of the state basic legislation on EIA according to which the EIA is performed by the state environmental authority when public projects are carried out by the state in the territory of the Autonomous Communities—e.g. those projects declared to be of general state interest. The Basque country claimed that the EIA of projects falling within its territory always belonged to the competence of its own environmental authority. The Constitutional Court declared, however, that the state basic legislation on EIA was constitutional and did not invade Basque country powers on environmental protection. Taking into account the fact that the provisions of this new Basque Law enshrined the principles defended by the Basque country in Ruling 13/1998, it is quite likely that the state government action will succeed.

[32] [1996] OJ L257/26.

[33] BOE No. 84, 8 Apr. 1998, 11918.

STEFAN RUBENSON*

A. INTRODUCTION

An extensive legislative process was brought to an end when the new Environmental Code (hereafter "the Code") entered into force on 1 January 1999. The main environmental provisions of 15 different Acts have been reviewed and combined into the Code while the provisions regarding environmental quality standards and environment impact assessment have been expanded. The Code integrates different pieces of environmental legislation such as nature conservation, activities harmful to the environment, protection of health, water resources, genetically modified organisms, chemicals, and waste. However, the Code has a wider scope than the total sum of the areas enumerated, since the fundamental rules of the Environment Code will apply to all human activities that may harm the environment. Essential parts of the Code, including provisions on precautionary measures and environmental impact assessment, have also been embodied in other pieces of legislation concerning land use such as the Roads Act, the Railway Construction Act and the Minerals Act.

B. AIR POLLUTION

According to the Environmental Code, the government may prescribe environmental quality standards. These standards specify levels of pollution that the environment may be exposed to in a certain area, without manifest impairment to the environment. Thus, the Ordinance on environmental quality standards regulates the maximum permissible level in the open air of dioxide, nitrogen and lead.[1] In a Supreme Court ruling, manufacturers and importers of motor cars were made liable for upgrading vehicles when their exhaust emission equipment did not meet Swedish requirements in this respect. However, this obligation does not apply to cars over five years old or with a mileage in excess of 8,000 kilometers. The Ordinance on car exhaust emissions has been amended following a European Court of Justice ruling to the effect that importers of cars into Sweden are not obliged to present a national certificate of exhaust emission approval in order to get the car registered in Sweden, assuming that the same model of the car already has been approved for registration in another Member State.[2]

Furthermore, the government submitted a Bill to Parliament on environmental quality objectives. The Bill contains guidelines for the next five to ten years. Regarding air quality, the Bill stipulates that emissions of carcinogenic

---

* Director and Head of Legal Services, Ministry of the Environment, Stockholm.

[1] Ordinance 1998:897.   [2] Case C–329/95, *VAG Sverige* [1997] ECR I–2675.

substances in urban areas should be halved by 2005, with 1991 as the baseline. Emissions of volatile organic compounds (VOC) from the transport sector should be reduced by 60 per cent by 2005. Another target is that emissions of nitrogen oxides from traffic must be reduced by 40 per cent by 2005 compared with the baseline year 1995. Sweden's emission of sulphur dioxides into the air must be reduced by 25 per cent by 2010 compared with the baseline year 1995. A climate change committee has been set up and is expected to put forward proposals on targets and an action programme.

C. CHEMICALS

The Treaty of Accession contained special provisions in the field of the environment and health care, which allowed continued application of national provisions for a period of four years.[3] The European Union committed itself to reviewing the relevant EU standards during those four years. Meanwhile, Sweden was allowed to maintain specific provisions for the classification of 67 dangerous substances and a number of dangerous preparations and different criteria for classification and labelling, including different criteria for the classification of carcinogens and specific requirements for the classification, packaging, and labelling of pesticides.[4]

Furthermore, the Treaty of Accession allows for restrictions on the marketing and use of cadmium, arsenic, PCP, and tin compounds to be maintained,[5] a prolonged limitation on the cadmium content of fertilizers and a different composition of alkaline manganese batteries with a mercury content of 0.025 per cent.[6] According to the Commission,[7] the review process resulted in the adoption of higher standards on an EU-wide basis in a number of cases, thereby raising the level of environmental protection.[8] In other cases solutions were found enabling new Member States to maintain national standards. Concerning Directive 67/548/EEC on the Approximation of Laws, Regulations and Administrative Provisions Relating to the Classification, Packaging, and Labelling of Dangerous Substances,[9] new criteria and a revised classification have been incorporated into the Annex. In addition, Sweden was allowed to maintain a derogation concerning the labelling of carcinogenic substances as well as a national classification system of categories of hazard until 31 December 2000, when the review

---

[3] Until the end of 1998.

[4] The derogations are related to Council Dir. 67/548/EEC on the approximation of laws, regulations and administrative provisions relating to the classification, packaging and labelling of dangerous substances [1967] OJ L196/1; Council Dir. 88/379/EEC on the classification, packaging and labelling of dangerous preparations [1988] OJ L187/14; and Council Dir. 78/631/EEC on the approximation of the laws, regulations and administrative provisions relating to the classification, packaging and labelling of pesticides [1978] OJ L206/13.

[5] These derogations relate to Council Dir. 76/769/EEC on the approximation of laws, regulations and administrative provisions of the Member States relating to the restrictions on the marketing and use of certain dangerous substances and preparations [1976] OJ L262/201.

[6] Council Dir. 91/157/EEC on batteries and accumulators containing certain dangerous substances [1991] OJ L78/38.

[7] COM(98)745 final.

[8] i.e. Council Dir. 99/51/EC [1999] OJ L142/22.   [9] [1967] OJ L196/1.

process will also be completed.[10] Regarding Directive 88/379/EEC on the Approximation of the Laws, Regulations and Administrative Provisions of the Member States Relating to the Classification, Packaging, and Labelling of Dangerous Preparations,[11] and Directive 78/631/EEC on the Approximation of the Laws, Regulations and Administrative Provisions of the Member States Relating to the Classification, Packaging, and Labelling of Dangerous Preparations (pesticides),[12] the Commission undertook a combined review and proposed a new and more ambitious directive. A common position was adopted in September 1998 and submitted to the Parliament. The new Directive, including amendments proposed by the European Parliament, was adopted by the Council on 31 May 1999.[13] The same procedure is expected with regard to Directive 76/116/EEC on the Approximation of the Laws of the Member States Relating to Fertilizers.[14] Directive 91/157/EEC on Batteries and Accumulators Containing Certain Dangerous Substances,[15] has been adjusted to technical progress resulting in a ban on mercury in all kinds of batteries except button cells, which answers Sweden's concerns regarding batteries. Moreover, Sweden has implemented Directive 96/59/EC on the Disposal of Polychlorinated Biphenyls and Polychlorinated Terphenyls (PCB/PCT),[16] through the Ordinance on disposal of PCBs.[17]

The Supreme Administrative Court delivered its judgment on the decision by the Inspectorate to prohibit the introduction of a pesticide, in *Rhône-Poulenc* v. *the National Chemical Inspectorate. Rhône-Poulenc* argued that the decision by the Inspectorate contravened the provisions of Directive 91/414/EEC Concerning the Placing of Plant Protection Products on the Market,[18] as well as Articles 28 and 30 (formerly Articles 30 and 36) EC. The Court declared that the pesticide in question contained substances not covered by the harmonized rules of Directive 91/414/EEC and that the substances might have characteristics that are so harmful that the Inspectorate was entitled to refuse approval according to Article 30 (formerly Article 36) EC.

D. NATURE CONSERVATION

Chapter 8 of the Environmental Code includes provisions for the protection of fauna and flora. A new Ordinance on the protection of endangered species of wild fauna and flora was introduced in 1998.[19] The Ordinance contains additional provisions supplementing the Environmental Code and Council Regulations (EC) No. 338/97 on the Protection of Species of Wild Fauna and Flora by Regulating Trade Therein,[20] and (EC) No. 939/97 Laying Down Detailed Rules Concerning the Implementation of Council Regulation (EC) No. 338/97 on the Protection of Species of Wild Fauna and Flora by Regulating Trade Therein.[21] Furthermore, the Ordinance includes elements to be found in

---

[10] [1999] OJ L199/57. [11] [1988] OJ L187/14. [12] [1978] OJ L206/13.
[13] [1999] OJ L200/1. [14] [1976] OJ L24/21. [15] [1991] OJ L78/38.
[16] [1996] OJ L243/31. [17] Ordinance 1998:122. [18] [1991] OJ L230/1.
[19] Ordinance 1998:179. [20] [1997] OJ L61/1. [21] [1997] OJ L140/1.

Directive 92/43/EEC on the Conservation of Natural Habitats and of Wild Fauna and Flora,[22] and Directive 79/409/EEC on the Conservation of Wild Birds.[23] The Ordinance includes a ban on keeping wild birds and animals in captivity and the gathering of wild flowers listed in an Annex. The same provisions apply to eggs, parts, and goods made from objects protected by the Ordinance. The Ordinance also contains some additional provisions regarding the CITES Convention.

E. WASTE

On 1 January 1999, a new Ordinance on waste entered into force.[24] The European Waste Catalogue as well as other EU instruments regarding the classification of waste have been annexed to the Ordinance, thus bringing Swedish waste legislation into conformity with Directive 75/442/EEC on Waste.[25] The Ordinance includes provisions concerning transport and final disposal of combustible and organic waste. Combustible waste must be stored and transported separately from other categories of waste. Combustible waste that has been separated at source may not be used for landfill or put into permanent storage. These provisions will apply from 1 January 2002. Similar provisions will apply to organic waste from 1 January 2005. A new Ordinance on batteries entered into force on 1 January 1998.[26] The municipalities are responsible for collecting used batteries, separation at source, and disposal according to their content. Batteries that contain hazardous components must be disposed of in a plant licensed for disposal of hazardous waste. A levy will be charged for the use of hazardous batteries. The levy is intended to finance information campaigns, but also to help cover municipal costs concerning separation at source of batteries. An Ordinance on producer responsibility for end of life vehicles entered into force on 1 January 1998.[27] This Ordinance aims at reducing the amount of waste arising from motor cars. Manufacturers and importers are responsible for the re-use and recycling of materials and components from motor cars. Parts of motor cars not designated for re-use or recycling shall be disposed of in an environmentally friendly way. Re-use and recycling must be promoted and a target of 85 per cent has been set for 2002. The target for 2015 is 95 per cent. Another target was presented in the Bill on environmental quality objectives stating that the total quantities of land fill waste (excluding mining waste) should fall by 50–70 per cent by 2005 compared with the baseline year 1994.

The Commission has been notified that Sweden intends to introduce producer responsibility with regard to waste from electrical and electronic equip-

---

[22] Dir. 92/43 [1992] OJ L206/7, as recently amended by Dir. 97/62 adapting to technical and scientific progress Dir. 92/43/EC on the conservation of natural habitats and of wild fauna and flora [1992] OJ L206/7.

[23] Dir. 79/409 [1979] OJ L103/1, as amended recently by Dir. 97/49 of 29 July 1997 amending Council Dir. 79/409 on the conservation of wild birds [1997] OJ L223/9.

[24] Ordinance 1998:902.   [25] [1975] OJ L194/47.   [26] Ordinance 1997:645.

[27] Ordinance 1997:788. See further the article by M. Onida in this volume.

ment. This will put commercial vendors of electrical and electronic equipment under an obligation to dispose of the products when they become waste. The obligation will apply to products listed in an Annex to the Ordinance. The proposal suggests that this responsibility shall enter into force on 1 January 2000.

The Commission has initiated an infringement procedure, starting with a letter of formal notice followed by a reasoned opinion, concerning implementation of Directive 94/62/EC on Packaging and Packaging Waste.[28] The Commission's main concern seems to be that, according to Swedish waste legislation, the municipalities are not obliged to include package waste in their waste management plans. Sweden is at present reviewing its waste legislation with regard to waste management plans.

F. WATER

With regard to Directive 80/68/EEC on the Protection of Groundwater Against Pollution Caused by Certain Dangerous Substances,[29] Sweden has undertaken to review some provisions in national legislation concerning "prior investigation", an obligation introduced in Article 3 of the Directive. Concerning urban waste water treatment, Sweden has submitted a report to the Commission in accordance with Article 5(6) of Directive 91/271/EEC Concerning Urban Waste Water Treatment,[30] regarding the identification of sensitive areas. With regard to eutrophication, in Sweden all water bodies as defined in Annex 2A(a) are to be considered to be sensitive areas. A target for ground water policy in the government Bill on environmental quality objectives is that all landfill sites should have achieved a uniform standard and should comply with more stringent environment standards by 2008. Furthermore, the government intends to introduce environmental standards applying to leisure boat engines.

---

[28] [1996] OJ L365/10.   [29] [1980] OJ L20/43.   [30] [1991] OJ L135/40.

XIV.   United Kingdom

Tim Jewell*

A.   AIR POLLUTION

The historic absence of strategic air quality planning and management in the United Kingdom has been much criticized. It is no wonder, therefore, that it has been the focus of considerable recent attention. As part of a more general trend towards the clearer articulation of strategic environmental targets,[1] the first UK National Air Quality Strategy was adopted in 1997 in conjunction with binding statutory air quality standards.[2] The latter are not themselves particularly new, and in any event were made in response to Community measures.[3] Of more recent significance have been localized initiatives intended to extend the range of regulatory options available for controlling air pollution in pursuit of these new, albeit limited, strategic objectives.[4]

B.   NATURE CONSERVATION

Key issues in UK conservation law currently include its practical effectiveness; the reform of conservation law; and the implementation of Community conservation measures. However, it is the emergence of bio-diversity as the central theme of UK conservation policy which underpins all of these issues. The legal problem is that the mainstay of conservation law is the protection of specific sites, which are designated on scientific rather than broader conservation grounds, and that those designations are easily circumvented either at the wish of affected landowners or through the land use planning system.[5]

The necessary implementation of Directive 79/409/EEC on the Conservation of Wild Birds (Wild Birds Directive)[6] and Directive 92/43/EEC on the Conservation of Natural Habitats and of Wild Fauna and Flora (Habitats Directive)[7] has lent protection to "European" sites additional to that enjoyed by their national comparators, despite the established designations being

---

* Lecturer at the School of Law, University of Southampton.

[1] T. Jewell, "Public Law and the Environment: The Prospects for Decision-Making" in T. Jewell and J. Steele (eds.), *Law in Environmental Decision-Making: National, European and International Perspectives* (Oxford: Oxford University Press, 1998).

[2] Cm. 3587, Mar. 1997.

[3] Air Quality Standards Regs. 1989, SI 1989/317, which were enacted to give effect to Dir. 80/779/EEC [1980] OJ L229/30, Dir. 82/884 [1982] OJ L378/15 and Dir. 85/203/EEC [1985] OJ L87/1; Air Quality Regs. 1997, SI 1997/3043.

[4] Department of the Environment, Transport and the Regions, guidance notes LAQM.G1–G4(97) and LAQM.TG1–TG4 (98), see (1998) 10 *Environmental Law & Management* 34.

[5] See, e.g., Wildlife and Countryside Act 1981 and C. Reid, *Nature Conservation Law* (Edinburgh: W. Green, 1994).

[6] [1979] OJ L103/1.   [7] [1992] OJ L206/7.

employed for Community purposes. For example, a reference made to the ECJ from the United Kingdom confirmed the limited factors which could be taken into account in the designation of special protection areas under the Wild Birds Directive,[8] a limitation which would *not* apply to "national" sites. The Habitats Directive itself has subsequently been amended to limit the impact of this decision.[9] Certain distinctions therefore do apply in UK law between European sites and other sites.[10] Yet with its apparent commitment to bio-diversity, the "new" UK government does now propose to give a greater coercive edge to conservation law,[11] although even if modified it will bear no comparison to industrial pollution law.

C. WASTE

The contrast between the first—surprisingly recent—waste-specific legislation in the UK (the Deposit of Poisonous Waste Act 1972) and the present regulatory scheme is striking. A well-developed, cradle-to-grave regulatory regime is now in place, which is complemented by market mechanisms, and which applies to both industrial and commercial waste, and domestic waste arisings. A new wave of reforms is now also imminent, in the context of the forthcoming adoption of the Landfill Directive.[12] The recent statutory obligation to prepare a national waste strategy[13] has prompted wide-ranging reform measures, planned for introduction in spring 1999.[14] These are premised on two conclusions: first, that previous UK governments have under-estimated the scale of the change necessary to reach targets for recycling and recovery; secondly, that there has been a failure in the past to place waste strategy squarely in the context of sustainable development and resource use. This has not been assisted by a recent judicial reluctance to impose binding weight on the obligations created by Council Directive 91/156/EEC amending Directive 75/442/EEC on Waste[15] in respect of public authorities' choice of waste disposal options.[16]

The revised UK approach is to adopt an "economic" approach to waste problems: it seeks to identify and address the market failures that act as

---

[8] *R. v. Secretary of State for the Environment, ex p. Royal Society for the Protection of Birds* [1997] QB 206.

[9] Habitats Directive, Art. 6(4) and (7).

[10] Conservation (Natural Habitats) Regs. 1994, SI 1994/2716.

[11] Department of the Environment, Transport and the Regions, *Sites of Special Scientific Interest: Better Protection and Management*, Sept. 1998.

[12] Commission proposal for a directive on the landfill of waste, COM(97)105 final. For a Parliamentary response to the draft dir. see: House of Lords Select Committee on the European Communities, *Sustainable Landfill*, 17th Report, Session 1997–8 (HL Paper 83).

[13] Environment Act 1995, s. 92; DoE, *Making Waste Work: A Strategy for Sustainable Waste Management in England and Wales*, Cm. 3040, 1995.

[14] Department of the Environment, Transport and the Regions, *Less Waste. More Value*, June 1998.

[15] [1991] OJ L78/32.

[16] Particularly Art. 4: *R. v. Bolton Metropolitan Borough Council, ex p. Kirkman* [1998] JPL 787; *R. v. Environment Agency, ex p. Gibson, R. v. Environment Agency, ex p. Leam, R. v. Environment Agency, ex p. Seller & Petty* (1998) 280 ENDS Report 49.

barriers to increasing the use of material recycling, composting and energy recovery services. One of the most important barriers that has been identified is the present immunity enjoyed by households from meeting the full social costs of their waste. As yet there is little indication of what legal measures might be adopted to address this, beyond encouragement of local authorities to seek waste minimization, perhaps through charging schemes for the collection of certain wastes.

i. Packaging and Packaging Waste

More marked legal developments are evident in the implementation of Parliament and Council Directive 94/62/EC on Packaging and Packaging Waste,[17] which also contributes to shifting the regulatory burden away from end-of-pipe treatment and disposal. The Directive was implemented in the UK by regulations at the end of 1997,[18] which were subject to a review in 1998.[19] This concludes that the Regulations' interim target of 32 per cent recovery (which is not contained in the Directive itself) was almost met in the first year. However, the waste recovery targets for 1999 may have to be raised by between 2 and 4 per cent, primarily to deal with an increase of materials entering the waste stream, and significant problems in making accurate assessments remain, as data are often not accurately reported.

D. WATER

In contrast to the position regarding waste management, water quality control is very well-established. The tasks of the Environment Agency for England and Wales and the Scottish Environmental Protection Agency have become more elaborate with the creation of further classification schemes and water quality objectives, by reference to which those bodies must exercise their functions.[20] This continues the familiar practice of super-imposing classification schemes on established licensing systems, in this case to give further effect to Council Directive 76/464/EEC on Pollution Caused by Certain Dangerous Substances Discharged Into the Aquatic Environment of the Community.[21] More complex still is the further superimposition of measures to protect groundwater.[22]

Community obligations to designate areas within which activities contributing to water pollution are controlled are a departure from the normal practice of UK water law. However, measures such as nitrate sensitive areas

---

[17] [1994] OJ L365/10.

[18] Environment Act 1995, ss. 93–95; Producer Responsibility Obligations (Packaging Waste) Regs. 1997, SI 1997/648.

[19] S. Tromans and M. Nash, "Packaging Waste Review" (1998) 48 *Environmental Law Bulletin* 8.

[20] Surface Waters (Dangerous Substances) (Classification) Regs. 1997, SI 1997/2560, and Surface Waters (Dangerous Substances) (Classification) Regs. 1998, SI 1998/389.

[21] [1976] OJ L129/32.

[22] Dir. 80/68/EEC on the protection of groundwater against pollution caused by certain dangerous substances [1980] OJ L20/43; Groundwater Regs. 1998, SI 1998/2746.

and now nitrate vulnerable zones (NVZs) are becoming increasingly signifi-cant. The Directive on nitrates from agricultural sources[23] was issued after the UK had introduced measures to designate nitrate sensitive areas,[24] hence the need to introduce new implementing measures. Extensive new controls have therefore been introduced, although their legality has been challenged.[25] A reference to the ECJ has subsequently been made concerning the relevance (if any) to designation of a NVZ of the contribution to pollution of non-agricultural sources as opposed to agricultural sources of nitrate pollution.

E.   HORIZONTAL INSTRUMENTS

i. IPPC

An "integrated pollution control" (IPC) regime has been progressively imple-mented in the UK since 1990.[26] Although subject to limitations, IPC has had a powerful influence both on industrial perceptions of the significance of indus-trial pollution regulation[27] and on EC initiatives themselves. The process of super-imposing Council Directive 96/61/EC Concerning Integrated Pollution Prevention and Control (IPPC Directive)[28] onto the UK's IPC regime is proving a complex one, however, despite the putative similarities between IPPC and IPC. There are, in fact, significant differences between the IPPC Directive and the IPC regime, including: the Directive's application to a wider range of instal-lations than the processes currently subject to IPC; the wider range of envi-ronmental impacts relevant under the Directive; and the more flexible institutional arrangements anticipated by the Directive than currently prac-tised in the UK. The need to introduce implementing measures promptly has also had important implications for their likely legal character.

The measures themselves have emerged from a series of consultation exer-cises and culminated in the presentation of a Bill to Parliament in November 1998.[29] That Bill would repeal the present IPC regime and replace it with an IPPC system whose underlying principles and details are to be determined by ministers under delegated powers.[30] Even for the UK, this is an unusually extensive delegation. This can be expected to create Parliamentary contro-versy, although this is likely to delay, rather than defeat, the Bill itself. A final

---

[23] Council Dir. 91/676/EEC concerning the protection of waters against pollution caused by nitrates from agricultural sources [1991] OJ L375/1.

[24] Water Resources Act 1991, s. 94 and Sched. 12.

[25] The Protection of Water Against Agricultural Pollution (England and Wales) Regs. 1996, SI 1996/888; *R. v. Secretary of State for the Environment, the Minister of Agriculture, Fisheries and Food, ex p. Standley* (1998) 10 Journal of Environmental Law 92.

[26] Environmental Protection Act 1990, Pt. I.

[27] A. Mehta and K. Hawkins, "Integrated Pollution Control and its Impact: Perspectives from Industry" (1998) 10 Journal of Environmental Law 61.

[28] [1996] OJ L257/26.

[29] Pollution Prevention and Control Bill, Session 1998–9 (HL Bill 3), 26 Nov. 1998.

[30] Draft Pollution Prevention and Control Regs. accompanied: Department of the Environment, Transport and the Regions, *Third Consultation Paper on the Implementation of the IPPC Dir.*, Dec. 1998.

feature of the implementation proposals is that different arrangements will apply in Scotland and in Northern Ireland. Major constitutional reforms are in progress in the UK, including a measure of devolution in Scotland, and certain delegations to Wales and to the English regions. Responsibility for the implementation of IPPC in Scotland will therefore be devolved to the Scottish Parliament in line with a general devolution of environmental functions effected by the Scotland Act 1998.

ii.   *Environmental Impact Assessment*

The implementation of Directive 85/337/EEC on the Assessment of the Effects of Certain Public and Private Projects on the Environment (EIA Directive)[31] has had continuing general impacts in land use planning, as well as particular impacts in respect of forestry. July 1998 saw the proposal of modifications to the principal regulations implementing the 1985 Directive, which generally form part of the land use planning system.[32] Those proposals have been made to give effect to the amendments to the Directive itself,[33] rather than to criticisms of the original implementation of the Directive which have emerged as a result of research undertaken by the UK government.[34] The revised arrangements are intended to come into force in March 1999,[35] however, they must also be viewed in light of the pragmatic approach taken by UK courts to compliance with the Directive in practice. There are two aspects to this. First, where there has been substantive but informal compliance with the Directive, the courts have shown a marked reluctance to overturn the relevant decision.[36] Secondly, there are signs of a converse willingness to extend the substantive application of the Directive beyond some earlier judicial limitations, even in the absence of a categorical statement from the European Court of Justice that the Directive is directly effective.[37] Indeed, at the end of 1998, the Court of Appeal implicitly accepted the direct effect of the Directive even in the absence of such a statement from the ECJ.[38]

However, there has been a major change of policy towards the regulation of forestry projects. In the past, afforestation projects have generally fallen outside the scope of land use planning controls, and thus also environmental assessment. Forestry planting has instead been regulated through grant schemes, and an environmental assessment obligation has attached not to

[31] [1985] OJ L175/40.

[32] Town and Country Planning (Assessment of Environmental Effects) Regs. 1988, SI 1988/1199, as amended.

[33] Council Directive 97/11/EC [1997] OJ L173/5.

[34] Department of the Environment, *Changes in the Quality of Environmental Statements for Planning Projects*, noted in (1996) 8 *Environmental Law & Management* 169.

[35] Draft Town and Country Planning (Assessment of Environmental Effects) (England and Wales) Regs., published in July 1998.

[36] e.g., *Twyford Parish Council* v. *Secretary of State for the Environment and Secretary of State for Transport*, (1992) 4 *Journal of Environmental Law* 273–88 (High Court); *Berkeley* v. *Secretary of State for the Environment, The Times*, 2 Mar. 1998 (Court of Appeal).

[37] Case C–72/95, *Aannemersbedrijf P. K. Kraaijeveld BV* v. *Gedeputeerde Staten van Zuid-Holland* [1996] ECR I–5403.

[38] *R.* v. *North Yorkshire County Council, ex p. Brown* [1998] Environmental Law Reports 385.

land use decisions but to the grant applications themselves.[39] This regulatory gap has been filled through a new obligation to secure formal consent before *any* planting takes place.[40]

iii.   Environmental Information

The UK's 1992 implementation of the Directive on the Freedom of Access to Information on the Environment[41] has also been reviewed, and amendments made. However, and as was the case in respect of EIA, it is not the practical shortcomings of the operation of the 1992 Regulations that have driven that amendment, but technical failures in the Regulations themselves. The amendments narrow the range of circumstances in which information may be withheld where the disclosure of that information would affect certain classes of interests, such as national security or international relations.[42] The practical problems with the Regulations, which are not addressed, include issues such as whether they apply to privatized utilities, the problems of securing physical access itself, and the suggestion that charging schemes undermine the basic right of access.[43]

F.   MISCELLANEOUS DEVELOPMENTS

It is in the emergence of certain general measures that the UK government's commitment to certain "alternative" instruments for environmental protection has begun to develop most clearly. That commitment dates from at least 1990, but practical initiatives remain unusual.[44] Innovation in regulatory technique is now becoming an important feature of UK environmental law, however. This is partly because of the need to adapt to complex and fast moving environmental problems; and partly because of changing perceptions of the relationship between the public and private sectors, and between Member States and the Community.[45] That innovation is exemplified in developments in the use of retrospective liabilities for historically contaminated land, reliance on the incentive effects of taxation to pursue environmental policy,

---

[39] C. Reid, "Environmental Regulation through Economic Instruments: The Example of Forestry" (1996) 8 *Environmental Law & Management* 59–63; Environmental Assessment (Afforestation) Regs. 1988, SI 1988/1207.

[40] Environmental Assessment (Forestry) Regs. 1998, SI 1998/1731.

[41] Council Dir. 90/313 [1990] OJ L158/56 implemented by Environmental Information Regs. 1992, SI 1992/3240.

[42] Environmental Information (Amendment) Regs. 1998, SI 1998/1447.

[43] House of Lords Select Committee on the European Communities, *Freedom of Access to Information on the Environment*, First Report, Session 1996–7 (HL Paper 9); C. Kimber, "Understanding Access to Environmental Information: the European Experience" in Jewell and Steele (eds.), n. 1 above.

[44] Department of the Environment, *This Common Inheritance* (Cm. 1200, London: HMSO, 1990). More recently, see: Department of the Environment, *Sustainable Development: The UK Strategy* (Cm. 2426, London: HMSO, 1994); and Department of the Environment, Transport and the Regions, *Sustainable Development: Opportunities for Change*, Consultation Paper on a revised UK Strategy, Feb. 1998.

[45] An analysis of these pressures is given in Jewell and Steele (eds.), n. 1 above.

greater emphasis on "economic regulation" (that is, arm's length state regulation of private or privatized industries) and reform of the land use planning system.

New powers to require the clean-up of contaminated land have been introduced, partly as a reaction against the Commission's 1993 Green Paper, *Remedying Environmental Damage*, and partly to provide greater certainty in property transactions. The UK government's rejection of the need for Community action in this field, let alone the detail of what was proposed,[46] will inform its reaction to new initiatives, which seems likely to include a proposal on environmental liability. In the meantime, extensive consultation has been undertaken over the new UK controls, and their implementation is expected in April 2000. In essence, those controls will impose liabilities for past environmental damage on those responsible for the contamination of land or, in some cases, the owners or occupiers of land, where the damage is quantified in terms of the cost of corrective activity.[47] In most cases the emphasis will be on voluntary remediation, premised on an assessment of the risks arising from particular contaminants in particular situations.

Whilst the contaminated land powers have yet to bite, we do now have some practical experience of another key economic instrument, the landfill tax. Established in 1996, the tax is payable by landfill site operators, and is charged on the disposal of waste by landfill.[48] Evidence in 1998 to a Parliamentary review of the tax reported that 1,879 sites are receiving taxable deposits, with 1,100 operators registered and accounting for the tax.[49] In the year 1996–7, the tax raised £361 million (approximately 566,662,000 Euros), although there has been a consequential, but apparently "modest", increase in illegal fly-tipping. Changes to the tax are anticipated as part of the review of the national waste strategy planned for early 1999, as well as in conjunction with the adoption later that year of the Landfill Directive. Further economic instruments are now also proposed in the context of water pollution and abstraction, the business use of energy, and the exploitation of primary aggregates.[50]

---

[46] That response was published on 8 Oct. 1993 as a Memorandum, reproduced as App. IV to *Remedying Environmental Damage*, Session 1993–4 (HL Paper 10).

[47] Environmental Protection Act 1990, Part IIA, inserted by Environment Act 1995, s. 57.

[48] Finance Act 1996, ss. 39–41; Landfill Tax Regs. 1996, SI 1996/1527.

[49] House of Commons Environment Select Committee, *The Operation of the Landfill Tax*, First Report, Session 1998–9, Joint Memorandum from the Department of the Environment, Transport and the Regions and HM Customs & Excise.

[50] Department of the Environment, Transport and the Regions Consultation Paper, *Economic Instruments for Water Pollution*, Nov. 1997; Task Force on the Industrial Use of Energy, *Economic Instruments and the Business Use of Energy: A Consultation Paper* (1998); and HM Customs & Excise Consultation Paper, *A Proposal for an Aggregates Tax*, July 1997.

Reviews of Books

Law in Environmental Decision-Making. National, European and International Perspectives edited by Tim Jewell and Jenny Steele. Clarendon Press, Oxford, 1998, xxxi + 294 pp. £50.00 hb. ISBN 0 19 826077 6

This book is a collection of essays examining the effectiveness of current regulatory and institutional frameworks of environmental law. The central theme of the book is the extent to which law can provide solutions to environmental challenges. The challenges identified include the nature of environmental harm, particularly its unpredictability and ability to cross national borders, the rival claims of participatory and representative democracy, and the changing role of the nation state in an era of globalization.

In chapter 1 the book's editors, Tim Jewell and Jenny Steele, draw together the often diverse contributions within a common framework. They explore the theme of integration that is implicit throughout the book. Integration is discussed in two respects: first, as a trend within environmental law, by which is meant the growing inclination of policy-makers to view environmental law in a more holistic way, incorporating controls, principles of action and agency structure and, secondly, the integration of environmental law into a variety of broader legal contexts. While the chapter acknowledges that integrating trends within environmental law are a relatively recent phenomenon, it also predicts that they are likely to be an increasingly common trend.

Jewell and Steele also identify the trend towards "innovation" as a common theme in the book, with evidence of a general proliferation of policy instruments beyond the traditional command-and-control approach. They identify the shift in decision-making to the private sector as being a key development in the "privatization" of environmental regulation, through mechanisms such as self-regulation, and conclude that innovative trends are becoming more common because the failures of traditional command-and-control mechanisms almost inevitably imply flexible, responsive and process-oriented approaches.

The structure for the remainder of the book reflects an emphasis on the ever increasing diversity of legal and political contexts for environmental issues. Within these contexts, the process of attempting simultaneously to achieve both regulatory effectiveness and significant participation poses considerable challenges for law.

David Robinson (chapter 2) explains the evolution of regulatory pollution control mechanisms, identifying regulatory responses to pollution in different national regimes and highlighting the limitations of the command-and-control approach. Recognizing the limitations of command-and-control mechanisms, Robinson identifies alternative strategies, based on economic instruments, self-regulation and innovative enforcement approaches, but concludes that they also have weaknesses. He instead advocates information-based initiatives, based on greater openness to all stakeholders, as being the key to environmental improvement.

Tim Jewell (chapter 3) examines the appropriateness of processes for making decisions with a direct environmental impact. This chapter is essentially a discussion of contemporary developments in UK environmental law from a public law perspective. Jewell locates the emergence of distinctively environmental considerations that influence the development of statute law. He identifies a number of new directions in public law and the environment, including greater administrative openness and the use of economic instruments and concludes with the pessimistic view that, although these developments may have been presented as being both environmentally and economically efficient, the key environmental decisions are likely to be characterized by less, rather than more, transparency.

Jenny Steele (chapter 4) examines the challenges brought through tort law by affected individuals and groups against a background which has been dominated by regulatory control of environmental risk. Steel examines claims based on foreseeability, causation, culpability, and nuisance. She engages in a lively discussion of a number of important cases. Despite the limited success experienced by the plaintiffs, Steele contends that these cases raise issues relating to the allocation of environmental responsibility and retrospective "blame". She concludes that the tort law raises issues concerned with the evaluation of risk that are potentially of great importance for environmental law more generally.

Cliona Kimber (chapter 5) assesses the role that an ideal model of access to environmental information can play in environmental decision-making. She then provides a critique of the Directive on Freedom of Access to Environmental Information, concluding that the system of access in the EU falls short of the ideal in a manner that may lead to frustration and resentment unless the system is reformed.

Han Somsen (chapter 6) undertakes a wide-ranging examination of the dynamics, processes, and instruments of environmental decision-making in the EU. Somsen re-assesses the effectiveness of environmental law by considering various points of the "regulatory chain" through which environmental legislation is designed, conceived, drafted, implemented, and enforced. His conclusion, that Community environmental law consists of numerous intricate relationships between Member States and supranational institutions, may not be novel, but his use of the "contextual" approach, taking into account both economic and institutional factors, provides a helpful framework within which further work will no doubt be undertaken to assess regulatory effectiveness.

Tony Evans (chapter 7) shifts the focus of analysis from European to international environmental law by examining the challenge of globalization. From a globalization perspective, Evans describes environmental degradation as a "crisis of modernity". Evans writes from a political science perspective and the chapter encompasses the realist tradition of international political theory, emphasizing the hegemonic influence of states over the global environmental commons. His conclusion, that globalization requires a re-evaluation of international law, acknowledges the limitations of current legal structures and identifies the establishment of environmental security as the challenge for transnational regime systems in the future.

Christine Chinkin (chapter 8) also addresses the challenges facing international environmental law. She examines how states have used and developed established legal techniques in response to the need for international action on environmental problems that transcend national borders. This examination highlights familiar problems of procedural constraint, absence of dispute resolution and lack of effective implementation. It concludes with the stark view that the emphasis on new processes of international law deflects attention away from important problems of international implementation and enforcement. As with Tony Evans, we are left with the impression that current legal structures may well be insufficient to meet the challenges of the global environmental agenda.

Overall, this well-edited book provides a valuable forum in which a clearly-defined set of national, European and global legal and environmental issues are presented in a thought-provoking volume which is likely to prove a valuable addition to any academic library. It does, however, leave the overall impression that law has thus far provided only limited solutions to environmental problems at national, European and international level. The need for innovative and effective legal instruments to tackle environmental harm appears all the more urgent in the light of the evidence set out in this book.

DUNCAN MATTHEWS

Trade and the Environment. A Comparative Study of EC and US Law by Damien Geradin. Cambridge University Press, Cambridge, 1997, xxiv + 231 pp.

Damien Geradin, assistant professor of law at the University of Liège (Belgium), undertakes the task of comparing EC and US law on trade and the environment. However, as the author himself acknowledges (at 202), the title of the book is broader than the subject treated, as it focuses exclusively on internal aspects of trade and the environment. All aspects of international trade, which increasingly dominate international legal discussions, are omitted. This omission is certainly regrettable, as both the USA and the EC seem at least in part to apply different standards at international level from those they apply internally.

The book has a second, very important limitation. The author discusses measures only in the area of products, processes, and waste. In particular tax issues, animal welfare, fauna and flora protection, and issues of implementation are not considered. The fact that all examples are taken from areas other than fauna and flora appears to indicate that the author differentiates between products and species of fauna and flora. The need for such differentiation seems obvious at international level. However, the GATT provisions ignore this distinction.

The book is divided into two parts, on negative and positive harmonization. Each part discusses EC law, US law and then undertakes a comparative analysis. A general conclusion tries to draw some lessons from this analysis.

For Geradin "negative harmonization" refers to the situation where no harmonized legislation has been adopted. The author examines, for EC law, the provisions of the EC Treaty as they were interpreted by the ECJ in trade and environment issues. He starts from the principle of free trade (Articles 28 and 30 (formerly Articles 30 and 36) EC), reviews the exceptions to this principle as established by the ECJ; and undertakes an application of these principles to waste, product standards, and process standards.

The parallel chapter on US law considers the "Commerce Clause" and, again, its application by the US Supreme Court to waste issues and product and process standards. For the European reader it is particularly interesting to learn that attempts to limit the import of waste from other states were turned down by the Supreme Court with the argument that such a limitation is discriminatory and contrary to the Commerce Clause. The author convincingly demonstrates, in his comparative analysis, how this reasoning differs from the ruling of the ECJ in *Wallonian Waste*. "Landfilling was seen by the Supreme Court as a natural resource that all states were under an obligation to share for the common good" (at 57). Community law attaches more importance to Member States' discretion to decide on questions of land use—including land filling.

Another interesting aspect is that the Supreme Court does not allow a state to protect the environment in another state, whereas the ECJ has never been obliged to be as specific. Geradin discusses this issue only in general terms. Personally, the reviewer feels that Member States' measures to protect the environment in another Member State may be possible under certain circumstances, in particular as regards fauna and flora protection.

As regards product standards, the author extensively discusses the principle of proportionality in the context of Article 28 (formerly Article 30) EC, which docs not have an express parallel in US law, where the criterion is whether a state measure discriminates against products from other states. However, the "balancing test" used by the Supreme Court (a state measure which affects inter-state commerce will be upheld "unless the burden imposed on such commerce is clearly excessive in relation to the putative local benefits" (at 37)) leads to largely identical outcomes.

Geradin observes that process-related trade restrictions have not yet been taken in the EC and that hence no case law from the ECJ exist. The same is true for the USA, where the Supreme Court has never had to decide on process-related trade restrictions.

In Part Two, "Positive Harmonization", Geradin examines EC law (chapter 5), US law (chapter 6), and once more compares the legal approaches (chapter 7). This is preceded by an analysis of the attributed powers to harmonize environmental standards. As regards Articles 95 and 175 (formerly Articles 100a and 130s) EC, this involves the principles of subsidiarity and proportionality, the ways of harmonizing environmental standards and the question of residual powers for Member States to adopt more stringent provisions, once the EC has legislated. To be sure, the author does not attempt to describe in full all environmental product standards elaborated at Community level. For product standards, he illustrates the procedure and problems through the example of air pollution emission limit values for cars. For process standards, Directive 88/609/EEC on Large Combustion Plants and Directive 76/464/EEC on the Discharge of Dangerous Substances Into Water serve this purpose. As for waste, the framework provisions (Directives 75/442/EEC and 91/689/EEC) and the shipment of waste take centre stage, whilst installations are briefly analysed.

Chapter 6 on US law follows the same pattern. Environmental matters are normally the responsibility of the states. The main basis for regulating environmental aspects at federal level is the Commerce Clause (Article 1(8), Clause 3 of the US Constitution). Besides, the Property Clause (Article IV(3), Clause 2 of the US Constitution), the clause authorizing the imposition and collection of taxes, duties etc. (Article 1(8) Clause 1 of the US Constitution) and the Treaty power (Article 2(2) of the US Constitution) serve this purpose. Of interest to European readers is the analysis of harmonization of environmental standards. As regards product standards, Geradin again uses the example of air emission standards for cars. Federal legislation adopted since 1967 provided for a uniform national standard, but allowed California to retain more stringent standards. This permission was extended in 1977 to other states. This two-tier system continues today.

As regards process standards, the USA has established, in order to control water and air pollution, uniform provisions for the major polluting sources, such as steel and chemical plants, paper mills, tanneries, and food-processing plants (at 163). However, as regards air quality standards, states might attract industry by applying less strict emission limits than other states. The Federal Clean Air Act attempted to prevent this by providing for the fixing of uniform emission limits based on the "best adequately demonstrated technology", and by establishing three classes of clean-air regions, for which specific ceilings ("increments") were fixed for air emissions.

As regards waste, federal legislation concentrated on hazardous wastes, leaving the regulation of non-hazardous waste to the states. Inter-state movements of waste have not been regulated by federal legislation, although efforts by states to limit the import of hazardous wastes from other states were declared constitutionally invalid.

In his comparative analysis, Geradin concludes that for product standards developments in the USA and in the EC have been largely similar, both jurisdictions trying to achieve uniform standards and preventing states (Member States) from adopting more stringent standards. A number of concessions, however, have to be made in both areas. For product standards the author detects a trend towards more uniform standards in the USA. In the European Community the introduction of majority decisions in Article 175(1) (formerly Article 130s(1)) EC increases the tendency towards uniform standards, but this is counteracted by Member States' political will to maintain national product standards within the Community.

Both the EC and the USA adopted rules for minimum environmental standards in respect of waste disposals. For the shipment of waste, different solutions were adopted: the Community controlled intra-Community shipment by way of prior informed consent procedures, but allowed Member States to ban all imports or exports of wastes for disposal. The USA opted for a free market for waste. The authority for states to restrict imports from other states might be granted, however, for hazardous waste (at 194). Despite these differences, the author believes that legislation on the movements of waste might eventually converge.

The book is very good reading. The author has a great capacity to present complex situations in a transparent and clear way. The descriptive as well as the analytical parts are carefully worked out and hence invite very few critical comments. My only significant observation is that, as regards harmonized US law, the author frequently refers to the writings of my friend Richard Stewart. He might have mentioned, however, that for several years Richard Stewart played a prominent role in the republican federal administration, which obviously affects the legal position he defends.

Overall, as an introduction to the problem of environmental policies and the internal market within the EC and the USA and the evolution of environmental legislation since the end of the sixties, the book is to be warmly recommended.

The author's analysis of likely future developments, however, is more contentious. Geradin departs from the principle of free trade to which the provisions on environmental protection constitute the exception without questioning this hypothesis (at 9 and 13). Historically, this is correct. However, the EC Treaty was revised in 1987, 1993, and 1999, and each time the position of environmental issues within the Treaty context was reassessed. Thus new Article 6 EC requires that the requirements for environmental protection must be integrated into the design and implementation of all other Community policies, which has no equivalent in the sphere of trade. The author could therefore have questioned the continued validity of this presumed hierarchy of norms. In this sense, his approach to this whole problem remains rathertraditional. The real challenge facing the Community in the years to come is the construction of a genuine internal market, based on high levels of environmental protection. This challenge, acknowledged in the

EC Treaty but not yet fully translated in legal policy, is not taken up by the author.

Neither does the author seem fully to realize the profound changes of the Community's policy on product standards since the early 1990s. Indeed, it seems that it is now generally accepted that product standard are minimum standards. The Community will have to be watchful not to increase the gap between Member States maintaining stringent product standards and those which tolerate lax standards.

Finally, the reader should be well aware of the limits of comparative law, which does not take heed of political considerations, which are particularly relevant in the setting up of the European Union. This may be illustrated by way of an example. The basic Community approach to wastes is that they should be moved as little as possible and that Member States should retain the freedom to ban shipments for disposal purposes. As a legal consequence of this approach, EC law provides for a ban of hazardous waste shipments to the Third World, in line with the Basel Convention. The USA treats industrial (hazardous) waste in the same way as a product, applies the Commerce Clause, and is critical of state import restrictions. It is for this reason that the USA did not ratify the Basel Convention and strongly opposes, at international level, restrictions to the free movement of hazardous waste, frequently invoking GATT rules. Clearly, different approaches are dictated as much by policy as by law. It is perhaps appropriate to recall Luther's observation that a lawyer who is merely a lawyer is a poor soul. Geradin's outstanding capacities as a lawyer would ideally be accompanied by a more passionate approach towards questions concerning the environment and trade dichotomy. However, the author's lucidity and understanding of both EC and US law make this book an indispensable source for all those interested in this fascinating subject.

LUDWIG KRÄMER

The Implementation of EC Environmental Law by Decentralized Authorities in the Netherlands by Johan van de Gronden. Kluwer, Deventer, 1998, 605 pp. (in Dutch, with a summary in English)

In this extensive volume, which was written as a PhD dissertation, Johan van de Gronden explores the Community law requirements for the transposition, embedment, application, and enforcement of EC environmental directives and regulations by provinces, municipalities, and water management boards in the Netherlands. Since in the Netherlands decentralized authorities play an important role in the implementation and application of environmental law, his study is highly significant for these decentralized authorities. Although only Member States are addressed by environmental directives and regulations, decentralized authorities also fall within the scope of the notion "Member State". Thus, the principle of loyalty to the Community laid down in

Article 10 (formerly Article 5) EC also applies to municipalities, provinces and water management boards. Until now, focus on the implementation of European environmental law by practitioners has largely ignored the role of decentralized authorities.

Van de Gronden discerns four aspects of implementation: transposition, embedment, application, and enforcement. "Transposition" is the incorporation of the Community norm in national legislation, such as the Provincial Environmental Ordinance, in which rules are laid down to ensure the collection of Packaging Waste, thus implementing Directive 94/62/EC on Packaging and Packaging Waste. In national legislation implementing this Directive, the province has been instructed to adopt such rules. "Embedment" means the creation of a legislative framework making EC environmental directives and regulations operational, such as rules in the same Provincial Ordinance to ensure implementation of Regulation 259/93 (EC) No. on the Supervision and Control of Shipments of Waste Within, Into, and Out of the European Community. "Application" means the application of a Community norm to a concrete case by competent authorities, such as applying an environmental quality standard to a permit on waste water by the competent authority of a water management board) or ordering an environmental impact assessment for a certain project. "Enforcement" simply means governmental action against non-compliance with Community norms, such as actions taken against an industrial business that does not comply with a permit granted under Directive 96/61/EC on Integrated Pollution Prevention and Control (IPPC Directive). As can be seen from these examples, all four aspects are relevant for decentralized authorities.

After the four chapters dealing with these four aspects of implementation, Van de Gronden considers the matter of liability for non-compliance with EC law as developed in Joined Cases C–6/90 and C–9/90, *Francovich* [1991] ECR I–5357 and Joined Cases C–46/93 and C–48/93 *Brasserie du Pêcheur* [1996] ECR I–1029. He concludes that in some cases decentralized authorities may be held liable for incorrect implementation by the central government, especially where the illegal act by the decentralized authorities is the consequence of a violation of Community law by the central government authorities at an earlier stage of the implementation process. To avoid such liability, decentralized authorities must in all cases refer to the relevant secondary EC law themselves; they cannot rely on national legislation implementing EC directives. In case of incorrect transposition, they must even refrain from applying national law.

This very thorough and well documented study on the subject of implementation of EC law by decentralized authorities clearly shows that the strict requirements for the implementation of secondary Community environmental law strongly influence the state structure within Member States. In the Netherlands, the current constitutional division of powers between national and decentralized authorities is being eroded as a result of EC law. Van de Gronden concludes that there are two fields of tension. First, secondary Community environmental law simultaneously restricts and expands the powers of decentralized authorities. On the one hand, the strict requirements in respect of implementation restrict the powers of the decentralized authorities. In most cases there is only very limited room for a discrete provincial or municipal environmental policy, where EC environmental law already exists. On the other hand, however, secondary Community law also provides decentralized authorities with an additional power, in that they must consider whether the national provisions which they are to apply and enforce are compatible with the relevant EC law provisions. Secondly, a decentralized authority may be held liable if it applies or enforces national legislation which may at a later date prove to be incompatible with an EC directive or regulation. The other side of the coin is that the national authorities may be presented with the bill in respect of defective implementation at the level of the decentralized authorities. Van de Gronden therefore concludes that the decentralization of implementation powers is a partial failure, as the responsibility and liability do not correspond with the powers.

To cope with these problems, Van de Gronden puts forward no fewer than twenty-five recommendations. He advocates, for example, the establishment of an advisory body, to be consulted by decentralized authorities in cases where there is doubt whether EC environmental law is applicable (national implementing legislation often does not clearly identify the underlying EC law provisions). Also, a special legal facility should be created to enable central authorities to intervene where decentralized authorities fail to perform their Community tasks. At Community level, Van de Gronden recommends that decentralized authorities should be given increased influence in the Community legislative procedure.

Van de Gronden's analysis has exposed the paramount importance of EC environmental law for decentralized authorities, which therefore would be well advised to take heed of the author's conclusions.

JONATHAN VERSCHUUREN

Protecting the European Environment: Enforcing EC Environmental Law edited by Han Somsen. Blackstone Press, London, 1996, 312 pp.

This edited collection by Han Somsen consists of fourteen thematic and analytical essays which address the question of Community environmental enforcement. These are topical essays, well written and carefully planned to provide the reader with an integrated study of the enforcement of European Community law in all its dimensions. The authors are well known and highly distinguished experts in their field. Environmental policy in the EU has been changing rapidly over the past few years and the essays track many of the changes that have transpired. It has also been a period of great change for environmental law and policy in Britain. Indeed, on the eve of the Warwick Conference, from which this volume originates, the government published in January 1994 a White Paper on sustainable development, which is being presently reviewed and revised. The Warwick conference also coincided with the development of the Environment Agency.

European Community policy on the environment had a long gestation period before it came of age. This has given rise to a degree of *ad hoc* development. The most well known examples are Directive 91/271/EEC on Urban Waste Water Treatment, Directive 76/160/EEC on the Quality of Bathing Water, and Directive 80/778/EEC on Drinking Water. DGXI is directly responsible for environmental matters but in matters of, for example, competition policy DGIV has a role to perform. The idea of a single market within the EU should provide the means to deliver common environmental standards and the means to enforce them. Delivering common implementation strategies throughout all Member States in the EU is not easy and gives rise to a systemic weakness in current arrangements.

In chapter 1, Lord Clinton-Davies gives a thematic overview to the collection as a personal perspective on enforcing EC environmental law. This chapter sends a clear message for greater powers for the Commission to take action against an offending Member State. His analysis is powerful and persuasive. He considers that it might be desirable that a Community Inspectorate should be set up under either the European Environmental Agency or DGXI. The essay is stimulating to read in perspective and analysis.

In chapter 2 Richard Macrory offers a rich analysis of the obligations contained in the EC's environmental legislation and the regime of enforcement. Beginning with a discussion of Article 226 (formerly Article 169) EC procedures, Macrory analyses the typical circumstances in which Member States fail to comply with a directive. Noting that the Commission has restricted powers of investigation, the author offers suggestions to enhance the effectiveness of handling investigations. Macrory rightly observes that increased involvement of national institutions in the enforcement of EC policy is required to supplement the activities of the Commission.

A similar theme is expressed in chapter 8 by Eckard Rehbinder who, in analysing the enforcement problem in EC environmental law, stresses the need to decentralize supervisory powers. The author argues that there are a number of reasons for the limitations of the court-based approach to the implementation and enforcement deficit (e.g. interest group activities, procedural position of actors, organizational structure and budgeting of agencies, culture of administrators). Despite the problems, Rehbinder argues that access to courts and administrative tribunals is an important source in limiting these politico-administrative implementation problems. To this end, the author assumes that proper implementation could be facilitated by the harmonization of national rules relating to standing. To be sure, the author acknowledges that without the harmonization of national standing rules, it is unlikely this procedural strengthening would be sufficient to enhance the position of environmental groups across Europe. Rehbinder has written an important essay which should influence more discussion.

The topicality and importance of the essays are in no doubt. Regulating the environment in the changing economic climate of the world's economies requires new strategies for managing scarce resources. Sustainable development is a key policy adopted by many governments in their approach to environmental problems. Increasingly, reliance is placed on the regulation of impacts on the environment.

Implementing and enforcing environmental law is a necessity. The pressure for industrialized nations to respond in a positive way to new environmental initiatives is intense. Equally clear are the economic conditions that intensify the dilemma facing many governments. Recession in many industries has forced changes in industrial policy. The cost of implementing environmental rules and standards has to be balanced in terms of jobs and employment opportunities.

Environmental law has developed new techniques. This collection of essays provides the reader with an insight into many technical workings of the law. It also highlights the importance of developing the appropriate cultural attitude to the environment. Perceiving the protection of the environment as essentially pollution control is misplaced. Prevention of environmental pollution in all its forms must be the starting point. Good enforcement techniques grounded in transparent rules must be the norm.

The answer to the criticism that the essays in this collection have become dated because of the rapid changes in the law in this area is to consider a revised second edition. The quality of the essays under review suggests that a second edition will be under way quite soon.

JOHN McELDOWNEY

Manual of European Environmental Law by Alexandre Kiss and Dinah Shelton. Grotius Publications, Cambridge University Press, Second Edition, 1997, 622 pp.

Although this *Yearbook* is hardly the place to wax lyrical about the significance of European environmental law, this work concerns one of the most consequential areas of the law of the EU. The book under review is in its revised second edition. Its authors are distinguished contributors to the literature on the subject. The authors have the case study support of 21 further listed and profiled expert contributors.

The previous edition was highly acclaimed in having made more accessible the ever-increasing volume of rules, policies, research, and regulations on the law in point to a mixed readership of academic lawyers and practitioners as well as anyone else directly or otherwise interested in the formulation and application of the law of the environment in the regional structure of the EU and indeed beyond, by adaptation and example. The main feature of the work is that it provides handy modestly encyclopaedic coverage of its much consolidated subject.

This present edition has notably involved an elaborate updating of the successful previous volume issued in 1993, with new chapters on the environmental protection and economic development aspects. Its 13 chapters are classified in three parts: "Overview", "Sectoral Protection", and "Transsectoral Issues", the classification itself being indicative of the focused and broad foresight required in proper consideration of the subject. The remainder of the present review adopts the format of the "Manual". Each chapter very usefully contains well-conceptualized questions and problems to bring home the reading, as well as further bibliographical detail.

The first Part consists of five chapters. Chapter 1 (at 3–34) explores the terminology, basic characteristics, and various documents of European environmental law from, and also provides a concise history about the 14th century. Chapter 2 (at 35–54) describes the fundamental concepts such as sustainable development, precaution, and apportionment of liability, as well as documents such as the Stockholm and the Rio Declarations. Chapter 3 (at 55–71) introduces the most important agencies and institutions at national, European, and international levels. The position of the wider public within the sectoral framework as it derives from human rights and from the participation of non-governmental organizations (NGOs) is examined in chapter 4 (at 72–97).

This fourth chapter on the public's role is, along with others presently identified in the course of review, central to the future of the subject in terms of law in action. It carries the first set of case studies, of NGOs in the EC and in Central and Eastern Europe, as well as relevant illustrative documents including Council Directive 90/313/EEC on Freedom of Access to Information on the Environment, followed by further pragmatising national constitutional provisions in similar vein, closing (at 101–9) with an addendum of the judgment of the European Court of Human Rights in *López Ostra* v. *Spain* (9 December 1994, Series A, No. 303–C). In this case Article 8 of the European Convention on Human Rights, providing for individual rights to home, private and family life, and freedom from degrading treatment, was recognized to subsist in view of prior exhaustion of local remedies. Spain was liable in substantial damages to the tune of some 24,040,48 Euros, and legal costs, in its failure to have struck a fair balance between urban economic well-being in having a waste treatment plant in the particular locality on the one hand, and on the other the applicant's effective economic and social (in effect, environmental) human rights. *Francovich and Bonifaci* v. *Italy* (Cases C–6/90 and C–9/90) had previously featured at pages 23–4 in the more general context of directives as a source, having considerable scope and potential, of applicable EC law.

Chapter Five ("Techniques of Environmental Law"), the last chapter of the first part introduces the ways and means of environmental law, which are more fully developed in the succeeding part:

— preventive methods and procedures: regulation; licensing; impact assessment (at 114–27);

— the protectionary economic and market devices: revenue; loans; insurance; grants and subsidies; "green" labelling (at 127–34);
— implementation measures, of surveillance, e.g. under Directive 82/883/EEC, state and Community agencies' data reporting, and monitoring, and the so-called environmental audit (at 136–8), and "negotiated agreements" between government and industry (at 138–9);
— enforcement and remedial measures (at 139–53) as are centred on the nature and scope of civil and criminal liability, and the remedies, actions and administrative procedures available to secure enforcement at the national level and under the European Convention on Civil Liability for Damages Resulting from the Exercise of Activities Dangerous for the Environment 1993; and
— prioritized international compliance mechanisms (at 153–5), via the general international legal principle of state responsibility, or state obligations (e.g. under Directive 91/692/EEC) to make environmental reports.

As is to be expected, several important documents are appended, including Britain's Environmental Protection Act 1990, Council Directive 85/337/EEC on the Assessment of the Effects of Certain Public and Private Projects on the Environment, the Convention on Environmental Impact Assessment in a Transboundary Context 1991 ((1991) 30 ILM 800), Council Regulation (EC) No. 880/92 on Eco-label Award Schemes, and the OECD Council Recommendation (1991) on the use of economic instruments in environmental policy.

Chapter Six (at 181–249) is entitled "Biological Diversity and the Protection of Nature". As in the preceding part, this and succeeding chapters all have questions and problems, and bibliographies, at their ends. The particular chapter begins with the nature of the threat to nature's balance, particularly in Central and Eastern Europe, as is combatted, e.g. by Council Directive 92/43/EC and by the UN Convention on Biological Diversity 1992 (such as these instruments' territorial definition might so permit), measures to protect species of flora and fauna (including, interestingly, gene banks: at 194–5), habitats and whole ecosystems. "Comprehensive and Integrated Protection" features between pages 203 and 206, taking in the Berne Convention on the Conservation of European Wildlife and Natural Habitats 1979, the Barcelona Convention for the Protection of the Mediterranean Sea against Pollution 1976 (and the 1995 revision of its Protocol Concerning Specially Protected Areas and Biological Diversity in the Mediterranean 1982), and the Convention on the Protection of the Alps 1991. The authors point out the difficulty in assessing the effectiveness of protective measures, partly arising from non-implementation or maladaptation of Community directives in point. "Biotechnology" takes up pages 207 to 211, and is followed by a selection of detailed case studies of nature conservation in Switzerland (Dr Gottesmann at 211–19), the Netherlands (Professors van der Zande and Wolters at 219–28), Finland (Mr Haapanen at 228–30), and the previously mentioned Berne Convention and the EC Habitat Directive respectively. The British

Environmental Protection Act 1990 resurfaces with the relevant provisions of Part IV thereof.

Chapter Seven (at 250–89) takes up soil protection in its relatively more recent crystallization, if one takes into account much earlier cognate national approaches from forestry and afforestation, as are being spearheaded, for example, by the UN Environment Programme's Environmental Guidelines for the Formation of National Soil Policies (1983) and the UN Convention to Combat Desertification in Those Countries Experiencing Serious Drought and/or Desertification, Particularly in Africa 1994. Case studies start comparatively early on in the chapter, with Professor Prieur, on legal protection for soil (at 254–61), setting out the distinct ecological (biomass) and human activity (including cultural heritage) functions soil serves, and engaging in an edifying comparison of national laws which, primarily from the viewpoint of environmental contamination, itself provides the justification for better defensive policy and strategy as is now being put in place through Directive 86/278/EC on Agricultural Sewage Sludge, Directive 80/68/EC on Groundwater, Directive 91/676/EC on Nitrate Pollution, and Directive 91/156/EC on Waste Control and Regulation (EEC) No. 2092/91 Concerning Biological Agriculture and Regulation (EEC) No. 2328/91 on the Efficiency of Agricultural Structures. Mr Harcourt's study (at 261–5) is concerned with the Council of Europe's soil protection activities, in particular the Draft European Convention for Soil Protection (featured as an appendiced document at 286–8) which throws up a duality of types of instrument: those that are general and in which soil protecting norms and principles are included (e.g. the UN General Assembly's World Charter for Nature 1982 and the 1987 Report of the Global Environment and Development Commission), and the soil-specific as are set out in the documents at the end of the chapter. There are also studies of the Italian law (Professor Lucarelli at 265–73), and of the Dutch programme (Professors de Haan and van der Zee at 274–85).

"Fresh Waters" is the topic of chapter Eight (at 290–337), and the discussion encompasses an introductory overview of some 12 pages, followed by case studies of Western Europe (e.g. Dr Burchi at 302–9; Dr Krämer at 309–14). Alexandre Kiss (at 322–7) himself studies the *Gabcikovo-Nagyamaros* case, which arose between Slovakia and Hungary in the circumstances of a water scarcity and environmental impact (thus non-navigational) dispute before the International Court of Justice in the early 1990s in the course of a planned project to build a hydro-electric dam on the Danube. The Helsinki Convention on the Protection and Use of Transboundary Watercourses and International Lakes 1992 is set out between pages 328 and 336, of particular general interest being (a) the classification of provisions as between all parties, and as between riparian parties, and (b) imperatives as to the use of "best available technology" to ensure water and environmental quality. The protection of the marine environment is discussed in chapter Nine (at 338–83), complete with the legal provisions' intersection with, e.g., the UN Conventions on the Law of the Sea as these develop the applicable standards in consonance with the categories of marine space recognized therein, and with the sources of harm. Professor

Scovazzi case studies the international legal rules themselves between pages 352 and 360, Dr Mahmoudi the Baltic and North Sea regulations (at 360–72), Ms Pol the Spanish Sea system (at 372–6), followed by documents including the Helsinki Convention on the Protection of the Marine Environment of the Baltic Sea Area 1992 etc.

Chapter Ten (at 384–434) concerns the ever novel problems raised by "the atmosphere", "the least stable milieu of the planet . . . with which the Earth's inhabitants have the closest contact . . . [T]he singularly genuine 'global common' " (Professor Ruiz, at 394, studying international law's protection of the atmospheric environment) to close the part. The chapter traces national and community measures against, and the international dimensions of, air pollution. The expository rubrics are national statutory air pollution regimes (including, e.g., those brought into being under Directive 85/337/EEC on Environmental Impact Assessment, Directive 89/369/EEC on Municipal Waste Incinerators, the regulation of specific pollutants, of air quality standards, of "zoning" (at 391–2) "to adapt standards, as much as possible, to geographic realities". The Trail Smelter Arbitration ((1911) 3 UNRAA 1) is explored at pages 392 and 395 in connection with state responsibility, as is the Geneva Convention on Long-Range Transboundary Air Pollution 1979 and its Protocols.

Much as the reviewer would wish to dwell on the discussion of the rules and principles, the constraints of space militate against doing so in the present review. Suffice it to identify the Vienna Convention on the Protection of the Ozone Layer 1985 ("a framework agreement of international scope, with only slight prescriptive content": Prof. Ruiz, at 399), the Montreal Protocol on Substances that Deplete the Ozone Layer 1987, and the UN General Assembly Resolution on "the protection of the world climate for present and future generations". He pointedly opines at page 405 that "the road that lies ahead is . . . long", mindful of the need "to combine wisely techniques of soft law (even ultra-soft law) with strictness in the standards which reflect the fundamental interests of the community as a whole", and that "[t]he basic rules for the protection of the atmosphere, which, like the evolution of the climate, are a matter of 'common concern of mankind' " (quoting from UNGA Res. 45/53), "[to] be looked upon more and more as norms of *ius cogens*, binding *erga omnes*". Dr Krämer's second case study (at 406–10) is of the EC threads beginning with the Treaty of Rome's omission of environmental issues and on to the Directive 70/220/EEC. It then moves on to a plurality of subsequent items of Community legislation. Thereafter, Professor Lomas presents the British case between pages 410 and 416, and deals with the early Alkali Act 1906, and then the Health and Safety at Work Act 1974 in the broader European framework. Some of the documents previously relied on in the book are found at the end of the chapter.

The last third of the "Manual" contains three chapters: "Regulating Sources of Environmental Harm" (at 437–511), "Environmental Planning and Integrated Protection" (at 512–614), and "Economic Development and Environmental Protection" (at 583–614). In several respects, this is where the true multidisciplinary orientation of the work properly picks up, in the sense that the part addresses those far reaching inter-relationships of environmental law with other non-environmental disciplines, e.g., integrated urban–rural protection and economic development (encompassing comparatively more recent directions from world trade, sustainable development, international competition policy, global and international financial institutions' responsibilities). There is a two-page rationalizing conclusion at pages 615–16. There then follows an index of some six pages.

One may occasionally question the choice of illustrative instruments, but this may be an inevitable consequence of the vastness and complexity of the subject area. Otherwise, one might as well be unjustified asking the authors to have produced an altogether different work from what they intended and have elegantly come up with. There are other multi-volume works on the same subject.

On a lighter soothing note, the front cover of the handsomely produced paperback edition reviewed bears a photograph detail of the landscape, birds, and beasts depicted in Roelandt Savery's "the Garden of Eden with Eve Tempting Adam". Without putting too fine a point on the book's content as described above and having succumbed to the different sort of temptation to have read it, it certainly is nothing but altogether wholesome in a greatly accessible and edifying way. It is an account of the law on the environment in its characteristic supranationalistic cast, so that the common lawyer in this reviewer pined, as he may have done elsewhere in reviewing other works on the subject (e.g. Katharina Kummer's *International Management of Hazardous Wastes—The Basel Convention and Related Legal Rules*), for conceptual and, if necessary, comparativist analysis or distillation in terms of harmonizing juridical analogues from the law of nuisance (cf. e.g. Professor Markesinis's *Foreign Law and Comparative Methodology* (1997), chapter 12, 240–4, the distinguished professor applying the context of "Policy Factors and the Law of Tort").

All the same, the book being reviewed delivers more than its authors' promise of "an overview of all the main aspects of environmental laws in Europe". It is an exceedingly good, thorough compendium of the material one should expect from its title, and it is strongly recommended on its authors' terms, and as an essential acquisition.

Some other interesting aspects of the work deserve to be noted, even at the close of these present comments. There are an appreciative Foreword (at page xix) by the Director-General of the UN Economic Social and Cultural Organization, Mr Federico Mayor, and a chronology of pertinent documents and cases drawn from international and EC sources from 1900 to 1996 between pages xxiii and xxxiv, followed by a "Table of National Laws" (at pages xxxv–xl) which includes the newer European state laws as well as those of countries yet or about to accede to membership of the EU, such as those which formed the former Soviet Union.

It is likely to be affordable even to students, and will probably outdo the preceding edition as it would convincingly appear to be set to do.

OLUSOJI ELIAS

Documents

LUDWIG KRÄMER*

I. Communications, Greenbooks and Whitebooks

A. COMMISSION COMMUNICATION ON ENVIRONMENT AND EMPLOYMENT (BUILDING A SUSTAINABLE EUROPE)

The Commission made this Communication in light of the Amsterdam Treaty on European Union which fixed, in Article 2, as Community objectives a balanced and sustainable development and a high level of employment.[1] The Communication concludes from that that employment aspects now need also to be integrated into all other Community policies.

The Commission underlines that Community economies are still characterized by under-use of labour resources and over-use of environmental resources. "As a whole, our patterns of production and consumption are far from sustainable." Member States are therefore called upon to shift from old, polluting technologies and end-of-the-pipe measures, to new and clean technologies. The sooner such new technologies are developed, the faster Europe will get a sustainable economy and more jobs. Environmental policy should be seen as a driving force for investment and the building of a sustainable Europe, creating both growth and employment.

After a short introduction, chapter two of the Communication explores the links between environment and employment. Chapter three calls for supportive policies, urgent tasks, territorial aspects, specific objectives for supportive policies, review of labour market policies and financial support. Chapter four indicates the way forward, for which the Commission suggests:

— encouraging public authorities and private and public enterprises in their re-orientation towards cleaner and eco-efficient production and consumption;
— promoting technology assessment and development and broadening the scope of existing Best Available Technologies (BAT) screening exercises so as to include employment effects;
— ensuring that Community funds and instruments support employment and sustainable development;
— incorporating environmental and resource costs into market prices of goods and services; and

* Head of Unit, Directorate General XI, E3, "Waste", of the European Commission.
[1] COM(97)592, of 18 Nov. 1997.

— promoting education and training to support the implementation of new environmentally friendly technologies and working practices.

The Commission is well aware that the realization of these actions largely depend on measures at levels other than the Community level. Thus, it suggests co-operation between all partners, "at EU, Member State, business, and local level, including the private sector, public authorities and NGOs".

B.   COMMISSION COMMUNICATION ON ENERGY FOR THE FUTURE: RENEWABLE SOURCES OF ENERGY. WHITE PAPER FOR A COMMUNITY STRATEGY AND ACTION PLAN

This Communication is a follow-up to a previous Communication (Greenbook) with the same title.[2] It is structured into four chapters and a number of annexes on the present situation, as well as scenarios for 2010. The first chapter places the discussion on renewable sources of energy into the general context of the discussion on climate change. It resumes the discussion on the Greenbook and states that "the strategy and action plan in the White Paper are directed towards the goal of achieving a 12% penetration of renewables in the Union by 2010—an ambitious but realistic objective", but calls this objective of doubling the present percentage of 6 per cent "indicative". A definition of renewables is not given. However, the annex lists as renewables:

— biomass, which is "woody biomass and the residues of the wood working industry, energy crops, agricultural residues and agro-food effluents, manures as well as the organic fraction of municipal solid waste or source, separated household waste and sewage sludge";
— hydro power;
— wind energy;
— solar thermal;
— photovoltaics;
— passive solar (solar and low-energy buildings);
— geothermal and heat pumps; and
— others, such as tidal power, ocean currents, etcetera.

The second chapter describes the main features of the action plan, which include access to the electricity market, fiscal and financial measures, and actions in the area of transport, environment, town and country planning, regional policy, agriculture, and research. Chapter three enumerates a number of national and Community campaigns designed to reach the objectives. Chapter four describes the follow up to and implementation of the action plan. The Communication indicates that essential parts of the action plan will have to be implemented by Member States which will have to adopt national goals and strategies on the use of renewable energies.

This Communication is reproduced in full, elsewhere in this volume.[3]

---

[2] COM(97)599, of 26 Nov. 1997.   [3] See p. 587 below.

C. COMMISSION COMMUNICATION ON A EUROPEAN COMMUNITY BIODIVERSITY STRATEGY

The Communication starts by indicating that "in some European countries, up to 24% of species of certain groups such as butterflies, birds and mammals, are now nationally extinct".[4] The Community strategy on biodiversity is a response to the challenges raised by the International Convention on Biodiversity. It tries to define a framework for action on biodiversity, centred around four major themes: (1) conservation and sustainable use of biological diversity; (2) sharing of benefits arising out of the utilization of genetic resources; (3) research, identification, monitoring, and exchange of information; (4) education, training, and awareness. The strategy then tries to define a number of, rather general, objectives for the conservation of natural resources, agriculture, fisheries, regional policies and spatial planning, forests, energy and transport, tourism and development, and economic co-operation. The paper finishes by announcing action plans for all these sectors, either in specific or in general form. The specific action plans will take the form of Commission Communications and, where appropriate, comprise proposals for legal instruments.

This Communication is reproduced in full, elsewhere in this volume.[5]

D. COMMUNICATION FROM THE COMMISSION ON TRANSPORT AND CARBON DIOXIDE—DEVELOPING A COMMUNITY APPROACH

The seven chapters of this Communication[6] concern, respectively:

1 the current situation, trends, and analyses;
2 the policy for different transport segments;
3 complementary measures for reducing CO_2 emissions from transport;
4 cost and effect assessment;
5 long term solutions;
6 information on an action plan and monitoring;
7 conclusion.

A statistical annex completes the Communication.

The Commission states that action plans would best be developed at Community, national, and local level. A Community action plan will only be able to be developed "when the overall Kyoto strategy is developed in more detail". It concludes that "on unchanged trends and policies, CO_2 emissions from transport—road and air transport in particular—will continue to rise strongly". The analysis shows that the increase in CO_2 emissions until 2010 can be reduced by 20 to 25 per cent, mainly by: action on car fuel economy, progress with fair and efficient pricing in transport, completion of the internal market in rail transport, and better integration of the various modes of

---

[4] COM(98)42, of 4 Feb. 1998.   [5] See p. 641 below.   [6] COM(98)204, of 31 Mar. 1998.

transport into inter-modal transport systems. After 2010, alternative propulsion systems and fuels hold, according to the Commission, the potential for radical reductions in transport CO_2 emissions, although these options are still too costly and have operational drawbacks. Furthermore, a bold research and development programme is needed.

E.   COMMISSION COMMUNICATION ON ENERGY EFFICIENCY IN THE
EUROPEAN COMMUNITY—TOWARDS A STRATEGY FOR THE RATIONAL USE
OF ENERGY

The Communication identifies an urgent need to promote better energy efficiency, in order to contribute to a reduction in CO_2 emissions.[7] The Communication indicates that saving energy has been a policy objective of the Community and its Member States since the first oil crisis, in order to reduce oil imports and to react to high oil prices. Since these pressures disappeared, efforts to improve energy efficiency have decreased. The Commission calculates that by 2010, 18 per cent of the 1995 consumption of energy could be saved.

This potential is not fully used. Indeed, energy prices do not reflect energy costs, though it is hoped that changing structures will improve this situation. Also, little or no information is available on the real price of energy. Furthermore, institutional and legal barriers exist, such as the "institutional energy planning mind", or the practice of selling energy in the form of kWh instead of as energy services such as heating and cooling, lighting and power. Another example is the practice of choosing and installing appliances with low initial costs but high running costs for energy. Numerous technical barriers exist, such as inadequate technical support, absence of market incentives, advantages for economies of scale.

Another section addresses the existing measures for energy efficiency, where the Commission is prudently critical of the achievements reached so far.

The Commission sketches a future energy-saving strategy, being well aware that all economic and public actors need to participate. It points to energy saving potentials in transport, taxation, research, and international activities. Particularly important is the building sector, which accounts for 40 per cent of the Community's energy requirements. Other areas concern household appliances and other end-use equipment. The Commission will try to reach agreements with manufacturers for better energy efficiency and to take a number of other measures to improve the present situation. It underlines that Member States will have to develop their own national strategies and outlines, in an annex, the national programmes and measures for energy efficiency. Finally, it announces its intention to elaborate, at a later stage, a comprehensive action plan to reduce energy use in the Community.

[7] COM(98)246, of 29 Apr. 1998.

F. COMMISSION COMMUNICATION ON ACCESSION STRATEGIES FOR THE
ENVIRONMENT: MEETING THE CHALLENGE OF ENLARGEMENT WITH THE
CANDIDATE COUNTRIES OF CENTRAL AND EASTERN EUROPE

This Communication focuses on the ten candidate countries of Central and Eastern Europe.[8] The Commission announces its intention to publish a separate document for Cyprus.

The Communication first specifies the legislative challenge (lack of comprehensive analyses of legal gaps between national law and the Community *acquis*; shortage of legal expertise and language barriers) and the institutional challenge (necessity to strengthen the administrative structure for environmental management; difficulties in co-ordination between administrations; necessity of developing local and regional implementation and enforcement structures).

On air pollution, the Communication notes that clean-up plans for polluted areas have the objective of assisting acceding countries in better orienting their national programmes to the adoption of Community environmental legislation. While it underlines that economical as well as ecological reasons require the taking over of the Community *acquis*, it also observes that a comprehensive strategy and careful planning are necessary, since the costs are very substantial.

"In the waste sector, much remains to be done in all the applicant countries." The Communication states that, in particular, many waste incinerators will need retrofitting and restructuring to meet Community standards. In the water sector, little progress to reduce contamination from nitrates of agricultural sources is noted. As regards drinking water quality, investment programmes are under way, or planned, in most countries. For industrial pollution control and risk management, more attention for accident prevention is asked for, as well as the clean up of industrial plants in industrial areas. "Based on first region-wide estimates, the total investment costs of meeting the environmental *acquis* are likely to be between 100 and 200 billion ECU for all the ten candidate countries."

The Communication then spells out priorities, which are country-specific. A second set of priorities concerns the legislative or administrative gaps which have to be filled, in order to meet the *acquis*. This concerns, in particular, horizontal legislation and framework provisions. A third set of priorities concerns economic implications, which suggests that provisions on drinking water supply, large combustion plants, and waste management be adopted first, since their full application requires huge economic investments.

Chapter three provides a general overview of the existing means for financial assistance which are available, and indicates the Commission's intention to increase these efforts.

---

[8] COM(98)294, of 20 May 1998.

G.   COMMISSION COMMUNICATION: PARTNERSHIP FOR INTEGRATION;
     A STRATEGY FOR INTEGRATING ENVIRONMENT INTO EU POLICIES

The Communication was prepared for the Cardiff summit of heads of state and governments in June 1998.[9] It seeks to promote ways to put the new Article 6 EC into practice. It begins by describing the challenge of integrating environmental issues into other policies, and argues that the development of new technologies and practices shows that the know-how exists to find solutions for sustainable development issues. This requires a strong commitment from all Community institutions. "In order to be able to measure our achievements and to adjust the adopted policies, as required, we will need a system of regular monitoring and review."

The guidelines for integrating environmental concerns into other policies remain rather general. The Commission should ensure that a detailed environmental assessment should accompany all key proposals where an important environmental effect is expected. Also, it should prepare strategies for action in key areas, which should "include the identification of policy and performance indicators and, where justified, indicative targets as a basis for monitoring". The Council should report on best practices in Member States, and identify, in key areas, priority actions for integration, and provide for monitoring mechanisms. It should also ensure that environmental requirements are explicitly reflected in its decisions on new proposals.

As concrete examples of integrating the environment, the Communication indicates cohesion policy, agriculture, enlargement and the implementation of the Kyoto Protocol. As potential candidates for future integration activities, the Communication flags the single market and industry, development and trade policies, tourism, fisheries, and taxation.

H.   COMMISSION COMMUNICATION ON CLIMATE CHANGE—TOWARDS AN
     EU-STRATEGY POST KYOTO

In this Communication, the Commission attempted to develop a Community strategy, in order to implement the obligations which the Community had accepted at the Kyoto conference on climate change.[10] The measures were to affect, in particular, the sectors of energy, transport, agriculture, and industry, but were to be complemented by measures of economic operators. The envisaged measures became obsolete, at least in part, when on 16 June 1998, without a corresponding proposal from the Commission, the Council adopted a list which fixed for each Member State the percentage by which the CO_2 emissions had to be reduced in order to implement the Kyoto requirements.

---

[9] COM(98)333, of 25 May 1998.   [10] COM(98)353, of 3 June 1998.

I. COMMISSION WORKING PAPER: TOWARDS A FRAMEWORK FOR THE SOLUTION OF THE ENVIRONMENTAL PROBLEMS CAUSED BY TRAFFIC OF HEAVY GOODS VEHICLES

The Communication attempts to clarify a number of issues concerning existing policies for heavy goods vehicles.[11] An introductory chapter describes the main problems caused by the operation of heavy goods vehicles. In addition, it describes the policy background and the purpose of the paper, which is to describe past, present, and possible future Community actions to reduce the environmental effects of heavy goods vehicles. After the enumeration of the principles which guide Community action, it discusses, in four sections, charges for road use, railway policy, and infrastructure, combined transport facilities and technical standards for vehicles.

As regards charges for road use, the paper estimates that the total amount of external costs for road use (congestion, accidents, noise, and environmental damage) amount to approximately 250 billion Euros per year. It argues in favour of the introduction of a framework concerning taxes and charges that gives users incentives to confront these external problems themselves, and of electronic road pricing through roadside equipment. To develop these and other aspects further, the Commission will publish a White Paper on infrastructure charging.

The chapter on railways largely reports on measures suggested in the past, but does not really develop new initiatives on how to proceed. This is understandable, since the primary responsibility for railway issues lies with Member States. The chapter on combined transport facilities also remains largely descriptive. As regards technical standards, the Commission reports on the progressive reduction of emissions from heavy goods vehicles and the progressive introduction of emission controls. Particulate emissions are controlled from 1993 only, and Member States were required to commence testing commercial vehicles' diesel smoke opacity as late as 1996. Other standards tested the road worthiness of trucks. A specific section mentions pollution of the alpine regions due to heavy goods traffic. The paper concludes by emphasizing that no single measure on its own is sufficient to achieve the objective of sustainable transport. Two annexes enumerate the proposals and initiatives which the Council has not yet adopted, and reproduce the section of Protocol 9 with Austria, that deals with road transport.

J. COMMISSION COMMUNICATION ON THE COMPETITIVENESS OF THE RECYCLING INDUSTRIES

This Communication addresses the major problems encountered by the waste recycling industries to achieve or maintain viability.[12] The first chapter describes these waste industries, including activities which concern the

---

[11] COM(98)444, of 14 July 1998.   [12] COM(98)463, of 22 July 1998

collection, dismantling, and sorting of wastes, in particular metals, paper, glass, plastics, and textiles. The second chapter identifies the key factors for competitiveness in recycling. It finds that at the supply side, recycling activities are facing growing cost for the collecting and processing of waste, and concludes that the efficiency of recycling could be improved by ensuring that product design takes into account the post-consumption collection, sorting and recycling of waste. On the demand side, the Communication states that there is a lack of preference for recyclables on behalf of processing industries. Also, industrial standards for recyclables have often not been created, or sometimes discriminate against recycled materials or products. The recycling markets lack transparency, which often prevents investments. Also, differences in the implementation of the EC definition of waste, in the provisions concerning the EC lists for various wastes and hazardous wastes within the Community, and at international level, and in the provisions on the shipment of waste, lead to difficulties for economic operators. The principles of proportionality and subsidiarity need to be accentuated in the area of recyclable wastes.

The third chapter proposes a number of actions to improve the present situation. These include actions in the area of standardization, of market development and transparency, the stimulation of innovation, the simplification and correct application of Community waste provisions, the development of market-based instruments to promote recycling, the minimum requirements for the content of recycled materials in specific products, and new provisions on the composting of biodegradable waste. The most important short-term proposal is to set up a recycling forum "with the widest possible participation of public and private stakeholders". This body will include economic operators, environmental and consumer organizations, and public administration. It will serve as a discussion point for all aspects related to recycling, in particular the creation of new markets, the improvement of economic structures and for the question of the opportunity to create a European recycling centre. The forum is to be set up around the turn of 1998 to 1999.

K.   COMMISSION COMMUNICATION ON IMPLEMENTING THE COMMUNITY
STRATEGY TO REDUCE CARBON DIOXIDE EMISSIONS FROM CARS:
AN ENVIRONMENTAL AGREEMENT WITH THE EUROPEAN
AUTOMOBILE INDUSTRY

This communication announces an agreement with the European Car Manufacture Association (ACEA).[13] This agreement is to take the form of a commitment formally adopted by ACEA (which is reproduced in the annex), a Commission recommendation on the subject, and an exchange of letters between the Commission and ACEA. The Communication tries to align the agreement with previous Commission communications, as well as Council

[13] COM(98)495, of 29 July 1998.

and Parliament resolutions on environmental agreements and on CO_2 emissions from cars. The Commission indicates that it will report annually on the implementation of the agreement. It also draws attention to the fact that a formal notification under Article 81 (formerly Article 85) EC might be necessary for the formal commitment of ACEA. The agreement refers only to European manufacturers. Similar agreements should be concluded with non-ACEA manufacturers and importers, in particular Japanese and Korean manufacturers, according to the Commission.

This Communication is reproduced in full, elsewhere in this volume.[14]

L. COMMISSION COMMUNICATION: STRENGTHENING ENVIRONMENTAL
INTEGRATION WITHIN COMMUNITY ENERGY POLICY

This Communication is designed to review overall progress and suggests actions for further integrating environmental considerations in energy policy, within the context of sustainable development.[15] Chapter one describes actions and measures that have been taken so far, and to what extent they have contributed towards a more sustainable energy policy. It concludes by stating that integration of environmental objectives into energy policy needs to take into account all energy policy priority objectives, including competitiveness and security of supply. It should be based on facts and analysis and be flexible. Chapter two discusses further actions to strengthen environmental integration within energy policy. This chapter discusses the need for Member State action and indicates as the only concrete example the need for an action plan to implement the Kyoto Protocol. The Community would in particular need to promote energy efficiency and saving and the use of cleaner energy sources. It should also reduce the environmental impact of the production and use of energy sources. Chapter three discusses the strengthening of the Commission's action. Chapter four clarifies that it "is clearly for the Council and the Parliament as co-decision makers, to establish a clear strategy for environmental integration in energy policy, identify priorities for action and allocate the necessary budgetary resources". The paper suggests a number of actions which could be taken, such as the adoption of the proposals for structuring the Community Energy Framework Programme (1998–2002) and for a directive on rational planning technologies in the electricity and gas sectors. The Communication pleads for the elaboration of a specific strategy for a sustainable energy policy, as requested by the Cardiff European Summit in 1998, with clear objectives and priorities, and a timetable for action.

It may thus be expected that the Commission will soon present a proposal for such a strategy.

---

[14] See at p. 573 below.   [15] COM(98)571, of 14 Oct. 1998.

II. Reports

A. COMMISSION REPORT ON THE APPLICATION OF REGULATION 2078/92
(EEC) NO. ON AGRICULTURAL PRODUCTION METHODS COMPATIBLE WITH
THE REQUIREMENTS OF THE PROTECTION OF THE ENVIRONMENT AND
THE MAINTENANCE OF THE COUNTRYSIDE

The agri-environment Regulation (EEC) No. 2078/92 provides for programmes to encourage farmers to carry out environmentally beneficial activities on their land, and for financial assistance for such activity.[16] The report gives an account of implementation up to 1997. The first chapter of the report describes the operation of this Regulation, which pursued the following goals: first, accompany changes brought by the 1992 reform of the Common Agricultural Policy to market organization rules; secondly, to contribute to the Community's policy objectives regarding agriculture and the environment; and finally, to contribute to providing an appropriate income for farmers who deliver the environmental benefits. The different measures which were eligible to receive help were to be comprised in national, regional, or local programmes. By the middle of 1997, the Commission had approved 127 programmes, which were extremely diverse in nature. Not one single programme was of a transboundary nature. The measures concerned essentially environmentally beneficial productive farming (84 per cent), non-productive land management (14 per cent) and training and demonstration projects (3 per cent).

Chapter two reports on the links between the measures that were financed as well as agricultural, and other Community policies. The chapter specifically mentioned that programmes designed to develop hunting and shooting areas are not eligible for support. Chapter three gives an overview of implementation up to 1997. The programmes are co-financed by the Community up to 75 per cent. During the 1993–7 period, the programmes' total financing was 6.2 billion ECU, out of which 3.8 billion ECU came from the Community budget. By the middle of 1997, 1,350,000 agreements had been signed with farmers, covering 17 per cent of all holdings and persons employed in agriculture. In Austria, this figure was nearly 70 per cent of persons employed in agriculture. In Finland, Germany, and Sweden this was approximately 50 per cent, compared to 3 per cent in Spain, 4 per cent in Italy (1996), and 0 per cent in Greece (1995). The agreements covered 22.3 million hectares, which is 17 per cent of the utilized agricultural area. This figure was more than 70 per cent in Austria, Luxembourg, and Finland, and 6 per cent in Italy (1996), 2 per cent in Spain, and 0 per cent (1995) in Greece. The average amount of premium per hectare was 117 ECU. The chapter also provides a first assessment of the efficiency of the measures.

---

[16] COM(97)620, of 4 Dec. 1997.

Chapter four outlines some tentative conclusions, under the headings of outstanding issues, and reflections on possible amendments of Regulation (EEC) No. 2078/92 and future developments. It is interesting to note the numerous other Community programmes which support environmental activities, which are carried out by farmers and which confirm the statement that "recognition of the role of farmers as protectors of the environment and stewards of the countryside is now established policy of the Community". Agenda 2000 provides for future expenditure for the measures specified in this Regulation of 2.8 billion ECU per year.

B.   COMMISSION REPORT PURSUANT TO ARTICLE 7(3) OF REGULATION (EC) NO. 1404/96 (LIFE)

The report describes activities under the environmental mini-fund LIFE, between 1992 and 1997.[17] In that period, LIFE has attracted about 6,500 proposals for projects. It co-financed 979 projects with an overall value of 542 million ECU. Of these projects 299 concerned the natural environment, on which 240 million ECU was spent. The contributions mainly benefited those Member States with the greatest number of natural habitats and species of Community interest. Spain, Greece, Portugal, and Ireland benefited from a level of co-financing far above the Community average. Public bodies and environmental organizations are the main beneficiaries of the funds.

A total number of 680 other projects were co-financed (14 per cent of all projects received). The four main types of projects, covering more than 90 per cent of all projects, were waste management and the clean-up of contaminated sites, promotion of clean technologies, methods of detecting pollution and monitoring networks, and land-use planning and urban problems.

Eighty projects were co-financed in third countries, mainly in the Mediterranean and the Baltic Sea region. The Commission points out that it receives about 900 requests per year. One third of these requests are eligible, and approximately 150 projects per year receive financial assistance.

C.   COMMISSION REPORT: MEASURES TAKEN PURSUANT TO COUNCIL DIRECTIVE 91/676/EEC CONCERNING THE PROTECTION OF WATERS AGAINST POLLUTION CAUSED BY NITRATES FROM AGRICULTURAL SOURCES; SUMMARY OF REPORTS SUBMITTED TO THE COMMISSION BY MEMBER STATES UNDER ARTICLE 11

According to the Commission, this report (on national actions[18] which must be read in conjunction with the Commission's implementation report on Directive 91/676/EEC Concerning the Protection of Waters Against Pollution Caused by Nitrates from Agricultural Sources[19]) in the Commission's own words, "highlights the lack of progress made by Member States in their application of

---

[17] COM(97)633, of 12 Dec. 1997.   [18] COM(98)16, of 20 Jan. 1998.
[19] COM(97)473, of 1 Oct. 1997 [1997] OJ C312/12.

the Directive and the status of legal proceedings against the Member States". The two reports are not in every respect consistent with each other.

Under Directive 91/676/EEC, the report on national actions should have been published in the middle of 1997. It was delayed, since the Member States' reports arrived late; only Ireland had reported on time. Information on national actions in Belgium, Italy, and Spain was still not available when the report on national actions was published. The Commission regrets, generally, the difference in the quality of the information received, which it believes is due to the vague drafting of the reporting requirements in the Directive.

The report is divided into two sections. The first provides a brief overview of the measures taken in the 12 Member States, for which information is available. The second section presents each Member State individually. Five Member States (Austria, Denmark, Germany, Luxembourg, and the Netherlands) designated the whole of their territory as vulnerable zones (these are, in particular, zones where the nitrate concentration in water exceeds or risks to exceed 50 mg/l), to which the action programmes for improving water quality thus apply. Groundwater monitoring led to the designation of vulnerable zones in Sweden and the UK only. Eutrophication is a problem in several Member States, in particular in coastal areas. Codes of good agricultural practice were drawn up in all reporting Member States except Portugal. Action programmes to reduce nitrate pollution were submitted by Austria, Denmark, Luxembourg and Sweden.

The implementation report states that Member States should have complied with their obligations under Directive 91/676/EEC by the end 1993, and new Member States by the start of 1995. Only Denmark and France had respected this deadline. By the end of 1997, only four Member States (Denmark, France, Luxembourg, and Spain) had fully transposed the Directive into national law. Codes of good agricultural practice were unavailable for Belgium, Portugal, and Spain, and had been adopted with a delay of more than two years in Germany, Ireland, Luxembourg, and Sweden. Vulnerable zones had, by the end of 1997, not been designated or been insufficiently designated in Belgium, Finland, France, Greece, Italy, Portugal, and Spain. The action programmes for reducing water contamination by nitrates should have begun to be applied by the end of 1995. By the middle of 1997, the Commission had received action programmes from Austria, Denmark, Germany, Luxembourg, and Sweden. The German and Luxembourg programmes were declared not to comply with the Directive; the other three were under examination. The implementation report gives some information on infringement proceedings, which is already outdated. It concludes by indicating that six years after its adoption, the status of the Directive's implementation is unsatisfactory in most Member States, "so much so that any revision of the Directive would be inappropriate".

D. COMMISSION COMMUNICATION ON THE STATE OF THE ENVIRONMENT IN THE SIX *LÄNDER* OF THE FORMER EAST GERMANY

The title of this Communication[20] is slightly misleading: the Communication deals with Germany's obligation to apply, according to Directive 90/656/EEC,[21] Community environmental legislation in the six new *Länder*, within a specified timetable and by the end of 1995 at the latest. Thus, the Communication does not describe the state of the environment in Eastern Germany. The Communication is a follow-up to Communication COM(93)295, of 29 June 1993.

The report is exclusively based on information which the German authorities have conveyed to the Commission. The Commission makes no attempt to assess compliance itself. The report consists of a summary of ten pages and four annexes which reproduce, in German, the voluminous information which was sent to the Commission by Germany.

Legislation has been implemented and measures have been taken in time to meet the obligations provided for by Directive 90/656/EEC, except as regards a range of directives in the water sector. There has been a failure correctly to implement the range of EC legislation as regards the setting up of systematic plans of action for surface water used for drinking water, and the implementation of legislation as regards bathing water, the discharge of dangerous substances and the quality of fish-farming waters. There are particular difficulties as regards the quality of drinking water in two *Länder*, SO_2 emissions in one and lead emissions in three specific areas.

E. FIRST REPORT ON THE IMPLEMENTATION OF THE CONVENTION ON BIOLOGICAL DIVERSITY BY THE EUROPEAN COMMUNITY

The report, drafted under the authority of the services of the Commission, describes Community activity in the area of biological diversity.[22] The introductory chapter explains the environmental policy-making in the Community. Chapter two gives a summary assessment of the importance and status of biodiversity. Chapter three describes the actions undertaken hitherto, subdivided into horizontal instruments and initiatives and measures in specific policy areas. A final chapter four on the future, in particular, outlines the biodiversity strategy and a new environmental action plan.

The report recognizes that in spite of past efforts, existing measures "are insufficient to reverse present trends" and points to the Commission's proposal for a Community biodiversity strategy. As regards the new environmental action plan, the report refers to the review of the fifth environmental action programme and, as regards the general context, the Commission's

[20] COM(98)33, of 2 Feb. 1998.
[21] Dir. 90/656 on the transitional measures applicable in Germany with regard to certain Community provisions relating to the protection of the environment [1990] OJ L353/59.
[22] SEC(98)0348–C4–0155/98.

Communication Agenda *2000: for a Stronger and Wider Union*.[23] The report
does not announce new concrete measures.

F.   COMMISSION REPORT ON THE OPERATION OF REGULATION (EEC) NO.
     2455/92 CONCERNING THE EXPORT AND IMPORT OF CERTAIN
                      DANGEROUS CHEMICALS

The first section of this report[24] describes the content of this Regulation, the
second section the obligations of industry, Member States, and the
Commission. Section three reproduces the points of view of the Commission,
Member States, industry, and environmental organizations on the effectiveness of the Regulation. These views were collected on the basis of a questionnaire. The report concludes that the Regulation was considered, in general, to
be very effective. Section four enumerates the Commission initiatives since
1993, and section five announces some likely or possible future developments.
A short conclusion follows, which underlines the excellent co-operation
between Member States and the Commission, lists the main achievements
since 1993, marks the fact that the prior informed consent procedure is at present only mandatory for the EU and Member States of the European Economic
Area. Finally, it announces the Commission's intention to modify the
Regulation in order to improve it further. Annex I lists the administrative
system in Member States, annex III the national designated national authorities.

   Of particular interest are the data contained in the report, in particular in
annex II. The Regulation covers at present 39 groups of chemical substances
concerning more than 200 chemicals, the export of which is banned or
severely restricted. Until June 1997, 488 export notifications had been registered (of which 309 came from the UK, 65 from Spain, 49 from Germany, and
46 from Italy). Mercury compounds (376), 1,2 dichlorethane (59) and ethylene
oxide (17) are the principal compounds. By the end of November 1996, 311
import notifications were notified. Exported or imported quantities are not
communicated. The report states that some exports have taken place where
the third country had prohibited the import for some uses, but not for others.
An eventual infringement of the importing country decision cannot be established, when the intended use is not known.

G.   COMMISSION REPORT: QUALITY OF BATHING WATER
                (1997 BATHING SEASON)

This report consists of an atlas of the measuring results for all 15 Member
States and an explanatory report.[25] The data are based on the reports submitted by Member States. Overall, the report covers 13,129 bathing areas in
coastal zones and 6,177 areas in fresh water zones. Of the coastal zone waters,

---

[23] COM(97)2000 of 15 July 1997.   [24] COM(98)245, of 28 Apr. 1998.
[25] (Luxembourg 1998), EUR 18166.

93.3 per cent comply with the mandatory values of Directive 76/160/EEC, as do 79.8 per cent of the fresh water zones.

The report underlines that there are considerable differences between countries, as to the number of beaches monitored, sampling frequencies and geographic situations. Though it does not have the objective of comparing various Member States, the report stresses that the reproduced data do allow comparisons.

The following data can be taken from the report:

Table VI: Member State compliance with Directive 76/160/EEC concerning the quality of bathing water

Member State	*numbers of bathing areas*		*% of compliance with mandatory standards*	
	coastal	*fresh water*	*coastal*	*fresh water*
Belgium	39	56	100	94.6
Denmark	1195	112	95.5	89.3
Germany	416	1723	91.1	89.7
Greece	1701	4	98.4	50.0
Spain	1588	251	96.5	67.7
France	1829	1587	90.0	78.8
Ireland	114	9	96.5	100
Italy	4836	740	94.6	88.5
Luxembourg	—	20	—	85.0
Netherlands	87	500	90.8	70.6
Austria	—	268	—	96.6
Portugal	336	24	89.9	25.0
Finland	94	360	58.5	60.6
Sweden	401	523	68.6	54.3
UK	492	—	88.3	—

H. COMMISSION: FIFTEENTH ANNUAL REPORT ON MONITORING APPLICATION OF COMMUNITY LAW

This fifteenth report contains interesting information on the monitoring of the application of Community environmental law.[26] At the end of 1997, 200 infringement procedures were pending against Member States. The Commission reports 33 cases where a judgment by the Court of Justice, based on Article 226 (formerly Article 169) EC, had not (yet) been complied with. The Directives predominantly at issue were Directive 76/464/EEC on Pollution Caused by Certain Dangerous Substances Discharged Into the Aquatic Environment of the community[27] (16 cases), Directive 79/409/EEC on the

---

[26] COM(98)317, of 17 May 1998 [1998] OJ C250/1.   [27] [1976] OJ L129/23.

Conservation of Wild Birds[28] (19 cases), and Directive 92/43/EEC on the Conservation of Natural Habitats and of Wild Fauna and Flora[29] (16 cases).

The Commission states that the quality of environmental impact assessments, under Directive 85/337/EEC on the Assessment of the Effects of Certain Public and Private Projects on the Environment,[30] is insufficient and that the assessments' conclusions are not sufficiently taken into consideration in the final decision on the project. Frequently, work on a project starts before the impact assessment is finished.

As regards water, the Commission reports pending infringement procedures against seven Member States (Belgium, Germany, Spain, France, Italy, Finland and the UK), which have not fully complied with Directive 76/160/EEC Concerning the Quality of Bathing Water.[31] As regards Directive 80/778/EEC Relating to the Quality of Water Intended for Human Consumption,[32] the report states that it is often particularly difficult to prove that the maximum admitted concentrations have been exceeded, as access to the data is often not easy.

In the waste sector, the Commission underlines in particular the absence of management plans for wastes (Directive 75/442/EEC on Waste[33]) and batteries (Directive 91/157/EEC on Batteries and Accumulators Containing Certain Dangerous Substances[34]). For this, as well as for the other sectors, the Commission describes, in some detail, the different procedures pending. It is noteworthy that the number of procedures seems to have decreased as a result of the more general character of the provisions of the directives, in particular in the sector of air pollution.

I.   COMMISSION COMMUNICATION CONCERNING THE IMPLEMENTATION OF REGULATION 259/93 (EC) NO. ON THE SUPERVISION AND CONTROL OF SHIPMENTS OF WASTE

The Communication reports for the first time on the implementation of this Regulation, in 1994–6.[35] Under Article 41 of the Regulation, Member States shall send annual reports on the implementation of the Basel Convention on the shipment of hazardous waste, to the Secretariat of that Convention, as well as a copy to the Commission. Based on these reports, the Commission shall, every three years, issue a report on the implementation of the Regulation by the Community.

For 1994, the Commission had received reports from all the Member States, except Ireland and Greece. For 1995, reports had not been submitted by France, Ireland, Greece, and Finland. For 1996, only Luxembourg and Portugal had sent reports.

The report assembles information on 19 different aspects of waste shipments, and comes to the conclusion that the information transmitted was incomplete. Thus, when asked to give their national definition of hazardous

---

28 [1979] OJ L103/1.   29 [1992] OJ L206/7.   30 [1985] OJ L175/40.
31 [1976] OJ L031/1.   32 [1980] OJ L229/11.   33 [1975] OJ L194/39.
34 [1991] OJ L78/38.   35 COM(98) 475, of 28 July 1998.

wastes, Member States usually answered that it conformed to Community legislation. Hardly any Member State gave information on statistics; seven Member States provided no information on the various disposal methods for waste; the rest *did*, albeit very briefly. Only six Member States answered the question on measures taken to develop technologies for reducing or eliminating waste generation, etc.

The Commission noted that the Basel Convention reports did not cover a number of provisions of Regulation 259/93, which made it impossible to draft a comprehensive report on Community waste shipments. In addition, it gave a considerable number of examples of such omissions.

The experience of this first report on the implementation of the Regulation shows that most Member States have failed to take the necessary steps to inform the Commission of the measures they have taken pursuant to the Regulation. On the basis of Article 41(2) of the Regulation the Commission intends to request additional information by means of a questionnaire.

COMMISSION OF THE EUROPEAN COMMUNITIES

Brussels, 29.07.1998
COM(1998)495 final

COMMUNICATION FROM THE COMMISSION
TO THE COUNCIL AND THE EUROPEAN PARLIAMENT

Implementing the Community Strategy to Reduce CO_2 Emissions from Cars: An Environmental Agreement with the European Automobile Industry

I.　Introduction
One of the elements of the Community's strategy to reduce CO_2 emissions from passenger cars and improve fuel economy (COM(95)689) is an environmental agreement with the automotive industry (the other elements being vehicle-related fiscal measures to promote fuel-efficient cars within an overall Community framework on vehicle taxation, and a consumer fuel-economy information scheme (fuel-economy labelling)). These three instruments will reinforce and add to each other when implementing the strategy. Following the outcome of its negotiations with the European automobile industry *(European Automobile Manufacturers Association*—ACEA) and its earlier consultations with the Council and the European Parliament on this matter, the Commission intends to conclude an agreement with ACEA (hereinafter "the *Agreement*"). The Community's strategy on CO_2 emissions from passenger cars was proposed by the Commission. The Council endorsed its overall approach. The Council specified that the objective of the strategy should be to achieve an average CO_2 emission figure for new passenger cars of 120 g/km by 2005, or by 2010 at the latest (Council conclusions of 25.6.1996). The Council

also indicated that an agreement should seek to commit the industry "to make the major contribution" to this objective.

The European Parliament for its part has so far objected to the principle of an agreement and has called on the Commission to propose CO_2 emission limit values for passenger cars, with even more ambitious objectives than those set by the Council, while supporting fuel-economy labelling and fiscal measures (resolution of 10.4.1997). However, the Commission understands that though maintaining its opposition to an agreement in principle, the Parliament might go along with an agreement under certain conditions. During the successful conciliation between the Parliament and the Council on the Auto-Oil I fuel quality directive on 29.6.1998, the Commission at the invitation of the European Parliament made the following declaration: "In the event of negotiations with ACEA not coming to a successful conclusion, the Commission undertakes to consider the introduction of binding legislation."

The Commission will shortly put forward a legislative proposal for a consumer fuel-economy information scheme.

The Commission believes that the terms of the *Agreement* which the Commission intends to conclude with ACEA correspond to the Council's expectations and the Commission's own original objectives (COM(95)689). Furthermore, they take account of the general criteria for environmental agreements contained in the Commission Communication on Environmental Agreements (COM(96)561). The *Agreement* will take the form of: a *Commitment* formally adopted by the Board of ACEA (see Annex); a Recommendation to be subsequently adopted by the Commission; and (as far as its practical implementation is concerned) an exchange of letters between ACEA and the Commission.[1] This Communication sets out the Commission's assessment of the terms of the *Agreement*.

II. The terms of the Agreement: The Commission's assessment

The Commission Communication on Environmental Agreements (COM(96)561) recommends a number of general guidelines for environmental agreements. The *Agreement* with ACEA takes account of these guidelines, and satisfies the requirements of the Community's strategy on CO_2 emissions from cars.

1. CO₂ emission objective:

The ACEA *Commitment* contains a clearly quantified CO_2 emission objective for the average of new passenger cars sold in the European Union, i.e. 140 g/km to be achieved by 2008, measured according to the Community's current

---

[1] See also the analysis by the Commission Services of ACEA's proposal for a *Commitment* of 2 June 1998 (SEC(1998)1047) which already contained most of the elements of the *Commitment*.

measurement procedure (Directive 93/116/EC). The scope of the *Agreement* are [*sic*] passenger cars of category M1 as defined in Directive 70/156/EEC, although innovative vehicle concepts and cars using alternative fuels or radically new propulsion systems will equally be counted towards ACEA's CO_2 objective (see the assumption concerning the acceptance of innovations in the *Commitment*). In the Commission's view, these specifications meet the requirement of a quantified objective and unambiguous definitions as a major criterion for a good environmental agreement.

The CO_2 objective of the *Agreement* for 2008 also corresponds to the Council's benchmark that an agreement should make "the major contribution" to the objective of the Community's strategy as a whole by covering about 70% of the gap between the current (1995) market average (186 g/km) and the Community's 120 g/km objective. The target year of 2008 is within the time-frame set by the Council, i.e. 2005–2010. In addition, ACEA commits itself in 2003 to review the potential for additional CO_2 emission reductions in the 2012 perspective.

Given that the Community's strategy on CO_2 from cars consists of instruments which complement each other in achieving the strategy's overall target, it is essential that the added value of the instruments is maintained. CO_2 emissions from cars can be reduced:

• by technological improvements. Technological improvements can furthermore induce changes in the market by increasing the attractiveness of certain categories of cars to the consumer and/or creating new market segments; and

• by changes in the market, and in particular by a shift towards smaller and more fuel-efficient cars ("downsizing"). Market changes can be the result of, *inter alia*, changes in consumer preferences, product policy and marketing efforts by the automotive manufacturers, and fiscal measures and fuel-economy labelling.

The added value of the different elements of the Community's strategy is ensured as ACEA commits itself in the *Agreement* to technological improvements and as its CO_2 target allows for CO_2 emission benefits from market changes in addition to ACEA's CO_2 commitments, which could be induced by fiscal measures and fuel-economy labelling.

ACEA's *Commitment* explicitly recognises the possible added value of fiscal measures, and does not contain any clauses which question the right of the Community or its Member States to exercise their prerogatives in the field of fiscal policy. At the same time, ACEA assumes that it can achieve its CO_2 objectives under the *Commitment* without additional fiscal measures. Furthermore, ACEA commits itself to achieving its CO_2 target for 2008 "mainly" by technological developments and related market changes which leaves scope for further market changes being induced by the other instruments of the

Community's strategy. The Commission will emphasise in its Recommendation the added value of fiscal measures. With the added value provided by the other instruments foreseen in the strategy, the Commission considers it desirable to build upon ACEA's commitment with a view to achieving the Community's 120 g/km objective.

2. Assumptions:

ACEA's *Commitment* contains certain assumptions. The assumptions reflect the fact that the automotive industry's ability to attain its CO_2 objective may be affected by developments outside its control, reflecting technical and economic constraints, and they are therefore justifiable. More particularly, the Commission sees the assumptions in the following context:

1. The availability of enabling fuels for the application of technologies required to achieve ACEA's CO_2 objective: The *Commitment* is based on the requirements resulting from the conciliation procedure between the Council and the European Parliament on 29.6.1998, notably the maximum sulphur specifications of 50 ppm in petrol and diesel and the maximum aromatic content for petrol of 35%, although ACEA expects that the market average fuel quality will be better than these legislative requirements for technical and market reasons. Any problems with respect to fuel quality would be considered in the monitoring of the *Agreement*.

2. No distortions of competition which disfavour the European manufacturers due to their efforts to reduce CO_2 emissions: This assumption is in line with the Community's strategy on CO_2 emissions from cars. (See also Section III below.)

3. The unhampered diffusion of fuel-efficient technologies into the market: It is the Commission's and ACEA's common understanding that this does not restrict the Community's and the Member States' freedom to use fiscal or regulatory measures. However, such measures would be considered in the monitoring of the *Agreement* and could be grounds for its review under certain circumstances.

4. Impacts of the strategy on the general economic situation of the European automobile industry to be taken into account: These would in any case be taken into account by the Community.

The Commission has no reason to believe that the assumptions[2] will not be borne out, and therefore it should not be necessary to review the *Agreement* at any stage. Furthermore, the Commission would agree to a review of ACEA's CO_2 objective only once both sides had jointly conducted a careful analysis of

---

[2] Another "assumption" besides those mentioned above is that innovative vehicle concepts, and cars using alternative fuels or radically new propulsion systems will be counted towards the CO_2 objective of the *Agreement*. However, this "assumption" relates more to the definition of the scope of the *Agreement* (see p. 573 ff. above), and as the Commission accepts the inclusion of such vehicles in the scope of the *Agreement*, it is not strictly speaking an assumption.

all relevant circumstances, having consulted other experts as appropriate, and once both parties had exhausted all other means to maintain the CO_2 objective. ACEA and the Commission will lay down the procedure to be followed in such an event in an exchange of letters at a later stage.

Overall, the Commission views the CO_2 emission objective of ACEA's *Commitment* as a firm and unequivocal basis for the *Agreement* which satisfies the requirements of the Community's strategy to reduce CO_2 emissions from passenger cars.

3. Intermediate objectives:

The Commission, the Council and the European Parliament have emphasised the importance of intermediate targets in an agreement with the automotive industry. A staged approach is also an essential guideline for environmental agreements generally (COM(96) 561). The *Agreement* with ACEA conforms with this criterion by setting the following two intermediate objectives:

1. Not later than 2000, some European manufacturers will begin to sell models emitting 120 g/km CO_2 or less in the EU market. This demonstrates ACEA's commitment to undertake efforts soon to reduce CO_2 emissions from cars.

2. An "estimated target range" for the average new car CO_2 emissions is provided for 2003. This target range, however, is indicative and does not represent an additional commitment by the industry.

The Commission recognises that the intermediate target for 2003 is of a purely indicative nature, which is in line with the guidelines in its Communication on Environmental Agreements (COM(96) 561). It nevertheless attaches special importance to this intermediate objective as a basis for verifying whether the *Agreement* is effective. This corresponds in particular to concerns expressed by the European Parliament. Against this background, the Commission would thoroughly review the *Agreement* should ACEA fail to achieve its target range in 2003, and consider drawing up a proposal for binding legislation. Of course, the Commission would in any event take measures to allow the target to be achieved should any circumstances arise at any point during the life of the *Agreement* suggesting that the *Agreement* is not being honoured. This intention should be included in the Commission Recommendation and will, as a result, form part of the *Agreement*. ACEA is fully aware of this clause. It should be noted that the Commission has already stated its intention to consider the introduction of binding legislation should the negotiations with ACEA fail (through its declaration made during the successful Auto-Oil Conciliation on 29 June—see above).

4. Monitoring, verification of results and reporting:

The Council conclusions of 25.6.1996 stressed the importance of a monitoring system to follow the development of the average CO_2 emissions of new passenger cars on the basis of data provided by the Member States. A monitoring system independent of industry data is the best basis for an independent verification of results (one of the criteria for environmental agreements recommended by the Commission (COM(96)561)). The Commission has presented a proposal for a Community monitoring system along these lines (COM(1998)348). It invites the Council and the European Parliament to treat this proposal rapidly so that the system can become operational as soon as possible. At the same time, the Commission welcomes ACEA's offer to provide its own data derived from official government sources, in particular with a view to monitoring progress before the future Community monitoring system is operational.

In addition to the statistical exercise of tracking the evolution of average new car CO_2 emissions, a broader, "holistic" monitoring system is established by the *Agreement*, to be administered jointly by the Commission and ACEA. This system would give particular scrutiny to the assumptions underlying the ACEA *Commitment*. ACEA has agreed to provide the necessary information in order to allow this monitoring system to function and to enable it to identify in a proactive way problems which might arise in the achievement of the CO_2 emission objective of the *Agreement*. It will allow the early identification of any circumstances which might facilitate or hinder the achievement of the objectives of the *Agreement*. The procedures for this joint monitoring system will be laid down in an exchange of letters between the Commission and ACEA. The future Community monitoring system and the joint monitoring mechanism with ACEA will, in the Commission's view, together provide an effective instrument for the monitoring of the *Agreement* and a basis for a broader co-operation between both sides in the area of CO_2 emissions from passenger cars.

Based on the future Community monitoring system on CO_2 emissions from cars, the joint monitoring system with ACEA and any further studies as necessary, the Commission will report annually to the Council and the European Parliament on the implementation of the *Agreement* and of the progress and impact of the Community's strategy on CO_2 emissions from cars overall in the light of the Kyoto commitments. If appropriate, it will involve technical experts from the Member States in the preparation of this report.

Together with the publication of the ACEA *Commitment* and the Commission Recommendation in response to this *Commitment* in the Community's Official Journal, the Commission's annual reports will satisfy the criterion of public information and transparency as set out in the Commission's guidelines for environmental agreements (COM(96)561).

5. *General provisions:*

The *Agreement* will also fulfil the other guidelines in the Communication on Environmental Agreements (COM(96)561) where applicable.

1. In the way of additional guarantees for ACEA's commitments under the *Agreement*, the Commission should make it clear in its Recommendation that it will consider regulatory measures should ACEA not honour its commitments. The *Agreement* does not affect the Commission's right of initiative under the Treaty.

2. ACEA's *Commitment* clearly declares the parties to the *Agreement* on the industry's side. The *Commitment* will be made by the President of ACEA acting on behalf of ACEA according to ACEA's statutes. Those members of ACEA which manufacture passenger cars support the *Commitment* and have agreed to make every endeavour to contribute to the achievement of ACEA's commitments.

3. In principle, the *Agreement* ends once its CO_2 emission objective has been achieved in 2008. However, the Commission warmly welcomes ACEA's commitment to review the potential for additional CO_2 reductions in 2003 with a view to moving further towards 120 g/km CO_2 by 2012. This could be the basis for an extension of the *Agreement*.

4. The terms of the *Agreement*, and in particular its CO_2 objective, may be subject to review, especially if any of the assumptions underlying ACEA's commitments are not borne out. Procedures will be laid down for such an event in the above-mentioned exchange of letters. In turn, the Commission maintains its prerogatives under the Treaty. Both parties to the *Agreement* will act in good faith in the implementation and any review of the *Agreement*.

5. As a general rule, the Commission's attitude towards co-operation as regards environmental protection is positive. However, the ACEA *Commitment* has to comply with Community competition rules. As far as the *Commitment* would contain or build upon certain restrictions of competition, a formal notification would be required under Article 85 [now Article 81] of the EC Treaty before the Commission can take a position on the *Agreement*. At this stage, the Commission has no reason to believe that the *Agreement* would not be in compliance with Community competition rules. The Commission Services will work closely together with ACEA in order to clarify this issue as quickly as possible.

III.   Non-ACEA manufacturers

The *Agreement* with the *European Automobile Manufacturers Association* (ACEA) represents the critical first step in implementing this element of the Community's strategy on CO_2 emissions from passenger cars. According to the strategy, similar agreements should be concluded with non-ACEA manufacturers and importers. The Commission welcomes the fact that ACEA has not made its *Commitment* conditional on these other agreements. At the same time it recognises that ACEA's assumption regarding distortions of competition will best be met by concluding agreements with the major (groups of) non-ACEA manufacturers present on the EU market, and in particular the Japanese and Korean automobile manufacturers and Chrysler (the status of the latter remaining under review in the light of recent developments).

The Commission has in the meantime begun negotiations with the *Japan Automobile Manufacturers Association* (JAMA) and is confident that an agreement with them can be concluded soon. The Commission has also invited the *Korean Automobile Manufacturers Association* (KAMA) and Chrysler to begin negotiations.

IV. Further steps in the follow-up to the *Agreement*

The *Agreement* foresees that innovative vehicle concepts as well as cars using alternative fuels or radically new propulsion systems are included in ACEA's CO_2 objective. This requires that their CO_2 emissions be measured and/or calculated according to a standardised procedure. Directive 93/116/EC will therefore have to be amended by the Commission accordingly. At the same time, the driving cycle in this directive should be aligned with the driving cycle according to Directive 91/441/EEC as modified by the outcome of the Auto-Oil conciliation procedure between the Council and the European Parliament on 29.6.1998.

V. Conclusions

In the Commission's opinion, the *Agreement* with the *European Automobile Manufacturers Association* (ACEA) on the table corresponds to the guidelines in the Communication on Environmental Agreements (COM(95)561) and to the benchmarks for an agreement with the industry according to the Community's strategy to reduce CO_2 emissions from passenger cars (COM(95)689; Council conclusions of 25.6.1996). The *Agreement* makes "the major contribution" to the overall objective of the strategy, as called for by the Council, and is based on sound terms which justify the expectation that it will be fully implemented. The Commission has entered into negotiations on similar agreements with non-ACEA manufacturers and expects to conclude these negotiations in good time. The *Agreement* will make a significant contribution to the achievement of the Community's greenhouse gas emission objectives under the Kyoto Protocol.

Against this background, and provided that the notification under Community competition law does not give rise to problems, the Commission believes that this *Agreement* with ACEA is satisfactory and intends to adopt a Recommendation to ACEA as its part of the *Agreement*. Before doing so, however, the Commission would like to give the European Parliament and the Council an opportunity to express their views on the ACEA *Commitment* and the assessment in this Communication, and will therefore defer the adoption of the Recommendation until the end of October.

<u>ANNEX:</u>

ACEA Commitment on CO_2 Emission Reductions from New Passenger Cars in the Framework of an Environmental Agreement between the European Commission and ACEA

ACEA

ACEA COMMITMENT

ON CO_2 EMISSION REDUCTIONS

FROM NEW PASSENGER CARS

IN THE FRAMEWORK OF AN

ENVIRONMENTAL AGREEMENT

BETWEEN THE EUROPEAN COMMISSION AND ACEA

INTRODUCTION AND PRINCIPLES

(1) This Commitment is based on an undertaking by ACEA itself and has the support of all its car manufacturing companies: BMW, Fiat, Ford of Europe, GM Europe, Daimler-Benz, Porsche, PSA Peugeot Citroën, Renault, Rolls-Royce, Volkswagen and Volvo, who have agreed to make every endeavour to contribute to the achievement of ACEA's goals.

This Commitment demonstrates ACEA's support for significant reductions in CO_2 emissions in line with the European Union's undertakings under the United Nations Framework Convention on Climate Change following the Kyoto Conference. At the same time it aims at preserving the diversity of the product offerings of the European car manufacturers and at maintaining their competitiveness, as well as their financial performance and employment.

(2) As long as its commitments (see below) are being honoured, ACEA is assuming that this Commitment provides complete and sufficient substitute for all new regulatory measures to limit fuel consumption or CO_2 emissions, and for any additional fiscal measures in pursuit of the CO_2 objectives of this Commitment. Any fiscal measures, including their added value to this Commitment, will be taken into account in the monitoring procedure and their potential effects will be assessed in good faith.

(3) The European automotive industry's CO_2 reduction commitments are very ambitious in the light of present and future technologies, and the industry is willing and prepared to commit substantial development efforts to implement the following commitments.

(4) Together with the European Commission, ACEA will ensure that the Commitment is implemented in a manner which complies with applicable competition rules.

ACEA COMMITMENTS

(1) Some members of ACEA will introduce in the EU market, not later than 2000, models emitting 120 g CO_2/km or less, measured according to Directive 93/116/EC (see Technical Annex, Point 1 Measuring Procedure).

(2) ACEA commits to achieve a target of 140 g CO_2/km by 2008, measured according to Directive 93/116/EC, on the average of the EU new car sales represented by ACEA classified as M1.

This target will mainly be achieved by technological developments affecting different car characteristics and market changes linked to these developments. In particular, ACEA will aim at a high share—to the point of 90%—of new cars sold being equipped with CO_2 efficient direct injection gasoline and diesel technologies.

Compliance with this target translates for the European automobile industry into an average CO_2 reduction of 25% for newly registered cars, compared to 1995.

(3) In 2003, ACEA will review the potential for additional CO_2 reduction, with a view to moving further towards the Community's objective of 120g CO_2/km by 2012.

(4) For 2003, ACEA considers an estimated target range of 165–170 g of CO_2/km to be appropriate.

This translates into a reduction of 9–11% compared to the reference year 1995. (See Technical Annex, point 3: Review in 2003/Estimated Target Range.)

(5) To assess compliance with these commitments, there will be a joint ACEA/Commission monitoring of all the relevant factors with regard to these commitments.

ACEA's commitments are based on the following:

A) *Availability of enabling fuels*
Given the outstanding importance of improved fuels for CO_2 reductions ACEA assumes the full market availability of fuels with a sufficient quality to enable the application of technologies needed for the industry to achieve its CO_2 commitments during the life-time of this Commitment (s. Technical Annex, Point 2 Fuel Specifications).

B) *Distortion of competition*
In order to ensure a level-playing field:

—non-ACEA member car manufacturers will be committed to equivalent CO_2 reduction efforts for their sales in the EU, in line with the Council Conclusions of 25.6.1996;

—the Community will use its best efforts to continue to seek that other car manufacturing countries, notably Japan, USA and Korea, will undertake equivalent car CO_2 reduction efforts, in line with the Kyoto Protocol spirit ensuring that the European automobile industry is not put at a competitive disadvantage in world markets by CO_2 reduction commitments in Europe.

C) *Promotion of car CO_2-efficient technologies*

European car manufacturers have high expectations for certain technologies, in particular those associated with direct injected gasoline and diesel engines, which are two of the most promising routes to achieve the central commitment of 140 g CO_2/km in 2008. This commitment is based on the assumption of an unhampered diffusion of car CO_2 efficient technologies into the market via competition amongst ACEA members and other market participants which is expected to result in market mix changes. Therefore it is fundamental that any measures which might hamper the diffusion process of either of the CO_2 efficient technologies will be taken into consideration in the monitoring procedure.

D) *Acceptance of innovations*

The acceptance by the Commission of innovative concepts for vehicles replacing conventional cars in short haul traffic and of cars not producing fossil CO_2 as well as a share of cars using alternative fuels or propulsion systems as contributing factors to comply with the Commitment.

MONITORING

The joint ACEA/Commission monitoring procedure should cover:

(1) The development of CO_2 emissions based on the collective achievement of reductions on the average EU fleet of new car sales represented by ACEA and according to the above commitments.

(2) The development of the CO_2 emissions of non-ACEA car manufacturers for their sales in the EU.

(3) Any developments regarding the underlying factors upon which ACEA's Commitment is based.

(4) The impact on CO_2 emissions of new regulatory measures.

(5) The development of new breakthrough technologies (e.g. natural gas, hydrogen, fuel cells, electric drive), which might be available for production in the next decades, and the impact of the Community's 5th R&D framework programme, which is expected to foster research in this area.

(6) The development and the promotion of other measures deemed to reduce fuel consumption, i.e. telematics and optimisation of the infrastructure reducing congestion; driver education for fuel efficient behaviour; driver information on fuel efficiency.

(7) The impacts on the financial performance, competitiveness and the employment within the European automotive industry associated with this Commitment.

The Commission's official reports on the monitoring results will not refer to individual companies' achievements, to avoid competition being distorted. ACEA is willing to provide the necessary data to achieve the objectives of the monitoring.

* * *

On the basis of the outcome of the monitoring, or if the impacts of this Commitment on the European automotive industry, particularly its employment situation and its global competitive environment, are detrimental, ACEA and the Commission will review the situation and make any necessary adjustments in good faith.

TECHNICAL ANNEX TO THE ACEA COMMITMENT ON CO_2 EMISSION REDUCTIONS FROM NEW PASSENGER CARS

(1) Measuring Procedure

ACEA's proposals have been established according to Directive 93/116/EC, which has been fully implemented as from 1.1.1997, and will be applicable for the coming years. The implementation of this new measuring procedure has led to an artificial average increase of 9% of the CO_2 emission figures, compared to the previously used directive, whereas the CO_2 emissions from cars in the real world have not changed.

(2) Fuels Specifications

Characteristics of the fuels are key factors in car CO_2 emission reductions:

A) to achieve further emission reduction together with lowered CO_2 emissions the fuel efficient lean burn technology will be combined with special exhaust gas after-treatment devices capable to reduce NOx under lean burn conditions. But those systems are only working with fuels meeting specific requirements, in particular a low sulphur content;

B) low sulphur fuels ease the NOx/CO_2 trade-off in favour of CO_2 emission reductions;

C) low aromatics in gasoline and a high cetane number in diesel lead to CO_2 emission reduction too.

ACEA acknowledges the outcome of the conciliation procedure between the Council and the European Parliament on 29.6.1998 and upholds its 140 g CO_2/km commitment by 2008. However, ACEA is expecting that fuels of the following better quality might be available in the market due to technical reasons, commercial competition as well as possible national policies:

A) Some gasoline (e.g. Super-Plus, 98 octane as agreed in Germany) and some diesel plus with a maximum sulphur content of 30 ppm are provided in 2000 on the whole EU market in a sufficient volume and geographical cover.

B) In 2005 full availability of fuels on the whole EU market which satisfy the following:

• gasoline with a maximum sulphur content of 30 ppm and of a maximum aromatic content of 30%;

• diesel with a maximum sulphur content of 30 ppm and a cetane number of minimum 58.

Any problems which might arise with respect to fuel quality will be considered in the monitoring procedure.

3. Review in 2003/Estimated Target Range

ACEA is willing to contribute to a periodic monitoring of its commitments, jointly undertaken by ACEA and the Commission, which it sees as the main tool to examine the evolution during the period of the Commitment. This should include a joint "Major Review" in 2003, covering both ACEA and non-ACEA developments. This would incorporate the results of CO_2 emission reductions up to and including calendar year 2003, including comparison of that year's fleet average to the estimated target range.

The reduction in CO_2 emissions will not be linear; the pace will notably depend on the timing of availability of the enabling fuels on the market as well as on the lead-times for new technologies and products and their market penetration. The reduction profile is therefore expected to be relatively slow initially and to gather pace later.

Given all the uncertainties and the lead-time necessary for introducing new technologies and models, ACEA considers an appropriate estimated target for 2003 to be within the range of 165–170 g CO_2/km. This is a reduction of 9–11% compared to the 1995 reference year.

ACEA provides this estimated target range for 2003 on the following basis:

A) it does not constitute a commitment of any sort by ACEA;

B) the provisions set out under "Monitoring" are fully implemented and any necessary adjustment to the 2008 commitment or the 2003 estimate are made in good faith;

C) in particular, fuels of sufficient quality are available—such that fuels issues do not constrain the application of technologies needed to improve fuel efficiency (see point 2 above: Fuels specifications).

COMMISSION OF THE EUROPEAN COMMUNITIES

Brussels, 26.11.1997
COM(97) 599 final

COMMUNICATION FROM THE COMMISSION

ENERGY FOR THE FUTURE: RENEWABLE SOURCES OF ENERGY

White Paper for a Community Strategy and Action Plan

TABLE OF CONTENTS

Chapter 1 Setting the Scene

1.1 The General Framework

1.1.1 Introduction

Renewable sources of energy are currently unevenly and insufficiently exploited in the European Union. Although many of them are abundantly available, and the real economic potential considerable, renewable sources of energy make a disappointingly small contribution of less than 6% to the Union's overall gross inland energy consumption, which is predicted to grow steadily in the future. A joint effort both at the Community and Members States' level is needed to meet this challenge. Unless the Community succeeds in supplying a significantly higher share of its energy demand from renewables over the next decade, an important development opportunity will be missed and at the same time, it will become increasingly difficult to comply with its commitments both at European and international level as regards environmental protection.

Renewable energy sources are indigenous, and can therefore contribute to reducing dependency on energy imports and increasing security of supply. Development of renewable energy sources can actively contribute to job creation, predominantly among the small and medium-sized enterprises which are so central to the Community economic fabric, and indeed themselves form the majority in the various renewable energy sectors. Deployment of renewables can be a key feature in regional development with the aim of achieving greater social and economic cohesion within the Community.

The expected growth in energy consumption in many third countries, in Asia, Latin America and Africa, which to a large extent can be satisfied using renewable energies, offers promising business opportunities for European Union industries, which in many areas are world leaders as regards renewable energy technologies. The modular character of most renewable technologies allows gradual implementation, which is easier to finance and allows rapid scale-up where required. Finally, the general public favours development of renewables more than any other source of energy, very largely for environmental reasons.

1.1.2 The Current Situation

Five years after the Rio Conference, Climate Change is again at the centre of international debate in view of the upcoming "Third Conference of the Parties to the United Nations Framework Convention on Climate Change" to be held in Kyoto in December 1997. The European Union has recognised the urgent need to tackle the climate change issue. It has also adopted a negotiating position of 15% greenhouse gas emissions reduction target for industrialised countries by the year 2010 from the 1990 level. To facilitate the Member States achieving this objective, the Commission, in its communication on the Energy

Dimension of Climate Change[1] identified a series of energy actions—including a prominent role for renewables.

The Council of Ministers endorsed this when inviting the Commission to prepare an action programme and present a strategy for renewable energy. In preparation for the international climate change conference in Kyoto, the Commission confirmed the technical feasibility and economic manageability of the Union's negotiating mandate. In a recent Communication,[2] the Commission analysed the consequences of reducing CO_2 emissions significantly, including the implications for the energy sector. In order to achieve such a reduction, the Union will require major energy policy decisions, focusing on reducing energy and carbon intensity. Accelerating the penetration of renewable energy sources is very important for reducing carbon intensity and hence CO_2 emissions, whatever the precise outcome of the Kyoto Conference.

The EU's dependence on energy imports is already 50% and is expected to rise over the coming years if no action is taken, reaching 70% by 2020. This is especially true for oil and gas which will increasingly come from sources at greater distances from the Union, often with certain geopolitical risks attached. Attention will therefore increasingly focus on security of supply. Renewable energies as indigenous sources of energy will have an important role to play in reducing the level of energy imports with positive implications for balance of trade and security of supply.

Much progress has been achieved towards completion of the Internal Energy Market. Agreement has been reached in the Council of Ministers on the first phase of liberalisation of the electricity sector and negotiations in the gas sector are well under way. Opening the markets for the network-bound energies will bring market forces into play in sectors which until recently were for the most part dominated by monopolies. This will provide a challenging new environment for renewable energies, providing more opportunities but also posing the challenge of a very cost-competitive environment. Suitable accompanying measures are needed in order to foster the development of renewables.

Renewable energy sources still make an unacceptably modest contribution to the Community's energy balance as compared with the available technical potential. There are signs, however, that this is changing, albeit slowly. The resource base is better understood, the technologies are improving steadily, attitudes towards their uses are changing, and the renewable energy manufacturing and service industries are maturing. But renewables still have difficulties in "taking off", in marketing terms. In fact many renewable technologies need little effort to become competitive. Moreover, biomass, including energy crops, wind and solar energy all offer a large unexploited technical potential.

---

[1] COM(97)196 final, 14 May 1997, "The Energy Dimension of Climate Change".
[2] COM(97)481 final, 1 Oct. 1997, "Climate Change—The EU Approach to Kyoto".

Current trends show that considerable technological progress related to renewable energy technologies has been achieved over recent years. Costs are rapidly dropping and many renewables, under the right conditions, have reached or are approaching economic viability. The first signs of large-scale implementation are also appearing as regards wind energy and solar thermal collectors. Some technologies, in particular biomass, small hydro and wind, are currently competitive and economically viable in particular compared to other decentralised applications. Solar photovoltaics, although characterised by rapidly declining costs, remain more dependent on favourable conditions. Solar water heaters are currently competitive in many regions of the Union.

Under prevailing economic conditions, a serious obstacle to greater use of certain renewables has been higher initial investment costs. Although comparative costs for many renewables are becoming less disadvantageous, in certain cases quite markedly, their use is still hampered in many situations by higher initial investment costs as compared with conventional fuel cycles (although operational fuel costs are non-existent for renewables with the exception of biomass). This is particularly the case due to the fact that energy prices for conventional fuel cycles do not currently reflect the objective full cost, including the external cost to society of environmental damage caused by their use. A further obstacle is that renewable energy technologies, as is the case for many other innovative technologies, suffer from initial lack of confidence on the part of investors, governments and users, caused by lack of familiarity with their technical and economic potential and a general resistance to change and new ideas.

Globally, Europe is at the forefront for several renewable energy technologies. Significant employment is associated with the industries concerned in the European Union, involving several hundred companies, mainly small and medium-sized enterprises, in primary assembling/manufacturing alone, without taking into account other service and supply needs. For the new renewable energy technologies (i.e. not including large hydro-electric power stations and the traditional use of biomass) the world-wide annual turnover of the industry is estimated to be higher than ECU 5 billion, of which Europe has more than a one third share.

1.1.3 The Need for a Community Strategy

Development of renewable energy has for some time been a central aim of Community energy policy, and as early as 1986 the Council[3] listed the promotion of renewable energy sources among its energy objectives. Significant technological progress has been achieved since then thanks to the various Community RTD and demonstration programmes such as JOULE-THERMIE, INCO and FAIR which not only helped in creating a European renewable

---

[3] [1986] OJ C241/1.

energy industry in all sectors of renewables but also in achieving a world-wide leading position. This technological leadership will be maintained by the contribution of the 5th RTD framework programme in which the renewable energy technologies will have a central role to play. With the ALTENER programme,[4] the Council for the first time adopted a specific financial instrument for renewables promotion. The European Parliament for its part has constantly underlined the role of renewable energy sources and in a recent Resolution[5] strongly advocated a Community action plan to advance them. In its White Paper, "An Energy Policy for the European Union"[6] the Commission put forward its views as regards Community energy policy objectives and instruments to achieve them. Three key energy policy objectives were identified, viz, improved competitiveness, security of supply, and protection of the environment. Promotion of renewables is identified as an important factor to achieve these aims. A strategy for renewable energy sources was proposed, and specifically cited in the "indicative work programme" attached to the Energy Policy White Paper.

At the same time some Member States have introduced some measures to support RES and related programmes. Some have set up plans and targets aimed at developing RES in the medium and long term. The share of renewable energies in the gross inland energy consumption differs widely between Member States, from less than 1% to over 25% (see Table 1). A Community strategy will provide the necessary framework and bring added value to national initiatives increasing the overall impact.

A comprehensive strategy for renewables has become essential for a number of reasons. First and foremost, without a coherent and transparent strategy and an ambitious overall objective for renewables penetration, these sources of energy will not make major inroads into the Community energy balance. Technological progress by itself cannot break down the several non-technical barriers which hamper the penetration of renewable energy technologies in the energy markets. At present, prices for most classical fuels are relatively stable at historically low levels and thus in themselves militate against recourse to renewables. This situation clearly calls for policy measures to redress the balance in support of the fundamental environmental and security responsibilities referred to above. Without a clear and comprehensive strategy accompanied by legislative measures, their development will be retarded. A long-term stable framework for the development of renewable sources of energy, covering political, legislative, administrative, economic and marketing aspects is in fact the top priority for the economic operators involved in their development. Furthermore, as the internal market develops, a Community-wide strategy for renewables is required to avoid imbalances between Member States or distortion of energy markets. The leading position of the European

---

4 [1993] OJ L235/41.   5 PE 216/788: fin.
6 COM(95)682 of 13 Dec. 1995, "An Energy Policy for the European Union".

renewable energy industry world-wide can only be maintained and strengthened on the basis of a significant and growing home market.

A policy for the promotion of renewables requires across-the-board initiatives encompassing a wide range of policies: energy, environment, employment, taxation, competition, research, technological development and demonstration, agriculture, regional and external relations policies. A central aim of a strategy for renewable energy will be to ensure that the need to promote these energy sources is recognised in new policy initiatives, as well as in full implementation of existing policies, in all of the above areas. In fact, a comprehensive action plan is required to ensure the necessary co-ordination and consistency in implementing these policies at Community, national and local levels.

The role of Members States in the implementation of the Action Plan is crucial. They need to decide on their own specific objectives within the wider framework, and develop their own national strategies to achieve them. The measures proposed in this White Paper must also be adapted to the particular socio-economic, environmental, energy and geographic situation of each Member State as well as to the technical and physical potential of RES in each Member State.

With a view to illustrating the potential effects of specific policy initiatives in the renewable energy field, the Commission sponsored an exercise referred to as TERES. The TERES II study[7] builds on one of the scenarios previously developed in the Commission's European Energy to 2020[8] report but goes further by adding various specific renewable energy policy assumptions to form three additional scenarios. These scenarios predict the contribution of renewable energy sources to gross inland energy consumption to be between 9.9% and 12.5% by 2010. The technical potential, however, is much larger.

The various scenarios clearly illustrate that renewable energy sources can make a significant contribution to the energy supply of the European Union. On the other hand the renewable energy component of the energy mix is very sensitive to changing policy assumptions. Unless specific incentives are put in place; the large potential for renewable energy will not be exploited and these sources will not make a sufficient contribution to the European energy balance.

1.2 The Debate on the Green Paper

As a first step towards a strategy for renewable energy the Commission adopted a Green Paper on 20 November 1996.[9] A broad public debate took place during the early part of 1997 focusing on the type and nature of priority

---

[7] TERES II (European Commission, Luxembourg, 1997).
[8] *European Energy to 2020. A Scenario Approach* (European Commission, Luxembourg, 1996).
[9] COM(96)576 of 20 Nov. 1996, "Energy for the Future: Renewable Sources of Energy".

measures that could be undertaken at Community and Member States' levels. The Green Paper has elicited many reactions from the Community institutions, Member States' governments and agencies, and numerous companies and associations interested in renewables. The Commission organised two conferences during this consultation period where the issues were extensively discussed.

The Community Institutions have delivered detailed comments on the Green Paper as well as opinions on what should be the essential elements and the major actions to be undertaken for a future Community strategy on renewable energy sources and the role of the Community in this process. The Council in its Resolution[10] on the Green Paper, affirms that adequate action on renewables is vital for achieving sustainable economic growth, the aim being a strategy that would lead to improved competitiveness and a substantial share of renewables in the long term. Thus, it confirms that Member States and the Community should formulate indicative targets as a guideline for this ambitious indicative target of doubling the overall share of renewables in the Community by 2010. The Council Resolution states that such a comprehensive strategy should be based on certain basic priorities: harmonisation of standards concerning renewables, appropriate regulatory measures to stimulate the market, investment aid in appropriate cases, dissemination of information to increase market confidence with specific actions to increase customer choice. It also takes the view that adequate provision for the support for renewables in the Fifth Framework Programme for Research, Technological Development and Demonstration is required, as well as effective co-ordination and monitoring of progress in order to optimise available resources.

The European Parliament in its Resolution[11] on the Green Paper recognises the important role that renewable energy can play in combating the greenhouse effect, in contributing to the security of energy supplies and in creating jobs in small and medium enterprises and rural regions. It believes that the European Union urgently needs a promotion strategy which will tackle the issues of tax harmonisation, environmental protection and standards, internalisation of external costs, and ensure that the gradual liberalisation of the internal energy market will not place renewables at a disadvantage. It proposes a goal of a 15% share of renewables for the European Union by the year 2010. It calls on the Commission to submit specific measures to facilitate the large-scale use of renewable energy sources and advocates certain specific measures. These include the setting of targets per Member State, the concept of a common energy-related tax model, free non-discriminatory access to the grid combined with a minimum payment by the utilities for the electricity supplied from renewable energies, the main features of a plan to establish a European fund for renewable energies, a strategy for a common programme to

---

[10] Council Resolution n/8522197 of 10 June 1997.   [11] PE 221/398.fin.

promote renewable energies to include a further 1,000,000 photovoltaic roofs, 15,000 MW of wind and 1,000 MW of energy from biomass.

Parliament's Resolution also calls for a buildings directive, a plan for greater use of structural funds, a strategy for the better utilisation of agricultural and forestry biomass and an export strategy for renewable energy technologies. It reaffirms its belief in the need to increase the Community budgetary appropriations in support of renewable energy sources to the level currently used for nuclear research. It also proposes the constitution of a new Treaty for the promotion of renewable energy sources. The Committee on Agriculture and Rural Development of the Parliament has also issued an Opinion in which it considers that the contribution of biomass-derived energy to the primary energy mix could reach 10% by 2010. It also calls for a better co-ordination of European Union energy policy and the common agricultural policy and emphasises the need to make the necessary arable land available under the latter.

The Economic and Social Committee[12] and the Committee of the Regions[13] have also presented detailed comments on all chapters of the Green Paper, which also stress, analyse, and support the overall goals relating to sustainability and the different ways the potential contribution of renewables can be maximised. Furthermore, these contributions set out ways in which the role and responsibilities of regional and local public authorities and other bodies could be best harnessed to facilitate renewables support and market penetration. Given the predominantly decentralised implementation of most renewable technologies, practical measures in this direction would allow recourse to the subsidiarity principle, in the framework of a Community Strategy and Action Plan, facilitating local authorities in their decision-making power and environmental responsibility. Moreover, this context is a prime example where energy policy aims and those of structural and regional policy can synergise with one another to great effect, as illustrated by the case of rural, island, or otherwise isolated communities where sustainable development and the maintenance of a population base can be actively supported by replacement of inefficient small-scale fossil fuel use by renewables plants. That leads to better living standards and job creation.

More than 70 detailed written reactions have been received from Member State agencies, industries, professional associations, regional associations, institutes and non-governmental organisations following the publication of the Green Paper. The extensive public debate on the Green Paper and the many contributions received have provided valuable input for the Commission in drafting this White Paper and in proposing the Action Plan.

[12] CES 462/97 of 23–24 Apr. 1997, Opinion of the Economic and Social Committee.
[13] CdR 438/96.fin, Opinion of the Committee of the Regions.

1.3   Strategic Goals

1.3.1   An Ambitious Target for the Union

In the Green Paper on Renewables the Commission sought views on the setting of an indicative objective of 12% for the contribution by renewable sources of energy to the European Union's gross inland energy consumption by 2010. The overwhelmingly positive response received during the consultation process has confirmed the Commission's view that an indicative target is a good policy tool, giving a clear political signal and impetus to action. The strategy and action plan in this White Paper therefore, are directed towards the goal of achieving a 12% penetration of renewables in the Union by 2010—an ambitious but realistic objective. Given the overall importance of significantly increasing the share of RES in the Union, this indicative objective is considered as an important minimum objective to maintain, whatever the precise binding commitments for CO_2 emission reduction may finally be. However, it is also important to monitor progress and maintain the option of reviewing this strategic goal if necessary.

The calculations of increase in RES needed to meet the indicative objective of 12% share in the Union's energy mix by 2010 is based on the projected energy use in the pre-Kyoto scenario (conventional wisdom, European Energy to 2020, see footnote 8) It is likely that the projected overall energy use in the EU 15 may decrease by 2010 if the necessary energy saving measures are taken post Kyoto. At the same time, the enlargement of the Union to new Member States where RES are almost non-existent will require an even greater overall increase. It is therefore considered at this stage, that the 12% overall objective cannot be refined further. It is in any case, to be emphasised that this overall objective, is a political, and not a legally binding tool.

1.3.2   Member States Targets and Strategies

The overall EU target of doubling the share of renewables to 12% by 2010 implies that Member States have to encourage the increase of RES according to their own potential. Targets in each Member State could stimulate the effort towards increased exploitation of the available potential and could be an important instrument for attaining CO_2 emission reduction, decreasing energy dependence, developing national industry and creating jobs. It is important, therefore, that each Member State should define its own strategy and within it propose its own contribution to the overall 2010 objective, indicate the way it expects different technologies to contribute and outline the measures it intends to introduce to achieve enhanced deployment.

Nevertheless, it should be emphasised that both the Community and the Member States have to build on existing measures and strategies, as well as tackle new initiatives. Some Member States have developed national Plans for

RES and set objectives for 2010, 2020 or even 2030. Annex III outlines the plans and actions of Member States for renewables development. Member States are indeed already making efforts to develop RES and the Community Strategy will provide a framework to encourage those efforts and to ensure their cross-fertilisation. Action at the level of the Community can provide added value in terms of the sharing and transfer of successful technological and market experiences.

1.3.3   Possible Growth of RES by Sector

Achievement of the average 12% overall indicative objective for the Union clearly depends on the success and growth of the various individual renewable technologies. Views expressed during the consultation process on the Green Paper confirmed that it is important to analyse how the overall objective can be achieved by a contribution from each sector, and hence to estimate the contribution each renewable source is likely to make. The potential sectoral growth of RES suggested in this Strategy has to be considered as a first attempt to identify a possible combination of renewable technologies that could allow the EU to reach the overall target, within technical, practical and economic limitations. However, renewable energy technologies may well evolve differently, depending on many factors, including market developments, options chosen by Members States and technical developments. The estimate share of different technologies are clearly indicative and will serve to help monitor progress and ensure that each technology makes its optimal contribution, within a clear policy framework.

The current share of renewables in the energy mix of approximately 6% includes large-scale hydro, for which the potential for further exploitation in the European Union, for environmental reasons, is very limited. This means that the increases in the use of other renewables will have to be all the more substantial.

In Annex II a set of indicative estimated contributions from each renewable energy source as well as for each market sector are outlined, as a projection of one way in which the overall desired growth of RES can be achieved. According to the particular, scenario outlined, the main contribution of RES growth (90 Mtoe) could come from biomass, tripling the current level of this source. Wind energy, with a contribution of 40 GW is likely to have the second most important increase. Significant increases in the solar thermal collectors (with a contribution of 100 million m² installed by 2010) are also anticipated. Smaller contributions are foreseen from photovoltaics (3 GWp), geothermal energy (1 GWe and 2.5 GWth) and heat pumps (2.5 GWth). Hydro power will probably remain the second most important renewable source, but with a relatively small future increase (13 GW), keeping its overall contribution at today's level. Finally passive solar could have a major contribution in reducing the heating and cooling energy demand in buildings. A 10% contribution in this sector, representing fuel savings of 35 Mtoe, is considered feasible. If the sectoral growth outlined in the scenario is achieved then the overall doubling of the current share of renewables can be achieved, as shown in the tables in Annex II. As far as the market sectors are concerned, the doubling of the current electricity and heat production from renewables plus a significant increase of biofuel in transport fuel use by 2010 are important elements in the scenario for achieving the overall Union objective.

1.4   Preliminary Assessment of Some of the Costs and Benefits

In order to assess the feasibility of achieving the overall Community objective, the necessary costs have to be estimated. Equally important, however, is the estimation of the related benefits. The doubling of the current market penetration of renewable energies by 2010 will have beneficial effects among others in terms of CO_2 emissions: security of supply and employment. In Table 6 of Annex II the estimated investment costs required to achieve the target together with the estimated benefits are presented. The total capital investment needed to achieve the overall target is estimated at 165 billion ECU for the period 1997–2010. What is more relevant, however, is the net investment which is estimated at 95 billion ECU.[14] However, it must be underlined that there are very significant avoided fuel costs.

In Table 5 of Annex II these figures are compared with the total investment of the energy sector for the same period, as projected by the Conventional Wisdom scenario of the "European Energy to 2020" study of the Commission. If we consider that in this scenario an amount for investments in renewable energies is already included, the additional net investment needed if the action plan is to have its full effect is then equal to 74 billion ECU. In the same table, it can be seen that the doubling of the share of renewables may require an increase of approximately 30% in the total energy sector investment but it could create an estimated gross figure of 500,000–900,000 new jobs, save annually (in 2010) 3 billion ECU in fuel costs and a total of 21 billion ECU for the period 1997–2010, reduce the imported fuels by 17.4% and the CO_2 emissions by 402 million tonnes/year by 2010.

This amount of CO_2 savings represents a significant contribution towards the CO_2 reduction needed to successfully combat climate change. The calculation of the figures in the table needs some clarification. In the recent Communication from the Commission "Climate Change—the EU approach to Kyoto"[15] it is estimated that the 800 million tonnes CO_2 emission reduction potential can be achieved with an annual compliance cost of 15 to 35 billion ECU and with a total (primary and secondary) benefit which might range from 15 to 137 billion ECU per year. From the analysis presented in Annex II, it is

---

[14] It has been calculated by taking the total investment and subtracting the investment that would have been needed if the energy from renewables was provided by fossil fuel technologies.
[15] COM(97) 481 final—see n. 2 above.

shown that doubling the share of renewables can reduce the CO_2 emissions by 402 million tonnes per year with respect to 1997. This corresponds to an additional reduction possibility of 250 million tonnes of CO_2 with respect to the 2010 "business as usual" Pre-Kyoto scenario used in the Climate Change Communication and one third of the expected CO_2 reduction target. The difference between figures (402 and 250) is due to the fact that in the scenario for 2010, an increase of 30 Mtoe in the use of renewables between 1995–2010 is assumed which corresponds approximately to annual savings of 150 million tonnes of CO_2 by 2010. Therefore, the estimates of CO_2 emission reduction from RES cited in this White Paper results from a technical assessment and represents the full expected reduction from a doubling of the current share of RES, whereas in the policy communication on Kyoto, the figure cited is the additional reduction in CO_2 emissions to be attained to reach a specific reduction target, over and above what may have been attained under the specific Conventional Wisdom pre-Kyoto scenario for 2010.

Net employment figures in the renewable energy sector are difficult to predict and calculate. Real figures exist in the sectors that have reached a certain level of development. Wind energy, for example, has already created more than 30,000 jobs in Europe. Each renewable energy technology has its own characteristics as far as the quality and the kind of employment generated. Biomass has the particularity of creating large numbers of jobs for the production of raw material. Photovoltaics creates a large number of operational and maintenance jobs, since PV installations are small and dispersed. Hydro is not expected to create more jobs than those already existing in Europe.

Detailed estimations of net employment have been made in the TERES II study using the SAFIRE market penetration model developed under the JOULE II programme. The model predicts for 2010 a net employment of 500,000 jobs directly created in the renewable energy sector and indirectly in the sectors that supply the sector. This is a net figure allowing for losses of jobs in other energy sectors. Sectorial studies—performed mainly by the industry give much larger employment figures. The European Wind Energy Association (EWEA)[16] estimates that the jobs to be created in 2010 by the wind sector will be between 190,000 and 320,000, if 40 GW of wind power is installed. The European Photovoltaic Industry Association (EPIA) estimates[17] that a 3 GWp installed power in 2010 will create approximately 100,000 jobs in the PV sector. The European Biomass Association (AEBIOM)[18] believes that the Biomass employment figures in the TERES II study are underestimated and that employment in the sector will increase by up to 1,000,000 jobs by 2010 if the biomass potential is fully exploited. The European Solar Industry Federation (ESIF) estimates that 250,000 jobs will be created in order to meet the solar collector 2010 market objective. While it is not possible to reach any hard

---

[16] *EWEA Strategy Paper '97* (ALTENER publication, 1997).
[17] EPIA, *Photovoltaics in 2010* (European Commission, Luxembourg, 1996).
[18] Statement of AEBIOM on the Green Paper of the European Commission, Feb. 1997.

conclusions as is the likely cumulative level of job creation which would derive from investments in the various forms of renewable energy sources, it is quite clear that a proactive move towards such energy sources will lead to significant new employment opportunities.

An important additional economic benefit not included above is the potential growth of the European renewable energy industry in international markets. In most technical areas, European industry in this field is second to none in its ability to provide the equipment and technical, financial and planning services required for market growth. This offers therefore, significant business opportunities for exports and possibilities for expansion of the European renewable technologies industry. A 17 billion ECU annual export business is projected for 2010, creating potentially as many as 350,000 additional jobs.

Considering all the important benefits of renewables on employment, fuel import reduction and increased security of supply, export, local and regional development, etc. as well as the major environmental benefits, it can be concluded that the Community Strategy and Action Plan for renewable energy sources as they are presented in this White Paper are of major importance for the Union as we enter the 21st century.

Chapter 2   Main Features of the Action Plan

2.1   Introduction

Without a determined and co-ordinated effort to mobilise the Union's renewable energies potential, this potential will not be realised to a significant extent, resulting in missed opportunity to develop this sector and to reduce greenhouse gas emissions significantly. If pro-active steps are not taken in a co-ordinated way within the Union, renewable energies are only likely to emerge slowly from today's niche markets to become more widely used and hence fully cost competitive in around 2020, with full market penetration perhaps still years beyond. The Action Plan set out below aims at providing fair market opportunities for renewable energies without excessive financial burdens. Increasing the current share of renewables significantly will not be an easy task, but the benefits to be obtained justify a major effort.

Investments will have to be made both by the private and public sectors, but these will provide multiple dividends as Europe's industry and service companies demonstrate their technological leadership in a globally competitive market. At the same time, the increasingly liberalised and globalised energy markets present a new situation, which will have to be used in a positive sense to provide new opportunities while new obstacles to RES growth in the electricity sector will have to be avoided.

The Community Strategy and Action Plan should be seen as an integrated whole, to be further developed and implemented in close cooperation between the Member States and the Commission. The challenge facing us requires a concerted and coordinated effort by the various players over time. Measures should be taken at the appropriate level according to the subsidiarity principle within the coordinated framework provided by this Strategy and Action Plan. It would be incorrect and unrealistic to assume that actions need only be taken at Community level. The Member States have a key role to play in taking the responsibility to promote renewables, through national action plans, to introduce the measures necessary to promote a significant increase in renewables penetration, and to implement this strategy and Action Plan in order to achieve the national and European objectives. Legislative action will only be taken at EU level when measures at national level would be insufficient or inappropriate and when harmonisation is required across the EU. The Strategy and Action Plan must be flexible and be updated over time in the light of experience gained and new developments including international commitments undertaken to reduce CO_2 emissions. For this reason, a system of continuous review is proposed (see section 4.1. below).

2.2 Internal Market Measures

The following is a list of priority measures aimed at overcoming obstacles and redressing the balance in favour of renewables, in order to reach the indicative objective of 12% penetration by 2010.

2.2.1 Fair Access for Renewables to the Electricity Market

Electricity is the single most important energy sector as it accounts for about 40% of gross energy consumption in the EU15. Access for renewables to the electricity networks at fair prices is therefore a critical step for their development. The basis for a Community legal framework largely exists and its implementation will have to provide for the necessary degree of legislative harmonisation. Experience of liberalisation elsewhere has shown that it can form the basis for a dynamic and secure role for renewables so long as adequate market-based instruments are provided.

At present Member States are transposing the internal market in electricity Directive[19] into national law. The Directive, in Article 8(3), permits Member States to require electricity from renewable sources to be given preference in dispatching. Further schemes for the promotion of renewables may also be compatible with the Directive, pursuant to Article 3 and/or Article 24. Most or all Member States are planning to include such schemes in their transposition of the Directive. The Commission is examining closely the different schemes proposed or introduced by the Member States in order to propose a Directive which will provide a harmonised framework for Member States to ensure that renewable energies make up a sufficient contribution to overall electricity

---

[19] Dir. 96/92/EC of the European Parliament and of the Council of 19 Dec. 1996 concerning common rules for the internal market in electricity [1997] OJ L27/20.

supply, both at the EU and at national level. Different preference schemes for electricity from renewables will be considered in this context.

Such an approach is an important element towards the creation of a true single market for electricity. Where significant differences exist between Member States regarding the extent to which renewable energy is supported and, possibly, the manner in which any consequent support measures are financed, this may result in significant trade distortions not related to efficiency.

Other issues to be addressed will include the following:

• the way in which transmission system operators should accept renewable electricity when offered to them, subject to provisions on transport in the internal market in electricity Directive;

• the guidelines on the price to be paid to a generator from renewable sources which should at least be equal to the avoided cost of electricity on a low voltage grid of a distributor plus a premium reflecting the renewables' social and environmental benefits[20] and the manner in which it is financed: tax breaks, etc.;

• on which categories of electricity purchases such measures fall;

• with regard to network access, avoiding discrimination between electricity produced from solar radiation, biomass (below 20 MWe), hydroenergy (below 10 MWe) and wind.

2.2.2 Fiscal and Finance Measures

The environmental benefits of renewable energies[21] justify favourable financing conditions. The so-called "Green tariffs" already offered in certain Member States by appealing to voluntary environmental solidarity on the part of those consumers—domestic or corporate—able and willing to pay higher rates are not sufficient, nor appropriate in all cases.

The Commission has already made or will make the necessary additional proposals for legislation and amendments to existing Directives before the end of 1998, including tax exemption or reduction on RES energy products on behalf of Member States "prerogatives" under art. 13 to 16 of the proposed Directive "Restructuring the Community Framework for the Taxation of Energy Products".[22]

---

[20] This premium could be above 20% of that avoided cost which is about equivalent to the average tax on electricity in the European Union. The avoided cost introduced here above refers to the cost at the "city gate", i.e. the wholesale price at which the grid operator of a municipal low voltage grid buys electricity from the transmission network. The premium is put equivalent to the tax rebate or tax exemption of renewable energy as it is currently implemented in those European Union Member countries which have introduced CO_2 tax. Renewable energy tax exemption is also requested in a recent commission proposal modifying the Directive on taxation of energy products.

[21] Environmental benefits as established by the EXTERNE project (see also Annex II.11).

[22] COM(97)30 final, 12 Mar. 1997, Proposal for a Council Directive on "Restructuring the Community Framework for the Taxation of Energy Products".

In some cases it will be appropriate and sufficient for Member States' authorities to enact the necessary legislation or other provisions, in areas such as

- flexible depreciation of renewable energies investments;
- favourable tax treatment for third party financing of renewable energies;
- start up subsidies for new productions plants, SME's and new job creation;
- financial incentives for consumers to purchase RE equipment and services.

The Commission however will also make a survey of the progress made throughout the Union in this regard by the end of the year 2000, and if this indicates a remaining need for Union-level measures in certain of the areas listed, the necessary proposals will be put forward.

Other financial measures, which are proving their value in some Member States, will also be examined and promoted more widely as appropriate such as:

- so-called "golden" or "green" funds addressed to capital markets. Such funds are financed from private bank accounts which in this case attract lower interest rates. The margin consented by the lower interest rate paid to the account holder is passed on by the bank to the renewable energies investor in the form of discount rates;
- public renewable energy funds, managed by regulated agencies. The facilities offered could include revolving funds as well as credit guarantees (renewable energies bonds) and should in any case conform to the Treaty provisions;
- soft loans and special facilities from institutional banks (see Section 2.5.3).

2.2.3   New Bioenergy Initiative for Transport, Heat and Electricity

Specific measures are needed in order to help increase the market share for *liquid biofuels* from the current 0.3% to a significantly higher percentage, in collaboration with Member States. The overall environmental effect varies from biofuel to biofuel and depends, amongst others, on the crop cultivated and the crops replaced. Promotion of biofuels has to be coherent with the *Auto Oil Programme* and the European policy on fuel quality, and should take account of the full cycle of environmental costs/benefits. The role of biofuels in the clean fuel specification for 2005 and beyond is being studied under the Auto Oil II project.

Two new directives, currently under negotiation, concerning transport fuel[23] and sulphur reduction in liquid fuels[24] already include provisions encouraging the use of biofuels for transport, i.e. alcohols and ETBE, vegetable oils and esters for biodiesel.

[23] COM(97)248 final, 18 June 1997.
[24] COM(97)88 final, 12 Mar. 1997—Proposal for a Council Directive on "Reduction of Sulphur Content in Certain Liquid Fuels" and modification of Dir. 93/12/EEC.

Given the fact that currently the production cost of liquid biofuel is three times that of conventional fuels, a priority effort needs to be placed on further research and other measures to reduce production costs of biofuels. An increased use of liquid biofuels at present can only be obtained if there is a high rate of tax relief and subsidised raw material production. Detaxation of biofuels is currently made on a limited scale, in the framework of the directive 92/81[25] on harmonisation of the structures of excise duties, allowing such detaxation on a pilot scale. The Commission proposes that a market-share of 2% for liquid biofuels could still be considered a pilot phase. This level may well be reached in the short or medium term in some countries (in particular Austria, Germany, France and Italy). The Commission has already made proposals for adjusting the relevant European legislation in order to allow a large scale liquid biofuels detaxation.[26]

For *biogas* promotion, production of landfill gas or biogas from the food industry or farms will be encouraged, in order to obtain with energy and environmental policy benefits. Fair access to the electricity market will be promoted as indicated in point 2.2.1 above. Measures for biogas will contribute to the achievement of the Commission's strategy on reducing methane emissions[27] from manure by using anaerobic digesters or covered lagoons as well as meeting the objectives on protection of waters[28] and on landfill.[29]

It is proposed under this strategy that demonstration programmes at European Union, national, regional and local level should be supported to install recovery and use systems for intensive rearing. In addition, the Commission will examine the possibility of integrating biogas actions in the structural funds.

In order for the markets for *solid biomass* to be further developed, the following must be actively promoted:

• co-firing or fossil fuel substitution in coal power plants and in existing district heating networks;

• new district heating or cooling networks as an outlet for co-generation with biomass;

• greater access to upgraded fuels such as chips and pellets and a more intensive exploitation of appropriate forest, wood and paper industry residues;

---

[25] [1992] OJ L316/12.

[26] (a) [1994] OJ C209/9—Proposal for a Council Directive on excise duties on motor fuels from agricultural sources; (b) proposal for a Directive on the taxation of energy products mentioned in para. 2.2.2 above—see n. 17 above.

[27] COM(96)557 of 15 Nov. 1996.

[28] [1991] OJ L375—Council Dir. 91/676/EEC concerning the protection of waters against pollution caused by nitrates from agricultural sources and [1997] OJ C184/20, Proposal for a framework Directive concerning waters protection.

[29] COM(97)105 of 5 Mar. 1997—Proposal for a Council Directive on the landfill of waste.

• new scaled up IGCC (Integrated Gasification in Combined Cycle) systems in the capacity range of 25–50 Mwe based on a mixture of biomass and waste derived fuels;

• Clean energy generation from municipal waste either by thermal treatment, landfill gas recovery or anaerobic digestion as long as energy generation from waste complements and does not replace waste prevention and recycling.

The Commission has recently published a strategy[30] *to promote combined heat and power.* CHP is of paramount importance for the success of biomass implementation. Almost 1/3 of the new additional biomass exploitation by 2010 could fall in this category. District heating and cooling is also vital to maximise the financial and economic benefits of cogeneration. Increased use of bioelectricity is linked, like that for wind and solar electricity, to European Union wide measures for fair access to the electricity market (see Section 2.2.1).

2.2.4 Improving Building Regulations: Its Impact on Town and Country Planning

Energy consumption in the domestic and service sectors can be significantly reduced by improving energy intensity overall in addition to more use—in retrofitting as well as for new buildings—of renewables such as solar energy. It is important to adopt a global approach and to integrate measures of rational use of energy (for the building envelope as well as for heating, lighting, ventilation and cooling) with the use of renewable energy technologies. Total energy consumption in this sector could be reduced by 50% in the European Union by 2010, half of which could be accounted for by introducing passive and active solar technologies in buildings for which concrete promotional measures are necessary. This could be facilitated by amendments to the existing Directives on improving energy efficiency in buildings[31] and to the Directive on building materials[32] in order to include new building materials for solar efficiency in the standards specifications.

In order to promote the use of RES in buildings, the following specific measures are proposed:

• incorporation of requirements on the use of solar energy for heating and cooling in building approvals under current legislative, administrative and other provisions on town and country planning should be considered;

• promotion of high efficiency windows and solar façades, natural ventilation and window blinds in new buildings and for retrofitting;

[30] COM(97)514 final, "A Community strategy to promote CHP and to dismantle barriers to its development".
[31] Council Dir. 93/76/EEC of 13 Sept. 1993 "to limit carbon dioxide emissions by improving energy efficiency (SAVE)".
[32] Council Dir. 89/106/EEC of 21 Dec. 1988 "on the approximation of laws, regulations and administrative provisions of the Member States relating to building materials".

- promotion of active solar energy systems for space heating and cooling and warm water, e.g. solar collectors, geothermal heating and heat pumps;

- promotion of passive solar energy for heating and cooling;

- encouragement of PV systems to be integrated in building construction (roofs, façades) and in public spaces;

- photovoltaic electricity sales to utilities from private customers should be priced so as to allow direct reversible metering;

- measures to encourage the use of construction materials with a low intrinsic energy content, e.g. timber.

2.3   Reinforcing Community Policies

The priority given to renewable energies in existing Community policies, programmes and budgets is mostly very low. There is much scope for reinforcement. It is also important to make the renewable energies potential better known and to increase awareness among all those bearing responsibility for Community programmes.

2.3.1   Environment

The Fifth Environmental Action Plan gives due consideration to renewable energies and proposes support measures including fiscal incentives.[33] The measures in the Fifth Environmental Action Plan referring to renewable energies, will be implemented by the year 2000, within the overall framework of the strategy proposed in this White Paper. The net environmental effects of different renewable energy sources will be taken into account when implementing different measures. It is important to underline that a significant increase in the share of renewable energy sources will play a key role in meeting the Union's CO_2 emission reduction objectives, in parallel to efforts for energy efficiency and other areas. Measures related to climate change will take into account the Community Strategy on RES.

2.3.2   Growth, Competitiveness and Employment

The Commission's White Paper on Growth, Competitiveness and Employment constitutes an important point of reference for further action on renewable energies.[34] There is indeed a great potential for renewable energies to contribute to the aims set out in that White Paper. Achieving the indicative objective of 12% in 2010 would lead to an increase in the market for European Industry and could create a significant number of new jobs as outlined in Section 1.4. The export market is particularly important as Europe, with its tra-

---

[33] COM(92)33, 11 Apr. 1992, Fifth Environmental Action Plan—"Towards Sustainability".
[34] COM(93)700 final—"Growth, Competitiveness and Employment—The Challenges and Ways Forward in the 21st Century".

ditional links with Africa, South America, India and lately South-East Asia, is in a very favourable position. The following actions deserve particular attention:

• strengthening the competitive edge of European industry in the global renewable energies market by supporting its ventures into technological leadership and supporting development of a substantive home market in addition to emerging export opportunities;

• investigating opportunities for the creation of new SMEs and jobs;

• introducing RES issues in the actions addressed to SMEs under the social fund;

• action for education and training relating to renewable energies within existing Community programmes.

2.3.3   Competition and State Aid

In considering the various ways in which to promote the development of renewable energy sources, the positive effects of competition should be taken into account. In order to make renewables more competitive, priority should be given to ways which let the market forces function to bring down the costs for producing renewable energy as rapidly and as far as possible.

When authorising State Aids, the Commission has to take into account the derogations laid down in Article 92 of the Treaty. The guiding principle for the Commission in assessing aid for renewable energies, contained in the Community Guidelines on State Aid for Environmental Protection[35] is that the beneficial effects of such measures on the environment must outweigh the distorting effects on competition. The Commission will consider appropriate modifications in favour of renewable energies in support of its policy in this area during the revision of the present guidelines taking into consideration the Council's Resolution on the Green Paper "Energy for the future: renewable sources of energy" which states that investment aid for renewables can, in appropriate cases, be authorised even when they exceed the general levels of aid laid down in those guidelines.

2.3.4   Research, Technological, Development and Demonstration

It is generally recognised that there is still great scope for Research, Technological Development and Demonstration to improve technologies, reduce cost and gain user experience in demonstration projects on condition that technological development is guided by appropriate policy measures for introduction into internal and third country markets and subsequent implementation.

---

[35] [1994] OJ C72/3.

Every kind of action, whether of a fiscal, financial, legal or other nature, is addressed to facilitate the penetration of the technologies into the market. The strategic goals presented under 1.3 above have to be reached at the end by the use of renewable energy technologies, and the role of RTD is to help the development of technologies which are continuously more efficient.

As research, development and demonstration on renewable energies is moving strongly into industrial development and higher cost intensity, the financial means to be earmarked for renewable energy sources should be increased significantly. The 4th Framework Programme for Research, Technological Development and Demonstration and more particularly the Non-Nuclear Energy RTD programme is giving a priority to Renewable Energies sources as they represent about 45% of its total budget. The 5th Framework Programme should offer the possibility to finance the necessary RTD efforts in this area. The specific programme "Competitiveness and Sustainable Growth" which will be part of the 5th Framework Programme, contains a key action on energy which indicates clearly the important role of renewable energies and decentralised production energy systems.

All RTD activities related to RES should take into account the present Strategy and Action Plan, including the socio-economic aspects. The complementarity between RTD on RES and RTD on other technologies should also be encouraged. The role of RTD is important upstream of the actions in the "Campaign for Take Off" described later in that it should provide the cost efficient technologies to be used in this Campaign.

2.3.5 Regional Policy

Renewable energies already feature to some extent in the European Union's regional policy. In 1999 new guidelines for 2000–2007 will be decided. The next multi-annual funds' negotiation package will be the occasion to extend, consolidate, and clarify the aid opportunities available for renewable energies and above all to increase the weight given to RES within the energy programmes. Decision-making criteria must reflect the importance of renewables' potential for less favoured regions (which are in general dependent on energy imports), peripheral and remote areas, islands, rural areas, in particular those lacking traditional energies. In those areas RES have a high potential for new job creation, for the development of indigenous resources and industrial and service activities (particularly in objective 1 areas). The latter also applies to industrial areas under reconversion and cities (future objective 2). New incentives should also be undertaken in the tourism sector as the great potential of renewable energies in this area is still largely unexplored.

The Community will give support to regional and local projects and planning in the framework of its promotional programmes such as ALTENER (see 2.5.1). However, it is essential to encourage the Member States to include RES implementation plans in the programmes that they will submit to the structural funds for co-financing (ERDF and accompanying Community Support Frameworks), so that the share of RES in energy programmes under the Objective 1 CSF could reach at least 12%. This would reflect fully the objective set out in this White Paper for renewable energy consumption by 2010. However, in order to stimulate a shift towards renewable energy use so that this objective can be reached at MS level, a considerably higher engagement of the structural funds seems appropriate. Since the demand for funding for RES projects has to be Member State driven, effort has to be put in explaining the possibilities for RES funding and raising awareness on their potential and benefits for the regions. Other programmes for Objective 2 regions should also contribute to the promotion of RES.

It is important for the Commission to highlight that regional funds invested in renewable energy sources development could contribute to increased standards of living and income in less favoured, peripheral, island, remote or declining regions in different ways:

• favouring the use of local resources and therefore indigenous development;

• being usually labour intensive, they could contribute to the creation of local permanent jobs;

• contributing to reduce the dependency on energy imports;

• reinforcing energy supply for local communities, green tourism, preserved areas, etc.;

• contributing to develop the local R&TD and Innovation potential, through the promotion of specific research-innovation projects adapted to local needs.

The CSF sub-programmes for R&TD and innovation should also give particular attention to projects aiming at the development of new technologies and processes adapted to local and regional needs in the areas of RES.

2.3.6 Common Agricultural Policy and Rural Development Policy

Agriculture is a key sector for the European strategy of doubling the share of renewable energies in gross energy demand in the European Union by 2010. New activities and new sources of income are emerging on-farm and off-farm. Among those, the production of renewable raw materials, for non-food purposes in niche markets or the energy sector, can represent a new opportunity for agriculture and forestry and contribute to job creation in rural areas.[36]

The reference in Agenda 2000 refers to the encouragement of renewable energies. In particular biomass should be fully implemented using all available policy instruments be they agricultural, fiscal or industrial. In the future CAP alternative use for agricultural products will be a major element. Member

---

[36] COM(97)2000 Vol. I, 26 (English).

States should be encouraged, in the context of the national aid regimes, to support renewable energies.

Within **the future rural development policy**, the Commission will encourage Member States and regions to give renewable energy projects a high priority within their programmes for rural areas. However, the regions will continue to assume their responsibility for the selection of the projects.

The Common Agricultural Policy could contribute by supporting the biomass energy sector to increase standards of living and income in different ways:

• developing energy crops and utilising agricultural and forestry residues as a reliable source of raw material, under the reformed common agricultural policy, negotiated in accordance with Agenda 2000, making full use of the results of the research and development policy;

• giving support for bio-based renewable energies under the rural development policy and other ongoing programmes;

• supporting the regions by co-financing innovative, demonstrative and transferable renewable energy projects, such as the installation of combined solar, wind and biomass heat and electricity production under a new Community initiative for rural areas, as it is already possible within the existing LEADER programme;

• applying the regulation 951/97 on processing and marketing of agricultural products in relation to renewable energy products wherever feasible;

• the Commission will table a proposal enabling Member States to make the granting of direct payments for arable crops and set-aside conditional on the respect of environmental provisions, allowing them to be increasingly used to pursue environmental objectives.[37]

The existing possibilities under Regulation 2078/92 will be reviewed in the context of Agenda 2000. In this context, programmes which reduce environmental pressures from biomass-production and other uses under the agri-environmental objectives should be developed. In particular, schemes where energy crops are produced using reduced water supply, low inputs, by organic methods or harvested in a way to promote biodiversity etc. could attract a premium. The Commission could envisage more agri-environmental schemes being developed by national authorities to support energy crops respecting the fact that priorities for programmes would continue to be set by regional needs and potentials.

On a European **forestry** strategy the European Parliament, in its "Thomas Report" has called on the Commission to put forward a legislative proposal. This report, inter alia, considers the need for adding value to biomass through

---

[37] COM(97)2000 Vol. I, 29 (English).

energy production including a wide range of instruments. The report is currently under examination by the Commission, and particular attention will be paid to this point.

Non-food policy should also provide for support for energy uses of agricultural products, by-products and short rotation forestry. The Commission intends to examine the adequacy of existing instruments particularly in the sense of the need to promote RES and to improve further harmonisation. Some support is in fact already provided for in the European legislation, such as 1586/97 (non food set aside) Regulation 2080/92 (forest measures), 2078/92 (agro-environmental measures) and 950/97 (improvement of efficiency in the agricultural sector). Full use should be made of those existing Regulations.

2.3.7   External Relations

Information on and promotion of RES is important for third countries, especially as they will also have to contribute to global CO_2 emission reductions. In that respect, it is important to promote RES in the European assistance programmes, such as PHARE, TACIS, MEDA, the European Development Fund and other Lomé Convention facilities, as well as in all relevant co-operation and other agreements with developing or industrialised third countries, taking into account the possibilities and constraints of each programme. For PHARE and TACIS, the promotion of renewable sources has to be considered in the context of the economic and energy sector reform priorities of these programmes.

A proactive co-operation and export policy to support renewable energies will be stimulated, by enlarging the scope and basis of the relevant European Union energy programmes such as SYNERGY, as well as the Scientific and Technological Cooperation components of the 5th RTD Framework Programme. The action list should include the following:

• support for co-operation on energy planning and integrated resource planning with emerging economies, in order to optimise exploitation of the available renewable energy potential;

• support for exporters, in the form of credit guarantees and "currency turmoil" insurance and in the organisation of trade missions, fairs, joint workshops etc.;

• collaboration in the implementation of the "Word Solar Programme 1996–2005" which intends to realize worldwide, and especially in the developing countries, high priority regional and national projects;

• cooperation with the international financing organisations such as the World Bank and the Global Environment Facility GEF.

Special action concerning ACP Countries :

- a special initiative to promote solar electricity (photovoltaics for deprived rural areas in third countries currently without electricity);[38]

- encourage increased use of alternative renewable energy sources to resolve the problems caused by overconsumption of fuelwood in both rural and urban areas of developing countries;

- encourage the development of suitable fuelwood species plantation;

- stepping up the ACP States' research and development activities as regards the development of new and renewable energy sources.

Special action concerning associated countries:

- a special initiative to promote the process of approximation of Community legislation on renewables in associated countries;

- implementation of Protocols concerning the participation of associated countries in promotional EU programmes such as ALTENER;

- involving associated and third countries in demonstration programmes under the 5th RTD Framework Programme, in addition to specific energy policy programmes such as SYNERGY and ALTENER.

2.4   Strengthening Co-operation Between Member States

For successful implementation of the European Union Strategy and Action Plan for renewable energies, effective co-operation between Member States is of paramount importance. At present serious discrepancies persist in levels of advancement both as regards renewable energy implementation in the different Member States, and between the technologies themselves. Co-operation within a Europe-wide implementation strategy offers considerable added value to Member States, as successful policies and experiences at national level can be shared, and national renewables goals better co-ordinated, with the result that the efficiency of overall policies as well as particular projects will increase.

The Commission adopted on 4 October 1996 a proposal for a Council Decision concerning the Organisation of Co-operation around Agreed Community Energy Objectives.[39] The draft decision identifies the promotion of renewable energy resources as one of the agreed common energy objectives and calls for supportive measures at both Community and national levels with the aim of achieving a significant share of renewables in primary energy production in the Community by 2010. Concrete measures will be proposed as part of the implementation of the Council Decision, once adopted.

[38] Today, an estimated 2 billion people worldwide lack access to modern energy sources. Photovoltaics technology is now cost-effective in stand-alone power applications remote from utility grids.

[39] COM(97)436 final, 26 Aug. 1997. Proposal for a Council Decision concerning the organisation of co-operation around Community energy objectives.

2.5 Support Measures

2.5.1 Targeted Promotion

The ALTENER II[40] programme, and the subsequent programme included in the proposed Energy Framework Programme[41] will have a crucial role to play as the basic instrument for the Action plan.

ALTENER II will continue to support the development of sectoral market strategies, standards and harmonisation. Support will be given to RES planning at national, regional and local levels and to information and education infrastructures. Support will also be given to the development of new market and financial instruments. Dissemination of information is also a major action in ALTENER II. In addition, promotion of innovative and efficient renewable energy technologies and dissemination of related information are also supported by JOULE-THERMIE.

In order to enhance the impact of ALTENER II in RES market penetration, new measures to help overcome obstacles and increase operational capacity for the production of energy from RES have been proposed. These actions will be targeted on assisting biomass, solar thermal and PV, buildings, wind, small hydro and geothermal to penetrate the market. Actions under ALTENER II will also be crucial for the preparation of the Renewables Campaign for Take-off (see chapter 3).

Monitoring the progress in the implementation of the RES Strategy in Member States and in the Community will be critical and measures in ALTENER II to support monitoring and evaluation are essential (see chapter 4).

In order to achieve the objectives for renewables, a major effort will be required to harness the potential, influence and experience of all manner of associations and bodies such as citizens' groups (grass-roots organisations), relevant non-governmental organisations, and pressure-groups including the international environmental protection organisations.

At local and regional level, the creation of energy agencies under the SAVE II programme allows local authorities to play an important role in the promotion of renewable energies, mobilising local partnerships, focusing on practical actions and of becoming a key initiator of policies at local level.

The setting up of effective networks is important in order to convey information on renewables at all levels—from the technological to the financial to the local public environmental concerns. A major feature of the Commission effort in this area will be the use of Internet websites.

---

[40] COM(97)87 final of 12 Mar. 1997, Proposal for a Council Decision concerning a multiannual programme for the promotion of RES (ALTENER II).

[41] COM(97)550, 18 Nov. 1997, Proposal for a Council Decision establishing a multiannual framework programme for actions in the energy sector, and associated measures.

Other public relations tools such as industry awards, renewable energy prizes, conferences and other open events can and already do have a strong promotional effect in the renewables field, but careful selection in the allocation of support is essential to avoid dispersion of effort.

2.5.2 Market Acceptability and Consumer Protection

The following actions are planned:

• consumer information on quality goods and services for renewable energies. This information is to be disseminated in such a way that customers can choose anywhere in the internal market the most appropriate European product and source at the least price;

• standards should be established at European level but also at a wider international level in order to support exports. Since standardisation work in the renewables field started only in 1995, an increased effort has to be made to extend standards to all commercial equipment; provisional certification has also to be promoted. The EU Joint Research Centre has an important role to play in this respect, giving technical support to the CEN and CENELEC in the framework of ALTENER;

• in order to respond to and mobilise the existing strong public support for renewable energies, products should be clearly labelled as such;

• best practice experience in particular for services, system operation (a typical field for this is passive solar applications) should be collected and widely disseminated;

• regional focal points for information and consumer advice should be set up. The existing regional and city energy centres—and those which continue to be set up under the SAVE II programme are in most cases ideally situated and equipped to take on this role.

2.5.3 Better Positioning for RES on the Institutional Banks and Commercial Finance Market

International financial institutions such as the EIB (incl. EIF etc.) and the EBRD and their national counterparts have already become involved in the financing of renewable energies, in particular hydro and wind plants. Their role can be strengthened considerably by:

• providing soft loans and credit guarantees;

• creating special facilities for renewable energies;

• developing schemes facilitating loans for small renewable energy projects.

Specific action focused on commercial banks will be promoted:

• guidelines and risk evaluation schemes to help banks to audit RES businesses applying for loans;

• EU support to packaged projects in order to facilitate soft loans access.

2.5.4 Renewable Energy Networking

Transnational co-operation in Europe is important in order to exchange experience and to increase effectiveness. As the scale of renewable energies implementation becomes more significant, the following initiatives should be taken:

• networks of regions, islands, and cities aiming at a 100% energy supply from renewable energies by 2010;

• networks of universities and schools pioneering renewable energies;

• renewable energies technology research and technological development networks;

• renewable energies twinning of cities, schools, farms etc.;

• temporary networks for specific tasks;

• the virtual centre "AGORES" for the collection and dissemination of information on: regulation, calls for proposals, Community and Member States programmes, technical state-of-art, training, financing, assistance, etc.

Chapter 3 Campaign For Take-Off

3.1 Introduction

Even though renewable energy technologies have reached a certain maturity, there are many obstacles to their market penetration. In order to assist a real take off of renewables for large-scale penetration, make progress towards the objective of doubling the EU renewable energy sources share by 2010, and ensure a coordinated approach throughout the Community, the Commission proposes a campaign for take off of renewables. This will need to be undertaken over a number of years and will require close cooperation between the Member States and the Commission. The proposed campaign aims to promote the implementation of large-scale projects in different renewable energy sectors and will send clear signals for greater use of renewable energy sources. In preparation for the Campaign, the Commission will catalogue and analyse all existing European Union and Member States' activities and programmes which could provide support for such a campaign. The conclusion of this preparatory survey will be reported to Council and to the European Parliament. Detailed guidelines for the campaign will then be drawn up, together with the Member States.

It is clear that the role of Member States is critical in this concerted action for promoting large-scale implementation of renewables. The Commission's role will be to establish the framework, to provide technical and financial assistance, where appropriate, and to coordinate actions. For such a major effort to succeed, it is also important to implicate all the interested parties and bodies in promoting renewables through the means available to them. The involvement of these actors can include the negotiation of commitments and voluntary agreements where appropriate.

Many parties can be potentially active in a campaign to promote renewables, including the following:

- the regions;
- municipalities and their distribution utilities;
- the oil and car industries;
- town and country planning bodies and architects;
- authorities in charge of public procurement;
- industry associations and utilities;
- farmers' associations;
- forest-based industries and cooperatives.

In the preparatory phase for the campaign, proposals will be made for their involvement and contribution.

3.2 Key Actions

The following key actions are proposed to be promoted during the campaign:

3.2.1 1,000,000 Photovoltaic Systems

Photovoltaics (PV) is a high technology with strong export potential in a very competitive global market and fierce competition with Japan and the USA. There is a very motivated PV industry in Europe which should be supported in its effort to bring domestic and export markets off the ground. Besides the leading European oil and other big companies, many SMEs are active in the field. There is much scope for their number to increase and for large numbers of jobs to be created.

An ambitious and very visible promotion campaign is needed in order to provide a sufficiently large market base to enable the prices to fall substantially, and so the Campaign will comprise an EU wide 500,000 PV roof and façade initiative for the domestic market and an export initiative for 500,000 PV village systems to kick start decentralised electrification in developing countries. The basic capacity for each of the systems (the integrated building systems in Europe as well as the solar village schemes overseas), is $1kW_e$, i.e. the total capacity to be installed in this Campaign by 2010 is $1 GW_p$.

A large part of the future PV market will be associated with building applications, especially in Europe where the electricity grid is omnipresent. A 500,000

PV roof and façade campaign or the European Union will represent, on the basis of 1 kW generators, a total capacity of 500 MW$_p$ and will make up one-sixth of the 3 GW$_p$ estimated implementation potential outlined in Annex II. This is a very significant campaign for the future of PV, even though it will affect less than 2% of the 30 million houses and non-residential units which will probably be built between now and 2010. This is without taking into consideration the equally large potential for PV retrofitting in existing buildings.

The rationale of such a goal in a global solar market is its consistency with the corresponding goals fixed in Japan and the United States. The first 1000 PV roof programme implemented in Germany at the beginning of the 1990s proved highly successful for market introduction of PV, quality assurance and cost improvements. Japan is implementing in 1997 a 10,000 roof programme which is funded for one-third from public sources. The total investment cost of a 500,000 roof programme would be 1.5 billion ECU (assuming 1kW generators at an average price over the 13-year period of 3 ECU/W). On average, it would mean approximately the installation of 40,000 systems per year. Total yearly investment costs would then be 120 million ECU of which one-third, i.e. 40 million ECU might be provided from public funds. The equivalent amounts will be used for the export initiative. Although there are virtually no regulations in place to promote PV in the European Union, there is a wide spectrum of funding and fiscal incentives for PV employed today. The most important ones are the 50% investment subsidy in some German Länder, Greece and other Member States, a full cost electricity tariff for PV energy supplied to the grid in some German cities and accelerated depreciation in the Netherlands. A less generous support of one-third of the investment cost from public funds which is currently applied in Japan may actually be sufficient to open up the commercial markets.

This campaign should incorporate specific actions such as:

• promotion of photovoltaics in schools and other public buildings. This action has not only an educational effect to increase knowledge and awareness at an early and receptive age, but it is technically sound as it minimises the need for storage capacity and in many cases can benefit from advantageous financing;

• incentives for photovoltaics applications in tourism, and sports and recreational facilities, which offers considerable potential due to strongly peaking seasonal demand in mass tourism and the fact that a large proportion of tourist sites are isolated and/or mountainous or otherwise expensive to supply from grids;

• incentives for financing from public funds and city utilities, for instance by spreading the extra cost for photovoltaics over the entire customer base as opposed to the sole purchasers for solar electricity.

3.2.2   10,000 MW of Large Wind Farms

Wind energy today is competitive and has already been widely installed at specific sites with favourable conditions. Areas potentially suitable for wind energy applications are dispersed throughout the European Union. At present, some have to bear additional costs due to their particular location which increases installation and/or operational costs (areas far from existing grids, in very cold, hot or dusty climates, offshore, islands, remote rural areas etc.). In particular, there is enormous potential for offshore wind farms. They have the advantage of higher wind speeds, although access is clearly more difficult. In order to achieve large-scale penetration of wind energy in the European Union these areas have also to be used. A specific campaign is thus required to support large wind farms in such locations and the development of such new or adapted technology as may be appropriate. This programme will clearly imply a major role for the utilities most concerned.

The 10,000 MW of wind farms proposed here represent 25% of the feasible overall wind energy penetration for 2010 outlined in Annex II. No public financing will be needed for the 30,000 MW remaining installed capacity provided that a fair access to the European grids for the wind turbines is guaranteed, as described in section 2.2.1. An additional help is needed only for the less favourable or unconventional applications described above.

The average ex-works cost of wind turbines for wind farms is today less than 800 ECU/kW of installed capacity. Project preparation cost depends heavily on local circumstances, such as condition of the soil, road conditions, proximity to electrical grid sub-stations, etc. For flat onshore sites the overall cost of an installed wind farm is about 1,000 ECU/kW. This cost could increase substantially for offshore and unconventional site applications. On the other hand, costs are expected to fall by at least 30% by 2010. It is then logical to assume the total investment cost of the proposed 10,000 MW will be in the order of 10 billion ECU. A public expenditure of 15% would amount to 1.5 billion ECU throughout the Union or a little more than 100 million ECU per year.

3.2.3   10,000 MW$_{th}$ of Biomass Installations

Bioenergy is among the most promising areas within the biomass sector, and combined heat and power using biomass has the greatest potential in volume among all renewable energies. Consequently, a campaign to promote and support decentralised biopower installations throughout the European Union is essential. Such installations could range in scale from a few hundred kW to multi-MW and combine different technologies, as appropriate to local circumstances, including fuel switching. Wherever possible use should be made of opportunities for rationalisation through regional and local level implementation.

The estimated contribution of biomass in combined heat and power plants, as outlined in Annex II.1, could be 26 Mtoe. This corresponds typically to an overall installed capacity of approximately 20 GW_e, or 60 GW_{th}. The promotion of 10 GW_{th} through this campaign represents 1/6 of the total estimated contribution biomass could make by 2010. It will in particular be important to take measures in the early years of this action plan in order to launch a bioenergy market.

The total installation cost of such an initiative would be in the order of 5 billion ECU, assuming an average cost of 500 ECU/kW_{th} of installed capacity. A public expenditure of 20% would amount to 1 billion ECU for the whole period for the whole Union or around 80 million ECU per year. The biomass feedstock cost would amount to 270 million ECU per year, if we assume a 100 ECU/ton.

3.2.4 Integration of Renewable Energies in 100 Communities

To optimise the available potential of renewable energy technologies requires them to be used together wherever this is productive either in integrated systems for local power supply or, on the other hand, in dispersed schemes for regional power supply. These obviously have to be adapted to the conditions of each specific location, so as to ensure reliable power supply to the required quality and continuity standards.

As part of this campaign action, a number of pilot communities, regions, cities and islands will be selected from those which can reasonably aim at 100% power supply from renewables. These pioneer collectivities, in order to feature as credible pacemakers, should be of varying size and characteristics. On a small scale, the units could be blocks of buildings, new neighbourhoods in residential areas, recreational areas, small rural areas, or isolated ones such as islands or mountain communities. On a larger scale, "solar cities" should be identified, as well as large rural areas, and administrative regions which can benefit from an existing sense of community. Large islands (e.g. Sicily. Sardinia, Crete, Rhodes, Mallorca, Canary Islands or Madeira) could also be used as pilot regions.

In order to specify the actions required and to monitor progress, a strategy including schedules, priorities and players must be defined. Local and regional authorities as well as regional energy centres have a central role to play in implementing this project.

Preference should be given to activities involving combinations of technology and application in such a way that such projects have the potential to cover the entire range from pre-feasibility study, through feasibility study and demonstration phase (mainly programme financed), to large-scale implementation with (mainly) commercial international financing.

The costs of this initiative are difficult to define with any precision at this stage due to the different size and nature of each possible action. Projects implemented in other sectors of the present campaign can also be a part of the actions promoted here. As a first estimate one may assume a yearly cost of 200 million ECU, with a public funding in the order of 20% or 40 million ECU per year throughout the Union.

3.3 Estimates of Some of the Costs and Benefits

Cost estimates and an investment plan to be financed by all partners, Community and Member States' programmes and funds and also by institutional and commercial banks, utilities and others, will have to be drawn up. The effects of this Campaign on CO_2 emissions and employment will also be analysed in detail. As a first estimate, the Campaign could involve 20.5 billion ECU of investments for the period 1998–2010. Public funding from all possible sources (European, national, regional, local), to stimulate the Campaign could be in the order of 4 billion ECU or 300 million ECU per year. At the same time, it must be underlined that 3.3 billion ECU will be saved in avoided fuel cost to 2010 and external benefits in the order of 2 billion ECU per year are estimated.

The following table summarises the figures related to the Campaign and estimates the direct benefits in avoided fuel costs and reduction of CO_2 emissions.

Campaign Action	Proposed New Installed Capacity billion EC	Estimated Total Investment Cost	Suggested Public Funding billion EC	Total Avoided Fuel Costs billion EC	CO_2 Reduction million tn/year
1. 1,000,000 PV systems	1,000 MWp	3	1	0.07	1
2. 10,000 MW Wind Farms	10,000 MW	10	1.5	2.8	20
3. 10,000 Mwth Biomass	10,000 MWth	5	1	—	16
4. Integration in 100 Communities	1,500 MW	2.5	0.5	0.43	3
Total	**20.5**	4	3.3	40	

Chapter 4   Follow up and Implementation

4.1   Implementation and Monitoring of Progress

During the period of implementation of the Strategy and Action Plan outlined in this White Paper, there is the need for a constant monitoring of activities in order to follow closely the progress achieved in terms of penetration of RES, and to ensure and improve co-ordination of programmes and policies under the responsibilities of the Community and the Member States.

There is, in this context a case for improving the co-ordination and data collection as regards the action on renewables undertaken within the various programmes of the Community and the activities of Member States, and for developing a unified acceptable system of statistics based on the substitution principle. The Commission, in the framework of the ALTENER II programme and in co-operation with the Statistical Office and the JRC will create a monitoring scheme which can register all Community support given to renewables as well as the action undertaken at national level and progress made in terms of renewables penetration in different sectors. In this way policies and programmes affecting renewables and progress towards increasing the share of renewables can be monitored reliably and effectively.

4.2 Internal Co-ordination of EU Policies and Programmes

A major added value of a Community Strategy is the proposed integration of the promotion of RES in several policy areas. In order to ensure the effective follow-up and implementation of this aspect within the Commission, the internal co-ordination will be strengthened to deal with all policy aspects of renewable energy integration in the Community's policies and areas of responsibility.

4.3 Implementation by Member States and Co-operation at EU Level.

The active participation of the Member States in the further development and implementation of the Strategy, as well as in the assessment and monitoring of progress is essential. Co-operation within an EU-framework provides added-value for the effectiveness of the actions and also offers considerable benefit to Member States, as successful policies and experiences on national and local levels can be disseminated and objectives and actions can be coordinated. Joint policies and transnational Projects will increase efficiency.

A working group involving Commission and Member States representatives will be established in order to monitor the measures undertaken and evaluate the impact of energy policy decisions at all levels with regard to the use of renewable energy sources. Member States need to adopt national goals and strategies, and these will be compared alongside European wide action discussed and to be put into effect. The Member States, as part of their contribution to this process, will be asked to report to the working group the feasible contribution they can realistically make to the 2010 target, including how they intend to promote renewables sector by sector. The working group should also co-ordinate responses and form "a view on the likelihood of the RES Community objective being achieved, and if necessary stimulate new measures.

4.4 Implementation of Action Plan—Next Steps

The Community Strategy presented above is the basic framework for action for achieving the indicative objective of 12% penetration of renewables by 2010.

In order to implement the Strategy, concrete measures are proposed in an Action Plan (Annex I), in which the Strategy sets out the individual actions by categories, and indicates the form of each action. Actions are attributed to the EU, Member States or both, depending on the nature of the action and in accordance with the principle of subsidiarity. Whole-hearted commitment will be necessary from all the players involved, EU institutions, Member States, regional and local authorities, industry and consumers, to implement this Action Plan and, in so doing, achieve the objective adopted for a significant increase in the share of renewable energies in the total inland energy consumption by 2010. If the objective of doubling the share is achieved it will have an important impact on reducing the EU's CO_2 emission as well as contribute to job creation and regional economic development.

A Communication to the European Parliament, the Council, the Economic and Social Committee and the Committee of the Regions will be produced every two years in order to evaluate the success of the strategy and recommend a revised direction and/or new actions if sufficient progress in the penetration of renewables does not appear to be made.

The European Parliament, the Council, the Economic and Social Committee and the Committee of the Regions are invited to endorse the EU Strategy and Action Plan set out in this White Paper, and to support its implementation over the period to 2010.

Annex I

PRELIMINARY INDICATIVE ACTION PLAN FOR RES 1998–2010
(Includes some actions already initiated)

ACTION PLAN	European Union
1. Objectives and Strategies	
Community Strategy and overall objective of 12% for the EU up to 2010	Communication of the Commission—White Paper—(1997)
Member States setting individual objectives to 2005 and 2010 and establishing strategies	
2. Internal Market	
Fair Access for RES to the Electricity Market Directive (1998)	Proposal for a transposition
Restructuring the Community Framework for the Taxation of revised Directive	Proposal for a transposition or (COM/97/30)
Energy Products	
Start-up subsidies for new production plants. SMEs and new job creation	
Development or/and harmonisation concerning "golden" or "green" funds of the Commission	1998 : Promotion 2000 : Communication
Progressive increase of the market share of liquid biofuels	

	European Union
ACTION PLAN	
Promotion of Biofuels in transport fuel Directive	Proposal for a transposition COM(97)248
Promotion of biofuels in low-sulphur liquid fuels Directive	Proposal for a transposition COM(97)88
Extend the scope of the SAVE Directive to passive and active	Proposal for transposition
Amendment of solar systems in buildings to take into account the energy gains for heating and cooling Extend the scope of the Directive to building materials with a low intrinsic energy content (1998)	Directive 89/106/EC

3. Reinforcing Community Policies

Inclusion of Actions on Renewables in the overall strategy for combatting climate change	Commission COM(97)481
Adoption and implementation of the 5th Framework Programme for RTD (1998–2002)	Decision of the EP —
RES to be included in the main priorities jointly with employment and environment in the regional fund new phase (2000–2006)	Council (. . . / . . . / . . .)
Promotion of biomass in CAP and rural development proposals 2000 for 2000–2006	CAP proposals/Agenda
Review of Reg. 2078/92 in context of Agenda 2000 2078/92 and	Decision awaited 1998 Review of Reg.
Examination of adequacy of existing instruments and possibility of further harmonisation	
Definition of an energy strategy for the co-operation with ACP countries, in the Lomé Convention Framework, emphasizing the role of RES	
Sufficient funding from TACIS and PHARE for RES in order to implement Protocols opening EU support programmes	Specific Protocols Communication
ALTENER and SYNERGY to associated countries. Appropriate agreements with Mediterranean area countries as well as other areas. Collaboration in the implementation of the World Solar Programme 1996–2005.	

4. Strengthening Co-operation between Member States

Strengthening co-operation between MS under Council Decision on the Organisation of Co-operation around Agreed Community Energy Objectives	Proposal for a implementation (COM/. . . / . . .)

ACTION PLAN	European Union

5. Support measures

EU programme to promote RES, open to CEECs and Cyprus, Council Decision aimed at creating the necessary conditions for the implementation of the Action Plan particularly the legal, socio-economic and administrative conditions and encourage private Framework	Proposal for a submission of "ALTENER II" Proposal for 1998–2002
and public investments in the production and use of energy from RES to include specific actions for the identification and promotion of business opportunities	
Consumer information campaigns. Targeted information action on the protection of environment with simultaneous energy recovery	EU actions
Development of European standards and certifications	CEN and CENELEC under ALTENER
Better positioning for RES on the institutional banks and projects	agreements and agreements
commercial finance market by developing schemes facilitating investments in RES projects	
Creation of a virtual centre "AGORES" for collection and dissemination of information	action under ALTENER

6. Campaign for take-off

1,000,000 PV systems half in EU, half in third countries. financial	EU promotion and co-funding contribution
10,000 MW of large wind farm financial	EU promotion and co-funding contribution
10,000 MWth of biomass installations financial I contribution	EU promotion and co-funding
Integration of Renewable Energies in 100 Communities financial	EU promotion and co-funding contribution

7. Follow-up

Scheme to monitor progress ALTENER	EU action under data
Improvement of data collection and Statistics	Commission action
Inter-services co-ordination group	Commission action
Creation of a Working Group involving Commission and Member States	Commission action
Regular reporting to the Union's Institutions	Commission action

Annex II

Estimated Contributions by Sector—A Scenario for 2010

In this Annex, the realistic potential for exploitation of the different renewable energy sources is presented within the framework of the Strategy and Action Plan. The contribution that the various renewable energy sectors could make by 2010 towards achieving the indicative objective of 12% share of renewables is estimated. These estimates present one particular scenario of RES development—it is clear that the market could evolve differently. Nonetheless, it is considered important to present an overall view of projected developments, in order to help orientate policy instruments and campaigns.

II.1   Biomass

Currently biomass accounts for about 3% of total inland energy consumption (EU15). However in the new Member States—Austria, Finland and Sweden—this renewable source already accounts for 12%, 23% and 18% respectively of primary energy supply. It is difficult to make estimates in this area on future development as regards the extent to which the biomass and its distribution sector will expand. Under the particular scenario followed in this Annex, use of three times the present amount of 44.8 Mtoe is considered to be a possible development for 2010, on condition that effective measures are in fact adopted. This would mean additional biomass amounting to 90 Mtoe, equivalent to 8.5% of the projected total energy consumption in that year.

Biomass is a widespread resource as it includes in addition to woody biomass and the residues of the wood working industry, energy crops, agricultural residues and agrofood effluents, manures as well as the organic fraction of municipal solid waste or source, separated household waste and sewage sludge. Energy from biomass is versatile in that it can produce electricity, heat, or transport fuel as appropriate, and unlike electricity it can be stored—simply and usually economically. In addition, production units can range from small scale up to multi-megawatt size.

The additional estimated bioenergy use of 90 Mtoe by 2010 would be derived from agricultural, forest, and forest industry residues, waste streams as well as from new energy crops. Biomass exploitation has the double benefit of exploiting an important renewable energy resource and also of improving the environment and climate. Clearly in the development of biomass particular care will need to be taken to safeguard bio-diversity in the EU. Strategies and approaches should be adopted that minimise the impacts on bio-diversity.

The advantages of exploiting biomass, based on new technologies, can be clearly seen in the case of biogas exploitation. This consists largely of methane, a gas with a large greenhouse impact. It is estimated that the total energy content of land fill gas and digestible agricultural wastes in the EU exceeds 80

Mtoe. The contribution that could be made by biogas exploitation from livestock production, agro-industrial effluents, sewage treatment and landfill by 2010 is estimated at 15 Mtoe. A stronger exploitation of the biogas resource is indeed in line with the Commission's strategy for reducing methane emissions on environmental grounds. This point has received particular attention in the preparation of a global agreement on greenhouse gas emissions. On the other hand, a new directive on landfill which is currently being discussed by the European Union institutions is rather going to limit the production of biogas from landfill: The directive plans a 75% reduction of biodegradable rubbish that can be dumped in landfill sites by 2010. However, the volume of the organic matter that could be used as feed stock for the production of biogas by anaerobic digestion would increase and the organic matter landfilled before 2010 will continue to produce methane by fermentation for several years after 2010.

As far as solid residues are concerned, there is first of all a huge potential so far unexploited in the form of wood and agricultural residues, straw etc. which exceeds 150 Mtoe per year. It is estimated that 30 Mtoe can be mobilised annually by 2010 for the power and the heating and industrial process heat market. Energy crops also need to be considered if the objective of doubling the renewable energies' share by 2010 is to be achieved. In total, the contribution for bioenergy production from crops by 2010 is estimated at 45 Mtoe i.e. an amount equal to that anticipated for bioenergy from residues and wastes. Of this 18 Mtoe could be in the form of liquid biofuels (including however liquid biofuels from non-energy crops such as wood residues, used vegetal oils, or biogas used as motor fuel) and 27 Mtoe as biomass for heat and/or power, under one particular scenario.

Liquid biofuels are currently the least competitive product from biomass in the market place, given the low oil prices. It is, however, important to ensure their continuing and growing presence in the fuel market since the short/medium term oil-prices are unpredictable, and in the longer term alternatives to the finite oil reserves are needed. The energy demand in the transport sector is expected to grow strongly in the future and so will the emission problems associated with it, and the external dependence on oil, if no alternatives are available. Biofuels have an overall positive energy balance, although this varies from crop to crop, and also depends on the crop replaced. Whether there is such an increase will depend crucially on closing the gap between production costs of biofuels and competing products.

Future development of biofuels will have to be based mostly on production in Europe. In 1993 the "utilised agricultural area" of EU15 was approx. 141 million hectares of which 76 million hectares were "arable land". It is doubtful that more than a maximum of 10 million hectares, i.e. 7.1% of the agricultural area would be sustainable for biomass crop production, the choice of crop species for liquid biofuels would need to be limited to the most productive ones with the maximum benefit and minimum environmental impact.

As far as the potential contribution of 27 Mtoe from solid cellulosic bioenergy crops is concerned, the options for production are manifold. This material can be derived from short rotation forestry (ex: willow), or non-wood, energy crops (ex: miscantthus) also good for combustion and gasification. There are various plant species suitable for specific types of agricultural land. There is a choice of crops for short rotation forestry on rather marginal land of lower value. At yields of 10 tonnes per hectare a year, a production of for example, 27 Mtoe of solid biomass by 2010 would imply a cultivated area of 6.3 million hectares of land. There exist also various options for high yield C4 plants, annual or perennial ones. They deliver about twice as much material as the short rotation forestry.

There are also plants which produce simultaneously cellulosic materials and feedstocks for liquid biofuels. An example is sweet sorghum which typically yields 5 m^3 bioethanol and 20 t of dry cellulosic material per hectare a year. It is important here to note that the fast-growing plants have several other attractions : many are annual and fit into conventional agricultural practice; they do not require the best arable land; they require less than half the water and fertilisers required by fast growing crops, such as maize. There is also a promising prospect for production of liquid biofuels from cellulosic matter. All options of species should be carefully examined with preference given to the high-yielding/low input crops, which respect biodiversity. In any case, it seems appropriate in any biomass development strategy to set an upper maximum a limit for land use. It is estimated, in this scenario approach, that if the maximum reasonable development of biomass is made by 2010, as much as 10 million hectares of land would be needed, much of it marginal land. Clearly, the environmental impacts of this development would need to be assessed, and the growth of the biomass sector would have to be compatible with sustainable development.

The overall volume of the solid vegetal biomass market is estimated at 57 Mtoe in 2010, the projected feedstocks being energy crops (27 Mtoe) and residues (30 Mtoe). If the market indeed develops in this direction, it is predicted that 25 Mtoe would be taken up by the market for direct heating and industrial process heat and 32 Mtoe would go to power generation. A portion of these 32 Mtoe, i.e. 6 Mtoe could be used in cofiring plants in combination with coal and the remaining 26 Mtoe in combined heat and power installations

Projected additional bioenergy use by 2010 under the scenario presented	90 Mtoe
* Biogas exploitation (livestock production, sewage treatment, landfills)	15 Mtoe
* Agricultural and Forest Residues	30 Mtoe
* Energy Crops	45 Mtoe

II.2   Hydro Power

Hydro power is a proven mature technology and its operation has been competitive with other commercial energy sources for many years. However, the existing technical and economic potential for large hydro power plants has either been used, or is unavailable due to environmental constraints. In contrast to this situation, only about 20% of the economic potential for small hydro power plants has been so far exploited. In addition many existing small hydro plants are out of operation, often as a result of a lack of specific incentives as to maintenance and other costs, as well as the overall grid pricing situation, but can be refurbished with relatively modest outlay, especially in the case of small typically rural and relatively isolated installations. European Union countries dominate the world market for small hydro equipment.

In 1995 approximately 307 TWh of hydro energy was produced in the Union from an overall capacity of 92 GW. Small hydro plants, i.e. plants smaller than 10 MW accounted for 10% of installed capacity (9.3 GW) and produced 37 TWh.

An increase of 10% in installed capacity of large hydro (8,500 MW) is likely by 2010 if one takes into account projects already planned, and some environmentally acceptable development. An additional installed capacity of 4,500 MW of small hydro plants by 2010 is a realistic contribution which could be achieved given a more favourable regulatory environment, since these small projects, if correctly planned, can have much lower environmental impact.

II.3   Wind Energy

Wind energy technology is developing fast. The average weight of wind turbines has halved in five years, the annual energy output per turbine has increased fourfold, and costs have decreased by a factor of ten in ten years. At present, the average size of new machines being installed is 600 kW, although there are a few machines as powerful as 1.5 MW on the market. About 90% of the world's manufacturers of medium and large-sized wind turbines are European. The largest machines are at present produced only by European manufacturers. Wind turbines give rise to some noise pollution, and research effort is being successfully undertaken to reduce noise emissions.

Wind energy is in some Member States currently the fastest growing energy source for electricity production. Europe is the world leader in wind energy, with more installed capacity than any other region of the world: 3.5 GW in EU15 at the end of 1996. There has been an average annual installation growth rate of 36% in the past five years, reaching, at present, an annual rate of 1 GW/year. If production continues to increase by the same rate, yearly production of turbines in 2010 will amount to more than 20 GW and the accumulated capacity will be more than 100 GW. A constant installation rate at this current value (~ 1 GW per year) would mean 18 GW of installed generation capacity in

2010. Therefore an estimated contribution of 40 GW wind power in the RES development by 2010 for the EU15, while ambitious, is realistic given the strength of these trends. The campaign for take-off for 10GW should provide a basis for wider implementation of wind-powered electricity generation under more difficult conditions.

A significant contribution from wind energy for 2010 can only be achieved if conditions of access to the European grids are fair for the wind generators. A major factor in the recent market success of wind energy in Member States such as Denmark, Spain, and in particular Germany, which now has the world's largest electricity generating capacity from wind, has been the price to be paid by utilities to wind generators for sale onto the grid. Any major changes that might be made to the existing regulatory structure should encourage and not jeopardise the appropriate development of wind energy.

II.4   Solar Thermal

Solar thermal heating technology is almost fully mature. There is nevertheless scope for further cost reductions from larger scale production and improvements in both production processes and marketing. At present in EU-15 about 300 small and medium enterprises are active in this sector, directly employing about 10,000 people. Solar thermal heating is cost-competitive today as compared with electric water heating, in particular in the southern parts of the European Union. Design is constantly being improved to minimise visual impact.

In 1995 there were 6.5 million m² of solar collectors installed in the European Union with a 15% growth rate over the preceding few years. The annual current installation rate is 1,000,000 m², concentrated in three EU member countries—Austria, Germany, and Greece. A growth rate of 25% could be achieved if the other 12 European Union member countries even partially followed this example. At a 20% annual growth rate, total installed capacity would be 100 million m² in 2010 which taking all relevant factors into consideration is an achievable contribution to RES development. Use of large collector fields in large-scale applications such as district heating systems—the most economically rational way of using solar thermal energy—would in itself stimulate a dramatic increase in collector production. Public awareness campaigns can effectively also boost the market as has been borne out by experience in Greece.

II.5   Photovoltaics

Solar photovoltaic electricity generation is very much a recent and close-to-state-of-the-art renewable energy technology. Costs have fallen dramatically with a 25% cost decrease over the past 5 years, but are still significantly higher than for electricity generated from conventional fuels. The European Union, currently accounts for about one-third of annual, more than 100 MW$_p$, world-wide photovoltaic module production and use. The European industry has built up a leading position in the field of photovoltaic incorporation in buildings. Europe also has the lead in applications of photovoltaics in developing countries.

Eurostat estimates that 32 MW_p of photovoltaic generation capacity was installed (EU12) at the end of 1995. The most recent estimate from the European Photovoltaic Industry Association (EPIA) suggests as much as 70 MW_p (EU 15). Photovoltaics is very much a global market. World annual module production is forecast at 2.4 GW_p by 2010. To attain an annual output of 2.4 GW_p world-wide, would require annual growth of 25%. Such an estimate is in fact compatible with the assumptions used in an EPIA study commissioned by the Commission.

Under the above assumptions a contribution of 3 GW_p installed capacity in EU15 from photovoltaics by 2010 seems ambitious but realistic. It is forecast that this would be accounted for mainly by grid-connected installations incorporated into the structure of buildings (roofs and façades) as well as a certain number of large-scale power plants (0.5–5.0 MW_p). Anyhow, PV technology should be considered in a more general way not just as a measure of GW_p installed. As it is the case for solar thermal applications, PV systems are always associated with Rational Use of Energy measures in buildings and can be evaluated as a part of the significant effort of reducing energy consumption, which always should accompany their utilisation. Grid-connected photovoltaic generation is not competitive at currently prevailing classical fuel-based generation costs and also compared with wind turbines, but it could be based on an average cost level of 3 ECU/W_p of installed capacity, which on the basis of current trends could happen around 2005. A sizeable initiative at European level for incorporating photovoltaic modules in roofs and façades can thus play a major part in definitively launching this technology. Secondary advantages of building integration such as lighting, heat supply, façade substitution should be valorised. The concept of energy system should take into account the "added value of PV". Integration of 2 PV in buildings can also convert any visual impact into an architectural design advantage.

The campaign for take-off promoting the installation of 1,000,000 photovoltaic roofs and façades would mean new capacity of 0.5GW_p in the Union and 0.5GW_p in third countries.

II.6 Passive Solar

Thermal energy demand (mostly for space heating) in the domestic and tertiary sector in EU15 represents 23% of total energy demand. It is estimated that 40% of energy actually consumed in this sector is in fact gained from solar energy through windows, but this passive energy supply is not taken into account in statistics. Consequently, the potential for further reducing the thermal energy demand in buildings with available passive solar techniques is very substantial. "Solar" and "low-energy" buildings cost almost no more to build than conventional ones. Experience in Austria has shown that passive solar construction increases overall dwelling costs by less than 4% while achieving 75% reductions in heating energy. Large gains can also be achieved in the existing building stock by retrofitting windows and façades to make more use of natural sunlight and simultaneously insulate. New materials for windows, daylighting and insulation are commercially available. Passive cooling techniques have also been developed during the last few years and could help reduce the fast-growing cooling demand in southern European countries.

Even conservative estimates show that a 10% reduction by 2010 in thermal energy demand for buildings is easily attainable by increased recourse to passive solar techniques. If it is assumed that thermal energy demand in the domestic and tertiary sector remains stable (at 23% of the total), then this represents fuel savings of 35 Mtoe. Switzerland has already committed itself to a 30% energy reduction for heating in buildings by the same year. These additional gains should be counted in the balance of the European Union's gross energy consumption.

II.7 Geothermal and Heat Pumps

Geothermal energy accounts for only a very small part of total renewable energy production in the European Union. Although power production is already viable from high-temperature dry steam, the risks associated with exploitation still present a disincentive to investment. The use of geothermal heat is thus growing slowly. However, the use of heat pumps to upgrade lower temperature ground heat is becoming much more common.

Currently installed geothermal power capacity in the European Union amounts to 500 MW. More electrical units are gradually coming on stream in France (above all overseas departments), Italy, and Portugal (the Azores). It is estimated that a doubling of the current installed capacity is an achievable contribution to RES growth by 2010.

Most low-temperature geothermal heat is employed in buildings applications. The current capacity of 750 MW_{th} is concentrated in France and Italy. This capacity could be more than tripled in 2010, to give 2.5 GW_{th}.

Turning to heat pumps, those installed to date mostly use electricity or fuel as the necessary driving energy input. A new generation make use of heat exchangers installed some 100m underground which thus exploit naturally stored solar energy and some intrinsic heat from the earth itself already at such a depth. A total of 60,000 geothermal heat pumps were installed in 1995 in the European Union, most of them in Sweden representing 8% of the capacity for all types. Assuming that this total installed heat pump capacity will be tripled by 2010 in EU15 and that the market share of geothermal heat pumps will double to reach 15%, gives an estimated achievable total capacity of 2.5 GW_{th} by 2010.

II.8   Other Renewable Technologies

There are a number of other renewable energy technologies, such as solar thermal power, tidal power, ocean currents, wave power, hot dry rock, ocean thermal energy conversion, for which the current market in the European Union is non-existent. Projections are difficult to make, but some of these technologies will undoubtedly offer significant potential in the future. It is reasonable to expect that at least one of these renewable sources will have started to be exploited commercially over the coming decade or so, which justifies assuming a marginal contribution of 1 GW by 2010.

II.9   Achieving the Overall Community Objective for RES

Table 1A summarises the estimated contributions by sector described in the present annex in the particular scenario chosen for projecting ways of achieving a 12% share of renewables in the Union by 2010. Table 2 compares gross energy consumption by type of renewable energy in Mtoe for the year 1995 with that projected for the year 2010, assuming that these contributions by the different RES are indeed made. On this basis the overall objective of doubling the current share of renewables to 12% by 2010 can be realistically achieved. The projected total gross inland consumption for 2010 is taken from the Pre-Kyoto scenario (Conventional Wisdom, "European Energy to 2020", see footnote 8). If post-Kyoto energy use turns out to be lower than that foreseen prior to Kyoto, this will have the effect of slightly increasing the current indicative objective to above 12%. On the other hand, enlargement to States with very little or no penetration of renewables may have the effect in practice of lowering the objective to below 12%. This will be taken into account in the monitoring and review mechanisms foreseen.

II.10   Estimated RES Contributions in Electricity and Heat Generation

In Table 3 the current and projected contribution of renewables to the electricity market is presented by type of energy. If appropriate measures are taken, electricity production from renewables could grow significantly by 2010, from the present 14.3% to 23.5%. The projected total electricity production for 2010, once again, is taken from the Pre-Kyoto scenario. Finally, the doubling of the heat produced by renewables is the projected development for 2010 for the heat sector as shown in Table 4 if the promotion strategy for RES is successful.

II.11   Assessment of Some of the Costs and Benefits

In Table 6 the estimated investment costs and the benefits related to, avoided fuel costs, and CO_2 emissions reduction, are presented by type of renewable energy while Table 5 provides estimates for the overall strategy to 2010. The first column of Table 6 shows the additional capacities needed to be installed in order to achieve the estimated contributions by different RES. In columns 2 and 3 the current unit costs by type of technology and the corresponding projected unit costs in 2010 are presented respectively. The fourth column shows an average reference unit cost, where the projected time frame for the deployment of each technology is taken into account. For those types of energy where installations are projected to grow steadily, such as wind energy, the average unit cost is nearer to the 2010 value. For those technologies, such as hydro, where the installations will be more or less evenly distributed in time, the mean value between 1997 and 2010 is taken as the average reference unit cost. In the 5th column the total investment needed for the installations is presented. Column 6 shows the expected annual business in 2010. Installation rate, operation and maintenance as well as fuel costs (for biomass) are included in the figures presented in this column.

Estimations on avoided fuel costs are presented in columns 7 and 8. Additional fuel savings from wind, hydro, photovoltaics and solar thermal collectors have been estimated to be 3 billion ECU in the year 2010. Assuming a constant rate of increase of installations during the period 1997–2010, a total amount of 21 billion ECU of additional fuel savings is calculated. Fuel substitution of coal and oil at 1997 prices has been assumed in all calculations. Biomass and geothermal are considered to have the same fuel costs as fossil fuel technologies and they are not included in the estimation. On the other hand, all renewables contribute to the reduction of fuel import supplies achieving a 17.4% reduction in 2010 with respect to the 1994 figures.

The last column shows the CO_2 emission reduction figures. For electricity production from wind, hydro, photovoltaics and geothermal, the displacement mainly, but not exclusively, of conventional coal-fired power plants is assumed. The CO_2 emissions, in this case, are calculated on the basis that one TWh produced by renewable saves one million tonnes of CO_2. As far as biomass is concerned, although it has a neutral effect on CO_2, the emissions generated during the feedstock production have been taken into account.

In addition, a significant number of additional jobs are expected to arise as a result of the doubling of the share of renewable energies foreseen in this Community strategy (see section 1.4).

The sum of these estimated figures shows that a total investment of 165.1 billion ECU could be needed in order to achieve the overall significant increase in renewable penetration aimed for in this strategy. As a result of this investment, an annual business of 36.6 billion ECU is estimated to be generated in 2010, creating a significant number of new jobs, avoiding fuel costs of 21 billion ECU, reducing imports by 17.4% and reducing the CO_2 emissions by 402 million tones per year with respect to 1997.

Annexe III Member States' Plans and Actions for the Development of Renewables

Austria has a share of 24.3% for RES. The Austrian government introduced in 1996 an energy tax on electricity and gas excluding RES. In 1994 a promotional tariff for power generation from solar, wind and biomass was introduced. Further development of hydro power, biomass in existing thermal plants and energy crops and solar energy are the main objectives.

In **Belgium**, energy policy has been decentralized. While there is no specific target for the energy sector, promoting RES is expected to see a reduction in CO_2 emissions of about 20 MT by 2000 in industry. In Wallonie the PEDD (Environment plan for sustainable development), adopted in 1995 is expected to be followed by a development programme for RES.

In 1996 **Denmark** elaborated an Energy Action Plan "Energy 21" including medium and long-term scenarios to 2005, 2020 and 2030. The assumptions to 2005 for RES include 200 MW offshore wind turbines, about 1 PJ landfill gas and about 1 PJ geothermal heat. After 2005 the assumptions include developing 5500 MW wind turbines (of which 4000 MW offshore), 145 PJ annually from biomass and biogas including energy crops and 25 PJ annually from geothermal and heat pumps in district-heating.

The **Finnish** government adopted in 1995 a decision on energy policy which includes increased use of bioenergy of 25% by 2005. A promotion programme for wind energy in 1993 set a target of 100 MW installed capacity by 2005.

France started in 1996 a five-year programme including 225 MW from wood combustion, 20,000 solar thermal panels for the DOM areas and 250 to 500 MW of wind turbines "Eole 2005".

In **Germany** the Act "Stromeinspeisungsgesetz" of 1991 has had a significant effect on new capacity from RES. A programme to support RES was adopted by the Federal Government with 100 million DM for the period 1995–98. Many of the Länder also have programmes. RTD is very important, with a 250 MW wind demonstration programme. 30% of the government's RTD programme is for RES. Solar thermal and PV campaigns (1000 Roofs) have had an important impact. In wind energy, Germany holds second place in the world.

The **Greek** government has a comprehensive approach to encourage RES. The law 2244/1994 was strengthened by the Decision 8295/1995 in order to remove restrictions on electricity production from independent producers up to 50 MW. The electric utility (PPC) has a ten-year programme to develop RES with the following targets : biomass (733 Mtoe by 2000 and 1400 Mtoe by 2005) wind (68 and 136 Mtoe) small hydro (15 Mtoe and 41) solar (156 Mtoe and 204) and geothermal (20 Mtoe and 40). In 1994 a second Support Framework of the Community earmarked 100 MECU for RES, 75% of funding will come from structural funds.

In **Ireland**, as a result of the AER 1 and 2 initiatives (Alternative Energy Requirement programme of 1994) and the RES Strategy, the additional RES generation will be 6% of installed capacity by 1999 bringing the total to 11%.

In **Italy**, if progress continues the PEW (National Energy Plan) expectations could be surpassed and RES could give a contribution of 2700 MW by 2000. Specific targets are 600 MW for wind and 75 MW for PV by 2000.

Luxembourg has no specific policy objectives for RES, nevertheless instruments include subsidies for solar, biomass, wind, small hydro and heat pumps.

The Netherlands has an Action Programme 1997–2000 for RES and has elaborated scenario for 2007 and 2020 which includes: development of wind energy (750 MW in 2000, 2000 MW in 2007) solar PV(119 MW 2007) biomass (residual flows 30–80 PJ/year and energy crops (12–70 PJ/year) solar Thermal (5 PJ in 2007 or 250,000 water heaters) and heat pumps (50 PJ in 2007).

In **Portugal**, the Energy Programme of 1994 had a target of about 170 MW for RES electricity. Traditional biomass is about 26% of energy needs in the residential sector. The biomass centre has a specific programme to develop biomass.

In **Spain** the PEW (National Energy Plan) for 1991–2000 had the following objectives: SMP 213 Mtoe, biomass 427 Mtoe, wind 35 Mtoe, PV 0.389 Mtoe, solar 34 Mtoe and geo thermal 10 Mtoe. At the end of 1996 the objectives were surpassed in SMP 1045%, wind 381.5% and PV 149%.

The **Swedish** Government Bill 1996/97: 84 on a Sustainable Energy Supply includes measures aimed at increasing the supply of electricity and heating from RES. The five-year scenario for RES includes an expansion of bio-fuel-based CHP of approximately the equivalent of 0.75 Twh of electricity per year, an annual increase ot around 0.5 Twh from land-based wind facilities and an annual increase of 0.25 Twh from small-scale hydropower.

The **United Kingdom** is currently reviewing its policy on renewable energy, consideration being given to achieving 10% of the country's electricity need from RES by 2010.

TABLE 1
Share of Renewable Energy Sources in Gross Inland Energy Consumption

	1990	1995
Austria	22.1	24.3
Belgium	1.0	1.0
Denmark	6.3	7.3
Finland	18.9	21.3
France	6.4	7.1
Germany	1.7	1.8
Greece	7.1	7.3
Ireland	1.6	2.0
Italy	5.3	5.5
Luxembourg	1.3	1.4
Netherlands	1.3	1.4
Portugal	17.6	15.7
Spain	6.7	5.7
Sweden	24.7	25.4
United Kingdom	0.5	0.7
European Union	5.0	5.3

Source: EUROSTAT

TABLE 1A
ESTIMATED CONTRIBUTIONS BY SECTOR IN THE 2010 SCENARIO

TYPE OF ENERGY	SHARE IN THE EU IN 1995	PROJECTED SHARE BY 2010
1. Wind	2.5 GW	40 GW
2. Hydro	92 GW	105 GW
2.1 Large	(82.5 GW)	(91 GW)
2.2 Small	(9.5 GW)	(14 GW)
3. Photovoltaics	0.03 GWp	3 GWp
4. Biomass	44.8 Mtoe	135 Mtoe
5. Geothermal		
5.a Electric	0.5 GW	1 GW
5.b Heat (incl. heat pumps)	1.3 GWth	5 GWth
6. Solar Thermal Collectors	6.5 Million m²	100 million m²
7. Passive Solar		35 Mtoe
8. Others		1 GW

TABLE 2
CURRENT AND PROJECTED FUTURE GROSS RENEWABLE ENERGY CONSUMPTION (Mtoe) FOR 2010

TYPE OF ENERGY	CONSUMPTION IN 1995		PROJECTED CONSUMPTION BY 2010					
	Eurostat Convention	% of total	Substitution Principle	% of total	Eurostat Convention	% of total	Substitution Principle	% of total
Total Gross Inland Consumption	1,366		1,409		1,583 (Pre-Kyoto)		1,633	
1. Wind	0.35	0.02	0.9	0.06	6.9	0.44	17.6	1.07
2. Total Hydro	26.4	1.9	67.5	4.8	30.55	1.93	78.1	4.78
2 a. Large (incl. pump storage)	(23.2)		(59.4)		(25.8)		(66)	
2 b. Small	(3.2)		(8.1)		(4.75)		(12 1)	
3. Photovoltaics	0.002	—	0.006	—	0.26	0.02	0.7	0.05
4. Biomass	44.8	3.3	44.8	3.12	135	8.53	135	827
5. Geothermal	2.5	0.2	1.2	0.1	5.2	0.33	2.5	0.15
5 a. Electric	(2.1)		(0.8)		(4.2)			
5 b. Heat (incl. heat pumps)	(0.4)		(0.4)		(1.0)		(1.0)	
6. Solar Thermal Collectors	0.26	0.02	0.26	0.02	4	0.25	4	0.24
Total Renewable Energies	74.3	5.44	114.7	8.1	182	11.5	238.1	14.6
7. Passive Solar			35		35	2.2	35	2.1

Table 3

CURRENT AND PROJECTED ELECTRICITY PRODUCTION BY RES (TWh) FOR 2010

	ACTUAL IN 1995		PROJECTED FOR 2010	
TYPE OF ENERGY	TWh	% of total	TWh	% of total
Total	2,366	2,870		
			(Pre-Kyoto)	
1. Wind	4	0.2	80	2.8
2. Total Hydro	307	13	355	12.4
2 a. Large (incl. pumped storage)	(270)		(300)	
2 b. Small	(37)		(55)	
3. Photovoltaics	0.03	—	3	0.1
4. Biomass	22.5	0.95	230	8.0
5. Geothermal	3.5	0.15	7	0.2
Total Renewable Energies	337	14.3	675	23.5

Table 4

CURRENT AND PROJECTED HEAT PRODUCTION (Mtoe) for 2010

TYPE OF ENERGY	ACTUAL IN 1995	PROJECTED BY 2010
1. Biomass	38.04	75
2. Geothermal	0.4	1
3. Solar Thermal Collectors	0.26	4
Total Renewable Energies	38.7	80
4. Passive Solar	—	35

TABLE 5 ESTIMATED INVESTMENT COSTS AND BENEFITS OF THE OVERALL STRATEGY IN THE 2010 SCENARIO

Total investment energy sector of which RES[42]	249 billion ECU
	39 billion ECU
Total investment RES in Action Plan	165 billion ECU
Net investment RES in Action Plan	95 billion ECU
Annual net investment RES in Action Plan	6.8 billion ECU
Additional net investment due to RES	74 billion ECU
Increase of total energy sector investment	29.7%
Employment creation	see Section 1.4
Avoided annual fuel cost in 2010	3 billion ECU
Total avoided fuel cost 1997–2010	21 billion ECU
Import reduction (ref. 1994)	17.4%
CO_2 reduction (with respect to 1997)	up to 402 million tn/ year
(with respect to the 2010 pre-Kyoto scenario)	250 million tn/year
Annual benefits from CO_2 reduction[43]	5 to 45 billion ECU

[42] European Energy 2020. A scenario approach, European Commission, 1996.

[43] COM(97)481 final—see n. 2.

TABLE 6

ESTIMATED INVESTMENT COSTS AND BENEFITS BY SECTOR

TYPE OF ENERGY	ADDITIONAL CAPACITY 1997–2010	UNIT COST 1997 ECU	UNIT COST 2010 ECU	AVERAGE UNIT COST ECU	TOTAL INVESTMENT 1997–2010 billion ECU	ADDITIONAL ANNUAL BUSINESS 2010 billion ECU	BENEFIT OF ANNUAL AVOIDED FUEL COSTS 2010 billion ECU	TOTAL BENEFIT OF AVOIDED FUEL COSTS 1997–2010 billion ECU	CO_2 REDUCTION million tn/year in 2010
1. Wind	36 GW	1,000/KW	700/KW	800/KW	28.8	4	1.43	10	72
2. Hydro	13 GW	1,200/KW	1,000/KW	1,100/KW	14.3	2	0.91	6.4	48
3. Photovoltaics	3 GWp	5,000/KWp	2,500/KWp	3,000/KWp	9	1.5	0.06	0.4	3
4. Biomass	90 Mtoe				84	24.1	—	—	255
5. Geothermal (+ heat pumps)	2.5 GW	2,500/KW	1,500/KW	2,000/KW	5	0.5	—	—	5
6. Solar Collectors	94 Mlo m²	400/m²	200/m²	250/m²	24	4.5	0.6	4.2	19
Total for EU market					165.1	36.6	3	21	402

COMMISSION OF THE EUROPEAN COMMUNITIES

Brussels, 04.02.1998
COM(98) 42 final

COMMUNICATION FROM THE COMMISSION TO THE COUNCIL AND THE EUROPEAN PARLIAMENT

ON A EUROPEAN COMMUNITY BIODIVERSITY STRATEGY

I. INTRODUCTION

A) The challenge

1. Biological diversity (biodiversity) is essential to maintain life on earth and has important social, economic, scientific, educational, cultural, recreational and aesthetic values. In addition to its intrinsic value biodiversity determines our resilience to changing circumstances. Without adequate biodiversity, events such as climate change and pest infestations are more likely to have catastrophic effects. It is essential for maintaining the long-term viability of agriculture and fisheries for food production. Biodiversity constitutes the basis for the development of many industrial processes and the production of new medicines. Finally, biodiversity often provides solutions to existing problems of pollution and disease.

2. It is estimated in UNEP's Global Biodiversity Assessment that, on a global level, biodiversity is decreasing at a faster rate now than at any other time in the past. The situation in Europe is also a cause for concern. The rich biodiversity of the European Union has been subject to slow changes over the centuries, due to the impact of human activities. The scale of this impact has accelerated dramatically in the last few decades. The Assessment by UNEP confirms that in some European countries up to 24% of species of certain groups such as butterflies, birds and mammals are now nationally extinct.

3. The reasons for this decline in biodiversity in Europe mean that it is likely to accelerate unless action is taken. The European Environmental Agency states in its "Dobris Assessment" that "the decline of Europe's biodiversity in many regions derives mainly from highly intensive, partially industrial forms of agricultural and silvicultural land use; from an increased fragmentation of remaining natural habitats by infrastructure and urbanisation and the exposure to mass tourism as well as pollution of water and air. Given the projected growth in economic activity, the rate of loss of biodiversity is far more likely to increase than stabilise."

4. In spite of past efforts by the Community and its Member States to address the problem of biodiversity reduction or loss, existing measures are

insufficient to reverse present trends. It is therefore both essential and urgent for the Community to develop a strategy and take action towards the conservation and sustainable use of biodiversity.

B)   The response

5. The global scale of biodiversity reduction or losses and the interdependence of different species and eco-systems across national borders demands concerted international action. The framework for this action is the Convention on Biological Diversity (CBD). The European Community ratified the CBD on 21 December 1993. The CBD pursues three objectives, namely the conservation of biodiversity, the sustainable use of its components and the fair and equitable sharing of the benefits arising out of the utilisation of genetic resources. Biodiversity is defined in the CBD as "the variability among living organisms from all sources, including, inter alia, terrestrial, marine, and other aquatic ecosystems and the ecological complexes of which they are part; this includes diversity within species, between species and of eco-systems".

6. Article 6 of the CBD specifically requests each party to:

• "develop national strategies, plans or programmes for the conservation and sustainable use of biological diversity or adapt for this purpose existing strategies, plans or programmes which shall reflect, inter alia, the measures set out in this Convention relevant to the Contracting Party concerned"; and

• "integrate as far as possible and as appropriate, the conservation and sustainable use of biological diversity into relevant sectoral or cross-sectoral plans, programmes and policies". The Conference of the Parties has provided additional guidance for the elaboration of such strategy.[1]

7. The European Union plays a leading role world-wide in furthering the objectives of the Convention. It does so to respond, not only to the legal obligations under the Convention, but also to the expectations and aspirations of its citizens, which in addition to the proven economic and environmental values of biodiversity, include the ethical principle of preventing avoidable extinctions.

8. The Community Biodiversity Strategy set out in this Communication will provide the framework for developing Community policies and instruments in order to comply with the CBD. The "First Report from the European Community to the Conference of the Parties of the CBD" provides a summary assessment of the importance and status of biodiversity in the European Union. It also provides a comprehensive overview of on-going and planned Community initiatives and instruments relevant to achieve the objectives of the CBD. This report therefore constitutes an important background document for the strategy.

---

[1] Decision II/7 of the Second Conference of the Parties to the CBD and Decision III/9 of the Third Conference of the Parties to the Convention on Biological Diversity.

9. The Council of Ministers in its conclusions of 18 December 1995 has considered that "with regard to matters within the field of its competence and in close co-operation with its Member States, the Community should elaborate a Community Strategy to identify gaps in the European Community conservation policy, and to promote biological diversity into the policies of the Community, complementary to strategies, programmes and plans of the Member States, in order to ensure the full implementation of this Convention".

10. All Member States of the Community are Contracting Parties to the CBD. As a consequence, they have either already developed their respective national biodiversity strategies or are in the process of doing so. By developing and implementing their national strategies Member States make an essential contribution to achieve the aims of the Convention. Many Member States have established a national biodiversity co-ordinating body, assembly or committee. All have integrated, or intend to integrate, conservation and sustainable use of biodiversity into relevant sectoral or cross-sectoral plans. Policy sectors concerned and the approach taken vary from country to country in response to the specific characteristics of their biodiversity and relative importance of pressures affecting them. Environment, agriculture, forestry and fisheries policies are generally perceived to have the greatest priority. Science and technology, energy, industry, transport, tourism and recreation, health, education and defence are also considered in many cases. In their national strategies Member States place different emphasis on various themes contained in the CBD. A first assessment on the implementation by the Member States of the different measures contained in the CBD has been made by the European Environmental Agency.[2] A more up to date review is contained in the Member States reports to the Conference of the Parties on the implementation of the CBD.

11. Successful implementation of the CBD requires co-operation both within Member States and at Community level. To develop and implement national strategies in all Member States is essential, but a number of Community policies and instruments also have an important impact on biodiversity. The Community therefore needs to take action in these areas to both complement and avoid frustrating national efforts. The Community strategy focuses on the further development and implementation of Community policies and instruments.

C) Scope and objectives of the strategy

12. As a key player on the international level, it is evident that the Community must ensure that its own policies and instruments, many of which impact significantly on biodiversity, reflect concerns about and contribute to the conservation and sustainable use of biodiversity.

[2] European Environmental Agency. The UN Convention on Biological Diversity. Follow-up in EEA Member Countries, Copenhagen, 1996.

13. The proposed Community Biodiversity Strategy therefore aims to anticipate, prevent and attack the causes of significant reduction or loss of biological diversity at the source. This will help both to reverse present trends in biodiversity reduction or losses and to place species and eco-systems, which includes agro-ecosystems, at a satisfactory conservation status, both within and beyond the territory of the European Union.

14. The Community Biodiversity Strategy is an element of the 5th Environmental Action Programme "Towards Sustainability"; and must be viewed also in the context of the obligations to integrate environmental concerns into other sectoral policies, in accordance with article 130R (2) [now Article 174(2)] of the Treaty. It is in line with the strengthened commitments to sustainable development contained in the Amsterdam Treaty which establishes that "environmental protection requirements must be integrated into the definition and implementation of Community policies and activities in particular with a view to promoting sustainable development". The strategy also takes into account a number of Council conclusions and the relevant objectives from the Pan-European Landscape and Biological Diversity Strategy.

15. The Strategy defines a framework for the actions necessary to fulfil the European Community's legal obligations under article 6 of the CBD. The relevant obligations of the CBD for the European Community are set out in section II of the strategy, in the context of four major themes. The objectives to be achieved in the context of the relevant Community policies and instruments in order to meet these obligations, are specified in section III.

16. The implementation of the CBD by the Community calls for a two-step process. The adoption of this strategy containing the general policy orientation is the first step. The second is the development and implementation of Action Plans and other measures by the Commission through its services responsible for the policy areas concerned. This second step will enable to translate into concrete actions the objectives derived from the Convention.

17. The Action Plans and other measures will develop further the links between the objectives under each theme and the objectives in each policy area. By establishing a mechanism to ensure the integration of biodiversity concerns into other policy areas and instruments the strategy contributes to fill a gap in existing Community conservation policy.

18. Action Plans and other measures to achieve the objectives should build on and complement existing policies and planned initiatives. The development of Action Plans will need to take into account the objectives and actions envisaged by Member States strategies to ensure real value added, consistency and complementarity. How this can best be done will only be clear once all Member States strategies are available.

19. As the Community and its Member States participate in a number of international conventions and agreements relevant to the objectives of the

Convention on Biological Diversity, this strategy provides guidance to ensure coherence in initiatives taken in different international fora. Implementing this strategy, therefore, will help achieve Community objectives under other Conventions.

20. Progress in the implementation of the strategy and the performance of the Action Plans and other measures will be monitored and assessed using biodiversity indicators and measurable targets in order to measure the effectiveness of actions taken and to provide guidance as to further actions needed. The process of further development, implementation and monitoring is described in section IV.

II. STRATEGY THEMES

1. The Community Biodiversity Strategy is developed around four major Themes. Within each Theme the specific objectives that will need to be achieved in the context of Action Plans and other measures are highlighted. These objectives emerge from and qualify the specific obligations relevant for the Community contained in the CBD.

Theme 1. Conservation and sustainable use of biological diversity

2. Under this Theme, the Community should seek the conservation and, where relevant, restoration of ecosystems and populations of species in their natural surroundings. It should also focus on the conservation of the ecosystems where crop species and varieties and domestic animal breeds have developed their distinctive properties. Conservation in situ needs in some cases to be complemented by additional ex-situ initiatives.[3] This Theme also refers to the measures required to ensure that use made of natural resources is sustainable.

In-situ conservation

3. The Community will continue supporting the establishment of networks of designated areas, particularly the EU NATURA 2000 network. However, for a large number of wild species, crop species and varieties and domestic animal breeds, the establishment of a system of protected areas alone is not sufficient or appropriate. Therefore, in-situ conservation requires that the Community within relevant sectoral and horizontal policy areas, considers impacts on the conservation and sustainable use of biodiversity across the rest of the territory outside protected areas. This aspect constitutes one of the major gaps in the existing Community conservation policies. The Community should therefore where appropriate seek:

---

[3] Art. 2 of the CBD defines "in-situ conditions" as the conditions where genetic resources exist within ecosystems and natural habitats, and, in the case of domesticated or cultivated species, in the surroundings where they have developed their distinctive properties. "Ex-situ conservation" means the conservation of components of biological diversity outside their natural habitats.

• to promote and support conservation of ecosystems characteristics.

• that the population size, structure, distribution and trends of wild species that occur naturally are in a satisfactory conservation status, and also to support recovery plans for the most threatened species.

• to take measures to maintain the genetic pool of wild and domesticated species and prevent processes of genetic erosion.

4. The presence or introduction of alien species or sub-species can potentially cause imbalances and changes to ecosystems. It can have potentially irreversible impacts, by hybridisation or competition, on native components of biodiversity. Applying the precautionary principle, the Community should take measures pursuing to prevent that alien species cause detrimental effects on ecosystems, priority species or the habitats they depend on and establish measures to control, manage and, wherever possible remove the risks that they pose.

5. Also, while biotechnology in general presents a number of potential benefits to society, the introduction of genetically modified organisms into the environment can have negative impacts on biodiversity. Applying the precautionary principle, the Community has established mechanisms notably under directives 90/219/CEE and 90/220/CEE to assess, regulate, manage or control the risks associated with the use and release of genetically modified organisms resulting from biotechnology which may affect biodiversity. Moreover, the Community takes the lead to finalise a Protocol on Biosafety under the CBD by the end of 1998. The Protocol should establish at the international level procedures in the field of safe transfer, handling and use of living modified organisms, specifically focusing on transboundary movement of any living modified organism resulting from modern biotechnology that may have adverse effect on the conservation and sustainable use of biodiversity, and should set out in particular appropriate procedure for advance informed agreement.

Ex-situ conservation

6. Gene banks, captive breeding centres, zoos and botanical gardens can play a very valuable role if their activities are integrated in the framework of co-ordinated re-introduction or integrated conservation schemes. For crop species and varieties, including plants used for forestry, as well as for domestic animal breeds, there is a need to avoid genetic erosion and maintain a diverse genetic pool to ensure the future viability and improvement of the qualities of the varieties and breeds involved. The maintenance of adequate gene banks within the Community will require, in some cases, the collaboration of third countries. The Community should:

• encourage within and outside the Community adequate ex-situ conservation of both wild species and genetic resources of wild crop relatives, wild plants and domestic animal breeds useful for food production, whenever they cannot be conserved in situ or whose conservation in situ is under serious threat.

• encourage zoos, aquariums, botanical gardens, gene banks and collections to keep species, crop varieties and domestic animal breeds, under satisfactory standards that guarantee their conservation and integrate their work in co-ordinated action plans which aim at the restoration of the species to a satis-factory in-situ conservation status.

Sustainable use of components of biodiversity

7. Human activities may have positive or negative impacts on the sustainable use of biodiversity. A good assessment of the impact of strategies, policies, programmes, plans and projects on biodiversity is key to the promotion of sus-tainability. In the first instance activities with a potential negative impact need to be identified in order to find solutions that will avoid or minimise such an impact. Secondly, the most efficient options for meeting the needs of biodi-versity should be identified. The Community therefore should:

• consider the objectives of this strategy in the environmental assessment of its sectoral and cross-sectoral strategies, plans, programmes, policies and pro-jects.

• develop where feasible cost-effectiveness analyses of relevant Community strategies, plans, programmes, policies and projects to ensure the achieve-ment of the objectives of this strategy.

• develop appropriate methods and techniques to enable stakeholders to par-ticipate in assessment procedures and in the implementation of remedial and preventive actions.

8. Economic and social incentives such as subsidies, taxes and duties may have a considerable effect on biodiversity. In some cases they may be used as instruments to change or maintain patterns of production and consumption relevant to biodiversity. The Community encourages methods to promote that well-informed consumers can take as much as possible individual decisions benefiting the conservation and sustainable use of biodiversity. The recent Commission Communication on Green Levies defines some proposals to achieve these objectives. The Community should therefore aim to promote where feasible:

• the internalisation of the values of biodiversity in costs/benefit analysis.

• eco-labelling schemes based on life cycle analysis for products whose pro-duction, distribution, use or disposal could affect biodiversity.

• the integration of biodiversity concerns into liability mechanisms.

9. Alongside the identification and introduction of incentives to support con-servation and sustainable use of biodiversity, it is necessary to consider

removing incentives which have a negative impact. This includes reviewing certain systems of property and use rights, contractual mechanisms, international trade policies, and economic policies. Therefore, the Community should in particular focus on:

• shifting incentives to encourage positive effects on the conservation and sustainable use of biological diversity, rather than negative ones.

• contributing to the social and economic viability of systems supporting biodiversity as well as to the removal of incentives with perverse effects on the conservation and sustainable use of biodiversity.

Theme 2.   *Sharing of benefits arising out of the utilisation of genetic resources*

10. The sharing of benefits arising out of the utilisation of genetic resources relates to the implementation of the CBD in a number of aspects, i.e. access to genetic resources and distribution of the benefits of biotechnology including research and commercial partnerships between providers and users of genetic resources; transfer of technology; technical and scientific co-operation; knowledge, innovations and practices of indigenous and local communities embodying traditional lifestyles.

11. In relation to genetic resources, the CBD reaffirms the sovereign right of Parties over their genetic resources. It also stipulates that Parties should not impose inappropriate restrictions and that access should be on mutually agreed terms. Correspondingly, a whole range of solutions regarding access to these resources needs to be considered. Therefore, the Community should:

• promote appropriate multilateral frameworks.

• promote guidelines for bilateral co-operation on a voluntary basis to be applied particularly in cases where only some countries have or need access to the genetic resource in question.

• support the countries of origin of genetic resources to develop national strategies on bioprospecting and access taking into account relevant multilateral frameworks and instruments.

12. Technology transfer should be understood in a broad sense encompassing technology co-operation with respect to access to and availability of technologies as well as institutional development and capacity building to identify and use appropriate technologies, including indigenous and local technologies. Objectives are based on the fact that useful technologies exist in the public as well as in the private domain and that an adequate legal and economic framework, including intellectual property regimes, is necessary in order to facilitate technology co-operation and transfer. The need for relevant technology is especially present in developing countries. The Community should therefore endeavour to :

• increase the development of technology for the conservation and sustainable use of biodiversity.

• facilitate transfer of technology for conservation and sustainable use of biodiversity to developing countries.

13. Technical and scientific co-operation should in particular aim at strengthening the basic capacities in developing countries for the conservation and sustainable use of biodiversity and its components and the establishment of joint research programmes, in particular as regards identification, monitoring and exchange of information. The Community should:

• promote both within and outside the Community the wider application of knowledge and technologies for conservation and sustainable use of biodiversity, including knowledge, innovations and practices of local and indigenous communities.

Theme 3.   Research, identification, monitoring and exchange of information

14. It is widely recognised that the current incomplete state of knowledge at all levels concerning biodiversity is a constraint on successfully implementing the Convention. This should not however slow down ongoing activities based on the existing state of knowledge. It is therefore necessary to strengthen efforts to identify and monitor the most important components of biodiversity as well as pressures and threats on them, paying special attention to the indicative list of categories of important components set out in Annex I of the CBD. It is also necessary to strengthen basic research into biodiversity, its principles, concepts and fundamental mechanisms.

15. Tasks and targets identified in the Action Plan and other measures in this area should be incorporated in the activities within the Framework Community Programme on Research and Development. The importance of data held by the NGO community, Member States, their agencies and private collections should be taken into account.

16. Research initiatives should build in particular upon the work of the Ad hoc European Working Group on Research and Biodiversity (EWGRB) established in the framework of the European Commission DG XII "Environment and Climate Research Programme" and could focus on:

• establishing a network between European centres of excellence in biodiversity research in order to foster basic research into the importance and functioning of biodiversity on all levels.

• promoting the implementation of appropriate research activities concerning the functional mechanisms of the natural evolution of biodiversity, including tools and methods needed to implement the biodiversity policy objectives.

• increasing knowledge about how to safeguard biodiversity in nature, agriculture, forestry and fisheries and its wider role in life-support systems;

• increasing the understanding of how the biosphere functions at different spatial scales: global, regional and local level and understanding of the effect of human activities on life-support systems.

• assisting in identifying the necessary changes in legislation, programmes and political actions for the conservation and sustainable use and equitable sharing of the benefits arising from the use of biodiversity. This should include addressing the policy, organisational and management factors affecting the sustainable use and conservation of biodiversity in third countries, in the context of economic globalization.

• promoting research activities using molecular methods in biodiversity measurement and validation of these technologies.

• promoting the creation of tools and choices for partners in the conservation and utilisation of biodiversity, including research on clean technologies and on ex-situ conservation technologies.

• promoting the evaluation of the various forms of biodiversity from the perspective of all societal actors.

• supporting the development of a global interface with third countries, addressing in particular the sustainable use and management of biodiversity in transition economies, as well as in emerging ones and developing countries.

17. With respect to identification the Community will promote further support activities by the European Environmental Agency and its Information and Observation Network (EIONET) including tasks to:

• develop a baseline study to identify and catalogue important components of biodiversity that exist—in situ or ex situ—or that have become extinct in the last 50 years.

• identify the conservation status and trends of components of biodiversity.

• identify relevant pressures and threats, together with their causes, on components of biodiversity.

• apply modern taxonomy to build scientific tools for policy on conservation and sustainable use, aiming, inter alia, to fulfil gaps in taxonomy knowledge.

18. As the monitoring and continuous assessment of all the components of biodiversity in the Community, as well as of the pressures and threats that may affect them would be impractical, it is proposed to promote the development of a system of indicators based on a species and ecosystems approach.[4]

---

[4] Examples of indicators at local level could be decline of a species, use of pesticides or change in pesticide use. Examples of indicators at Community level could be percentage of threatened species per known species, fragmentation of habitats by linear transport infrastructure or sites designated under NATURA 2000.

19. The Community will support research on this system in its research programme and such work will be included in the new Multi-annual Work Programme of the European Environmental Agency and its Network. In addition, Eurostat is developing indicators of pressures affecting biodiversity in the context of its Pressure Indices Project.[5] The identification of these indicators and the monitoring of their evolution is an essential element of this strategy because it will provide the required information to assess the performance and impact of the Action Plans and other measures. They should therefore include:

• the identification of a set of indicators to assess how components of biodiversity are affected by the sector and assess progress on the implementation of the strategy.

• the mechanisms for monitoring the evolution of the indicators having regard, inter alia, to activities causing habitat degradation, unsustainable harvesting, emission of pollutants and release or spread into the environment of alien species and genetically or living modified organisms.

20. The importance of assessments and of international exchange of information for achieving the objectives of the CBD is underlined by the cross-border nature of many ecological processes, the interdependence between ecosystems, the migratory behaviour of various wild species, the need for international collaboration to maintain genetic pools of crop varieties and domestic animal breeds as well as the cross-border nature of many pressures and threats affecting biodiversity. The strengthening of cross-border co-ordination in between Member States as well as with other Parties to the CBD, on a bilateral or regional basis, is therefore an important objective.

21. This includes support for consolidation and further development of the Clearing House Mechanism[6] (CHM) which is established as the prime vehicle for international information exchange on biodiversity. The European Environmental Agency and its Information and Observation Network (EIONET) should consolidate and further develop the Community CHM in order to become an efficient vehicle for promoting and facilitating technical and scientific co-operation. This should be needs-driven, decentralised and allow for provision of information useful for meta-data levels of analyses. The provision of information by the CHM is of particular importance for the compilation of national and Community reports and for information on progress in implementing concrete measures for biodiversity. The Community CHM will establish links to the Member States CHM focal points.

---

[5] Described in the Communication from the Commission to the Council and the European Parliament—Directions for the EU on Environmental Indicators and Green National Accounting—the Integration of Environmental and Economic Information Systems, COM(94)670 final, 21 Dec. 1994.

[6] The concept, aims and objectives of the Clearing House Mechanism are established in Art. 18 of the CBD and developed through decisions I/3, II/3 and III/4 of the Conference of the Parties.

22. Consequently Action Plans and other measures should help to:

• identify and review existing mechanisms to facilitate the exchange of relevant information through the Community Clearing House Mechanism.

• establish or strengthen systems for the exchange of information at national and international level and make existing knowledge of biodiversity available and useful to the public and decision makers.

Theme 4. Education, training and awareness

23. Many of the pressures and threats on the conservation and sustainable use of biodiversity have their origin in human perceptions, attitudes and behaviour. Similarly, the biodiversity strategy could be difficult to implement if actors involved are not aware of the problems affecting biodiversity and their possible solutions. Changing these factors requires long-term concerted efforts in education and public awareness.

24. Public awareness is essential to ensure the success of many actions in favour of biodiversity, e.g. a consumer policy promoting the conservation and sustainable use of biodiversity. Therefore, public awareness campaigns and the main instruments available to achieve the CBD objectives should be considered. In all these aspects NGOs play a very important role.

25. Finally, the implementation of any strategy on biodiversity will require specific up-to-date technical expertise on the part of the various actors involved. This expertise can only be obtained if relevant training schemes are adequately adapted to scientific, technical and technological progress.

26. The Community should therefore encourage the development of:

• programmes for public information, education and awareness raising on conservation and sustainable use of biodiversity.

• programmes to ensure the training required for the human resources involved in the implementation of this strategy at Community, National and local levels.

• capacity building to monitor, assess and report on the impact of Community strategies, plans, programmes, policies and projects on biodiversity in third countries.

III. POLICY AREAS

1. In the following paragraphs the importance of different policy areas and sectors for the conservation and sustainable use of biological diversity are highlighted, and objectives for the Community are identified in order to achieve the objectives of the Convention as described in section II.

1) Conservation of Natural Resources

2. The conservation and sustainable use of natural resources involves specific measures for wild species, including the establishment and management of NATURA 2000 ecological network:

OBJECTIVES:

• *To fully implement the Habitats Directive,[7] as well as the Birds Directive[8]*

• *To support the establishment of networks of designated areas, particularly the EU NATURA 2000 network, and to provide adequate financial and technical support for their conservation and sustainable use.*

• *To develop management plans for selected threatened species and some hunt-able species.*

• *To implement the EC CITES[9] Regulation and to adapt it to reflect further decisions by the Conference of the Parties to CITES.*

3. Initiatives for biodiversity across the rest of the territory outside protected areas need to be developed and promoted. The Community does not have a comprehensive legal instrument in this field but efforts have been made as part of the implementation of the 5th Action Programme to promote the integration of environmental considerations into sectoral and cross-sectoral policy areas. In this context, the Commission's recent proposal for a Council Directive establishing a framework for Community action in the field of water policy is especially relevant. Water quantity and quality (particularly in relation to pollution by pesticides and fertilisers) are essential parameters for the functioning of all ecosystems. The competing and potentially conflicting demands of this limited resource from different sectors, make water policy highly strategic to the conservation and sustainable use of biodiversity. Wetlands also have outstanding importance for the conservation and sustainable use of biodiversity, as recognised in the Ramsar Convention and in the Commission's Communication on wetlands.

OBJECTIVES:

• *To develop in co-operation with Member States instruments to enhance the conservation and sustainable use of biodiversity across the territory outside protected areas.*

• *To use the Water Framework Directive as a tool for the conservation and sustainable use of biodiversity and in this context to develop analyses of water quantity and quality versus demand for every river basin including agricultural irrigation, energy generation, industrial, drinking and ecological uses.*

---

[7] [1992] OJ L206/1.   [8] [1979] OJ L103/1.   [9] [1997] OJ L61/1.

• *To enhance the ecological function of land cover, including riparian and allu-vial vegetation, to combat erosion and maintain the water cycle supporting ecosystems and habitats important for biodiversity.*

• *To protect wetlands within the Community and restore the ecological charac-ter of degraded wetlands.*

4. A number of global processes have serious impacts on biodiversity in par-ticular climate change, desertification, ozone layer depletion. The impact of climate change on some sensitive ecosystems and crop varieties as well as the effects of some actions to combat climate change, for example, can be relevant to the objectives of the CBD, these reforestation and afforestation initiatives should incorporate measures that ensure additional benefits for biodiversity. Moreover, policies related to the conservation and sustainable use of biodi-versity should take into account changes that could occur in ecosystems as a consequence of the accelerated rate of change in climate. The effects of ozone layer depletion on marine productivity and on fisheries, as well as on some crop varieties and the impact of the use of some ozone depleting substances on local biodiversity are equally important. Desertification has significant impact on soils, the maintenance *of the* hydrological cycle and the conserva-tion of different ecosystems. It leads to decreasing soil productivity and the potential local extinction of wild species. Problems caused by desertification are particularly relevant in the Mediterranean and other regions outside Europe.

OBJECTIVES:

• *To promote better co-ordination between different initiatives in the inter-national fora in the field of climate change, ozone layer depletion and desertifi-cation to avoid duplication of efforts, in particular with respect to reporting procedures.*

• *To identify interactions between the CBD and activities under other existing international agreements in order to optimise the opportunities for synergy.*

2) Agriculture

5. Land use patterns and practices have a major influence on biodiversity in Europe and around the world. In some cases land use patterns and practices support the conservation and sustainable use of biodiversity, while in others they cause serious threats. In this context, agriculture generates both benefits and pressures on biodiversity depending, in many cases, on practices, bio-geography, grazing periods, etc.

6. The agricultural sectors are heavily influenced by varying degrees of gov-ernment intervention, employing measures that have often led to levels of commodity production and the adoption of farming practices that have not been conducive to sustainability, or have discouraged more sustainable prac-

tices. The increase in productivity is being achieved in many cases at the cost of degrading natural capital (fertile soil, clean water, natural and semi-natural ecosystems). In addition, the factors behind the decline of biodiversity can be understood by considering the incentives and disincentives facing a country or an individual farmer with regard to sustainable use of genetic resources

7. On the other hand, some externalities generated by agriculture have positive characteristics of a "public good". Fields and pastures, along with forests and natural areas, form part of the rural landscape. Agricultural land often provides and creates important habitats for wildlife. Land, or the soil itself, plays an important function in the hydrological cycle and in cleansing the air of noxious gases, such as ammonia.

8. Farming communities have an intrinsic interest in ensuring that land use practices are sustainable and contribute to the conservation and sustainable use of biodiversity. Some semi-natural habitats can be preserved only if appropriate farming activities are continued. In many situations where agriculture production is a key element of sustainable ecosystems, abandonment of agriculture would lead to the irreversible degradation of different habitats. There has been an increasing awareness among farmers on the gains to be made by adopting environmentally sound agricultural practices, which have been underpinned by rapid advances in "green technologies". However, such practices will not be adopted to the extent necessary unless agricultural and environmental policies give farmers complementary signals.

9. Because of the interaction of sustainable agriculture and rural development, with the conservation and sustainable use of biodiversity and the need for integrated land-use planning as mentioned in Agenda 21, the conservation and sustainable use of agro-biodiversity should be based on the combination of two mutually coherent approaches:

10. First, the conservation and sustainable use—in situ and ex situ—of the genetic resources of species, varieties, domestic animal breeds and microbial life-forms with actual or potential value as agricultural commodities and the equitable sharing of benefits arising from the utilisation of genetic resources in agriculture requires a wide range of in and ex-situ actions. Firstly, in-situ conservation of local species, varieties and domestic animal breeds requires an adequate system of economic and social incentives, combined with increased consumers awareness. Some farming and breeding activities help to maintain endangered plant and animal species. Secondly, gene banks in the Community are not as well developed as elsewhere and action should be taken to improve the situation. These initiatives would help to meet present and future requirements for global food security and they should focus on the key elements of the Global Plan for Action for the Conservation and Sustainable Use of Plant Genetic Resources for Food and Agriculture.

In the Action Plan for agriculture, Community initiatives in the field of genetic resources should, inter alia, build upon the existing legislation.

OBJECTIVES:

• *To formulate policy measures, programmes and projects which promote the implementation of the Global Plan of Action for the conservation and sustainable use of plant genetic resources for food and agriculture.*

• *To promote the development of technologies assessing levels of diversity in genetic resources.*

• *To reinforce the policy of conservation—in situ and ex situ—of genetic resources of actual or potential value for food and agriculture.*

• *To promote the development of adequate gene-banks useful for the conservation in situ and ex situ of genetic resources for food and agriculture so that they will be available for use.*

• *To endeavour to ensure that legislation does not obstruct the conservation of genetic resources.*

11. Secondly, the conservation and sustainable use of agro-ecosystems and their interface with other ecosystems. Agriculture is an important element of the ecosystems where it takes place. Sometimes it also influences other ecosystems in the surroundings or downstream. In both cases interactions could be positive or negative for the conservation and sustainable use of biodiversity. Agriculture has played and continues to play a major role in the diversity of ecosystems and in the creation and maintenance of semi-natural ecosystems. Therefore the conservation and sustainable use of agro-ecosystems require:

a) The maintenance and further development of farming with a view to optimising its positive impact on the conservation and sustainable use of biodiversity; recognising and supporting the role of farming communities in the creation and maintenance of semi-natural habitats; taking into consideration the positive role of non-intensive agricultural systems for wildlife and wild plants habitats; and optimising the positive impacts of agricultural practices and production systems on the conservation and sustainable use of biodiversity. In particular, the maintenance of some well-established traditional methods of extensive agriculture, sometimes in marginal areas, is essential to preserve the value that such areas have for biodiversity.

b) The mitigation of negative impacts of agricultural activities on biodiversity. In particular, certain land use practices, the use of agro-chemicals, the overgrazing and pollution consequences of excessive livestock intensity, monoculture, the elimination of wetlands and hedgerows, and the use of heavy machinery, has serious effects for biodiversity. Pesticides, for example, can have a negative effect on the conservation of biodiversity not only in the place where they are applied but also in other ecosystems (i.e. by pesticide run-off).

12. In this context, the Action Plan on agriculture should build upon the existing policies and those foreseen in Agenda 2000 and complement them so that they contribute to biodiversity.

13. *OBJECTIVES:*

• *To encourage the ecological function of rural areas.*

• *To integrate biodiversity objectives into the relevant instruments of the CAP.*

• *To promote farming methods enhancing biodiversity, by linking agricultural support to environmental conditions where appropriate.*

• *To promote good agricultural practice standards with a view to reducing the risk of pollution and of further damage to biodiversity.*

• *To increase awareness among all producers of the polluting potential of specific agricultural practices both short and long term and the need for all producers to be protectors of both environment and biodiversity. This includes the development of an integrated strategy for the sustainable use of pesticides.*

• *To promote and ensure the viability of those crop species and varieties and domestic animal races which have to be farmed to conserve the ecosystems of priority wild species.*

• *To promote and support low-intensive agricultural systems especially in high natural value areas.*

• *To further develop the agri-environment measures to optimise benefits on biodiversity by:*

1. *reinforcing targeted agri-environment measures*

2. *assessing its performance against a specific set of biodiversity indicators*

3. *increasing the relevant budget and resources, as proposed in Agenda 2000*

14. The impact of trade policies on agricultural commodity production and land use is particularly relevant for biodiversity conservation. Direct investment by producers should be a strong force in promoting sustainable development and biodiversity. Implementation of global, regional and bilateral trade agreements is certain to have effects on land use in many countries. The global process of trade liberalisation leads to important changes in existing subsidies and protective mechanisms. Together with changes in the pattern of trade, changes in global and regional patterns of agricultural production are likely to entail displacement or abandonment of some long-established local production systems, or lead to their intensification to maintain competitiveness, or to supply new markets.

15. In this field legislation on quality labels can also contribute to biodiversity. It helps to maintain a genetic pool of rustic domesticated species and plant

varieties contributing to prevent genetic erosion. It also helps to maintain land use practices beneficial for biodiversity. Organic farming should also be supported by certification systems. Protection of geographical indications and designations of origin and specific characters for agricultural products and foodstuffs is also important and can contribute to the conservation of special agro-ecosystems enhancing biodiversity.

16. *OBJECTIVES:*

• *To promote trade related agricultural policies and disciplines which respect the needs for conservation and sustainable use of biodiversity as well as the principles of the World Trade Organization.*

3) Fisheries[10]

17. The increasing pressure exercised by human activities on marine and coastal environment stresses the importance of integrating biodiversity concerns into marine resource policies, including fisheries, and into agreements on the protection of coastal and marine environment and on fisheries. The conservation and sustainable use of marine and coastal ecosystems is essential to maintain the livelihoods of fishermen and fishing communities.

18. Indeed, while fisheries policies have a major impact on the conservation of biodiversity and sustainable use of biological resources, the Common Fisheries Policy has not yet fully achieved the objective of sustainable fishing. Achieving this objective requires implementation of upper limits of exploitation rates (fishing mortality rates) and minimum levels of stock biomass, so that there is a high probability of ensuring viability and sustainability of fishing for a species or group of species. Once the maximum exploitation rate to be allowed in respect of each species is defined, the mechanisms to keep it below the critical level will need to be defined. The tools to limit exploitation rates should be defined, as appropriate, as maximum levels of fishing effort, as total allowable catches or as combinations of these two instruments. The Common Fisheries Policy provides the necessary operational tools to define both allowable exploitation rates and the associated ancillary measures.

19. Research efforts should ascertain how to ensure that irreplaceable genetic resources are not lost by genetic contamination affecting indigenous populations by hybridisation or competition. Moreover, the integration of CBD objectives within the fisheries policy sector requires action at three different levels: a) the conservation and sustainable use of fish stocks, b) the protection of non-target species from fishing activities; and c) the prevention of impacts of aquaculture on different ecosystems. These different levels should also be considered in the context of Community fisheries agreements with third countries.

---

[10] In this section the words fisheries, fishing and fish stocks make reference, where appropriate, not only to fish species but also to moluscs, crustaceans, marine mammals and other marine or estuarine animals.

20. *OBJECTIVES:*

• *To promote the conservation and sustainable use of fish stocks and feeding grounds.*

• *To promote the establishment of technical conservation measures to support the conservation and sustainable use of fish stocks. Measures available include inter alia fishing exclusion areas (mainly for the protection of dense aggregations of juvenile fish), and mesh sizes. Each measure should be applied according to its merits and expected conservation effect.*

• *To reduce the impact of fishing activities and other human activities on non-target species and on marine and coastal ecosystems to achieve sustainable exploitation of marine and coastal biodiversity.*

• *To avoid aquaculture practices that may affect habitat conservation through occupation of sensitive areas, i.e. mangroves in third countries and inter-tidal areas within the Community, pollution by inputs and outputs from fish farms and genetic contamination by possible releases or escapes of farmed species or varieties.*

4) Regional policies and spatial planning

21. The Commission's Communication "Europe 2000+: Co-operation for European territorial development" highlights how spatial planning can contribute to conservation and sustainable management of ecosystems. Indeed, spatial planning can play an important role, in the conservation and sustainable use of biodiversity across the entire territory:

a) at the local and regional level, by pointing out the benefits to be expected from sustainable land-use—notably in socio-economic terms—when it can facilitate partnership between the local/regional authorities, economic actors, local and indigenous communities, NGOs and biodiversity conservators; and

b) at the strategic level, spatial planning highlights the inter-linkage between the different tiers of Government and between different policies competing for the same natural resources. Spatial planning means setting out a common set of longer term objectives to be carried out through mutually compatible measures tailored to the socio-economic and environmental characteristics of the space to which they apply.

22. Spatial planning should promote sustainable land use while ensuring a more balanced geographical distribution of economic activities. It should help avoid excessive pressure on certain parts of the territory and take account of ecological requirements everywhere. The Commission has incorporated and integrated spatial planning approach into its Demonstration Programme on Integrated Coastal Zone Management which is considering, among other things, biodiversity. In order to further develop a European-wide approach to spatial planning, the European Spatial Development Perspective is being

drawn up and the first official draft was endorsed at the Nordwijk informal ministers meeting in June 1997. It addresses biodiversity under the heading "Continuing pressure in Europe's natural and cultural heritage". It underlines that specific local factors should be taken into account when implementing policies with a spatial impact to avoid further losses of biodiversity.

23. In general, in the context of regional aid, a comprehensive and integrated approach is the best way to ensure the long-term conservation and sustainable use of biodiversity. In eligible regions, in particular those characterised by high biodiversity, the promotion of sustainable development could be included in regional development strategies and Structural Funds programmes.

24. In this context, particular attention should be given to the rural areas where, in many cases, the continuation of agricultural activities is necessary to avoid losses of biodiversity and habitat degradation. A rural development policy has the potential to protect and enhance these environmental assets. By encouraging land conservation and higher environmental standards of land use, the agri-environmental measures are an essential instrument for the sustainable development of land use, enabling conservation and sustainable use of biodiversity.

25. *OBJECTIVES:*

• *To promote the policy options identified in the spatial planning initiatives which can assist in conserving and enhancing biodiversity throughout the European territory. Particular attention should be paid to:*

—*Ecological corridors and buffer zones*

—*Unprotected, sensitive areas with high level of biodiversity such as mountains, coastal areas and islands.*

—*Rural areas in order to ensure a better synergy between the objectives of economic development and conservation of biodiversity needs.*

• *In coastal zones, to develop integrated management and planning of both land and sea, including fisheries, shipping, coastal infrastructure and impacts from agricultural and forestry activities in the hinterland.*

• *To promote sustainable development based on an integrated spatial planning approach.*

• *To encourage sustainable regional development within the Operational Programmes as well as transnational co-operation programmes including measures to conserve and make sustainable use of biodiversity. These could be supported under the Structural Funds to preserve environmental quality particularly in eligible areas with high biodiversity.*

• *To ensure that interventions co-financed under the Structural Funds and the Cohesion Fund, which are mainly aimed at economic and social cohesion, do not infringe upon Community legislation of relevance for biodiversity.*

5) *Forests*

26. Globally, forests contain the greatest proportion of biological diversity in terms of species, genetic material and ecological processes and have an intrinsic value for the conservation and sustainable use of biodiversity. Furthermore, forests are important to combat climate change and minimise its impact on the conservation of other ecosystems. The livelihoods of many rural communities are based in the conservation and sustainable use of forests and they represent essential national resources for present and future generations. While recognising the importance of reforestation schemes to increase the forest cover, measures should be taken in relation to the afforestation or reforestation of areas to avoid endangering important and/or valuable ecosystems (e.g. wetlands, steppes, heathlands, etc.) or the use of inappropriate tree species. It is therefore important to take into account in a balanced way, the need for ensuring the conservation and appropriate enhancement of biodiversity in forests, the need for the maintenance of forest health and ecological balance, the sustainable production of raw material for forest industries as well as of goods and services sought by society.

27. Conservation and sustainable use of biodiversity in forests can be considered at three different levels:

a) On the global scale, tropical as well as some boreal forests are currently facing greater threats than at any time in history, with many areas undergoing rapid deforestation, degradation or loss of quality as a result of human activity. The Community has recognised the critical importance of halting and reversing this cycle of destruction, making sustainable forest management one of its focal points in development co-operation policies (see the chapter on development co-operation below). In particular the implementation of the recommendations of the Intergovernmental Panel on Forests (IPF) are important for the objectives of the CBD. Also, the Community has promoted in the IPF and continues to support the development of a legally binding instrument on forests, aiming among other things to integrate biodiversity conservation objectives with sustainable management of forests at national, regional and global levels.

b) At Pan-European level the Community is a signatory party to the resolutions adopted at the ministerial conferences on the protection of forests in Europe. In this context general guidelines for the conservation of the biodiversity of European forests are defined in Resolution H2 of the Helsinki Conference for the protection of forests in Europe. Reference to conservation and appropriate enhancement of biodiversity is also made in Resolution H1 in which general guidelines for the sustainable management of forests in Europe are set out.

In this context the participation of the European Community in the Third Ministerial Conference "Environment for Europe" which was held in Sofia in

October 1995 is also especially relevant. It endorsed the Pan-European Biological and Landscape Diversity Strategy. A close co-ordination was subsequently established between both processes. A Common Work-Programme on the Conservation and Enhancement of Biological and Landscape Diversity in Forest Ecosystems has been proposed for the period from 1997 to 2000.

c) Within the Community, forest policies are basically developed at national level. The Community has, however, taken a number of initiatives to promote forest conservation, in particular initiatives to protect forests against atmospheric pollution and fire, afforestation, the improvement of woodlands, the protection of forests, the development of forest infrastructure and the initial transformation of forest products, the conservation of genetic resources of forest collections and, where necessary, making comparable or complete forestry information from the Member States and forestry related research supported through specific European Community research programmes on agriculture, environment, biotechnology and energy.

28. The European Union Forestry Strategy called for by the European Parliament in its Resolution of 30 January 1997 should include actions to promote the conservation and enhancement of biodiversity in forests.

29. *OBJECTIVES:*

• *To promote the conservation and appropriate enhancement of biodiversity as an essential element of sustainable forest management at the national, regional and global levels.*

• *To further develop the Council Regulation 2080/92 to enhance its benefits to biodiversity.*

• *To ensure that, while promoting a net increase in forest extension as a means of maximising their carbon sink function to combat climate change, afforestation is conducted in a manner that does not negatively affect ecologically interesting or noteworthy sites and ecosystems.*

• *To promote sustainable management of forests which respects the ecological characteristics of the areas affected and to promote the restoration and regeneration of areas that have suffered deforestation. Native species and local provenances should be preferred where appropriate. Wherever introduced species are used to replace local ecosystems, sufficient action should be taken at the same time to conserve native flora and fauna.*

• *To promote the development of specific, practical, cost effective and efficient biodiversity appraisal systems and methods for evaluating the impact on biodiversity of chosen forest development and management techniques.*

• *To promote international research into the impact of possible climate change on forest ecosystems, the possible adaptation of forest ecosystems to climate change and the mitigation of adverse effects of climate change by forest ecosys-*

tems as detailed in Resolution n°4 of the Helsinki Ministerial Conference on the Protection of Forests in Europe.

• *To promote the implementation of the general guidelines for the conservation of the biodiversity of European forests (Resolution H2 of the Helsinki Conference) and the recommendations of the IPF in relation to the conservation of biodiversity.*

6) Energy and Transport

30. The energy and transport sectors have a global and regional impact on biodiversity through climate change and acidification. Additionally, the development of infrastructures for transport and for energy production may have a more local impact on biodiversity.

a) Emissions from fossil fuels have led globally to an increase in atmospheric concentrations of greenhouse gases. These changes are projected to lead to regional and global changes in climate. This will add an additional stress to ecological systems already affected by pollution, increasing resource demands and unsustainable management practices. Composition and geographical distribution of ecosystems will shift more rapidly than they have previously according to natural processes. Subsequently, the limited capacity of some species for adaptation to these changes will pave the way for increased losses in biodiversity.

b) Regional effects of fossil fuel use are acidification of inland waters and soils (with effects also on vegetation and forest health) and degradation of forests. Acidification of lakes and water courses make them unsuitable for the survival of some species. Additionally, acidification of soils leads to changes in their chemical composition and structure and affects the ecosystems of which they form part.

c) There may also be local effects due to the spatial impact of the development of infrastructures for the production and distribution of energy not only from conventional fuels. Any potential side-effect from the use of renewable energy sources (e.g. hydropower plants, unsustainable use of biomass or large-scale energy plantations) should also be taken into account. In this context, attention should be paid to the links with water management policy because of increasing water demands for energy production. Transport, road and airport infrastructures may have a direct impact on spatial occupation of ecosystems and habitat fragmentation and have indirect impacts—including genetic isolation—and disturbances—including the presence of people, charges in light, wind, temperature, humidity and soil nutrients—on wild species. In addition, transformation of rivers into channels to allow fluvial transportation may increase the pressures on aquatic and fluvial ecosystems by spatial occupation and disturbance, habitat transformations and pollution. Sea transport and infrastructures also have an impact on marine pollution.

31. *OBJECTIVES:*

• *To implement acidification and climate change strategies with a view to minimising negative impacts on biodiversity.*

• *To minimise the impact on biodiversity of the development of infrastructures for energy from conventional and renewable sources.*

• *To assess the best options for biodiversity when deciding which energy sources are used to match demands at regional level.*

• *To minimize the impacts on biodiversity of transport infrastructure by optimizing the capacity and efficiency of the existing infrastructure and, for new infrastructure, giving full consideration to environmental concerns.*

7) Tourism

32. Tourism is closely linked to the preservation of a healthy environment, which in turn is an essential element of tourism development and helps to raise public awareness on some biodiversity issues. Tourism policies are developed at national and regional level and may have an important impact on biodiversity and sustainability. On the one hand, tourism places direct and indirect pressures on, and threats to, the conservation of species and habitats, may cause disturbances on wildlife and increase pollution caused by transportation. On the other hand, sustainable tourism, in many areas, is providing extra resources and employment to local communities giving them additional motivation for the conservation of nature and protection of the environment.

33. Sustainable development in touristic areas needs to reconcile the interests of the tourism industry, tourism satisfaction and the conservation and sustainable use of biodiversity.

34. In this context it is important to identify to what extent some sensitive areas should be protected from additional human interference caused by tourism and the tourism-carrying-capacity of some habitats and ecosystems. It is also important to understand the limitations of a system of transfer of resources based on few tourists providing additional income to many members of local communities.

35. Tourism activities which directly or indirectly contribute to the conservation and sustainable use of biodiversity should be promoted. The public and the private sector have also much to gain by the exchange of best practice in this field. The private sector should be encouraged to apply guidelines and codes of conduct for sustainable tourism.

36. While policies on tourism are Member States' responsibilities, particular attention should be paid, to the impact of tourism on potential NATURA 2000 areas. Tourism also has important interrelation with the development of regional and spatial planning policies and some of these concerns could be

reflected in the development of Action Plans for different sectors. On a global scale, the Berlin Declaration sets out the basis for the development of global guidelines for the sustainable development of tourism within the framework of the CBD.

37. The Community should in particular pursue the following objectives:

• *To encourage the assessment of the tourism carrying capacity of different ecosystems and habitats.*

• *To encourage the exchange of best practice among public and private tourism interests.*

• *to promote the development of international guidelines for sustainable tourism.*

8) Development and economic co-operation

38. Developing countries and economies in transition offer a wide spectrum of habitats and ecosystems, of which forests, grasslands and marine/coastal ecosystems are generally the most significant. Various kinds of human activities are harming biodiversity in terms of habitat loss and degradation. The underlying causes are numerous, and include poverty. Biodiversity in small island developing states is a particular problem because of the extremely small area of some local habitats, the high incidence of endemism throughout the islands, and the high vulnerability to natural disasters and habitat destruction.

39. The CBD recognises in Article 20 the principle of common but differentiated responsibilities of the Convention parties and the role of development co-operation. Furthermore, Article 3 of the CBD recognises the national sovereign right to exploit natural resources pursuant to their own environmental policies. In this context the Community development aid co-operation is an important instrument to support third countries in their efforts to achieve conservation and sustainable development of biodiversity. In particular, capacity building schemes are important to enable third countries to develop expertise for the development and use of technologies, including indigenous and traditional technologies, for the conservation and sustainable use of biodiversity. It will be equally important to explore ways to repatriate taxonomic information housed in collections in the Community.

40. Moreover, activities funded under the PHARE programme should pay attention to maintain areas of high value for biodiversity, in particular by stimulation of the adoption of the acquis communitaire in that area by the candidate countries.

41. <u>*OBJECTIVES:*</u>

• *To mainstream biodiversity objectives into Community development and economic co-operation strategies and policy dialogue with developing countries and economies in transition. Biodiversity objectives should be integrated in development projects across different sectors of the economy of the recipient countries ensuring greater coherence between Community development co-operation policy and other Community policies, such as international trade, agriculture and fisheries.*

• *To support sustainable use of natural resources, particularly in relation to forests, grasslands and marine/coastal ecosystems.*

• *To strengthen capacity of relevant agencies involved in conservation and sustainable use of biodiversity.*

• *To further integrate EIA practices into development and economic co-operation.*

• *To co-ordinate the implementation of this strategy and the Action Plans emerging from it, with third countries' strategies ensuring coherence between Community support to third countries and the objectives of those countries' own biodiversity strategies.*

• *To ensure complementarity and co-ordination of policies and approaches in Community and Member States' aid programmes, as well as with other donors and international institutions, particularly the Global Environmental Facility, for a coherent implementation of the CBD.*

• *To provide sufficient funding for biodiversity on bilateral aid programmes as well as for international mechanisms (e.g. CBD)*

• *To promote schemes for the integration of biodiversity objectives into agriculture in accession countries.*

IV. THE DEVELOPMENT AND IMPLEMENTATION OF ACTION PLANS AND OTHER MEASURES

1. Within the framework of this strategy set out in this document, Action Plans of a sectoral and a cross-sectoral nature will have to be elaborated to ensure the implementation of the objectives set out in sections II and III.

2. Specific Action Plans are envisaged for conservation of natural resources, agriculture, fisheries, regional policies and spatial planning and development and economic co-operation. For the other policy areas, the objectives formulated under III will be taken directly into account for their further development and implementation. In the case of regional policies and spatial planning the specific Action Plan will have to ensure that the objectives pursued by the biodiversity strategy are directly incorporated in the future programming guidelines as well as relevant Community initiatives and this will not imply the development of specific new instruments. Proposals for action on forestry will be part of the proposal for a EU Forestry strategy. Energy and transport do not require new specific action plans as the development and implementation of

the Community strategies on climate change and acidification, which have a focus on ecosystems, together with the implementation of adequate environmental assessment procedures should be adequate to achieve the biodiversity objectives in these policy areas. For tourism, the implementation of environmental assessments and initiatives to be taken in the field of regional policies and spatial planning should help achieving the biodiversity objectives.

3. These Action Plans should be practical tools to achieve the integration of biodiversity into sectoral and cross-sectoral policy areas and instruments relevant to the conservation and sustainable use of biodiversity within the Community. Taking into account Article 3 of the CBD, the Action Plans should also ensure that Community policies and instruments do not cause damage to the environment of third countries or of areas beyond the limits of national jurisdiction and help third countries in their efforts to achieve conservation and sustainable use of biodiversity.

4. Taking into account the assets that some of the associated countries of the Community in Central and Eastern Europe have with respect to biodiversity it should be ensured that Action Plans and other measures include a specific focus on enlargement issues.

5. Action Plans and other measures will pursue the respect, preservation and maintenance of knowledge, innovations and practices of indigenous and local communities embodying traditional lifestyles relevant for the conservation and sustainable use of biodiversity and promote their wider application with the approval and involvement of the holders of such knowledge, innovations and practices.

6. To implement this strategy, the relevant actors in the policy areas mentioned above will have to develop the Action Plans and other measures in view of the specific goals they are pursuing and with the specific mechanisms and procedures to which they are subject. The actors requested to elaborate or contribute to the elaboration of Action Plans and other measures are in the first instance the relevant Commission services responsible for the policy area concerned, working in close co-ordination with each other as well as in co-operation with other European institutions and bodies (such as the European Environmental Agency, the European Investment Bank, etc.) and together with the national authorities where the responsibility for the definition and implementation of measures is shared. The Action Plans will take the form of Commission Communications to the Council and to the Parliament and, where appropriate, comprise proposals for legal instruments.

7. Action plans should be an integral part of the existing sectoral policy agendas and should make use of the existing agreements and international undertakings. Action Plans and instruments should implement the objectives indicated for the policy sectors in question and the objectives indicated under the different Themes of this strategy. In this way biodiversity concerns will be taken account of, inter alia:

- in the current review of the arrangements for the Structural Funds.

- in the CAP reform process announced in Agenda 2000; and

- in the new arrangements for development aid to be decided in 1998, especially through the new framework agreement between the EU and the ACP beyond the year 2000.

8. Action Plans should enhance collaboration and partnerships as well as a more efficient use of available resources. Interest groups such as industry associations and NGOs will be associated in the development and implementation of the Action Plans.

9. The development of the Action Plans normally will require a review of existing policies and instruments to determine how they affect species and ecosystems. They should identify the extent to which the aims and objectives indicated in this strategy are already incorporated and any gaps and additional initiatives that may be necessary. They should also set priorities for action. In the development and implementation of the Action Plans a precautionary approach should be taken in cases where incomplete knowledge exists. Socio-economic aspects of the implementation of the measures contained in the Action Plans should be evaluated. In order to set priorities and to justify chosen options when different alternatives are available. Action Plans should incorporate the necessary cost-effectiveness information.

10. Each Action Plan should as a general rule set out clear tasks, targets and mechanisms to assess their performance and to evaluate progress in the implementation of the strategy. The Commission will in co-operation with relevant bodies identify indicators in order to enable an evaluation ex ante and ex post of the implementation of the Action Plans. Species and ecosystems likely to be affected by each policy area mentioned in section III, and for which action is needed to ensure their conservation and sustainable use, will be the basis for the establishment of indicators. Economic indicators will also be considered.

11. Following the adoption of the Action Plans, it will be the responsibility of the relevant actors to ensure their implementation. The different sets of indicators will help the focal points to be established to follow the development, implementation and review of the strategy and Action Plans and ensure co-ordination and consistency on cross-sectoral issues.

12. Assessments on the implementation of the strategy and the effectiveness and appropriateness of the Action Plans will normally be made on a three-year cycle basis or in accordance with the planning cycles of the relevant policy. On the basis of these assessments the Commission will present a report to the Council and to the Parliament.

13. The development of Action Plans should be completed within two years after the adoption of this Communication by the Commission.

Table of Cases

NUMERICAL LIST

Table of Legislation

Denmark

European Treaties

Decisions

Regulations

Index